Douglas A. Russell

Stanford University

STAGE
COSTUME DESIGN

Theory, Technique, and Style

Second Edition

PRENTICE-HALL, INC., Englewood Cliffs, New Jersey 07632

Library of Congress Cataloging in Publication Data

Russell, Douglas A.
    Stage costume design.

    Bibliography: p.
    Includes index.
    1. Costume.   I. Title.
PN2067.R78 1985   792'.026   84-9926
ISBN   0-13-840349-X

Printed in the United States of America

10   9   8   7   6   5   4   3   2   1

Editorial/production supervision and interior design: Paul Spencer
Cover design: Diane Saxe
Manufacturing buyers: Ron Chapman and Barbara Kelly Kittle
Page layout: Jill S. Packer
Jacket photo courtesy Hirmer Fotoarchiv, Munich

ISBN   0-13-840349-X   01

Prentice-Hall International, Inc., *London*
Prentice-Hall of Australia Pty. Limited, *Sydney*
Editora Prentice-Hall do Brasil, Ltda., *Rio de Janeiro*
Prentice-Hall Canada Inc., *Toronto*
Prentice-Hall of India Private Limited, *New Delhi*
Prentice-Hall of Japan, Inc., *Tokyo*
Prentice-Hall of Southeast Asia Pte. Ltd., *Singapore*
Whitehall Books Limited, *Wellington, New Zealand*

To Marilyn, Malcolm, and Andrea

Contents

Part II: Theory and Style

Outline History of Western Costume

Foreword

The fact that Doug Russell got me my first job as an actor in the theatre thirty years ago has absolutely nothing to do with the great and thoroughly justified praise I intend to lavish on his book.

This book answers a tremendous need in the professional theatre, for it gives a complete definition of the role of costume designer, covering every aspect of training, professional relationships, research, studies in fabric, patterns, budgets, shop personnel—in short, it provides a statement of what professional directors expect in their artistic and practical relation to the stage designer. This comprehensiveness is the book's glory and principal value. In his own right, Doug Russell is one of the brilliant American interpreters of clothes for the stage. He has incorporated here the high standards of work that he requires of himself. His language is direct, concentrated, and extremely clear for any member of the professional theatre. It will be a joy to read. He puts into engaging prose many aspects of

the designer's work that have hitherto, to my knowledge, remained unsaid.

The art of design for the stage requires of the artist a tremendous sensitivity to the life of the play. The costume designer must be sensitive to styles of literature, to the art of acting, and to the coordination of visual effects with the stage designer and the lighting designer; must have a tremendous sympathy and understanding for the actor who is creating a role; must be a leader and an inspirational force among the shop crew; must have a deep personal responsiveness to the art, music, and architecture of all historical periods; must have a passionate belief in the power of individual and composed color; and most important, must have a vivid sense of the "theatrical."

This book unfolds as a series of revelations to the young designer. Of great importance are Russell's detailed observations about relations with the director, preliminary discussions of the play, the ever-important budget, scheduling, and charts. He provides invaluable information on how to prepare the most readable costume sketches, what medium to work in, and how to reveal significant details without losing the overall production tone. His discussions of color control and color relationships are unmatched.

The pages are bursting with information that must be part of the working kit of any professional. At the same time the writing and illustrations are sure to prove tremendously fascinating to the imagination of the beginner.

With an inspirational vividness, this book plants in the minds of readers many imaginative questions that will lead them to go on in the profession, to test and explore techniques in order to develop and shape their own styles. With absolute conviction I say that this book is a must for all students who intend to make costume design, stage design, or directing their profession.

In the theatre we rarely come upon a book that sets forth standards that will command the respect of the profession. This is such a book and it is my hope that the principles presented in this volume will awaken new standards and an enlightened approach to costume design throughout the profession in our country.

William Ball,
American Conservatory Theatre

Preface

This is the second edition of an introduction to the study of costume design. Its aim is to arouse interest in the subject on a variety of levels—critical, aesthetic, practical, and historical—and to give a well-rounded view without attempting to dwell on any one area in great detail. For instance, it does not attempt to examine the history of dress except briefly in the Appendix, since that has been well covered by my book *Costume History and Style*, also published by Prentice-Hall. The present book is intended primarily for courses that introduce the student to the problems of sketching, principles of design, practices of costume construction, and style in period plays. It should also be of general interest to actors, directors, and teachers in general theatre.

Part I (Chapters 1–8) includes an analysis of what is meant by costume design and the nature of the field as it exists today. A discussion of sketching and a presentation of costume plates follow. Design principles and the use of color are briefly discussed, and the complex area of patterns and fabric follows. Part I closes with two chapters on costume construction and the organization of the wardrobe and wardrobe personnel. Part II (Chapters 9–20) is devoted to the problems of style in costume design and begins with a chapter introducing the problems of style in relation to the history of art. Succeeding chapters treat each major period of art and drama in Western history and generally discuss its art and culture, the theatre, the drama, and at least one representative play, including the problems of costume design for production. An appendix, "Outline History of Western Costume," is devoted to a capsule review of the periods of dress in Western history, each with a representative male and female costumed figure, a list of costume terms used, and a representative list of useful books for each period. Part I and Part II are independent of one another and can be used separately in a course or combined and used with other related sources.

In the discussion of plays in Part II, a method of play analysis has been used that should lead the designer to consider the structure of the play as well as its story line as the basis for the costume designs. The plays were selected as famous and frequently anthologized representative dramas from the periods in which they were written, and each was chosen to reinforce the discussion of visual style in a particular chapter. Each is intended as a clear and direct example of a particular period style or a particular aspect of that style. The aim is to provide the student designer with a foundation scheme for planning the style for his costume designs from script to production.

The Bibliography, though not exhaustive, attempts to indicate useful books for each chapter. Additional reading suggested under each chapter heading will give greater dimension to the particular subject under discussion.

This book is based on many years of experience as a costume designer and teacher of costume history and design. Ideas have come from students, teachers, other designers, historians, the costume examination of the United Scenic Artists of America, other colleagues in the field, and many books.

A book such as this could not be written without the aid of students and colleagues directly or indirectly involved during the period of writing and the collecting of illustrative material. I am indebted to my teachers, Virginia Opsvig, Hubert Heffner, and Frank Bevan, for the will to do the original book and to Lewis Spitz of the Stanford University History Department for getting me to sit down and begin the actual writing of that first edition. I also want to thank the staffs of the Stanford University Library, Department of Art, and Department of Drama for assistance along the way. I also wish to acknowledge specialized help from Robin Coon, Ruth Henderson, and Barbara Cleveland, patient checking of the original manuscript by my typist, Carolyn D. Hill, and the kind help of all the people who are credited with providing sketches, photographs, and other illustrative material. I also wish to thank those who have kindly written critiques of the first edition and made suggestions for incorporation in the present revision. Thanks are particularly due to Norman Philbrick, both for the very kind use of illustrative materials from his extensive theatre library, and for his careful, patient reading of the original manuscript for content, balance, and style. His service has been invaluable. Finally, I wish to thank my wife, Marilyn, for her helpful advice and editorial assistance with both the original and the present edition of the book.

D.A.R.

1

Introduction

The Visual Environment of a Production

The art of the theatre is often understood to consist of two parts: the literary and the visual or, more specifically, the writing of the play and its presentation before an audience. The playwright tells a story and creates characters in words, while the theatre artists must recreate the play on the stage in concrete visual terms. They must make the ideas, characters, story, and dialogue visible and audible by translating the playwright's words into acting, music, dancing, costumes, scenery, and lighting. The theatre artists must create a visual and aural equivalent on stage for what occurs in the script. If the interpreters are fine artists, and if they have understood the text and have been intelligent in their interpretation, the same thought and spirit should govern the recreated vision that governed the original. Words, however, are only symbols for ideas, and it is possible to interpret symbols in a number of different ways. Theatre artists who are expert in dance, pantomime, speech, stage design, costume design, and lighting may each gain very different ideas about stage presenta-

tion from an author's stage directions and dialogue. If the approach of any one of these artists is placed on the stage, an audience will probably feel that what it sees is a true interpretation of the script; but if the views of the various artists are combined in a single production, the result will be complete confusion, like an orchestra without a conductor. The recreation of a script's imagery in visual and aural terms must, therefore, be unified in all its elements, and the effect of a performance on an audience must be one. The conductor of this orchestration of dance, acting, music, costume, scenery, properties, and lighting is the director, and it is through the director's eyes that the audience should see the production of a play.

The most important element in this recreated vision is action: not just the physical action of pantomime and speech but the spirit of "man in action," that vital flow of dramatic movement that brings a play to life on the stage through the medium of rhythmic speech and gesture. As Sheldon Cheney said in *The Theatre: Three Thousand Years of Drama, Acting and Stagecraft* (1972):

1

. . . the art of the theatre has to emphasize the presentation of a play by actors on a stage, through a flow of action, with that fusion of all the contributive stage arts which makes the drama live for its audience at its highest possible emotional intensity. Within this larger definition there should be special emphasis on action as the essential theatric core of the arts; . . . action in the sense of movement (as in early ritual drama and in . . . highly developed dance drama), or in the sense of the unfolding of a story or drama by actors using speech largely for expressiveness.

Scenery and costume, as the re-creation of the text, must always serve the play's dramatic action, developing and enriching it, but never dominating it or distracting from its flow and movement. Scenery and costume should be the visual expression of the play's dynamic spirit—an environment for the action. It was Robert Edmond Jones, the famous American scene designer, who used the word "environ-ment" to describe the function of scenery and costumes (Figure 1-1). Although theatre ideas have changed greatly since Jones wrote *The Dramatic Imagination* (1941), the term "environment" is still useful if one thinks of it not as used in psychology and sociology, but rather as an envelope for the mood and ideas of the playwright—a visualization in color, line, and texture of the actors' actions and emotions. Seen in this way, environment can be as broken and inconsistent as the action in the script, and absurdist dramas and dramas of multileveled reality will not remain outside the definition.

The Function of Environment

The most obvious use of environment is to place or illuminate the dramatic action. In setting the place and time of the play *realistically*, costumes and sets may try to re-create fully the

Figure 1-1. A costume sketch by Robert Edmond Jones for the 1945 production of *Lute Song.* From *The Theatre of Robert Edmond Jones* by Ralph Pendleton, Wesleyan University Press, Middletown, Conn., 1958, p. 137. Photograph courtesy of The Museum of Modern Art, New York.

places and times of the action, although not in as much detail as if actual properties and costumes were used. Costumes and setting may also be used to suggest the locality and period, as in a production on the Elizabethan stage. With a few simple scenic forms, a few properties, costumes of strong silhouette and not too much detail, the audience is made to feel the presence of a much larger and fuller action than is shown. The environment also may be used to *express* an idea through the presentation of distorted or abstract forms in which some inner vision of the playwright is projected with little or no reliance on forms in nature. Finally, there may be no specific environment except the space formed by stairs, platforms, and plain wall surfaces. These are very broad statements about the visual environment of a play and will be examined historically and conceptually in the second part of this book when we begin to discuss the great periods of the drama and the visual styles they engendered.

Aside from placing the action, a second function of the visual environment is to reinforce the action by reflecting the characters' personalities. A number of little touches about a room, a property or two, or an individual costume may tell the audience more about a character than does the dialogue. The visual environment may reinforce the action through the use of symbols—for example, in a Shakespearean historical play, red costumes and banners showing the Lion of England for the British forces and blue costumes and banners showing the gold Fleur de Lis for the French forces. The visual environment frequently sets the weather, time of day, or year. The geographical location of the action may be indicated by the texture and weight of clothing, the use of hats and outer wraps, or the inclusion of lamps and fireplaces in the setting, while the social and economic state of the characters may be shown by the quality and style of clothes, furniture, walls, and properties. Or more broadly still, the visual environment may reinforce the dramatic action through the creation of mood and atmosphere. Costumes and settings can become emotionally charged through

the subtle and careful use of color, line, and texture and can suggest loneliness, sadness, joy, fear, or laughter and thereby put the audience in the appropriate mood for the action of the play. In the last act of *Cyrano de Bergerac,* for example, the soft fall of leaves, the quiet movement of the darkly gowned and crisply hooded nuns, the light slowly fading through the trees together help the audience sense how the aging poet's life is finally drawing to a close. Such scenes attune the audience to the emotional mood of the action.

A third function of environment is to make a play visually attractive through an appealing use of line, texture, and color. The environment may be beautiful, ugly, harmonious, disruptive, or shocking, but it should not be flat, monotonous, dull, or boring. In addition to its functions in placing the action and reinforcing the play symbolically and atmospherically, the environment must be interesting as an abstract work of art created in time, one that achieves its effect during the two to three hours of action onstage. No matter how disconcerting the visual picture, nor how many levels of visual reality are used, an artistic design or plan behind the entire visual presentation must capture and hold the attention of the audience.

Elements of the Visual Scene

The four elements that comprise the visual scene or environment of a production in the modern theatre are scenery or stage space, properties or stage furniture and incidental objects, costumes and makeup, and lighting or illumination. Scenery gives the physical placement, background, and shape to the action, and sometimes the relation of the action to the audience viewing it. The properties have a strong dramatic value in that they are the objects that the actors handle, talk about, and on which they lie and sit; they frequently place the action without the aid of scenery, and they are part of the color and composition of the total scene. Costumes are the moving scenery of a production, and when worn by the actors, who are the center of all dramatic action, they are the strongest element of the visual scene; they project personality and individual emotion and obtain the strongest audience focus. Costumes usually are the most pronounced accents of color, line, and texture on stage. Lighting is the strongest element in unifying and composing the various visual effects through the manipulation of color, highlights, shadows, and focus. It is lighting that can most fully intensify the dramatic values in the total stage scene.

Three functions of the environment of a play's action are, as we stated earlier, to locate or place the play, to express its spirit or mood, and to make the play visually interesting. Regarding this last category, more should be said about the concept of the well-composed visual scene. In teaching design for the theatre, for many years great stress was placed on the fourfold concept of *unity, variety, balance,* and *harmony.* The *unity* of a well-composed scene meant that all of the parts—mass, line, color, texture in costumes, properties, scenery, and lighting—should appear to belong together. Achieving unity in a design depended on (1) selection of only those elements that could properly be related to one another to gain the specific environment required; (2) arrangement of the chosen elements into a plan that emphasized those features or motifs most clearly expressing the environment; and (3) maintenance of a single style throughout the entire design. A unified scene was said to be a scene with a sharp focus on central details. *Variety* was thought of as a subcategory; a unified scene always avoided monotony by means of successful contrasts. The design should be alive and interesting, but still subordinate to the dominant motif or mood of the production. *Balance* was also thought of as being integral to the unified or well-composed scene. Each costume, each piece of scenery, each property, and the stage as a whole was designed to weigh certain elements of mass, color, line, or texture against other elements so that a certain equilibrium was established. Finally, the well-composed scene was said to have a *harmony* in

which all of the different elements combined together to make an attractive whole, the result achieved through skilled application of the principles of unity, variety, and balance to the work of scene composition.

In recent years, however, many plays have deliberately distorted or violated these principles and often seemed to give the designer license to place anything on the stage without regard for principles of composition. But no matter how confused, distorted, or disunified a work may seem, a plan underlies its construction, even if the audience has difficulty discovering it. The plan must be found and expressed by the designer; for once he has the unifying thread running through the work, he will be able to use a variety that may seem to verge on violent and excessive contrast, a balance that may seem to be all imbalance, and a harmony that may appear to be shockingly inharmonious; but the final impression, though not creating "an attractive whole," will have a unity of opposites, contrasts, and confusions—a logic underlying what at first may have seemed incomprehensible or meaningless. In Jean Gênet's *The Blacks,* the audience sees the action of the play as if in a set of reflecting mirrors, each distorting the image previously reflected. Each image may for a moment be mistaken for reality; but upon examination it always proves to be an illusion. Truth, or the beginning of the set of reflections, can never be found. The characters assume roles, but when the disguises are removed, the true persons are never discovered; each appearance is only a new disguise. But two or three unifying threads weave through the play: the concept of life as a series of reflecting mirrors or disguises; the idea of what would happen in Western imagery if white became black and black, white; the contrast between a black, African civilization and a white, Western one. A play such as *The Blacks* demands as much care in arrangement of artistic elements as does a more conventional and outwardly logical play. By concentrating on two or three unifying images, the designer can create unity—the unity of the absurd and irrational.

Requirements of the Visual Scene

In addition to the aesthetic problems of unity, variety, balance, and harmony, a number of physical requirements should be a part of the well-conceived visual scene or environment. The visual scene should be clear—designed to be seen and understood at a distance. Most of the audience may be anywhere from twenty to seventy-five feet away from the action, so all parts of the scene must be simplified and exaggerated. Indeed, the motto "Simplify and exaggerate" is used in most classes in costume and scene design; it is the basic concept behind turning source material into stageworthy costumes or scenery. One is always leaving out details from the painting or print used as a source while strengthening and exaggerating certain lines and motifs for the finished stage costume. Simplicity does not mean bareness or meagerness. It means the use of essentials, those elements that contribute to the main idea of the costume's design. In this way, the design becomes uncomplicated in the best sense and can easily be grasped by the spectator.

Another important physical requirement in the visual scene is that sets, costumes, and properties must be designed to be used efficiently and effectively by the actors. They must be safe enough and strong enough to weather the problems that arise in dress rehearsals, in the course of the play's action, and throughout the run of the production. Scenery, costumes, and properties must be practical. They must be clearly and easily translatable from sketch to final form, must fit within the budget limits of the production, must be capable of being constructed within the required time limitation, must satisfy the demands of costume changes or scene shifts, must be practical for the size of the stage, and must be able to be packed and shipped easily if the production is to travel. In short, the designs for sets, costumes, and properties must be the work of an efficient craftsman's mind as well as of an artist's imagination.

Finally, the visual scene must be part of the organic whole that is the entire production.

The designers of sets, of costumes, and of properties must not try to occupy first place in the audience's attention. They must not be swept away by the picturesque nature or decorative aspect of their work; they must not lose sight of the living, human element that is the actor, the dancer, or the singer. The visual scene must never be thought of alone, but only in conjunction with the directorial lines of the dramatic action. In the organic design of any theatrical presentation, the visual scene is the servant rather than the master of "man in action."

Costume as Part of the Visual Scene

Now that we have looked in a general way at the total visual scene or environment and discussed briefly how it functions in relation to the dramatic action of a play, we can introduce a specific discussion of costume design as one of the key elements in the formation of the total visual scene. The concept of costumes as moving scenery has already been mentioned. What does costume include and what does it do for the actor?

Costumes include all the body garments worn by actors, all the accessories they carry as part of their characters, all the items related to hairdressing, and everything associated with face and body makeup, including masks if they substitute for facial makeup. Costumes tell us many things about the characters played by the actors and about the nature of the play in which they appear. The list of things costumes can tell us about characters and the play is lengthy.

Costumes can provide identification of the period in which the play occurs. If a play is placed in a period other than that envisioned by the playwright, the costumes become more important than usual in bringing out new themes and ideas that have been sought by the director in consultation with the designer.

Costumes can establish the locale of a production, that is, whether it is set in the city, the country, a particular nation, or in the north, south, east, or west of a particular continent or country.

Costumes can point up the time of day and thereby clarify the nature of the occasion taking place, such as an informal morning at home, a dinner party, a midnight rendezvous.

Costumes can establish the social class and economic stature of the characters by distinguishing between rich and poor, aristocrats and peasants, those on the way up and those on the way down.

Costumes frequently establish occupation, especially when a type of uniform is used to indicate that a character is a maid, a mail carrier, a police officer, or a soldier.

Costumes can establish the ages of the characters, since certain garments are appropriate only to the aged, others only to the young. Costumes can indicate that characters are trying to appear older or younger than they are.

Costumes help to clarify character relationships; they can tie together members of a family, group, faction, or party through identifying elements of ornament, line, and color. Sympathetic and antagonistic relationships can be shown through similarities and contrasts in costume elements. Changes in costume can indicate alteration in the relationships among characters or in the psychological outlook of a character.

Costumes can point out the importance of the various characters through emphasis and subordination—for instance, the use of strong colors against weaker ones or the placement of a solid black costume in the midst of color.

The items above give us information about the characters and the play. But, more important, as a visual art, costume design can express intangible ideas that can strengthen the visual mood, style, and theme of the play. Costume design functions on two levels: the aesthetic or formal level, as pure art; and the associative or symbolic level, where it suggests by stimulating an audience's visual experience and sense of association.

On the aesthetic or formal level, the costume designer organizes and composes various media to appeal to the eye of the audience. The designer exploits the sensuous values of material and textural surfaces and their ability to reflect light; develops the formal relationships among colors, lines, and shapes; and works with fabric, ornament, color, and line to develop a costume or a group of costumes that create an interesting visual picture—a combination of line, texture, and color that will attract and hold the attention of the audience. Even if the desire is to shock the audience's visual sensibilities, the artist always works for just the right aesthetic balance to obtain the audience reaction the artist and the director desire.

But one cannot design on the aesthetic level alone. There is also the associative or symbolic level. Any visual experience will play in some manner on the audience's associations—a given set of shapes, colors, textures, and lines will evoke certain symbolic meanings. Jean Gênet probes this fascinating area in *The Blacks* when he tries to suggest through varying images the shock to Western sensitivity that takes place when one poses such reversals as virginity as black, devils as white, evil as white, and purity as black. The visual connotations or associations in the symbolic meaning of white and black or any other color have been ingrained in Western culture for so many centuries that any designer who deliberately defies them will be in grave trouble, and must expect to disturb the audience. In any visual experience there are, of course, two levels of association; the primary level sets certain shapes, colors, and textures as having more or less the same meaning for everyone in Western culture, and the secondary pertains to the background and experience of each member of the audience. Designers cannot design for individual association, but, unless they wish their work to be clichéd, they would be advised not to follow every cue leading to the stock associative responses of our culture; for example, red for the fallen woman, white for purity, the gray flannel suit for the businessman. Designers should learn to balance primary associative values with secondary ones from their own imaginative experience. This associative or symbolic level is a very difficult one for the teacher and the student of costume design, since it is easier to talk about formal and aesthetic values than about the personal, shifting nature of associative values. As society changes, these also change. But it is through associations and their symbolic use that the most exciting and the most deeply felt audience reactions are achieved. In a production of Ibsen's *Ghosts,* a designer, through a dusty, darkened palette and controlled use of braid and lace, can awaken in a middle-aged audience childhood memories of Victorian clothes and furniture seen in the photographs and interiors of a grandparent's home.

On the intangible and expressive level then, costumes can establish the overall mood of a play or the atmosphere of a scene. They can express a play's style; much more will be said of this in chapters to follow. But even at this point, it can be readily seen that the costumes

for an Ibsen drama such as *Ghosts* demand a closer fidelity to real-life garments than do the costumes for *The Tempest* (Figures 1–2 and 1–3). It can certainly be said that the costumes should always reflect the level of reality embodied in the script.

Finally, we can also say that the structure of a play should be subtly revealed through costume, so that the rise to climax and the fall from it to denouement are paralleled in dress. If the same costumes are worn throughout, they must sustain interest over a long period of time and be as effective in a certain combination at the climax of a play as they were in a different combination at its beginning.

Costumes can and do bear a great weight of fact and suggested meaning to an audience. It takes an accomplished and experienced costume designer to meet fully the demands of a complex production.

Figure 1–2. A scene from *Ghosts* by Henrik Ibsen as produced by the American Conservatory Theatre, San Francisco, 1980. Directed By Allen Fletcher, scenery by Ralph Funicello, costumes by Martha Burke. Photo courtesy of the American Conservatory Theatre. Photo by Ron Scherl.

Figure 1–3. The final scene from Shakespeare's *The Tempest* as produced at the Memorial Theatre, Stratford-upon-Avon, England, in 1951. Courtesy of the Harvard Theatre Collection. Photo by Angus McBean.

The Meaning of Costume for the Designer, the Actor, and the Director

Now that we have discussed the meanings and suggested effects resulting from well-designed costumes, let us consider the meaning of costume design for the various artists most closely involved with it. Do the scene and costume designers, the director, and the actor think of costume in the same way? Is each aware of all the meanings we mentioned when he or she thinks about the designs for a play or for a character? The answer is obviously no. Each artist thinks of costume subjectively, as a means of artistic expression, rather than as an artistic effect on the audience.

The designer, whether in charge of the whole visual scene or of the costumes alone, wishes to see a certain emotion or mood made manifest in fabric of a certain shape and color on an actor moving in and out of light on a stage. Sometimes the aim of the designer is to astonish and excite an audience by exaggeration and distortion of the actor's body; at other times, the aim is to beautify and enhance the human form. The designer may wish to hide an actor in a visual character creation that is so unlike the actor's real self that the individual will seem transformed, or may wish to find the actor's best points, the qualities of personality, form, and movement unique to that actor and to design all the actor's costumes, no matter what the character, subordinate to that personal image. There are times when the designer is not interested in actors at all but only in the creation of rich, sensuous effects in movement on a stage; while at other times he or she is interested only in textural and draped effects as they are actuated by light. All costume designers recognize in themselves these urges to expression. Because of their own personalities and experience, they find certain spurs to expression stronger than others, and many work in only one or two of these directions. In fact, a designer flexible enough to work in all directions may become too facile and eclectic, while a designer who concentrates on expressing himself in one or two modes may develop greater depth and artistry.

For the actor, the costume is at the same time a mask for his or her everyday character and personality and a release into the world of the play and the character being portrayed. Some actors subordinate the characters they play to their own strong personalities; such actors want their costumes always to express both the personality of the character and their own stage personality. Some actors subordinate their own personalities to their roles; for them, each costume for each role is very different, a mask that conceals the player behind the character. But actors will always want their costumes (even if uncomfortable and unfamiliar at fittings and first dress rehearsal) to become part of them and their roles. Ideally, the actor and the designer can share a vision of a character and its relation to the play and work cooperatively toward a common goal. However, friction may arise if the designer has some mood vision of the particular costume in the visual scheme and the actor can see only that the costume seems uncomfortable and wrong for his or her interpretation of the character. The actor feels unable to perform in such a costume, unable to relax fully into the role, while the designer feels that to fulfill the actor's idea the overall visual view of the play will have to be sacrificed. At this point, the more objective view of the director must effect a compromise.

In what way does costume act as a form of expression for the director? Ideally, it combines both the actor's and the designer's ideas in a broader, more objective view of the visual scene. If the director is a *régisseur,* all the visual ideas emanate from his or her overall view of the production, and the designer refines and embodies these ideas in the finished costumes. However, there have been many instances in the history of the theatre when an actor became the manager of production and supervised design of all the costumes to suit his or her taste as a star; conversely, there have been other cases, like that of the early twentieth-century design theorist, Gordon Craig, when all phases of the production were in the hands of the designer, and actors were but visual puppets in the hands of a great master. The ideal director should have as much knowledge of the visual arts of the theatre as of the art of acting, but should remain on a plane above both, working with actor and designer to release them artistically and to translate their ideas into concrete form. The most successful productions are those in which actors, director, and designer collaborate—when only a directorial outline of a role or a visual idea is given to actors and designer, when each brings to the director ideas that they mutually explore, and when the final effect can truly be said to be the creation of all the artists involved in the production.

The Meaning of Costume as Personal Expression

Unless the actor and designer communicate, there is danger that the actor will think of costume only as a means of expressing the character, while the designer will see it only as one part of the visual expression of the play. Although the director must keep the balance, all three need to understand the function of clothing in society, the way in which costume expresses people's ideas of themselves. Only then can the actor, the director, and the costume designer translate clothing into theatrical costume.

Since people first painted themselves and wore primitive adornments, clothing has been one of their best means of self-expression. Clothing is also one of the clearest ways in which people can show their relationship to their society. The two most obvious poles of expression in a society are *conformity* and *rebellion,* and clothes speak more clearly about them than any other social custom. If a person wishes to seem securely a part of the culture, for each social occasion he or she will choose only the dress prescribed by the leaders of society. Conformity gives security and relieves a person from thinking about why he or she chooses certain clothes for certain occasions. If a person wishes to establish a personality independent from the social ideals of the surrounding culture, he or she will choose dress that is opposed to that enjoined by the culture. Sometimes rebellious dress remains on the fringes of a culture; at other times it modifies the styles of a culture or overthrows them in favor of a modified form of the original fashion. T-shirts, tight trousers, uncontrolled hair, and boots are often seen as symbols of rebellion against the business suit and the afternoon dress. Such dress speaks loudly for a simpler, more natural way of life, and it attempts to brand the business suit and the afternoon dress as the uniforms of social robots trapped in a machine-made society.

We have talked about a deliberate rebellion against society in one's choice of clothing; but there is also the person who wishes to be comfortable at any cost, even if he or she appears unconventional. Or there is the person who may look ridiculous because he or she is preoccupied with work and completely unconscious of dress. Or there is the person who is genuinely careless in dress, who does not look well groomed by society's standards because of slovenly personal habits. A variation on these latter two is the person who is indifferent to clothing and its meaning in society. Still another type is the self-effacing person who dresses in a nondescript, anonymous way; clothes for this person are a means of hiding. Then there is the person who moves in the face of conformity to become a style innovator. And so it goes into ever more subtle breaks with or

interpretations of the accepted fashions of the day. It is a fascinating study, this picture of people's relationship to their society as expressed by clothing.

There are other basic dress instincts in humans, and one of the most important for the theatre is the instinct to *dress up,* to don rich fancy dress garments for special occasions. We have gowns for the opera ball, uniforms for lodge groups, special costumes for weddings, inaugurations, and funerals. We are excited and satisfied by observing the rich ecclesiastical robes in church ceremonies, the brilliant uniforms of a coronation, or the rich costumes of opera, ballet, and the theatre.

Another basic instinct, perhaps the most basic following the use of clothing as protection against the elements, is dress used to enhance a certain *sexual ideal* of manhood or womanhood. The history of feminine dress in particular can be read as an ever-changing game of revealing and concealing certain portions of the body. There are periods when the arm is bare, others when it is completely concealed; periods when the decolletage is so low that it creates the imminent danger of an accidental overexposure; others when not even the neck is left uncovered. In some periods, bare arms and decolletage for evening wear alternate with complete covering for day wear, as in the late nineteenth century. In some eras it is shocking to uncover the ankle, while at other times the legs are revealed above the knee. The changing image and sexual ideal of manhood is more related to silhouette or figure outline than to revealing or concealing parts of the body. One can contrast those periods that use the decorated codpiece with other periods when all trace of the sex organs is hidden. The male image shifts from padded shoulders or balloon sleeves to tight-fitting torso coverings, from loose garments to tight ones, from grotesque exaggerations of key parts of the body to a stress on the natural.

Personal expression through dress may appear in the way individuals use clothes to clarify their relations to others in a particular *social situation.* Choice of a business suit, riding habit, tuxedo, sport shirt, slacks, or swimsuit are ways in which people place themselves clearly in a particular social situation. People set their social level and the social occasion by how they select their wardrobes and how their garments correspond to the other garments at a particular function.

Closely related to social expression is society's use of uniforms and vestments to express a person's authority, position, and expected duties. Such clothing may also appeal to our sense of fancy dress, but in its basic form it gives station and identity. We know what to demand and expect of a person dressed as a nurse or a police officer, of a youth garbed as a choirboy.

The director, actor, and designer must understand dress as an expression of human personality, identity, and position before stage costumes can be created that are both aesthetically and psychologically appropriate to a play and its characters.

The Structure of Costume as Personal Expression

We have discussed how costume is more than mere body covering; the way it is made and the shape it takes are the psychological and aesthetic results of the individual's interaction with society. The designer, the director, and the actor must have some idea of how and why costume structure has changed through the centuries, even if the designer alone has full knowledge of the intricacies of costume history.

From the beginning of human history, when skins or leaves were used as a protection against the elements and for adornment, people had choices about how they would dress. If the skins or leaves were wrapped tightly around the body, they were used primarily for protection; if they were hung or draped from the body, the intention was more adornment, prestige, and display. For example, if a full animal skin is wrapped tightly about the human form it merely warms the figure, but if

the head is placed on the human head, the skin of the forelegs hangs over the arms, and the hind legs and tail fall behind, then a grand image of control over the animal world is created as well as a suggested fusion of the power of man and beast. From this difference come two widely used costume structures that are still the basis for much costume design: the wraparound effect and the hanging or draped effect. These two structural forms, of course, took on new significance when the art of weaving developed in the Neolithic or New Stone Age, for many more variations are possible in wrapping or draping woven fabric. It is also in the Neolithic period that humans invented the third basic structural form in dress, cutting fabric to fit the form of the body and sewing, pinning, or belting it into place. If one contemplates these three primitive structural forms, one realizes that with the addition of the distorted, artificial silhouette, all costume since has been a refinement of these four structural methods.

In pre-Greek times, most garments were either of the wraparound or hung variety, although Near Eastern dress showed a tendency toward the cut-to-fit. Then, if one follows through from Greek to late medieval times, one sees the gradual change from the fully draped line of the fifth century B.C. to the more fitted costume of the fifteenth century. In the sixteenth century a rigid and distorted human silhouette was added to Western dress, and since that time there have been recurring cycles that have moved from a soft, indistinct, draped silhouette to a rigid, fitted, and even distorted costume line. Since the Renaissance there has been a much greater reaching back to the past for costume effects than in previous centuries. Looking at the history of costume, one can see four general structural types that have continued in the later history of dress: *the draped costume, the semifitted costume, the fitted costume,* and *the artificial or distorted costume.*

The draped costume stresses a maximum amount of free movement of the human body under the draped fabric and a minimum amount of sewing and pinning. Draped dress

Figure 1-4. Example of a costume structure based on draping. Statue of L'Arringatore, first century B.C. Archaeological Museum, Florence. Photo courtesy of Alinari/Art Resource, Inc.

is dependent on the supple grace and movement of the wearer, and is usually stressed in periods such as the Greek, where there is openness, belief in natural movement, and admiration of the human body (Figure 1-4).

The semifitted costume applies to most T-shaped tunics and gowns, kimonos and pajamas, and loose shirts and trouser combinations of all kinds. It is basic to the Romanesque and early medieval period, most oriental dress, costumes for *commedia* clowns, and most modern men's clothes. It is often a transition from a draped to a fitted costume period or structural relaxation from a heavily artificial and distorted costume period (Figure 1-5).

The fitted costume strives to clothe the figure in a smooth-fitting outer skin of interesting texture that both limits body movement and reflects its strain in the pull and stretch of the fabric surface. This least frequent of all costume structures is often coupled with elements of the artificial or the semifitted structural approach. Again, an ideal form is demanded beneath the tight-fitting skin of fabric. The fitted costume is difficult to cut and fit correctly. In our own day, the fitted costume appears in tight-fitting trousers and knitted blouses, and it was boldly used in the fourteenth-century tight-fitting cotehardie (Figure 1-6).

Figure 1–5. Example of a costume structure of the semifitted variety. A gentleman's spring costume for 1823. From Max von Boehn's *Menschen und Moden im 19 Jahrhundert,* Bruckman, Munich, 1905.

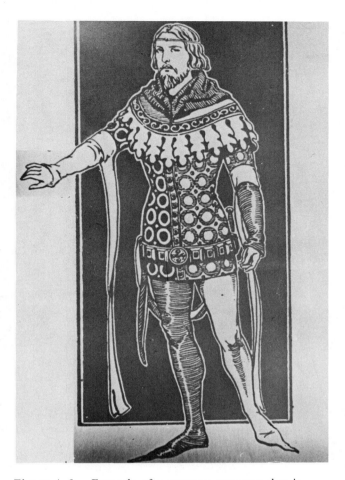

Figure 1–6. Example of a costume structure that is form-fitted. A cotehardie from the middle of the fourteenth century. Drawing by Herbert Norris from *Costume and Fashion* by Herbert Norris, E. P. Dutton, New York, 1927, Vol. II, p. 220. Courtesy of J. M. Dent & Sons Ltd., London.

Finally, there is the *artificial or distorted structural costume.* Fabric is forced to fit an arbitrary shape created by padding and boning the human figure, and the silhouette produced is unlike the form of the human body. The costume of the late sixteenth century is the most obvious example of the artificial approach, but it can also be seen in the bustles of the late nineteenth century and the grotesque wigs of the late seventeenth century (Figure 1–7).

In general, one can say that any of the four structural types are related to the general view of the human body and nature in a particular society. If the society is not too rigid, the body accepted, and nature admired, then fabrics will be used for their sensuous value. Costume structure will usually be of the semifitted or draped variety. If unrest, repression, and inhibition prevail and the normal human form is not admired, costume structure will cover and distort the human figure.

Figure 1–7. Example of a costume structure that is completely artificial. A portrait of Queen Elizabeth from an engraving of 1589 by William Rogers in the British Museum. Photo reproduced by courtesy of the Trustees of the British Museum.

Stage costume falls into the artificial structural category more often than civil dress because it must exaggerate for effect and must be built on a solid foundation; folds, puffed effects, and draped lines must stay in place through the performance. But the theatre artists involved in stage costume must understand the various psychological and social reasons for the structural methods used throughout costume history before they move to the artificial methods of the theatre workshop.

Historic Use of Costume in the Theatre

We have now seen how costume functions as part of the visual scene, as a means of expression for the director, actor, and designer, as a statement about an individual in relation to society, and as a structure in fabric that reveals much about people's view of themselves. Let us now turn our attention to what costume tells us about society's view of the theatre.

We have already noted how a costume designer can treat the formal and sensuous values of his or her work as abstractions to be presented in a purely visual manner. We have also talked of the symbolic or associative values of costume; a designer can suggest all manner of moods, ideas, and feelings by playing on the audience's primary and secondary associations. In the history of stage costume, the pendulum swings from costumes that are symbolic to those that are close to civil dress, from costumes that suggest cultural and religious ideals to costumes that express personality and social position.

In Greek plays, heroes and gods represented idealized humankind, while comic figures and humanized birds and animals represented the unregenerate aspects of human nature. The masks, enlarged costumes, and symbolic ornaments used were

Figure 1-8. Statue of Melpomene, Muse of Tragedy, from the Vatican Museum, Rome. Photo courtesy of Alinari/Art Resource, Inc.

more than extensions or enlargements of civil dress; all were based on traditions inherited from archaic times (Figure 1-8).

Roman stage costume borrowed from the Greek, although there was more stress on realistic or melodramatic touches in masks, wigs, and garments, as there was in Roman plays and art. Medieval stage costume was a marvelous mixture of the real and the symbolic—at one moment saying something obvious about the psychological and sociological position of a character and the next commenting symbolically on the character's religious significance. The dualism apparent in all the visual aspects of medieval theatre, and, of course, in medieval art, is nowhere more obvious than in the costumes of the mystery, miracle, and morality plays.

In the Renaissance theatre, costume came much closer to civil dress, overlaid with accessories and ornamentation that still acted symbolically to lift a character or a scene above an ordinary psychological or sociological situation (Figure 1-9). In the Elizabethan theatre, the audience was willing to accept an actor as a king of France, a Roman leader, or a Moorish general if he wore a few symbolic or exotic accessories on his rich contemporary dress (Figure 1-10). In the eighteenth century, cos-

Figure 1-9. A pageant costume from the original drawing by Leonardo da Vinci at Windsor Castle. Copyright reserved. Reproduced by gracious permission of Her Majesty Queen Elizabeth II.

Figure 1-10. An original drawing for a theatrical costume by Henri Gissey. Crown Copyright Victoria and Albert Museum (Theatre Museum), London.

tume was still rich and decorative, with symbols of position, nationality, and historic period added to fancy dress (Figure 1-11).

At the end of the eighteenth century and the beginning of the nineteenth, a new, scientific view of history developed, and for the first time in the history of the theatre, historical accuracy appeared in stage dress (Figure 1-12). But historical accuracy limited the designer, director, and actor. With the new stagecraft of the late nineteenth and early twentieth centuries, stage costume once again became aesthetic and picturesque as well as unified, simplified, and controlled.

Figure 1-11. Mrs. Baddely as Joan la Pucelle in Shakespeare's *Henry VI,* Part 2. From Bell's Edition of Shakespeare's Plays, 1776.

Figure 1–12. An original sketch by James Robinson Planché of Leopold of Austria for a production of Shakespeare's *King John,* 1823. Courtesy of the Stark Collection, University of Texas Library, Austin.

Costume Design as a Profession

The new stagecraft brought designers to one of the strongest positions they had ever held in the history of the theatre. In the past, the actor, director, or person in charge of stage wardrobe was responsible for costume. Rarely did the set and costume designer control all the visual aspects of a production. In the Renaissance, the great painters designed *intermezzi;* in the seventeenth century, Inigo Jones designed masques; and in the Baroque period, Jean Berain designed *divertissements,* and all gave a certain unified personal vision to their productions. But only in the last seventy-five years has a person trained in the visual arts and the theatre had control of the visual presentation of a production.

Today there are various opportunities for work in the field of stage costume. In Europe, Latin America, Canada, and the United States, the field of professional costume design includes films, fashions, legitimate theatre, opera, extravaganza, and dance, and is usually controlled by labor union practice. In Europe and Latin America, there is a much less rigid pattern than in the United States, but the person who makes a living as a professional is usually a member of an organization, if not a union, that sets standards, wages, and hours and usually provides some form of benefits. Sometimes the costume designer merely pays a fee to join the organization, sometimes he or she is invited to join or is elected to membership, and sometimes an examination must be passed in order to become a member.

Probably the most lucrative area for the costume designer today is in films. In large-scale film epics, a costume designer assisted by an army of specialists may design a thousand costumes or more and control the costume effects on movie sets that cover acres. Costume design on this scale becomes an industry, and there are many people involved in research, sketching, choosing fabric, cutting, fitting, sewing, and accessory making. The work is carefully controlled by a union that oversees the settings, costume design, and art direction, and the fees paid to the designer as well as funds available for costuming a production are handsome.

Fashion design is only indirectly related to costume for the theatre, but it is one of the most publicized aspects of our present culture. In the great urban centers, fashion designers who have been apprenticed to great fashion houses or designers develop a line of clothes each season to fit all social occasions. These styles are meant to attract the attention of society's fashion leaders through a combination of shocking, eye-catching, or strikingly different ideas. It is a multimillion dollar business, and if a particular line attracts widespread attention and filters down to the mass buying public in adapted form, the design house sponsoring the line may have tremendous control over the fashion industry and the visual aspects of our culture. Only when a play requires high fashion does fashion design come close to costume design, and even then the high-style garments must be designed to be viewed at a distance rather than in the close proximity of a drawing room. Few designers have achieved a reputation in both the fields of stage costume design and high fashion.

The major area that captures attention in costume design is the legitimate theatre and opera, and although this is a rather limited profession, in many ways it offers more challenge to the talented costume designer than other fields. In Europe and Latin America, costume designers belong to loosely organized groups that only occasionally approximate our design unions, but in the United States, most stage work is controlled by the United Scenic Artists of America, Local 829 of the Painters and Decorators Union of the American Federation of Labor. Two other unions, Locals 350 and 816 in Chicago and Los Angeles, respectively, work closely with the parent organization in New York (and at this writing 350 in Chicago is in the process of merging with 829 in New York). The United Scenic Artists is divided into several divisions: there are the full scenic designers who design sets, costumes, and lighting, and there are costume associates, lighting associates, mural artists, and display associates who work only in those areas. Membership in the union is limited, and a thorough examination must be passed for admittance. Entrance fees and dues are fairly high, but the union does excellent work in gaining benefits and fees for the designer and in seeing that employers do not default on payments. In the professional theatre, many costume designers who belong to the union work as resident designers for a theatre company or a television network; others work as assistants to major designers and as off-Broadway costume designers, while a top few are employed designing the individual plays that make up the New York theatre and opera season and national touring companies. Many of these designers do work in other fields or have incomes from other sources; however, with the increasing number of resident professional companies, there is more opportunity for the costume designer in legitimate drama today than in the past.

Another design area is extravaganza. Although the challenge may be more limited, the richly decorative aspect of extravaganza appeals to many designers. Ice shows, circuses, night clubs, and dance revues demand costumes that emphasize purely decorative effects. Such costumes use strong color, brilliant ornamentation, and such light-reflecting surfaces as sequins, beads, and metallic fabrics. Extravaganza is a well-paid professional area that demands of the designer a minimum of subtlety and a maximum of surface effect.

In the related area of dance, there are a number of established ballet companies and a smaller number of dance troupes that need a costume designer; and although the opportunities are limited, the challenge to the designer interested in ballet and dance problems is exciting. The costume problems of the dancer are complex and very different from those of the actor or the entertainer, and the costume designer who can solve them brilliantly is always in demand.

Connected to the design field is the costume-servicing profession. This includes the great costume houses, the costume workshops for large theatres, and all the persons who work at wardrobe maintenance in theatres around the world. Most of the costume-servicing profession is also unionized, and its union is usually affiliated with the seamstresses of the garment industry. In the large costume houses and the costume shops for large theatres, the personnel include cutters, fitters, designers and makers of accessories, milliners, makers of footwear, dyers, and finishers, as well as the people employed to maintain the wardrobe, handle its movement in and out of the shops, and handle its rental after its original use in production. The same operation on a larger scale occurs in the film industry. This field, usually known as wardrobe, appeals to those people who do not wish to design, but who are fascinated by costumes of all kinds and usually have a craft or skill that can be used to excellent advantage in building or maintaining a wardrobe.

There are a number of opportunities in education for those interested in costume design. In the large universities and professional schools with a school of fine arts, the theatre department usually gives training in costume design, and has a designer-teacher to supervise the work and teach the courses, a small core of professional wardrobe personnel, and well-equipped shops. Each season the department usually presents a number of productions that make use of student talent, and it often helps place the graduating student in a beginning professional position. In departments of drama that are part of a liberal arts college or a small university, stress is on teacher training and there is less orientation toward the profession. Positions open after graduation are usually in other university and college drama departments. In small colleges and high schools with no emphasis on theatre, there is usually a production course that includes material on costume for the stage, or there may be a strong extracurricular drama society that gives training and experience in the arts of production.

Finally, there are the community theatres and many amateur groups around the country where much practice and training in costume for the stage is available, usually without cost but also without pay. Sometimes a large community theatre with city support will hire the services of a full-time person in costume; at other times a person may be hired to design and supervise a particular production. Although the quality of design work varies greatly in community theatre as it does in schools and universities, at its best it may reach a near-professional level. Opportunities here are usually for the person with some training who has not followed costume design as a career. Housewives and people in business who may have done costume work in college are often called upon to give their time and talent to community theatre productions.

2

Planning and Presentation
of the Costume Sketch

Reading the Script

The first order of business for the costume designer, as for the other artists collaborating on a production, is reading the script. For an opera or a musical, the designer may listen to the music before reading the libretto; for a ballet, he or she may see part of the choreography before reading the story outline. The script may be a full play or it may be an outline of music and movement in a dance presentation, an ice show scene, or a circus sequence. If there is no dialogue or story line, the designer must look for other clues to suggest a costume scheme. Perhaps music or a historical theme will indicate the mood. If the script leaves matters open, the designer must bring a sense of the occasion and the theatrical effect required to the visual solution of the problem. When the designer creates a visual sequence in a musical or dance presentation, he or she is limited only by a choreographer's or director's ideas and by the patterns of motion and gesture that have

been developed for the sequence. But most often there is something to read besides an outline of music and movement, and it is usually from this first reading that many of the designer's deepest visual reactions to the play are developed.

During the first reading of the script there should be no thought of costume changes, problems of period, or methods of construction. The designer should absorb as much as possible of the author's story, mood, characterization, imagery, and pictorial intent before addressing the challenge of design. The designer may wish to make notations about the play's progression or rhythmic development, the underlying pattern, the prevailing atmosphere, the nature of the verbal imagery and how it suggests visual effects, and especially the level of reality in the script. This last is a delicate problem, since the designer's response to the level of reality may be quite different from that of the various members of the audience. As we shall see in Part II, the visual style

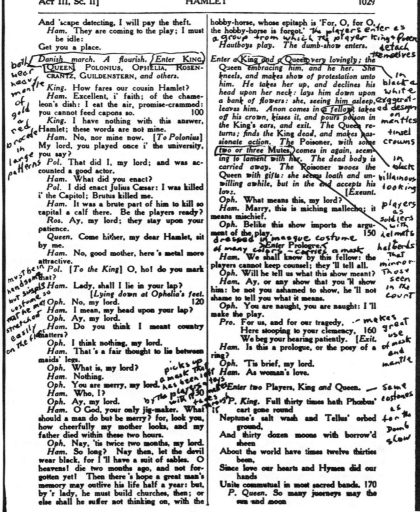

Figure 2-1. Costume notations in a playscript. A page from Shakespeare's *Hamlet* as printed in the Globe Edition by William Clark and William Wright, 1864.

in a production depends on an understanding of the plot, character, thought, language, rhythm, and spectacle in the script. Only after analyzing the entire play should the costume designer continue with a closer appraisal of its costume demands.

During the second reading of the script the designer will read specifically for costume data. First, there are the factual questions: Where and under what circumstances will the play be performed? How much time has the designer for design and execution? How large is the theatre? What is the distance from the stage to the first row of seats? How many people will the house hold? What backstage facilities are available? What is the nature of the audience? How long with the play run? At what time of year will the production take place? If the play is to tour, perhaps many of these questions cannot be answered. It may only be after conferences with the producer and director that the designer will know the date and the theatre for the opening.

Second, the costume designer will want to know if any casting has taken place or if the production is being built around a particular star. Ideally, all casting should be completed before the designer begins work, but it seldom is; often he must do his preliminary planning without knowing full casting. If some actors have been cast, the designer should meet them, understand their methods and personalities, and try to envision them in their parts during the second reading. If the designer knows none of the actors cast, he or she may read with certain people or types in mind, but this is frequently dangerous until after a first conference with the director.

Third, the designer should mark anything in the script that pertains to costume. He or she should make notes on the geographical location, the historical period, and the time of day and year for the play and for each scene, and should list any indication of a costume item or accessory and any costume description or image in the dialogue. Any action that would affect the construction or wear of a costume should be written down, and all possible changes of a full costume or parts of a costume should be clearly charted. Also, the time needed and time available for such changes should be estimated (Figure 2–1).

Finally, before attending conferences, the designer should make a rough estimate of the number of costume changes, the number of costumes, and the costs involved, assuming that he or she has some idea where the costumes will be constructed and where and under what circumstances the buying will be done.

Conferences

Obviously, much of the preliminary planning during the second reading of the script may be drastically revised or nullified by subsequent conferences with the producer, the director, the set designer, the lighting designer, and sometimes the playwright, but it is still wise to come to the first conference with a full understanding of the play and its costume problems and with an estimate of cost and numbers. At the first conference, the director should set forth as clearly as possible his or her interpretation of the play. The costume designer must listen carefully to determine whether the director is visually oriented or not. If the answer is yes, there may be a fruitful collaboration on the designs for the production; if not, the director will prefer to wait to see the sketches and will then accept or reject them. There must also be a preliminary understanding among the other visual artists about the general direction in which each will work, although there is seldom immediate agreement about all the visual matters discussed, and seldom does one meeting serve to elucidate everyone's ideas of the production's aims. Sometimes the costume designer makes almost no contribution to the discussion, or may have an approach that in no way agrees with that of the author or the director. Sometimes the playwright and the director cannot develop a common interpretation of the script. Sometimes the principal actors desired by the producer or the playwright do not envision the characters as the director does. Many times misunderstandings or breakdowns in communication at the conferences can ruin the unity of effect in the final product. And there are times when disagreements or failures to reach mutual understanding result in the cancellation of contracts or even of the production. The importance of communication at the start cannot be stressed too strongly. Many a disaster is due to a failure of a group of theatre artists to reach a candid interchange of views before the production opens. Prominent and experienced theatre artists must not ignore what they know to be basic differences of opinion merely for appearance's sake, or as the work progresses, each person will set out to achieve a separate end at the expense of the artistic production.

True, it is difficult for the various workers to reach an understanding: Each is a specialist in his field; every production is in many respects unprecedented; and there are often as many opinions, theories, experiences, and schools of thought as there are theatre artists. But misunderstanding and vagueness must be eliminated as completely as is humanly possible from the proceedings. For example, in later conferences with the director, the costume designer must have certain key visual sources to show, rather than merely verbal descriptions. The designer must do thumbnail sketches or small figure layouts for the director to see, and must urge the director to articulate his or her reactions to each item. The costume designer must learn to watch the director's face to see if he or she is really reading the sketch as a costume or is merely viewing it as an illustration, and the designer must never leave a conference feeling a lack of clear contact with the director.

At the first conference, the costume designer will want to know the budget available, the amount of time available for design and construction, the final acting version of the script, and the director's changes, special interpretations, or specific requests.

At later meetings, the costume designer should have ready all the sketches, color plates, costume charts, accessory lists, and fabric swatches to make the visual concept as clear as possible to the director. Unless the costume designer is specific, the director may discover at dress rehearsal that many elements do not operate as envisioned. This may still occur, but one should try to avoid it. Last-minute changes are costly and sometimes impossible.

After all sketches and plans have been approved, the designers and technicians move on to building the production while the director turns full time to rehearsals, and although there may be further conferences at regular or irregular intervals, the work of the designers and the director and actors progresses more or less independently until the first technical and dress rehearsals.

Research

We have said that the costume designer, like the other artists in a production, must make a thorough study of plot, character, dialogue, thought, rhythm, and spectacle, in order to have a secure grasp of the whole play as well as an understanding of the individual characters. But costume designers can seldom go directly from the script to their imaginations to produce the finished designs. Even in a play that seems to have few ties to reality or period, background research is still necessary, if only to learn more about the playwright and the playwright's ideas. If it is a period play, the designer should have a solid background in the social history of the period and should be thoroughly familiar with the garments worn in the age: the characteristic silhouette, the typical textures and materials, the favorite colors and ornamental motifs, and the key accessories.

What are the usual sources from which the costume designer works? Obviously, this depends on the play and its interpretation; there are productions in which the costume ideas have come from books on marine life, texts on biology, treatises on zoology, or manuals on flower arrangement. Most frequently, however, a script presents some aspect of historic or present-day society that demands careful study. The resource material for such plays is usually located in the following places.

Books on the history of dress, especially those of the past few years, are fully documented with excellent original visual sources. If the books use modern drawings and sketches rather than original sources such as paintings and sculptures, there is a danger that one will miss the facts and quality of a past era. (See the recommended sources in the Bibliography).

Magazines of the period (for the past two centuries) give the true flavor of the times, although with certain limitations. If one concentrates on fashion drawings, the costumes will follow the fashion ideal rather than what was actually worn; if one concentrates on illustrations, one comes close to the truth, but the information will be filtered through the illustrator's view; if one is able to use magazine photographs for periods after 1850 or 1860, one will get at the truth of the period but not at how people saw themselves.

Prints, paintings, engravings, etchings, and sketches of past periods are often difficult to locate, since the most frequently reproduced artistic products of the past may not provide insight into costume styles and accessory details. Often, much detective work must go into unearthing primary source material that is not to be found in volumes on fashion history.

Books on the plastic arts are another source: works on sculpture may be useful, and so may works on architecture if one is pursuing a certain artistic idea behind the costume and architecture of a period. Because it is three-dimensional, sculpture is more helpful than painting in giving a sense of the form inside a costume.

The minor arts of jewelry, mosaics, pottery, textiles, and glassware provide information about accessories and details of costume. They also provide a more general kind of information: the color, line, and texture favored by a society. Sometimes the inspiration for a whole production may evolve from a small bit of tableware, a piece of furniture, or an item of jewelry.

Original garments from past periods can be found in museums or private collections. These usually date back only to the eighteenth century, but there are some from the Middle Ages. Original garments are particularly useful for learning the methods of cutting and fitting period costumes.

Finally, source material may be obtained from anything that strikes a response. No area should be closed; the designer should keep an eye open for possible inspiration and information from everything in the surrounding world.

Most of the material listed above will be found in the visual arts sections of libraries under the 700s in the Dewey decimal system, although books on the history of dress are frequently placed with social customs under the 390s. Books on theatre costume are often found under 809. In the Library of Congress system most costume books are under GT, with some under N and NK. Books on costume for the theatre are under PN and those specifically on design are under TT. Many libraries have picture files that are useful if certain paintings or a phase of an artist's work cannot be found in art books, and some libraries have slide files that cover the history of the visual arts far more fully than do volumes on the subject. A fine arts library is an ideal place for research.

Much material will be found only in museums, especially original garments, paintings, sculpture, and minor arts. If excellent museums are within easy reach during the design period, they should certainly be visited; if not, material can be sent in slide or print form. Certain large museums, like the Metropolitan Museum of Art in New York City and the Victoria and Albert Museum in London, have a separate costume library and museum in addition to their larger collections, and here people trained in costume history can help the designer find the needed sources.

Most designers also develop their own files of pictures from magazines, newspapers, and journals, and some keep detailed files of costume fabrics that can be used in texture layouts.

Another source the designer uses is background reading. Social histories give the broadest view of a society, while biographies provide detailed portraits of people and the age in which they lived. Memoirs, reminiscenses, and diaries are helpful in giving a direct, spontaneous, informal view of a period. For example, no book offers subtler insight into Restoration England than the diary of Samuel Pepys.

But what about the use of source material in developing a costume approach? The designer has collected much valuable information in the course of doing research and is tempted to use all of it. It takes great discipline and self-criticism to pare away material as one works to the core of a particular approach. Repeatedly, one sees productions in which all the costume designer's research is still on the stage on opening night; one sees an illustration of a period, a pageant of dress from past times, an unrolling of historical facts that are fascinating in themselves but stand in the way of the audience's concentration on the mood of the play. The more creative costume designers neither lift costumes from books and source material nor copy the dress of past times; they are not obsessed with historical accuracy, but attempt to get at the essence of the period as seen through the eyes of the dramatist and the director and to make this ordered artistry operate in terms of the theatre. Theatrical appropriateness to the character and play are far more important than historical accuracy and an abundance of historical detail.

Schedules, Lists, and Charts

We noted earlier that the designer should mark the script with notations about any matters pertaining to costume and should start recording this material in chart form while doing research. To make a chart, divide a large sheet of paper or cardboard into squares. Down the left side, in each square, write the name of each character in the production along with the name of the actor playing the role. Then, across the top of the chart, list each act or scene, with one square allotted to each character (or actor if an actor plays a variety of roles). In each square, indicate the costume item worn by the actor in that scene, including all accessories. Some designers attach color samples for the costumes. The color range and overall color scheme can thus be seen at a glance, and the list of costume items can be used as a guide in dressing the actors and in keeping the costumes organized in the designer's, director's, and actors' minds (Figure 2–2). A costume chart may also be used by a designer to gain insight into the structure and rhythm of a play. By noting the way a character weaves in and out of the action, the way crowd scenes are grouped, which characters appear when, and how large and small scenes

relate or alternate, the designer gains a subliminal sense of the nature and development of the script as a plan for stage action and stage pictures.

Similar in scope, and usually used to present a breakdown of costs to the producer, is the costume list. The characters in the production are listed in categories, the men divided from the women and the principals from the supporting cast and from the chorus or extras. After each character's name is written every item of clothing worn or accessory carried for each costume change. There are two sets of numbers to the left of the costume changes: the first set runs consecutively from the first to the last full costume in each category and tells the designer and the producer exactly how many full costumes he has in each grouping and in the play as a whole. The second runs consecutively for each character and gives only that character's total number of costumes. After each name, there is usually the character's age and a brief identification. At the end of the list are totaled the number of costumes in the production; the number of women's costumes; the number of men's costumes; the numbers for principal men and principal women; and, finally, the numbers for men chorus or supers and women chorus or supers (Figure 2–3). The costume list is invaluable when the designer talks with a producer about costs or negotiates with a costume house that may build the wardrobe. It is also helpful when filing the Costume Designer's Contract with the United Scenic Artists, which sets a certain fee for the costume designs of featured or principal players, another fee for the costume designs of supporting players, and a lesser fee for repeats of a costume design, for instance, for a chorus or an army.

Another chart, used later in the production preparation period to help actors keep the parts of their costumes in order, is the character or actor costume chart, which gives at the top the dresser, the dressing room, and the title of the play. The body of the chart lists the character, the actor playing the role, and a notation of footwear, garments, headgear, and accessories (Figure 2–4). A chart like this should

	ACT I							ACT II						
	Lonely Landscape	Sarastro Palace	A Grove	Palm Grove	Court or Temple	Garden	Hallway	Inside Pyramid	Garden	Wild Mountain Spot	Small Garden	Rugged Cliffs	Temple of Sun	Comments
Sarastro			✓ 1st cost	✓		✓ 2nd cost		✓					✓ 3rd cost	
Tamino	✓		✓		✓		✓	✓		✓			✓	
Papageno	✓	✓	✓		✓		✓	✓			✓			
Queen of Night	✓					✓						✓		
Pamina		✓ 1st cost	✓			✓ 2nd cost	✓	✓	✓	✓			✓ 3rd cost	
Monostatos		✓	✓			✓					✓			
Papagena						✓ disguised as old lady/disguised					✓			Throws off disguise on stage
1st Lady	✓				✓							✓		
2nd Lady	✓				✓							✓		
3rd Lady	✓				✓							✓		
1st Boy Genie			✓				✓		✓		✓			
2nd Boy Genie			✓				✓		✓		✓			
3rd Boy Genie			✓				✓		✓		✓			
1st Priest					✓			✓		✓			✓	
2nd Priest				✓	✓		✓	✓		✓			✓	
3rd Priest					✓			✓		✓			✓	
Speaker			✓	✓	✓		✓	✓					✓	
Slave		✓												
1st Man In Armor										✓				
2nd Man In Armor										✓				
Female Chorus Slaves			✓	✓				✓					✓	
Male Chorus Slaves		✓	✓	✓				✓					✓	
Chorus Guards			✓	✓				✓					✓	
Chorus Priests			✓	✓				✓					✓	
Chorus Priest-esses			✓	✓				✓					✓	

Figure 2–2. Example of a costume chart for Mozart's *The Magic Flute*. From the notebooks of the author.

Principals – Male

Sarastro – age 50 – High Priest of Isis
(1) 1. fantastic headdress, corselet, overskirt, tonnelet, tights, boots, mantle, jewelry.
(2) 2. headdress, gown, robe, tights, boots, staff, jewelry.
(3) 3. turban-headdress, cuirass, gown, sash, underskirt, mantle, tight boots, jewelry, staff.

Tamino – age 25 – An Egyptian Prince
(4) 1. plumed helmet, corselet with labels, arm guards, tights, boots, mantle.

〰〰〰〰〰〰〰〰〰〰〰〰〰〰〰〰〰〰〰

Principals – Female

The Queen of the Night – age 40 – Mother of Pamina
(14) 1. fantastic headdress, corsage, overskirt, underskirt, mantle, staff, petticoats, corset, stockings, slippers, jewelry.

〰〰〰〰〰〰〰〰〰〰〰〰〰〰〰〰〰〰〰

Chorus – Male

1st Male Guard
(26) 1. headdress, robe, tonnelet with belt, tights, boots.

2nd Male Guard
(27) 1. headdress, robe, tonnelet with belt, tights, boots.

3rd Male Guard
(28) 1. headdress, robe, tonnelet with belt, tights, boots.

〰〰〰〰〰〰〰〰〰〰〰〰〰〰〰〰〰〰〰

Chorus – Female

1st Priestess
(55) 1. headdress, corsage, skirt, mantle, jewelry, petticoats, corset, stockings, slippers.

〰〰〰〰〰〰〰〰〰〰〰〰〰〰〰〰〰〰〰

TOTALS

Total Number of Costumes	75
Total Women's Costumes	37
Total Men's Costumes	38
Principal Men's Costumes	13
Principal Women's Costumes	12
Chorus Men's Costumes	25
Chorus Women's Costumes	25

Figure 2–3. Excerpts from a costume list for Mozart's *The Magic Flute.* From the notebooks of the author. (Zigzags across the page represent missing sections in the list.)

COSTUME CHART

Dresser _____

Dressing Room _____   Play _____

Character	Actor	Footwear	Basic Garments	Outer Garments	Wigs & Headdresses	Accessories

Figure 2-4. Example of a character-actor costume chart. From the no

28

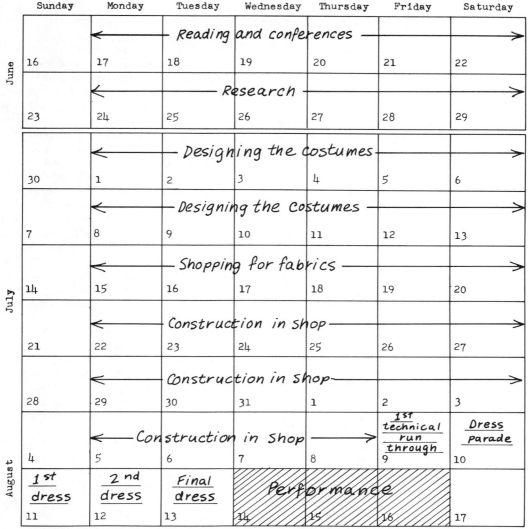

	Sunday	Monday	Tuesday	Wednesday	Thursday	Friday	Saturday
June		←———————— Reading and conferences —————————→					
June	16	17	18	19	20	21	22
June		←———————— Research ————————→					
June	23	24	25	26	27	28	29
July		←———— Designing the costumes ————→					
July	30	1	2	3	4	5	6
July		←———— Designing the costumes ————→					
July	7	8	9	10	11	12	13
July		←———— Shopping for fabrics ————→					
July	14	15	16	17	18	19	20
July		←———— Construction in shop ————→					
July	21	22	23	24	25	26	27
August		←———— Construction in shop ————→					
August	28	29	30	31	1	2	3
August		←———— Construction in Shop ————→			1st technical run through	Dress parade	
August	4	5	6	7	8	9	10
August	1st dress	2nd dress	Final dress	Performance			
August	11	12	13	14	15	16	17

Figure 2-5. Example of a costume calendar for design and construction periods. From the notebooks of the author.

eventually be in each actor's dressing room, but earlier in the design period it is useful to pin it to the back of the sketch.

One final chart the designer should have for private use is a work calendar. Here the periods for each phase of the work can be penciled, and the designer can see how to budget time and perhaps minimize the emotional crises that frequently accompany the pressure of production. The calendar should be divided generally into six periods: (1) reading the play; (2) conferences; (3) research; (4) design; (5) shop-

ping and construction; and (6) the rehearsals and previews leading up to opening night. The calendar always gives the designer a guideline and an added confidence in planning (Figure 2-5).

Other charts related to construction and handling will be explained in a later chapter, but the overall costume chart, the costume list, and the individual actor's costume chart are aids that are best prepared when one is in the final stages of preliminary sketching and layout.

Preliminary Sketching and Layout

Once the research period has ended and the designer has clarified the costume requirements on the overall costume chart, preliminary sketching begins. Obviously, each designer will have a personal method of working, but almost everyone, with research fully in mind, goes through a period of doodling with pen and ink, pencil, or paint in an attempt to bring into focus various ideas for the production. Sometimes research material is laid near the drawing board, sometimes sketches and inspirational notations from a research notebook are displayed nearby as the designer develops early sketches. The designer may use swatches of fabric at this point if he or she thinks of texture and draped line before thinking of form.

Figure 2-6. Idea sketch from a designer's notebook. From the notebooks of the author.

The preliminary sketching period is one of the most exciting periods of the entire design process, because now the designer attempts to take hold of the vague concepts that have seemed intriguing since the first reading of the play. At this point, the designer must not force a design to appear, but must let ideas and research join at the subconscious level before surfacing on the pages of a notebook or sketch pad. Sometimes the idea for a costume will come quickly and remain intact even after later criticism, while another costume may remain elusive for days, and the designer will cover pages of a sketch pad or notebook in an effort to crystallize a sense of exactly what is required for the role. These pages of doodlings and half-ideas are often meaningless to anyone but the designer, for whom they are a trail leading, often with many false starts, to the final costume form (Figure 2-6).

In plays where an abstract idea has been conceived as the key to all the costumes, the designer may work for every possible variation that can be drained from the original idea before becoming ready to piece together the individual costumes for character. In a production of *The Tempest,* if the designer wishes to use the basic costume forms of the English masque in conjunction with the visual imagery of the sea, the first step will be to do research into the masque designs of Inigo Jones and then into books on sea life; the doodling period may then be devoted to pages and pages of masque forms combining, contrasting, and recombining the shapes of seaweed, crustaceans, and fish fins until masque design principles become a part of the designer's inner consciousness. Only then will it be time to move to the more concrete level of preliminary sketches for the characters.

When the preliminary sketching begins to approach its final form, the designer should again consult with the director so that each is assured that their ideas are developing in the same direction. At a consultation like this, one or two costumes will usually create a problem. If there seems to be no immediate solution, the designer can either keep working at the preliminary designs or bypass those costumes and do a layout for the remainder of the play, hoping that by further clarifying the overall concept for the production a solution to the problems will arise.

The layout is usually a string of small figures in pen and ink, sketch pencil, colored pencil, or pigment that shows the director at a glance what the entire costume concept will look like. Sometimes, especially if the layout designs are in pen and ink with no indication of color, swatches of fabric will be pinned above each sketch. If the layout is in full color, then samples of the textures to be used are included at the side. The figures themselves may be strung out horizontally on several sheets of drawing paper or mat board; they may be on small individual pieces of sketch paper or mat board; or they may all be grouped on a large board or sketch sheet so that all changes for one character are clustered together and characters are grouped according to visual relationships in the play. Whatever the layout method, the small sketches should be simple and clear so that one will not waste time explaining one's intentions to the director (Figure 2–7). The layout is only an aid to the director and designer, not a finished statement to show actors, producers, backers, and interested friends.

Figure 2–7. Example of a costume layout for Molière's *Les Fourberies de Scapin.* From the notebooks of the author.

The Costume Sketch

One should be careful to make the final sketches clear and large enough so there is no confusion about detail. Some designers' sketches are so vague that much marginal information is necessary for the cutters and seamstresses. Other designers make their sketches so detailed that the mood they wish to convey is lost. Obviously some middle ground is preferable: the designer should retain the original feeling that he or she had about the costume idea when it was conceived, yet also be able to convey the fact that the costume is a wearable garment. This is a difficult balance to achieve, and many designers do not try; they use whatever sketching style suits their personality and is easiest for them to achieve. One solution developed by the great American designer Lee Simonson was to do a set of beautifully vague and imaginative color sketches for the producer, actors, and lobby display, and another set—three or four simple, small, face-front figures on board surrounded by detailed construction information—for those who were to make the costumes.

The average size of a costume figure should be about ten to fourteen inches high; the male figure should be approximately 8½ heads tall, the female about eight heads tall (Figure 2-8);

Figure 2-8.   Male and female figure proportions to aid in developing the costume sketch. Based on ideas in *Costume Drawing* by Doten and Boulard, published by Pitman Publishing Corporation.

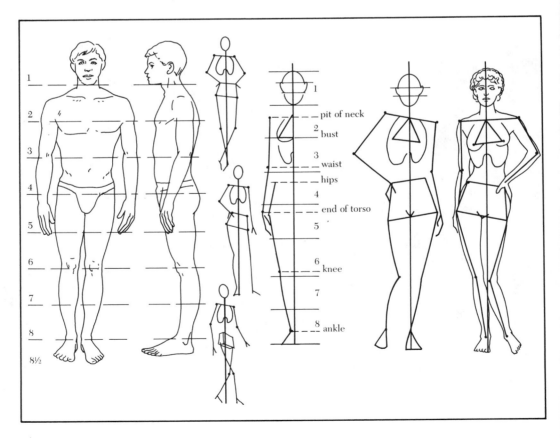

and the costume figure should be either in full-front or in three-quarter view with a minimum of foreshortening. To give a feeling of the possibility of movement (since costumes on stage are seldom frozen in place), it is often wise to place the weight of the figure on one leg to give it the famous *contraposto* stance, notable in many classical and Renaissance statues. To achieve this easily, drop a straight line from the center of the head to the floor and make this the line of gravity for the figure, with the weight-bearing leg following this line and the other moving out to one side (Figure 2–8). In gaining a sense of body proportions for costume sketching it is important to divide the male and female figures into ''heads'' and then memorize where these divisions fall. In the male figure the first head ends at the chin, the second at the chest, the third just above the navel, the fourth just above the genitals, the fifth midthigh, the sixth just above the knees, the seventh at midcalf, and the eighth at the ankles. In the female figure the first head ends at the chin, the second at the bust, the third just above the waist, the fourth just above the crotch, the fifth just above midthigh, the sixth just below the knee, the seventh just below the calf, and the eighth at the toes (Figure 2–8).

In most costume sketches it is wise to place at least one of the arms in an open position so that sleeve detail is visible. Other possible positions for the arms are: one hand at the neck with the other held away from the side; both arms opened wide; one or both hands on hips; hands folded in front of the figure; one arm on the chest, the other at the side; and, occasionally, the hands behind the back, if this is appropriate to the character and will not obscure important cuff detail. Kneeling, sitting, strong bending, and side views are usually inappropriate for costume sketches, as they will call attention to the position rather than the costume and will obscure important costume detail (Figure 2–9).

Figure 2–9. Costume diagrams to aid in sketching. After sketching ideas in *The Art of Costume Design* by Marilyn Sotto. Courtesy of The Walter Foster Art Service, Inc., Tustin, Calif., and Marilyn Sotto.

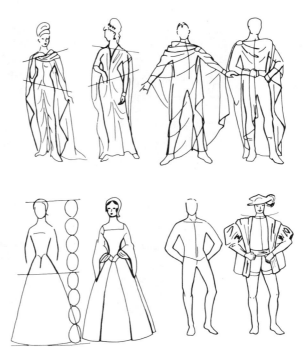

Each sketch should also carry the following four items of information: (1) the name of the production; (2) the name of the character; (3) the act and scene in which the character wears the costume; (4) the designer's signature. Although there is no hard and fast rule about the placement of this information, the production name most often goes in the upper left-hand corner, the character's name with the act and scene number on the lower right, and the signature or initials of the designer at the left foot of the costume figure (Figure 2–10).

Figure 2–10.   Example of the labeling and placement of the costume sketch. From the notebooks of the author.

Queen and the Rebels

Act II sc3

Surfaces for the Costume Sketch

It is always difficult to decide on what surface to present the finished costume sketch. Mat board will not bend, can be easily stood against a wall, and will wear far better during shop use than watercolor or sketch paper. But mat board will seldom suit the watercolorist, who uses the surface and texture of the paper for the effectiveness of the sketch, and many mat board sketches together make a heavy portfolio. Some designers choose a surface and texture to suit each play; there are no limits to presentational possibilities. The designer may always use the same medium, surface, and technique as a sort of personal signature, or may try to suit the presentational approach to the atmosphere of the play and its costumes.

Here are some of the surfaces that can be used:

Watercolor paper is used most frequently, because watercolor is still the most frequently used medium for costume sketching. Watercolor paper comes in many weights and textures, from very stiff and rough to quite light and smooth. Most designers prefer the medium to heavier weight, which holds up better, wrinkles less easily, and takes a heavier use of water and pigment. The costume designer whose original watercolor sketches will be used in the shop needs a sketch that will not deteriorate easily, and unless the sketch is going to be fastened to a solid mat board surface, a fairly sturdy surface background will be necessary. (Suggested watercolor papers: Andrews-Nelson-Whitehead; Bainbridge Sons; Grumbacher; Strathmore; Winsor & Newton.)

Mat board is another favorite background surface, since it is sturdy, does not easily bend or deteriorate, and is available in a variety of surfaces, from rough to smooth. It is not as ideal for watercolor as watercolor paper, but for gouache, pen and ink with wash, colored pencil, acrylics, or colored inks it is satisfactory if the appropriate surface texture is chosen.

Mat board usually comes in sheets 30 by 40 inches or sometimes 32 by 40 inches, which can be divided into eight sketch surfaces, each 10 by 15 or 10 by 16 inches. If gouache or any kind of opaque color is used, great variety of effect can be achieved by choosing colored or tinted boards that will suggest the background mood of the play. Black is a favorite, since it allows the designer to paint in only what the audience will see under stage lighting; the shadows are provided by the board surface. Black board is especially fine for presenting costumes if a play requires much shadow onstage and lighting from specific rather than general sources (Figure 2–11). Rough-surfaced mat board lends itself well to dry-dragging or dry-brushing with opaque color for a soft, fresco-like surface. (Suggested mat boards: Bainbridge Sons; Grumbacher; Crescent.)

Drawing paper, which comes in various weights and qualities, is useful for the artist who prefers to work dry, with pen and ink or colored pencils. The choice of a surface depends on how it reacts to the artist's pen or pencil stroke. If colored surfaces are required, the designer may use colored construction paper, which takes soft colored pencils effectively. (Suggested drawing paper: Bainbridge Sons; Strathmore; Winsor & Newton.)

Velour paper is usually chosen for pastel renderings, but the sketches must be protected with plastic spray or they will smear and disappear. Black velour paper gives a beautiful velvety background of great depth, and pastels or thick dry-brushed opaque colors can be effective in bringing out what the audience will see of the costume under stage lighting (Figure 2–12). One can choose colored velour paper to suggest the mood of the play. (Suggested velour paper: Grumbacher; Strathmore; Winsor & Newton.)

Other surfaces can certainly be used. Some designers use a paste-up technique; that is, they paste various cut-out colored surfaces onto a roughly indicated human form placed against a fabric background, metallic paper, a

Figure 2–11. A costume sketch for the Duke in a production of Shakespeare's *Measure for Measure,* showing the use of black mat board as a background; as produced by the Stanford Players, 1962. From the collection of the author.

patterned wallpaper background, or a thin rice paper surface. Even when a designer uses pen and ink, he may choose surfaces ranging from thin rice paper to heavy metallic paper, and some artists will also attempt to paint on these backgrounds. Certainly nothing should be

Figure 2-12. A costume sketch for the Baroness in Anouilh's *The Cavern,* as produced by the Stanford Repertory Theatre, 1967, showing the use of black velour paper as a background. From the collection of the author.

ruled out if it projects the designer's feeling about a production and how he or she would like to work during the sketching process. But if the same design is to be used by shop personnel, the design must be readable and capable of having construction information attached to it.

Rendering the Costume Sketch

The sketch surface the designer chooses depends on the medium for the final costume rendering. The media usually include pencils, inks, transparent color, opaque color, casein, acrylics, or cut-out or paste-up materials.

PENCILS. Drawing, as opposed to painting, is usually the first step in rendering the costume sketch. The designer clarifies ideas in the preliminary design stages and then sets down the forms and outlines of the final sketch before moving to the painting process. Very few designers rely exclusively on the drawing process, but all will use it at one time or another. Drawing is usually divided into three modes: (1) delineation or line drawing; (2) form drawing; and (3) color-value drawing. Line drawing is rare even in preliminary sketching stages, since some indication of dark or light is usually given, even if unconsciously. Often a designer mixes all three modes without being aware of it. All steps in the drawing process can be done either with pen and ink, with pencil or, as in the Orient, with a brush. When beginning the finished renderings, the designer who feels most at ease with a pencil may draw the figure with great detail, bringing in all elements of form and light, and then tint the results with color. Or the designer may wish to use pencil for the entire sketch, even to adding color with colored pencils. (Suggested drawing pencils: No. 1 or 2 Eagle; Eberhard Faber; Grumbacher; Winsor & Newton.)

Colored pencils usually come in hard and soft varieties; the hard are useful for linear effects such as crosshatching, clustered diagonal strokes, and thinner and thicker lines to bring out form, but one cannot merge color strokes into a smooth, colored form with them. Soft colored pencils are like pastels, but without their softness and their tendency to blur and smear. With soft colored pencils one can approach the softness of conté crayon as used by the eighteenth-century French artist Jean-Antoine Watteau. Blended color is possible, and on the correct surface a nonlinear result can be achieved. Colored pencils, both hard and soft, work best on tinted or colored surfaces, where highlights can be placed with a white pencil (Figure 2-13). (Suggested colored pencils: Eberhard Faber; Eagle Prismacolor— highly recommended.)

Figure 2-13. A costume sketch for Parolles in Shakespeare's *All's Well That Ends Well,* showing the use of soft colored pencils and black felt pen on tan parchment paper. Note the photocopy of the engraving source for the design in the upper right corner; for a production at the Berkeley Shakespeare Festival, 1982. From the collection of the author.

Figure 2-14. A costume sketch for M Perrichon in Labiche's *The Voyage of M Perrichon,* showing the use of a pen-and-ink drawing filled in with gray value washes of ink or watercolor. From the collection of the author.

INKS AND DYES. In costume sketching, inks are used mostly for setting the line and form before adding color washes, although colored inks can be used in place of watercolors. For costume sketches without color, black indelible ink sets a clear, flat outline with any width of line from very thin to quite heavy, in preparation for a value wash in grays that is usually done with washable black ink. Fabric swatches must be attached to costume sketches without color (Figure 2-14). (Suggested drawing inks: Pelikan; Carters; Higgins.)

Another possibility is a flat ink outline with shadowed or receding areas inked in with indelible ink. This gives a stronger effect than the line and flat tone washes (Figure 2-15).

Still another quick and interesting technique that gives a feathery, soft result—ideal for fairy tales and impressionistic plays—is to lay in the sketch in three full dimensions with a pilot pen, then to brush water over the sketch. The pilot pen markings will bleed and soften into a very appealing, artistic sketch before the desired tints of color are added (Figure 2-16).

Figure 2–15. A costume sketch for Bernardo in Shakespeare's *Hamlet* set in 1820, showing the use of indelible ink crosshatching and shadow used under watercolor washes to give depth to the sketch; as produced by the Stanford Players, 1963. From the collection of the author.

Figure 2–16. Costume sketch for Allmers and Asta in Ibsen's *Little Eyolf,* showing the use of a pilot pen technique overlaid with a water wash; tints of color were added while the sketch was still damp. As produced by the Stanford Drama Department, 1980. From the collection of the author.

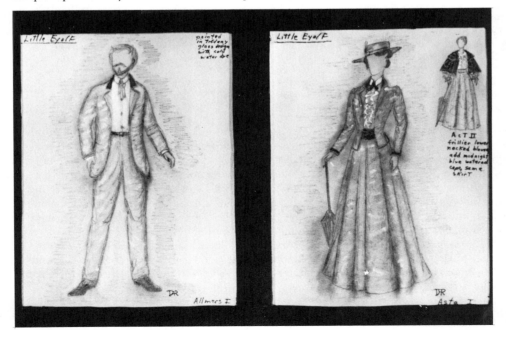

If one varies the thickness of the sketch lines when drawing with indelible ink, as did the fifteenth-century Italian artist Antonio Pollaiuolo, one can get form without shadowing or working in value washes. Color swatches will provide the color. Or one can use a thick diagonal-point felt pen to make strong shadows down one side of the figure; the whole is thus given a strong three-dimensional quality when painted.

One can also develop a sense of three-dimensional form through crosshatching and clustered horizontal, vertical, or diagonal stroking.

Finally, we have the method of most Japanese art and also much poster art: the flat indelible ink outline with flat color washes added. The washes can be either watercolor, colored ink washes, or the famous Dr. Martin's dyes, which give wonderfully deep and rich transparent color washes. If opaque color is used with strong, flat ink outlines, the result will be very like poster art (Figure 2–17).

Although the brilliant transparent results of colored inks and dyes are exciting, there is not much possibility for variation. They must be used as a transparent wash, although varying amounts of the surface beneath may be allowed to show. Occasionally, inks used with a dry-brush technique can be effective. (Suggested colored inks: Arthur Brown; Grumbacher; Higgins; Winsor & Newton.)

Finally, there are colored felt pens available in scores of varied colors. The colors cannot be easily mixed, of course, but they can be blended somewhat through crosshatching. For students who feel insecure with watercolors and liquid paints of any kind, felt pens are ideal—especially for any flat, posterlike sketches. Metallic pens or markers have recently come on the market and are excellent for rendering armor and jewelry. (Suggested felt pens: Magic Marker; Eberhard Faber; Pentel.)

WATERCOLORS. The most common way to use watercolors in the preparation of a costume sketch is to execute a pencil drawing and then quickly brush in watercolor to suggest texture

Figure 2–17. A costume sketch for the Doctor in Hindemith's *Hin und Zurück,* showing an indelible ink sketch filled in with flat opaque color; as produced by the Stanford Opera Theatre, 1962. From the collection of the author.

and color (Figure 2–18). If the drawing is complete in pencil form, the designer may color in the areas with a minimum of brushwork; if the drawing is vague, the folds, highlights, shadows, and accessory details can be suggested by the brushstroke. Watercolors are most effective when the paper beneath the costume is

Figure 2–18. An original sketch by Leslie Hurry for Richard III in Shakespeare's history play, showing a rich and complex watercolor technique. From The Norman Philbrick Library. Courtesy of Leslie Hurry.

allowed to show through. If the surface of the paper or board used is rough, a dry-brushing or dragging technique can be effective, and with heavy pigment one can draw rather than paint with the brush. Always remember that watercolor sketches must retain their transparency and must give a feeling of spontaneity and rapid execution to be effective; the artist must paint in color and shadow, leaving highlight to the white surface beneath the sketch (Figure 2–19). Probably the simplest use of watercolors is as flat color washes that fill in areas of ink or pencil drawing with an indicated color, with no attempt at brushstrokes, feathering, bleeding color, or more complicated techniques. (Suggested watercolors, tube: Grumbacher; Weber; Winsor & Newton; cake: Grumbacher; Pelikan; Winsor & Newton.)

OPAQUE COLOR. In many ways, gouache colors or opaque watercolors are easiest for a beginning designer with little experience of the transparent media. Opaque color gives an excellent flat surface and a true sense of color, since one is not confused by surface effects in transparent color. With opaque color, highlights can be painted into the sketch, and one can make excellent use of colored and tinted backgrounds.

The most common use of opaque color and the simplest is to draw in the full, strong figure outline with indelible ink, and then fill in the areas of the costume in flat color. The result is like poster art. One can sometimes allow small amounts of the paper to show through the gouache application to give variety and a fuller sense of the sketch process (Figure 2–20). One may also use a dryer brush, and especially if a rough surface is used, one can achieve a pleasing rough plaster or fresco-like effect. Still another variation is to draw rather than paint with the brush. This works best on a dark or black surface, and with a full range of values from white to the black of the board, one can create vivid figures. Shadowing and highlighting in opaque color can become quite an art; and, on a dark or black surface, one can develop a figure as if seen in theatrical spotlighting, achieving a three-dimensional effect with a minimum of effort. One can also outline one side of the figure in white and the other in black to indicate a light source (Figure 2–21). An interesting surface on which to work with gouache is velour paper; here great thick pigment strokes give a rich, soft, textural sketch (see Figure 2–12).

Figure 2–19. An original sketch by Alix Stone for Katharina in Shakespeare's *The Taming of the Shrew,* showing a watercolor technique combined with sepia ink drawings. From The Norman Philbrick Library. Courtesy of Alix Stone.

Figure 2–20. A costume sketch for Figaro in the Rossini opera *The Barber of Seville,* showing a mat board background containing a sketch in opaque color; as produced by The West Bay Opera, Palo Alto, 1980. From the collection of the author.

 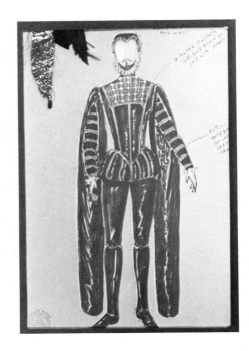

Figure 2–21.   Costume sketches for the Duchess and Ferdinand in Webster's *The Duchess of Malfi,* as produced by the Berkeley Shakespeare Festival, 1979, showing the use of white highlighting on the left sides of the figures, as well as the placement of fabric swatches; sketches are also matted to set them off. From the collection of the author.

In general, opaque color is easier to use than transparent watercolor, because it can be used in a drier way, allows for more control, does not puddle and grow muddy the way beginners' watercolor sketches do, and gives a better idea of possibilities in fabric colors than does watercolor. (Suggested opaque or gouache colors: Grumbacher; Shiva; Winsor & Newton.)

CASEIN, OIL, ACRYLICS.   Although used by commercial and professional artists, oil and casein are usually not used by the costume designer because they take a long time to dry. However, plastic acrylics offer the designer another choice because of the wide range of effects they can achieve and the speed with which

they can be used. With water as a thinner, the designer can move all the way from the impasto and glaze of oil to the transparency of watercolor; impasto can be used without a drying time; and colors will not fade, crack, or age. When dry, they are water resistant, and various transparent layers may be overlaid in any sequence without erasing or obliterating the layer below. Many designers have abandoned the older media for the possibilities that can be achieved with acrylics (Figure 2–22). (Suggested casein and oil colors: Grumbacher; Talens; suggested acrylic and polymer colors: Grumbacher; Shiva; Talens; Liquatex; Bocour.)

CUT-OUTS AND PASTE-UPS.   Some designers

Figure 2–22.   A costume sketch for Lady Macbeth in Shakespeare's *Macbeth,* as designed for a class project by Jean Schultz Davidson, showing the use of acrylic paints. Courtesy of Jean Schultz Davidson.

use collage, a cut-out and paste-up method, instead of a sketch. They choose an interesting background, such as fabric, metal, wallpaper, construction paper, or velour paper, and construct the figure on it by pasting fabrics or colored or patterned papers to the background in appropriate shapes. Ralph Koltai used this method in his designs for the Royal Shake-speare Company production of *The Merchant of Venice,* and John Blomberg in his sketches for the television series *The Six Wives of Henry VIII* used crinkled paper, paper lace, fabric, and paint (Figure 2–23). The artist may draw or paint on top of the paste-up to clarify the design, but frequently the cut-out and paste-up method is used alone.

Figure 2–23. Costume sketches for the Prince of Aragon and the Duke of Morocco by Ralph Koltai for Shakespeare's *The Merchant of Venice,* showing the use of cut-out paper and paint against a metallic paper background. From The Norman Philbrick Library. Courtesy of Ralph Koltai.

Backgrounds, Framing, and Preservation of the Costume Sketch

Many designers will not be content to present a simple figure on a blank sheet of paper. They will wish to help the viewer see better how the designer envisions the particular costume and the play as a whole. We have already mentioned that an interesting surface can help enhance a particular rendering technique, and that colored or tinted surfaces can contribute to setting the mood of the play. Many designers use brush or colored pencil to lay in a colored area behind the costume figure to give it further importance on the sketch surface. Some use a pen-and-ink stroke to build up a

background or frame for the figure or they may cover the surface behind the figure with an interesting texture and color pattern laid in with brush, pen, or pencil, or by spattering with a toothbrush, or even by pressing crumpled paper into a wet wash background (Figure 2–24 and see Figure 2–15). Whatever choice is made, the designer must be certain that the background does enhance the sketch and does not distract from or blur its artistic effect or make the construction notes surrounding it difficult to read.

If a designer's sketches are intended to be used in the shop, that is, to be handed about instead of hung on a wall, they should be preserved under a covering of polyethylene or

Figure 2-24. A layout of sketches for Ibsen's *Peer Gynt,* showing the use of pen-and-ink cross-hatching to set off sketches from the background; as produced by the Missouri Repertory Theatre, 1974. From the collection of the author.

plastic. If pastels or soft pencils have been used, the designer should spray the sketch thoroughly with a plastic preservative before covering it. If the sketches are to hang on the walls of the costume room or be shown in public exhibition, the designer may wish to consider matting—adding a 2- to 3-inch border of mat board in an appropriate color and texture to set off the effect of the original rendering (see Figure 2-21). Framing in mat board also gives a border on which to clip any typed information that might be needed if the sketch is exhibited.

Construction Notes

One of the dilemmas facing the designer is whether to treat the rendering as a sketch plan for the costume shop staff with full construc-

tion notes surrounding the sketch, or as an artistic idea that only suggests the finished product and is intended to sell the costume and the artistic approach to the actor, director, producer, and public. It has already been mentioned that the leading American designer Lee Simonson made two sets of sketches, one an artistic evocation of the mood of the play, the other a set of figures and plans for construction. Most designers try to strike a balance, and many still prefer construction drawing on a separate sheet or on the back of the sketch.

If the construction notes and drawings are on a separate sheet, they are usually attached to the left-hand side of the sketch and fold over it when it is carried or fold behind it when it is shown (Figure 2-25). A separate sheet gives more space for notations than does the space around the costume figure, but one cannot

Figure 2–25.   A costume sketch for the First Priestess in Mozart's *The Magic Flute,* showing construction notes appended to the sketch. From the collection of the author.

draw arrows or lines from the sketch to the notation or detail drawing. The same is true if the costume information is on the back of the sketch. It is certainly easier to relate the sketch to the detail drawing or construction notes if the information surrounds the figure (see Figure 2–13).

Costume construction notes generally explain something that cannot be seen clearly in the sketch. They do not need to show the patterns for basic garments; the experienced people in the costume shop should know the patterns. In fact, conferences with an expert cutter will often teach the designer a better

way to make a garment or costume detail. But anything in a costume sketch that is not self-explanatory to trained people should be blown up in a small construction sketch with accompanying notes. A hat shape or hairdo; a form of collar; the way something is to be draped, laced, or belted; small ornaments such as bracelets, buckles, brooches, and pins; patterns on fabric or elsewhere; and armor, complicated headdresses, swords, canes, or snuff-boxes should be shown if they present any problems in construction, purchase, or rental. Most designers tend to limit their clarifying notes and drawings to two or three major items if the information surrounds the sketch (see Figure 1-1).

Finally, although more will be said of this in Chapter 5, the costume sketch in the upper left-hand corner should contain sample swatches of the fabrics to be used in building the costumes. Sometimes swatches from the designer's collection will be placed on the sketch for the director to see or for the designer to refer to when buying, but the swatches should be replaced by the fabrics to be used when the renderings reach the shop (Figures 2-11, 2-13, and 2-21). Some suggested books on rendering methods and materials are *The Craftsman's Handbook* (New York: Dover, 1970); Rutherford J. Gettens and George L. Stout, *Painting Materials: A Short Encyclopedia* (New York: Van Nostrand Reinhold, 1966), a paperback; Ralph Mayer, *The Artist's Handbook of Materials and Techniques* (New York: Viking, 1981); also see the Bibliography at the end of the book.

3

Principles of Characterization and Design

The Fundamentals of Design

Although preparing the costume sketch is in many ways the most rewarding part of the design process, it is only a means to an artistic end. The costume sketch is the plan for the finished costume, which will involve an interplay of line, form, texture, and color. The beginning designer often thinks of the sketch merely as a picture or an illustration of a costume to be built, rather than as a design formed consciously or intuitively from a knowledge of certain common design principles.

In this book we shall view costume design not merely as a set of techniques for dressing plays, but as an art form. In developing an approach to costume design, now is the time to say something about art and about the principles of artistic theory. The study of aesthetics has usually produced a great many questions such as: What is art? How do we perceive it? Is there such a thing as beauty? For our pur-

poses, such philosophical questions are far less important than a pragmatic look at how artistic principles work in various artistic media and how the designer works with limited concepts such as line, proportion, mass, shape, and balance.

Philosophers of art have divided art into three categories or fields of value: sensuous, formal, and associative. The responses aroused by each of these values is distinct, and even a beginning student of design should have no difficulty in distinguishing one from the other. *Sensuous* values are those that arise from a perception of and response to colors, textures, and tones of light and shade, independent of the formal organization, the story, or the meaning of the work. For example, fabric surfaces of a costume may have visual or tactile appeal without creating in us an involvement in the period of the costume or the nature of the character wearing it. *Formal* values are less obvious, more complex, and more difficult to understand than the sensuous. Here we respond to the intellectual relationships that can be perceived in the work. In costume, one is particularly aware of the parts of the individual costume, how they relate to each other, and how each costume in the production relates to the total design concept. In this chapter we shall consider formal values as we look into the nature of line, the problems of repetition and balance, the nature of proportion, and the concept of unity. Finally, as mentioned in Chapter 1, there is an important category of symbolic or *associative* values, in which art objects gain meaning by reminding the viewer of things, ideas, or events outside the work itself. Such values are usually tied to memory, to past experiences, to a general cultural inheritance, and can be divided into two levels: primary and secondary. Primary associations are those that have universality and appeal to all people, while secondary associations are personal and are not necessarily understood by others.

If the costume designer were to design only for circus, dance, and extravaganza, it would be possible at this point to move directly from an introduction of the three types of aesthetic value to a discussion of the formal values or the principles of design, but most designers are involved with costume designs for specific characters with specific functions in a play. Therefore, before discussing the problems of formal design, it is important for us to establish how the designer develops a costume for a character in his or her visual imagination.

Principles of Characterization

The character costume develops from what characters say and do and what others say about them. It may or may not deal with what the playwright has indicated in the stage directions, depending on the director's approach to the play. Just as people dress according to the many influences on them in daily life, so does the dress worn by an actor playing a specific character reflect the influences of the script. Sometimes the character is not well delineated

and remains two-dimensional and obvious, but the leading characters must project the many subtle sides of their personalities through what they wear.

The designer usually begins to develop a costume by covering pages and pages of a notebook with idea sketches that attempt to solve the problems of characterization. During this preliminary sketching, the designer puts aside for the moment the results of research and concentrates on the size, shape, posture, and silhouette of each character, trying to visualize the habits and gestures of the characters, the things they handle, the physical actions demanded of them by the director and the script, and to relate these things to the characters' ages and social stations in the play. Often, the designer may sketch an actor (or a human form) without clothes or in a leotard and then gradually add the minimum clothing necessary to create the characterization (Figure 3–1). If any roles have been cast, the designer may wish to see the actors in leotards performing basic movements and gestures required in the play. At this stage of the idea-sketching process, the designer should think of each piece of clothing not as moving scenery or period decoration, but as something that will further underline an aspect of character. For each piece of clothing added to the sketch, the designer should ask: How will it move? How will it work? How will it help the actor on the stage underline some aspect of the characterization? There *may* be an intellectual reason for a piece of clothing to appear on a character, but one must always remember that the audience will see the costume before knowing the reason that the character is wearing it. One must avoid clothing that is false to the visual image the character should project. A production of *The Cherry Orchard* comes to mind in which Madame Ranevsky appeared in an ugly wrapper that was alien to her visual personality. The director chose to have her wear it because it was a gift from Madame Ranevsky's lover in Paris, and reflected the lover's taste, not her own. If the wrapper gave a subtle insight into her personality, it did so through in-

Figure 3–1.   Padding under a leotard used to emphasize pose and character. Drawings by the author.

tellectual, not visual, means. For the audience, the wrapper did not relate to the mood of the scene, the dramatic needs of the action, or the character of Madame Ranevsky.

A slightly different situation developed in a recent production of *Twelfth Night* that the director wanted costumed in the style of the eighteenth-century Directoire. I became excited by the possibility of presenting Sir Andrew as an Incroyable—a dandy—and Malvolio in another version of this style when he appeared in his yellow stockings. I also thought it would be interesting to have Olivia and Orsino move from the older court styles into the youthful Directoire styles as the play developed—all interesting ideas but more intellectual than visual. The final production presented an interesting historical moment grafted onto the play rather than a true visual evocation of the drama (Figure 3–2).

The production that has all parts cast by the time the preliminary design period begins in-

variably presents an easier and more rewarding experience for the designer, who can get to know the actors personally and learn how they wear costume and makeup on the stage. If older actors are playing younger parts, or if the actors are of established reputation and feel they must always appear handsome onstage, the designer may have to make an extra effort to hide less desirable points and stress the best points of their physical appearance. In this regard, much attention must be placed on the hairdo or wig and the makeup, and although specialists other than the costume designer may be in charge here, the designer must supervise and be responsible for the final results. In designing for well-known actors, the designer must attend more than usual to the comfort, fit, and perfection of costume lines. This means that the preliminary idea sketching must explore every possibility for creating just the right effect, and the designer may require several conferences and even working

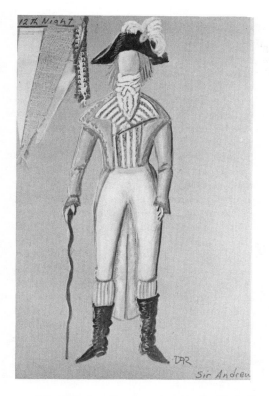

Figure 3–2. Costume sketches for Sir Andrew and Olivia in Shakespeare's *Twelfth Night,* showing intellectual period style choices taking precedence over visual solutions to the character problems; as produced by the Drama Department, Stanford University, 1981. From the collection of the author.

periods with the leading performers before the right level of subtle character delineation is achieved.

One cannot stress too fully the need to build the costume characterization from the inside out, no matter who the actor performing the role. It is in the basic structure underneath the costume that the secret of success is to be found. A little padding at the shoulders, at the bustline, or at the hips, a little cinching in at the waist, the upper arm, or the hips, a little boning of the torso and the back, and one can often achieve exactly the right combination of period line and personal characterization. Each item of underclothing worn in a period

should be analyzed for its function, not its looks or its charm, and nothing should be worn or discarded until its necessity for the final physical characterization is established. As we said in Chapter 1, most theatrical costume is of the artificial structural type rather than the fitted, semifitted, or draped variety; and it is the structural foundation that makes possible the variety of subtle changes in silhouette, movement, and gesture that cannot be achieved when clothing is worn directly over the human form.

Accessories must also be considered when making preliminary sketches of costume silhouette and line, and all adornments and ornamentation should be a reflection of the basic character line inherent in the costume. By character line, it should be clear by now that we mean the importance of a character in a play, the posture and stance of a personality, the height of a figure, and the other ways in which we take in a character at first glance. The only times the basic character line is relatively unimportant is when a character in a play is less a personality onstage than a moving decoration for the stage scene. Once a character has been developed, and if the character is not to sustain major physical changes (such as aging, injury, or illness), the designer is well advised to have as few costume changes as is consistent with the play's action. A dazzling display of costume changes may be rewarding for the audience and challenging for the designer, but many changes will weaken the physical characterization established at the beginning of the play.

There are a number of basic costume lines that designers, through many years of experience, have found helpful in stressing the actor's best physical attributes, although the use of these will vary with the general physical ideal in vogue at the time.

First, beginning at the top of the figure, an actor will profit by having his or her face show clearly. Hats should not cover the forehead and shade the eyes, wigs should not hang across the sides of the face, collars should not hide the jawline and chin. Second, the neck should be lengthened so that the head does not appear to sit directly on the shoulders, although overly long necks can also present problems. In Figure 3–3 a number of variations in women's necklines are shown, each accomplishing something quite different. The V neckline (a) will draw the eye down from the neckline and will stress the area from the neck to the center of the bust. The square neckline (b) will widen the shoulders and the figure below the neck and the area above the bust. The U-shaped neckline (c) will give a gentle line to the area below the neck and draw little attention to the area above the bust. A boat or crescent neckline (d) will give the same soft line but with more stress on the width of the shoulders and will not draw attention to the

Figure 3–3.   Line problems in necklines. Drawings by the author.

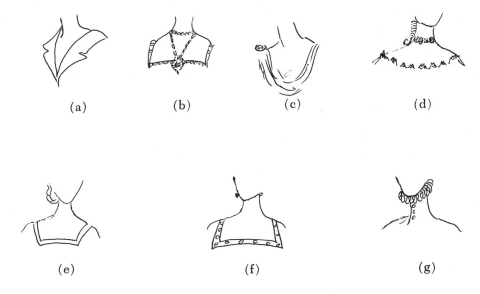

bust. A keystone neckline (e) is used infrequently even in period dress, since it is not particularly flattering; it tends to widen the shoulders and narrow the bust. The trapezoidal neckline (f), usually associated with the sixteenth-century Tudor style, tends to draw attention from the shoulders and give great breadth to the bust. A high neckline (g) of any kind appears to enclose and suppress the area below the chin.

Third, although we have seen how the bust can be greatly influenced by the neckline, it should usually be shaped by careful padding or boning on a foundation garment or in the foundation of the bodice or gown. It can be remade to suit any period ideal or characterization. The waist is always seen in connection with the bust, and it can be pulled in by a foundation garment, or the area between hip bone and rib cage can be stretched out by boning. For some periods and for some personalities, the waist must be balanced with the bustline to give a boyish or straight line to the torso; at other times, it must be especially small in contrast with an exceedingly large bust. The same is true of the hips; they will need to be enlarged or contracted depending on the proportions desired in a particular period or character silhouette. They can be large in contrast to a small waist or slimmed so that bust, waist, and hips are all more or less equalized. These proportion changes also apply to men; chest, waist, and hips can be built up or contracted for a particular character or period line. For example, the male silhouette of 1830 had a padded chest, cinched-in waist, and padded hips comparable to the feminine ideal of the period.

One must decide whether it is best to expose or cover the arms. If they are exposed, they must not be overbalanced by the remainder of the costume; if they are partly covered, three-quarter-length sleeves may make them look too long or the sleeves too short. If the sleeve is full length, one must decide whether the line is to be broken at several points by decoration, puffs, or an over- and an undersleeve, be all of one piece, or be sharply divided at the elbow

into an upper and lower sleeve. If great puffs are used on the upper arm, will the lower arm and hands seem too small? Can the arm be enlarged without looking grotesque against the rest of the costume? The same is true of legs: they can be left uncovered to the hips, covered to below or above the knee, or covered all the way to the floor, including or excluding the feet. In each case, the covered and uncovered areas must be balanced against one another to gain the right balance and proportion and the particular character silhouette desired.

Thus the costume should give as much meaning to the character as possible, but it must not try to usurp the job of the actor. The actor, not the costume, is the primary instrument of communication between the character and the audience; the designer should help in this process, but not try to do all the work. Once in a while, when a character is more a symbol than a flesh-and-blood reality, the designer may create a costume that completely symbolizes the character's position in the drama, but it is dangerous and wrong to try to do this in all situations.

There is also a problem of designing so many subtle nuances into a character costume that they cancel each other out and confuse the audience. Always design the central line of a character's costume, keep the underlying contradictions in dress under careful control, and do not let indications of subconscious desires take focus or distract from the central action line of the scene.

Finally, there is the great challenge of designing individual character costumes into large group scenes. The designer must clearly establish the overall goal and mood of a scene with the director before designing a group of very specific character costumes that will add up to a related overall visual picture. The key to good group design is to establish mood and overall scene effect clearly before developing the individual character costumes. Then design the individual costumes—even those of minor supporting characters—with a full sense of their individuality and uniqueness within the group. Even when the script tells us nothing about the people in a street scene or at a ball, the designer should create for each actor or actress a costume that allows that person to become an individualized character. Large scenes that look like a miscellaneous assemblage of clothing always indicate poor design.

Elements of Design

The next step in developing a design consciousness involves a more formal, abstract, and less subjective approach to theatrical costume. A study of the elements and principles of design will develop the designer's ability to see with the mind as well as the feelings. Twentieth-century art has taught us to see abstractly. We have learned to see lines, colors, shapes, and textures in themselves, unrelated to a story, scene, or particular subject matter. We have learned to look at one or two things at a time, and as we look up and down and across an arrangement of color, line, and texture, we find that subtle differences create in us emotional responses often as great as those we feel when we see great religious or historical paintings.

Line, shape, measure, mass, position, color, and texture are the elements of design. They make up what are usually referred to as the form of a work of art—the ''design form,'' which implies that a composition has been created using these elements of design. A costume designer must learn what these terms mean and make them part of the way he or she sees.

LINE.   We might say that line is a record of the movement of the eye when it examines an object. In primitive drawings and in children's sketches, we can see the visual shorthand that may allow a single line to stand for a full, complex shape. Even the simplest lines have mood, meaning, and emotional associations, and thus we feel a strong difference in the effect of vertical and horizontal lines, of curved and serpentine lines. Line in costume is manifested primarily in the silhouette of garments, but it may also be seen in seams, darts, and ornamentation. It may be complex, with zigzags, scallops, and intricate patterns of brocade and embroidery. The line used in one costume must relate to the overall pattern of line used in the other costumes in a production and to the line pattern used in the visual setting for the production.

SHAPE.   One role of line is to define an object as a shape. Line can define and limit the size of a particular area, but it also does more; as soon as an outline for an area has been established, the line that surrounds the shape will appear to have movement, rhythm, and emotional connotations. In costume, shape refers to the area of a garment—dress, shirt, doublet, cloak, coat—or to the area of a particular ornament or pattern decoration.

MEASURE.   One of the most important characteristics of a trained eye is the ability to measure without the aid of tapes or yardsticks. One must be able to judge sizes and the distances between shapes and lines. For the costume designer, measure is one of the most vital elements in the creation of quality designs. It involves the size of buttons, the distance between buttons or ornaments, the width of a collar, the length of a skirt, and a host of other sizes and distances that must be correct in any design.

MASS.   The effects of line, shape, and measure are combined so that an area of a certain size is seen to have bulk and depth; in other words, mass is three-dimensional shape. In costume, attention must be paid to the mass of a particular garment that an actor wears, the mass of an entire costume in relation to other costumes, and the entire spatial arrangement of the stage. We can see the importance of mass as a design element when we view a stage full of costumes at a distance that allows us to take in all the costumes at once.

POSITION.   Position indicates not just the distance between shapes, but the placement of a shape in relation to another shape and in relation to the area around it. If a shape is not symmetrical, then the strongest or most important side of the shape can lead the eye in a particular direction. Thus, the position of an asymmetrical brooch or decorative ornament can be extremely important in a costume. For example, a rectangular shoulder brooch for a medieval mantle can be placed horizontally on the shoulder to give more width to the figure, or it can be placed vertically to stress the vertical line of the mantle.

COLOR.   Color is obviously one of the most important design elements, because it generates associative and emotional responses in an audience. We shall discuss color more fully in Chapter 4, where it will become evident that color can be used to create effects in all three areas of aesthetic value: the sensuous, the associative, and the formal. Rich, thick, intense colors can elicit a sensuous response from a viewer, and color can be used to organize and direct the eye's response to a stage full of costumes.

TEXTURE.   Costume design is different from other arts because it uses fabric as its major medium. Texture refers to the tactile response the surfaces and folds of the fabric arouse in the viewer. Texture is usually thought to be a sensuous value, but it can also be viewed associatively and, to some extent, as a formal series of arranged relationships. In costume design, one of the major factors in the choice of textures is the effect of a surface under light. Textures with a thick, fuzzy surface such as velour or heavy woolen will absorb light; shiny, smooth surfaces such as satin or metallic armor will reflect light. It is the interplay of texture and light that creates the complex subtleties of tactile response in an audience. The distance between the viewer and the stage often requires that texture be simulated or artificially enhanced through painting, scraping, polishing, brushing, or other processes. A detailed discussion of texture will be found in Chapter 5 and at the end of Chapter 7.

Principles of Design

Having looked briefly at the elements used in producing a composition with a "design form," let us now look at the terms that describe the principles of organization used to create the artistic product. By these principles of organization a designer seeks to manipulate ideas and visual material in such a way as to bring unity, interest, and meaning to a design. Although in the work of the experienced costume designer many of the principles are used unconsciously or instinctively, it will be helpful to the beginning designer if we discuss them here.

UNITY.   Probably the key word in any discussion of design principles is unity, or the linking of the separate parts of a composition in such a way as to create a whole that is greater than the sum of its parts. In costume design, unity involves organizing the parts of a single costume and the total costumed stage picture into an overall plan. If disunity, not unity, seems to be required in many modern productions, one merely has to reverse one's thinking; the planning is the same. One has to calculate just as carefully the correct balance of clash and opposition, the right proportion of disparate elements, so that the final design approach has the "unity of disunity" correct for the production.

HARMONY.   Unity is achieved through the use of harmony and contrast. Harmony is the pleasing grouping of lines, textures, and colors with certain similar characteristics. When similar effects are repeated and sequences of effects are created, an artistic organization and control can be achieved that we feel to be harmonious. However, if there is too much repetition, or too obvious a sequence, the result may be monotonous. For example, too many closely related colors, or too few variations of line in a set of costumes, may produce results that are dull and unexciting because they lack variation and contrast.

CONTRAST.   Diversity in the grouping of the design elements creates contrast and gives interest and life to a design scheme that may lack variety because it has a strong harmony. Without contrast, form cannot be revealed: in war, for example, soldiers and weapons are concealed from the enemy—camouflaged—by the use of color harmony. In the theatre, sharp contrast is obviously preferred to the color harmony that can occur accidentally when a green costume sinks into a green chair. What is needed in a production is the right balance between harmony and contrast.

VARIATION.   When repetition produces monotony, regularly introduced variation will add interest to the composition. A variation in the shape of every third ornament on a doublet sleeve or the space between every third appearance of a particular motif in a pattern is more interesting than identical forms or identical distances between forms in a sequence. To create variation in a sequence, a motif can be alternated so that it shifts its position in relation to its central axis without changing the direction of the pattern; it can be placed in opposition so that every other repetition of the motif opposes the preceding one; or it can be inverted so that the direction of the pattern keeps reversing as the sequence of motifs moves in a particular direction. As can be seen in border or overall fabric patterns (Figures 3–4 and 3–5), the different means of variation can be used in many combinations.

BALANCE.   When one creates a sense of stability by the careful distribution of the forces or weights within a composition, the result is said to be balanced. A costume will appear balanced when one has distributed color, line, and texture in such a way that those elements that attract the most attention are spread evenly over the figure. In a stage scene, one group of costumes must not attract all the attention; it may have to be weighted against another group. The visual tension between individual costumes and groups of costumes gives a production a feeling of balance. There are tensions of balance between upstage costumes and downstage costumes, between costume groups right stage and left stage, and in a single costume between head and toe and arm and arm.

The stage has an element that a painting does not have: movement, or the change of the composition in space and time. It is the harmonious maintenance of different balances as the eye of the audience is led through changes in color, shape, size, and texture that gives the theatre its particular fascination. Even the

Figure 3–4.   Variation in patterns. (a) Repetition of elements. (b) Variation of shape. (c) Variation of measure. (d) Variation of position. (e) Variation of color. (f) Variation of texture. Drawings by the author.

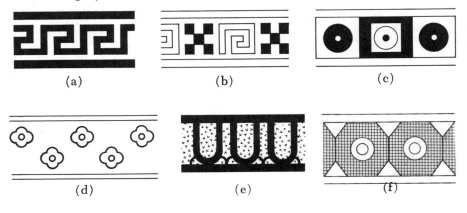

(a)   (b)   (c)

(d)   (e)   (f)

a   b

c   d

Figure 3–5. Variation in a pattern composition. From *Scene Design and Stage Lighting* by W. Oren Parker and Harvey K. Smith. Copyright © 1963 by Holt, Rinehart and Winston, Inc. Reprinted by permission of Holt, Rinehart and Winston, CBS College Publishing.

balance of the individual costume is ever-changing as an actor sits, raises the arms, runs, or falls.

There are two kinds of balance: symmetrical and asymmetrical. In the individual costume, the more common form is symmetrical balance, where both sides of the costume are alike. But asymmetrical balance is not to be neglected, for there are many costumes in which a drapery may pass across the figure and trail at one side, or ornamentation and accessories may follow diagonal lines across a figure rather than balance horizontally or vertically. Sometimes an entire sleeve or a leg covering may be a different cut or color from the one opposite (Figure 3–6).

PROPORTION.   The relationship of one element of a design to another is proportion. A young designer with an innate sense of scale and proportion will be on the way to good costume design. Although much can be learned by training, and the eye can be sharpened by continual analysis, a great part of one's sense of proportion is intuitive.

Figure 3–6.   Symmetrical (left) and asymmetrical (right) balance in costume. Drawings by the author.

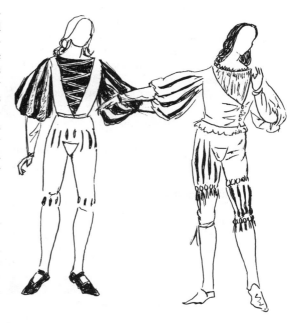

Figure 3–7. Proportion (left) and disproportion (right) in costume. Drawings by the author.

In the theatre, the human form is the measure of all decisions of proportion. Even in a large theatre presenting an operatic production, the designer cannot overlook the human form of actor or singer in developing a scale of proportions in costume and setting. To exaggerate or overscale costumes and accessories may achieve a heightened size or grandeur for the human form, but it also may weigh the actors down, hide their movements, and inhibit their expression. To underscale a production may be to present an audience with a blur of textures, lines, and details that never make their point because they are too small and weak.

Proportion is especially important in the individual costume. The designer must give attention to the amount and distribution of color, the length of a bodice in comparison to a skirt, and the width of shoulders in relation to hips, waist, and bust. Through the manipulation of proportions, one can improve an actor's appearance. For example, by emphasizing vertical lines, a plump actor can be made to appear more slender, while horizontal

lines will increase his width. In short, what we consider to be beautiful, graceful costumes usually come from right proportion, awkwardness, ugliness, and humor from disproportion (Figure 3–7). In modern drama, much use is made of disproportion for the sake of shock, surprise, violence, or ugliness.

EMPHASIS.   As does a painting or a piece of sculpture, a costume design needs a focus or center of interest, a point to which the eye is first directed (Figure 3–8). Emphasis may be created by a patch of color, converging lines, a change in texture, or ornament and accessories. Through emphasis, a good costume designer can direct attention to an actor's good points and minimize or disguise poor ones. In the full-stage picture of grouped costumes, some should obviously be more important than others; the eye should be led to the principal rather than the subordinate characters.

RHYTHM.   A sequence of visual impressions that has been ordered into a recurring pattern with certain accents and emphases cre-

Figure 3–8. Emphasis in costume design: emphasis below waist (left) and emphasis at neck (right). Drawings by the author.

ates a sense of rhythm. Rhythm is one of the most deeply felt, innate responses that human beings have, since its pulsing quality is related to the two fundamental life processes of the heartbeat and breathing, as well as to the rhythms of the sexual act and the progression and decline of human life. As John Dewey said in *Art as Experience* (1934): ''So far as nature is to us more than a flux lacking order in its mutable changes, so far as it is more than a whirlpool of confusion, it is marked by rhythms.'' An audience in a theatre responds instinctively to the rhythm of music in a production, to the rise and fall of the plot, and to the recurring patterns and accented groups of visual stimuli projected by sets and costumes. It reacts both emotionally and physically, usually at a subconscious level.

In costume design, a unifying rhythm is achieved by the way lines, shapes, textures, and colors of a costume direct the eye from the major points of interest to the subordinate parts and from one grouping of costumes to another throughout the play. The rhythm of the costume designs should support the play's action, visual atmosphere, and emotional climate.

Problems in Line

The designer must remember that the two-dimensional lines in a costume sketch will be translated into the three-dimensional costume of a moving actor onstage. It is important to know exactly how each linear effect in the sketch will appear in the finished garment, and how the use of line will be carried throughout all the costumes in the production.

Some designers stress line, some stress color or texture, and some combine the three; after designers have worked for many years, they become aware of their preferences and learn their strengths and weaknesses. Ideas for designs may come from the line treatment of fashion illustrations, from the work of other designers, and from the art of the past, but the designer always attempts to see the two-dimensional linear effects as they will appear in three-dimensional garments.

In the outer lines of a costume, the designer can work for a harmony of long lines, short lines, or medium lines. While he or she will usually try to avoid the clash of too sharp a contrast of line, there are many modern plays in which a disproportionate effect is needed.

Figure 3–9.   Short-line (left), medium-line (center), and long-line (right) costumes. Drawings by the author.

Most period fashions are a harmony of lines that do not contain too sharp a contrast. For example, a modern suit is a harmony of medium straight lines; a Roman soldier's costume is composed primarily of short lines; ecclesiastical vestments usually involve an interplay of long lines (Figure 3–9). Mid-nineteenth-century women's costumes, which call for tiers of fabric and small pattern pieces, are a play of short lines.

The outer lines of a costume may show a play of curved lines, such as one finds in eighteenth-century dress or in the costume lines of the Romantic period. The curved line of the upper puffed sleeve is contrasted with the curved lines of the skirt and underskirt, and in the eighteenth-century costume, the harmony of curves is further accentuated by the draped curves of decoration on the outer skirt or by the draping of the outer skirt itself in a series of curves over the panier. Often, such harmonies of curves have contrasting accents of angles at the bodice front, in the trim, or even at the neckline, so that the lines of the costume do not become too monotonous. A costume based more on a harmony of angles than on curves is the early sixteenth-century Tudor gown. Here angularity is apparent in the neckline, waist, overskirt, and gabled headdress. Minor accents of curves are sometimes added by a necklace or in the shape of the sleeves (Figure 3–10). In such a contrast the curved-line harmony is soft, full, and graceful, while the angular harmony is strong, solid, and harsh.

A harmony of direction is achieved when the major lines of a costume are horizontal, vertical, or diagonal; if the lines go equally in all three directions, complete confusion and fragmentation of effect result.

Let us consider the possibility of a harmony of curves and angles. If we take a dress that has almost all of its exterior lines as curves, and add a series of scalloped flounces also in curves, we have a harmony of curves. If we then add a zigzag bottom flounce, we destroy the total effect by destroying the expectation set up by the three curved flounces. Unless we

Figure 3–10.   Angular-line (left) and curved-line (right) harmony. Drawings by the author.

can include a series of repeats for the zigzag line as a subordinate accent, the one strong zigzag must be left out. The strength of the curves and the zigzags cannot be equal or they cancel each other.

Or, let us take the example of a strong circular pattern down one side of a costume and a triangular pattern down the opposite side. Each side has a strong harmony through repetition, but the two sides are opposed in their decorative patterns; the result is an opposition between the two sides of the costume.

Compositional Problems in Shape and Measure

Problems of shape and measure have to be solved during every step of the design process. Designers must train their eyes to judge proportion and shape in the objects about them and the clothes they see in the street. Just how large and what shape should a belt, sleeves, neckbands, and wristbands be? Only when one achieves a fine eye for shape and measure can one tell immediately that a belt is too large or the wrong shape, or that the shape of a

bodice and its length are disproportionate to a particular female form.

The most common decorative harmonies with a definite shape and measure are the circle, the band, and stripes. There are any number of variations derived from them. When the designer repeats a shape three or more times, the size of the shape and the space between the repeats become a problem to be solved in relation to the rest of the costume. One must not overdo repetitions, but should work to achieve the correct placement, shape, size, and space between shapes so that a focus or accent is created instead of a monotonous repetition of decorations.

Compositional Problems of Sequence and Repetition

The designer who works with simple geometric shapes is doing something basic to the most primitive societies: abstracting pattern from nature, and ordering and controlling it. Looking at Neolithic wall paintings and decorative pottery, one is aware of how much importance human beings have placed on the abstraction and ordering of objects taken from the apparent disorder of nature.

When one repeats a shape more than twice, a sequence results. If the decoration on a costume is subtly done, a sequence permits the eye to move from point to point rather than to remain focused on a single motif. The problem with a sequence is that it must not be too obvious, and the eye must follow from point to point easily (Figure 3–11a); it must not confuse the eye by too large a jump from one point to the next, nor must some larger and differently shaped motif interrupt in the middle of the sequence to destroy its effect (Figure 3–11b). When two sequences in a costume are about equal in interest and strength, they fight for dominance and cancel each other. The costume can never achieve a unity or a single focus until one sequence is subordinated to the other (Figure 3–11c). The designer who sees a conflict in a sequence must learn the simplest

method of correcting the focus so that the original idea for the costume need not be discarded. One area of the body that often causes trouble is the waistline. Frequently, a sequence of motifs that runs up the figure from floor to neck can be blocked by a belt that is too wide or has a sequence of horizontal direction that is too strong. One has to pay particular attention to the width and decoration of a belt. When a sequence of decoration is involved, any transition from one area to another can cause difficulty and must be handled with great care.

A sequence is more interesting if it is a sequence of alternation rather than mere repetition. In Western art, some of the great basic sequences of alternation are those used by the Greeks and Romans as architectural ornament. The egg and dart, bead and reel, and leaf and dart moldings are excellent examples of rhythmic alternations of shape. The accent

Figure 3–11.   Problems in sequence and repetition. Drawings by the author.

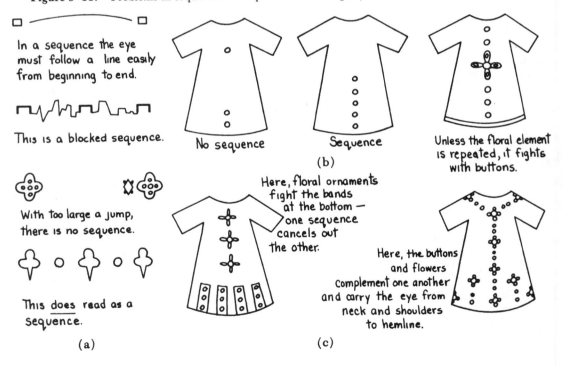

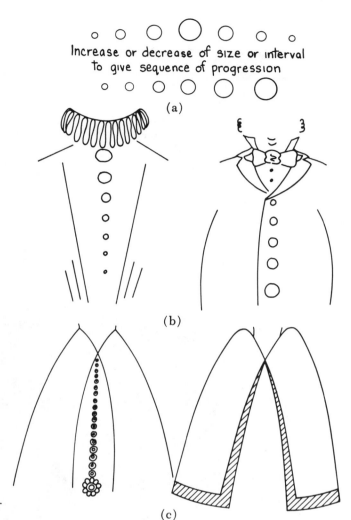

Increase or decrease of size or interval
to give sequence of progression

(a)

(b)

Figure 3–12. Sequences of progression. Drawings by the author.

(c)

comes at regular intervals, and one can sense oneself reacting rhythmically when one looks at the sequences or when one develops them as an artist. An even more interesting use of sequence, but one often difficult to work into a design without creating too obvious an effect, is a sequence of progression. Here the designer works to increase or decrease the size of the shape or the interval between the shapes so that a sense of growth or decay, a sense of enlargement or contraction is added to the sense of movement in the sequence (Figure 3–12a). For example, buttons can become larger and farther apart as they march up the torso to a climax in a large collar or ruff; or they may en-

large and grow farther apart as they come down from the neck to a very portly stomach (Figure 3–12b). Most progressions run downward; it is always easier to come down the figure than to go up it because of our sense of the pull of gravity. Another important use of the sequence is in enlarging the size and space between motif shapes as they go down a skirt front or edge a divided overskirt, since the expanding lines of the costume are complemented by the expanding progression of the decoration (Figure 3–12c).

Sometimes, especially in certain comic costumes or in classically simple costumes, the entire design scheme is based on a calculated

63

play of curved versus straight lines, bands of decoration in exactly the right proportions, and sequences of motifs that expand and contract to fit the expanding and contracting lines of the costume. It is a rational rather than an emotional kind of design, and the results can give the audience a sense of controlled humor.

Let us use as an example a comic costume designed for Sir Andrew Aguecheek in a production of *Twelfth Night.* To make the figure look taller and thinner and to make the lines of the body contract and expand in an exaggeration of the typical Elizabethan figure, the braiding on the doublet might deliberately get smaller toward the waist, the bands on the leg might outline the thighs as separate parts, and the bows at the shoulders and knees might make the whole figure look like a tightly packaged gift. All would give a calculated play of linear effects using repetition, alternation, and progression to exaggerate the human figure (Figure 3–13).

Figure 3–13. Harmony, sequence, and balance in a costume design for Sir Andrew Aguecheek in *Twelfth Night;* as produced by the Actor's Workshop, San Francisco, 1962. From the collection of the author.

The Dangers of "Obesity" in Costume Design

> Lack of faith in the value that lies in limitation and proportion . . . is the undoing of all good ideas which are born in the minds . . . of designers.
>
> —Edward Gordon Craig,
> *On the Art of the Theatre,* 1911

This quotation from the statements of the "New Stagecraft" designer Gordon Craig enunciates a basic principle of good costume design that should be heeded by the raw novice and the experienced professional alike. One should work for the large impression based on the structure of the play itself, not for an overly detailed period reality. Every designer should learn the value of simplicity and the need to work for limitation and proportion in costume design as in all other works of art.

Much contemporary costume design has lost touch with these basic principles and is heavy-handed, overdone, excessively complex, and lacking in a clear design mood or image. Looking at this kind of design is like eating an overly rich confection or a dish of ice cream with multiple toppings—the visual effect may be dazzling, but one cannot distinguish the individual flavors because they are so many and so varied that they cancel each other out. Simplicity flies in the face of materialistic consumerism, but if we think that art should lead rather than follow, then should we not attempt to change this trend in our school, university, and professional repertory productions rather than fall in with the worst habits of television and movie spectacle?

This same point was vividly reinforced by the actress Shirley Knight in talking to a group of students at the American Conservatory Theatre in San Francisco. Discussing her role in *Kennedy's Children,* she explained that in her early performances she had developed a careful, exact, overly motivated, and highly complex portrayal in which there were no loose ends. The audience understood it and accepted it, but found it too much to absorb and so did not reach out to get inside the role with her. As she became more secure in her part,

she removed some of the clarity, complexity, and detail, making the audience strain and guess about certain of the character's aims and motivations. Immediately she felt that the members of the audience were no longer acting as mere observers or consumers but were working with her to get inside the role, seeing relationships and finding answers along with her.

Perhaps these precepts seem all very well when applied to paintings or the performance of an actress but a little vague when applied to the specifics of costume design. Solid, three-dimensional garments with buttons and braid are not as easily transformed from materialistic reality into theatrical impression as are paintings or even the design sketch on which the finished costumes are based. One way to decrease some of the complexity and clarity of detail is to apply the techniques used in painting or in the design sketch directly to the costume. Too many people still think of costumes as items of clothing to be put into the wardrobe, and thus they seldom go beyond the dressmaking and tailoring process. Spraying, painting, highlighting, and shadowing are equally, if not more, important in the creation of stage costumes and should be used with much greater frequency than they are at present to achieve simple, striking design impressions or images.

Another important factor in good but simple design is the line of the costume and its overall silhouette. One of the classics of dramatic literature, frequently overdesigned, is *Faust.* Its costumes should have a larger-than-life quality without being distracting—a simplicity and strength that will concentrate attention on the play's themes and ideas, not on period spectacle. *Faust* is a great dramatic poem and philosophic parable, not an excuse for costume display.

When the late Frank Bevan, one of the great teachers of costume design, designed *Faust* at Yale in 1949 (see Figure 15–12), the costumes were simple and strong, reflecting none of the facile richness and technical display that one so frequently finds in this play or those by Shakespeare. Bevan chose clarity of silhouette, a careful sense of balance and proportion, and striking contrasts of dark and light over a display of period styles. The resultant designs are classics.

As for Shakespeare, there was a design in the preceding chapter (see Figure 2–15) from a post-Napoleonic production of *Hamlet* in which the figure of Bernardo is seen primarily as a mood silhouette rather than as a complex of period details. Silhouetted against the night sky, the costume would suggest the coldness of the night and the mystery of the moment, while in movement it would give a muffled size and larger-than-life dimension to the actor. But to the designer interested in technical virtuosity and display, the concept would seem simpleminded or unfinished. Why not a carefully researched, richly ornamented Napoleonic officer's uniform that would attract the eye with the variety of its line and the richness of its detail? Because it is the play and the mood of the moment that count, and the audience should not be distracted by a complex period costume.

Thus it is wise to recall those precepts set down by Edward Gordon Craig seventy years ago. It is the first impression that counts with an audience, and if that impression is of an overfrosted cake or a masquerade party, that is the image that will remain in mind throughout the evening. Brought up in a theatre tradition in which spectacle was always placed above the script, Craig argued for designs—particularly for Shakespeare—that supported the mood and structure of the play. Yet seventy years later two-thirds of the Shakespearean productions that one sees are excuses for heavy, ornate, complicated, materialistic spectacle— something for audiences to watch like television extravaganzas in case they are bored with the play. Designers and directors seem to fear their audiences' voracious visual appetites and feel that they must give them something else to digest every few moments during the production.

There is obesity in design today as there is in everything else in the United States—government, bureaucracy, inflation, deficits, waste, pollution, and all the rest. It is time to return to the concept that less can be more if it is the right effect in the right place at the right time. Memorable design moments are always simple, and too much design cancels them out. Designers should once again place their "faith in the value that lies in limitation and proportion."

Characterization and Design When Costumes Are Rented or Taken from Wardrobe

Ideally, costumes are designed for each production and "built from scratch" in a well-equipped shop, but a word or two should be said about the more common necessity of renting costumes or choosing them from the costume wardrobe.

First of all, a few costume houses will build costumes to a designer's specifications at a price that is well below that which they would charge to a commercial management; this may prove helpful when a designer does not have the trained personnel to build frock coats and other tailored garments. Costume houses will send out design layouts that include sketches for an entire production, but do not assume when you rent a production that all the costumes will mirror the lines in the sketches. The layout is primarily a promotional device to increase rentals, although when a costume house owns the costumes from a professional New York production, one may receive all the costumes designed for the original presentation. Usually, when renting, one receives a coordinated group of costumes related to the sketches in a costume layout but chosen to fit the measurements of one's actors.

For the best results, the designer or costume coordinator should go to the rental house and pick out the costumes with the company personnel. Only in an emergency should costumes be rented sight unseen on the basis of a description, a thumbnail sketch, and a few measurements. In preparing to visit a costume house, the designer or coordinator should do a complete layout as described in Chapter 2. To each small sketch colored fabrics in the appropriate textures may be attached as a reminder of the preferred costume scheme. Then the designer's plans will not be frustrated if he or she cannot find exactly the color scheme desired for each costume. The designer should have a clear idea of the unified result he or she wants to achieve in the production, and must keep it in mind throughout the trying process of choosing rental items. There will always be some costumes or parts of costumes that will not be satisfactory and will call for a compromise in the design plan.

Measurements usually needed by the rental house are bust or chest, waist, hips, shirt size, collar size, hat size, shoe size, inseam, over-arm, and possibly the shoulder measurement. Costume rental houses that will usually give competent service will be found in the section ''Sources of Theatrical Supplies'' at the back of the book.

When the designer receives costumes from a rental house, he or she will be allowed certain changes in the garments as long as they do not basically alter the costume. New buttons and trim may be applied if the original ones are replaced before the costumes are returned, and garments may be altered to fit more smoothly.

When a designer works with costumes from the wardrobe or from local thrift stores, army surplus stores, or secondhand stores, the procedure is about the same as that used in choosing from a rental house, except that now any amount of change and alteration is possible. Often, disparate items from a wardrobe may be brought together by trim, buttons, or the way waistcoats, ties, or costume accessories are used. Color will help to give a unified feeling to a production in spite of great varieties in cut, line, and texture. Items also can be dyed or a felt pen or textile paint can be used to strengthen patterns or outlines of trim. One method of establishing a unity of atmosphere among a ''grab bag'' of wardrobe items is to texture the costumes with spray paint, dye, or dry-brushing. In this way the designer can still control the effect of the costume even though he must use ready-made items from the wardrobe.

The Costume Portfolio

Something must be said at some point about the costume designer's portfolio and the organization and presentation of this important aid to securing employment. The close of a chapter on the principles of design seems as logical a place as any for a discussion of this portable gallery devoted to the designer's work.

First of all, the portfolio should include no more than half a dozen productions in a carefully chosen breadth and variety of style. The designer should not overwhelm a potential employer with material. Secondly, all sketches should be amply supported by swatches, early-stage thinking sketches or ''doodles,'' small figure layouts, and above all photographs of the costumes in production (not lined up in the back hall). Portfolios should be presented in person if possible and not sent through the mails. If the latter is absolutely necessary then photos or slides of sketches should be sent—not the originals. Finally, remember what the portfolio is for. It is to portray and give insight into the way the designer works and solves artistic problems. It is not meant to be a gallery of lovely sketches and pretty pictures.

4

Color

Color Theory

An audience will generally react more readily to color than to line or texture. Thus, the strength of color as a part of design demands that the designer have full control of its use. The costume designer, like the scene designer, must know color theory before working with color. Knowledge of color theory does not inhibit imagination; it gives the designer control over color effects in fabric. Color theory is something that is learned, becomes a part of one's approach, and is forgotten as a series of rules, although it is retained as a critical way of seeing.

A color has three properties that can be varied: hue, value, and intensity.

HUE. When the radiant energy from the sun passes through a triangular prism of glass, the light beam is broken up into various wavelengths and a series of colors is seen by the eye, like the spectrum one sees when one looks at a rainbow. Hue is the name given to the various colors that are formed from the refraction of sunlight. Objects, or, in our case, fabrics, do not actually contain color; they have the capacity to absorb some wavelengths and reflect others so that only certain wavelengths reach the viewer's eye. It is the psychological and physical responses to these wavelengths that make a viewer call an object or fabric a certain color. There is, of course, great variation in the human response to color: what is red to one person is purple to another.

Many systems attempt to codify the basic colors of the spectrum in relation to each other and to black and white. But for our purposes, it is necessary only to know the standard color wheel used in grade school and introductory color theory classes.

The full color wheel is made up of twelve colors or hues: three primaries, six basic colors that include these primaries, and six intermediate hues. The three primaries are yellow, red, and blue. From the three primaries all the other colors of the wheel can be achieved by mixing. The secondary colors, orange, violet, and green, can be obtained by mixing equal amounts of two primaries. The intermediate colors, yellow-green, blue-green, blue-violet, red-violet, red-orange, and yellow-orange, can be obtained by mixing a primary color and a secondary color. Colors that are next to each other on the color wheel are said to be *analogous* colors, those directly opposite one another are *complementaries*. The center of the wheel is neutral or gray and, theoretically, if one mixes equal parts of two complementaries, one will achieve a neutral gray. An axis or line running up through this center neutral point of the color wheel will, in four even steps of gray, reach white above the color wheel and black below. By drawing lines from each of the colors on the wheel to the central axis that contains black and white, two cones are created, one above and one below the color wheel. Thus, one can see what happens to a color when it is mixed with black and white; it is both grayed and lightened or darkened at the same time. One can also understand that when two colors are mixed, they produce a color that is somewhat closer to the center of the wheel than any single color on the outside of the wheel; thus, all mixtures are less intense in color than a pure color (Figure 4–1).

VALUE. The lightness or darkness of a hue or color is its value. Lightness or darkness is determined by the amount of black or white mixed with a basic hue. A color of high lightness is known as a *tint,* one of low lightness or darkness is known as a *shade.* The color wheel, when viewed as the circular base that divides the two cones—one leading upward to white, the other leading downward to black—is not quite perpendicular to the axis through the two cones. It is tipped at a slight angle, and yellow is therefore lighter than blue, violet is darker than orange, blue is darker than green. One can arrange the twelve colors of the wheel on a scale that travels up the axis of the wheel from black to white. Since the untutored eye can see only so many different levels of gray, the scale of grays or neutral values up the axis of the wheel from black to white is usually limited to seven steps: low dark, dark, high dark, medium, low light, light, high light. It is important to realize that all the hues on the wheel, if grayed, do not correspond to medium gray

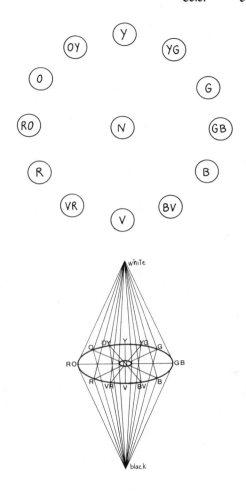

Figure 4–1. The color wheel (above) and the color solid (below). Drawings by the author.

or medium neutral. In other words, in the diagram of the wheel with the neutral axis through the center, the wheel is tipped so that yellow corresponds to high light, yellow-orange and yellow-green to light, green and orange to low light, blue-green and red-orange to medium, blue and red to high dark, blue-violet and red-violet to dark, and violet to low dark (Figure 4–2).

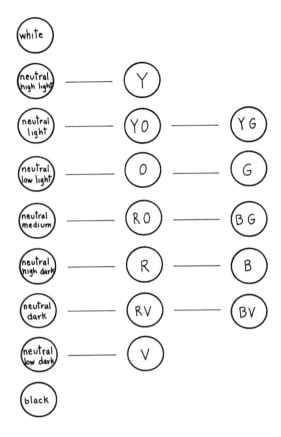

Figure 4–2. Value scale and value relationship of the twelve principal hues. Drawing by the author.

neutralization. If we crossed the full wheel from, let us say, orange to its complementary hue of blue, we would have seven full steps—three on each side of the axis of neutralization.

When one changes the value of a hue toward a tint or a shade by adding white or black, and thereby raises or lowers the value of a color, one also changes and lowers its intensity. In other words, one can change the intensity of a hue without changing its value, but one cannot alter the value without lowering the intensity. One can see from the diagrams that accompany this explanation that in going from a hue on one side of the wheel to its complement on the other side, the line from one to the other is not direct unless, as in the case of red-orange and blue-green, the complements meet at the same neutral value on the axis of the wheel (Figure 4–3).

Color theory both helps to explain color relationships and to describe in comprehensible terms the nature and appearance of a particular hue under particular conditions. If someone asks you to produce a red-orange color that is at one-fourth intensity and at a low light value, you can reproduce this tint without a great deal of difficulty. In short, color theory is not just an accurate way to describe color, but a tool artists and scientists use to reproduce color precisely.

Color Mixing

In practice, colors seldom do exactly what they are supposed to do according to color theory. Particularly in pigment mixing, color theory cannot take into account the effect of chemical reactions among ingredients, the purity of the pigments, or the variations in the textures on which the pigments are used.

There are two basic methods of color mixing: additive and subtractive. Both have to do with the way color is created by light. When a ray of light strikes any object, it is broken up into wavelengths that are reflected, absorbed, or transmitted. If the object on which the light

INTENSITY.   The saturation or intensity of a color is determined by its purity as a hue. If a color is pure and has full brilliance, it is said to have full intensity. It loses intensity if it is mixed with another hue or grayed with black or white. Usually, three steps are shown in moving a hue from full intensity to its value of neutrality or gray on the axis of the color wheel. These three steps are three-fourths intensity, one-half intensity, and one-quarter intensity; or, if they are read as steps toward neutralization and away from full intensity, they are labeled one-quarter neutralization, one-half neutralization, and three-quarters

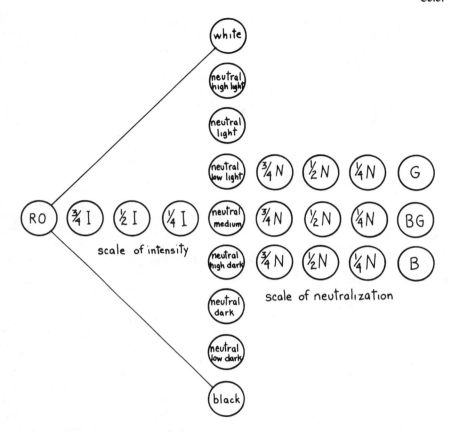

Figure 4–3. Intensity-value steps for red-orange and scale of neutralization for green, blue-green, and blue. Drawing by the author.

falls is transparent, then the resultant pattern of absorption and transmission is known as a subtractive color mixture. For example, when a small amount of white light falls on a red fabric, a small amount of white light is reflected (the exact amount depends on the angle at which the light strikes the surface), and this reflected light is dominated by the red wavelengths. Thus, red is transmitted to the eye of the viewer, and the remainder of the white light is subtracted. Theoretically, if one placed a green filter in the path of the red light, nothing would be transmitted because the red would be absorbed by its complementary hue of green.

When two different beams of light, each with a different composition of wavelengths, fall on a surface and are reflected to the eye, what the eye sees is a single hue or color. For instance, if a green and a red beam were reflected to the eye from the same surface, the viewer would theoretically see yellow. In other words, one color is added to another color to form a third color; this is called additive mixing.

ADDITIVE MIXING. Additive mixing is usually considered to be mainly the province of the lighting designer, who mixes colored light instead of pigments, but additive mixing can be extremely effective for the costume and the set designer, too. When a surface is spattered with dots of varying hues, the eye will mix the dots. At a distance, the dots will appear as a single hue, but with more intensity than a single hue achieved by colors mixed before painting. This was discovered by the nineteenth-century French pointillist painters, particularly the scientifically oriented Seurat. Additive mixing can enhance the appearance of a costume onstage by giving more depth to fabric, more three-dimensionality to form, and stronger contrasts between highlight and shadow.

SUBTRACTIVE MIXING.   Subtractive mixing is the mixing of color, usually pigment of one kind or another, before the rays of light are reflected to the eye. Here the designer is mixing hues directly, as when attempting to achieve subtle tints and shades in sketches. As any art student knows, when colors are mixed on a palette or in paint tins, the colors added subtract from the intensity and from the color of the original hue. When red paint is poured into yellow and the result is orange, all other wavelengths are subtracted except the orange one. The impressionists and the pointillists discovered that subtractive mixing grayed and neutralized the brilliance of primaries and secondaries. That is why they shifted to additive color mixing. By applying primary colors in dots or strokes, and allowing the eye to do the mixing, they retained a much greater intensity of color. In painting sketches or in preparing paint or dye for costumes, the costume designer sometimes uses the pointillist technique, but far more frequently employs the subtractive method and develops a palette from a large array of commercial pigments.

Color and Light

When a color in a fabric or in paint is seen onstage under light, the color is modified or changed by the light that strikes it. The costume designer not only has to consider the color and texture of the costumes in relation to

their background, but must know how the color of the costumes will be modified by colored light. The appearance of color under stage light is a particular problem if there is unusual lighting in a scene, such as that produced by a fire, moonlight, or some supernatural source. The basic principle here is similar to that in subtractive mixing: a red light makes a red fabric look redder, grays or neutralizes a green fabric, and makes a yellow fabric look orange or at least have an orange quality.

One way to visualize color modification is to view the costume color scheme through a sample of the gelatin or color medium to be used in the production. Well-equipped theatre plants may have a viewing room or a miniature theatre stage where the costume designer can check various fabrics under a duplication of the lights to be used onstage. The costume designer can get some idea of color effects under stage light by using two spotlights in a darkened room, one with cool and one with warm gels. The real challenge is to have colored light that is equally effective for both sets and costumes. It need hardly be noted that color planning for a stage production demands the closest cooperation among the light designer, the scene designer, and the costume designer. Some useful reference books on color theory are Ralph M. Evans, *The Perception of Color* (New York: John Wiley, 1974); Maitland Graves, *The Art of Color and Design,* 3rd ed. (New York: McGraw-Hill, 1951).

Color Consciousness for the Designer

One approach to color is not superior to another, nor are the color schemes of one age to be preferred to those of another. The art of each age has its own color formulas and restrictions, and so does the costume of an age. In taking any color usage for stage costume, the designer, whether using strong primaries or neutralized secondaries, must work for the control and unity that is right for a particular play. Bright colors may please the color sense of the average viewer, but they should be used only if they support the mood of the play to be produced. A musical comedy done in bright hues is often a visual success, not because of subtlety or color control, but because the bright colors have the same appeal as those on banners, flags, or heraldic emblems. Red, white, and blue for a musical can be designed just as effectively as grayed hues for *Pelléas and Mélisande,* even though the grayed hues may look more controlled because of the subtlety of color used.

One essential for the designer in developing a keen sense of color is the ability to separate color from the line, form, and texture that contain it. The designer must learn to see color as an isolated phenomenon of a certain hue, intensity, and value. This is often difficult to do with clothing, because one tends to see color as part of a garment rather than as an area of blue or green or red of a certain shape. We are all too conditioned to see intellectually rather than visually, to register the facts and associations about an object rather than to see it without preconceptions. Modern abstract art has attempted to teach people to see in a new way—to see color for its own sake and not as part of a preconceived idea. For example, the early twentieth-century French fauvists, revolting from the muddied and neutralized colors of nineteenth-century academic art, painted only with primary colors. They revived the viewer's pleasure in vivid colors for their own sake (Figures 4-4a and 4-4b). But many beginning designers, as well as most audiences, connect color with associations or facts. They do not see color visually. Thus, the designer always tries to balance the visual and intellectual ways of seeing, attempting to plan color in terms of hue, value, and intensity, while still fitting it to people's associations and preconceptions. To stress the latter without full control of the former is to produce color clichés.

As one develops as a designer, one may find, as did the great artists of the past, that one is either a linearist or a colorist. Either one will instinctively stress line and form over color, or vice versa. We know, for example, that Michelangelo stressed line and form,

while Titian stressed color (Figures 4-5a and 4-5b). Delacroix stressed color, while Ingres concentrated on line. The instinctual preference for line or color can be found in most costume designers, and designers must become aware of their biases. They may then perfect their work or broaden their feeling for color or line, depending on which receives the weaker emphasis in their work. A well-trained designer will take pleasure in working with both line and color, but one will probably always seem more interesting than the other. This has been true of artists through the ages, and it is certainly true of costume and set designers in the theatre today.

In developing a color sense, a costume designer, unlike the easel artist, must develop a sense of color in movement. While the set designer sees color move or shift with changes of lighting on the stage, the costume designer observes the entire color palette moving and shifting with each new grouping, each new picturization, each small cross or large gesture. This is difficult for the designer to remember when sketching, since he or she is then working like any other draftsman or painter. Before bringing color to a static costume on paper, the designer should experiment with colored cut-out swatches on a miniature stage, or with colored fabrics draped or hung over the actors in rehearsal, to get a clear picture of the color palette in movement, developing and shifting with the progress of the production. Eventually, a designer may be able to see color movement in his or her imagination; but in the beginning, anything that will assist in making the designer aware of the problem is helpful.

Developing a Color Palette

In developing a color palette for a production, there are two avenues of approach. One, the technical approach, is based on color theory. The other is an emotional approach based on some strong image, mood, or association that struck the designer during the first reading of the play. One of the favorite schemes for the beginning designer is the use of monochromatic color in a costume. By working with a gray-blue dress with rich blue trim and a pastel blue accent, a designer is assured of a costume that will be pleasing and harmonious without difficult color balances to be solved. Sometimes a whole scene will be designed monochromatically, with a possible accent of another hue. For example, the Edward Gorey designs for the 1977 Broadway revival of *Dracula* were all in black, white, and gray, but each scene had a tiny dynamic accent of red in either the sets or the costumes (Figure 4–6). A designer will often find that a fascinating game can be played with the variations on a single hue through shifts in intensity and value, or with the limited palettes that can be devised through the use of neutrals and a single color.

In *Macbeth,* the color palette can be all grays and blacks with an accent of red, and one can bring color movement to the production by increasing the amount of red in the costumes as the play progresses. Or one can do a play completely in black and white, the black creating the silhouette or form and the white creating the accents, or vice versa. A production of Webster's *The Duchess of Malfi* that was intended to stress the mannerist silhouette of Spain and Italy in the late sixteenth century might use all black and gray costumes with white accents in ruffs and cuffs and a few accents of red related to the deep burgundy color demanded by the Cardinal's costume—all against changing lighting on a back screen of arches suggesting the Doge's Palace in Venice.

Figure 4–6.   The use of black, white, and gray in costume and scenery for a Broadway revival of *Dracula,* 1977, designed by Edward Gorey. Each scene had a tiny, dynamic accent of red in sets, costumes, or props to create a point of focus for the audience and remind them of vampire blood. Photo courtesy of Martha Swope.

Figure 4–7. The use of black, white, gray, and red in costumes gives a controlled limitation of color based on late sixteenth-century paintings of Tintoretto and El Greco; a scene from a production of *The Duchess of Malfi* by John Webster, as produced by the Berkeley Shakespeare Festival, 1979. Costumes and photo by the author.

It would be a limited concept, but effective (Figure 4–7).

Another possibility is to have a repressed mannerist world in black, white, and gray come in contact with a developing world of soft tie-dyed colors—as if mannerism were about to be transformed into the early Baroque period, with its expansiveness and color. This was used in a production of *The Tempest* to contrast the courtiers and the islanders (Figure 4–8).

Many designers with a developed color sense like to use a palette that plays with intensity and value variations in analogous colors.

Figure 4–8. Figures of the shipwrecked courtiers in black and silver meet Prospero in a developing palette of tie-dyed color in a production of *The Tempest;* as produced by the Berkeley Shakespeare Festival, 1980. Costumes and photo by the author.

For example, a pleasing scheme of warmth and gaiety can be achieved by taking orange as the key color and working out a series of variations in red-orange and yellow-orange. For the band of exiled courtiers led by the banished Duke in *As You Like It,* one might develop a scheme that ranges from red-orange darkened to brown, orange-brown, and dark yellow-orange to the pure intense hues of each color, and on into accents of lighter red-orange, orange, and yellow-orange. Carefully done, it would be limited but still give a feeling of variety.

One may also expand this scheme into the cool or warm palettes so often used by designers. Here one group in the production is dressed only in warm colors, the other in cool. One frequently sees productions of *Romeo and Juliet* in which the Capulets wear warm hues—reds, oranges, warm browns, and golds—while the Montagues wear blues, greens, and blue-violets. *Antony and Cleopatra* is frequently designed with the forces of Egypt in the warm hues associated with that climate, while the forces of Rome wear much gray, white, and purple, the cool colors that seem appropriate to coldly intellectual Rome.

Finally, there are the schemes that can be developed using contrasting colors. The most obvious is found in complementary hues: orange and blue, yellow and violet, green and red. But such color contrasts are difficult to create without harshness and unpleasantness, unless there is a careful play of intensity and value in the way the colors are used together and a careful proportioning of the amounts of the complementaries used. To use equal amounts of full-saturation complementaries is to arrive at a scheme that would be acceptable only in band or football uniforms. However, in a production of *Twelfth Night,* Orsino's costume for the scene in which he listens to music and dreams of Olivia was designed in purple with accents of yellow and neutrals of black and white. There were lavenders and grayed purples with touches of pale yellow among the lords, all leading to the bright yellow costume of Feste. It worked as a use of the violet-yellow complementary contrast, even though it did not seem appropriate to the

particular scene. A variation of the complementary scheme is the split complement, in which, instead of using the hue directly across the color wheel, the designer selects two hues that lie on either side of the complementary hue. Instead of using yellow and violet, the split complement would use yellow with red-violet and blue-violet. The split complement gives a slightly greater range of color play and is effective when used with many variations in intensity and value. The expanded contrasting-complement scheme could have been used in the *Twelfth Night* production to give further variety to the courtier costumes surrounding Orsino.

Another use of contrasting colors is the triad. Colors that are equidistant from each other on the color wheel are used together, for example, yellow-orange, red-violet, and blue-green. The triad gives a variety of color effect when there is wide play of intensity and value variations, but proportion is again important. One hue should probably be dominant, and the others remain secondary or act as accents. Such a scheme might be useful in a play that had a triangular grouping of characters or an interplay of three forces. For *Antony and Cleopatra,* one might work out the Egyptian forces in the orange-yellow area, Rome in the red-violet area with neutrals, and the forces of Pompey in the blue-green area. Sometimes an obvious contrast such as red-blue is useful, even necessary, to differentiate between opposing forces. There are scenes in Shakespeare's history plays, where French forces are pitted against English, in which the French could be costumed in variations of blue with accents of white, black, gray, and metallic gold, and the English in variations of red with accents of black, white, gray, and gold. Such an obvious scheme is sometimes necessary for identification and clarity.

All of the above schemes are based on some limitation on the value-intensity scale or the color wheel itself, and are arrived at technically or intellectually rather than emotionally. The usual impetus for a designer's color scheme is his or her emotional response to the play, although the designer may later translate the color images into a technical scheme. For example, in Shakespeare's tragedies, such as *King Lear, Macbeth,* and *Hamlet,* one thinks of color of low value and intensity, of costumes seen in darkness or by flickering torch or sconce. There are almost no full daylight scenes in these plays. But the designer's color palette must be developed from more specific visual images in the play, from the period chosen in which to present the play, and from ideas about or characterizations of key personages. What the designer and the director arrive at first is a color image, even if only for one character or one scene that is for them important. Once a color image is set, the designer is free to work out a scheme that may use any or all of the technical schemes already mentioned to support and expand the color image. If the color image that strikes both director and designer in *Macbeth* is blood, then the color scheme might work out similarly to the technical scheme we mentioned, but it might also lead to more variety in low-keyed neutral colors than would be the case with grays, blacks, and whites used with red. In *Hamlet,* Hamlet's costume is black, since there is reference in the play to an inky coat of black. Black becomes a color image of strong emotional association and has great influence on what one does with the color of the other costumes in the play. Must the court be rich and gaudy, dark and austere, limited or varied in color? The answer lies in the director's and the designer's image of Hamlet as he stands against the court. There is no easy, step-by-step process for working out a color palette from emotionally felt color associations. In the beginning it is instinctive, and only after the key image for a play has been set can the designer's keen eye and knowledge of color theory be brought into play to develop a full color scheme for a whole production.

Color Associations

The first images that leap to mind as the designer reads the script must be sifted, rearranged, or revised many times during the preparation of a color scheme for a production, but the original color associations are usually valid and useful. Yet everyone has color associations that are clichés. We recognize the red and green of Christmas, the red for stop and the green for go, the red, white, and blue of Uncle Sam immediately. These colors must be developed carefully in relation to other colors if they are to achieve an artistic effect. Color clichés are useful for pop art effects, where the banality of our culture is exaggerated and satirized, and they are useful in expressionist productions, where the red, white, and blue of Uncle Sam or the American flag is made to dominate the audience and overwhelm it with this symbol of patriotism.

As we said in Chapter 1, a designer must be careful to distinguish between primary and secondary color associations. The primary color associations, such as the red, white, and blue of the American flag, the white of virginity, the red and green of Christmas, will mean the same to everyone in Western culture, but secondary color associations are personal. They come from events in a person's past in which a color has been associated with an event or emotion. The designer who uses personal color images is in danger of having the audience miss the color idea. The designer must use the associations carefully, must lead the audience into them in the same way he or she was led into the experience that set up the association in the first place. A designer may have a vivid remembrance of clothing of a certain color that he or she grew to hate as a child, and the sight of that color in any garment of a similar kind may still stir up a strong emotional reaction; but to use the association effectively on the stage, the designer would have to lead the audience along the same emotional path he or she had traversed as a child, or the color association would fail.

Besides personal color associations, there are those connected with theatrical productions seen in the past. If a designer has seen a particularly exciting color scheme in a production of a play he or she is later asked to design, it is often difficult for the designer to break with the remembered scheme when beginning the color layout for the new production. There is no harm in using a scheme one has seen work well in a previous production, but one must make it one's own. One must not just borrow a color scheme and repeat it second-hand.

Source of Color Images

Color images for a production must come from the feeling for the time and place of a play. If, after reading a script for the first time, one analyzes the nature of the color images or associations that have been aroused, one can usually trace them to a response to the play's setting, or the particular period demanded for the production. Think how the Scottish setting, the barbaric period, and the number of night scenes set up specific color images in *Macbeth,* or how the ancient English setting and the storm scene set up color associations for *King Lear.* Color associations arise from social levels in a play as well as age levels. We usually associate neutralized, earth colors with the lower classes and brilliant, rich colors with the aristocracy, just as we associate bright colors with young people and grayed and muted tonalities with age.

Most costume designers have a thorough knowledge of period fashions; the color usage of a period will come to mind by the very choice of a period for a play. Since each period has its color schemes, designers will often unconsciously be influenced in the colors they use by their knowledge of period clothes. Yet too close a reliance on period color usage may inhibit the color statement for the modern audience. Colors in period clothes should follow accurate period usage only when such a scheme helps the play to work for a modern audience. The designs must not exhibit a period color scheme that has no relation to audience taste. The designer is not demonstrating historical knowledge of period color, but attempting to make a particular play and a particular set of characters come vividly to life for the audience. A costume historian may object that

certain hues were not available in fabric dyes at the time that the play is set, but this should not inhibit the designer, who is designing for today. The actors must play before an audience that generally does not know period color schemes. Accurate period color schemes are useless if the audience loses contact with the visual scene.

One of the great sources for color schemes that truly reflect a period is painting, since it is an artistic expression of period color rather than a reflection of the fashion colors of the time. Many times a single painting, by being from the same period and by having the same mood as the play, will give the designer an entire color scheme for a production. While a color scheme based only on the fashion colors of a period may be charming but unrelated to the play, a color scheme based on a painting from the period may give a visual equivalent to the play's verbal style. A good example of this may be seen in the paintings of Paolo Veronese, an Italian contemporary of Shakespeare's. Veronese's canvases, which depict a Renaissance idea of the richness and sumptuousness of classical times, are analogous in many ways to Shakespeare's *Antony and Cleopatra.* A color scheme for this play from *The Feast at Cana* or *The Feast in the House of Levi* may not follow the fashion colors of the period, but it works easily and effectively without great alteration. Also, because Veronese is a great colorist, a modern audience can appreciate his effects, whereas they might not follow the color vagaries of late sixteenth-century fashion (Figures 4–9a and 4–9b).

Still other sources of color are the minor arts of a period: the tableware, lamps, furniture, tapestries, mosaics, jewelry. An interesting Victorian lamp may inspire a color scheme that is more valid than a scheme borrowed from the fashion plates of *Godey's Lady's Book,* or a set of Baroque tableware may be the key to a color layout for a play by Molière. Fine artifacts may be closer to the spirit of a period than its fashion because fashion is often personal, set by influential people who are not artists, while fine artifacts are the work of craftsmen-artists who have a deeper insight into the culture of the period.

Architecture can also be a source of color imagery, if color as well as form are important in a particular structure. For example, a richly decorated Romanesque church interior might suggest colors for a medieval production.

Certainly a designer should never overlook nature as a source of color imagery. In many productions, intricate and beautiful color schemes have come from marine life, flower gardens, rocks, insects, animals, and other natural sources. If the natural source is appropriate to the play, such a scheme has a freshness that cannot be found in mechanical use of color theory or borrowing from painting and the minor arts. For example, *The Tempest,* which stresses sea and marine imagery, can be beautifully costumed in a color scheme taken from the hues of undersea life, while *Twelfth Night,* which centers around a formal garden, can effectively take a color scheme from a flower garden (Figure 4–10).

There are many other possible sources for color images, and any of them, when matching the mood of the play, may provide a brilliant scheme. The designer must always be alert to all sources of color images.

Color Layouts

With color images in mind, the designer must try the proposed scheme to see if it will encompass all the individual costume requirements in the production. By taking colored cardboard (like that found in the Coloraid swatch book in art stores), cut-out colored papers, or colored fabric swatches, or by building a color collage in paint, the designer can develop color groupings for the various sets of characters. One should work on layout technique until one feels comfortable with the scheme. The scheme should be flexible enough to adjust if extra characters are added, if further courtiers and guards are needed by the director, or if a cast change calls for a different colored costume for a lead. In working with a layout, a designer

should always leave enough room in any direction for fairly full groupings of characters, or the result may be to create a scheme that backs the designer into a corner. For example, a children's play or a comedy that tried to rely completely on full-intensity primaries and secondaries would run into difficulty if there were many characters. Either colors would have to be repeated after all the primary and secondary colors had been used, or neutrals would have to be introduced with primaries and secondaries acting as accents. One should always allow for a fairly wide range of variation in value and intensity, even if the color scheme is limited to only two or three hues plus neutrals.

As we mentioned earlier, many designers prefer to do their color collages or color layouts in fabric. They keep extensive files of color swatches in carefully marked intensity and value steps for each hue. The swatches are arranged until a color scheme is developed that follows a particular color image and yet also shows the amount of each color to be used in the production.

While developing a color layout, a designer must remember that no matter how carefully a scheme is planned, it is the integration of the scheme with the other design factors—the costumes, the textures of the fabrics, the movement of the actors—that is the test of the scheme's workability.

Color Planning in a Play

There are a number of ways to proceed with color planning and the allocation of color groupings when developing a color layout. First, one must determine the script requirements. A change of scene or the passage of time may require a change of color. Perhaps a key character must wear a certain color, and groupings around the character will have to take this into account. A cardinal in full red robes for *The Duchess of Malfi* or *Henry VIII* is an insistent color block onstage, and all surrounding costumes must coordinate with his robes.

Perhaps class divisions must be indicated in color: aristocrats must be distinguished from the bourgeoisie and from the servants. In *Der Rosenkavalier,* it is important to set off the aristocratic Marschallin household from the upper-bourgeois Faninal home, and to distinguish both of these from the lower-class atmosphere of the third-act inn scene. Colors are important in making these distinctions. We have already mentioned the color schemes of opposing armies, such as red for England and blue for France. Even though the script may not demand such color division, confusion results if the two forces are not differentiated.

Should the designer stress the mood and atmosphere of the total production, or design in terms of character? Often a color scheme that is appropriate for the play is not appropriate for a particular character. For example, in a production of Gluck's opera *Iphigenia in Tauris,* I chose to use a color scheme based on the colors of Wedgwood ware. The soft blues, the light seaweed green, the earth red in the vases were appropriate for the cool, sophisticated, neoclassical mood we wanted for the production. None of the Wedgwood colors seemed right for the hero, Orestes. For his costume, I moved beyond my color sources and chose the standard gold and white of the typical late eighteenth-century operatic hero. Thus, there is no one answer to the problems of mood and atmosphere versus character. It all depends on the production, the direction, and the designer's ability to integrate character designs into the overall mood of the production.

A second method of color planning is the "big scene" approach. The designer works out the colors for the most important scene, and then works backwards and forwards to take in the smaller scenes and the characters that do not appear in the important scene. The climactic scene in *Hamlet* is the mousetrap scene. If one can achieve the appropriate color image for the key characters in this scene, with a color range for the surrounding courtiers, small changes for the earlier and later scenes will often solve the color scheme for the entire production. In a production of the play presented at the Oregon Shakespeare Festival in 1961, the color scheme for the mousetrap scene was based on the famous El Greco painting, *The Burial of Count Orgaz.* By taking the young child in black who acts as the "presenter" in the painting as Hamlet, the nobles behind the body of the Count as courtiers, the church fathers in their gold and red robes as Claudius and Gertrude in their court robes, and color accents from the heavens as the color accents for Polonius, Ophelia, Rosencrantz, and Guildenstern, the color layout for the scene was established. In earlier scenes, Claudius and Gertrude wore tight, quilted black costumes with a few jewels; in the mousetrap scene, they added to their costumes the court robes; in later scenes they wore dressing gowns. Changes were kept to a minimum, and it was possible to keep El Greco's color scheme intact throughout the play.

In another method of color planning, the designer follows the changing emotional climate of the play, or the emotional progress of the leading character. By having costumes that project a character's psychological development in color, one develops a scheme around which colors for the supporting characters can be grouped. In *The Heiress,* there is the progress from a cherry red dress in the first scene to the heavy, dark, almost colorless dress of the last scene. In *Richard II,* Richard's costume changes from the flamboyant colors of the early scenes to the simpler, more reserved colors in the deposition scene to the coarse-textured black of the death scene, while Bolingbroke's costume changes from somber hues in the early scenes to full royal colors at the end of the play. The colors of the other characters can be developed around the changes for Richard and Bolingbroke.

The most difficult kind of color planning is the contrast and coordination of three or four equally important characters. It is difficult to get the right color balance in *Agamemnon* for Agamemnon, Clytemnestra, Cassandra, and Aegisthus so that color will set character and position, yet so that all four will relate to one another according to the emotional demands of the play. In opera, a similar problem occurs with four singers in a quartet: each of the four should be equally important and yet each should reflect the character's relationship to the other three. In Verdi's *Otello,* it is difficult to obtain the right color scheme for the Otello–Desdemona–Iago–Emilia quartet and still keep their characters, personal relationships, and social stations in the correct balance. Once such problems have been solved, however, the colors for the costumes in the remainder of the production will usually fall into place.

The methods for approaching the problem of color planning can be as complicated or as simple as the play being designed. There is no single best way to plan the color scheme within a production. Each designer must work out an individual approach for each production. As one's experience increases, one will find a half-dozen methods that one uses most frequently and that serve one's design needs best (Figure 4–11).

Color Relationships between Costume and Scenery

Thus far we have talked about the planning and development of color schemes without reference to the background against which the costumes will appear. Yet it is important for the costume designer's color scheme to be coordinated with that of the set designer.

The most obvious approach to color coordination between sets and costumes, and the one most frequently used on open stages, in Shakespearean unit sets, and in formal staging, is to keep the backgrounds primarily neutral in tone and allow the costumes to provide the color accent. On the Greek stage, the background was architectural, and color accents came primarily from costumes and secondarily from decorated panels. In the medieval theatre, the interior of the church, the town square, or the front of the cathedral provided a neutral background; the color was provided by the costumes and the decoration of the little booths or mansions that were used as settings. On the Elizabethan stage, the facade against which the plays were presented was neutral. The color was provided by the costumes, banners, and hangings. Only with the arrival of the proscenium stage did a complex color coordination have to take place between sets and costumes. The new stagecraft of the late nineteenth and early twentieth centuries returned to the neutral background for many productions. Sketches by Adolphe Appia and Gordon Craig indicate a neutral architectural arrangement of space against which the costumes would provide the color. This is still a workable and effective method today for Shakespearean and classical productions and has been used for many years for the Wagnerian operas at Bayreuth, Germany. It leaves the costume designer free to choose a color palette; color coordination with the set designer is thus not as important as coordination of line and form (Figure 4–12).

If the background is not to be neutral, then there should be contrast between sets and costumes, not so much that unity is destroyed, but enough so that costumes do not blend into sets. If the settings are done primarily in cool colors, then the costumes might be in warm hues. If the background is relatively dark, then the costumes might be lighter in value, or the reverse effect might be used. If a setting is grayed, then more brilliant or intense colors in costume might be used against it; but if the set is bright, the reverse, the use of grayed colors in the costumes, is not particularly effective. Obvious but often effective in achieving a high style and mannered color coordination is the subtle interaction of color from sets to costumes; a color accent in each costume is reflected in value and intensity variations in the setting. This can often turn comic, however, if upholstery, draperies, and wallpaper are too obviously color-keyed to costume. Probably the most effective color interaction between sets and costumes is a mood-evoking palette in the setting that is insistent but not obvious, in

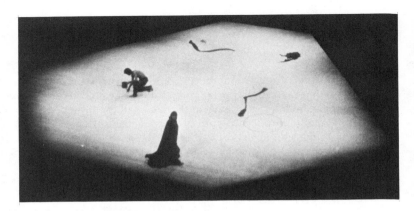

Figure 4–12. Four examples, from a 1980 Missouri Repertory Theatre production of Euripedes' *Medea,* of the importance of lighting in relation to costume and its ability to change the entire look of a production from scene to scene. Setting by Richard Hay, costumes by Douglas Russell, staging by Erik Vos. Photos by Richard L. Hay.

Figure 4–4a. Example of the use of neutralized color and its mood effect in painting: *The Angelus* by Jean-François Millet, The Louvre, Paris, 1857–1859. Photo courtesy of the Musées Nationaux, Paris.

Figure 4–4b. Example of the use of intense color and its mood effect in painting: *The Houses of Chatou* by Maurice Vlaminck, Chicago Art Institute, Chicago, ca. 1904. Photo from the Collection of The Art Institute of Chicago.

Figure 4-5a. Example of the linearist approach in Renaissance painting: *The Doni Madonna* (Holy Family) by Michelangelo, Uffizi, Florence, ca. 1506. Courtesy of Alinari/Art Resource, Inc.

Figure 4-5b. Example of the colorist approach in Renaissance painting: *The Rape of Europa* by Titian, Isabella Stewart Gardner Museum, Boston, ca. 1559. Photo courtesy of the Isabella Stewart Gardner Museum.

Figure 4–9a. Example of a painting used as a source for a rich sixteenth-century color scheme: *The Feast at Cana* by Paolo Veronese, The Louvre, Paris. Photo courtesy of the Musées Nationaux, Paris.

Figure 4–9b. A production of Shakespeare's *Antony and Cleopatra* on an Elizabethan stage, using Veronese as a color source for the costumes; as produced by the Oregon Shakespeare Festival, 1959. Photo by the author.

Figure 4–10. Example of color imagery based on marine life: a scene from a production of *The Tempest* by Shakespeare as produced by the Oregon Shakespeare Festival, Ashland, Ore., 1960. Photo by the author.

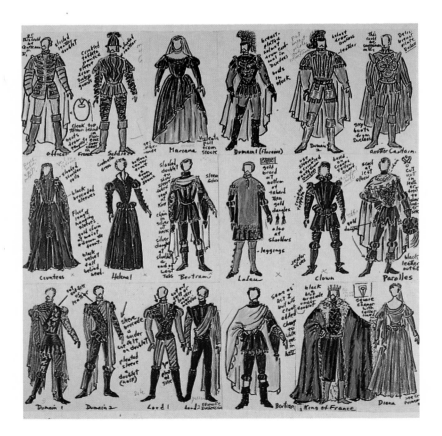

Figure 4–11. Example of the first layout of costumes for a production: a color layout of small figures for a production of Shakespeare's *All's Well That Ends Well* as produced by the Berkeley Shakespeare Festival, 1982. From the collection of the author.

which individual colors stand out less than all-over tonality of mood. If costumes are of the same general range but stronger and more intense, they both accent the scheme and blend into it as a part of the atmospheric whole.

It is important that costume color and scenery color complement one another, that each is made stronger by the addition of the other, that the entrance of a costume strengthens rather than disrupts the color scheme of the setting. A red dress on a figure seated in a red chair of the same hue or a blue costume lost against a blue wall must be avoided at all costs.

The lighting designer's scheme must work for both sets and costumes, and the gel plan used must not kill but enhance colors in both sets and costumes. Many thrust or open-stage theatres have now given up colored gels altogether in favor of white light that sculptures the form of the actor in costume and brings out the true color of the fabric. Usually, the gel colors are adjusted to the costume colors instead of fabric colors being selected to fit a certain gel scheme. But the lighting designer and the costume designer should certainly confer well in advance of costume construction about colors to be used. A costume designer who knows what each of the major gel colors will do to fabric colors on the stage can avoid the problems that may arise when a scene must be lit by firelight or moonlight.

The watchword is coordination between the lighting designer, the costume designer, and the set designer. Each must try to visualize in advance what will happen in each scene onstage, and each must strive to create the unified visual scene conceived by the director.

Unity Through Color

In closing this chapter on color, we must stress again how important it is to set up a color limitation for a production that will give a unity of effect. To say that a production is colorful is not to say that it is well designed. Unless a scene is supposed to look like a riot, the color layout should be carefully composed to give the correct accent and focus to the right characters and to the desired part of the individual costume. A riot of color onstage is just that; color fights color, character relationships are blurred, major and minor character contrasts are lost, and confusion reigns. Everyone has at one time or another seen a production in which a jumble of color prevented the principals from being seen among the chorus, a lead character had so many colors in his costume that an overall view of his costumed form was impossible, or the audience was unable to tell to which group or social class a character belonged.

Color cannot be divorced from the texture and the shape of the garment of which it is a part, nor can it be divorced from the movement of acting and the blocking of a scene. The designer is always working with color in movement and must never design as if color, as in a painting, will stay in repose.

5

Fabric

Fabric for the Stage

The designer must know a great deal about fabrics, the basic element of stage costume design. He or she must be sensitive to draping quality and to surface texture—to how the fabric drapes on an actor's moving body and how the surface of the fabric appears under stage lights. The costume designer always considers these two aspects of fabric when making choices for stage costumes.

Fabrics can be divided into two groups according to their draping qualities: limp fabrics, which hang in soft folds; and stiff fabrics, which hang in angular folds. For example, chiffon is a soft fabric with light, fluid draping lines, while organdy, which has the same weight and transparency as chiffon, is quite stiff. Of course, there are many variations within these two fabric groups, but in most productions the costumes will fall into one group or the other.

Fabrics can also be divided according to their surfaces into dull and shiny. Dull fabrics have no reflective quality and absorb light; this group comprises woolens and cottons. Shiny fabrics have a smooth surface such as one finds in satin and chintz; this group comprises silk, rayon, nylon, and other synthetics.

Surface texture is the quality that first attracts the beginning designer and untutored lay person. Many period plays are done in velvets, satins, and brocades, not because the surfaces or the draped lines of these textures are appropriate for character or visual mood but because the effect is rich and sensuous. In many ways, these are particularly difficult fabrics to use. Brocades are frequently effective at close view but ineffective at a distance, while velvets must be used with restraint or the various surfaces chosen will war with each other onstage.

The Basic Fabric Fibers

Before one can use fabrics effectively onstage, one must have an understanding of the nature and composition of fabrics. A beginning designer shopping for fabrics may look at the surface and feel the weight without knowing much about the content; but gradually the beginner will develop a knowledge of fabric composition and of how fabrics are woven, treated, and finished.

One of the first phrases that the young designer or costumer will learn is "fiber content." A fiber is the basic unit of the fabric, a filament of the raw material from which cloth —cotton, wool, silk, nylon—is made. To see what a fiber looks like, unravel a thread, called a *yarn,* from a piece of fabric. The tiny hairs you see when the yarn is untwisted are the fibers. Cloth can be constructed from fibers or yarns in a number of different ways:

Weaving. Two sets of yarns are interlaced at right angles, the warp threads running lengthwise and the woof or weft threads (sometimes called the filling) running crosswise. The woof or weft threads are carried over and under the warp threads. The outer finished edges of the fabric are known as the *selvage.*

Knitting. Rows of loops formed by the yarn are drawn through another series of loops of a single yarn by needles, the loops supporting one another like chains. An elastic, porous fabric results.

Crocheting. A looped fabric is made from a single yarn with a hook that creates a chain of loops.

Braiding. Yarns are interlaced one over another at an angle of less than ninety degrees to form a flat, tubular fabric. Braiding can be done over a core of another yarn.

Knotting. An openwork fabric is made by knotting threads or yarns together into a pattern. In tatting, which is a variation, a knotted lace is formed by a shuttle filled with yarn passing through loops of yarn to form knots.

Felting. Fibers are pressed together by heat, steam, and pressure to create a matted fabric.

Laminating. Fibers are pressed together into a sheet of fabric and held together by adhesives. Frequently, several layers are held together by adhesives.

Fabrics are known as textile fabrics when they are made from fibers by one of these methods. (Leather is therefore not a textile fabric.) Textile fibers used to create textile fabrics fall into two major categories: the natural fibers from vegetable and animal sources, and the synthetic fibers that have become so important since World War II. Cotton, wool, silk, and linen are the most-used natural fibers for clothing. Ramie, jute, and hemp are sometimes used for certain coarse, rough-textured fabrics.

First, let us look at the vegetable fibers.

COTTON. Cotton comes from the cotton plant, which is a small bush whose blossoms become cotton balls or pods that produce cotton fibers. Unless treated, it has no pronounced luster of its own, yet its strength, compared to that of other fibers, is considerable, increasing when wet, decreasing when dry. It is not nearly as elastic as silk or wool; it conducts heat better than silk or wool, although not as well as linen. Cotton fades and loses strength under prolonged exposure to the sun, but it can take heat up to 300 degrees Fahrenheit without injury. When it does burn, it smells like burning paper. It takes dyes less well than wool or silk, but still presents no great problems when dyed and can be bleached fairly easily without injury to the fibers. It can be made up into a tremendous variety of fabrics with greatly varied surface effects, but because of its lack of elasticity and weight per square inch of fabric, it does not drape particularly well. As a fabric, it ranges in price from most reasonable to very expensive.

LINEN. Linen is a vegetable fiber taken from inside the stalk of the flax plant. It has been one of the most basic fibers since early Egyptian times. The fibers are longer and wider than those of cotton, and their strength and natural luster are greater. Linen is even less elastic than cotton; it feels hard and smooth and wrinkles very easily. Accordingly, it irons into creases and folds beautifully. It conducts heat away from the body more readily than cotton, and is often used in hot climates. It has a poor affinity for all dyes, and is usually seen bleached or in its natural buff color. Linen will take about the same amount of heat without burning as cotton, and when it burns it smells like burning rope. When made up into fabric, it has an uneven thread, a shiny, hard surface, and costs more than cotton.

RAMIE, JUTE, AND HEMP. Ramie, jute, and hemp are used more often for rope and heavy matting than for fabric. Ramie is sometimes used in place of flax, and it has many of the same characteristics as linen when made up into fabric. It is more often seen in upholstery, mats, draperies, and rugs than in clothing. Jute comes from a tall, flax-like plant, and when made up into fabric it resembles linen, although it is much weaker, coarser, and does not take well to dye, bleach, or sunlight. It is usually seen in bags, sacks, rugs, and coat interlinings. Hemp comes from a tall, fibrous plant that produces a fiber stronger than linen, jute, or cotton. It is less elastic and coarser than linen, and is usually seen woven into heavy webbings or gauzes. The most common fabric that comes from these three fibers is burlap, which is usually woven from jute.

Some seldom-used fibers are sometimes mixed with the standard ones. Paper can be used in conjunction with cotton threads in very cheap fabrics. It is not washable, and the paper fibers disintegrate in water, leaving only the cotton. Kapok is a fluffy fiber used for stuffing, but it is not adaptable to spinning into cloth. Fireproof minerals are also mixed with cotton yarn and then woven into fireproof cloth. Metal threads that make up lamé fabrics usually consist of a thin ribbon of metal wound over a core of cotton yarn. Lamés are popular for rich, light-reflecting fabrics used in theatrical costumes and evening wear.

Now let us examine the natural animal fibers.

SILK. Silk originated in China, reached the Mediterranean basin after the birth of Christ, and for centuries was the most costly and prized fabric of princes and kings because of its scarcity. It is the product of the silkworm, of which there are two varieties: the wild and the cultivated. The fibers of the wild silkworm are brown and have a coarse hard texture. The wild silkworm feeds on the scrub oak, and the resultant fabric is known as wild silk. The cultivated silkworm requires much care. It feeds on the mulberry leaf and its fibers are yellow to gray. During the two months that it lives it goes through four stages: the egg, the worm, the cocoon, and the moth. The fine, gummy filaments that exude from under the worm's mouth and from which it spins its cocoon are eventually made into silk. Three thousand cocoons will make one yard of silk. There are two ways of removing the filaments from the cocoon: by spinning and by reeling. In reeling the filament, the longest threads are retained and a minimum of twisting takes place. In spinning, the shorter threads are used and much twisting takes place. Reeled silk is stronger and more lustrous than the spun variety. When made up into fabric, silk can be woven into the lightest of all the natural fiber fabrics, although raw silk fabrics can also be woven to be relatively heavy, depending on the amount and weight of the fiber used. Light weaves are sometimes weighted with metallic salts, but the fibers are thereby weakened and the resultant fabric cannot be called pure silk. The basic characteristics of silk are lightness of weight, great elasticity, and a high, subtle luster. It is smooth, soft, pliable, dyes beautifully, holds heat, making it excellent for warmth, absorbs moisture without appearing damp, and if it burns it has no animal odor. Because for centuries it was so scarce and costly, silk has a certain value in the history of Western culture, and people will usually choose it over less costly rayons or cottons with comparable surface effects.

WOOL. Wool comes from the fleece of sheep and goats and has been a staple fiber since human beings first began to weave. There are three categories of woolens: new wool, which has never been processed before; reprocessed wool, which often comes from felting cuttings from the garment manufacturer's cutting room; and reused wool, which is made from discarded woolen garments that have been remade into fibrous form. Wool is also mixed with cottons, as well as rayons, nylons, and many other synthetic fibers. Today the term wool often includes such exotic fibers as camel's hair, alpaca, llama, and vicuña. Wool comes in a great many yarn variations, in two-, three-, and four-ply layers of thickness, some heavily twisted, some combed and fluffed. When it is made into fabric, it offers great surface variety, from a hard, tightly woven fabric to a soft, pliable, loosely woven pile surface. Wool is quite strong, very elastic, and takes dyes well if it has been treated so that it will not shrink. Water or moisture makes wool give off a damp animal odor; the same is true if the fabric is burned. Wool wears very well and is excellent for warmth.

Finally, let us consider a few of the synthetic fibers.

RAYON. Rayon was the first of the synthetic fibers; the name applies to all textile fibers derived from cellulose. Cellulose comes from wood pulp and cotton linters (the short hairs covering the cotton seed) treated with a variety of chemicals. Until 1924, rayon was called artificial silk, but in that year the National Dry Goods Association invented the name rayon to apply to all synthetic fibers, since the luster of the fabrics was like the reflecting rays of the sun. When it was first produced, the fibers were exceedingly lustrous, and one could clearly see the harsher effect of a rayon surface compared with that of silk, but today rayons are woven in almost every subtlety of surface texture formerly reserved for silks. Rayon is not as elastic as silk, nor can it be woven into as light a fabric as china silk; it also burns more rapidly than silk. Acetate is made from the same raw materials as rayon, but the chemical process is completely different; with too much heat, rayon will burn, but acetate will melt (as will most synthetics). Both acetate and rayon dye relatively well, although acetate requires a special dye treatment, and both usually sell at prices far less than silk.

NYLON. A synthetic textile fiber with a chemical base, nylon was created by E. I. du Pont de Nemours and Company in 1928. Nylon is derived from coal, air, and water by a complicated process, and although it seems similar to rayon in many ways, it is the strongest fiber yet made into fabric. It does not dye well, but it dries very quickly, irons easily, holds a crease well, and holds bodily warmth very well. In fact, its major problem when warm is that it does not breathe, but holds in perspiration and heat. It is often mixed with rayon, cotton, and wool to obtain many textile variations. Like acetate, it will melt rather than burn.

POLYESTER. This synthetic fiber was developed in England during World War II and was first marketed under the name Terylene. Du Pont introduced it into the United States under the name Dacron. Other less common trade names are Avlin, Fortrel, Trevira, Kodel, and Vycron. All the polyesters are noted for their resistance to creasing and wrinkles, and the fabric is very strong. Polyesters breathe better than other synthetics, but even so, polyester is often blended with cotton (65 percent polyester to 35 percent cotton and 50 percent to 50 percent are common blendings) to give cool comfort combined with easy care properties. When there is less polyester than cotton, a drip-dry finish is usually added, which makes the surface somewhat shiny. A blend of wool and polyester gives much greater wrinkle resistance and crease retention than is possible in 100 percent woolen suits. Polyester burns slowly and shrinks away from flame.

ACRYLIC. Du Pont perfected acrylic fiber after World War II and in 1950 began production of Orlon, which is also known by other trade names, such as Acrilan, Dynel, Creslan, and Verel. This fiber carries to a new high the process of setting the shape of garments by heat. It is nearly impossible to alter the original line of the garment by washing or cleaning. Also, acrylic yarns can be woven to look remarkably like wool, even though the feel is very different. Acrylic sweaters hold their shape much better than woolen ones, but the absorbency is greatly inferior. Acrylics are also used as the basis of most fake furs, and although these sometimes will look very much like the real thing at a distance, the cheaper ones never approximate the look of real fur.

Acrylics burn and melt when a flame is applied.

Synthetics as a group are somewhat uncomfortable to wear owing to their lack of absorbency, but this in turn makes them easy to wash, and they dry very rapidly. Waterborne stains are easily removed, but oily stains are sometimes difficult even with dry cleaning. Synthetic fibers when woven in soft woolenlike surfaces tend to pill, producing little balls of fiber on those areas of the surface that get the most wear, and unlike natural fibers these fiber balls cannot be brushed away. Finally, synthetic fabrics build up large amounts of static electricity, which makes clothes cling to the body or hang poorly. Fabric softeners help reduce static electricity on washable garments somewhat.

The Basic Weaves

Now that we have listed and briefly discussed the basic textile fibers, let us discuss the weaving and processing of the fibers into finished fabrics. Weaving developed as people experimented with weaving grass mats and baskets; when people learned how to twist short fibers together into yarn and to work the yarn into a fabric, the art of weaving was born. The first hand looms were crude and simple, while today's machine looms are very complicated, but the process is basically the same. The warp threads are the threads running lengthwise in a piece of fabric. The filling or weft or woof threads are carried between the warp threads in an in-and-out pattern known as *picking*. Each time the filling is carried across the cloth, one pick is made. Each filling is pushed against the previous filling, and this is called *battening*. When the warp threads are released from the warp beam, the finished cloth is said to be *let off* and *taken up*. The outer edges, or *selvages*, are finished off with more closely spaced warp threads than the rest of the fabric.

The ways in which the warp thread and the filling yarns are interlaced change the appearance of the fabric and produce many intricate designs. Weaves are named according to the system or design followed in interlacing warp and filling yarns. The basic weaves are plain, twill, satin, pile, jacquard, dobby, leno, and the ornamental weaves.

PLAIN WEAVE. Plain weave is the simplest weave. The yarn filling is passed over one warp yarn and under the next, alternating in this manner across the cloth. The second time across, the filling passes over the warp yarns it previously went under and under the warps it went over on the row above. Alternation takes place throughout the remainder of the fabric piece (Figure 5-1a). Cottons are the textiles most often woven in the plain weave, and they are usually simple in effect, inexpensive, and long wearing.

Variations on the plain weave can produce many more interesting surfaces. By using fillings much heavier than warp threads, a *ribbed weave* can be produced, while a *patterned rib* can be produced by alternating a fine and a coarse warp thread at regular intervals. A *basket weave* results when two or more filling threads are passed alternately over two or more warp threads; Oxford cloth and monk's cloth are good examples (Figure 5-1b). If uneven threads are used at irregular intervals, a roughened, bumpy texture is produced, as in shantung; if the number of warp and filling threads is varied, a tight or loose weave is produced. A tight weave, such as cotton broadcloth, is called a high-count cloth; a loose weave, such as cheesecloth, is called a low-count cloth. One can get variations in the surface by changing the amount of twist in the yarn, as in crepe, or by mixing different fibers, or by dyeing the fibers different colors before weaving. Finally, the yarns may be printed with a design before weaving, the cloth may be dyed after it has been woven, or a pattern may be stamped on the cloth after it has been woven.

TWILL WEAVE. Twill weave is the most durable of all weaves. The filling yarns are interlaced with the warp yarns so that diagonal

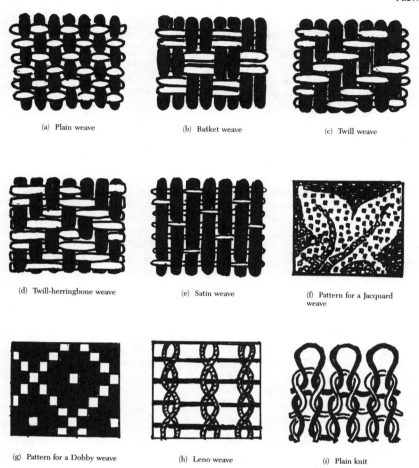

(a) Plain weave   (b) Basket weave   (c) Twill weave

(d) Twill-herringbone weave   (e) Satin weave   (f) Pattern for a Jacquard weave

(g) Pattern for a Dobby weave   (h) Leno weave   (i) Plain knit

Figure 5–1.   Diagrams of weaves and knits.

ridges are formed across the fabric (Figure 5–1c). These diagonals, called *wales,* may run from upper right to lower left, from upper left to lower right, or both ways in the same cloth. There are uneven twill weaves, even twill weaves, and a variation called herringbone in which the diagonal reverses direction at regular intervals (Figure 5–1d). The diagonals may also be formed so that diamond patterns appear. Different effects are made possible by varying the yarn sizes and qualities, mixing fibers, varying yarn colors, and adding special finishing processes. Twill weaves usually give a close texture that is heavier and stronger than plain weaves; this is why twill is the most common weave in men's clothing. Twills do not show dirt readily, but when dirty they are difficult to clean. Twills are usually found in woolens and cottons rather than in silks, rayons, nylons, and linens.

SATIN WEAVE.   When one touches the surface of a satin, the hand slips more easily lengthwise than crosswise because more warp threads than filling threads are exposed on the right side (Figure 5-1e). In satin weaves there is a semblance of a diagonal pattern, and the satin weave is sometimes considered rearranged twill; but the interlacings of the warp and filling are placed far apart to avoid the forming of wales. In satin the warp may not interlace with the filling for from four to twelve yarns. Varying lengths of warp are thus left exposed on the surface, and if a warp or "float" (an exposed warp thread) skips twelve fillings before it interlaces, it is called a twelve-float warp satin. Obviously, a long-float satin is not a strong fabric, although it is lustrous. A short-float satin is much stronger. Creped yarns can be used in the filling to produce a satin crepe; twists in the warp and filling threads can be varied; and filling threads can vary in color or in yarn fiber. Satin is used primarily in coat linings, vests, and in lustrous gowns for formal wear.

PILE WEAVE. Fabrics such as velours, velvets, and plush, with a soft, downy texture that absorbs a great amount of light, are examples of the pile weave. The pile weave uses the plain or twill weave as a ground. A third or extra yarn is woven or tied between each warp and filling thread, projecting up from it as a cut end or loop. The third threads can be cut off at any length to give a high or low pile. The pile effect can be achieved in a number of ways, but only in the terry weave method is the pile uncut and formed from loops rather than cut ends. Silk, rayon, and nylon are at their richest and most luxurious when pile construction is used. Silk pile appears rich and deep in color when one looks directly into the pile or up the nap. (The nap is the direction in which the third or pile thread lies when woven into the ground of the fabric.) If the pile is pressed down or one looks directly down the nap, the color is lighter and the fabric has a silvery sheen. Piles must be brushed and steamed, not ironed, and many cannot be washed, but must be dry cleaned. A pile weave is used in silks, rayons, cottons, and wools; in wools it is the basis for most rug and upholstery surfaces.

JACQUARD WEAVE. Complex patterns are not possible in the weaves that have been dis-cussed. After the invention of the jacquard loom in 1801, elaborate designs could be woven into fabric (Figure 5-1f). In the jacquard weave, cards are punched with a pattern of holes (similar to the holes on the rolls of player pianos), and needles going through the holes bring the warp threads to the surface to create the pattern. It is a complex process, and large amounts of yardage in a pattern must be run off to keep the price of the finished fabric within a reasonable range. The jacquard weave uses elements of the satin, plain, and twill weaves in the ground of the fabric, so one might say that a combination of weaves is used to bring out a pattern. In cotton, jacquard weaves are usually called damasks or tapestries; in linen, they are called damasks; in silk and wool, they are called damasks, tapestries, or brocades.

DOBBY WEAVE. The dobby loom does small, uncomplicated designs in a simple way by using a chain of narrow wooden strips instead of the cards of the jacquard loom (Figure 5-1g). The strips or pegs pick out the design as the filling threads are worked through the warp threads. Small geometrical patterns are the result, as are found in toweling, shirts, and tablecloths.

LENO WEAVE. Lace-like or open effects like those in curtains are made by a loom with a leno or tying attachment and are called leno weave (Figure 5-1h). Adjacent yarns are twisted around each other, usually in pairs, the filling threads passing through the twisted warps. Sometimes the leno weave is combined with the plain or basket weave to produce a lacy mesh called lace cloth, or a fabric of plain weave may have strips of leno weave. Considering their open construction, cloths of leno weave are durable; the twist not only adds strength but prevents the filling from slipping. The leno weave is usually found in cotton and rayon or a mixture of the two; occasionally it is found in silk.

ORNAMENTAL WOVEN WEAVES. Patterns similar to embroidery can be woven into fabric when it is made, but the result differs from the dobby or jacquard weaves because the embroidered effects can be pulled out by hand without injury to the rest of the cloth. In the *swivel weave* an extra shuttle on the loom for each figure in the cloth works the embroidery threads into the fabric with the raw end left loose on the back side. In the *lappet weave* the embroidery threads are carried from one figure to another across the back of the fabric by a needle attachment. The swivel weave is done with extra filling yarns, the lappet with extra warp yarns.

KNITTED CLOTH. Knitted cloth is not a woven fabric, since knitting uses one continuous thread rather than two. Knitted cloth is constructed of rows of loops, each row caught into the previous row and depending for its support on the row below and the row above (Figure 5–1i). The yarns are more loosely twisted than they are for weaving, and the result is a very elastic, porous fabric. Cottons, wools, rayons, and silks are all knitted, but linen seldom is. There are many variations in the knit stitches that can be used to achieve interesting surface effects, and the size of the yarns and the size of the stitch can be widely varied.

Dyeing and Printing

Although the problems involved in dyeing fabrics for the stage must wait until Chapter 7, something should be said at this point about dyeing and printing fabrics for the textile market. (What is said here is compressed and necessarily brief. A fuller statement may be found in a du Pont booklet, *Modern Dyestuffs and Their Properties.*) Although the costume designer may not have to worry as much as the average consumer does about colorfastness in washing and under long exposure to sunlight, the designer should be sure that all colored fabrics he or she buys are resistant to perspiration and at least reasonably fast to washing and dry cleaning.

Until 1856, all dyestuffs were natural; that is, they were obtained from insects, minerals, plants, shellfish, and woods. In 1856, aniline dyes were derived from coal tar. But the great developments in chemical dyestuffs came after World War I. Dyestuffs may be classified according to their dyeing properties or according to how they take on various fibers. The principal synthetic dyestuffs are

1. basic colors
2. acid dyes
3. sulfur dyes
4. direct dyes
5. developed colors
6. mordant and chrome dyes
7. naphthol or azoic dyes
8. vat dyes
9. acetate dyes
10. pigment dyes

Basic colors are chemically alkaline, and *acid dyes* are chiefly acid. Both will dye animal fibers directly with no prior chemical treatment, but vegetable fibers must be treated with a mordant or chemical that has an affinity for both dyestuff and fabric. For a basic dye the mordant is acid; for an acid dye the mordant is alkaline salt. *Sulfur dyes* are used almost exclusively on vegetable fibers and appear most frequently in the dyeing of automobile upholstery. *Direct dyes,* such as acid dyes, are salts of colored acids. They are usually applied directly, are used mostly in the dyeing of cottons, and are usually not as brilliant as basic dyes. *Developed colors* are dyestuffs applied directly to fabrics and then treated with chemical developers that change, deepen, and set the color. Silk does best with these dyes; other fabrics tend to lose color in laundering. *Mordant and chrome dyes* are colored compounds that become insoluble when metallic salts are added, combine well with the fiber of wool or silk, and are colorfast. *Naphthol* or *azoic dyes* are used almost exclusively on cotton. The cotton is impregnated with a beta-naphthol that has been dissolved in caustic soda and then immersed in a basic dye. The name *vat dyes* originated in the making of the old indigo dyes, which had to steep for days. Modern indigo is still the most famous of the so-called vat dyes. The dyes usually come in powder form and are mixed with water, sulfonated oil, and caustic soda, with sodium hydrosulfate added when the dye is heated. It is difficult to match colors with these dyes, because the color changes sharply when dry. *Acetate dyes* are certain insoluble compounds of azoic or vat dyes kept in a gelatinous suspension and used almost exclusively on rayon and nylon fibers. *Pigment dyes* are usually printed or stamped into cloth using dry color pigments mixed with a synthetic resin solution.

Dyeing can be done in the original raw state of the fiber, after the fiber has been carded and combed, in the yarn, or in the final fabric. Printing of colored patterns into a fabric is usually done by large stencil rollers, although colored patterns are occasionally stenciled or even hand blocked on expensive fabrics. Hand-painted designs, silk-screen printing, and the new process of photoprinting a design onto fabric are also seen on the market. Today, most designs are set into the fabric so that they will remain after washing and extended usage, but some printed patterns obviously retain their original look much longer than others. Without a microscope it is difficult to tell which printed patterns have been set into the fabric most deeply, although one can tell something by unraveling some of the yarns in the pattern.

Fabric Finishes

The stiffness of organdy, the smooth, silky feeling of batiste, the colored print on cretonne, the watered or moiré effect on silk are all the result of finishing treatments to which fabrics are subjected after they are made. Finishes are mechanical (the older processes) or chemical (the newer ones), depending on whether they are done by machine or by dipping.

Permanent and nonpermanent finishes. Finishes that will stand wear, washing, and sunlight are called *permanent*. They include bleaching, glazing, printing, dyeing, napping, water-marking, beetling, and preshrinking. Surfaces that rub off when a fabric is brushed or washed, such as sizing, certain kinds of glazing, weighting, some forms of creping, embossing, and some forms of moiréing, are called *nonpermanent*. Today, more and more of the finishes that used to be nonpermanent are treated to withstand wear, washing, and sunlight.

Pretreatments. Before regular or functional finishes can be applied, fabrics are usually given pretreatments. The most common is *bleaching,* in which the natural color of the fiber is bleached to a pure white. *Scouring* and *carbonizing* are preliminary processes that remove oil and dirt from the natural fiber before dyes are applied. *Degumming* removes the natural gums from silk yarns by boiling before dyeing, while *immunizing* is a process whereby cottons can be made to take the same dyes as rayons, thus giving a much greater variety of color. *Mercerizing* is another such process in which cottons are given greater strength, a greater affinity to dyes, and a greater luster.

Regular finishes. Regular finishes include both treatments that enhance a fabric for the eye and those that add weight, body, warmth, or appeal to the sense of touch. Those that enhance the look of the fabric are as follows:

Perching is an examination of cloth to catch defects in the weave.

Burling removes knots or irregularities from the weave.

Crabbing tightens up and sets the weave (for wool fabrics only).

Brushing removes all loose fibers by revolving fabric through cylinders covered with bristles so that a smooth surface results.

Singeing burns off all loose fibers to give a clean, clear surface.

Shearing removes raised fibers or fuzz or cuts a pile to a certain length.

Beetling subjects fabric to a pounding by steel or wooden hammers to flatten fibers and make them glossy and is a common finish for linen napkins and tablecloths.

Decating is a process in which steam is forced through a fabric in tension to add luster and set nap.

Tentering makes all fabrics on the bolt the same width.

Calendering is the final process, after all chemical and mechanical finishes have been applied, which smoothes and presses the finished fabric.

Moiréing, related to calendering, is a process in which the roller in the calender process is engraved with lines to give a watered pattern to the finished fabric.

Embossing imprints a design from the calender rollers to the fabric as it is pressed.

Creping uses steam or caustic acid to pucker or shrink fabric in a pattern in the calendering process (such creping should not be confused with the permanent creping process done at the weaving stage).

Glazing uses starch or a form of glue to polish a fabric with rollers to give the hard, shiny finish of glazed tarlatan or chintz.

The following finishes appeal primarily to one's sense of touch:

Fulling shrinks wool to close its weave and give the fabric further weight, compactness, and softness.

Gigging and *napping* raise the fuzz from the fiber with brush rollers to cover the weave (for woolens, cotton flannels, and duvetyns).

Steaming conditions the fiber and makes the fabric more compact.

Shrinkage control or *sanforizing* preshrinks fabrics so that they will not shrink after washing.

Weighting adds weight and substance to a fabric by adding a chemical component to silks or a steamed flocking to wool.

FUNCTIONAL FINISHES. Functional finishes are applied to fabrics to make them better suited for particular purposes. Most of them resulted from experimentation during World War II. They are as follows:

Absorbent finishes result when a fabric is treated with an ammonium compound to make it hold moisture (towels, washcloths).

Crease-resistant finishes result from ex-periments with various resins (cotton, linen, and rayon meant for clothing).

Flameproofing makes a fabric fire-resistant by dipping it in a solution of boric acid and borax (draperies and curtains and even much fabric for clothing).

Germ-resistant finishes, mildew-resistant finishes, and *moth-repellent finishes* aid in the storage of fabrics and clothes.

Permanent starchless finishes make stiff, firm fabrics that do not require starching after washing (collars, cuffs).

Waterproofing or *water-repelling finishes* are used for rainwear or bathing suits.

It can readily be seen that in the present fabric market as much is achieved through finishes as through the weaving of the various textile fibers, and new finishing processes are appearing every day.

A Basic List of Standard Fabrics

Before discussing the problems that arise when shopping for material, it may be helpful to list the standard fabric names that one will meet.

BROCADE. Brocade comes in widths of 36 to 54 inches in many colors and patterns, usually of rayon or silk in dress, drapery, or upholstery weights. The patterns woven into the brocade may be of one color or a combination of colors, and a background and pattern that have different textures on one side will reverse on the other. In choosing brocades for period plays, one should try to suit the pattern to the period so that the effect will not be too modern. There are some inexpensive brocades, but imported silk brocades are often the most expensive fabrics sold.

BUCKRAM. Buckram comes in rolls of light, medium, and heavy weight in black and white. It is an open-weave material sized with glue, stiffer than crinoline or Pellon, and is used as a foundation for hats, headdresses, stiff collars, and other costume pieces needing stiffening. One of its prime attributes is that it can be dampened and shaped over a headblock and then allowed to dry back to stiffness. It can then be painted and covered. The edges of buckram will wear and shape better, especially in hats, if they are wired with milliner's wire.

BURLAP.   Burlap comes in 36- to 54-inch widths in a limited number of colors. It has a very coarse texture, is rather stiff, and works well for homespun effects, peasant costumes, and beggars' outfits. It is rough and scratchy and is usually lined or worn over a protective undergarment.

CALICO.   Calico comes in 36- to 44-inch widths and is a plain-weave, smooth-surfaced cotton fabric, usually carrying small printed designs in sharp contrast to the color of the background. In the past the name referred to a wide assortment of basic cottons in bleached white, plain colors, stripes, and prints.

CANVAS.   Canvas usually comes in 27-, 36-, and 45-inch widths and is a strong, heavy, usually plain-weave fabric, useful for heavier linings in its natural state. It is usually of cotton, though it sometimes contains a mix of synthetic yarns. It also comes in a variety of colors, and garments made of it will have a very crisp line and will take the heaviest wear. It is sometimes used in outdoor productions in which a nonrealistic effect is desired because the fabric is durable in all weathers. Canvas is heavier than *sailcloth* or *duck,* though the names are sometimes used interchangeably. All are invaluable as interlinings for stiff period bodices.

CHALLIS.   Challis is a soft, lightweight, plain-weave fabric often printed with strong floral patterns on a dark background or with a paisley design. It may be made of cotton, rayon, or wool, which provides the most beautiful (and most expensive) texture.

CHIFFON.   Chiffon usually comes in 45-inch widths in a variety of colors and is more practical and less expensive when made from rayon or nylon than when made from silk. It is a transparent, filmy fabric that is excellent for soft, floating, draped costumes. It is

difficult to handle, since it creeps and puckers during costume construction. It is excellent for veils, clinging transparent dresses, scarves, fairy costumes, and impressionistic effects.

CORDUROY.   Corduroy comes in 36- to 54-inch widths in a variety of colors and printed patterns. It is usually woven of cotton in pile ridges that form wales. A wide-wale corduroy is more lustrous and more expensive than a narrow-wale. Corduroy is inexpensive and widely used in costume construction, but only at great distances will it pass for velvet, and on the whole it should be used only for garments that would logically be made of corduroy.

CREPE.   Crepe usually comes in 45-inch widths in colors and some patterns. It has a crinkled surface achieved by using high-twist creped yarns, by twisting during the weaving process, by chemical means, or, on synthetics, by embossing. The cost varies from cheap to expensive. Crepe has a softer draping quality and less sheen than taffeta and is excellent for lingerie, blouses, and flowing costumes with draped folds. Wool crepe is especially rich, and rayon crepe is excellent for bias-cut garments.

CRÊPE DE CHINE.   Crêpe de Chine was originally an expensive silk fabric in a plain weave with a soft twist to the warp threads and a more tightly twisted set of filling threads. It was the tight filling threads that caused the crinkle. Today, a cheaper blend of rayon and acetate is manufactured for linings and some lingerie.

CRINOLINE.   Crinoline usually comes in black and white only in 36-inch widths. Originally it had a sizing that washed out when laundered, and even today permanent-finish crinolines lose some stiffness when washed. Its use as a stiffening agent for petticoats, sleeves, bustles, and paniers has mostly been taken over today by nylon nets.

DENIM.   Denim usually comes in 36- to 44-inch widths in many colors and some patterns, including a variety of stripes. It is a twill-weave cotton (or cotton and polyester blend) that is heavier than percale or muslin and has a rougher texture. It is durable, launders well, and is excellent for lower-class and peasant costumes and for crisp, flat, stylized effects. Its colors are never deep and rich, but always slightly grayed.

DRILL. Drill is a strong, hard-wearing fabric similar to denim but of a better quality and smoother appearance. It is made in a twill or satin weave of cotton or cotton-polyester and is often used for uniforms, bush jackets and other tropical wear.

FAILLE. Faille is a plain-weave fabric with tiny ribs made from filling threads. It is woven in silk, rayon, and sometimes of synthetics, usually in 36- to 44-inch widths. When the ribs are quite prominent and are made of cotton filling threads, the name is usually changed to *bengaline* or *bengaline faille*. Bengaline and faille are useful for costumes that need a crisp silhouette, body, and a subtle sheen, as in the seventeenth-century garments for a Molière production.

FELT. Felt usually comes in 72-inch widths in a variety of bright colors. It is made of fibers that have been pressed rather than woven, and it can thus be cut in any direction without the edges raveling. It comes in wool, cotton, or rayon. Wool felt is used for flat, stiff, bulky costumes and trimmings, and for hats; it will also steam and shape into headdresses and armor.

FLANNEL. Flannel is a soft, plain-weave fabric with a napped surface that usually comes in 36- to 54-inch widths. It is most often woven in wool for men's suits and casual jackets and trousers, where it is admired for its softness and easy drape.

FLANNELETTE. Flannelette is a thin cotton version of flannel napped on both sides that usually comes in 36-inch widths in a fair variety of soft colors. It will dye well, is inexpensive, and is often used by amateur groups to replace light woolens. It does not drape well and

on the market is usually made up into sleepwear.

GABARDINE. Gabardine is a twill-weave fabric with a tight, hard surface that comes in light, medium, or heavy weights, usually in 44- to 54-inch widths. Though traditionally of wool, it now also comes in cotton, rayon, and synthetics. It is much used for rainwear.

GINGHAM. Gingham is a traditional plain-weave cotton fabric with dyed checks, stripes, and plaids. Today, the fabric is woven from a variety of cotton and synthetic blends, with checks as the preferred pattern.

GROSGRAIN. Grosgrain is a plain-weave fabric with rounded ribs that is usually seen in ribbons but is also available in 28- to 36-inch widths. Once made entirely of silk and very expensive, it is usually a mixture of rayon and cotton or acetate and cotton today. Though difficult to find, it is very useful for nineteenth-century period costumes.

JERSEY. Jersey usually comes in 36- to 44-inch widths or in tubular form in many colors and has great drapability, since it is knit rather than woven. It is available in cotton, wool, rayon, and nylon in weights from light to heavy, with wool the preferred choice, if affordable, for certain Greek, Roman, and medieval garments.

JEWELS, SEQUINS, AND SPANGLES. These are not fabrics but are listed here as items used in the trim and finish of costumes. They can be found in junk stores, secondhand shops, or by the gross or dozen in theatrical supply houses, as well as in limited supply in fabric stores.

LACE. Lace is a linen or cotton material with a decorative openwork pattern that is light and rich in effect. It usually comes in 36-inch or trimming widths in a limited variety of colors. Dress lace is used for complete dresses, especially the elaborate gowns of the early twentieth century, while lace trimming can be purchased in narrow widths for edges and borders on costumes.

LEATHER. Leather—which is animal skin and not fabric—can be obtained from old leather clothing if new leather is beyond the budget or by the skin in a leather store. It can be cut in any direction that will give maximum use of the skin and is available in many colors, weights, and surfaces. Leather is priced by the square inch, but it is often worth the cost to have a genuine leather look in boots and jackets.

LINEN. Linen is the name of a fabric as well as a fiber and was originally made exclusively from flax, but today it is often a mixture of flax and synthetic fibers, which give it more wrinkle resistance. Its somewhat irregular yarns give interest to its surface, and it reflects heat, which makes it excellent for tropical garments. It is a costumer's necessity for early twentieth-century motoring dusters, summer jackets, and sporting skirts.

MARQUISETTE. Marquisette usually comes in 45- and 50-inch widths in pastel colors, and it may be made up in rayon, nylon, or cotton. It is transparent and can be found in a medium-stiff to a very soft texture. It is used primarily in blouses, kerchiefs, and scarves.

METALLIC FABRICS AND LAMÉS. Metallic fabrics usually come in 36-inch widths in silver, gold, and copper, sometimes mixed with another color. Theatrical fabric stores have wider selections than yardage houses and often have inexpensive choices that look good but do not wear well. Metallic fabrics can be either stiff or fluid, with the latter the most costly. Cottons and synthetics mixed with metallic threads are often theatrically effective and cost less. Metallics are widely used in musicals, circuses, ice shows, and nightclub acts.

MONK'S CLOTH. Monk's cloth is a basket-weave cotton that usually comes in 50- to 54-inch widths in a very limited number of colors. It is used primarily as a drapery fabric and comes in a fine or coarse basket weave. In its natural tan color it can be easily dyed, and though it does shrink it can be an inexpensive substitute for heavily draped woolen garments.

MUSLIN. Muslin is a plain-weave cotton that usually comes in 45-, 54-, and 72-inch widths, either in a bleached or an unbleached state. The unbleached is the standard fabric for lining costumes, and when the size has been washed out it dyes well. It is one of the staples of the costume shop for making up the first approximation of a costume, and when it is bought in bulk it is quite inexpensive.

NET. Net comes in 45- to 72-inch widths in a variety of colors in cotton, rayon, or nylon. All nets are quite stiff, though some will soften after washing. The nylon net is excellent for ballet skirts, ruffled gowns, stiff veils, Elizabethan ruffs, and other such effects, and is relatively inexpensive.

ORGANDY. Organdy is a thin, transparent fabric, originally of plain-weave cotton treated with a special finish to add stiffness. In recent years, permanent press finishes and synthetic yarns have been added to remove the objectionable creases and wrinkles of the past. Organdy is used mostly in blouses and bouffant evening gowns.

PELLON. Pellon is a brand name for a pressed-pulp stiffening agent that comes in black and white rolls that can be cut in any direction. It is often used in place of crinoline as an interlining or a petticoat, since it is easier to handle and does not lose its stiffness until after many cleanings.

PERCALE. Percale usually comes in 36- or 44-inch widths in many colors and some patterns. It is used wherever muslin would be appropriate, and often substitutes for muslin in cases when the designer does not wish to dye or pattern muslin. Percale launders well and is only slightly more expensive than muslin. It is often used in summer shirts, blouses, and dresses.

POPLIN. Poplin is a closely woven cotton (or cotton and synthetic) weave with a fine horizontal rib that comes in 36- to 54-inch widths. It has a crisp feel and a slight reflectivity and is important for nineteenth-century women's suits and skirts.

SATEEN.   Sateen is a strong, semilustrous satin-weave cotton fabric in 36- to 44-inch widths. The filling threads are on the right side, as opposed to satin, in which the warp threads are on top. Sateen is usually used as a lining fabric.

SATIN.   Satin comes in 40- to 45-inch widths. The term refers to a weave as well as to a group of fabrics done with a satin weave. It can be made up in silk and in rayon, nylon, and other synthetic fibers, and is more lustrous than taffeta. It must be checked carefully to be certain that it is not too reflective under lights. *Antique satin* is a double-sided fabric with a right side that is smooth and lustrous and a wrong side that is like shantung. It is used for period garments and is purchased in drapery shops. *Crepe-backed satin* has a smooth satin side and a creped side; it is lighter than antique satin and is used for linings. *Double-faced satin* is a dress-weight fabric that has a shiny satin look on both sides. *Duchesse satin* is the heaviest and richest of the satins and is widely used for wedding gowns. *Slipper satin* is a very tightly woven satin of a lighter weight than duchesse and was originally used for evening slippers.

SERGE.   Serge is a basic suiting fabric in a woolen twill weave that usually comes in 54- to 60-inch widths. It is a hard-wearing fabric that today is often blended with synthetic fibers.

SILK.   Silks are once again in great demand and are in ready supply with the opening of Chinese mainland sources. *China silk* is a lightweight, filmy, inexpensive silk used for kerchiefs and banners. *Pongee* is a fairly lightweight silk fabric with a slight irregularity in the yarns. *Raw silk* is a dull, rough, tan fabric woven from filaments from which a glue-like substance has been removed. It is often used for women's suits and jackets. *Shantung* is a plain-weave fabric with irregularities in the

yarns that give an uneven texture. Originally woven only in silk, it is sometimes seen today in synthetics, with the yarns made to look irregular. *Surah* is a silk fabric with a twill weave and a high sheen. *Thai silk* comes from Thailand and is of fairly heavy weight in brilliant iridescent colors. *Tie silk* is a somewhat less lustrous silk used for making men's ties. *Tussah* is made from the secretions of wild silkworms and is naturally tan in color and rough in texture. It cannot be bleached and is excellent for creating peasant rags.

SUEDE CLOTH OR COTTON DUVETYN.   Suede cloth has a soft brush-napped surface and comes in 36- to 44-inch widths. One side is like cotton flannel; the other has a hard, plain-weave effect. It is relatively inexpensive and is sometimes used to approximate wool for winter garments, servants' outfits, breeches, short capes, and coats. It does not drape well.

TAFFETA.   Taffeta is a plain-weave fabric and usually comes in 40- to 50-inch widths in many colors and several degrees of stiffness. Originally, it was always of silk and moved with a rustling noise, but today it is usually of rayon. It has a smooth surface and a fairly high sheen, wears well, drapes crisply, and is much used for eighteenth- and nineteenth-century clothing. *Moiré taffeta* has a watermarked pattern rolled and pressed into the fabric.

TERRYCLOTH.   Terrycloth, an uncut, looped pile weave, comes in 36- to 44-inch widths in white, colors, and patterns and can sometimes be used as a substitute for heavier woolen fabrics if carefully dyed and textured. When used in large amounts it drapes well even though it is a cotton, and it is relatively inexpensive.

TRIMMING BRAIDS.   Trimming braids, both cloth and metallic, can be purchased by the yard in bolts of varying amounts and widths and can be found in upholstery, theatrical, and yardage supply stores. The cost depends on the quality and the width. Braids are essential for giving the proper finish to the borders and edges of costumes.

VELOUR.   Velour is a heavy pile weave that comes in 50-inch widths in a limited variety of colors. With a much heavier pile than corduroy or velveteen, it is used chiefly for draperies but is sometimes useful for bulky costumes or heavier outer garments.

VELVET.   Velvet, a fabric with a short, closely woven pile, usually comes in 36- to 45-inch widths in a variety of colors. It is made of silk or of rayon, nylon, or other synthetics and has more sheen and drapes better than cotton velveteen. Silk velvet is very rich in texture and very expensive. Velvet can be woven plain or in a figured design produced by weaving a pattern into the pile or by cutting and shearing the pile into designs. *Panné velvet* is produced by flattening the velvet pile in one direction. *Crushed velvet* is produced by crushing the pile in different directions.

VELVETEEN.   The term velveteen refers to unribbed, closely woven cotton pile fabrics that usually come in 36- to 44-inch widths in a variety of colors and patterns. It can often be used in place of velvet, though it does not drape as well and in black is never as rich as velvet. It is more expensive than corduroy with its ribbed pile and about the same or slightly less expensive than synthetic velvets.

VINYL.   Vinyl is produced when plastic film is laminated to fabric. It comes in 36- to 60-inch widths in various weights and colors. Usually used in upholstery, it can sometimes approximate leather at a distance and can be used as a special effect when a shiny, synthetic, stiff look is required. Vinyl does not breathe and is very hot when worn.

VOILE.   Voile is a plain weave made of hard-twisted, two-ply yarns in cotton, silk, rayon, or wool in 36- to 44-inch widths. It is easily dyed, fluid, and (in cotton) semitransparent. It is relatively inexpensive and useful for lightweight summer dresses.

WHIPCORD.   Whipcord is a twill-weave cotton or wool worsted that comes in 44- to 54-inch widths. It is heavier than gabardine and is used for uniforms, riding clothes, and other sturdy outdoor garments.

WOOL.   Wool is both a fabric and a group of materials made from the fleece of sheep or other animals. It comes in 54- to 60-inch widths in wonderful colors and geometric woven patterns and is the best fabric for heavy draped costume lines. Considering the width of the fabric, prices are high but not prohibitive, and there are no substitutes that will give the same soft, absorptive, rich, elastic, draped effect.

Buying Fabrics

The designer wants to spend the least amount of time possible buying fabrics for a production, yet too much haste may mean costly changes later on. Every minute must count, and every decision must be the right one.

First, the designer must have a good idea of fabric prices before going shopping, so that he or she can estimate the cost to the producer or director and can plan the price range for each costume. Even though the designer may not know what specific fabric will be used, he or she should have a general group of fabrics in mind. The added expenses of trimming, lining, and finishing must also be estimated along with the cost of the main fabric.

The designer must also know yardage, since one cannot estimate cost without knowing how much fabric will be needed. The designer must know in what widths fabrics come: How many yards of 54-inch wool will be needed for a costume? How many more yards of 36-inch cotton would be needed for the same costume? It is a good idea to prepare a chart of the general garments used in stage costume and the amounts of fabric they require in the various fabric widths. This will save time in purchasing and prevent mistakes. If one does not buy enough fabric, one may find that it is not always possible to get more of the same; if one buys too much, one may not be able to find a use for leftover material. If there is time, the designer should note the estimated yardage and trim needed in the corner of the costume sketch before going shopping.

The designer will usually find it difficult to tell from a bolt how a fabric will look onstage, but must nonetheless be able to imagine the effect of a fabric in movement before ever seeing it at a distance under stage lights. One should never rely on the look of the fabric on the bolt, but should unroll a fair amount, drape it in various ways over other fabrics or an arm, or let it fall to the floor to check its elasticity and folds before judging its effectiveness at a distance. Even if store clerks are aghast at these peculiar procedures, the designer should not be intimidated into buying any fabric without checking its textural and draping qualities thoroughly. To be rushed into buying a fabric without being convinced of its effectiveness for a particular costume is usually to invite a mistake. Even if one is rushed for time and does not wish to look further, it is unwise to buy a fabric that is acceptable but not exactly what one had in mind. It is important to be absolutely clear about what the fabric is supposed to do: Is it to be lined and tailored? Is it to be soft and flowing? Is it to be heavy but soft?

There will, of course, be times when the designer will despair of finding the right fabric in the right color. In such cases one should always buy the right fabric in white and dye it rather than buy another fabric merely because it is the right color. If one has to buy a fabric that is not exactly right, one can often treat it in the shop. For example, a fabric may have to be washed a number of times, its stiffness or fiber tightness broken down by heavy brushing, or its pattern brought up by outlining. In such cases the designer may wish to buy a very small amount of the fabric and test out such treatments on it before buying the fabric for the entire costume.

But even with the greatest of care in the shopping process, what about the problems faced by the designer who is shopping for several productions at the same time? I am indebted to Jeannie Davidson of the Oregon Shakespeare Festival for sharing her method of shopping for several large Shakespearean productions at the same time. The key, which Frank Bevan of Yale also espoused for careful control in the shopping process, is to do all the swatching for a series of productions in advance, with no buying until a later date.

Thus the *first step* is a swatching trip by the designer and/or the design assistant, with all possibilities from all possible stores for all of the productions included. Each swatch is given a color-coded "sticky spot" (purchased at a stationery store), the colors representing various stores or fabric sources. On each colored spot is recorded the yardage price of the fabric, and the swatches are placed in envelopes according to production. The *second step* is the sorting and selecting process. All the sketches for a production are spread out on the floor for coordinating and matching. This may take several days, and trade-offs may have to be made to keep a production within budget. Finally, when there are several fabrics still competing for a place on a sketch, each sketch is dealt with individually until a final choice is made. The *third step* involves making a chart or sheet for each production, with the swatch on the left side, next to it the name of the character, the garment, the yardage to be purchased, notes about later treatment or dyeing, and lastly a blank box to be checked when the fabric has actually been purchased. The sketches will probably still go with the shopper, but they are no longer absolutely essential to the shopping process. The *fourth step* is the shopping process itself. First, all the fabrics selected from a particular store are brought out and checked off. If there is damage or not enough yardage, substitutions may be made on the spot; if not, the swatch is marked to be solved later. When all the fabrics in a particular store have been cut and purchased, the checks at the right of the swatch card are crossed or double checked. (These checks can also be used as a shipping list to be checked off if fabrics are mailed.) The *final step* is to prepare five- by eight-inch cards for each costume in a production, containing all the swatches for that costume with information about dyeing, washing before cutting, what part of the garment the swatch is for, and how the fabric is to be handled in the sewing process. The dyer may receive a similar card with the swatch and the color it is to be dyed.

Needless to say, this shopping system is for a large shop that contains a full complement of costume personnel. For the small operation, careful on-the-spot buying by the designer is still possible.

Like casting, buying for a production is one of the key moments of decision in the whole design process, and mistakes made at this time will cost in time, money, and nerves later in the building and rehearsal period. Through experience a designer must develop a sharp eye, the ability to envision fabric on a bolt made up into finished costumes, and the ability to make purchases that decisively solve his fabric problems for each costume in the production.

Fabric Images

To help set up the textural or fabric image for a play, the designer should create a fabric layout for a production before shopping. A fabric layout can readily be made if a designer keeps small swatches of fabric in white or in color in as many weaves and finishes as can be found. The designer can file the swatches in small boxes or drawers under weave and fabric names and then select and arrange them until the right balance of textures for a production is achieved. A fabric layout or collage may help in discussions with the director, who will be able to see and touch the fabrics and react to texture even though he or she may not be able to estimate the fitting and draping effect of the fabric in large masses. It may also help the designer and the director to clarify the feeling they wish to achieve in the fabric usage for the production. Is the production to have the light, soft, fluid, draped, transparent effect that one

Figure 5-3. Example of hard, sculptural folds: *The Charioteer of Delphi,* bronze, ca. 470 B.C. Photo courtesy of Hirmer Fotoarchiv, Munich.

Figure 5-2. Example of crinkled fabric folds: woodcut *The Three Bishops* by Albrecht Dürer. Photo courtesy of the Stanford University Department of Art.

might wish for an impressionistic piece such as *Pelléas and Mélisande?* Or is it to have the heavy, dull-surfaced, deeply sculptured folds that one might use in *Macbeth?* Should the fabric reflect light and have the crisp, lustrous, hard, rich quality of taffeta and satin that one associates with many eighteenth-century paintings and with plays such as *The School for Scandal?* Or should the fabrics have the deep, thick, rich, subtle, absorptive qualities of heavy velvet and velour that one associates with Jacobean tragedy? By showing the director a fabric collage and asking careful questions, the designer can often get a much clearer idea of the director's feeling for texture and for fabrics under light than can be obtained from discussions alone. Sometimes reproductions of paintings or sculpture with particularly strong emphasis on texture are also helpful as a departure point for discussion. Compare the crinkled folds of a Dürer woodcut with the hard, sculptural folds of *The Charioteer of Delphi* or the soft transparency of the fabric on the Three Graces in Botticelli's *Allegory of Spring* (Figures 5–2, 5–3, and 5–4).

Fabrics in Movement

We have already mentioned how important it is for the designer to know before buying fabric the effect desired from the costumes in movement. If some of the basic fabrics are on hand in a costume shop or in the designer's studio, the designer can gain a clearer idea of how the costumes will move onstage by draping the fabrics over someone in a manner that may approximate a particular gown, sleeve, or mantle. If the actor who will play the role is available, the designer can work with him or her and a large piece of fabric to refine the costume line and determine the amount of fabric and the weight and texture that will be needed.

If there is a key costume whose lines in movement are important to the play, the designer may refrain from buying the fabric until the production is well into rehearsal and the designer can understand the directorial demands to be made on the costume and see the blocking of the movement. Using a rehearsal skirt, gown, or cape, or even an uncut piece of draped fabric of approximately the right size,

Figure 5–4.   Example of soft, light transparency: the Three Graces in Botticelli's *Allegory of Spring.* Photo courtesy of Alinari/Art Resource, Inc.

and working with the director and the actor, the designer may be able to determine the fabric requirements for a costume. Stairs, ramps, and platforms, the width and depth of steps, the width given for the passage of a flowing garment, surfaces and corners will affect the way a costume makes its point. No one should think of designing great flowing robes for Lady Macbeth's sleepwalking scene if the stair she descends to enter the scene is so narrow that it inhibits the effectiveness of her costume; no one should design a costume for Romeo without knowing the nature of the ladder and how the actor is going to use it in the scene in which Romeo leaves Juliet's bedroom.

It will save time and money if all the problems of the costume and its movement over the set can be solved before the final costume fabric is purchased. If this cannot be done, and the costume has to be built before the set and movement problems have been solved, the director, actor, set designer, and costume designer should go over sketches, models, fabric swatches, and the script in an attempt to foresee any problems.

Fabrics Under Light

In choosing a fabric, the designer must visualize what is going to happen to it under stage light. At this point the designer is not thinking of what happens to the colors of the costumes under the colored gels of the lights, but of the reflectivity and the absorptive qualities of the surface texture, and the highlights and shadows that will come from the costume folds.

The first consideration is certainly the reflective quality of a fabric. A lustrous, high-sheen satin under a full barrage of light can be blinding; the light bounces off the fabric so sharply that the fabric seems to leap off the stage. However, in a dimly lit production, fabric surface that is too absorptive may make a costume all but disappear at a moment when it should have at least a subtle strength. A designer must balance reflective surfaces so that they are neither all exactly alike nor too sharply contrasted. There should be a range that is varied and interesting without being so great that it causes certain costumes to jump out of the general grouping. Violent contrast should be used only when a violent effect is desired.

The second consideration is the effect of lights on folds. Should there be form-fitting costumes without folds, in which highlights come from the raised areas of the body? Or should there be semifitted garments with some folds, or draped costumes with many folds, where the highlights are on the edges of the folds or drapes? Thick fabrics give deep folds with strong highlights and shadows; thin fabrics give many small highlights and shadows. In a production that stresses folds, the lights should usually be arranged at angles that will give the maximum sculptured effect to the ridges and valleys of the folds to make the strongest contrasts between highlights and shadows. The lighting designer and the costume designer should confer as carefully about the angle and placement of lighting as about gel colors, and if possible the costume designer should check the fabrics for folds, highlights, and shadows under an approximation of the stage lights before beginning final construction of the costumes. Some of the most exciting costume effects in the theatre come from the subtle interaction of light on fabric in movement, and such effects should not be merely accidental but carefully planned in advance.

6

Patterns

Introduction

After selecting and purchasing the fabrics for a production, our next concern is drafting the patterns, or adapting existing patterns to suit the requirements of the costume designs. It would be simple if the designer could buy patterns in stores the way one buys clothes. Unfortunately, except for a few standard, traditional garments or masquerade costumes, patterns for theatrical costumes are not manufactured. The designer and the shop personnel must expand patterns from diagrams in books or must draft patterns to suit the design lines. A well-equipped costume shop, whether educational, amateur, or professional, will have a file of patterns that will make even the most exotic and complicated costume possible. But a costume designer should know how to draft a basic pattern from an actor's measurements and how to adapt specialized patterns from these basics. There are times when a designer may have untrained personnel, no access to store patterns, and limited time available, yet have to translate the costume sketches into complete sets of simple patterns quickly so that construction can commence. At such times all the designer needs, aside from a basic knowledge of measurements and pattern layouts, are a T-square, triangle, ruler, tape measure, pencil, eraser, and the paper from which the patterns are to be cut. Often it is a good idea to draft on heavy wrapping paper and then transfer the finished pattern to muslin. A muslin pattern is easier to lay out on fabric, will last longer, and can be stored more easily than a paper one. Patterns of any kind must, of course, be fitted to the individual, even though both the person and the pattern are a size 38. No one in the theatre depends on store sizes to fit perfectly; the costume designer must design and fit costumes to the actors the way the tailor or the seamstress fits garments. A pattern to be included in a permanent file may be drafted to fit the standard measurements of a store size and altered to fit an individual, or it may be designed from the first to fit a particular person's measurements. If several costumes in different sizes will be made from one pattern, it saves time to draft one pattern in a medium size and then alter it for the different measurements. If only one costume is to be made from a pattern, it is easiest to use the actual measurements of the actor to be fitted.

Measurement Chart

Play

Name of Player

Role

Height-- stocking feet	Men only-- trouser size
Weight	-- shirt size
Head-- around the circumference at the widest point	-- sleeve length
	-- inseam
Head-- forehead to nape of neck	
Head-- ear to ear over the top of head	Women only-- bra size
Hat size	-- stocking size
Neck-- loose to top center of collarbone front	-- dress size
	-- underpants size
Neck-- around center	
Chest or bust	Women only-- shoulder to bust point
Waist	-- bust point to bust point

Across the shoulders-- front   -- back

One shoulder-- across the top

Armseye to armseye-- narrowest point above chest and below shoulders
                    in front

Shoulder to waist-- front   -- back

Shoulder to floor-- front   -- back

Armpit to waist

Arm length outside-- to elbow   -- to wrist over bent elbow

Arm length inside-- to elbow   -- to wrist with arm straight

Around the biceps of the arm   -- around the forearm

Wrist-- tight   -- loose so that hand can slip through

Armseye-- loose so that the tape does not bind under the arm

Waist to floor-- front   -- back

Waist to thigh-- front   -- back

Waist to above knee-- front   -- back

Waist to below knee-- front   -- back

Around knee-- above   -- below

Inseam from crotch to floor

Crotch-- waist through crotch to waist

Hips

Thigh

Calf

Ankle   Stocking foot size for tights

Shoe size   Trace foot on separate sheet and attach

Figure 6-1.   A measurement chart.

Measurements

A permanent workshop where many plays are costumed must have mimeographed measurement blanks with a space for the name of the play, the actor's name, and the role played in the production. Include every measurement the costume shop will ever use on this blank, even though all the measurements may not be needed on any one production. Such a measurement blank places an actor's measurements on file, and if the acting company is a permanent one, then only minor adjustments need be made on the measurement card for each new production. The cards or sheets are filed alphabetically in a cabinet or file box, or sometimes in a binder or folder for each production. Sometimes the designer fastens the actor's measurements to the back of the sketch. Figure 6–1 shows a typical measurement blank with explanatory comments. The underlined items are those especially necessary to know when renting.

The garment industry has standard measurement charts which are simpler than those used in the costume shop because they give measurements for the standard sizes of manufactured clothing. These charts are good for drafting basic patterns to fit a standard size rather than a particular individual. The measurements follow average figure proportions. A pattern can usually be altered by several inches in each direction, so that standard patterns in small, medium, and large would be adaptable to all the shapes and sizes in a cast. Commercial patterns, which are primarily for women, usually give only the bust, waist, hip, and back (base of neck) to waist measurements. Some time ago, the whole system of sizing for patterns was revised, so that a woman may now buy patterns by bust measurements alone in any of the six categories into which women's patterns fall: young junior teen, junior petite, junior, misses, women's, and women's half-sizes. The "new sizing" equates all the other measurements to the bust measure once the correct choice within the six categories has been made. The categories are based on age and build, and the "new sizing" attempts to provide patterns that correspond more closely to the standard ready-to-wear sizes of the store.

See Figure 6–2 for a typical set of proportions useful in pattern drafting for a man and a woman of average build, the man with a 38-inch chest and the woman with a 36-inch bust.

Figure 6–2. Measurements: male and female average sizes.

Measurement	Average Sizes (inches) Male	Female
Chest or bust	38	36
Waist	31	26
Neck	15	13
Shoulder	5	4½
Width of back	15	13½
Width of chest	16	14
Hip	40	40
Back from neck to waist	17	16
Front from neck to waist	16	15
Underarm to waist	9	8½
Armseye	17	15
Sleeve from shoulder to elbow	14	13
Sleeve from elbow to wrist	11	10
Underarm to wrist	20	19
Wrist	8	6½
Front from waist to knee	26	25
Front from waist to hip	8½	7¼
Front from waist to ankle	41	40
Inseam	32	31

Standard Commercial Patterns

Although a designer will always prefer to have patterns drafted to his or her sketch requirements by a trained cutter, there are times when it may be useful to know about commercial patterns that can be adjusted to a desired costume line. All patterns from past productions should be on file, so that when a particularly useful pattern has been developed it can readily be produced and adapted to the requirements of the moment. If a limited number of commercial patterns are to be kept on file they should be in three sizes: 32, 36, and 38 for women and 36–38, 39–40, and 42–44 for men. Some possibly useful commercial patterns are as follows (note that patriotic patterns such as George Washington and Uncle Sam have disappeared since the first edition of this book):

Men

A standard pajama pattern with a V-neck, a cossack neck, and a side opening.

A cassock: Butterick 6765.

A surplice and choir robe: Butterick 3194.

A classic overcoat: Vogue 7407.

A classic vest: Butterick 4005 and Vogue 2112 and 1129 along with jacket and pants.

A classic smoking jacket: Butterick 3566.

Knee pants (male and female knickers): McCall's 7670.

Clown: Simplicity 7162, Butterick 3372 (with angel, rabbit, and animal).

Fantasy (buccaneer, harem girl, genie, Dracula): McCall's 7739.

Women

Standard patterns for a kimono nightgown and a fitted bodice with tight long sleeves and a high or low neckline.

Centennial (eighteenth- and nineteenth-century dresses): Simplicity 9616.

Frontier: Butterick 4585.

Fantasy (see under *Men*).

Witch and princess: Simplicity 7684.

Children

Children's nativity (kings, angels, shepherds): McCall's 7733.

Dracula and witch: McCall's 7316.

Clown and angel: McCall's 7230.

Devil and princess: McCall's 7231.

There is also in many yardage stores a specialized pattern book called Folkwear Patterns. Aside from many ethnic dance costumes, the book contains many period patterns including the following, at $4.50 to $6.50 a pattern: prairie dress, Victorian shirt, Edwardian female underwear, Gibson Girl blouse, hooded cloak, 1927 tea frock, Empire dress, and others.

The fancy dress costumes listed above are modern versions of period or traditional garments evolved from a superficial study of sources and sharply modified to give simplicity of construction and a pleasing modern look. They almost always call for less material than one should use to give a period feeling, but they can give basic structure and save time in the drafting process in certain situations. They should usually be used only as a guide, not as the finished pattern.

Expansion of Patterns Drawn to Scale

There are many sources where the designer can find reproductions of period patterns in a reduced scale. Many designers and cutters prefer to expand period patterns to full size because they achieve a more authentic line than they would if they drafted without a guide. A small-scale pattern may be expanded in many ways. It may be enlarged by using an opaque projector and tracing the outline; it may be enlarged with the mechanical enlargers used in mechanical drawing; or it may be enlarged by extending a series of lines outward from a single point until the original can be drawn full size. This last method, which is simple and requires no equipment, is as follows: If the scale for a particular set of small printed patterns is 1/16 inch to 1 inch, from any given point (A) ex-

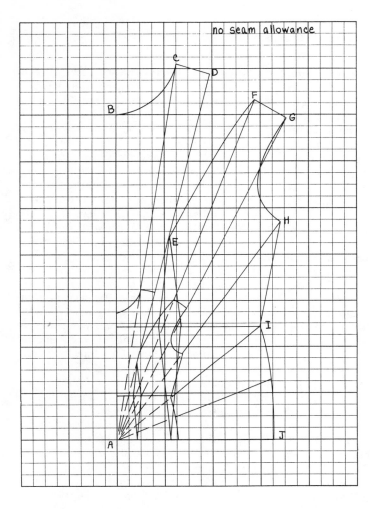

no seam allowance

Figure 6–3. One method of expanding a pattern diagram.

tend a line 16 times the original length in all directions until enough points (B, C, D, E, F, G, H) have been established to retain the original cut (Figure 6–3).

Readily Available Sources for Costume Patterns

In recent years many books have been published that present a wide variety of period patterns, some exactly as they were used originally, some simplified for the costume shop, and some originals that have been adapted to today's sizes. No matter how exciting a pattern may look on paper, no matter how accurate it may seem to be, it cannot be recommended for theatrical use until it has been cut, sewn, and fitted for an actor. Many period patterns will not fit today's male and female figures, even with the appropriate underpinnings. In the past century, because of changes in diet and health habits, men and women have become taller and broader. Therefore, even though the reproductions of some patterns may appeal more than others, and some may look more professional than others, each pattern must be tested before it is approved and filed in the workshop or in the designer's file.

First let us mention a few books with easy-to-read, simplified patterns for costumes that are not authentic. These patterns are intended to suggest period line and are meant for the amateur costume workshop. *Costume Design and*

Making by Mary Fernald and Eileen Shenton gives patterns for English costume from Saxon times to the end of the nineteenth century. The patterns are easy to understand but overly simplified. *Dress the Show* by Daty Healy presents similar diagrams but concentrates on tunics, vests, trousers, jackets, skirts, and bodices. Fitted coats and complex gowns are not included. *Stage Costume Handbook* by Berneice Prisk gives clear diagrams and directions for basic bodice, sleeve, skirt, and trouser patterns, and for some basic costume shapes from Egyptian times to the late nineteenth century. Miss Prisk's book with Jack Byers, *The Theatre Student: Costuming,* also has simple, clear patterns. *Dressing the Part* by Fairfax Proudfit Walkup has tiny pattern diagrams with the line drawings that illustrate the book, but they give little more than the general shape of the pattern piece. Two fine new books on constructing costumes with clear instructions on patterning are Rosemary Ingham and Elizabeth Covey, *The Costumer's Handbook,* and Joy Spanabel Emery, *Stage Costume Techniques.* Two other new books on costume design that contain pattern information are Rosemary Ingham and Elizabeth Covey, *The Costume Designer's Handbook,* and Barbara and Cletus Anderson, *Costume Design.*

Few books present original patterns edited and adapted for stage use and adjusted to present-day sizes. *Period Patterns* by Doris Edson, with commentary by Lucy Barton, is intended as a supplement to Miss Barton's book, *Historic Costume for the Stage,* which is a text on the history of dress. Although *Period Patterns* presents only a sampling of patterns from each period, and these are taken from items available in this country, each is clearly presented and has been thoroughly tested on models before inclusion in the book. The *Costume and Fashion* series by Herbert Norris, which includes Vol. I: *The Earlier Ages;* Vol. II: *From Senlac to Bosworth;* Vol. III: *The Tudors,* Books 1 and 2; and Vol. VI: *The Nineteenth Century* by Norris and Oswald Curtis, is a monumental series intended for the costume designer. Although the many costume diagrams are not ac-tually patterns, they give an accurate picture of original pattern shapes, and costume patterns can be easily drawn from them. Mary G. Houston's series, *Technical History of Costume,* including *Ancient Egyptian, Mesopotamian, and Persian Costume; Ancient Greek, Roman, and Byzantine Costume;* and *Medieval Costume in France and England,* does much the same thing. Diagrams show the cut of a particular garment, and from these it is not too difficult to devise a full-size pattern. *A History of Costume* by Carl Köhler, a standard work for almost sixty years, is now available in paperback and includes many pattern diagrams. Unfortunately, the measurements are in the metric system. Mary Evans' *How to Make Historic American Costumes* has a set of simple, clear patterns for male and female American dress from the early seventeenth through the nineteenth centuries. *Masterpieces of Eighteenth and Nineteenth Century Women's Costumes* by Aline Bernstein, the American costume designer of the 1920s, has detailed patterns of some beautiful examples of feminine fashion. Blanche Payne's *History of Costume* has an appendix of costume patterns. *Medieval Theatre Costume* by Iris Brooke has helpful Gothic patterns.

A number of books contain patterns taken from old tailors' manuals, patterns derived from period garments, and patterns reproduced from those in private collections and museums. *The Cut of Men's Clothes 1600–1900* by Norah Waugh is a good example. Its companion is *The Cut of Women's Clothes 1600–1930.* Both contain many illustrations and contemporary quotations explaining the patterns, and almost every major style from 1600 to the present is included. Another is *Patterns of Fashion* by Janet Arnold, in two volumes. The first volume gives patterns from 1660 to 1860, the second, patterns from 1860 to 1940. The patterns are large and readable, without too many complex markings and complicated information. A third excellent volume is *The Evolution of Fashion: Pattern and Cut from 1066 to 1930* by Margaret Hamilton Hill and Peter A. Bucknell. It has large, easy-to-read patterns of an excellent size. *The Blue Book of*

Men's Tailoring: Theatrical Costume-makers Pattern Book for Edwardian Men's Costumes by Frederick T. Croonburg is a must for cutting late nineteenth- and early twentieth-century men's garments. A standard work is still *Costume Patterns and Designs* by Max Tilke, which includes patterns for national costume around the world as well as the usual survey of patterns for the history of Western dress. *The Vogue Sewing Book* is also very useful, as is Clarence Poulin's *Tailoring Suits the Professional Way.*

Patterns may also be found in a number of nineteenth- and twentieth-century periodicals with sections on women's fashions, such as *The Delineator, Godey's Lady's Book, Good Housekeeping, Harper's Bazaar, Illustrated London News, Journal des Dames et des Demoiselles, Ladies' Home Journal, Ladies Tailor, McCall's, Peterson's Magazine, The Studio,* and *Vogue.* Certain museum costume collections, such as those at the Metropolitan Museum in New York City, the Brooklyn Museum, and the County Museum of Los Angeles, have extensive pattern files.

Once patterns are copied, traced, or drafted, they should be carefully labeled and filed, in a manila folder, in a filing cabinet. In this way the designer or costume shop supervisor gradually will build up an extensive file of period patterns that are accessible at short notice. It is best to use heavy wrapping paper or muslin for the patterns, because the tissue-thin paper on which commercial patterns are printed soon deteriorates.

The Layout of Basic Pattern Shapes

When time is of the essence, or when books with diagramed period patterns are not available, the designer may have to draft a basic costume shape from measurements alone. Simple items such as a basic bodice shape, a basic sleeve, or a basic pair of trousers can be drafted quickly, and any lack of precision can be remedied in fitting. Often, when chorus members are added to a production or supers must be readied to fill up the stage, the designer must produce a finished costume directly from an actor's measurements without the luxury of a cutter and still achieve the look of a carefully prepared pattern. Here is a simplified procedure for drafting basic patterns from a set of measurements.

Basic bodice or waist front—male (Figure 6–4a)

1. Lay out the neck-to-waist front measurement vertically in the center of a large sheet of paper, AB.
2. At the bottom of this line at A, lay out one-fourth the waist measurement to either the right or the left, AC.
3. Assuming that we have laid out one-fourth the waist measurement to the right of this center line, measure approximately 3¼ inches to the right of the neck- to waistline, AB, and lay out the shoulder-to-waist measurement, DE.
4. Draw in the curve of the neckline, BD, with right angles at neck and shoulder.
5. Making sure that there is a right angle where the shoulder line meets the neckline, D, lay out the measurement of one shoulder, DF.
6. Lay out one-half the armseye-to-armseye measurement front, GH, approximately 3 inches below the base of the neckline.
7. Lay out one-fourth the bustline or chest measurement, IJ, approximately 3 inches below the armseye-to-armseye measurement.
8. Lay out the underarm-to-waist measurement, JC, so that it connects the end of the bustline measurement with the end of the waistline measurement.
9. Draw in the armseye so that its curve, FHJ, creates a right angle with the shoulder line at F and the underarm-to-waist measurement at J, so that it makes a deep curve between the armseye-to-armseye measurement and the bust- or chestline.

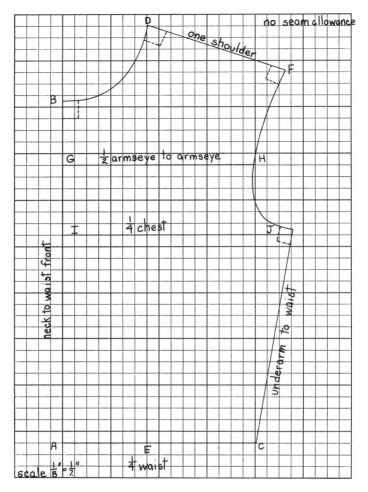

Figure 6–4a.   Basic bodice or waist front—male.

Basic bodice or waist front—female (Figure 6–4b)

1. For women, add approximately 1½ to 2 inches to the waistline, AC, and redraw the underarm-to-waist line, as JK; take this 1½ inches out of the center of the side waist front in a triangular slice, ELM, to create a dart rising to a point 2 inches below the bustline.

Placement of darts (Figure 6–4c)

1. The 1½ to 2 inches taken out at the waist, ELM, may be transferred either to the side under the armseye, PNO, or to the shoulder seam, SQR, either completely or partially, thus giving a fitted bust with darts at waist or darts at waist and side, darts at side and shoulder, darts at shoulder and waist, or darts at all three places.

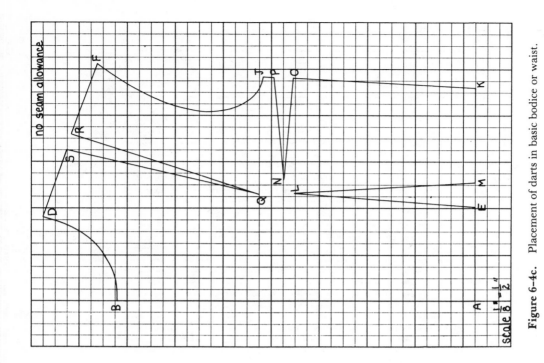

Figure 6–4c. Placement of darts in basic bodice or waist.

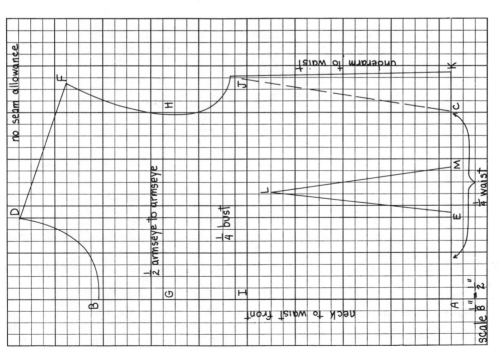

Figure 6–4b. Basic bodice or waist front—female.

111

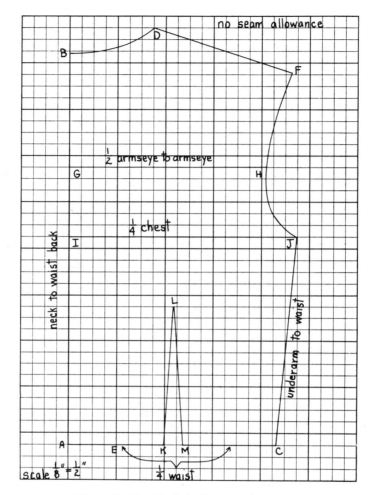

Figure 6-4d.   Basic bodice or waist—back.

Basic bodice or waist—back (Figure 6-4d)

1. This is laid out in the same manner as the front, except that no bustline darts are necessary, although small darts at the center of each side, KLM, may be needed in fitting.

2. It requires a more gradual curve to the armseye, FHJ, and a neckline, BD, that is not as deeply cut in back as it is in front, since the neck-to-waist measurement, BA, is longer in the back.

One-piece sleeve (Figure 6-5)

1. In the center of a large piece of paper, lay out a vertical line the length of the over-arm measurement, AB.

2. At B, lay out a horizontal line, CD, equal to the wrist measurement.

3. Lay out the underarm measurement, BL, on the vertical line up from the wrist, and lay out a horizontal line, ELF, at L. EL is 6½ inches, LF is 7 inches.

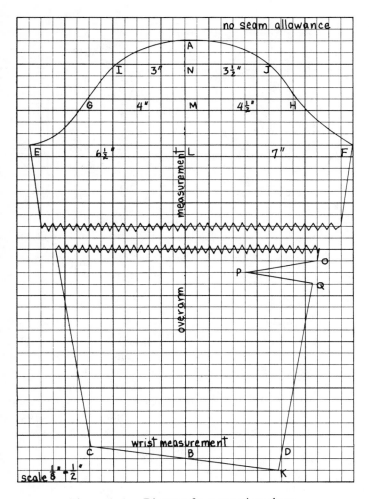

Figure 6–5. Diagram for a one-piece sleeve.

4. At M, 2 inches above this horizontal line, lay out a second horizontal line, GMH. GM is 4 inches, MH is 4½ inches.

5. At N, 1½ inches above this, lay out a third horizontal line, INJ. IN is 3 inches, NJ is 3½ inches.

6. Connect the ends of these lines, EGIA-JHF, with a gradual curve, making adjustments until the length of the curve approximates the armseye measurement.

7. Connect the ends of the armseye curve, EF, with the ends of the wrist measurement, CD.

8. Take a 1-inch dart at the elbow, OPQ, halfway down the right underarm-to-wrist measurement, FD.

9. Extend FD 1 inch to K and redraw the wrist line along a new line, CK.

10. For more curve, curve the two underarm-to-wrist lines, EC and FD, to the left 1 to 1½ inches and again connect their lower ends with the wrist measurement.

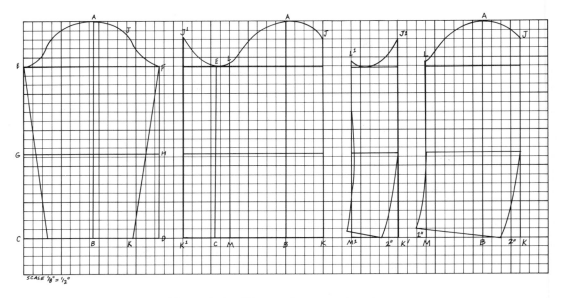

Figure 6–6. Diagram for a two-piece sleeve.

Two-piece sleeve (Figure 6-6)

1. Trace the one-piece sleeve onto another sheet of paper, and construct new side seams, EC and FD, parallel to the center line, AB.
2. Lay out elbow line, GH, perpendicular to AB, using shoulder to elbow measurement.
3. Construct back seam, JK, parallel to AB, halfway between AB and FD.
4. Cut patterns along JK and tape FD to EC.
5. Measure 1½ inches to the right of the taped edges, EC and FD, and construct a line, LM, parallel to the center line, AB.
6. Cut along this line, LM, and reverse the undersleeve section, EC and JK, so that the back sides of each pattern piece, EC and LM, are to the right.
7. Curve both back seams, EC and JK, from the elbow to a point 2 inches to the left of the bottom of points K and K′.
8. Slightly curve front seam, L′M′, of the undersleeve, as shown.
9. Curve the front seam of the top sleeve sec-

tion out from the original seam line, LM, from elbow to 1 inch at bottom and tape on the extension.
10. Measure the length of the front inside seam and adjust its length until it matches the length and line of the outside seam.

Basic pair of trousers (Figure 6-7)

1. In the upper third of a large piece of paper, lay out a horizontal line, ADB, one-half the hip measurement.
2. At A, raise a perpendicular vertical line of 9 inches, AC.
3. At D, raise a perpendicular vertical line of 8½ inches, DE.
4. At B, raise a perpendicular line of 7½ inches, BF.
5. Lay out a horizontal line, GH, 7½ inches below the hip line, ADB.
6. At G, extend a horizontal line 5 inches to the left, creating IG.
7. At H, extend a horizontal line 3 inches to the right, creating HJ.

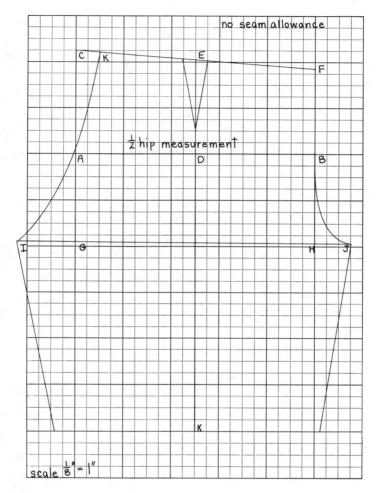

Figure 6–7. Diagram of a basic trouser top.

8. Connect points CEF.
9. On this new line, measure in 2 inches from C and establish a point K.
10. Connect this point K with A and I in a gentle curve.
11. Connect F, B, and J with a deep curve.
12. With the crotch line, IC and FJ, now established, the inseam or the waist-to-knee measurements may be laid out below IJ and the desired width of the trouser at the bottom or at the knee (in knee breeches) established. A dart may be

taken at the side seam of the trousers at the waist, at E, or a seam may be put in between E and K and a dart added at E to give the desired fit.

Basic gored skirt (Figure 6–8)

1. In the upper third of a large piece of paper, lay out a horizontal line, AFB, one-half the hip measurement.
2. Mark point C 6½ inches directly above point A and point D 7½ inches directly above point B and connect, CD.

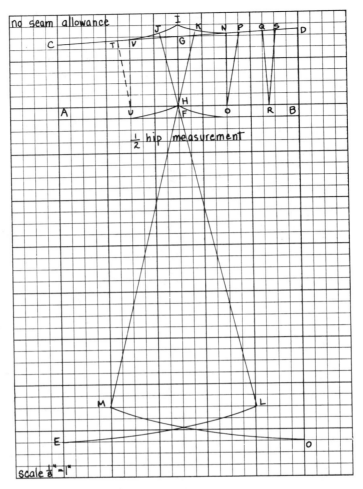

Figure 6-8. Diagram of a basic skirt.

3. At the middle of AB at established point F, draw a vertical line through it intersecting CD at G.

4. Mark point H 1 inch directly above point F.

5. Connect AH and BH with gentle curves.

6. Mark point I 1 inch directly above point G, and connect CI and ID with gentle curves.

7. Through point H, lay out a straight line, HJ, to make a right angle with CI at J and with AH at H.

8. Through point H, lay out a straight line to make a right angle with HB at H and with ID at K.

9. On KD, take two small darts, NOP and QRS, so that CJ and KD add up to one-half the waist measurement.

10. A single dart, TUV, on CJ may be necessary to keep the side seam at JHK centered on the side of the skirt.

11. CE may be laid in as the front waist-to-ankle or waist-to-floor measurement, while DO is the back waist-to-ankle or waist-to-floor measurement.

12. EL should follow a gentle curve to meet

the extension of JH at L in a right angle.

13. OM should follow a gentle curve to meet the extension of KH at M in a right angle.

14. OM and EL may be shortened in length to gain a narrowed, pencil-line skirt.

15. OM and EL may also be lengthened to form a fuller gored skirt, as long as JL and KM continue to make right angles with CJ and KD.

These layouts are not accurate patterns; they are ways to make basic garment shapes from measurements and a few numbers that establish general proportions. The refinement must take place in the fittings. If accuracy is desired from the beginning, the designer should obtain patterns from the appropriate source books and adapt them to the actors' measurements before cutting. Only when under pressure, when there is no time to refine a pattern, or when a costume is simple in line should the designer use a basic layout.

Pattern Adaptation

Changing a pattern size is simple if the designer remembers not to make changes all in one place or all on one edge of the pattern. Only in lengthening or shortening skirts, trousers, or sleeves should one edge, the bottom edge, be used for the adjustment. If 2 inches must be taken from the bustline of a bodice pattern, then ½ inch should be taken from each half of the front and the back pieces of the pattern. Often it is best to split the pattern pieces down the middle and overlap them to reduce size or spread them apart to increase size. If one does not wish to cut the pattern, then trace halfway around it, move the pattern the necessary amount to add the extra width, and trace around the other half. The proper relationship between the two halves of the pattern must, of course, be kept.

To develop patterns for period garments for which one does not have pattern sources, or for fanciful garments for which there are no pat-

terns, the designer needs a good set of basic patterns. These patterns can be drawn and reshaped until they suit the sketch. If a commercial pattern is copied on heavy brown paper, it can be cut, spread apart, compressed, worked over, and new seams added until the right line is achieved. Much experimentation may have to take place before the right line is obtained. The pattern may have to be transferred to muslin and pinned together on the actor or dress form a number of times before the fabric can be cut for the final costume.

Pattern Pieces

Figures 6–9 through 6–15 illustrate the variety of pattern shapes that have resulted from experimentation with basic clothing lines through the centuries. The diagrams are drawn ¹⁄₁₆ inch to 1 inch, and no seam allowance is shown.

Figure 6–9 shows the basic male waist pattern for such fitted garments as the cotehardie, certain doublets, and certain male foundation garments for a size 38. With it are two waistcoat variations and a sixteenth-century doublet layout.

Figure 6–10 shows further variations on the basic waist pattern for men for a seventeenth-century cassock with pleated skirt, an eighteenth-century coat, an Empire coat, and a late nineteenth-century evening coat.

Figure 6–11 shows the layout of the basic woman's waist, with measurements for a size 16. Variations include the bodice of a Spanish gown of the late sixteenth century, the bodice of a mideighteenth-century court gown, an Empire bodice, a bodice used with the hoop skirts of 1863, and a bodice of the last decade of the nineteenth century.

Figures 6–12a and 6–12b show a basic trouser pattern, with measurements for a size 38 man's suit and including cutting lines for eighteenth-century knee breeches. Other diagrams are for trunks, Elizabethan trunk hose, and tight-fitting trousers of the early nineteenth century.

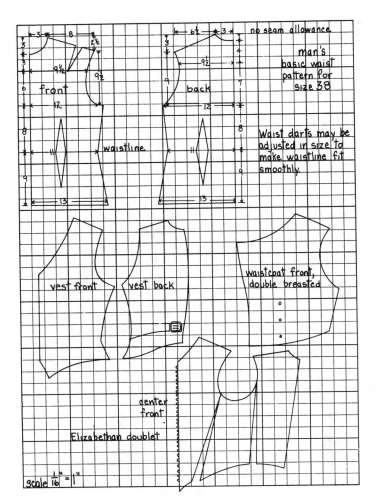

Figure 6–9. Diagrams of men's doublets and vests.

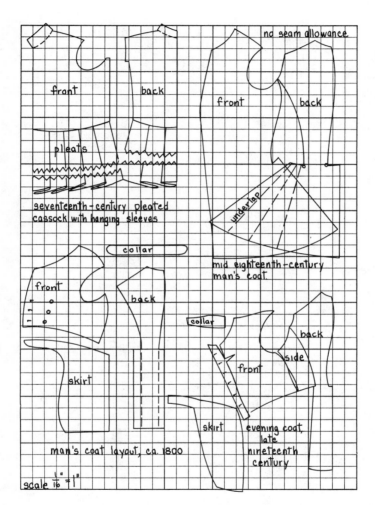

Figure 6–10. Diagrams of men's jackets and coats.

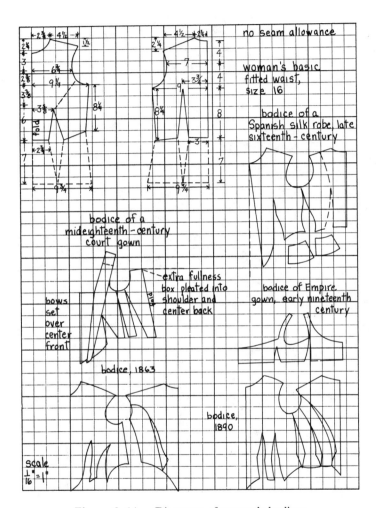

Figure 6-11.   Diagrams of women's bodices.

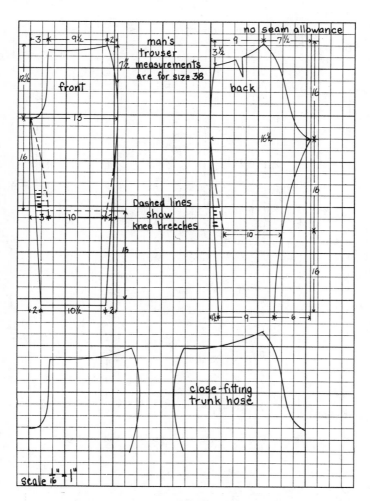

Figure 6–12a.   Diagrams of breeches and trousers.

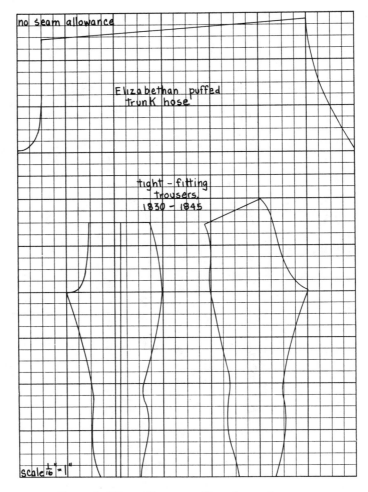

Figure 6–12b.   Diagrams of breeches and trousers.

The sleeve patterns in Figures 6–13a and 6–13b show the basic layout of a woman's one-piece fitted sleeve and a two-piece sleeve, both with measurements for a size 16. Other diagrams show how to expand the sleeve for added width and fullness at the top, with variations that include a bell-shaped Gothic sleeve, a Renaissance bagpipe sleeve, an eighteenth-century cap sleeve, a Renaissance open-hanging sleeve, a slashed hanging sleeve, and a tiny Empire cap sleeve.

In Figure 6–14, a basic woman's skirt, size 16, is shown with measurements and dashed lines to indicate the method for making the skirt more circular. With this diagram are layouts for an Empire skirt and a skirt of the 1890s.

Figure 6–15 shows variations on the basic half-circular cloak pattern by the addition of shoulder capes, sleeves, collars, and facings.

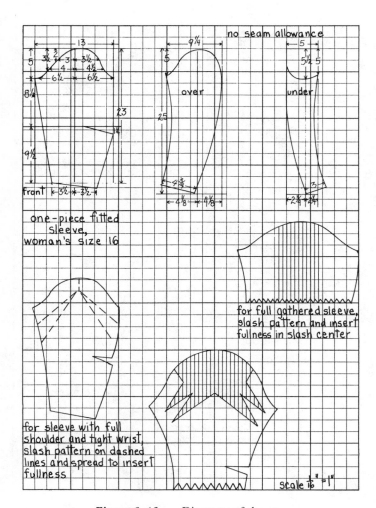

Figure 6–13a. Diagrams of sleeves.

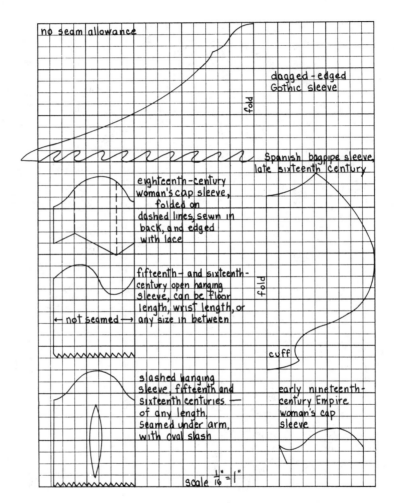

no seam allowance

dagged-edged
Gothic sleeve

fold

Spanish bagpipe sleeve,
late sixteenth century

eighteenth-century
woman's cap sleeve,
folded on
dashed lines, sewn in
back, and edged
with lace

fifteenth- and sixteenth-
century open hanging
sleeve, can be floor
length, wrist length, or
← not seamed → any size in between

fold

cuff

slashed hanging
sleeve, fifteenth and
sixteenth centuries —
of any length,
seamed under arm,
with oval slash

early nineteenth-
century Empire
woman's cap
sleeve

scale $\frac{1"}{16} = 1"$

Figure 6–13b.   Diagrams of sleeves.

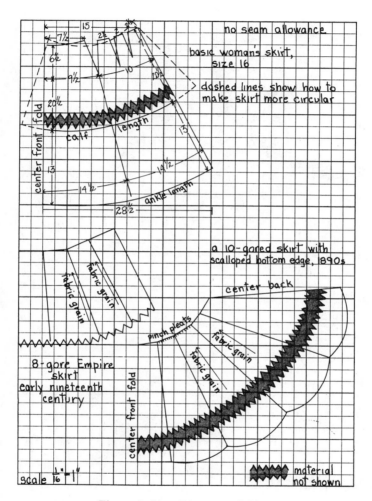

Figure labels (as shown in diagram):

- no seam allowance
- basic woman's skirt, size 16
- dashed lines show how to make skirt more circular
- center front fold
- 7½
- 15
- 2½
- 6½
- 9½
- 10
- 20½
- 20½
- calf length
- 13
- 15
- 13
- 14½
- 14½
- ankle length
- 28½
- a 10-gored skirt with scalloped bottom edge, 1890s
- center back
- fabric grain
- pinch pleats
- fabric grain
- fabric grain
- 8-gore Empire skirt early nineteenth century
- center front fold
- scale 1" = 1'
- material not shown

Figure 6–14. Diagrams of skirts.

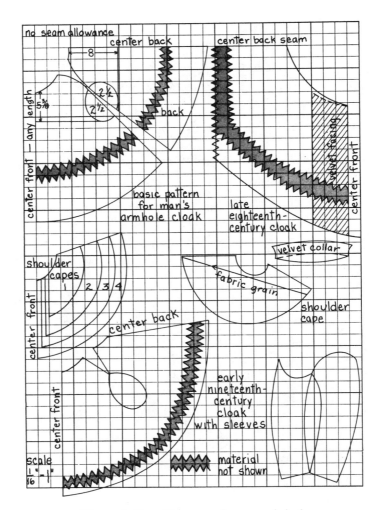

Figure 6–15.   Diagrams of capes and cloaks.

7

Construction and Ornamentation

Costume Construction

When the designs for a production have been completed and the patterns for the costumes devised, the actual construction of the garment begins. During this period the designer's time is occupied by countless details; and even the designer who is fortunate enough to have an excellent shop foreman and trained cutters, seamstresses, and personnel for dyeing, ornamentation, painting, and finishing must always be everywhere at once. No matter how carefully the sketches and working drawings have been prepared, no matter how carefully the patterns have been worked out, unless the designer spends time with each cutter and seamstress, he or she will find at dress parade that the original ideas have not been fully executed. Robert Edmond Jones used to write little poems and inspiring notes to his construction staff to give them his feeling about the costumes, in hopes that the workers would capture some of his imaginative vision in the finished products. There is no one way to work with a staff, but one must try to encourage and inspire them to do more than turn out a machine-like product. Each costume must be given that extra thought, that extra personal touch that keeps the original vision of the designer alive through long and grueling hours of work. Especially at the fittings, from the first one in muslin to the final one before dress parade, one must make known to the actor and the fitter one's hopes and desires for the costume. Even though a busy professional designer is not always in the shop during costume construction, one must spend as much time as is necessary on the fittings to ensure that the final result fulfills one's design image for the play.

Workshop and Storage Facilities

Although the university or repertory theatre designer seldom sets up costume workshop facilities, he or she will be consulted about workshop and storage space and costume equipment when a new theatre is being designed. Therefore, in this section we shall discuss the space and equipment requirements for the ideal costume department.

The proper facilities for the construction and storage of costumes are of great importance if a theatre is to produce plays in a professional manner. Nothing is more important in a continuing operation, whether repertory or run of the show, than the storage space to house costumes on hand and store new ones. It is best if the storage room and the workshop can be close to each other. Only if the storage is easily accessible from the workshop is the transfer of costumes from storage to workshop easily manageable. If the rooms must be on different floors, there should be a large elevator for rolling racks. The ideal is to have adjoining workshop and storage space areas, both easily accessible to the dressing rooms and the stage.

The Costume Storage Area

The room used for storage must be dry, because dampness can cause considerable damage to stored clothes. Its size must be determined by the extent of its use, but it should always be larger than what is at first apparently needed. After a theatre has presented several seasons of shows, wardrobe costumes will need a much larger area than would have been anticipated. A good average size is 1200 to 1600 square feet. The space should be divided between hanging space and shelves or drawers. Shelves are cheaper to build than drawers, and labeled boxes can be used on the shelves in the sizes needed, while drawers once built cannot be expanded. Costumes should be hung to avoid folds and wrinkles. The hanging space can either be open space equipped with pipes, or built-in wardrobes. The latter is preferable if the storage space is not completely dust free. If open racks are used, it is best to cover them with dust covers. The hanging space needs to be only the width of a coat hanger plus clearance for large padded sleeves or unusual bulk. A six-foot height will accommodate the length of most costumes, except gowns with long trains and large mantles. Long garments can usually be pinned up to clear the floor. A very

good arrangement is two low-ceilinged rooms, one for hanging space, the other for shelves. High shelves that require one to climb a ladder to reach a box should not be used.

It is difficult to state exactly what the height between the shelves for storage boxes should be, but there should be several inches' clearance above the storage box. Shelves should generally be three feet deep, with two feet between shelves. The storage box should be about 27 inches by 15 inches by 15 inches so that it can be conveniently handled by one person even when the box is fully packed. The box should be constructed of durable cardboard with detachable overlapping covers. Edges and corners that become worn with handling can be reinforced with gummed cloth tape. At least 1 inch of space should be left between boxes. All boxes and all racks of costumes should be clearly labeled so that items can be easily located on demand.

The Costume Workshop

The workshop size should be determined by the number of people most likely to be working in the room at the same time, the amount of work to be done, and the size of the largest productions costumed. The number of productions done during a season is another determining factor.

The room should have windows for natural lighting (and a pleasant view, if possible, for worker morale). The room should usually be arranged so that the bank of sewing machines is under the windows, the cutting tables are in the center of the room, the fitting area is at one end, ironing boards are in a corner or area removed from other activity, and shelves, cupboards, and dress forms are placed along the far wall away from the windows. If one has a choice of lighting, it is best to request incandescent light instead of fluorescent light, because fabrics look different under fluorescent than they do under stage light (Figures 7–1 and 7–2). A separate connecting room with a sump in the floor should be reserved for all dye

Figure 7–1.   An example of a costume workshop. The arrangement of the equipment and facilities in the new work space at the Department of Drama, University of Texas. Courtesy of Paul Reinhardt. Photo by Alan Smith.

Figure 7–2.   Another view of the costume workshop at the University of Texas, showing the arrangement of cutting tables and storage cabinets. Courtesy of Paul Reinhardt. Photo by Alan Smith.

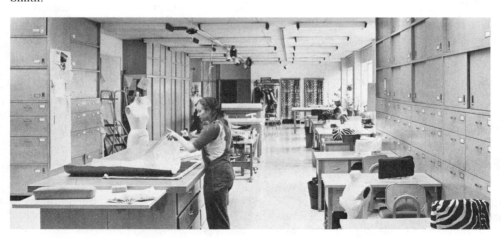

equipment. Part of this room or a third room should be reserved for washing equipment.

The following alphabetical list of equipment includes everything commonly used in the construction of stage costumes. Some items are essential, others are merely conveniences.

Cutting

BINS OR WASTEBASKETS. Receptacles are needed to hold the daily accumulation of trash.

CUTTING TABLE. A 50-inch width allows for convenient cutting of 45-inch material with a margin on which to lay shears and other tools. Although a wider table is helpful for 54-inch fabrics, it is difficult to reach across its width. A table can be as long as the room will conveniently allow, up to ten feet, but it is preferable to have several tables, each about eight feet long, if the room will accommodate them. It is then possible to have three tables six to eight feet long and in heights for short, medium, and tall people. It is very important to have tables the correct height to ease back strain. For short people, 32 to 34 inches is best; 36 inches is best as a general height; and 38 to 40 inches is best for tall people. The surface of the table should be smooth so that fabrics will not catch on it. One of the most practical surfaces is cork, because fabrics can be pinned directly to it and slippery fabrics will not skid on the surface.

DRAFTING TOOLS. These include a large plastic right-angle triangle; a rectangular ruler 15 inches by 4 inches in clear plastic, known as the tailor's square; and the standard yardstick for measuring and laying out straight lines.

DRESS FORMS. Commercial padded tailor's dummies on heavy-duty adjustable stands are to be preferred. They are easier to obtain in women's sizes than in men's, but a well-equipped shop will have three female forms, sizes 10, 12, and 14, and two male forms, sizes 38 and 42. To make a moldable form, wrap a well-built actor wearing a T-shirt in six or seven layers of gummed paper tape; cut the actor out of the finished form; put the pieces back together; set the form on a wooden template with a strong dowel through the center to the neck; and place it on a solid wooden stand. Moldable forms are recommended only when there is not enough money to buy commercial forms. Inexpensive adjustable forms sold for the domestic market are not recommended.

DRESSMAKER'S SHEARS. These shears come in 8-, 10-, or 12-inch lengths; they should always be well sharpened and should be used only for cutting fabric.

FABRIC BINS. A workshop should have fabric drawers or bins marked by color or fiber into which all large scraps should be placed for future use.

FILING CABINETS. These are essential for filing patterns and measurements.

MANILA FOLDERS. These are useful as holders for patterns and measurements.

PAPER SCISSORS. There should be several pairs of medium-sized scissors for cutting paper patterns. Fabric scissors should not be used to cut paper.

PUSH PINS. These are used for putting up sketches, pinning wigs to wig blocks, putting patterns and swatches on walls, and securing patterns to the cutting table.

ROLL OF BROWN PAPER. Wrapping paper is used for cutting patterns and for covering tables.

SCRAP BOXES. All the scraps from a production in progress should be placed in a large scrap box marked with the name of the production. When the production is over, small scraps should be thrown away and the large ones placed in fabric drawers or bins for future use.

SQUARED PATTERN PAPER. This is very useful in drafting or blowing up small patterns from books.

STEPLADDERS. Small or medium-sized ladders may be necessary to reach items on high shelves or on top of cupboards.

STOOLS. It is very helpful to have one or two high stools around each cutting table to allow cutters to change position and rest their backs and feet while doing small detail work on the cutting table.

TAILOR'S CHALK. The flat wax-type chalk —available in black, red, yellow, and blue—is superior to the pressed powder variety. The wax chalk is used to mark pattern lines and alterations and can usually be removed by melting with a hot iron.

TAPE MEASURE. Tape measures are of plastic, 60 inches in length; they should have large numbers and should be reversible so that they can be read from either end.

TRACING PAPER. This is a heavy waxed paper with a colored surface and is used to transfer pattern markings. It comes in packages of assorted basic colors.

TRACING WHEEL. A small saw-toothed metal wheel on a handle, this tool is used with tracing paper to transfer pattern markings from a paper pattern to muslin.

Sewing

BEESWAX. This is used to wax thread to keep it from knotting.

NEEDLES. There are two types of *machine needles,* the standard or sharp-pointed needles for regular fabric and the ball-pointed needles for polyesters and knits. Machine needles are sized to fit a particular machine, so one must be careful to use only the correct size indicated for a specific machine. Never sew with a bent needle. There are also a variety of *hand needles.* Long-eyed needles in sizes 5 to 10 are convenient for ordinary sewing. Carpet, darning, upholstery, and heavy embroidery needles are necessary for heavy work. Needles can be bought in bulk quantity from a wholesale supply house to save money and cover a full season of work.

PINS. Straight pins for pinning patterns and fabrics together should be rustproof, bought in quantity in boxes, and of a medium size that will easily penetrate fabric, yet not small enough to be lost during cutting and sewing.

RAZOR BLADES. Single-edged blades set in a holder are useful for cutting leather, fur, and other tough substances. They should not be used to rip seams.

SEAM GAUGES. These are tiny measuring devices with a marking gauge for keeping seam markings in line.

SEWING MACHINES. Three sewing machines are usually the minimum needed for a small shop. At least two of these should be the standard cabinet models, which are easily operated and repaired. At least one of the cabinet models should do zigzag work, buttonholes, edgings, and bindings. The third machine should be of the industrial variety to do very heavy seams and leatherwork. Singer, Union Special, and Pfaff are the most popular industrial brands; Bernina, Viking, and Pfaff are the most popular domestic machines.

SEWING MACHINE OIL. Lightweight sewing machine oil is essential for lubricating the machines and is available from sewing machine retailers.

STITCH WITCHERY. This is a brand name for a material used to laminate fabrics together. It is cut to the shape desired and then pressed with an iron between the pieces to be laminated. The heat melts the stitch witchery and bonds the fabrics.

TABLES AND CHAIRS. These are needed in a quiet corner of the costume shop, where the hand-sewers and finishers can do their work removed from the bustle of the major construction area.

THIMBLES. A thimble is a metal or plastic guard that protects the fingertip when a hand needle is pushed through fabric. Thimbles come in a range of sizes.

THREAD. In medium- and large-sized theatres, only black and white thread is usually used, since thread color cannot be seen from a distance. In intimate productions, colored thread is necessary. Only a few sizes are needed: mercerized #40 and #50 for machine and ordinary sewing, heavy button and carpet thread for buttons and leather, and mending thread for hose.

THREAD NIPPERS. These are small scissors for cutting thread. They have only one finger hole, and the two blades are fastened together at the end rather than at the center.

THREAD STAND. The most economical way to buy machine thread is in 1200-yard cones, but these cannot be used on the regular spindle on a sewing machine. A thread spindle or stand, secured from industrial machine suppliers, is useful for feeding thread through the machine without tension.

Fittings and Fastenings

BUTTONS. Boxes of buttons in various sizes and colors should be accumulated over a period of time. There should always be on hand a range of button forms, from small to large, for making fabric-covered "self buttons."

HEMMING PLATFORMS. It is useful to have an 18-inch-high platform on locking casters on which actors may stand when having hems taken.

HOOKS AND EYES. Hooks and eyes should be kept on hand in black and silver in sizes #2, #3, #5, and #12. Metal pants hooks for heavy costumes are also necessary. There is also hook-and-eye tape that can be sewn on by machine, thus saving the trouble of sewing on individual hooks and eyes.

PINCUSHIONS. These tiny padded cushions, which often come with a bracelet attachment to clip to the wrist, are essential for the storage of straight pins during a fitting.

PINKING SHEARS OR A PINKING MACHINE. Pinking shears trim seam edges in a zigzag, saw-toothed pattern to keep them from raveling. There is also a hand-operated machine

that can be attached to a table to do the same thing.

SAFETY PINS. These are closed pins that will not stick the fitter or the actor and should be on hand in assorted sizes purchased in bulk.

SCISSORS. Medium-sized to small scissors should be on hand for clipping seams, cutting threads, and trimming.

SEAM RIPPERS. A single-pronged blade set in a handle is best for ripping seams and unwanted stitches. It is to be preferred to a single-edged razor blade.

SNAPS. Snaps should be kept on hand in black and silver in sizes #000, #00, #1, and #2.

THREE-WAY MIRROR. A full-length three-way mirror is essential for the actor and costumer during fittings. It helps in removing wrinkles, setting seams, checking proportions, and observing hem lines.

VELCRO. Velcro consists of two pieces of tape with napped surfaces. When pressed to each other, these surfaces hold tightly to form a garment closing. Velcro comes in widths from ½ inch to 1 inch in black and white and some colors. It is relatively expensive, makes a tearing sound on opening, and is useful primarily for fast changes.

ZIPPERS. Metal zippers are available in a range of lengths, strengths, and colors and are to be preferred for costumes over nylon zippers. *Dress zippers* are the nonseparating kind most used in costume shops in lengths from 7 to 22 inches. A variety should be kept in black and white and the white dyed to match the costume. *Separating jacket zippers* are heavy, open at the bottom and top, and used in waist- or hip-length garments. *Placket zippers* are connected at the top and bottom and are used primarily in underarm side seams.

Dyeing

DYE VAT. For large amounts of fabric, there are large steam vats that can be purchased at a fairly high cost. Often these are too large for a costume shop and a commercial steam-jacketed soup kettle may be used instead. They have a thirty- or forty-gallon capacity and may either generate their own steam or be tapped into an existing steam pipe.

DYES. Dyes can be purchased in bulk or in dime-store packets, but the latter is expensive. It is better to buy dye by the pound and have both the salt-added Tintex dyes and the non-salt union dyes. Other specialized dyes should be bought for specific projects.

GLASS AND PLASTIC CONTAINERS. These are essential for storing and mixing dyes, both dry and liquid.

HOT PLATE. A gas or electric two-burner hot plate is essential for boiling dye solutions when the vat is not used.

KETTLES. Granite, enamel, or stainless steel kettles are essential for boiling fabrics in dye solutions on the hot plate.

MEASURING CUPS AND SPOONS. These are needed to do the appropriate measurement of dye pigments or salt when mixing dye solutions.

SINK. A stainless steel sink with running water is an essential part of the dye-room equipment.

WASHING MACHINE. An automatic washing machine and dryer are needed for dyeing (or more properly tinting) when the dye solution is not boiled during the dyeing process.

Pressing

IRON CLEANER. This liquid cleaner should be kept on hand to remove dirt and burned-on discoloration from steam irons.

IRONING BOARDS. In the area of the shop set aside for pressing there should be an industrial ironing board or ironing table, or, if this is unavailable, one or two regular ironing boards. All should be placed on a carpeted area so that fabric that touches the floor while being ironed will not get soiled.

IRON REST. There should be a metal or rubber iron rest on which to place the commercial steam iron when it is not in use.

IRONS. Heavy-duty steam irons with portable tanks that hold up to three gallons of distilled water are to be preferred, as they can be left running through a full working day without damage. The steam from these irons is more concentrated than in domestic irons, and unlike the latter, the iron seldom has to be replaced. To avoid having a spitting or drizzling steam iron, be certain that distilled water is used and that the water is hot enough before setting the iron to release steam.

PRESSING CLOTHS. These are soft, firm cloths placed over very delicate fabric to keep the iron from touching it.

SLEEVE BOARD. This is a small ironing board designed to slip inside sleeves and other tubular shapes for easy ironing.

SPRAY STARCH. Applying commercial starch from a spray can is the simplest way to starch fabric before ironing.

STEAMER. A portable steamer that generates a jet of steam is useful for velvets and velours, for shaping felt hats, and to help in distressing woolen garments.

Crafts and Miscellaneous Equipment

ARMOR AND MASK-MAKING SUPPLIES. These include clay, materials for papier mâché, Celastic, softener or acetone, plaster of paris, glue, fixative spray, muslin, paint, and trims.

BINS OR WASTEBASKETS. Receptacles are needed to hold the daily accumulation of trash.

BULLETIN BOARDS. The workshop should have fiberboard- or cork-covered wall space for the display of costume plates and other items.

CURLING IRONS, COMBS, AND HAIRBRUSHES. These are all necessary for the dressing of wigs.

GLUE (FABRIC AND ALL-PURPOSE). There should always be two forms of glue in a costume shop: a fabric glue that is so flexible that even jewelry and patterns can be glued to fabric without cracking under heavy use, and an all-purpose glue for fastening solid objects firmly together. The spray-trim adhesive made by 3M is useful for quickly gluing fabric or trim to other fabric surfaces.

GLUE GUN AND GLUE PELLETS. These are must items for gluing things together but more importantly for creating decorative trim. The pellets are pushed through the hot gun and the resultant drizzle of glue can be used like the frosting in a cake decorator. Hot glue, however, will not withstand dry cleaning.

GROMMETING EQUIPMENT. This is a kit for setting large eyelets. It is very useful for making lacing holes in boots, jackets, and vests. Eyelets and grommets come in various sizes and colors and are essential for certain period costumes.

HAMMERS, SCREWDRIVERS, AND PLIERS. Such hand tools are very important for working with armor, leather rivets, jewelry, and costume properties.

HOOP WIRE. Flat, flexible spring steel is essential, along with crimping clips, for constructing hoop skirts.

HORSE-GROOMING RAKE. This saw-toothed circular tool is excellent for distressing the outer surface of fabrics.

MAT KNIFE AND BLADES. These are very useful for cutting Celastic, heavy cardboard, leather, and other substances that do not respond to scissors.

PAINTS AND PAINT BRUSHES. The variety of paints for crafts include fabric paints, dry scene colors, metallic powders, and a selection of matte and glossy spray paints. A small selection of good paint brushes (six) in various sizes is essential, and these should be kept in good condition by proper cleaning with the appropriate solvents or soap and water.

PAPER TOWELS. These are needed for blotting, wiping, and cleanup in the various craft processes.

RAZOR BLADES. In single-edged form, these are useful for a variety of cutting tasks in craft processes.

RIVETS. Pop rivets are used in leatherwork and come in various sizes.

SPRAY GUN. A spray gun that operates with a pressure canister is often useful in place of spray paints bought in cans, as it allows you to mix your own spray or dye colors.

STAPLE GUN. This is useful in putting up things on the shop walls and is sometimes necessary for fastening decorative items to surfaces like leather and heavy felt.

TAPE (MASKING AND TRANSPARENT). Tapes have many applications, from putting swatches on sketches to piecing patterns to covering cutting tables with brown wrapping paper.

THUMBTACKS AND PUSH PINS. These are used for putting up sketches, pinning wigs to headblocks, and putting patterns and sketches on walls.

WIGBLOCKS. These blocks in wood or styrofoam are essential for the constructing and the dressing of wigs.

WIRE CUTTERS AND TIN SNIPS. The first is needed for cutting various sizes of wire that may be used, the second for cutting sheets of metal or even for trimming Celastic.

WORK TABLE. Finally, a large work table is needed on which to work with the various crafts, preferably out of the way of the sewing, cutting, and fitting areas of the shop or, even better, in an adjoining room.

Maintenance

BROOM AND DUSTPAN. These mundane items are essential for keeping a shop clean if there is no daily outside maintenance.

CLEANING SUPPLIES. Usually these consist of various dry-cleaning solvents in bottles and cans for stain and spot removal on costumes.

One should look for nonflammable fluids, and it is most convenient if one can find one all-purpose grease and dirt remover.

CLOTHES BRUSHES.   These are essential for removing lint from wool costumes.

DETERGENT.   This is essential for washing shirts and cotton accessories between performances and after the strike of a production.

DRYER.   A second clothes dryer not used for dyeing is very useful for drying the washing done during the run of a production and after the strike.

DRYING RACKS.   These are not essential but are useful for drying hand washables during the run of a production or after the strike.

SHOE POLISH KIT.   A fully equipped kit with a variety of polishes, brushes, and buffing cloths is needed to keep footwear polished.

TACKLE BOX.   Several of these should be fully equipped with hand-sewing supplies for backstage maintenance during the production.

VACUUM CLEANER.   An industrial vacuum cleaner is invaluable for keeping the shop, storage area, and dressing rooms clean if there is no daily outside maintenance.

WASHING MACHINE.   This should be used for maintenance washing, not for dyeing, and, if possible, should not be in the same area as the washer used in the dye process.

Organization of the Shop Personnel

A minimum staff for the costume shop should include the costume designer, assistant designer, the shop supervisor or foreman, the costume crew head, and the cutters, sewers, dyers, milliners, footwear and wig makers, and those involved with specialized items and accessories. Often the shop personnel must double up in their responsibilities. It is only in the best professional situations that one has separate personnel for each specialized area of costume construction. The major duties for

which each member of the shop personnel is responsible may be summarized as follows:

COSTUME DESIGNER.   The designer is responsible for all the artistic aspects of the costume designs.

ASSISTANT DESIGNER.   If a production is done under a union contract, the assistant designer is usually a beginning professional designer who is already a member of the union and is becoming established in the profession through work with an older and more experienced designer. In schools and universities, the assistant designer is usually an intermediate design student working either with the professor of design, if he or she is the designer of the production, or with a more advanced design student. The assistant designer's responsibilities, aside from helping the designer in any way possible, usually include preparing working drawings from the designer's sketches, procuring various colored fabric swatches from which the designer can make final fabric choices, and finding and purchasing all fabrics not supervised directly by the designer. In addition, the assistant designer helps the designer buy the many small items for trim and ornamentation and acts as a liaison between the designer and the shop, supervising all fittings and checking on all construction that cannot be directly overseen by the designer. If the designer makes good use of the assistant designer's services, the position is an admirable one from which to learn all aspects of costume design. It is also a very demanding job in the amount of time and energy that must be expended.

SHOP SUPERVISOR.   In the profession, the shop supervisor may be either the person in charge of all construction for a costume house or the person in charge of the entire construction operation in a repertory theatre organization. The shop supervisor must know all aspects of costume construction, be able to read and interpret a designer's sketches, and be able to work with actors and designers and supervise the shop personnel. In schools, universities, and amateur theatres, the shop su-

Costume Construction Chart

	fabric bought	costume cut	first fitting	second fitting	final fitting	costume complete
Actor:_____ Character:_____ Act:____Scene:____ Construction by:_____						
Actor:_____ Character:_____ Act:____Scene:____ Construction by:_____						
Actor:_____ Character:_____ Act:____Scene:____ Construction by:_____						
Actor:_____ Character:_____ Act:____Scene:____ Construction by:_____						
Actor:_____ Character:_____ Act:____Scene:____ Construction by:_____						

Figure 7-3. A costume construction chart.

pervisor is the keystone of the entire costume operation. In a school or university, the supervisor must grade students on their crew work, teach inexperienced people their craft, keep accounts of all expenditures and have accurate books to show on each production, and oversee all aspects of the construction process. In an amateur operation, the shop supervisor may be a volunteer or a paid position, but his or her assistants will usually be volunteers. The supervisor must command the loyalty of the volunteer staff, do much of the work personally, keep the wardrobe and shop in order, plan for the running of the production, and he or she may even have to serve the staff morning coffee or afternoon tea.

CREW HEAD. In the profession, the crew head, who is an employee of the costume house or the repertory theatre staff, is in charge of the hours the shop personnel spend on the job. The crew head must know the intricacies of union contracts and make sure that the shop personnel are paid for as much work as is needed, while overtime costs are kept to a minimum. In school, university, and amateur theatrical organizations, the crew head may also carry out many of the costume designer's plans, although he or she does not have full supervision of sewers and cutters. In schools, universities, and in large amateur organizations, the crew head is responsible for all the crew work done by the shop staff. He or she must make a costume chart based on the one made by the designer (see Figure 2–3), and a costume list that will show all the costume items in the production with the estimated and final cost of each costume (see Figure 2–4). The crew head usually has a chart that shows the order of costume construction and indicates the stage of development of each costume from fabric purchase through the final fitting (Figure 7–3). Unless a time clock is installed in the shop, the crew head records on the crew time sheet the time crew members spend on shop duties, and their absences and tardinesses. Personnel changes are noted fully on this chart (Figure 7–4). A costume measure-

Figure 7–4. A crew time sheet.

CREW TIME SHEET

Play: Hamlet	Aug. 8	Aug. 9	Aug. 10	Aug. 11	Aug. 12	Aug. 13	Aug. 14	Aug. 15
Crew Member: **Sam Penn** Assignment: **jewelry**	in 4:15 out 6:15	in 2:15 out 4:15	in 4:15 out 6:15					
Crew Member: **Bert Mall** Assignment: **footwear**	in 4:15 out 6:30							
Crew Member: **Sally Small** Assignment: **hats & headdresses**								
Crew Member: **Bella Gann** Assignment: **under garments**								
Crew Member: **Robert Pace** Assignment: **armor**								
Crew Member: **Cynthia Cole** Assignment: **wigs**								
Crew Member: **Bertha Gale** Assignment: **accessories**								

COSTUME MEASUREMENT
CHART

Actor's Name	Hd	Nk	Sh	Ch	Wst	Hip	Arm	WtF	NtW	UAtW	Ins	WtK	Ft
Sam Barclay	22	16	16	39	31	40	24½	45	19	10	32	16½	11½
Julius Kurtz													
Brigid Neils													
Patsy Samson													

Figure 7–5.   A costume measurement chart.

ment chart is also useful, and the crew head is expected to take the measurements from the actors' file cards and prepare a large chart that will give a quick rundown on the measurements for each role to be costumed (Figure 7–5). The crew head is usually in charge of keeping the workshop clean and in order during costume construction.

CREW MEMBERS. In the profession, the crew members usually include a head cutter, assistant cutters, and sewers, the head cutter having a position of authority second only to the shop foreman's and the designer's. The cutters are responsible for all patterns and cutting of garments and for much of the fitting.

Sewers are hired to do only the sewing and finishing and are usually divided into those who do machine work and those who do handwork. Then there is always a person or two who does dyeing, others who do nothing but painting and texturing, and still one or two more who do armor, accessories, jewelry, and footwear.

In schools, universities, and amateur groups, there is seldom such careful division of work, although in a large production it is certainly better to have some people assigned only to armor, footwear, wigs, headdresses, and accessories. However, seldom is there a division of work between the cutter and the sewer. Usually the person assigned to a costume does cutting, sewing, and fitting under the supervision of the foreman and the designer, with hand sewing and trim left to less experienced hands. All crew members or shop personnel must keep their belongings away from the work area; they must not smoke or eat on the job, but only in designated places away from the work in progress; they must return all tools to the proper places in the shop; they must report to personnel in charge when supplies are low; they must use only the designated shears for cutting things other than fabric; they must turn off electrical appliances after use; and they must leave the shop in good order at the close of each day's operation.

Cutting and Fitting the Costumes

With a fully equipped workshop available for the execution of the costume designs, the designer is next faced with the supervision of the costume construction process. Supervision may mean anything from full-time presence in the shop during the weeks before the dress parade to supervision of only the first and final fittings of each costume; but whichever it is, the designer must know the basic problems involved in the cutting and fitting of costumes.

The costume patterns cut from actors' measurements must be exact; they should have a full inch or more of seam allowance; they should be cut on the straight grain of the fabric; patterned or figured fabric must be cut so that the figure in the fabric is not unduly distorted at the seams; pieces of fabric with nap must all run in the same direction; sleeves, trousers, and skirts must all be cut 2 to 3 inches longer than necessary to allow for last-minute changes, alterations, or recasting.

The first fitting of a costume should be done in muslin to allow the designer to see and comment on the cut and fit of the costume before it is cut in the actual fabric. The muslin costume should be machine-stitched with a loose, long stitch before being fitted carefully to the actor's body. In fitting the muslin, the designer

should take into account the thickness of the fabric to be used in the final costume.

THE FIRST OR MUSLIN FITTING.   At this fitting, the actor should wear the undergarments he or she will wear under the finished costume. This includes all padding, corsets, girdles, brassieres, and petticoats.

First, let us take the problems that may arise in fitting jackets, bodices, and doublets. The muslin garmet should be slipped onto the body, the front or back opening should be centered so that it is straight, and then the garment should be pinned closed.

The neck and armholes should be trimmed so that the garment fits smoothly, and the side seams should be adjusted, working from the top down so that the same amount is taken in or let out on each side of the garment and the pinning is symmetrical from underarm to waist.

Next the shoulder seams should be adjusted by pinning from the outside of the shoulders to the neck. Darts should be pinned, keeping them equidistant from the center back, the center front, and the sides of the garment. Darts can be taken under the arms, halfway between the sides and the center of the back or front, on the center back seam, or in the front in the center of the two shoulder seams. Allow for the thickness of the finished seams when pinning seams and darts.

The neckline should next be sketched in with tailor's chalk from center front to center back on one side only, and, with the appropriate seam allowance, the neck should be cut out, the second half of the neck matching the first. This must be done while the garment is still on the actor, because the fit of the neckline affects the fit of the entire garment. Enough material should always be left in the neckline so that it can be finished off without problems.

One armseye should be trimmed to give the actor freedom to move the arm easily, again providing adequate allowance for seams; the other armseye should be cut out to match the first. The first fitting for the jacket, bodice, or doublet is then complete, but the garment should not be removed until the other parts of the costume have been fitted and the waistline and the placket opening have been clearly marked.

Next let us look at the problem of fitting sleeves.

Check the bodice or the doublet sleeves at the underarm and the shoulder seams, making sure that the actor can stretch easily. If a dart is to be taken at the outside of the elbow, it should be set into place, and the sleeve seam or seams (if it is a two-piece sleeve) should be adjusted to the correct fit. Have the actor move the arm in all the gestures required for the role in order to check the fit.

A tightly fitted sleeve may require a placket opening at the wrist. The placket opening should be long enough for the actor's hand to fit through before the sleeve is removed. The approximate length of the sleeve should also be marked, allowing for the reaching and bending that an actor may do in performance.

Now let us look at the problem of fitting a skirt.

A gathered or a pleated skirt will usually not need a first fitting, since it can be set onto a waistband or bodice that has been built to a certain waist measurement without trying it on the actor.

As with a bodice or doublet, a fitted skirt can be fitted in muslin and pinned to a correct fit. The placket opening should be pinned together first, whether it is at the side of the skirt or in the back, and the skirt should be carefully centered front to back so that the side seams are symmetrical.

The side seams should be taken in or let out the same amount on each side of the skirt, and the length of the placket should be marked carefully on both sides of the opening. The seam into which the placket is to be placed can then be opened to that point, and the skirt can be removed. The length should be marked not at this fitting but at the second fitting.

Finally, let us look at the problem of fitting trousers.

The trousers should be adjusted so that the crotch is in the appropriate position for the ac-

tor's comfort when moving. In fact, unless the crotch fit is exactly right from the beginning, all other fitting adjustments will be off.

The center front, the center back, the side seams, and the inseam should be taken in or let out, working evenly from waistline to hips so that the trousers will stay in place while the adjustments are made on the lower part of the leg. The length should be tentatively marked when the actor is standing straight. Knee breeches should be marked several inches below the knee with the knee bent to ensure adequate length. Trunks should be marked at the back of the leg, with the actor bent to a ninety-degree angle.

Both sides of the placket opening should be marked with tailor's chalk, and the trousers should be removed, testing to see that this can be done easily with the placket opened as marked.

Before completing any first fitting, the designer should remind the crew to check all special items that go with the costume, such as collars, belts, cuffs, peplums, shoes, hats, and gloves, so that all such accessory items will be available to be tried with the costume at the second fitting.

After the first or muslin fitting, the designer should see that the shop personnel mark all new seam lines in tailor's chalk, and if many changes have been made, a second muslin should be cut to reflect the changes. The actor may have to be called again briefly to be checked in this new muslin mockup. The muslin can now be opened to become the exactly fitted flat patterns from which the actual pieces of the garment will be cut in the fabric purchased for the costume. If an interlining is to be used in the costume, the pieces of the muslin pattern can be pinned and sewn with the costume fabric. If not, the muslin used for the first fitting can either be discarded or used as a basis for any other similar costume to be worn by the same actor.

With the actual costume now pinned together for sewing, all darts should be checked to see that they are equidistant from the center, symmetrical, and correctly placed. When all seams have been marked and pinned, the garment should be stitched together, with care taken to see that all plackets are left open. The seams should then be pressed open on the wrong side, with the seams stretched as they are pressed. Each seam should be pressed open before crossing it with another seam. Curved seams should be notched if on an outside curve, clipped if on an inside curve.

Neckline trimming should be checked, and the neck finished with bias tape, a bias facing of the same material, or a collar, as indicated in the costume sketch. On a curved edge, the second inside sewing should be done by hand. The armseyes should also be checked to see that they have been trimmed symmetrically before the sleeves are set in.

The sleeves should be finished off at the bottom if the length is correct; if there is still doubt, bias tape may be stitched to the bottom and the sleeve then turned up and hemmed after the next fitting. A sleeve gathered into a cuff or band can now have the cuff set on. The cuff should be cut three times larger than the wrist measure and twice as wide as the finished cuff, with a ½-inch seam allowance. The placket edges of the sleeve can be finished with a narrow hem or bias facing, and the sleeve can then be set to the cuff with right sides together, gathers or pleats being adjusted in the process. The cuff should usually extend ½ inch beyond the placket edges for ease in fastening. The cuff should now be folded in half, turned right side out, pinned, and sewn by hand to the inside edge of the cuff, with the edge turned under about ¼ inch. The sleeves should then be pinned carefully into the armseye, starting at the underarm seam, making certain that the right sleeve goes into the right armseye. If the sleeve is to be larger than the armseye or a full sleeve, pin it flat for 3 inches on both sides of the underarm seam and then distribute the fullness with gathers or pleats over the top of the sleeve. For a pleated sleeve, start with a box pleat at the shoulder seam, with additional pleats going down in either direction from the shoulder. Be sure that sleeves are symmetri-

cally pinned into place before stitching the sleeves to the armseyes with a ½-inch seam allowance. If the costume is to see a great deal of action, double-seam it.

In attaching a skirt to a bodice, pin it to the waistline marked at the first fitting, setting center back and center front first and then distributing the fullness, if any, according to the design. If a zipper is to extend to the skirt from the bodice, there should be no fullness at the waistline for 1 inch on either side of the closing line. When the skirt has been accurately pinned into place on the wrong side, it should be checked from the right side, then stitched, and the seam pressed up or down, whichever works best with the particular fabric.

If a zipper must be set in a garment, the lines of the opening marked at the first fitting should be checked; and the side of the costume which would be the underside of the zipper (left side on women, right side on men) should be folded back and pressed so that the fold is ¼ inch beyond the original closing line. On the top side of the closing, fold the fabric on the line and press. Pin the zipper into place with the top side overlapping the bottom fabric by ¼ inch, which is adequate covering to hide the zipper in period garments. The zipper should then be basted, but not finally stitched until after the second fitting.

If hooks or snaps are used on skirts and trousers, waistbands and plackets should be finished with a narrow hem or bias tape; if a zipper is preferred, it should be set in before the waistband is added. Cut a waistband double its finished width and at least 3 inches longer than the finished waist. Put on the band in the same way as collar and cuffs, distributing fullness according to the costume sketch, allowing less fullness across the front than across the back.

Other parts of the costume, such as ruffles, collars, belts, stoles, and drapes, should be finished and ready to pin into place during the second fitting. Footwear and headgear should be fully prepared, except for final adjustments, so that they also will be ready for the second fitting.

THE SECOND FITTING. The actor must wear the underpinning that will be worn under the final costume. By the second fitting the actor should know all the action that takes place when he or she wears the costume.

This time the actor tries the costume on and runs through the actions he or she will perform onstage. All seams and openings should be checked for strength and appearance. All fastenings should be checked for security, and zippers should be examined for defects or improper installation.

Belts and waistbands should be marked for fasteners, and hems, including the bottom edge of skirts, trousers, sleeves, jackets, gowns, and mantles, should be marked with a careful line of pins. For skirts and gowns, a yardstick should be used to ensure that all parts of the hem are the same distance from the floor. Pins marking the lengths of skirts, mantles, gowns, and robes should be about 2 inches apart.

Finally, all pieces of the costume should be carefully checked to be sure that no accessory has been overlooked, and all items to be sewn to the costume should be pinned into place.

After the second fitting, the costume can be finished completely, taking into account the corrections that have been made. Zippers can now be stitched firmly in place and checked to see that nothing can get caught in them. All hems can be taken by hand and the garment trimmed so that the amount taken up is the same all around, unless the garment has a train. The easiest place to pin a hem is on an ironing board or table, with the skirt laid out flat and wrong side out. The edge should be trimmed and folded under 1/4 inch before the hemline is pressed into place. If the edge of the hem on a circular skirt is much wider than the area of the skirt to which it is being sewn, then evenly distributed tucks must be taken along the edge of the hem to keep it flat. On heavy fabrics, it is better not to fold under the extra 1/4 inch but to use tape or seam binding to avoid the extra thickness.

The trim can now be added to the costume by hand or machine, although trim at the bottom of a skirt should be put on before the hem is turned up. All fasteners, buttons, and ties should be finished, dress shields should be tacked in place, and the costume should be given a final steam pressing; or, if necessary, it should be sent out to be pressed professionally.

THE FINAL FITTING. The final fitting is a last check on the fit of a costume and is usually made a day or two before the dress parade.

The actor should now run through the sequence of costume changes in order, checking each costume with the designer and the costume shop supervisor, so that every item needed is ready with the costume, and so that the actor feels able to execute every action required during the performance.

The actor should check the itemized list that accompanies each costume in the dressing room so that there is no question about what is worn when and with which costume props and accessories.

Lining and Finishing

The costume is usually lined in muslin, the lining stitched together with the outside fabric. If the inside of the costume will never be seen, this may be enough; the seams need only be bound off with tape. A separate lining such as that in a suit jacket or overcoat is essential, however, if the inside of the garment is to be seen onstage. This lining must be stitched in by hand.

When finishing a costume, all the seams should be securely stitched and the threads tied, if they are not backstitched, to guard against ripping. Except in skirt hems, cuff facings, and collar facings, machine stitching should be employed, unless there is too much bulk to pass through the machine. In this case, hand stitching with very heavy thread should be used. It is wise to stitch all places of extra stress, such as armseyes and crotches, with a double stitch for strength and security. The object of the inside stitching should be security and comfort, not appearance. If an armseye scratches, it must be bound off; if material ravels, then the edges must be pinked, overcast, or bound off. If hooks and eyes are used as fastenings, they must be sewn carefully and securely, not forgetting the shanks, and sufficient overlap must be left in the garment so that there will be no gap between the hooks. Hook-and-eye tape may occasionally be used, but it is difficult to sew by machine and the hooks are usually too widely spaced for stage costumes. To get the best fit with hooks and eyes, alternate them so that the hook is first on one side, then on the other side of the opening. The hooks must be placed very close together. Snaps are very risky except on garments and accessories that are given no strain at all. They may open if used on cuffs, waistbands, and bodices. Zippers are the most expensive fasteners, but they can be put on with minimal hand sewing and give a neat appearance and a secure feeling to a costume, although one must be certain that they do not show. There are two schools of thought on zippers. The careful actor will find that they make for ease and rapidity in costume changes, but the impetuous actor may jam them, and the crisis that results is more than the use of the zipper is worth. Trouser flaps should use pants fasteners above the fly zipper as is done in men's ready-made trousers. All zipper openings profit by having a hook and eye or a pants fastener at the top. Another closing device is Velcro, which consists of two strips of tape with textures that mesh together when one is pressed against the other. Such tape holds firmly and is useful for fast changes. It does, however, make a ripping sound when the tapes are separated.

Trousers, breeches, and sometimes tights should be equipped with suspender buttons, since tight-fitting nineteenth-century trousers and cotton tights will wrinkle unless held up from the shoulder. Even knee breeches look better if they are worn with suspenders. An actor who becomes accustomed to the feel of suspenders will be more secure and comfortable wearing them. If garments lack suspender buttons, the actor may use the old stage trick of twisting six pennies along the top of trousers or tights and then buttoning suspenders over them. Clip suspenders are dangerous; they have a tendency to come unclipped. Care

should also be taken in fastening separate doublets to trunks and skirts to bodices so that they will not separate when the actor raises his or her arms.

BONING AND CORSETS. Since corsets no longer contain boning made from whalebone, steel corset stays are now the standard for theatrical costumes (not home-sewn featherboning, which is not firm enough). Such steel stays come in a variety of widths and lengths and may be purchased in bulk from corset manufacturers or wholesalers dealing in dressmakers' supplies. Stays should run the full length of the boned garment, and if a stay has to be shortened with tin snips, the cut end should be covered with cloth or dipped in a tipping solution sold by corset supply firms. Stays may also be tipped with adhesive tape. One can also buy continuous rolls of steel boning from which lengths can be cut to measure and then tipped with tape, fabric, or corset-tipping solution.

Stays are fastened to garments only after being placed inside strong casings. Such casings are available from corset supply firms or may be constructed from double layers of twill tape. The casing should be on both sides of the stay for light garments, but on only one side, with the bone between the casing and the lining, for heavy garments. Stays may also be sandwiched between two layers of fabric when a garment has an inner and an outer lining. A totally enclosed stay should be cross-stitched by hand in a zigzag pattern to the lining of a garment. If it is placed between two linings, it can be slipped into a machine-stitched, tight-fitting pocket. If a single-layer casing is used, this can be machine-stitched into place and again the stay can be slipped into a snug pocket.

For the appropriate patterns and placement of stays for period corset construction, one should consult historical pattern sources such as Norah Waugh's *Corsets and Crinolines* (1970). Since corset shapes are devised to create very specific bodily shapes, it is essential to follow pattern sources closely. In order for the corset to lace tightly, it should be constructed an inch or two smaller in circumference than the actor measures. For best results, corsets should be constructed from canvas in two layers to allow the stays to be channeled into fitted pockets between the layers. A diagram of the stays should be drawn on the canvas, the garment stitched, casings sewn, grommets set for lacings, and then the finished corset fitted to the actor (who must be firmly encouraged to rehearse in the corset so that movement problems do not come as a surprise at dress rehearsal).

It is sometimes difficult to decide between using a full corset and using boning set into a bodice. The boned bodice is easier for the actor to wear, but the full corset is usually required for those historical periods in which the body must be completely reshaped.

Trim and Ornamentation

In choosing suitable trim and ornamentation to carry out the artistic spirit of the original design, the designer must always choose items that will show up at a distance and suggest the trim of a particular period without being too complicated. Braid is excellent if it is used to outline and accentuate the period lines of the garment and is not used to overdecorate and obscure the costume lines. Fine braiding is wasted on the audience, as are most embroidery effects. If braiding is done by machine, it should be done with a long stitch; but it is usually best to stitch it on by hand. When sewing braid on by hand would take too long and produce tension in the fabric surface, braid can be glued on with flexible fabric glue. Sometimes the glue itself or silicone caulking used in sealing shower stalls can be used as a kind of braid if it is painted after the raised line of the glue application has dried (Figure 7–6). An even more effective use of the same technique can be made with an electric hot glue gun (made by Sears and by USM Chemical Company). As one writes or draws patterns with it, one presses pellets of glue into the gun. Before the glue has completely dried, gold and silver leaf can be pressed onto the design, and when the excess is brushed away, the metallic pattern is

Figure 7–6. Painted ornamentation made from fabric glue and silicone caulking. Detail from costumes for Racine's *Andromache* as designed by Regina Cate for the Stanford Repertory Theatre, 1968. Photo by the author.

Figure 7-7. Ornamentation created with a hot-glue gun by Ann von Kanel for a costume designed by the author for *Richard III,* produced at the Old Globe Theatre, San Diego, 1972. Reprinted by permission, The San Diego Union. Copyright 1972.

quite permanent. This technique gives great flexibility and speed, and very complex raised patterns can be applied (Figures 7-7 and 7-8).

A still newer material is Puff Tex, put out by Rosco Labs. It is a textural latex modifier that, when exposed to radiant heat, will rise to create a low relief. It is useful in creating braids, damasks, and embroidered fabrics.

When still wet, flexible fabric glue can have flocking or metallic glitter dusted over its surface so that a complicated pattern of decoration can be achieved without braid. Flocking is a finely ground fabric fiber that is often commercially sprayed on metal surfaces to give a finish that has fabric texture.

Appliqué takes time, but it is both effective and durable. A decorative pattern shape is cut out in fabric, usually in felt since the edges do not ravel, and then sewn or glued into place on the costume. To give added definition, the pattern can be outlined in braid. If the result is too flat, the pattern can be given depth by dry-brushing in paint on the highlights and shadows suggested by its shape. Some of the most

Figure 7-8. A sample of glue gun ornamentation showing various thicknesses, lines, and metallic surfaces that can be achieved with the glue gun. Note also how gems have been given a setting with the hot glue. From the collection of the author.

Figure 7–9. Braid and pearls glued to a costume and highlighted with paint. Detail from costumes designed for Shakespeare's *All's Well That Ends Well* by Jean Schultz Davidson for a production by the Stanford Repertory Theatre, 1966. Photo by the author.

effective ornamentation of stage costume uses this combination of appliqué, braid, and painted accents (Figure 7–9).

When jeweled pins and clasps are used as accents and points of focus, items should be chosen that are large and relatively simple, with strong lines that will carry at a distance. Buttons must be larger and slightly farther apart than in everyday dress. For accenting necks and cuffs, use lace that is coarse by everyday standards but fine when viewed at a distance.

Dyeing and Painting

The use of dye and paint creates in the finished costume onstage a richer and more theatrical effect than can be gained by the use of fabric and braided trim alone. At close range, dyed and painted effects may look crude and inartistic, but under stage lights, and at a distance, the result may be very effective. When fabrics are available in a limited range of colors, only dyeing will give the subtlety and variety required by the original sketch. Often elaborate patterns are not available in modern fabrics, and only through painting can desired effects be achieved.

Dyeing and painting involve a considerable amount of time and expense, but the subtlety of the result will often repay the designer for the extra effort. Dyeing and painting are usually used to change or deepen the color of a costume, to age a costume, to create embroidery or appliqué designs, or to strengthen the lines of a costume and its decoration. There are no fixed rules by which any of these processes can be executed, and a certain amount of experimentation in mixing and applying is advisable before a craftsman in the shop or the designer himself begins a full-scale project.

DYEING. Before the process of dyeing fabric begins, the fabric should be thoroughly washed and rinsed, and if it is heavily sized it may have to be soaked in a light soda ash solution before it is rinsed again for dyeing.

Before beginning the dye process, the shop dyer should present the designer with a series of small dyed swatches in a variety of subtle intensities and values surrounding the color to be achieved. In this way, the designer will be able to make a very careful and informed choice before the actual dyeing begins. The dyer should start by measuring a small amount of dye into a one-quart glass measuring cup, carefully recording the amount, whether teaspoons or grams. (One-quarter to one-half a gram of dye to a quart of water is the usual ratio.) When the dye has been measured, add a few drops of hot or boiling water and stir to make a paste. Add more water until the full quart measure has been reached. Then strain the dye through a nylon stocking into a stainless steel dye pan and add a small swatch of the fabric to the dye bath. Stir the swatch around until it is several shades darker than desired and then remove it.

Rinse it and iron it dry and then pin it to a piece of cardboard together with a record of the dye amount. Continue this process with other swatches and with slightly varying dye amounts until a range of color is achieved surrounding the color desired by the designer or indicated in the costume sketch. When the right swatch has been chosen, then the actual fabric can be dyed by expanding the dye-to-water ratio to the level necessary to cover the piece of fabric in a dye kettle or washing machine. It takes three to four gallons of water to make a dye bath for one pound of fabric.

As to the dyes to be used, any of the commercial dyes on the market can be used for most fabrics. The package will usually give directions and indicate the type of fabric on which the dye can be safely used. If dye is used frequently, it is cheaper to buy dyes by the pound, no less than a pound of each color. All-purpose or unified aniline dye will adhere to most fabrics, and only a few basic colors are necessary. Bright red, yellow, blue, brown, and black can be combined to make almost any color. The formula for mixing is enough water to cover the fabric and one teaspoon of powdered dye to each pound of dry fabric. A half cup of salt or vinegar for each teaspoon of dye can be used as a setting agent to prevent the dye from rubbing off. If one has nonunified aniline dyes, either an aniline meant for cotton fibers or one meant only for animal fibers, then each must be used only on the appropriate fiber. For nonunified aniline dyes, the cotton or basic dyes are set with salt; the silk-wool or acid dyes are set with vinegar.

In preparing a dye solution, bring to a boil enough water to cover the fabric completely. Dissolve the dye thoroughly and add the setting agent. Lukewarm water should be used for wool, warm water for synthetics, hot water for cotton. The dye must be completely dissolved before the fabric is added, and it is always wise to test the solution on a small fabric sample. The fabric should be rinsed in cold water before being added to the dye bath, and all folds should be shaken out so that the fabric does not form creases and tight wrinkles. If the water does not have to be brought to a boil, the best place for dyeing is in a washing machine, which will stir the dye solution automatically. The automatic top-loading washing machine is best for dyeing larger quantities of fabric, because the fabric can be inspected more easily during the dyeing process than when boiled in a pot or tub. If dyeing must be done on top of a burner or stove, then crockery, glass, copper, porcelain, or enameled receptacles should be used, because tin and other metals may corrode in the dye solution. All receptacles should be large enough so that the fabric can be stirred easily without knotting. While it is boiling, keep the fabric moving by stirring the solution with wooden paddles. Check the fabric from time to time by squeezing the dye out of one corner to ascertain the color. If additional dye must be added, the fabric should be removed from the dye bath, the dye added with the setting agent, the solution stirred until all powder has been completely dissolved, and the fabric added once again to the dye bath. When the fabric has reached the correct color, it should be lifted from the bath with the wooden paddles and rinsed in cold water until the water runs clear. In a washer, this usually means the full automatic cycle of rinses. The fabric should then be dried in a dryer or hung without folds. Finally, it should be pressed flat so that it is ready for cutting.

There are a few tips to remember about dyeing fabrics for the stage. First, if some small wrinkles are left in a dyed fabric, the fabric will look heavier and have more depth of color than if pressed completely flat. Second, if two colors of dye are to be mixed to achieve a certain hue, then a deeper, richer effect can sometimes be achieved if the fabric is dipped first in one dye bath and then the other rather than in a dye bath of mixed dyes. Finally, richer effects under light can frequently be achieved by dyeing fabric unevenly so that the shadows in the folds of the fabric show darker than the highlights. Sometimes the shadows can be brushed in with a slightly darker solution of the dye when the fabric is still wet. Dye may be sprayed onto a fabric after it has been dip-dyed to deepen and enrich the surface effect under stage lights. Either a hand spray or a small electric spray gun may be used.

Cotton fabrics dye readily, and almost any color can be achieved easily. Woolens can be dyed as long as cool water and the correct type of dye are used. Closely woven fabrics will not absorb dye as easily as those that are more loosely woven, and hard fibers are less absorbent than soft fibers. Synthetics are especially unpredictable, some absorbing easily, others shedding dye almost completely, but recently Rosco Labs has produced Poly dyes, a safe, water-soluble coloring system that works with most polyester and thermoplastic fibers to gain full color saturation.

Never begin fabric dyeing until samples have been thoroughly tested in the dye solution. All fabrics containing a starch or size should be thoroughly washed with soap and water before they are dyed, and all fabric must be rinsed in clear water before being placed in a dye solution. Many fabrics may shrink a bit in the dyeing process, and allowance must be made for shrinkage in the amount of fabric purchased. Obviously, it is better to dye fabric before cutting it, although it is possible to cut out the various pieces with enough seam allowance for shrinkage and then dye the individual pieces. Loosely woven fabrics shrink the most and usually become tighter and stiffer in the process. Cotton flannel and muslin will usually shrink about 1 inch to the yard, terrycloth as much as 2 to 3 inches, monk's cloth about 4 inches. Synthetics will shrink very little; wool will shrink only slightly in cool water but as much as 3 inches a yard in hot water.

CREATING PATTERNS WITH DYE.   There are three ways to apply patterns to fabric with dye.

The first is an old process called *tie-dyeing,* which acquired a new lease on life during the 1960s because of the fad for psychedelic swirls, blobs, and bursts of blending color in the fashions seen in the boutiques of the Sunset Strip and Madison Avenue. The first step in tie-dyeing is to tie the fabric into any of the five basic shapes known as rosettes, bunches, gathers, pleats, and marblings. String or dental floss can be used, but elastic bands are bet-

ter since they are not permeated by the dye and can be easily clipped to free the fabric after dyeing.

After the fabric has been tied, it is immersed in a simmering dye solution for a time that varies with the fabric. Cotton soaks up the dye slowly, while silk takes it very quickly. The fabric is then rinsed in cold water. The process may be repeated up to five times with different colors or weaker or stronger dye solutions. Shadings of color can be achieved by painting or spraying on chlorine bleach when the fabric is wet. Other variations can be created by dropping dye into the bunched or twisted folds of the ties or knots with a medicine dropper or a squeeze bottle, while larger effects can be developed by squirting dye onto the damp fabric with a poultry baster.

Tie-dyeing is time consuming, but its rich, sensuous, seemingly spontaneous results cannot be achieved in any other manner.

A second method of producing patterns with dye is the *wax-resistant* or *batik* method. A pattern is drawn on the material with tailor's chalk or a soft marking pencil and the material is stretched on a frame. Melted paraffin or a mixture of paraffin and beeswax is painted on with a small brush, outlining the pattern which has been drawn on the material. If the material is transparent, then the pattern can be drawn on paper and the paper placed underneath the material. Within the edges of the waxed lines, dye can be painted without fear of its running. Many colors can be applied one next to another if there is wax to hold the dye within the edges of the patterns. After the patterns have been worked in, they can be covered in wax and the whole piece dyed to get the desired background color. The wax is removed by ironing the cloth between blotting paper, and if the cloth is still stiff, a little gasoline or naphtha will take out the remaining wax. While this method is most often used on silk, it can also be done on cotton with good results.

A third way to apply patterns to fabric is with a *stencil* through which dye is sprayed onto the fabric. The stencil must be thumbtacked to the fabric against a smooth upright surface, and one must make sure to cover all surfaces adjoining the stencil with paper. Usually the dye sprayed on should be warm rather than hot or cold, and if the patterns can be ironed while damp this will help to set the color.

PAINTING WITH DYE. Many of the costume shops in the United States, Canada, and England have developed the technique of texturing and aging costumes to a fine art. Using this technique, painterly richness and sculptural form under light are added to stage costumes by the artistic highlighting and shadowing of costumes with paint or dye. Although there are many variations, the dye solution most frequently used is something known as FEV or French enamel varnish, which is a mixture of one part dry pigment and one part white shellac thinned with alcohol. The exact proportions are best found by experimentation. Recently Rosco Labs has produced Sprila Glazing Fabric Dyes, which can be dry-brushed or sprayed onto fabric and will remain fast when washed or cleaned. Sprila comes in sixteen colors and three mixing media. The best method of application for dyes is with a small, easily controlled aerosol-can hand spray, or a small motorized air compressor with interchangeable air brushes of varying sizes that can produce anything from a ¼-inch line of sprayed dye to mass coverage of large areas. With the artistic and controlled use of an air brush technique, exciting effects of depth, richness, age, and an overall tonality can be added to costumes that normally might appear too new, flat, or direct in their effect. The air brush technique has great possibilities as a way to unify large and complicated productions.

TEXTURING AND PATTERNING WITH PAINT. Fabrics with smooth textures, such as muslins, percale, rayons, and most synthetic fabrics, will be easier to use as a base for painted effects than napped fabrics, such as wools, flannel, corduroy, and velour. Even with napped fabrics, textured effects that bring out shadows and highlights can be very effective. If hand-painted designs are to be used, fabrics may be laid out flat on paper that will absorb any paint that may seep through, or the fabrics may be fastened to a frame that will stretch them flat while painting.

There are a number of paint mixtures that may be used: textile paints, designers' colors, emulsion and acrylic paints, and French enamel varnish are all possibilities. A textile paint called Versatex is a specialized product for painting on fabric. It comes in a variety of colors, is permanent, and stiffens the fabric very little. There is also a set of seventeen Fabric Colors sold by Rosco Labs that is very useful. Other possibilities are metallic powders mixed with bronzing liquid or thin glue, and dry scene pigment or tempera mixed with shellac thinned with a little alcohol. These media are usually best used on a fabric that is already rather stiff, since they will stiffen it further. Silk-screen ink thinned with water and Inko dye used commercially in creating flat patterns on fabric can also be used, and they will not stiffen the fabric to any appreciable extent. Spraying can be done with the above paints if textile colors are thinned with turpentine, emulsions and acrylics with water, and French enamel varnish with denatured alcohol.

There are three ways paint can be used: (1) freehand application, which will not have the stiff formality of a stencil; (2) stenciling; or (3) freehand texturing, which ages or brings out highlights and shadows. In the Memorial Theatre, Stratford, England, the costume shops seldom use a stencil even when applying complex patterns. It is felt that a more imaginative, artistic effect is achieved if an artist-craftsman decorates an entire costume freehand than if he or she uses the more mechanical stencil method. Another freehand method is that of accentuating or outlining a pattern that already exists in the woven fabric. This can be done with paint or with a crayon or thick pencil. If a stencil is used, one section of the design is drawn on stencil paper, and the parts that are to be colored are cut out with a stencil knife or razor. Enough bridges must be left between the various parts of the design so that the stencil will hold together during long and rough use, and the effectiveness of the stencil design should be tested on paper before application to the fabric. In applying the design to the fabric, a stencil brush is usually used with textile paint in a stippling rather than a brushing motion. The stencil should be wiped after each pattern application so that no excess paint rubs off where it is not desired. The third painting method, which is usually referred to as texturing or dry-brushing, is very much used today to give age and textural variety. It has become synonymous with the ''Brechtian technique'' of production. Coarse woolens and burlaps are dry-brushed in textile paint or sprayed with leather dyes (Magix leather spray dyes come in scores of colors) to bring out the wear lines of the garment, accentuate highlights and shadows, and give an overall patina of age (Figure 7–10). This brings the scene painter's art to the costume shop. The costume craftsman who really understands and has mastered the effects of painting costumes is a most valuable asset to the costume shop and to the theatre. In many modern productions, more than 50 percent of the visual effect of the costumes onstage comes in the final painting and texturing process.

AGING AND DISTRESSING COSTUMES.   In addition to painting and texturing, the aging and distressing of garments can be achieved by washing them several times; rubbing elbows and knees with beeswax; using a cheese grater or horse-currying rake on cuffs, knees, hems, and any other places that should look frayed; and placing weights in jacket and pants pockets to stretch them out of shape. Buttons can be sanded down, the entire surface can be scraped with a wire brush, edges can be sanded, filed, or cut, and stains can be added with shoe polish, a paste of tempera and water, or by spraying with leather dyes. Mud can be added by mixing sawdust, dry brown pigment, and a thin glue solution. Bleach, either diluted or undiluted, is useful for breaking down fabrics, making strong discolorations, and even eating holes through the fabric surface.

Figure 7–10.   Costumes from the Stanford Repertory Theatre Wardrobe that have been sprayed and spattered to give depth and age. Photo by the author.

8

Accessory Construction and Wardrobe Organization

The Construction of Special Costume Parts and Accessories

During costume construction, the designer will have to supervise work besides sewing and fitting. We have already discussed painting and texturing of finished costumes as an art closer to scene painting than sewing. There are also other items, such as hoops, masks, armor, headdresses, wigs, jewelry, and footwear, that demand knowledge and craft techniques often not related to the art of the sewer or the tailor. In fact, in many of these areas the most creative work of the designer and his or her associates may take place. It is interesting to note how many costume designers, such as Desmond Heeley at Stratford, England, and Brian Jackson at Stratford, Ontario, began their careers in the property department, involved in the construction of ornamental furnishings, tableware, and jeweled accessories. A designer

who has mastered the art of ornamental design—jewelry, costume accessories, furniture, interior set ornament, and sculpture in miniature—has an excellent foundation for moving on to the larger areas of scene design and costume design. Often in the history of the fine arts, individuals such as Cellini and Ghiberti have begun as goldsmiths and developed into brilliant sculptors.

Mask and Armor Construction

Certainly the most challenging and exciting decorative accessories with which the designer must deal are masks, armor, and certain ornaments developed in deep relief. All require some form of molding to create the right surfaces and decorative shapes. In the past, molding meant making a clay mold and covering it with papier mâché. The clay mold was covered with six or seven layers of paper torn into strips and dipped in glue or paste. After the entire object was dry, the final layer was sanded and painted (Figure 8–1). Although papier mâché is inexpensive to make, it takes time, and the mask is at the mercy of wear and rodents, who love to eat the glued paper. Since World War II, a fabric with the brand name Celastic has been much in use for masks and armor in the theatre. It can be dipped in a special solvent, shaped, and dried in a short time, and it is very strong when finished.

The materials required for making articles of Celastic are modeling clay, metal foil, cheesecloth, a parting agent or separator, the Celastic fabric, solvent, and paint for finishing the object. To begin, a model of the object to be molded is made in clay. The entire object need not be created in clay if it is built over a form and the outside surface to be reproduced

in Celastic is fully detailed. When building headdresses or helmets, a wooden head block is an ideal base on which to shape the clay. Because Celastic has a tendency to shrink while drying, particular care must be taken so that the finished object will fit the head of the actor. Just as one allows for shrinkage in dyeing fabric, one should also allow for shrinkage in working with Celastic. If a small object is being created, then the entire mold is usually formed in clay; a layer of cheesecloth may be pressed into the wet clay so that the mold does not crack and break as it dries.

Many objects can be created directly from the clay mold by applying metal foil to the clay and then covering it directly with the Celastic, but for certain masks and articles in relief in which detail and smoothness of surface is important, a concave mold in plaster are necessary. This is made by covering a clay model

Figure 8–1. Herman George and the author making masks. Photo courtesy of News and Publications, Stanford University.

with plaster of paris. Since the plaster hardens almost instantaneously, it must be handled very quickly. The plaster is mixed with cold water until it has the consistency of thin cream, and it is poured over the model. Any bubbles that form as it is applied should be punctured. After the model has been covered with a thin layer of plaster, a second, thicker layer can be added, until a fine mold of about an inch in thickness is achieved. The mold must be thoroughly dry before it is removed from the clay, and it should be thoroughly washed inside. If any bubbles remain on the inside, they should be filled in with plaster of paris and allowed to dry before the mold is prepared for application of the Celastic.

If the clay model is to be used directly as a base for the Celastic, it should be carefully covered with metal foil pressed down into all crevices and cracks until the surface is as smooth and as like the surface of the clay model underneath as possible. If a plaster of paris or other nonabsorbent mold is used, the foil can be eliminated and the entire surface covered with the parting agent or separator.

The Celastic fabric is prepared by tearing Celastic into strips 1 to 4 inches wide. The narrow strips should be used for areas of intricate detail. The Celastic solvent should be placed in a shallow pan. Moderate amounts should be used at a time, as it evaporates rapidly. Celastic comes in thin, medium, and heavy weights. It is best to use the heavy weight for armor and helmets, and the thin and medium weights for subtle effects. The Celastic strips are dipped in the solvent and then applied to the mold until the entire surface is covered. The strips should be overlapped. Be certain that the strips remain wet on all the edges in the area on which you are working. Sometimes certain edges or strips will have to be redampened with solvent as the work proceeds. When the entire area has been covered, special shaping can be done. If a helmet with a crest is difficult to build completely in clay or to cast in plaster of paris before the Celastic is applied, the crest can be cut of three-ply veneer board, set in place, and covered with the Celastic.

Ears, noses, and other features for full masks can be formed by building up or by molding subtly with the dampened Celastic while attaching the features to the rest of the mask. Usually the Celastic should be allowed to dry on the mold for at least twenty-four hours. Even after it has been removed from the mold it will continue to dry and to shrink.

When a Celastic article is removed from the mold, it should be fully loosened around the edges and lifted carefully from the foil or the plaster of paris. If there are undercut edges, as in the neck part of a headdress, which is smaller than the large part of the head, cut the article with a knife from the edge up to its largest circumference, then pull it off, being careful not to break the edges. The edges can be seamed together with strips of Celastic dipped in solvent. Be certain that both surfaces of the Celastic are damp when this is done.

When the Celastic article is free of the mold, its edges should be trimmed and the item checked on the actor for fit. When this has been done, the edges can be bound off with bias cuts of the Celastic about ¾ inch to 1 inch wide. Both the binding piece and the edge must be damp, and the binding must be done very smoothly so that there are no folds or bumps.

At this point in making a mask, holes for ventilation and vision must be cut or designed into the Celastic. If the eyes of the mask will not be those of the actor, then wire screening may be set into the cheeks of the mask through which the actor can see. The screening is not seen by the audience because the paint on the outside blends into the rest of the mask area. Certainly the openings through which the actor is to see must be carefully checked so that vision is not hindered, and all openings for ventilation should be placed so that there is a crosscurrent of air through the mask. Any ventilation holes large enough to be seen from the audience should be masked with screen or net before the mask is painted.

After the mask or piece of armor is smoothed with sandpaper, its edges bound, and all ornamental parts checked for clarity of

Figure 8–2. A Spanish sixteenth-century helmet made for the Stanford Repertory Theatre Wardrobe by Robin Coon from Celastic, braid, and heavy lace. Photo by Keeble and Shuchat.

projection, the article should be painted. If it is to be a metallic surface that is to appear aged, a ground coat of flat or semigloss black should be laid on the mask or armor before the metallic paint, which will act under lights as a highlight. This method is particularly helpful in adding to the three-dimensionality of the object. The dry metallic pigment is usually best mixed with shellac, and it can then be rubbed into the object or dry-brushed over the surface. A realistic aged metallic surface can be achieved with the use of graphite instead of aluminum paint to highlight the raised areas of the armor. In armor with intricate patterns of linear ornamentation that cannot be maintained in the final Celastic surface, sections of heavy lace can be used. These are glued into the appropriate places, the entire surface of the armor, including the lace, is painted black,

and then the highlights are brought out in gold, graphite, or silver (Figure 8–2). The effect is rich and complex and cannot be easily achieved in any other manner. Another decorative possibility is the use of white or clear silicone caulking (or glue from a hot-glue gun), squeezed from the tube into the raised pattern desired. This allows the designer to draw a design on the surface of the mask or helmet. Masks are often painted with oil paints so that an effect close to that of stage makeup is achieved, although a long drying period is necessary. If the final effect need not be realistic, then the mask can be given an even more durable surface finish with shellac.

A thermoplastic sheeting known as Polysar, used for masks, armor, and accessories, appeared in the 1960s and was described in the first edition of this book; it has since been withdrawn from the market. Similar but superior to Polysar is a new product with the overall name of Hexolite. It is marketed in a strong mesh form as Hexaform Mesh and in a solid sheeting form as Hexoplast. When either of these is heated to 140 degrees Fahrenheit (usually with hot water), it becomes flexible, providing the designer with a material that can be shaped, molded, folded, tucked, and stretched. Upon cooling, it firmly holds any configuration that has been created (Figure 8–3).

Another addition to molded plastics is Vacu-Form armor, in which a piece of chalky, opaque plastic is pressed over a breastplate or helmet by a machine that is a kind of waffle iron. Most theatres will not have Vacu-Form equipment, since it is very expensive and will be used only occasionally in production. Therefore, the variously shaped armor and helmet pieces are usually purchased inexpensively from a number of theatrical or costume supply sources. A large selection of helmets and breastplates, decorative plaques, and complete suits of body armor can be ordered from Costume Armor, Hangar E, Post Office Box 6086, Stewart Airport, Newburgh, N.Y. 12550.

From the variety of Vacu-Form pieces

Figure 8–3. An example of Hexaform Mesh and Hexoplast used in molding the armor for the ghost in *Hamlet* as produced at the Oregon Shakespeare Festival, 1983. Designed by Jeannie Davidson. Photo by courtesy of Jeannie Davidson.

available from the supplier, a form should be chosen that approximates the lines of the armor in the costume sketch, and the piece or pieces should be ordered well in advance of the dress parade. When the pieces arrive, they should be fitted to the actor and trimmed to get the correct line. Markings should be made for straps and buckles on breastplates.

As for decorating such pieces, there are a number of stock Vacu-Form pieces that can be added to give raised decoration, or decoration can be created with braid, rope, cork, buttons, heavy crochet pieces, or coarse lace. The hot-glue gun can also be used to add intricate borders and decorative twists and swirls. When the decoration is complete, give the en-

tire surface a flat undercoating of brown, if the surface is to simulate leather, or bronze or black, if it is to simulate silver, iron, or steel. If a rough surface is required, a bit of sand or sawdust in a thin mixture of flexible glue should be applied to the entire surface. After this, highlights should be rubbed or dry-brushed in with FEV, graphite, metallic bronzing powders mixed with alcohol and shellac, or a commercial product known as Rub and Buff that is used in jewelry crafts. This latter product, though fairly expensive, can give Vacu-Form armor a marvelous burnished metallic surface that will make it pass as real armor at close range.

When the armor pieces have been completed, leather straps and buckles should be added with rivets or leather laces put on. The armor is now ready for use, unless you want the edges reinforced from behind for comfort and longer wear.

Another substance from which armor may be made is sized felt. As with Celastic armor, a clay mold, an existing helmet or breastplate, or a built-up form in cardboard or papier mâché is needed on which to build or mold the felt armor. In this case, the mold should be covered with sheet plastic rather than aluminum. The felt used should be of industrial weight with a high percentage of wool fiber and should be cut in pieces that approximate the measurements of the actor's body. The pieces should be fairly accurate but with allowance made for the shrinkage that will take place during the molding process. The pieces should be soaked in a mixture of two parts flexible white glue to one part water and then placed over the mold and worked until there is a smooth fit without wrinkles over the entire surface of the mold. The felt should be pinned to the mold with T-pins and allowed to dry—a process that may take several days. When dry, the pieces should be removed, edges trimmed and smoothed, and a thin coat of shellac applied inside and out. Raised decoration in rope, braid, buttons, balls, glue gun patterning, coarse lace, and crochet is then applied, and a base coat is again given to the finished piece. Highlighting and finishing may follow, with straps and buckles added to make the armor ready for wear. Felt armor is the thickest of the substances from which to make stage armor and is best used for a heavier, more primitive look.

A lighter molding material recently imported by Rosco Labs from Haussmann in Germany is Hatomold K50, which can also be used to mold helmets, headdresses, and armor.

There is another process, stronger than Celastic, Vacu-Form, and felt, that uses fiberglass. There are both advantages and disadvantages to fiberglass for molding masks and armor, but fiberglass masks are heavier, stronger, and usually smoother than masks made from the other two plastics. Fiberglass comes in semitransparent sheets that are stiff until painted with fiberglass resin, which melts the fiberglass into every crevice and cranny of the plaster mold so that absolutely no detail is lost in molding (Figure 8–4). The fiberglass process excludes the use of clay as a positive mold over which masks and helmets can be formed. It demands a negative mold of plaster of paris before casting of the final forms can be undertaken. Fiberglass is in many ways more difficult to use than Celastic and sized felt, but the final results when sanded, painted, and finished are handsome, durable, and exact reproductions of an original mold or article (Figure 8–5).

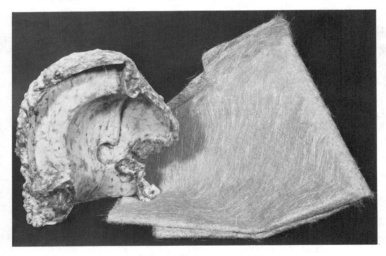

Figure 8–4.   Fiberglass before use, and the inside of a plaster mold. Items used in the workshops of the Stanford Repertory Theatre. Photo by Keeble and Shuchat.

Figure 8–5.   A group of finished masks and helmets of fiberglass from the wardrobe of the Stanford University Theatre. Photo by Keeble and Shuchat.

Decorative Jewelry and Raised Ornaments

Decorative jewelry and other types of raised ornaments, including buckles, clasps, orders, crowns, and brooches, can be manufactured in papier mâché, Celastic, molded felt, or fiberglass into which are set glass beads, bits of metal, or pieces of glazed ceramic. Another method is to cut out the shape of the clasp, buckle, or brooch in wood and build up the decorative shape by gluing on bits of cording that has a strong twist in it. The end product is painted black and highlighted in silver, bronze, gold, or copper—only the raised areas of the cording pick up the metallic highlight—and a rich, three-dimensional metallic surface is achieved. Such pieces may also be set with glass jewels and beads, and by linking groups of these shapes together, one can devise decorative link belts and royal orders. In designing such decorative accessories, historical accuracy is far less important than the overall clarity and richness of the design, and its depth and ability to pick up and reflect light. Simplicity and the right amount of exaggeration are the key to good stage jewelry and ornament (Figure 8–6).

Celastic, papier mâché, or plastic wood can be used as a base on which to build small bits of glass, beads, earrings, and other decorative materials into a rich-looking order, pendant, or brooch. Finger rings can be created out of Celastic or a bit of soft wire built up with tiny cord and a large jewel. The result at close hand will be gaudy and cheap, but the effect onstage will be rich.

Another useful substance is foam rubber, which can be carved or cut with a sharp knife or scissors into bold decorative shapes for lightweight jewelry and accessories. Foam rubber takes dye, paint, or metallics and is very durable and quite inexpensive.

A collection of junk jewelry should be kept in a workshop, separated according to size and use. Then, when the time comes to prepare the jewelry for a production, there is no need to rush about to locate the required items. The most satisfactory stage jewelry is that manufactured for the production rather than that purchased from costume supply houses. An excellent source of supply for odd bits of jewelry is the local stores of the Salvation Army and Goodwill Industries.

Chains for necklaces or large period pendants and orders can sometimes be bought at the hardware store, although they may be too heavy. Bamboo chain, sold in garden shops and import stores, is very light and, when textured with the appropriate metallic surface, is a substitute for metal chain. Specialty shops, import stores, and theatrical supply houses

Figure 8–6. Work in progress on the ornamentation for the coronation robe worn by Brian Petchey in the title role of the Stratford Festival production Shakespeare's *Henry VI,* 1966, directed by John Hirsch, designed by Desmond Heeley. Courtesy of the Stratford Festival, Ontario, Canada.

often carry light aluminum or plastic chain that has been made to look heavier by the addition of a gold or silver surface. Aluminum or plastic chain can be useful onstage if the surface is properly textured. Small chains for necklaces usually must be purchased from shops specializing in costume jewelry.

An actor's personal jewelry should not be worn onstage unless it is absolutely right for the character and the period and style of the production. It is usually better to create from the junk jewelry on hand the desired items for each character. Additional dangles can easily be added to earrings with heavy thread, extra jewels can be appended to bracelets and necklaces, and bracelets can be fabricated to fit a number of wrist sizes if jewels are sewn to a metallic thread elastic rather than to a rigid bracelet. One thing that must always be checked is the light reflectivity of jewelry. Large rhinestones or fake diamonds may reflect too much light and blink at the audience in a distracting way. Their surfaces can be soaped, or they can be gone over with a thin dry-brushing of water-based paint. Flat metallic surfaces without decoration can present problems in light reflection; if they cannot be dry-brushed, they may be covered with a thin layer of black net, which will diffuse the light hitting the surface. Soaping, dry-brushing, or black net may also be necessary with shoe and vest buckles.

Footwear

Footwear is one of the most expensive accessory items on the professional stage. Usually some firm other than the house making the costumes is responsible for it. If the footwear is important to the look and feel of a production and the producer's budget allows a footwear firm to be contracted to provide shoes and boots that match the original designs, then this is the best arrangement for the designer. However, often the designer must include the footwear in the total costume construction budget.

The style of shoe that an actor wears makes a great difference in the actor's stature and movement. In many period plays, the style of the actor is determined by his or her movement in the correct footwear. The height of the heels is particularly important in men's and women's shoes; the proper movement of hoop skirts, mantles, soft drapes, and other such items often depends on the correct footwear. Excessively high heels should never be worn onstage unless the style of the period demands them; this means that only in twentieth-century plays are high heels appropriate. For all other periods, medium and low-heeled shoes or slippers should be worn. If an actress has a floor-length dress it is often possible to find a plain low or medium-heeled shoe in lines that approximate those of the period and to allow these to be worn without great alteration. If the shoes are to be seen, they may be covered with the appropriate period brocade, recolored to match the costume, or decorated with bows, buckles, ties, or jewelry. For men's heels, one can buy either some of the more exotic present-day men's styles that have heels and resemble seventeenth-century shoes, or large-sized women's shoes. The shoes can be color-keyed to the costume, have tongues added, and bows, rosettes, and buckles set on to add the right period touch. Having a regular pair of men's shoes raised by having the shoemaker add height to the heel is usually not successful.

House slippers are useful and inexpensive items of footwear for the costume designer. They are available in soft and hard soles, with or without heels, in leather or in cloth, in black and brown and often in colors. More varieties are usually available for women than for men, but if the men have small feet they may be fitted with large-sized women's slippers. Slippers can often be recut and reshaped on top, covered by gluing fabric over the basic lines, or dyed and trimmed to match the costume. The old-fashioned elastic-sided leather slippers for men are especially good. They are strong and durable and can be covered and cut down to make period shoes that can be worn for more than one production.

Various types of dance shoes (particularly

rhythm or tai-chi shoes) are extremely useful when no heel or a very low one is desired, and many modern summer shoes or sandals are excellent for Roman, Greek, or Egyptian footwear with little alteration. Sometimes sandals may have to be manufactured from pieces of hard-sole leather and soft leather thongs, but if no one on the staff has experience in making sandals, it is probably better to have the sandals made by a sandalmaker. If soft shoes or slippers must be made, it is always better to build them over a pair of soft house slippers than to take the time to make them completely. Once the actor has been fitted with the slipper, it can be covered without another fitting. The covering can be cut and fitted over the slipper wrong side out, so that the seams can be easily stitched in the right places before the covering is sewn or glued to the slipper right side out. It is often easier to glue the covering to the slipper with flexible glue than to sew it around the edge of the sole, but if it is sewed, the stitches should be kept above the sole line so that they will not wear out quickly. A covering that has a center back and a center front seam is undoubtedly the easiest and quickest to make.

Boots may be made by making the boot top and then sewing or preferably gluing it with Barge cement to sturdy slippers with a hard sole or to low boots (unless a soft-soled boot is desired). Real leather, imitation leather, felt, or suede cloth can be used for the desired effect. If the part of the boot covering the shoe or low boot is carefully cut and sewn and the fabric is pulled tightly over the slipper or boot when it is glued, a realistic and wearable result can be achieved. If the boot is of a material that is too limp, it may have to be lined to give it more stiffness. Boots that are supposed to fit the leg must have a hidden zipper opening, preferably on the inside of the leg. If boots are to be laced, then either the center front or the outside of the leg is usually used. One should not rule out the use of real boots today, when it is easier than at any time in the past half-century to find in the stores boots of all shapes and styles for men and women. A costume shop should have boots in stock, especially if they are high enough and simple enough to be adapted to a number of different styles and uses. Sometimes a good buy can be arranged for many boots, or they can be purchased through a discount house or outlet store. Sometimes a shoemaker can be coaxed into using a medium grade of leather to make boots for a production at a price that is not prohibitive. Boots are an invaluable addition to a costume collection (Figure 8–7).

Figure 8–7. Leather over a slipper and leather over a short boot as a means of boot construction. From the Stanford Repertory Theatre Wardrobe. Photo by Keeble and Shuchat.

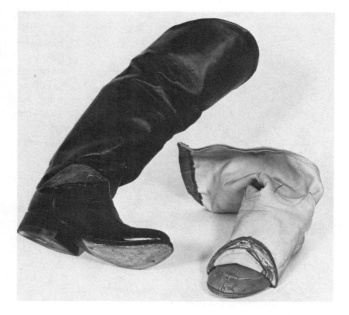

Hoop Skirts

The farthingale or hoop skirt must usually be made for a production in a number of sizes. It is usually made of flat, flexible hoop wire purchased at a theatrical supply house, heavy wire from a hardware store, or the ½-inch spring steel used in clock springs. Although this light hoop is not really like the heavier farthingale of the sixteenth century, it is a practical stage device to be used for any bell-shaped skirt. The flat, flexible wire or the spring steel is by far the most serviceable and easiest for the actor to handle, because it collapses when she goes through doorways or sits and will fall back into place again no matter how much it is pushed out of shape. If the hoop must be oval or elliptical, the less flexible hardware wire will retain the shape more readily than the flexible hoop tied into an elliptical line.

An average nineteenth-century hoop is usually made by a series of four to six hoops of wire, depending on the length of the skirt,

Figure 8–8.   Hoop skirt or crinoline construction.

placed 4 to 8 inches apart and topped by a muslin waistband. The largest hoop is at the bottom, and each succeeding hoop should be enough smaller to make a smooth line from the bottom edge of the skirt to the hipline. The hoops are fastened together with cotton tape 1 to 1½ inches wide, running vertically from the waistband to the bottom hoop. To make an average-sized hoop that measures 109 inches at the bottom, the six lengths of wire should be 111, 100, 89, 78, 67, and 56 inches, and they should be overlapped and riveted or overlapped with clips that can be cramped with pliers until the hoops cannot spring open. The muslin waistband should fit the actor comfortably. Ties are preferable to hooks for fastening the waistband. Nine floor-length tapes can be fastened to the waistband, and then, with the waistband on a dress form, the bottom hoop can be pinned in at the ankle position and the other hoops pinned in at equal intervals until the hip hoop is reached. If the skirt is not to stand out over the hips, the top hoop should not be pinned in. The hoops must be level before they are sewn firmly into place. If the hoop wire is covered with cloth tubing or tape, it will make the finished hoop easier to handle and more comfortable to wear (Figure 8–8).

The hoop can be worn easily under a petticoat and dress, with the effect but not the weight of many petticoats, and it can be stored by coiling and hanging on a hook. A ruffled petticoat is desirable over the hoop to smooth out the ridges and weigh down the hoop for easier handling. Wearing hoop skirts requires much rehearsal, and an actor should have her hoop and petticoat several weeks before the first dress rehearsal, because hoops not only take up extra space but affect all stage business.

Chain Mail

Chain mail is often required in medieval plays, and although it can be rented easily, it can also be simulated in a number of ways. If the production is not a realistic one, then a number of heavy-yarn open-weave fabrics can be used to suggest mail. If the weave is very open, a black jersey lining may be necessary, but the important things are that the outside surface is rough and the weave pattern is symmetrical. The open-weave fabric should be dyed a very dark gray or even black, and the entire surface can then be dry-brushed in silver. The resultant metallic surface can be pounded to give an even more metallic finish to the crossovers in the strands of yarn. Sometimes a cable-knit sweater and long stockings can be dyed and silvered in this way if the torso is fully covered by a surcote or tabard.

One can often buy from theatrical supply houses a knit metallic fabric that can be used for chain mail if its high reflectivity is removed by dry-brushing the brilliant metallic surface with black or gray. The problem with metallic knits is that the metallic surface is flat compared to the broken surface of actual mail.

The best way to make chain mail if you have the time and the help is to knit suits of mail out of heavy cord with the largest size knitting needles that are available. It is difficult to devise a pattern for arms, legs, and hood that all the knitters can follow, but once this has been done the pattern can be saved and new suits of mail added to the wardrobe whenever time permits. Use black cord for knitting or dye the finished suits black (although dyed suits tend to shrink). The suits can be silvered by dry-brushing and the knots pounded down to give a more metallic surface. Knitted mail will defy detection even at close quarters (Figure 8–9).

In Roman and early medieval times, the torso was covered with overlapping metal disks sewn to a base tunic. Here the base can be leather or imitation leather painted or decorated before the patterns in disks are set on or before the whole surface is covered with disks, scales, rings, or metal studs. The metallic pieces can be real metal or they can be manufactured from plastic.

Figure 8–9. Chain mail knitted from heavy string. From a production of Shakespeare's *Richard II* as produced at the Oregon Shakespeare Festival, 1960. Courtesy of the Oregon Shakespeare Festival, Ashland, Ore. Photo by Dwaine Smith, Classic Studio, Medford, Ore.

Wigs

Wigs are an important part of the costume designer's concern, even though a wig department, hairdresser, or "wig man" may have the responsibility for obtaining, dressing, and caring for the wigs. The designer must make the final decisions about the hairdressing styles and hair colors that complete a costume design. No designer should allow the wigs and hairdressing to be worked out between the actor and the hairdresser.

If wigs must be of real hair and there is not a full range in stock, the wigs must be rented or purchased from a house that supplies wigs for the stage. It is always difficult to make a decision between renting and buying, but in any permanent theatrical organization it is important to build up a large stock of real hair wigs in excellent condition. If someone in the organization is appointed full time to supervise wigs, and has training or can be trained in professional wig making, over a period of time a permanent collection can be added to the wardrobe. It would be impossible to give anything but a brief description of professional wigmaking methods here. The wig maker works on a reinforced, carefully fitted net cap with small amounts of hair that he or she attaches to the cap with a stocking darner. It is a slow and laborious process, but if the person has been trained by professionals, the result is a wig that can match the designer's sketch exactly.

Many different materials can be used for wigs that are supposed to be nonrealistic. Wigs for seventeenth- and eighteenth-century productions, for clowns, for animals, for fantastic characters, and for highly stylized effects can be made by unskilled labor with relatively inexpensive materials and equipment.

The best material for stylized wigs of the seventeenth and eighteenth centuries is probably a synthetic hair known as *rayon horsehair*. Rayon horsehair is manufactured for store mannequin wigs and comes by the pound in black and white, which can be dyed other colors. Sometimes it can be purchased in a wide range of natural colors. It takes about half a pound to make a male eighteenth-century wig, while a full-bottomed seventeenth-century wig will use up to two pounds. *Dynel* is another soft synthetic wig material that gives a realistic effect at a distance and comes in a great range of natural colors, but it is expensive. For children's plays or stylized effects, *felt* can be cut in wavy or straight strips and sewn to a cap, *cellophane fringe* can be purchased at a theatrical supply house and used to give a wet, glistening effect, *metallic ribbon* can be looped into curls for nonrealistic sculptural effects, sheets of *plastic* can be cut into strips and tacked into curls, and *frayed rope* can be used for animal hair, horses' manes, and fringes of hair on clowns' skull caps.

The one piece of equipment that must be on hand before any work can begin on a wig is a *head block* (Figure 8–10). The blocks made of soft wood or styrofoam are probably best because they take push pins easily, even though they do not wear as well as those of hard wood. The wig department of a costume shop should always have at least a half-dozen such blocks in sizes ranging from 21 to 25 inches. A *revolving stand* is another useful item of equipment, because it allows the wig block to be easily revolved while one is working on the wig. *Heavy-duty mercerized thread,* an *ordinary needle,* a *long needle,* and a *curved upholstery needle* are also required, as well as *cotton net* for the basic wig cap. Cotton net is better than fabrics such as buckram, which can be shaped to the head but does not provide ventilation and is too hot for the actor to wear comfortably.

To begin construction, pin a piece of elastic around the head of the actor for whom the wig is being made so that it rests just above the hairline and the ears. If the actor has long hair, it must be pinned smoothly in place, because it will be under the wig. It is usually best to part the hair from front to back and wrap it smoothly about the head with a nylon stocking cap to keep it in place. Then take a piece of net a little longer than the head measurement and wide enough to cover the head and put it around the head, pinning it at the center back where the elastic is fastened. Pin the net to the

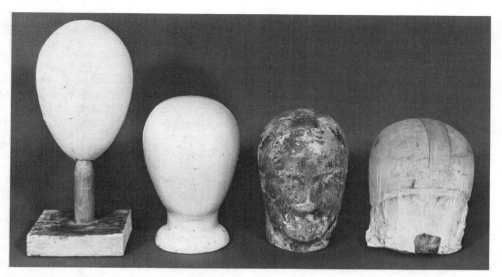

Figure 8–10. Wig blocks. From the Stanford University Theatre Wardrobe. Photo by Keeble and Shuchat.

elastic all the way around the head and fold the surplus net smoothly over the top of the head, pinning it in place. Cut off the excess net to keep the cap from being bulky, and trim off the extra net ¼ inch below the hairline. A new hairline can be drawn in, but care must be taken not to stretch the net. When the cap is removed from the actor's head, it should be handled by the elastic at its edge, not by the net.

The cap should then be placed on a wig block of the correct size and the seam sewn up the back and on the top. Edges should be sewn down flat, and when the cap is removed from the block, the net should be catch-stitched to the elastic on the inside. The elastic should be able to stretch and still not shift position inside the cap. The wig material with which the cap is to be covered should be measured out to double the wig length, and the hair should be placed on a piece of paper and sewn across the center with a long stitch on the machine. The paper is then pulled away and the line of stitching can be used as the part, or the hair can be folded along the line and pinned in place. The hair must be securely pinned to the cap on the wig block, and the cap must not shift and change shape as the hair is pinned to it. The hair should now be sewn to the cap in sections

so that it follows the direction of growth of the real hair, and the hair must be applied thinly enough so that it covers the cap but does not enlarge the normal head size. Rayon horsehair is best pinned in place while wet and sewn after it is dry. It shapes easily when wet, and curls can be set that will remain in place when dry. For eighteenth-century wigs, it may be wise to put a thin layer of cotton on the cap before adding hair, as this will cut down the amount of hair needed and will not allow a dark head of hair to show through from beneath. Cotton can also be used to build up a wig before the outer layer of hair is added. When all curls and styling have been set and sewn into place, the wig should be given a final fitting on the actor before being sprayed with a stiff hair spray and placed on a wig stand for transport to the actor's dressing room. Wigs must be carefully maintained during performance; loose waves and curls must be reset and sprayed with hair lacquer.

A method that can be used in place of sewing is gluing the hair into place with a flexible glue. The cap must be of a stiffer and firmer net or sometimes even of shaped buckram, and the wig may be warmer to wear, but a more satisfactory hairline can often be achieved by gluing groups of individual hairs into place.

Headdresses and Millinery

Hats and headdresses should also be made on a head or wig block if they are to fit properly. Allowance must be made if a wig is to be worn under the headdress. In fact, an old wig from stock that has the same thickness as the one to be worn onstage can be used on the block when the size of the headdress is being decided.

One of the most usable items for hats is the one-piece felt hat with a deep crown. Sometimes old hats that have been given to the wardrobe can be used. Felt hat shells sold in a millinery supply house can be purchased in the desired colors and brim sizes and reshaped by steaming on a hat block and possibly stiffening with lacquer or shellac. One can also use two pieces of regular felt soaked in water and then stretched and shaped over the appropriately shaped block. Even top hats can be made in this way, with one block for the crown and another for the brim. The resulting shapes can then be stitched together to complete the hat. Shaping a hat on a block is time consuming but not difficult if an electrically heated hat block is part of the costume room equipment. This heated block will make the felt soft and pliable when dampened. Adequate steam must be available to make the felt really soft and pliable. The hat must be pulled and stretched slowly so that it does not break or tear in shaping, and the full shaping must take place while the felt is damp. Even some period helmets may be shaped out of felt in this way, shellacked inside and out, and then painted to obtain a metallic surface. Shellacking inside and out also protects the hat or helmet from perspiration and makes it more durable. If a very heavy felt is used, hats without too high a crown or too wide a brim can be steamed and shaped in one piece from a flat piece of the fabric, but only a trained milliner will know all the subtleties and tricks that will achieve intricate and professional results.

For other styles of hats and headdresses, buckram, crinoline, or Pellon may be used as a foundation, depending on the degree of stiffness desired. Buckram is the most common foundation used in millinery because it can be cut and used stiff if the edges are overlapped at darts and seams, or it can be moistened and shaped over a head block and then allowed to dry. A great variety of hat crowns can be shaped in this way over a block and then painted or covered with fabric. Buckram softens when painted with dye, tempera, or oils, and it shrinks a little, but it can be stiffened again with shellac or glue. Its raw edges will scratch and fray and should be bound with bias tape, and it can only be sewn successfully by hand or machine before it has been painted or stiffened with glue. When a buckram foundation is covered with fabric, millinery wire sold at any milliner's supply house should be sewn around the brim. If the hat is tall, it should be sewn around the top of the crown before the cloth covering is added. If the brim is wide, a series of concentric circles of hat wire may have to be run around the brim to give the desired stiffness. In covering the buckram frame with fabric, care must be taken to remove all wrinkles and pulls so that the final result is absolutely smooth. The fabric should be kept tightly pulled over the foundation at every step of the sewing process.

Other materials may be used as headdress foundations, including wire frames of various kinds and even lampshade frames, but most headdresses can be built with a combination of wire, felt, buckram and glue, or plastic materials such as Celastic. Stiff but flexible cardboard with wire taped to the edges can also be used if it is necessary to keep costs to a minimum.

Specialized Surface Textures

For certain fantastic, nonrealistic productions, modern synthetics can be used to excellent effect when surfaces are burned and melted, and then painted with acrylics or plastic-based paints. For example, in a production of *Prometheus Bound*, described in Chapter 20, in which all characters were intended to look prehuman, the chorus and the character of Io

unique and unlike the usual concept of what constitutes a stage costume (Figure 8–11 and see Figures 20–3, 20–4).

Through experiments with new synthetic materials, many of which will at first seem unrelated to the construction of stage costumes, a variety of new and interesting effects can be achieved. The designer must experiment with all forms of plastics for theatrical textural effects and must be ever alert to new possibilities of craftsmanship in costumes and costume accessories. At the same time the designer must not neglect simple obvious effects like spattered paint and dry-brushed surfaces (Figure 8–12).

Figure 8–12. Textural effects achieved with spattered canvas for a production of *Hamlet,* 1963. From the Stanford Repertory Theatre Wardrobe. Photo by Keeble and Shuchat.

Figure 8–11. Textural effects achieved with melted nylon highlighted in white, for a production of *Prometheus Bound,* Stanford Repertory Theatre, 1966. Photo by Keeble and Shuchat.

were dressed in overlapping petals made of muslin covered with melted nylon chiffon. Other costumes were made of burned styrofoam balls glued to a muslin background, foam rubber was burned to create rock-like shapes and set with pieces of chipped resin, sisal hemp was burned and added to surfaces of melted nylon, and overlapping scales were pressed out of plastic sheets with a child's Vacu-Form play set. All finished costumes were heavily painted or spattered with plastic paints. The finished textural effects and the costume shapes were

Sources of Theatrical Fabrics and Supplies

As most designers and costumers know, finding sources for the wide variety of fabrics and supplies needed in production sometimes presents a problem. One can always start with the classified telephone directory of the nearest large city, but it is helpful to have a basic list of sources for the purchase of theatrical supplies and fabrics that cannot be purchased in the local department store or dry goods house. A basic list, to which firms can be added as sources are discovered, will be found on p. 464.

The Organization of a Wardrobe Running Crew

Now that the specialized items and accessories that complete the costume designs have been briefly dealt with, something should be said about the wardrobe personnel who will take over from the costume shop and handle costume problems during dress rehearsal and production. Only too often there is chaos and confusion backstage in the dressing rooms at dress rehearsal and dress parade. With a little planning and organization, many of the headaches and problems of dress rehearsals can be avoided. If final fittings of all parts of an actor's costume have been completed during the week before dress rehearsal, and the actor is aware of all his or her costume problems, a smoother dress rehearsal period will result and all major costume problems will have been solved before the opening of the production.

The wardrobe personnel are in a different union from those who work in the shop. They are separated from the construction process, and usually do not see the costumes until the dress parade. Once the costumes leave the shop, the wardrobe personnel are in charge. During the run of the production, they see to mending, ironing, cleaning, and general maintenance. In the nonprofessional, educational, and semiprofessional theatre there is seldom a clear-cut division; it is often advantageous if the person who has headed the costume crew also heads the running crew for the production. In this way there is a follow-through from the beginning of the construction process until the closing of the production; one person organizes the time and hours in the shop while the production is in preparation and the costumes and personnel backstage during the run of the production. This is, of course, a long and time-consuming job, and it may well be impossible for one person to devote so much time to it, especially if the run of the production is extended.

In a theatrical organization that is part of a school, college, or university, the crew, crew head, and the designer and his or her assistant usually come from a costume or a production class, and the work for crew members, heads, and assistants must be based on individual experience and the experience to be gained from the current production. The professor or teacher in charge of the costume division of the theatre department must plan so that all those assigned to crew or head positions have adequate experience to carry out their duties smoothly and at the same time handle a job that is part of a larger learning process. One of the faults with much crew work in universities and colleges is that it is often easier to use the same people in the same positions in production after production. This may make for a smoothly running show, but it does not provide the changing experiences so desirable in a learning situation.

In a theatrical organization on the amateur level in which the crew heads and crew members are volunteers, the designer or the costume supervisor, who oversees the running of the production, may have to spend a good amount of time stressing the importance of each crew member to the success of the final production. Some effort should be expended to develop in volunteer crew members a sense of responsibility to fellow theatre workers and to the theatre in general, even though the volunteer may have joined the organization as a leisure-time activity.

The organization of the backstage costume operation should be based on the following general plan:

MASTER OR MISTRESS OF WARDROBE OR THE CREW HEAD. The wardrobe master or mistress is in charge of the entire wardrobe personnel for a production. All other dressers work under the wardrobe master's supervision. In many small productions, especially those that tour, one person may be able to handle maintenance, but usually the leading actors will require a dresser if there are any costume changes during the production.

In schools, universities, and amateur groups, the title "crew head" is usually used instead of wardrobe master, and the people working under this supervisor are usually labeled "crew members" rather than dressers, but the duties of the crew head and wardrobe master are similar. Before dress rehearsals begin, the crew head must have a list of the costumes and accessories worn by each actor in the production (Figures 2–3 and 2–4) and the name, address, and telephone number of everyone on the running crew; must know who is assigned to each of the actors in the company for each change; and must have a time sheet on which each crew member can check in and out before and after each call. The crew head must meet with the staff, stress the conduct to be followed backstage, give information regarding the clothes and footwear to be worn, and work out the placement of each member of the crew during the course of the play.

During the dress rehearsal period the crew head, with the stage manager, should post the dressing room assignments for the actors. Information should include the names of the dresser or dressers who will help each actor, a list of any items the actor may have provided for his or her characterization, any makeup instructions that may affect the dressing process, and a statement about the location of quick changes that cannot take place in the dressing room. The crew head must also arrange with the stage manager for space for quick changes. During the dress rehearsal period the crew head is responsible for all work done by the crew members, both during the production and in maintenance between rehearsals, although for major changes or alterations the costumes must go back to the shop. The crew head should make sure that neither crew members nor actors make costume alterations nor change the appearance of a costume without the designer's permission.

During the performances the crew head is responsible for seeing that the routine established during dress rehearsals is maintained and that precision in changes and dressing does not slacken. The crew head must also see to laundry and cleaning during the run and check to see that costumes are pressed and repaired as needed. If a production tours, then the crew head or wardrobe master must be dependable and resourceful, since he or she is primarily responsible for the visual freshness of the production.

After a production has closed, the costumes are returned to the costume workshop or a central location from which they can be disposed into a storage wardrobe, sent to the cleaners, or returned to the costume house in which they were constructed. In schools, universities, and amateur groups, the costume "strike" usually takes place directly after the final curtain on closing night, and before this period the crew head should determine and then list the disposition of all parts of every costume. Rented costumes must be packed and returned, borrowed costumes must be cleaned or laundered and returned, and all items that were worn next to the body should be cleaned or laundered before they are stored. No soiled or used garments should be placed into a costume storage area. The "striking" of costumes after the closing of a production should be done in a minimum amount of time, with the costume running crew carefully organized so that no time is wasted and each crew member knows exactly what to do. The costume crew head should make a final check to see that everything has been accomplished; then that person's duties for that production are terminated. Professionally, this means that the contract stipulations of the wardrobe master have been completed and that he or she is now free to take another wardrobe position.

DRESSERS OR CREW MEMBERS. In general, the dressers or members of the running crew are expected to remain on duty in or near their assigned dressing rooms throughout a dress rehearsal or a performance unless they have been assigned jobs elsewhere by the wardrobe master or crew head. They are also responsible for checking to see that all the costumes and accessories are in the dressing rooms assigned to them between rehearsal and performances and for having a full costume list for each actor posted in his or her dressing room. Dressers or crew members are usually expected not to eat, drink, or smoke while on duty, in order to avoid accidents with the costumes, and not to have friends visit them backstage while they are working. Crew members are expected to arrive when called and leave only when they are released; substitutions should be accepted only when a crew member has an excused illness.

In assembling the costumes for the dress rehearsal period, the crew members are expected to hang up and label each costume in each dressing room until a complete group of costumes for each character has been checked off and every item has been marked off on the costume list provided by the crew head. Costumes should be grouped together by character and hung carefully so that they all face the same way. No one hanger should be overburdened; skirts should be hung on skirt hangers or by clothespins, trousers on pants hangers or by clothespins, and all costumes should be easily seen and easily removable for wearing. Shoes and boots should be pinned together in pairs and placed under the costumes or on dressing room shoe racks. Headdresses should be placed on shelves above the dressing table or above the costume rack. Small accessories such as jewelry should be placed in small cloth bags pinned to the costumes or in small boxes in the drawers of the dressing tables. Assuming that each part of a costume has a label tape sewn inside before it is brought from the shop, a paper label should be pinned to each costume in the dressing room so that dresser and actor will have a complete picture of all costume parts and accessories as they are lined up in order on the costume rack. All nonwashable items should be equipped with dress shields, and protective dust catchers should be pinned and basted on all floor-length costumes and those with trains. The crew member should fold in half a strip of muslin or inexpensive cloth 12 to 18 inches wide and long enough to go around the hem, press the crease, insert the hem so that it fits inside the fold and touches the crease, and baste along its top edge through the skirt, catching the inside of the strip. The dust catcher protects both the inside and outside bottom edge of skirts and mantles while the actor is rehearsing. The dust catchers can be removed before the last dress rehearsal. Finally, in preparation for the dress rehearsal period, the crew members should equip each dresing room with a tool or supply box, which should include shears, razor blade or seam ripper, straight pins, safety pins, black and white thread, needles, hooks and eyes, a clothes brush, and dry cleaning fluid. All should then be ready for the period of dress rehearsals, but each crew member should have his or her dressing room checked out with the crew head before the first dress rehearsal.

During dress rehearsals the crew members must see that costumes are in place in the dressing rooms before each performance. If the company is performing in repertory, it is usually impossible to keep the costumes for all the productions in the dressing rooms at the same time. In that case movable racks must be rolled into the dressing rooms before each performance with the costumes for the production carefully arranged in order of use during the performance. The racks for the other productions should be stored in some central area or near the dressing rooms unless maintenance work is necessary. The crew member should see that actors are in full makeup before dressing in costume in order to minimize makeup stains, and the costume labels should be neatly placed so that they can be replaced on the costumes after the performance. The actor should be encouraged to hang up his or her own clothes in an area removed from the costumes. When dressed, the actor should check with the crew member the line of the costume, the security of fastenings, the angle of wear for accessories and headgear. The actor should be encouraged to check his or her appearance in a full-length mirror before every entrance. All changes during the performance must be carefully planned in advance with the actor, and if there is not enough time to return to the dressing room, arrangements must be made with the stage manager for space close to the actor's stage exit. The crew member must be responsible for having the space equipped with all emergency repair items and all the costume parts to be worn by the actor after the change, and for getting all items back to the dressing room after the performance. The crew member must also be responsible for any costume item used as a stage property, even if the property person accepts responsibility for picking up and returning the item before and after its use onstage, and must also see to it that no actor deposits any costume or costume accessories anywhere backstage during a performance and that no actor makes changes, alterations, or additions to costumes without the designer's consent. Any additions or changes in the costume list for an actor should be made as they take place, and after each rehearsal the crew member should check the list to see that each item is in the dressing room and in its proper place. The crew member should help the actor undress at the end of each dress rehearsal, but should not act as a valet. He or she should question the actor regarding any repairs that must be made before the next dress rehearsal. Crew members should also see as much of the production as possible when they are not performing specific duties so that they have a clear idea of how the production and the actors should look from the front of the house, but no crew member should be in the audience during the final dress rehearsal, previews, or performance. Dust catchers should be removed, a final check on the accuracy of the costume list and the order of the costumes in the dressing room should be made, and a final conference should take place with the head of the crew before the final dress rehearsal or first preview.

During the run of a production the routine established during the dress rehearsal period should be followed, and careful maintenance should take place each day after one performance and before the next. Cleaning and pressing should take place whenever required to maintain the costumes through the run in a condition approximating that on opening night.

When a production closes, the costume crew is responsible for carrying out the "strike" as smoothly and as efficiently as possible under the supervision of the crew head. Dress shields should be removed, pins should be taken out of costumes, zippers should be closed, trim that cannot be cleaned or laundered should be removed, shoes and boots should be pinned or laced together in pairs, and all pockets should be completely emptied. Laundry and cleaning lists should be made in duplicate, and items such as hats, wigs, and headdresses that are not going to the cleaners should have all makeup removed and be labeled for storage. Laundry should be sorted and labeled by color and be placed in bags ready to be sent out, while rental items should be checked, packed, and labeled for return to the company from which they were rented. Dressing rooms should be emptied of all items except what permanently belongs there, and any personal items left by actors should be turned over to the stage manager. The crew is finished with its work only when the crew head has checked on each crew member's work and has released the person from further responsibility on the production.

Release from responsibility can bring a sigh of relief to crew head and crew member alike, but also a sense of loss—of friendships, of commitment and contribution to an artistic enterprise, and of routine—and if the run has been an extended one, the leave-taking may be sad and poignant.

9

The Problem of Style in Costume Design

What Is Style?

The word "style" is often an obstacle in discussing a design plan for a theatrical production. Theatre people say that a production should have a unified style, and they will frequently talk about finding the right style for a presentation without knowing exactly what is meant by the term or how an overall style should be achieved. The term is treacherous, as are terms such as "form" and "content." But if we accept costume design as an art form that can be approached in the same way as we approach painting, architecture, sculpture, and the minor arts, then we must make some attempt to define what is meant by "style."

First, we must distinguish between the style of the individual artist and the style of the period in which the artist lives. The artistic style of a period is a reflection of the social and political history of the times, and the changes that occur in society are eventually reflected in the patterns and shifting artistic trends of the period. Artists contribute to these overall patterns, some directly, some indirectly, and

some by working in an opposing direction; no one work by an artist fully reveals the style of the period in which it was created. A period style is not an absolute, and it is almost never fully operative in a poem, play, painting, or theatrical production. Each work generates its own style, and we must analyze an entire lifetime of work to assess an artist's overall style. The compilation of all the creativity of an entire era is what finally gives us an overall sense of a period style.

An analogy given by James S. Ackerman, in an essay entitled "A Theory of Style," gives an excellent picture of the development of style:

> We might visualize a style as a great canvas on which generations of artists have painted. The earliest ones sketch a composition, later ones keep some of it, rub some out and add some of their own, the next do the same and so on. At any moment in the process there is a complete picture, but no indication of what it will look like after the succeeding artist has done his share. At the close of the process, when some artists have started on another picture, this one is aban-

doned. But the final image, although composed of contributions from every artist, cannot be said to represent the aims of the earlier ones, nor to represent a solution to the problem posed by the first of them.

Reality and Style in Costume Design

If Ackerman's picture of the formation of period style is true for the literary and the visual arts, it is also true for a more limited art such as costume design. But what is the relation of period style to visual reality? As with painting and sculpture, the finished work of the costume designer does not reproduce period reality. What is presented, even when designers or artists insist that they are merely recording and presenting facts, is a personal interpretation of a period's visual reality. The public is freed from actuality by the artist's approach—the artist's scheme for a painting or a set of costumes, the things he or she chooses to stress or ignore, and the form his or her visual statement takes. In costume design, the designer's style, influenced by the surrounding culture, makes it impossible to set on the stage the visual phenomena of another era. Art filters life, and the artist or designer always places the technique of representation between actuality and the public. Designers should put aside the idea that they can recreate the past in their costume designs. No matter how honestly they try, they are doomed to failure. No matter how objective and self-critical they may be about their work and no matter how much time they spend studying every possible visual source from the past, what is finally presented to the public is a personal interpretation, colored by training, personality, and culture.

Particularly in the nineteenth century, many theatrical designers believed that absolute fidelity to the past was possible. In every case their failure was complete. Examine, for example, the case of the actor-manager Charles Kean. In his overly serious way, he was determined to make his Shakespearean revivals complete, annotated tableaux of the eras suggested in the plays. His program notes boasted that it was more worthwhile to see a Kean production of Shakespeare than to spend time doing research in the British Museum. Pages of program notes and production footnotes explained in detail how each costume, each property, and each bit of scenery was based on careful research and documented fact, and how the whole production was intended to give the public a visual experience of a past era. The more astute critics of the day often teased him about his methods, and they would announce that they had heard Kean was about to contract with the zoo for two alligators to appear in *Antony and Cleopatra,* or that he had sent an archeological crew to find the sea coast of Bohemia for a production of *A Winter's Tale* (Figure 9–1). The fact that Kean was one of

Figure 9–1. Charles Kean as Leontes and Ellen Terry as Mamilius in Shakespeare's *A Winter's Tale,* The Princess Theatre, London, 1856. An example of archeological accuracy in nineteenth-century theatrical design. Photo from Clement Scott's *The Drama of Yesterday and Today,* Vol. I, Macmillan, London, 1899, p. 282.

the first to have photographs taken of his productions merely added humorous proof that his production method was misguided. The photos are deadly serious but the results are amusing, since even Mrs. Kean would not remove her Victorian corset from under an authentic Greek costume, and Kean could not persuade Victorian actresses to give up Victorian makeup and hair styles, or get nineteenth-century players to look, even in a general way, like people from the first century. But Kean never learned, and he thought the critics and the public equally ungrateful. Only a membership in the Royal Society of Antiquarians soothed him and made him feel that at least in archeological circles his theatrical efforts had been appreciated.

Other theatrical producers followed the same method, although usually admitting that reality had to take second place to theatricality when box office receipts were at stake. From David Belasco to Cecil B. de Mille, the same mistaken idea was put forward: that one could actually create the reality of the past for an audience. What was achieved was always a transparent falseness of feeling and effect, a secondhand production that was neither artistic nor unified and that had no overall sense of style.

Thus one is always brought back to the necessity for a unified style or, to put it another way, a unified technique for presenting one's interpretation of real life, past and present. The word "technique" is important because all art is limited, controlled, and defined by the technical experience of the artist. Nature offers the artist only the materials for style, and these materials are modified by the craft, the medium in which the artist creates. The working methods of the modern costume designer are strongly influenced by modern fabrics, certain methods of machine sewing, and certain forms of pattern layout, which always result in period costumes having a modern look, that is, a relationship to modern styles. Designers cannot escape their time and place; they cannot send themselves back in time so that they can design with the fabrics, patterns, and sewing techniques of the period to be placed on the stage. I have often heard a set of costumes ignorantly praised as "authentic," and seen publicity and advertising people use the same term. Even though twentieth-century design has tried to kill the chimera of historical accuracy in design, there are still people who confuse art and archeology, who allow the nineteenth-century belief in the scientific approach to interfere with their intuitive response to an artistic experience.

Stylization in Art and Costume Design

If costumes cannot be authentic, what can they be? This is obviously a complicated question to answer, but it can be said at this point that they can be as close to reality or as far from it as the director, the designer, and the playwright wish, as long as they do not attempt the impossible: the recreation of a period on the stage. Many a brilliant, unified artistic production has costumes that give the audience the illusion of period reality, but careful analysis and examination will show that the costumes are actually limited in line, texture, and color, are seen from the artist-designer's point of view, and create a world of the play and of the production before they create a world of the past. Any well-designed "realistic" production will create the world of the play before it creates place and time in some past era, just as a "realistic" painter such as Velázquez creates a world of pigment and light before he creates the brilliant illusion of Spanish court life in the seventeenth century. It is a matter of the artistic choices an artist makes. One artist will stress an illusion of reality rather than the line, texture, and color of the medium for its own sake, while another artist will manipulate these abstract values of the medium with little or no regard for reality. As for the gallery- or theatre-going public, one can never be certain whether they will be more attracted by an artist's abstract manipulation of artistic values or by his or her interpretation of reality. It depends on the visual values stressed in the general culture, the amount of knowledge the viewers have about visual processes, and the educational and intellectual level of the audience to which the painting, sculpture, or theatrical production is being presented. A designer may think he or she has designed a "stylized" production—that is, sets and costumes that stress line, texture, and color more than visual reality—only to find the audience accepting the entire scheme as authentic period reality. Today, many theatrical presentations are almost completely abstracted from visual reality without the audience feeling that this interferes with their appreciation of the characters' psychological reality, while a half-century ago the audience would have been distracted by such designs (Figures 9-2 and 9-3).

The problem of reality in art and the visual aspects of theatre is a very complicated and relative matter. One must know about the visual values of a culture and of an audience within that culture before one can estimate how an audience will respond to a particular visual approach.

Figure 9-2.   A scene from *The Return of Peter Grimm* by David Belasco, as produced by the Stanford Players, 1949. An example of a completely realistic production. Photo courtesy of the Stanford University Archives, Stanford, California.

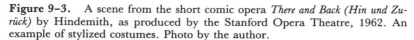

Figure 9-3.   A scene from the short comic opera *There and Back (Hin und Zurück)* by Hindemith, as produced by the Stanford Opera Theatre, 1962. An example of stylized costumes. Photo by the author.

Form and Content in the Visual Arts

Any discussion of the level of reality in a theatrical presentation or in a work of art must certainly take into account the way in which each age has viewed reality, and especially how much stress, and what kind, has been placed on the content of a work of art versus the form that it takes. At this point let us discuss briefly the arguments that have been formulated by art critics and commentators down through the centuries about the importance of form and content in art, and then let us see how these broad concepts can be narrowed to specific ways of seeing. A student of visual design for the theatre will have a better picture of how this art is tied to the history of the visual arts if he or she understands the progress of the artistic pendulum that swings from abstraction to reality and back again.

There has always been a tendency for human beings to turn from an emotional to an analytical and abstract approach in the visual arts, from the wish for submission to the reality of an impenetrable, natural world to the desire to organize and control nature. In fact, the great contrast between Paleolithic and Neolithic art is based on the swing from one of these poles to the other. In the famous cave paintings in northern Spain and southern France, which provide some of our best records of Paleolithic art, there is a striking naturalism, an attempt to counterfeit the animal portrayed in a ceremonial, mysterious, magical way—to identify with the animal in order to capture and kill it. In the cave paintings, art is a form of sympathetic magic with which humans identify and become a part of the mystery of the natural world (Figure 9-4).

With the rise of Neolithic culture, art assumed a different form. During this period, people began to control nature, organize life, and exert their will against the forces of the universe. Their art reduced nature to simple, often abstract patterns. The artist stressed structure and layout, certain accidental effects

Figure 9-4. A polychrome bison from the Caves of Altamira in northern Spain, ca. 80,000—8,000 B.C. An example of naturalism found in Paleolithic art. Photo courtesy of the Spanish National Tourist Office.

Figure 9-5. Stylized figures on painted fabric from a tomb at Chanchan, Peru, 1200–1400 A.D. An example of the abstract geometric qualities in Neolithic art. Photo courtesy of the Museum für Völkerkunde, Munich.

in the artistic process became regularized, and a geometric clarity or formal repeat of patterns replaced the irregularities of nature. Art became a matter of planning; it celebrated the new power of humans over nature (Figure 9-5).

Whenever a particular culture develops a high level of humanistic values, a balance may develop between the values to be found in nature and the values of pattern, organization, and structure developed by humans. When fear has been subdued, when optimism about cooperation between people and nature is at its height, we observe a period that balances the formal and the natural, the analytical and the sensational. These periods are called "golden ages" in the history of art and culture. They are often followed by periods of decadence, excess, and distortion. From Greek times to the present, we can observe cycles that build from a formal, geometric style to a balance between the analytical and the sensational and thence to a style that is dominated by exaggeration and excess. We find this in Greece as we proceed from archaic to classical to Hellenistic art. We find it in medieval times as we move from Romanesque to high Gothic to late Gothic; we

find it in the Renaissance as we move from early to high Renaissance and then on to Baroque. Whether this cycle is or will always be operative is certainly open to question, since one cannot force neat patterns on the history of art any more than one can on human history; but art is usually in the process of swinging from one pole to the other or is attempting to balance the two competitive outlooks. We can see this in modern art, where the sensational effects of expressionism are matched by the analytical and formal effects of hard-edged abstraction. With our strong nineteenth-century inheritance, we are inclined to talk of the opposition between romanticists and classicists, but analysis of a classicist will show an artist who places structure first; analysis of a romanticist will show an artist who places sensation and the mystery of nature first.

In recent years, much study has been given to the two sides of the brain—the left side, which processes analytical data, and the right side, which is the seat of creativity, intuition, and imagination. The ideal is a perfect balance between the two, but in most people there is a tendency toward either the intuitive or the analytical; the history of art as well as human history has seen a continuous attempt to reconcile these polar opposites. In great souls as in great artists, the right balance is sometimes achieved; but this balance is based on a precarious foundation, and it seldom can be continued beyond the life of a single person or artist, or beyond a limited time in the history of a culture. Today, in our increasingly complex civilization, there are much stronger attempts to achieve this balance than ever before. When the attempts fail and either reason or emotion becomes disconnected from humans and nature, chaos results.

Major Polar Opposites in the Visual Arts

The dividing line between the analytical and the sensational view of life and nature is never simple and clear, any more than is the political line that divides liberal and conservative, but critics often try to explain a particular period in art by using this method of comparison. One widely known attempt to do this is Heinrich Wölfflin's *Principles of Art History* (a comparison of the Renaissance with the Baroque), which sets up five opposing forms of representation. These opposites may also be used to explain and organize the art of other periods, literary as well as visual. They are useful to the student of theatrical design who is attempting to create visual equivalents for a playwright's mode of seeing and organizing material.

The first polar opposition is the distinction between the painterly approach and the linear approach. A linear style emphasizes clarity of contour, sharp edges, clear-cut boundaries, and the decorative isolation of ornamental details, while a painterly style blurs the limits and boundaries, merges objects and forms, and gives an illusory and shifting appearance to objects and forms. For example, if Botticelli is linear, then Rembrandt is painterly; if Bramante's architecture is linear, then that of Borromini is painterly; if classical Greek statuary is linear, then Hellenistic Greek statuary is painterly—or, to be more specific, if Michelangelo's *David* is linear, then Rodin's *Balzac* is painterly. If you apply this concept of

polarity to the visual theatre, then the plays of Racine require a linear visual style in sets and costumes while the plays of Maeterlinck require a painterly approach (Figures 9–6 and 9–7).

The second polar opposition is the distinction between depth in plane and depth in recession. With depth in plane, space is organized as a series of receding planes, one behind the other, until a horizon is reached or a vanishing point is located. In painting, this leads to one- or two-point perspective backgrounds; in sculpture, to the several planes located one behind the other, as in Ghiberti's second set of bronze doors for the Baptistry in Florence; in architecture, to the several planes of relief placed one on another in the interior and exterior of early Renaissance palaces. In a recessional use of space the plane is broken, and

Figure 9–6. *Judith with the Head of Holofernes* by Botticelli. Uffizi, Florence, ca. 1475. An example of a painting based primarily on a linear compositional method. Photo courtesy of Alinari/Art Resource, Inc.

Figure 9–7. *Self-portrait* by Rembrandt. The Frick Collection, New York, ca. 1656. An example of a painterly approach in brushwork and compositional method. Photo copyright The Frick Collection, New York.

visual space goes back in depth on diagonal and sharply foreshortened lines. Here, real depth replaces the several planes that stand one behind the other and hold close to the surface. Recessional depth is seen in paintings by Tintoretto and Rubens, in Baroque buildings that have a strong forward and backward movement and lead the eye up stairs and through arches to create an illusion of great depth, or in Baroque sculpture that has great movement and leads the eye backward and forward along imaginary lines of progression and recession. In the theatre, depth in plane and depth in recession can be seen by comparing *Romeo and Juliet,* with its suggestion of horizontal movement on a series of shallow planes against a flat, planar background, with *Hamlet,* in which the Prince moves directly from a forward soliloquy back into the depth of a full court scene in a recessional manner, while the space and background around him create a labyrinthine illusion of great depth. In *Romeo and Juliet* one thinks of a shallow series of horizontal planes, while in *Hamlet* we see Hamlet move backward and forward on lines of great recessional depth (Figure 9–8 and see Figure 12–5).

The third polar concept is a closed versus an open composition. In a closed composition things are rigidly framed and enclosed, and boundaries are the absolute limits of the composition. In an open composition there is no limit but a flow, a merging with the space outside the design. In a closed composition vertical and horizontal balance usually predominates, while in an open composition such stability is lacking, and a balance is achieved only by imagining a continuation into space. One suggests a stable, unchanging world, the other a world in flux that flows toward infinity. Raphael's *School of Athens* is certainly closed, while Tintoretto's *Last Supper* is open (see Figures 12–14 and 12–5). A building such as the Tempietto by Bramante is closed, while a church such as Borromini's San Carlo alla Quatro Fontana is open. Donatello's *David* is closed, while Bernini's *David* is open—it leads one beyond the statue to the imagined figure of Goliath. In the theatre one can compare the rigidly framed proscenium picture to the production scheme that breaks through the frame, moves out toward the audience or even down into it. It is the difference between rigidly

Figure 9-8. The "Solomon and Sheba" panel from *The Gates of Paradise* by Ghiberti, Baptistry of the Cathedral of Florence, ca. 1430–1450 (bronze). An example of action in a series of shallow, receding, horizontal planes. Photo courtesy of Alinari/Art Resource, Inc.

classical comedies of the Renaissance, carefully framed and limited, and operatic Baroque productions, in which the ballet comes down the steps onto the floor of the auditorium.

In the fourth polarity, one can make the distinction between multiplicity of incident and a compressed unity. In the first, individual details retain their identity even though they fit harmoniously together into the design, while in the second, the details disappear in the overall effect and one cannot distinguish the individual elements. This contrast is particularly clear when we compare any early Renaissance painting with a Baroque painting. In Botticelli, all parts are separate yet fit together harmoniously; in Rubens, one cannot separate the clouds from the whipped-up details of drapery. In Donatello's *St. George,* all is clearly seen as separate interlocking parts; in Bernini's *David,* it is only the overall impres-

sion of action that is seen. Most classical plays demand costumes and sets in which each part is seen for its own effect, while in romantic drama the details are intertwined to create a rich and complicated overall effect (Figures 9–9 and 9–10).

Wölfflin's fifth and last polarity is a distinction similar to that between painterly and linear, but it stresses light rather than composition. In this contrast between absolute clarity and relative clarity, the light and color of a painting, statue, or building may be used to clarify and illuminate, or they can be used to blur and distort until strong images are reduced to flickering subjective symbols or objects that stir the sense of mystery and the imagination. In the theatre such contrasts are evident in what the lighting designer does in a production, or how the set and costume designers use surfaces and textures to reflect light (Figures 9–11 and 9–12).

Figure 9–9. *St. George* by Donatello in the Bargello Gallery, Florence, 1415–1416. An example of multiplicity of individual details. Photo courtesy of Alinari/Art Resource, Inc.

Figure 9–10. *David* by Bernini in the Borghese Gallery, Rome, 1623 (bronze). An example of a compressed, complex unity in overall effect. Photo courtesy of Alinari/Art Resource, Inc.

Figure 9–11. *The City* by Léger, Philadelphia Museum of Art, A. E. Gallatin Collection, 1919. An example of absolute clarity in a painting. Photo courtesy of the Philadelphia Museum of Art: The Louise and Walter Arensberg Collection.

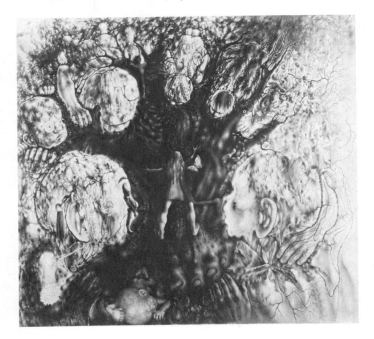

Figure 9–12. *Hide and Seek (Cache-cache)* by Pavel Tchelitchew, The Museum of Modern Art, New York, Mrs. Simon Guggenheim Fund, 1940–1942. Oil on canvas, 6′6½″ × 7′¾″. An example of relative clarity in painting. Photo courtesy of the Museum of Modern Art.

Other Polar Opposites in the Visual Arts

In *Four Stages of Renaissance Style,* Wylie Sypher develops other polar opposites based on concepts and ideas to be found in the critical works of a number of twentieth-century art historians. One very basic and quite simple contrast is that between rest and motion. Gothic architecture creates a feeling of restless motion, while Houdouin Mansard's additions to Versailles are heavy and static. Poussin's paintings are static, while those of Rubens are in full motion. In the theatre, we can compare the slow and static rhythm of Racine with the swift motion in most Shakespearean drama (Figures 9–13 and 9–14).

A distinction can be made between artists who are either in or out of phase with their culture and reality. The "in phase" artist frequently presents a design that follows an easy circular pattern in a unified composition, while the "out of phase" artist presents a design that is confused, violent, and broken. Raphael's *School of Athens* is cyclical and calmly

rhythmic, while El Greco's *View of Toledo* is broken and distorted. This is a major contrast between most high Renaissance art and most mannerist art, between much nineteenth-century and midtwentieth-century art. In the theatre, the violent rhythms and sharp shifts of mood in *Measure for Measure* can be contrasted with the relaxed and unified cyclical rhythms of Greek tragedy.

The polarity between representational (natural) and nonrepresentational (abstract) art is a major consideration in all theatrical approaches. Abstract art usually occurs when people sense that the natural world is hostile or beyond their power to comprehend and control, while natural art results when people read into nature their own sense of assurance and power. Abstract art is transcendental, crystalline, often geometric, and sometimes distorted, while natural art shows people submitting to or identifying with a nature and a natural world they find pleasing. The high Renaissance uses and loves nature, the mannerist period distorts and rearranges it to suit inner

Figure 9-13. The *Triumphal Entry of Henry IV into Paris,* oil sketch by Rubens, The Metropolitan Museum of Art, ca. 1621. An example of motion in painting. Photo courtesy of The Metropolitan Museum of Art, New York, Rogers Fund, 1942.

Figure 9-14. *Holy Family on the Steps;* Nicolas Poussin; National Gallery of Art, Washington; Samuel H. Kress Collection, ca. 1656. An example of immobility in painting.

Figure 9–15. *Good Morning Monsieur Courbet (Bonjour M Courbet),* Musée Fabre, Montpellier, France, 1854. An example of representational painting. Courtesy of the Musée Fabre, Montpellier. Photo by Claude O'Sughrue.

Figure 9–16. *Girl Before a Mirror* by Pablo Picasso. Collection, The Museum of Modern Art, New York, gift of Mrs. Simon Guggenheim, 1932. Oil on canvas, 64″ × 51¼″. Example of the nonrepresentational in art. Photo courtesy of The Museum of Modern Art.

subjective patterns. In the theatre one can see the contrast between the realism of the nineteenth century and the abstraction of the absurdists (Figures 9–15 and 9–16).

Another distinction one can make is between the visual and the tactile approaches to art: art that stresses only optical effects and art that stresses the surface of things, the feel of forms. Paintings that stress textural surface as much as the optical scene are tactile; some statues, such as those by Rodin, are far more tactile than those by classical Greek sculptors. Some modern buildings project no sense of surface, while others, like many Baroque structures, place great stress on tactile surfaces. We find that some playwrights stress tactile images; for example, Shakespeare's images are more tactile than Racine's. In stage design we often contrast the painted set on a flat surface with the rich, textural effects of solid-built scenery. In costume design tactile contrasts are achieved through varied fabric surfaces, and one can easily distinguish designs that primarily stress texture from those that stress line and color (Figures 9–17 and 9–18).

Ortega y Gassett made the distinction between near seeing and far seeing, which is based on the contrast between early Renais-

Figure 9–17. *Suprematism* by Kasimir Malevich, Stedelijk Museum, Amsterdam, ca. 1915. Example of the intellectual-visual in modern art. Photo courtesy of the Stedelijk Museum, Amsterdam.

sance landscapes, such as those by Sassetta and Gozzoli, and landscapes such as those by El Greco and Cézanne. In far seeing, a wide horizon is covered, embracing a whole field of distant objects with sharp clarity, whereas in near seeing, the eyes focus onto a single close-in area in which all edges of surrounding areas become blurred and indefinite. In El Greco's *View of Toledo,* for example, the space about the fringes of the composition seems to curve away from the central focus. Over the past few hundred years there has been a gradual retraction from the clearly seen object to the close-in subject and finally to the interior focus on the subjective or abstract. In plays we can see the same contrast between those that view everything from a clear but removed point of view and those that concentrate so much on one personality or one subjective idea that the surrounding characters and atmosphere are distorted or out of focus. In costume design this is the distinction between costumes that are designed to give a clear picture, in which all characters are treated equally and no subjective touches are added, and costumes that are designed to assault the senses through subtle or strong distortions that surround the central character. It is possible to envision *Hamlet* this way, and one would tend to design Brecht's *Man Is Man* in this fashion.

Figure 9–18. *Cow with the Subtile Nose* by Jean Dubuffet. Collection, The Museum of Modern Art, Benjamin Scharps and David Scharps Fund, 1952. Oil with enamel on canvas, 35″ × 45¾″. Example of the emotional-tactile in modern painting. Photo courtesy of The Museum of Modern Art.

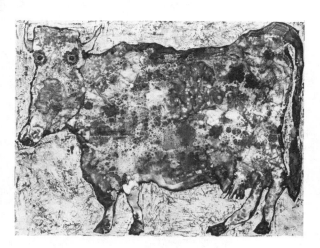

Similar to the contrast between multiple and unified vision is the discrimination between intensified seeing and relaxed seeing. It is the difference between the tense, wire-like vision of Botticelli and the sweeping, relaxed, saturated vision of Rubens. It is the difference between a statue by Rodin and one by Maillol. It is the intensified vision of Racine in *Phèdre* versus the exuberant story telling to be found in *Antony and Cleopatra.* In costume design it is the contrast between strong texture, with intensified highlight and shade painted into the surface of a garment, versus a smooth, flat texture with a minimum of highlight and shade (Figures 9–19 and 9–20).

Then there is the contrast between dark vision, as in the art of Rembrandt and the play *Macbeth,* and light, uniform illumination, as in Botticelli or in a play such as *Two Gentlemen of Verona.* The contrast of lightness and darkness is a major element in costume design and one of the first considerations in planning designs for a production (Figures 9–21 and 9–22).

When one sees the balance between horizontal and vertical energies in high Renaissance composition and the oblique and spiraling imbalances of mannerist art, one realizes that this contrast between stability and imbalance is also apparent in both art and theatre. In two realistic interiors, one by Degas and one

Figure 9–19. *Burghers of Calais* by Rodin (bronze), Rodin Museum, Philadelphia, 1884–1895. An example of intensified vision in art. Photo courtesy of the Rodin Museum. Gift of Julius E. Mastbaum.

Figure 9–20. *The Mediterranean* by Aristide Maillol. Collection, The Museum of Modern Art, New York, gift of Stephen C. Clark, 1902–1905. Bronze, 41" high, at base 45" × 29¾". An example of a relaxed vision in art. Photo courtesy of The Museum of Modern Art.

Figure 9-21. *The Birth of Venus* by Botticelli, Uffizi Gallery, Florence, ca. 1485. An example of a uniform lightness of tonality in painting. Photo courtesy of Alinari/Art Resource, Inc.

Figure 9-22. *The Education of the Virgin* by Georges de la Tour. The Frick Collection, New York, ca. 1645. An example of a dark tonality in painting for dramatic effect. Photo copyright The Frick Collection, New York.

by Winslow Homer, one can see the difference in effect between the tipped-up floor and oblique table angle in the Degas and the balanced and stable symmetries of the Homer. In the theatre, the raked stage, which was a device for projecting a geometric and stable recession into space, has been used in recent years to tip the action toward the spectator and project a heightened and rather unstable equilibrium. In a costume one can replace the balanced symmetries of horizontal and vertical line with diagonal and spiraling lines that give an unsettled feeling to the viewer (Figures 9-23 and 9-24).

Figure 9–23. *The Country School* by Winslow Homer, The Saint Louis Art Museum, 1871. An example of a balanced equilibrium in composition. Photo courtesy of The Saint Louis Art Museum.

Figure 9–24. *The Absinthe Drinkers* by Degas, The Louvre, Paris, 1876. An example of unbalanced equilibrium in composition. Courtesy of the Musées Nationaux - Paris.

Analogies between Visual and Literary Style

How does one determine style in theatrical art—specifically in costume design? How does one transform the literary style of the script into the visual style of the stage production? It has always been tempting to form parallels between art and literature, but because they are so different one often feels that the parallels must be false. However, if stage designers or costume designers hope to be true to the scripts they are called on to interpret, they, above all other artists, must believe that analogies can be developed between the literary and visual arts, or they will always feel that they are imposing their visual artistry on a play. Many critics have noted that compositions in different media resemble each other in technique. A style will usually express itself in similar ways in many media. If, for example, we find that the organizational scheme for a Renaissance play appears to be similar to the organizational pattern in a Renaissance painting, building, or sculpture, it should be useful for the designer to study the way both are organized in order to create a visual scheme for the play. There is no problem in designing a direct and simple play in a direct and simple manner, nor in taking a play with sharp, staccato dialogue rhythms and short scenes and designing sets and costumes made up of short lines, small changing forms, and sharp dashes of color. But more complicated plays demand a more varied and complex development of the visual scheme. Every artist—whether literary, plastic, or visual—thus begins with a concept or a scheme, and the subject matter is then molded by it.

The idea of approaching the design of a play on the basis of content, story line, and period setting is not enough. One must also design a play from the point of view of the director's and the author's plan or scheme for projecting the story onto the stage. Old arguments about whether one should always play Shakespeare in Elizabethan dress disappear, and the discussion moves to how one can relate the use of line, texture, and color to the way the playwright has organized and presented the plot, characters, dialogue, theme, rhythm, and spectacle. When one designs a production of *Oedipus Rex*, it is the tone and structure of the drama that should affect the designs far more than the story (Figure 9–25).

With this approach in mind, a costume designer would no longer design costume only for storytelling and character values, but would analyze the structure of the plot to see how various scenes were developed, how many lines of action were intertwined, whether tran-

Figure 9–25. Douglas Campbell as Oedipus in the Stratford Festival production of *Oedipus Rex*, 1955. An example of line, texture, and color related to the structure and organization of a drama. Courtesy of the Stratford Festival, Ontario, Canada.

sitions were abrupt or smooth, whether contrasts among scenes were sharp or subtle. The designer would look to see if one character dominated, two antagonists rose above the other characters, or whether a group or a series of paired individuals were the key to the play. He or she would analyze dialogue to see whether it was spare or rich, full of imagery or sharply telegraphic, tightened into sharp give-and-take character exchanges or expanded into long, full individual speeches. The theme and the rhythmic progression of the play would also be explored for qualities that could be translated into visual terms. Finally, the designer, with the help of the visual information given by the author, would prepare a design scheme for costumes that took into full consideration the choice of line, texture, and color.

As already established, when the director and the designer discuss the costumes for a play, both the story and the structure must be evaluated in making visual decisions. However, the story line frequently takes precedence, and the subtler visual needs suggested by the play's structure are frequently overlooked. For instance, while complicated, fashionable costumes for Molière may indicate the designer's knowledge of Louis XIV costuming, it is the spare, simple, clean-cut plotting and direct characterizations in Molière's plays that are important (Figure 9–26). In productions of *Le Bourgeois Gentilhomme,* designers frequently attempt to show M. Jourdain's lack of taste through extravagant and tasteless decor and costumes rather than rely on the strong unity and simplicity in the play's structure. Also, when a producer or director chooses, for the sake of novelty, to set a play in a period other than the one for which it was written, the superficial change will usually distort the script; but if the structure of the play is

Figure 9–26.   A scene from Molière's *Tartuffe,* as produced by the Stanford Repertory Theatre in 1965. An example of strong unity and simplicity in costume and setting based on the structure of the drama. Photo by the author.

kept in mind and an instinct for the line, texture, and color required by the play's composition is retained, then the new period can be interestingly and successfully fitted into the drama. Certain plays are so tied to specific dress styles and cultural mores that to change the period is extremely difficult, if not impossible; but for those plays that have a human or philosophic universality, one can often achieve new and exciting visual effects by a shift of period or a move to abstraction—if the designs are closely related to the structure of the play. By attempting to attune one's "fundamental brainwork," as Dante Gabriel Rossetti said, to that of the playwright, the theatre artist should be able to achieve, through planning and layout, effects analogous to those achieved by the playwright.

Such a statement may seem overly simplified because it does not consider how a director is going to interpret a playwright's work to the designer and actors. The excitement and interest for theatre artists occurs during these discussions in which it may be determined that the audience is to see a "new" play in place of the one read in an anthology. It is then for the audience and critics to discuss whether the "new" play is better than the old one, a distortion of the playwright's intent, or a fascinating but not necessarily helpful new look at an old script. But even in the wildest deviation from what the play seems to be on the printed page, the designer cannot stop analyzing the basic compositional method of the script, even though he or she must, of course, see the scheme through the eyes of the director.

Although we are always looking for new ways to present old plays or exciting theatrical devices for producing new plays, no designer can afford to be superficial or arbitrary in de-

veloping a visual concept for a play. The more one studies how playwrights gain absolutely different effects from the same subject, how the same story is changed by playwrights in different cultures, how even the poorest play with the least planning is still strongly imbued with the world outlook or artistic style of the times, the more one develops as a designer. Only when a designer has a healthy respect and a secure feeling for the relationships between the visual arts of an age and the playwrights of that era is he or she ready to work with a director in presenting an old play in a new light.

The plan for the remainder of this book will be guided by the fact that since theatrical design must transform a literary work into a visual work, a designer—specifically a costume designer—must understand the relationship between the literary and artistic developments in the period that shaped the play. This relationship should influence the visual concept and presentation of that play. Since one can find parallels between the literary works and the artistic works of a period, a costume designer should make a careful study of a play's plot, character, dialogue, theme, rhythm, and spectacle. The designer should devise the costume scheme so that the use of line, texture, and color will support the play's construction. One cannot use a rigid methodology and one's plan of attack has to be personal. It has to come from one's sensibility, and the result cannot be called right or wrong. Theatre costume design is far more than a vehicle for developing a talent or an opportunity to design period clothes—it is an artistic and intellectual challenge, and one must approach the job well fortified with a background in cultural and social history and dramatic structure.

10

Classical Plays

Ritualistic Beginnings of Theatre

Much has been written about the origins of the theatre, and much speculation has taken place about where and at what time aspects of nature worship and religious ritual entered the realm of drama and theatre. Certainly theatre grew out of ritual forms in which early humans, fearful of the changes in nature and the unpredictability of life, offered sacrifices to influence the powers of the unknown and the forces behind nature. The more these ritual sacrifices were performed, the more they became complex ceremonies displaying many theatrical effects, including body movement, vocal chanting, recitations, and special items of dress, accessories, and hand properties. Those persons who were especially effective in performing the rituals became the priests who planned the presentation of the rites and led in their performance. With the ability of men and women to disguise themselves as animals or gods and perform before others, the seeds of theatrical presentation had been sown; and with the acting out of a hunting scene, the death of an animal, or the cure of a tribesman, the priest assumed many of the characteristics of the actor (Figure 10-1).

Gradually, stories grew up around the rituals that attempted either to explain them or to veil them in awe and mystery. As such tales grew in complication and character, the origin of the stories was often lost and the material itself became supernatural and mysterious, while the characters became either gods or people closely connected with gods. Links were established from one legend to another through the reappearance of the same character, part of the story carrying over into another, or a series of stories being grouped together. The mythology that resulted was both fascinating as story telling and deeply symbolic —it intended to illuminate many of the unanswerable questions about human beings in their universe. Because primitive humans made little distinction between religion and life, work, and play, there was a close relationship between the myths' rhythmic, sequential, and verbal development and the way the tribe or social group lived. Hence, the rituals or rites performed in the presentation of such myths embodied the customs, beliefs, and life rhythms of the society.

There is an innate histrionic sensibility in every human being—an instinct to imitate— that makes people enjoy imitating others and

Figure 10–1. A wall painting of a medicine man wearing the antlers and skin of a deer, ca. 25,000–15,000 B.C. From a cave in the southern Pyrenees, France. Reproduced from *Theater Pictorial* by George Altman, Ralph Freud, William Melnitz, and Kenneth Macgowan, University of California Press, Berkeley, 1953. Photo courtesy of William Melnitz.

Figure 10–2. A mask of the Southern Dan style from northeast Liberia. From the Ralph Altman Collection. Photo courtesy of the Stanford University Art Department Slide Files.

seeing such mimicries performed by others. The use of imaginative masks, mystical properties, and exciting ornamental costumes are all combined in primitive theatre to project this histrionic instinct (Figure 10–2). It is the love of mimicry and imitation that sustains the theatrical instinct in society even when interest in myth and ritual begins to pale. It is one of the most basic of human instincts, and with those members of society who become actors it is merely a much deeper, stronger drive. Couple this with the story-telling instinct, which is another basic human impulse, and the result is

two of the strongest psychological reasons why theatre and drama, from primitive times to the present, have remained such powerful forces, even in ages when both theatre and drama were heavily frowned upon, if not prohibited, by society.

Greek Art and Drama

Although there is some indication that a static form of drama existed in Egyptian ritual ceremonies during the period of the Empire, it was in Greece that the first great drama of the Western world developed. In the festivals honoring the Greek god Dionysus, the god of wine and fertility, drama was born and gradu-

Figure 10–3. Model of the Parthenon, Athens, 447–432 B.C. An example of the Greek high classical style in architecture, which balances highly subtle and sophisticated proportions with very simple and natural forms. Photo courtesy of The Metropolitan Museum of Art, purchase 1890, Levi Hale Willard Bequest.

ally matured to the written form we now find in the great plays of the fifth century B.C.

Although the Dionysian festivals were dedicated to a god of irrationality, Greek drama and philosophy clearly reflected the Greek belief in balance—that a failure to do honor to any part of nature may lead to destruction. One of the great precepts of Greek art and culture is that humanity must achieve a balance and harmony among all the conflicting forces of nature. It is this drive for balance and moderation that gives Greek Golden Age culture its unique character.

The fifth century B.C. is one of the great periods in the development of naturalism, and the Greek impulse to be true to nature is almost as strong as the desire for proportion and balance (Figure 10–3). It is this balance that distinguishes Greek art from the later styles derived from it, and it is also closely tied to the political and social balance between the old aristocratic organization and the new democratic individualism. When individualism and particularism began to triumph, at the close of the fifth century, classical perfection in art began to falter and disappear.

One cannot separate the two forces or opposing stylistic trends in Greek art and theatre; naturalism and formalism are one. With the exception of Greek classical art, one cannot find elsewhere the human form presented with such complete relaxation combined with complete control, simplicity achieved through complexity, freedom and lightness combined with poise and serenity (Figures 10–4 and 10–5).

Figure 10–4. *Poseidon (Zeus?) of Cape Artemision,* ca. 460–450 B.C. (bronze), National Museum, Athens. One of the finest transitional or severe classical statues from fifth-century Greece. Photo courtesy of Hirmer Verlag, Munich.

Figure 10–5. Roman copy of *The Diadoumenos* by Polyclitus, 430 B.C. The Metropolitan Museum of Art, New York. One of the finest examples of high classical Greek sculpture in the fifth century B.C. Photo courtesy of The Metropolitan Museum of Art, Fletcher Fund, 1925. All rights reserved, The Metropolitan Museum of Art.

Classical Greek Tragedy

Tragedy is a primary creation of fifth-century Athenian society, and only in theatre are the inner conflicts of the social order seen so directly. Whereas the external presentation of the dramatic festivals to the masses was democratic, the tragiheroic content was strictly aristocratic. The plays treat questions of current politics in connection with a mythical background, and the religious basis of the story uses tragedy as an excellent mediator between religion and state policy, between religion and

art, between the irrational and the rational in the Greek spirit. The rational factor, called *Apollonian*—Apollo was the god of reason—is almost as fundamental to tragedy as the irrational or *Dionysian* element of religious ecstasy; and as tragedy developed, it was the rational element that became paramount. Those elements in the story that had been dark, confused, mystical, and ecstatic were brought into the light of experience, meaning, and logical thought. Drama, more than any of the other classical arts, shows the major part played by rationalism and naturalism and clearly demonstrates that the two principles are not incompatible.

Greek tragedy, like the fine arts of the fifth century B.C., is divided into three phases, represented by the playwrights Aeschylus, Sophocles, and Euripides. During the first forty years of the century aristocratic conservatism was dominant in art and drama, and it is this so-called severe style that we find embodied in the plays of Aeschylus. A supreme example of the final phase of this style in art may be seen in the *Poseidon (Zeus?) of Cape Artemision,* dating from about 460 B.C. (Figure 10–4). Though vital, human, and strikingly natural, the statue retains a severity, aloofness, and dignity that seem to raise it above the more relaxed and graceful figures that follow in the high classical period. Compare it to the graceful, idealized naturalism of *The Diadoumenos* by Polyclitus, from about 430 B.C., which may be taken as representative of the high classical style and analogous to the plays of Sophocles (Figure 10–5). The artist has broken from the restraints and aloofness of the severe style to create a perfect balance between motion and stasis, the individual and the ideal, the specific and the general. There is the same serenity and balance in this sculpture that one finds in the plays of Sophocles—the humanity, lyric harmony, flexibility, and relaxation to be found in a tragedy like *Antigone.*

Though Euripides died the same year as Sophocles, his plays are very different—less balanced, more cynical, less ideal, more violent and exaggerated, like the postclassical art of the fourth century and the subsequent Hellenistic Age. The full integration and balance found in the art of Periclean Athens was swept away by the Peloponnesian War, to be replaced by social and political unrest, individualism, melodramatic theatricalism, and skeptical cynicism. This world—the world of Euripides' plays—may be represented by the famous *Old Market Woman* of the second century B.C. (Figure 10-6). The figure is strongly

Figure 10-6. *Old Market Woman,* second century B.C. Illustrates the melodramatic theatricality and detailed individualism of the Hellenistic period in Greek art and culture. Photo courtesy of The Metropolitan Museum of Art, Rogers Fund, 1909. All rights reserved, The Metropolitan Museum of Art.

Figure 10-7. The tragic actor studying his mask. Wall painting, Naples, first century A.D. National Museum, Naples. Photo courtesy of Alinari/Art Resource, Inc.

individualized without a trace of idealization—particular rather than general, without a touch of the classical beauty and simplicity of the fifth century.

Thus the designer of costumes for Greek tragedy can learn much from looking at visual representations of severe classical, high classical, and postclassical art when designing plays by the three Greek tragic playwrights (Figure 10-7).

Greek Theatre

The theatre for tragedy began as a hillside grouping of spectators seated above a flat terrace, usually located near a temple dedicated to Dionysus, on which was placed a central altar and a chorus. In the case of the famous

Theatre of Dionysus located on the slopes of the Acropolis in Athens, many changes took place from the sixth century B.C. to Hellenistic and Roman times; but basically the theatre was made up of a three-quarter circle of seats, first wood, later stone; a flat, circular orchestra or dancing place around the central altar or *thymele;* and a scene house or *skene* opposite the circle of seats, which was first used as a changing room for actors and later used as a background for the play's action—certain props were utilized to suggest a temple, palace, or some other dwelling. Later this scene house or skene building was elaborated into a second story with side wings, machinery was added for mysterious appearances and other special effects, and the possibility of acting on a level above and away from the chorus developed. It is also supposed that scenic effects became much more complex (Figure 10–8).

The chorus was the backbone of the Greek tragedies and, in unison or in groups, delivered opinions, expressed sympathy, deepened the mood, and, most important, reacted to the events and characters as the author would wish the audience to respond. The chorus also added color and movement and a sense of spectacle to the proceedings; through the chanting and movement, with the help of accompanying music, it kept the rhythmical development of the drama organized, changing the pace, allowing for the deepening of audience reaction, and establishing mood pauses in the development of the tragedy.

Besides the chorus, there were three actors in each tragic trilogy, with "extras" brought in if they were needed. The three actors played numerous roles, male and female, and used lightweight masks of linen, cork, or wood and costumes based on the full draped folds of the

Figure 10–8. Drawing of a reconstruction of a fifth-century Greek theatre. From a drawing in the Stanford University Art Department Slide Files.

Greek chiton and himation of civil dress (Figures 10–9a and 10–9b). These costumes were often decorated with large symbols and ornaments to increase theatrical effect. The high-topped boot or *cothurnus* was the standard footwear. As a whole, the costume allowed for great flexibility and freedom of movement, and only at a later date did enlarged masks, raised shoes, padded shoulders, and violently exaggerated masks develop (Figure 10–10).

Figure 10–9a. Head of *Poseidon (Zeus?) of Cape Artemision,* ca. 460–450 B.C. One of the finest examples of the severe classical style and a model for what a classical tragic mask may have looked like in the fifth century B.C. Photo courtesy of Hirmer Verlag, Munich.

Figure 10–10. Ivory statue of a tragic actor; probably Roman, but similar to the dress worn by tragic actors in Hellenistic times, with high headdress, distorted and exaggerated mask features, thick-soled shoes, and a heavy robe. Photo courtesy of The Archives Photographiques, Paris. © Arch. Phot./VAGA, New York/SPADEM, Paris, 1984.

Figure 10–9b. Terra-cotta mask of King Priam, third century B.C. Illustrates the melodramatic, theatrical expressions used in the masks for tragic actors in the Hellenistic period. Photo courtesy of the Staatliche Museum, Berlin.

Oedipus the King

PLOT AND STRUCTURE. The story of *Oedipus* may be complex, but the plot is simple, the events are inevitable, there are no subplots, the time on stage is actual time, and all action takes place in one location. Sophocles, the author, keeps the distilled ritual rhythms inherent in the myth and merges them with the rational organization of his dramatic form so that the tragic rhythm, common to both, becomes as one and gives a deeper vision of life than is possible with either alone. On one level, the situation at Thebes as the play opens is analogous to the withering of winter in the ancient ritual of the seasons, followed by death and the hope for renewal. On a rational level, the play can be understood as an exciting murder mystery, with Oedipus as a prosecutor who eventually convicts himself in a marvelous theatrical resolution. As with Greek architecture and sculpture, the concentration on a simple and rational form leads to a heightened sense of the natural world around us and the mysterious world beyond.

CHARACTERIZATION. In matters of characterization, the playwright pays little attention to age and appearance; we know only that the leading characters are mature, while the other characters are labeled simply as old, blind, or children. The same is true of levels in society; we need only know that Creon, Jocasta, and Oedipus are rulers, that the other characters are a Priest, a Herdsman, a Messenger, and a Seer. It is clear that the playwright is interested only in the psychological and ethical content of his characters, not in their looks and social positions, and even here he is interested only in those psychological and ethical attributes necessary to the story. It is well to remember that all the speaking roles would originally have been played by three actors: one playing Oedipus, another probably playing Creon and the Messenger from Corinth, and the third probably playing the Priest, Tiresias, Jocasta, the Herdsman, and the Second Messenger. The first actor would have required the most sustained power, but the third actor would have needed great range and the most help from masks and costume. Numerous extras were required, and they could also double in roles.

THEME. There are a number of themes in the play. One lies in the final lines of the drama: "Count no mortal happy till he has passed the final limit of his life secure from pain." Human vision is limited, and a sharp contrast is drawn between human beings seeking their own destiny and the relentless fate or "will of the gods." Oedipus accepts his fate, yet sees himself as responsible for Laius' death and his own downfall. It is implied that people must submit to their fates, that to attempt to avoid it is to become more deeply entangled in a web of evil and wrongdoing. Behind this lies the one strong note of irrationality within the play: that the gods represent an unknown force in the life of humans over which none can triumph.

A minor theme is that of Oedipus as a symbol of the dismembered god-king, and on this plane an audience in classical times would have viewed the play as a ritual atonement—a pre-Christian passion play celebrating the mystery of human destiny. Still another motif is the contrast of sight versus blindness. The strongest statement of this is the comparison of the blind Tiresias' inner sight with Oedipus' physical sight: the blind see truth while the one with sight lies in darkness.

DIALOGUE. The language makes great use of images based on these key themes; it creates a "life" that lies below the surface of the play. It is in the dialogue of the play that we find action continuously moving between passion and reason. It is this complex histrionic usage that creates the power of the play. The simplicity, directness, and beauty of the speech can all be appreciated rationally, but the mystery, the suggestion of primitive roots, the stream of feeling and subjective imagery can only come through emotion.

RHYTHM. The rhythm or music of the play is tied to the carefully alternating structure of the script, which swings from forward movement to backward-looking exposition broken by choral interludes that serve to deepen the mood and atmosphere. The play's

Figure 10–11.   Creon returns triumphantly from the Shrine of Apollo in the Tyrone Guthrie Theater's production of *Oedipus Rex*, 1972, directed by Michael Langham, translated and adapted by Anthony Burgess, designed by Desmond Heeley, with music by Stanley Silverman. Photo courtesy of the Tyrone Guthrie Theater, Minneapolis, Minn.

choral passages would have been performed to musical accompaniment, and the dancing of the chorus would have been a direct reaffirmation in visual terms of the pattern and movement of the playwright's structural method.

SPECTACLE. The visual spectacle originally involved in a tragedy such as *Oedipus* was really quite limited. The play calls only for the stage house to represent the palace, no machinery or changes are called for, and an altar, in addition to the one at the center of the orchestra, is required. Costumes need only suggest the station of the character and the nobility of his or her personality, and the masks would indicate the age and personality of each character, with a change of masks required when Oedipus enters blind. Most of the visual effects in the drama would come not from scenery and costumes but from the patterns of movement of the actors and chorus (Figure 10–11).

Old Comedy

While tragedy was developing in the hands of Aeschylus, Sophocles, and Euripides, Old Comedy matured under Aristophanes, the only Greek comic poet whose complete plays we have. The plays in general are both allegorical and topical and deal with the political and social problems of the day. Although his comedies defy full translation, Aristophanes' genius for bawdy, sophisticated satire was so strong that his best plays, with their original spirit of exuberance and wild humor, still captivate audiences. Many of the plays took their names from the disguises assumed by the chorus— *Knights, Wasps, Birds, Clouds,* and *Frogs*—and it was primarily through the songs of the chorus that Aristophanes projected his satire. The basic idea in each play was comic in itself (for example, the staging of a sex strike to bring an end to war in *Lysistrata*) and was reinforced by a series of separate humorous scenes that gave

Figure 10–12. Old Comedy terra-cotta figurines, ca. 400 B.C. Illustrates the padded costumes, exaggerated movement, and exuberant action in the comedies of Aristophanes. Photo courtesy of the Staatliche Museum, Berlin.

great scope to both the comic inventiveness of the playwright and the acting abilities of the individual performers. A modern playwright could not hope to be accepted by a popular audience if he or she combined the personal invective, social satire, slapstick comedy, and obscenity that we find in a majority of Aristophanes' plays. Although modern audiences cannot appreciate all of Aristophanes' political and social allusions, they can enjoy his outrageous and universal sense of fun and bawdy physical comedy if the play is performed by superior actors (Figure 10–12).

The basic structure of the plays was simple.

A prologue established the mood and presented the comic idea, such as stopping a war by having all the women go on strike in *Lysistrata*. The chorus then entered, often wearing grotesque masks and costumes to suit their roles, and a debate then took place about the merits of the comic idea. In a choral ode the chorus directly addressed the audience about some current political or social problem and urged the members of the audience to take a particular stand. The second part of the play consisted of a series of loosely connected episodes that demonstrated the results of accepting the comic idea. The last scene reconciled all the characters before they exited to a banquet or feast.

By the middle of the fourth century B.C., New Comedy replaced Old. Social and political themes were rejected in favor of romance and personal and domestic problems, and characters became coarse, common types drawn from contemporary society.

Visual Presentation of *Oedipus*

In making a decision about a visual approach to *Oedipus* today, one quickly has to answer a major question: should the emphasis be placed on the rational or on the irrational elements in the play? Throughout this discussion of the nature of Greek classical tragedy and Greek classical art, it has been noted that the balance between the formal and the natural, the rational and the irrational, the direct and the mysterious created a precarious equilibrium in fifth-century drama. Today, with our fragmented view of life, it would probably be impossible to present a live and vital production of *Oedipus* that managed to achieve this balance in all aspects of production. Usually a director decides to take an approach to *Oedipus* that will bring out a wide spectrum of the play's meaning and moods without trying to encompass them all. Should one choose the formality, the classic restraint, the structural pattern of the play, the Apollonian elements? Or should one choose the primitive, ritualistic, violent Dionysian qualities of the script? Seventy years ago, when the Gilbert Murray translations of the Greek classics were in vogue, productions frequently stressed the sonorous and rather removed beauties of the script, while today, especially since the great Olivier production of *Oedipus* in 1946, the stress has more often been on the violence, primitivism, ritual, and unseen forces working behind the play's structure. Given this basic choice, even though a near balance may still be a goal, the director usually has to choose between symmetry and balance and the more mysterious and evocative qualities of the original myth. Should the palace be placed squarely and absolutely symmetrically before the audience or should there be an off-center placement that disrupts and unbalances this basic formality? The first choice presses on the director patterns of formal movement, balanced arrangement of chorus, and a great symmetry in the overall action of the play; the second gives room for ambiguity and imbalance, for achieving mystery and sharper contrasts in placement and movement. These latter elements are the ones that the early twentieth century, with its interests in African masks and primitive art forms, placed against the *beaux arts* tradition of the nineteenth century. This may appear to be too clear-cut and obvious a choice, but a director of *Oedipus* will finally make this choice regarding every aspect of the production to a greater or lesser extent.

In planning costumes for *Oedipus,* the choice must be made as to whether the characters should look like fifth-century statues brought to life or whether it is desirable to stress the archaic, mysterious aspects of the play in order to make the production less remote, less connected with book illustrations, and more related to current artistic and visual values (Figure 10–13).

Figure 10–13.   A scene from the Stratford Festival production of *Oedipus Rex,* 1954–55, directed by Tyrone Guthrie, designed by Tanya Moiseiwitsch. Courtesy of the Stratford Festival, Ontario, Canada.

The decision the designer and director reach regarding masks will set the tone for everything else done with movement and costume. The use of masks, whether exaggerated or subtle, will move the production away from psychological realism, no matter what the director's approach. Masks immediately establish the illusion that the actor and the character are not one; they create the illusion of the play as ritual, ceremony, a working out of forces behind and beyond reality. Masks obviously work best in a theatre that is not too small, since the removal of the actor's personality from the audience seems to require that the audience be at a distance from the action of the play. In a small theatre, seating about 300 people, it might be best to use makeup that would remove the character to a plane above the personality of the actor, but in the average or large theatre, holding 700 to 1200 persons, masks may become an important and integral part of the ritualistic mood in a Greek tragedy.

In creating masks one must establish the right sense of balance between the outer form of the mask and the expression of personality through the mask. Fifth-century busts, statue heads, and statuettes are excellent sources as well as inspirations. The famous statue of Poseidon from Cape Artemision (Figure 10–4) is an excellent work from which to gain a sense of the strength, severity, and careful form that weigh as heavily with the viewer as the personality projected. This monumental head sums up the great balance between form and content, ritual and mystery, and naturalistic statement that provides the key to the great Greek tragedies by Sophocles—especially *Oedipus*. For this tragedy, to create masks that are too naturalistic is to neglect the sense of structure at work in the play; but to concentrate too much attention on the formal, archaic aspects of the mask is to lose the sense of individuality that is so important to the play. A compromise that is a balance between the formal and the naturalistic, carrying the best qualities of both, is the ideal. One of the problems with the famed Guthrie production of the play at Stratford, Ontario, in 1955 was that the masks tended to stress the theatrical aspects of archaism and formality at the expense of character. It is better to use fifth-century sculpture as source material rather than the theatrical masks in the sculptural interpretations of theatrical performance from Hellenistic or Roman times; these later sources indicate a self-conscious piling up of theatrical effect that is not compatible with *Oedipus* (see Figures 10–9a and 10–9b).

In designing the masks, one should be careful to keep them as lightweight as possible, fabricating them out of leather, light plastic, or fiberglass; and usually, for modern performance, it is wise to cut the mask entirely away around the mouth and chin for a three-quarter rather than a fully masked face. Visibility must be as full as possible, even if areas around the eyes must be made of open screening painted to look opaque; and the mask must fit the head to allow air to circulate within the mask for proper ventilation.

Next in order of importance to the costume designer of *Oedipus* is the question of the weight and line in the costumes. With the use of masks, the costumes must be fuller and scaled larger than in Greek civil dress, and the folds and draped lines must be of a scale that matches the masked face of the actor, not the actor without the mask. This often means shoulder padding to give the appropriate support to the draped lines of the garments, and possibly gloves to keep the hands from looking like tiny naked appendages appearing from the folds of a huge Greek chiton. Although garments for certain characters may have to show bare arms or legs, these should be kept to a minimum, and wherever possible the body should be treated as a completely covered and whole design. Great importance should be given to the correct weight and softness of the fabric so that the folds of the garments will have the size and monumentality that will suit the formal aspects of the play's structure and yet have the ease and pliability to make movement and characterization perfectly natural. Woolens are the obvious choice, but they must be exactly right if they are to capture a balance between formality and flexibility. One should guard, in particular, against relying for inspiration only on the subtle, soft beauties of late fifth-century sculptural draping. Although the draping may conjure up a picture of Greece, it does not take into account that *Oedipus* is a Greek tragedy. Costumes executed in nylon or rayon jersey will be beautiful but too feminine. It is also wise to forget actual Greek practice in the cut and drape of the chiton and to build the folds and draped lines into the costume when it is constructed. This will free the actor from any need to pose like Greek statuary, strengthen the form of the total figure when masked, and ensure that the costume retains its original designed form from one performance to another.

In matters of texture, there is a choice between a rougher texture that may take light with more interest and give a slightly more primitive feel to the production, or a flat and smoother texture that will reflect more light and give a more civilized atmosphere to the play. Something that is a balance between the two effects, perhaps wool with a maximum of drapability and a minimum of texture, is probably most desirable as long as the choice does not result in a dull textural surface that has no

character. Textural variety among the costumes may be very desirable, but it must not confuse the overall visual plan for the production (Figure 10–14).

Color is often thought to be unimportant in costumes for Greek tragedy. Because the statuary that has remained from Greek times lacks color, we tend to see the plays in some neutral tone, with color appearing only in the ornamentation. We know, however, that Greek statuary was originally brilliantly colored, and we know that theatrical and civil dress used strong colors even during the fifth century. However, in tragedy the tendency is usually toward somber or neutral hues; and although more concentration on the strength of form and line in costume can come from less color, rich color can be very effective in small areas of ornamentation, borders of garments, and accessories. Color in the costumes is more effective if it is kept to a single hue for each costume and if color is within a limited scale of value. Despite the bright color used on Greek statuary, sharp contrasts of strong color from costume to costume are probably a mistake if one thinks about the way the script is written and the characters are developed.

In choosing ornament for the garments one

Figure 10–14. Creon, Oedipus, Antigone, and Ismene in the Tyrone Guthrie Theater's 1972 production of *Oedipus*, directed by Michael Langham and designed by Desmond Heeley. Note the heavy emphasis on texture. Photo courtesy of the Tyrone Guthrie Theater, Minneapolis, Minn.

must decide whether to concentrate on simple flat patterns, which are usually best derived from Greek vase painting, or whether to stress three-dimensional ornamental accessories, including brooches, belts, bracelets, tiaras, and pins. The strong three-dimensionality of the masks tends to suggest three-dimensional ornament, especially if the lighting is to give strong three-dimensional form to each actor. The flat, decorative effects of Greek vase painting do not seem compatible with the structural nature of *Oedipus*. Three-dimensional accessories of lightweight plastic can be painted to give a sense of weight and substance, and, with appropriate highlighting and shadowing, when properly lit these ornamental accessories can give great strength and focus to those areas of the costume on which they are used.

Thus, the costumes for *Oedipus* should cre-

Figure 10–15. Design by Tanya Moiseiwitsch for Tiresias in the Stratford Festival production of *Oedipus Rex,* 1954–55, directed by Tyrone Guthrie. Courtesy of the Stratford Festival, Ontario, Canada.

Figure 10–16. Donald Davis as Tiresias in the Stratford Festival production of *Oedipus Rex,* 1954–55, directed by Tyrone Guthrie, designed by Tanya Moiseiwitsch. Note the change in sleeves from the sketch in Figure 10–15. Courtesy of the Stratford Festival, Ontario, Canada.

ate a world larger, older, and more severe than the world of fifth-century Greek statuary. They should be both ritualistic and mysterious —natural in the use of simple, severe masks, formal yet natural in the draped folds of the chiton. Color should be simple, subordinated to and complemented by the lighting. Ornament should be strong, severe, simple, and used to focus attention on one or two key areas of the human figure (Figures 10–15 and 10–16).

Roman Art and Drama

Although tradition reports that Rome was founded in the eighth century B.C., the culture was for a number of centuries overshadowed by the Hellenistic influences of the Eastern Mediterranean. But Roman art did have a character of its own, just as did Roman drama. One way to contrast the two civilizations is to compare their respective sculpture. The Romans tended to use sculpture as portraiture in private homes or palaces, while the Greeks designed sculpture primarily for public monuments. Thus, Roman sculpture is more naturalistic and exaggerated and less idealized than the Greek (Figure 10-17); and in the Roman Empire, when painting became a more important art than sculpture, the stress was also on naturalistic, momentary illusionism.

The Romans adopted for their drama most of the practices of the classical and Hellenistic theatre, yet they made many fresh and original contributions. At the time of Plautus and Terence in the second century B.C., the stages were temporary and probably consisted of bleachers arranged around a semicircular orchestra and backed by a five-foot wooden platform that was long and narrow and bounded by a wooden frame stage house at back and ends. The back wall probably had three open-

Figure 10-17. *Head of a Man*, Lateran Museum, Rome, first century A.D. An excellent example of the solid realism in Roman sculpture. Photo courtesy of the Stanford University Art Department Slide Files.

ings, used in comedy as the entrances to houses. The stage usually became a street in front of the houses. This basic plan remained in force in the later permanent theatres, but there was a great increase in size and architectural elaboration (Figure 10-18). For exam-

Figure 10-18. A reconstruction of the threatre at Ostia, 30-12 B.C. From D'Espouy, *Fragments d'architecture antique,* Vol. I, 1901.

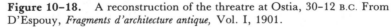

ple, the theatre at Orange in southern France, with a "scaenae frons" 118 feet high and 338 feet long covered with niches, statues, and columns, is obviously not suited for small comedies but only for the grandeur of the imperial spectacles that were so admired during the period of the Empire.

Costumes and masks in the Roman theatre of Plautus and Terence were based on those used in Greek New Comedy, but other playwrights, who stressed Roman settings and characters, used more native costumes and accessories. Most of the characters in the comedies are types or stock personalities, such as the old man, the young lover, and the parasitical servant, so costumes tended to be standardized, reflecting in color and line the occupation and age of the character. Even wigs were usually conventionalized in color, and masks completed the sense of exaggeration based on type. As in Greek theatre, masks allowed a full range of parts to be played by a limited number of actors (Figure 10–19).

In the plays themselves a number of changes took place during adaptation from the Greek. There was no chorus and no division into acts and scenes. Those divisions that appear today were added at a later time. Music was scattered through the action as in a modern musical rather than being placed in a formal manner. As in Greek New Comedy, the themes were everyday domestic affairs rather than political or civic problems; plots were based on mistaken identities, misunderstandings, lost children, lovers' problems, and parental obtuseness. In Plautus, a single relatively complicated plot is introduced by an expository prologue, while in Terence there is frequently a double plot and no prologue. The characters usually varied from about seven to fourteen; the most important figure was the rascally servant or slave, and the action invariably took place in the street in front of characters' houses.

The Menaechmi

PLOT AND STRUCTURE. In his plot structure, Plautus subordinates everything to his main purpose of gaining comic effect from mistaken identity, and the story is very con-

Figure 10–19. Red-figured Calyx-Krater, Italiote, early fourth century B.C. The scene from the *Phylakes* comedy of southern Italy deals with the ribald travesty of mythological subjects and heavily influenced Roman comedy. Photo courtesy of The Metropolitan Museum of Art, New York, Fletcher Fund, 1924. All rights reserved, The Metropolitan Museum of Art.

trived in motivation, exits, entrances, and final resolution. In performance the inconsistencies go unnoticed, however, and only in retrospect do they become obvious. The playwright develops his material with great economy, eliminating everything that does not contribute to his principal aim.

CHARACTERIZATION. The characters are two-dimensional types, and this is often suggested by their names: Peniculus (the Broom), who cleans up the house; Erotium (Sensual Beauty), who is the courtesan; Cylindrus (Rolling Pin), who is the cook. All the characters are limited in motivation: the Menaechmi desire sensual gratification, the wife wishes to reform her husband, the father desires to keep peace in the family, and the doctor wants a patient on whom he can practice his quackery. The limitation in character portrayal makes for sharp, clear, uncomplicated roles, and the actors required to perform the roles would need to be highly trained in movement, timing, stage business, and rapid dialogue. The ability to portray a wide range and depth of human emotion is not required.

THEME. The idea behind the play is not deep or penetrating, since the play is contrived purely for entertainment. It uses the simple device of twin brothers mistaken over and over again for one another until comic confusion dominates. There is no goal to educate or moralize. When the characters indulge in adultery, stealing, and deception, they merely contribute to the overall tone of good-humored cynicism that seems to lie behind the play.

DIALOGUE. The dialogue in the play is direct and utilitarian. It is used for comic descriptions, to further the narrative action, and to make bawdy or boisterous jokes. It is not subtle and does not grow out of character; it is employed to keep the plot moving and to evoke laughter from the audience by matching an expression, a word, or a brief description to some physical action in the play.

RHYTHM. The rhythm in the play is fast paced and furious, with few stops for reflection. Only if a rapid-fire rhythm in the dialogue and a fast tempo in the physical action is maintained throughout will the audience be swept along with the boisterousness and general mood of merriment. The music, now lost, originally accompanied more than half of the dialogue, and a number of songs were interspersed.

SPECTACLE. The scenery and costume requirements for the play are minimal. The original platform with a house for changes and properties at the rear is sufficient to suggest a street backed by a number of houses. The frequent eavesdropping that goes on suggests alcoves or projections in which characters can be concealed. The costumes are based on those from everyday Greek life, although seen through Roman eyes; and there is a strong stress on simplification and conventionalization according to social class, occupation, age, and sex. Although not required by the script, wigs and masks were, of course, part of the original production.

Visual Presentation of *The Menaechmi*

After looking briefly at the Roman comedy *The Menaechmi,* one is struck by its close similarity to a certain kind of modern American musical comedy. The use of song, the flute accompaniment to action, the coarse jokes, the flimsy plot, the juxtaposition of sentiment and vulgarity—all of these elements are reminiscent of the musical comedies of the 1920s and 1930s, which made use of the best vaudevillians and burlesque entertainers and reused hackneyed plots that had been serviceable for centuries. In fact, one of the best-remembered musicals of that era is *The Boys from Syracuse,* which is based on *The Menaechmi.*

Given the one-dimensional plot and characters and the similarity to certain early twentieth-century American musicals, the designer of *The Menaechmi,* even if asked to transpose the play to another period, will be inclined to use flat colors, sharp outlines, exaggerated forms, and lack of textural interest. If it is a Roman street, a modern street, or a street from some other era, the designer will tend to treat it in the exaggerated contours of the cartoon and the comic strip (Figure 10–20). The play has even been done as a "Peanuts" cartoon, and the designs were very successful.

But what does this mean to the costume designer? First of all, it means that texture is not of major importance in the choice of fabric. In a script that has a strong sense of design and contrivance, it would be a mistake to stress fabric texture; as a result, light reflection and a tactile sense would take precedence over outline and color. In the costumes for *The Menaechmi,* one would not want reflected light on the costumes to alter the texture, mood, or atmosphere of the play. To return to our earlier discussion of polar opposites, the category of absolute clarity would be most suitable to this play. Line, form, and color must be simple and direct—not distorted, muted, or disguised by

shifts in the effect of light on texture. Even the massed folds and draped lines of Greek and Roman statuary would be out of place in Roman comedy, since the depth and weight of fabric folds are analogous to depth and weight in the structure of the script. Whether one chooses soft or stiff fabrics—and this choice depends on how exaggerated and cartoon-like the production is to be—the fabrics should be almost without texture and cut and fitted with a minimum of folds and draped lines. To take a group of flat but relatively soft textures is to give a more natural look to the human form and to make the characters seem more human; to select a stiff set of fabrics that will tend to distort and exaggerate the human form, if cut and fitted for this purpose, is to make the play far less realistic and to approach more closely the modern cartoon strip.

The lines of the costume should be simple and sharp in effect, with an emphasis on short broken lines rather than long, unbroken verti-

Figure 10–20.   A sketch for a setting of *The Casina* by Plautus, by Donald Oenslager. From *Scenery Then and Now* by Donald Oenslager, W. W. Norton, New York, 1936. Courtesy of Donald Oenslager.

cal, diagonal, or horizontal lines. Only in this way will the lines of the costumes reflect the sharp, simple, direct characterizations and the short, broken nature of the rapid-fire dialogue. Also, there is a good deal of rough-and-tumble physical action. Only with costumes that make little or no use of long lines will the full movement potential in the play be achieved. Every costume should be as simple and as easy to work in as possible.

The matter of color has already been suggested by relating the play to the modern musical and the cartoon strip. This loud, hot, and boisterous comedy obviously requires colors that are direct, strong, and primary—the colors that are printed in cartoon books and Sunday supplements or the harsh, strong pigments in much abstract modern art. Subtlety of color is no more called for in this play than is subtlety of characterization.

In ornament, one might choose a few simple, exaggerated, flat forms and use them with little variation throughout the costumes. Again, linear design should take precedence over contour and three-dimensional depth of form. Often such ornamental decoration can be in linear black rather than color to act as an accent and an outline for the exaggerated movements of a character or the distorted outlines of a costume. Such use of a heavy black line in ornamentation is very like the black outlines in a cartoon strip, a flat print, or an illustration. Ornamentation, such as three-dimensional jewelry, buckles, and headdresses, should definitely be subordinate to the strong use of linear ornamentation. The best inspiration for this kind of ornamentation as originally used in *The Menaechmi* comes from the vase painting, statuettes, and illustrated manuscripts that show Roman and Greek

Figure 10–21.   Costume sketch for *The Menaechmi* by Plautus, by Betsy Leichleiter. Prepared as a class assignment in the Department of Drama, Stanford University. Courtesy of Betsy Leichleiter.

comedy figures in action. Vase paintings dealing with comic subject matter are particularly helpful in suggesting the strong, linear ornamentation appropriate for this play; statuettes showing figures from Roman comedy are especially helpful in indicating the effectiveness of the short lines in the costumes.

For the accessories, one would have to take a long look at the statuettes still available to us before deciding whether to use masks, wigs, and built-up areas of the human body. The masks would be effective for exaggerating the character of the actor but would hide any effective facial expressions. They would also create a problem when viewed at close hand, since they would make the already stereotyped characters seem even more unreal. To perform *The Menaechmi* in a large theatre would defeat the purpose of having audience and actors in close contact throughout the play for asides and direct statements to the audience. If masks are not used, then one should use a stylized makeup that will make the human faces match some of the distortions and exaggerations in the sets and costumes. Even if masks are not worn, it might be advisable to use wigs occasionally, just to have another major item near the actor's face for strong linear exaggeration

in line and form. The same is true of built-up padding on the human figure. If one uses a hunchback, enlarged buttocks, exaggerated feet, and a protruding phallus, one approximates the spirit of the original and makes the comic exaggerations in costume line and form fit the nature of the body wearing the costume.

Finally, there is the key technical question that must be answered by the costume designer: can the twins be made to look exactly alike if no masks are used? If the two people are exactly the same size and have similarly shaped faces, it is usually possible with the use of hats, wigs, and carefully exaggerated makeup to make them look enough alike to fit the demands of the play.

In looking at *The Menaechmi,* then, as a problem for the costume designer, one is struck forcibly by the direct connection between the play's structure and characters and their visual equivalent in line, texture, and color. No matter what the period of the costumes or what the approach used in the direction of the play, the visual equivalents to the plot structure and characterizations are so insistent that the range of variety in visual choices is quite effectively limited (Figure 10–21).

11

Medieval Plays

Medieval Art and Thought

It has long been fashionable in brief surveys of medieval art and theatre to speak of the Dark Ages as a barbaric backsliding from the naturalism, logic, and organization of Greece and Rome. However, it has also often been written that there were several rises to cultural peaks that did attempt to reestablish classical culture during the thousand years following the fall of Rome, and that the Italian Renaissance was the final full return to the ideals of Greece and Rome. Although there are many similarities, the Italian Renaissance was more than just a return to the ideals of antiquity, and the Carolingian and Ottonian revivals of the ninth and tenth centuries and the classical Gothic of the thirteenth century were not classical in method, although they did borrow classical images. As was brilliantly pointed out by Henry Adams in *Mont St. Michel and Chartres* (1904), the thought behind the art of the medieval period is so opposed to the logic and rationalism of classical art that it is illogical even at its most logical—unless the dual world of heaven and earth presented by Aquinas and Dante is

completely understood. The Italian Renaissance really was different from both the medieval period and classical antiquity in its nostalgia for the classical past and in its self-conscious desire to affirm the dignity of humankind in a universe of beauty and logic. And the medieval period, even when it copied directly from antiquity, had a logic that related its art neither to the Renaissance nor to Greece and Rome. Medieval thought always attempted the impossible balance between the world of nature and the world of the spirit, and the subtleties of the scholastic method devised to bring order to this double world could not reduce the degree of contradiction between flesh and spirit. The strain in Dante is severe, and every ledge of Purgatory is a theatre for human beings striving to master their human passions and reconcile them with God's will. Dante clearly presents the two poles: the ideal order of a universe expressing God's unchanging will, and the changing life of each human being who lives and feels the pain of existence. This double vision of reality in the Middle Ages is reflected in the great Gothic cathedrals, in which the aspiring leap to overcome the so-

Figure 11–1.   Notre Dame Cathedral, Paris. Example of transitional to high Gothic architecture, 1163–1250. Photo courtesy of the French Government Tourist Office.

lidity of the walls and the enclosure of space is opposed by the reality of strain and instability—a sense of danger in those soaring towers and overreaching vaults (Figure 11–1).

The Gothic period differs from the Romanesque and Carolingian periods in giving human beings a more central location in art; but even though a certain growing humanism gives much more emphasis to humankind in nature in this world, it always sees humankind in relation to the hereafter and the divine. In looking at any aspect of art in the late medieval period, one is aware of the conflict between the personal and the abstract, the logical and the transcendental, the historic and the timeless. Only when full reliance had been placed on human abilities and powers can we say that the Gothic was superseded by the Renaissance. It arrived when the artist and scientist succeeded in imposing mathematical and aesthetic theories on the loose discoveries of medieval empiricism. It is this empiricism, however, that created the great Gothic cathedrals and their negation of the inert, solid, block-like structures of Romanesque architecture. Gothic architecture rejected the idea of architecture as the enclosure of space. By forming and penetrating space rather than defining and encom-

Figure 11-2. *The Flight into Egypt,* a sculptural detail from the facade of Notre Dame Cathedral, Paris, late thirteenth century. The scene shows the combination of realism and idealism in Gothic art. Photo courtesy of Jean Roubier, Paris.

Figure 11-3. *Annunciation to the Shepherds,* two scenes from the Sacramentary of Fulda, Bamberg Library, Germany, second half of the eleventh century. The scene shows the use of properties and framing devices to present the subject matter as scenes from a play. Photo courtesy of the Stanford University Art Department Slide Files.

passing it, the Gothic cathedral became a frame for sculpture and stained glass—an illustrated book of knowledge for the religious community. Illuminated manuscripts and missals could be deciphered only by monks and scholars, but everyone went to the House of the Lord to worship and learn. One "read" a Gothic cathedral inside and out, in glass or wood, gilded metal or stone, and this Gothic world of flesh and spirit is crowded with intensely human anecdotes, stories, and details presented in a simple linear fashion (Figures 11-2 and 11-3). In the medallions of a stained glass window, in the statues arranged within a cathedral porch, or in the movement of figures in a manuscript there is a simple, linear progression. Gothic literature also accepts this arrangement of episodes (as in the Mystery plays) in which compartmentalized scenes are presented one after another until the cycle is complete (Figure 11-3). This one-dimensional story telling is often referred to as processional, because the scenes, dramatic as they may be, do not fit into a unified plot or scheme. The stories lack a dramatic focus, a point of crisis to which all characters and acts converge to form a climax. Gothic art gives us dramatic episodes with very human actors, but it cannot furnish the real space for sustained human interaction.

Medieval Theatre and Drama

Although records show actors and mimes wandering from place to place in the early Middle Ages, the revival of the drama as a part of medieval culture came only with the use of dramatic interludes within the services of the Church. It has never been clear why the Church began to use these dramatic interludes, but the answer seems to be that the Church leaders hoped to make the lessons and the stories more vivid and interesting. Also, since the majority of parishioners could not understand Latin, such dramatizations were added to the already important use of ritual and spectacle to give Church doctrine simplicity, directness, and power.

The two most important dates in the Christian calendar were quite naturally Christmas and Easter, and it was in connection with the services devoted to these holidays that the first short dramatizations developed. By the time the Church moved these dramatized episodes outside to the square in front of the cathedral, the placement of the scenes within the cathedral had become the standard plan that was to remain for most outdoor presentations of religious plays. The altar remained the key point of focus, with little booths or *mansions* set up in the two aisles of the cathedral to mark the place and character of the individual dramatized episodes. These mansions are identical in many ways with the little compartments or framing niches that appear as a framework for the religious scenes and characters that adorn the inside and outside of the cathedral, and they indicate vividly how strong was the influence from art to drama and from drama back to art (Figure 11-4). The area around the individual mansions, which became much more open when the drama moved outdoors, was called the *platea* or "place" and was the neutral playing space within which actors could move from one mansion to another as the action demanded.

In the staging of these plays, there came to be three or four widely used variations besides the open layout in the cathedral square: there was the rectangular platform arrangement on which the various mansions were arranged in an actual linear progression from left to right; there was the pageant wagon method by which each mansion, built on a wagon, moved from corner to corner and square to square throughout the city until all the mobile mansions had stopped and the playlets had been played to the full audience; while still another variation was to use Roman or other primitive amphitheatres as a setting for a circular arrangement of mansions around a central platea. But in all medieval staging there were certain elements that remained basically the same: there was always a series of mansions surrounded by a generalized area; the performances were composed of a series of plays, each more or less complete but tied to the preceding and succeeding play by the position of the story in the Bible or in other Church literature; each cycle

Figure 11-4. *The Angel Appearing to St. Anne* by Giotto, Scrovegni Chapel, Padua, ca. 1306. An example in painting of the use of theatrical mansions used to stage a scene from the Bible. Photo courtesy of Alinari/Art Resource, Inc.

Figure 11-5. The stage for the Passion Play produced at Valenciennes, France, in 1547. The various mansions, reading from the left, represent Paradise, Nazareth, the Temple, Jerusalem, a palace, the golden door, the sea, and the mouth of Hell. From a manuscript in the Bibliothèque Nationale, Paris. Photo courtesy of the Bibliothèque Nationale, Paris.

Figure 11-6. Scene from the Valenciennes Passion Play, showing the simultaneous depiction of several scenes involving Christ's curing of the paralytic and the woman with dropsy. Photo courtesy of the Bibliothèque Nationale, Paris.

of plays made use, in one or more of the plays, of three planes of action, Heaven, Earth, and Hell; and finally, there was a great attempt to make special and miraculous effects as convincingly realistic as possible (Figures 11–5 and 11–6).

To achieve these special effects a considerable amount of stage machinery was invented, and there was a real determination to make the miraculous events from the Bible as real as possible, so that no doubts about Church doctrine would be raised in the minds of the audience. The major area of concentration in special effects was the Hellmouth, with its fire and smoke and the horrific reality of the devils who emerged from Hell equipped with terrifying masks, tails, claws, cloven hoofs, and exploding fireworks. The costumes and equipment for such devils can be easily seen in the gargoyles of the great cathedrals and in the sculptural programs dealing with the Last Judgment. One can imagine how artists delighted in depicting these monsters, and producers of the cycle plays took inspiration from the figures they found carved on the exteriors of the churches. In costumes there was a mixture of everyday wear with elaborate overlaid accessories, and when saints and important Biblical personages appeared they usually car-

ried a specific visual symbol that was associated with them throughout the presentation. The costumes of heavenly figures were supposed to inspire awe and reverence, those of Hell were to arouse scorn and terror. Only the common person in such plays appeared as he or she would in everyday life, a representative of the common person of medieval society caught between the supernatural forces of good and evil.

There were, of course, in the late medieval period, plays other than the liturgical dramas or Mystery plays. The best known of these are Miracle plays, about the lives of the saints; secular farces such as *Master Pierre Pathelin;* and Morality plays such as the famous *Everyman.* Morality plays were allegories about the moral temptations that beset human beings on their journey from life to death, and the protagonist was advised by such personifications of good and evil as the Seven Virtues, the Seven Deadly Sins, Mercy, Good Deeds, Knowledge, and Death. Though many Morality plays cover a person's entire life, *Everyman* deals only with the preparation for death as the protagonist asks former companions to accompany him to the grave. Because only Good Deeds will go with him, Everyman comes to understand the meaning of life on earth in rela-

Figure 11-7. Banquet scene from *The Salzburg Everyman* by Hugo von Hofmannsthal; produced by the Goodman Theatre, Chicago, Ill., 1957. Translated and directed by John Reich. Illustrates the rich costumes, properties, and accessories required in this late medieval drama. Photo courtesy of John Reich.

tion to salvation. It is a simple, moving drama with universal appeal. In the German version, dramatized afresh by Hugo von Hofmannsthal in 1911, there is a brilliant banquet scene during which Death calls Everyman to his final Judgment. The scene allows a full display of late medieval costumes, properties, and customs (Figure 11–7).

The Second Shepherd's Play

Probably the single play that is most widely read and seen from the list of English cycle plays is *The Second Shepherd's Play* from the Wakefield Cycle of Mystery dramas. It is the thirteenth play in a long group of thirty-two short playlets dramatizing key Biblical events from the Creation to the Last Judgment.

PLOT AND STRUCTURE. The plot is based on the simple statement in the Book of Luke about the shepherds who watched over their flocks near Bethlehem when the angel of the Lord came to announce the birth of the Christ child. The author elaborated and enriched this idea with comic detail, farcical humor, and a strong feeling for contemporary medieval peasant life. This short narrative puts together what may seem to us opposing ideas of supernatural spirituality and earthy, farcical reality. With our religious outlook we cannot envisage placing a scene about the farcical problems of a stolen sheep in the same context with a scene depicting the Nativity, but such a juxtaposition of elements typifies the completely unselfconscious religious thought of the medieval peasant and also vividly illustrates the duality of thought in all medieval art.

CHARACTERIZATION. There are only seven roles in this short play, and all the parts would, almost certainly, have been played by men. In fact, the actor playing Gil may well have doubled in the part of the Virgin Mary, and the Christ child was probably a doll. The shepherds and Mak are simply but effectively characterized as peasants, and the age for all characters is indeterminate except for one shepherd who is a boy. There is little psychological development of character aside from one or two obvious traits for each person. The three shepherds are differentiated merely by the personal problem each indicates at the opening, and all are shown to be basically kind and generous. In fact, it is the generous instinct to give Gil's baby a gift that finally unmasks Mak and his deed. Mak himself is portrayed as a simple but clever thief who is rather cowardly and henpecked. The part must be played by an actor of great skill who can communicate one thing to the audience and another to the shepherds, while making expert use of comic timing. His wife, Gil, who is both clever and shrewish, must be a close second to his action and comic timing. The religious figures of Mary and the Angel of the Lord are seen as typical religious stereotypes.

Physical action throughout is reasonably realistic, although transitional actions such as the shepherds' falling asleep and the trip to Mak's house are missing. Thus, many details that are not indicated in the script would have to be supplied by the actors. There are also several demands for song, so the shepherds, Mak, and the Angel must all be capable singers.

THEME. The most important theme is, of course, humankind's basic sinfulness and the need for a Saviour. The play's structure is two-part—a demonstration of sin followed by the possibility of redemption. The shepherds represent the audience personality, Mak represents the sinners who need to be saved, and the Christ child is the symbol of God come to humankind.

DIALOGUE. The dialogue is very simple and has a naive chanted rhythm through its persistent use of obvious rhymed endings. Yet the play contains some beautifully simple, unpretentious phrases that completely illuminate a scene or a character with a minimum of effort. Although probably written by an unlearned author and consequently containing many crudities, the dialogue has an easy and elastic quality that allows it to follow all of the shifts in inflection, pace, and mood.

RHYTHM. The rhythm is the same processional, linear unrolling of action that we have discussed as being the basis for most medieval art, while the music that is included in the action highlights this simple, linear rhythm. The musical requirements are quite simple: the first song would undoubtedly be a contemporary popular song, while the Gloria and the shepherds' final song would have been taken from contemporary Church music.

SPECTACLE. The play calls for three scenes—the fields, Mak's house, and the stable at Bethlehem. Whether three mansions would have been required is doubtful; probably the same mansion was adapted for Mak's house and the Nativity, while the fields would have been in the open surrounding area. The mansion for the house would need a curtain to hide Gil and Mak when they were not on stage, as well as a door, a cradle, and a bed. If the mansion were placed on a pageant wagon, it is logical to assume that it would pull up to another flat-bedded wagon, or a stationary platform, which could then act as the open area of the fields.

The costume demands are minimal: the shepherds and Mak would wear the tunics or smocks of the medieval male peasant, Gil would wear the skirt and blouse of a lower-class woman, and only the Angel and Mary would require some richer ecclesiastical garments as symbols of authority. The Angel would certainly need wings, while Mary would require an upper-class medieval garment embellished with the symbols usually associated with the Mother of God.

Visual Presentation of
The Second Shepherd's Play

The mood created by any physical arrangement for one of the medieval Mystery plays should approximate the small-scale, naive, realistic method of the medieval artisans, even if strong modern stylization is employed. The craftsmen who did the settings for the medieval Mystery plays were the same ones who adorned the cathedrals, chapter houses, and monasteries; over and over again, as one looks at a sculptured Nativity or Last Judgment, one is struck by the theatrical groupings of character and a sense of a recorded moment in a playlet or drama. In a modern production this same sense of vivid, personal, naive decorative reality should be the ideal.

Since the medieval artisans gave full attention to ornamental detail and the individual pieces of stage property, no attempt was made to unify figures and background in a single space-time perspective. The modern designer should stress the discontinuity between the size of the characters and their backgrounds, the decorative unreality of ornamental detail, the continual shift from the real to the unreal. Just as Gothic art places very human actors in realistic "business" in an unrealistic framework, so should a modern production work diligently to capture the very real duality between the worldly and the unworldly that is operative in the Mystery plays.

Obviously, there is an abundance of source material to use as á basis for one's choice of line, texture, and color in the re-creation of a medieval Mystery play, but the danger is in becoming too involved with some specific source (stained glass, manuscript, or sculpture) and allowing the designs for a production to be quaint re-creations of some historical art form. One must capture the essence of the medieval usage of line, texture, and color within the duality of effect mentioned above. In medieval times color was used very directly and without complicated gradations and mixtures of hue. One usually thinks of the chalky colors of a Giotto fresco or the bright, clear, undiluted colors of stained glass, manuscript illumination, or heraldry. Line is the all-important item in medieval art, culminating in the fascinating arabesques and decorative linear effects of the international Gothic style of the late fourteenth and fifteenth centuries. Here depth, shadow, and highlight are all subordinate to the fascinating, delicate play of a serpentine line that creates pattern before it creates reality. Texture is secondary to line in medieval art and comes forward only as a surface of the particular media being used: the flat shiny surface of the manuscript, the hard surface of stone, the brilliant transparency of stained glass.

With these abstract elements in mind and the plan to use one or possibly two mansions to represent Mak's cottage and the Nativity scene, what would be the specific design problems involved in a modern presentation of *The Second Shepherd's Play?*

The most important visual idea to be borrowed from medieval art is the processional or linear unrolling of the play so that the various locales are visible at once and characters move from episode to episode without leaving the stage. Usually the physical re-creation of the pageant wagon would be unnecessarily academic, and the more practical arrangement would be to have the mansions (if separate frames are needed for Mak's house and the Nativity) arranged on a rectangular platform stage or grouped in an open "in the round" arrangement.

In producing some of the Mystery plays, one might wish to make use of the double-level arrangement found in so many medieval manuscripts and tympana sculpture; but, for this play, a mansion with a single level (and a roof for the angel) is all that is required, and a traverse curtain could be used to indicate the move from outdoors to indoors. One also has to make a decision about the nature of the mansion or mansions to be used. Is it to be a structural pavilion that has no decoration and can be used for any number of scenes, or is it to have a specific interior and exterior design, which would make it imperative to have a different mansion for Mak's house and the Nativity scene? If it has decoration, can it be abstract enough so that the same pavilion can be used for both interior scenes, and what should be the nature of the decoration? Is it relatively rich and architecturally decorative like the frames around a manuscript scene or the pavilion above a cathedral sculpture, or does its decoration suggest a shed or hut as in a Giotto fresco? The designer and director need to make the choice between architectural decoration (which may contrast with the realistic action) or a simple frame for the action.

However, there would seem to be no problem with the few properties and set pieces required. By the very nature of the play and the nature of medieval play production, it would be best to make them all simple and realistic. The costume requirements are so simple that a mere catalogue of the script's demands would be enough to guide one in choosing from a wardrobe of tunics, tights, and simple gowns. But if the subtle ideals of medieval art are to be projected by the costumes, careful planning and designing must take place.

The costumes for Mak and the Shepherds would require tunics, tights, soft shoes, and possibly a hood for one and a short cloak for another; the youngest shepherd should probably be without cloak or hood. As to how these clothes should look, there is a famous section of the royal portal from Chartres Cathedral that depicts two shepherds with their sheep, and here we can get an excellent idea of the simple costume requirements for this play (Figure 11–8). Note that the most important item that strikes the eye after one absorbs the overall simplicity and naiveté of the scene is the stress on line to achieve decorative effect. The draping of the hood and collar on the shepherd to the left, the folds on the sleeve of his tunic, the wrinkles in the hose of the cloaked shepherd— all make a decorative linear statement. This means that in choosing the fabric for such simple costumes and in cutting them to fit the actor, great pains should be taken to re-create these decorative wrinkles and folds. A very soft and pliable wool would be the most appropriate fabric choice, and linings in the sleeves and under the tights and torso might be necessary so that certain drapings and folds could be sewn permanently in place. The period during which these statues were carved has often been called classical Gothic because of the great formal beauty of the cathedrals and their decora-

Figure 11–8. *Shepherds in the Fields*, west portal, Chartres Cathedral, early thirteenth century. An example of the naive simplicity and faith to be found in early Gothic sculpture. Photo courtesy of Jean Roubier, Paris.

Figure 11-9. Scene from *The Second Shepherd's Play* from the Wakefield cycle of Mystery plays, produced at the Parish Church, Stratford-upon-Avon, England, 1950, under the direction of Henry Clark. Photo courtesy of Margaret Clark.

tion; it is the simple yet often detailed beauty of the sculpture of this period that gives it a classical note. This balance of naive simplicity and beauty can be admirably adapted to the costumes for the shepherds, and in this way the naive charm of the opening, the farcical humor of the middle scenes, and the religious beauty of the final scene can all be met (Figure 11-9).

12

Renaissance Plays

Art and Culture in the Fifteenth and Sixteenth Centuries

Traditionally, the Renaissance is thought to have begun in Florence at the beginning of the fifteenth century as a reaction against medieval modes of thought. It was an age of burgeoning thought about all aspects of the natural world and an age of rebirth of interest in the art and ideas of antiquity. The historians and philosophers of the nineteenth and early twentieth centuries conceived of the Renaissance as an age that rediscovered human beings and their world, an age that rose to its highest achievement in Italy at the time of Michelangelo, Raphael, and Leonardo, only to fall gradually into decadence during the following century. A few moments of distinction, like those in Cervantes' Spain and Shakespeare's England, brightened the decline. Today, this is considered to be a romantic and oversimplified view of the Renaissance, and the two centuries from 1400 to 1600 are usually divided into three very separate and distinct artistic periods.

First, the fifteenth century, until approx-

imately 1485 or 1490, is considered to be an age of experimentation—a period of conscious, consistent, objective analysis of the natural world. It was not that naturalism suddenly burst on the scene for the first time, but rather that a new and scientific view of reality triumphed in fifteenth-century Italy. The beautiful curving lines and flat decorative patterns of the international Gothic style gave way to the art of Masaccio, Donatello, and Brunelleschi, who stressed tactile form, mathematical precision, dignity, simplicity, and compactness (Figures 12-1 and 12-2, and see Figure 9-10). The primary feeling of this new art was unmetaphysical, unsymbolic, and unceremonial—a symbol of the youth and adolescence of a new culture.

Second, the period known as the high Renaissance, which lasted only about a generation (from 1490 to the death of Raphael in 1520), was a period of innovation led by several men of genius who were given great scope for their artistic ideas by the popes in Rome. Several powerful and worldly popes, including Alexander VI, Julius II, and Leo X, were determined to use the full resources of art

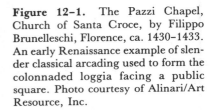

Figure 12-1. The Pazzi Chapel, Church of Santa Croce, by Filippo Brunelleschi, Florence, ca. 1430–1433. An early Renaissance example of slender classical arcading used to form the colonnaded loggia facing a public square. Photo courtesy of Alinari/Art Resource, Inc.

Figure 12-2. Donatello, *David* (bronze), ca. 1430–1432. The first life-sized, fully freestanding nude statue since antiquity. It symbolizes the adolescence and youth of the Italian Renaissance culture in the first three quarters of the fifteenth century. Museo Nazionale, Florence. Photo courtesy of Alinari/Art Resource, Inc.

Figure 12-3. *David* by Michelangelo, The Academy, Florence, 1501–1504 (marble). An example of the heroic scale, monumental grandeur, and unified emotional power of the high Renaissance. Photo courtesy of Alinari/Art Resource, Inc.

to achieve the strongest possible statement of Church authority. The works of Michelangelo, Leonardo, Bramante, and Raphael (in many ways a culmination of the artistic experiments of the fifteenth century) were also something new, based on the absolutism, unity, and power exercised by the towering figures of authority (Figure 12-3).

Third, the years following the death of Raphael are today seen not as a decline in art but as a move toward personal interpretation and even distortion of reality, derived from the inner feelings of artists. The optimism of the early Renaissance waned at the beginning of the sixteenth century with the many invasions of Italy, the rise of the Reformation, and the

final horror of the sack of Rome in 1527. A malaise and disillusionment arose among certain artists, who are today labeled *mannerists.* These artists deliberately distorted and exaggerated many artistic ideals of the high Renaissance in order to gain disturbing psychological effects (Figures 12-4 and 12-5). And because the ideals of the sixteenth-century Renaissance in Italy spread to the rest of Europe, the art of

Figure 12-4. *The Rape of the Sabines* by Bologna, Loggia dei Lanzi, Florence, 1583 (marble). An example of the self-conscious, artificial, choreographed exercise in spiral movement and force emotion that characterize much late sixteenth-century mannerist art. Photo courtesy of Alinari/Art Resource, Inc.

Figure 12-5. *The Last Supper* by Tintoretto, The Church of San Giorgio Maggiore, Venice, 1592–1594. The exaggerated perspective, brilliant night light, and self-consciously choreographed action create a sense of mystery and theatricality in the work of Tintoretto, El Greco, and other late mannerist painters. Photo courtesy of Alinari/Art Resource, Inc.

England, France, Germany, and Spain naturally adopted a mixture of Renaissance precepts and mannerist interpretations. The artists who moved north from Italy after Raphael's death were only nominally of the Renaissance. Although they knew its methods, they were psychologically mannerists, creating and teaching an art that was personal, distorted, ambiguous, and unnatural. During the late years of Henry VIII's reign and most of Elizabeth's reign, this art sifted north to England, and conditioned the artistic and cultural setting in which Shakespeare flourished.

Theatre and Drama in the Fifteenth and Sixteenth Centuries

ITALIAN COURT THEATRE. With the revival of interest in classical antiquity during the early years of the fifteenth century in Italy, an interest in the plays and theatres of Greece and Rome also developed. This interest is clearly evident even in Shakespeare, in plays such as *Julius Caesar* and *Antony and Cleopatra.*

The books of the Roman architect Vitruvius included much information about the theatre of classical times, but they were first published in 1486 without supporting illustrations. By the beginning of the sixteenth century, with illustrations added, his books were known throughout Europe. This interest in classical staging soon led to a demand for production, and by the late fifteenth century most of the cultured princes and dukes of the small Italian states were using festivals of plays to demonstrate the high development of art and culture at their individual courts (Figure 12-6). In many artistic centers there were academies of intellectuals organized solely to study the arts of antiquity, and they too staged plays to demonstrate their knowledge of the classical past. Both courts and academies used their own members in performance, costumes and scenery were usually done by a local court

Figure 12–6. Perspective scene from *L'Ortensio*, Siena, 1560: from the woodcut by H. Bols after B. Neroni in the Victoria and Albert Museum, London. An example of perspective scenery in Italy in the middle of the sixteenth century involving a raked stage, canvas wings of diminishing size, and a painted backcloth. Crown Copyright Victoria and Albert Museum (Theatre Museum).

painter or architect, and the plays were written, adapted, or translated by authors under royal patronage. Actors at court were aristocratic members of the royal household, while in the academies they were chosen from the membership (Figure 12–7).

The staging in these theatres stemmed from two sources—the permanent theatre background described by Vitruvius and the contemporary fascination with perspective in painting. Productions were usually staged in a hall where the stage and auditorium were specifically designed and built for each new production. Although we have many sketches and engravings of such court presentations, the first treatise on the subject did not appear until the architect Serlio devoted a section to theatre in his great work on architecture in 1545. His scenes for both comedy and tragedy are the street scenes of Roman comedy translated into a perspective setting; with no thought of a per-

manent theatre, there is no proscenium frame. No provision for shifting is indicated, since the background is seen as being continuous for each production.

The first permanent theatre to be built for the production of classical plays was the Teatro Olimpico in Vicenza. Designed by the renowned architect Andrea Palladio for the Olympic Academy, it opened in 1585 with a performance of *Oedipus Rex.* Here Vitruvius' plan for a Roman theatre was followed quite closely, and the influence of perspective is very evident in the alleyways designed in sloped perspective behind the doors of the facade. These fixed streets could not be shifted, and, in face of the growing demand for shifting scenery and more spectacle, this structure was old-fashioned even at the time it was built (Figure 12–8).

The final form of the Renaissance theatre does not appear until the dawn of the Baroque

Figure 12-7. Designs for costumes in the Florentine court "Intermezzi" of 1589, from the original drawing by Bernardo Buonalenti in the Victoria and Albert Museum, London. An example of the fantasy of design and ornament, based on the classical chiton with overfold, that developed in mannerist theatrical designs during the sixteenth century. Crown Copyright Victoria and Albert Museum (Theatre Museum).

Figure 12-8. The stage of the Teatro Olimpico at Vicenza with Palladio's *scenae frons*, 1580, and Scamozzi's added perspective vistas, 1585. An example of the strong interest in the theatre of classical antiquity coupled with the Renaissance preoccupation with perspective. Courtesy of the Norman Philbrick Library. Photo by Keeble and Shuchat.

era, when a permanent framing device (proscenium) was built into the Teatro Farnese in Parma in 1618. A combined inheritance, the proscenium uses an enlargement of the central doorway of the Roman theatre in conjunction with the picture-frame idea derived from the perspective school of the Italian Renaissance. By restricting the audience's view with perspective scenery, the stage machinery for shifting scenes became more effective; with the possibility of full stage illusion, the Baroque age of opera was ushered in.

COMMEDIA DELL'ARTE. Alongside the dramas of court and academy, Italy nurtured the *commedia dell'arte*—groups of itinerant professional actors who toured the countryside playing standard stock characters from an improvised script. The lovers (the straight parts in the action) were handsome, sympathetic, and did not wear masks. The three most famous older characters (who wore masks) were the Pantalone, a miserly Venetian merchant; the Dottore, a long-winded pedant or lawyer who loved long speeches filled with bad Latin; and the Capitano, a boasting soldier who talked of conquests in love and war only to prove the craven coward in the end. To complement these older comic types there were the servants or *zanni*—witty rogues who thought up every conceivable trick and deception to discomfit the older "masks." Usually one or two female servants, with names such as Colombina, Rosetta, Franciscina, and Olivetta, attended the young girls in the scenario and furthered the love complications of the plot. They usually received the amorous attentions of the zanni. All of the actors developed set speeches as well as clever bits of business, known as *lazzi,* which were used to spark audience interest whenever the plot or action began to lag (Figure 12–9).

The *commedia dell'arte,* which literally means comedy done by professionals, may well have descended from the farce comedy of ancient Rome, preserved in some limited way through the Middle Ages. It sprang into prominence in the middle of the sixteenth century and spread to all of Europe by the second or third decade

Razullo.   *Cucurucu.*

Figure 12–9.   A sketch of two figures from the *commedia dell'arte* by Jacques Callot, ca. 1620. Callot's sketches of Italian comedy figures vividly capture the gay, exuberant crudity of early seventeenth-century Italian popular theatre. Photo courtesy of the National Gallery of Art, Washington, Rosenwald Collection.

of the seventeenth century, appearing as an influence in Shakespeare's comedies as early as the last decade of the sixteenth century. It continued as a powerful influence on literary drama and formal stage presentation up to the opening of the nineteenth century.

POPULAR THEATRE IN SPAIN AND ENGLAND. In two European countries where there developed a strong national spirit and a native culture not affected by the limiting rules of neoclassicism, a native drama and a popular theatre grew up that rivaled the Golden Age of Greece. In both England and Spain, by the middle of the sixteenth century, small groups of wandering professional actors, although treated as outcasts from society, were patronized for the exciting if limited theatrical fare they had to offer. Such actors were not recognized legally in the two countries until after the founding of permanent theatres in London and Madrid in the last quarter of the century.

In England the drama that began to emerge

was a mixture of influences: school and university plays, which had been performed by amateurs since the beginning of the century; dramas staged by the young lawyers training at the Inns of Court; and the popular playlets derived from the medieval interludes and folk dramas that toured the country. The new plays were frequently a curious mixture of elements from early native drama and the new classical

Figure 12–10. Drawing of The Swan Theatre, London, by Johannes de Witt, 1596. The only contemporary drawing of the Elizabethan stage, showing a partially covered platform projecting into the yard, which was surrounded by balconies for spectators and backed by two doors and a stage balcony. From Johannes de Witt's sketch as copied by Arend van Buchell.

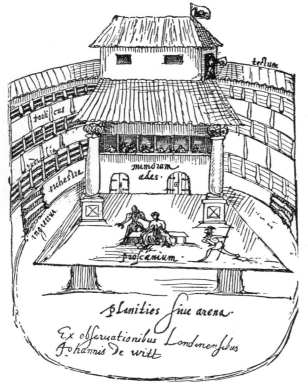

learning. In Spain the dramatic inheritance was similar, although in the plays of one of the most prolific of Spanish playwrights, Lope de Vega, the scope of subject-matter—the Bible, saints' lives, mythology, romance, history, and folklore—was far broader than in Shakespeare.

The physical theatre in England in the late sixteenth century was of two types: the outdoor public theatre and the indoor private theatre. Although both were open to the public, the indoor theatres charged higher prices and played to a more select audience. A number of famous public playhouses were built in London between 1576 and 1615, but aside from limited information about The Globe, The Fortune, and The Swan, few concrete facts survive to guide us in building reconstructions of the Elizabethan stage. Usually round, square, or polygonal, the theatres held between 2000 and 3000 persons, who stood in the central yard or pit or sat under roofed balconies surrounding the yard. The stage, a raised platform, projected into the center of the yard. A roof supported by pillars partially covered the stage, which was backed either by a wall with doors, or by an open inner stage flanked by large doors. An upper stage above this inner stage could be used for scenes requiring a second level. Scholars still disagree as to whether the inner and upper stages were permanent features of the theatre, or whether they were constructed only for specific productions. Despite disagreements about specific forms, the basic layout can be deduced from the plays: a large platform reaching out into the pit audience; a door on each side at the rear of the stage; a pavilion or curtained inner stage for "discovering" actors at the opening of a scene; an upper area or stage; windows above the doors on each side of the stage; and a third level for musicians that could be used for supernatural appearances (Figure 12–10).

The lists of a theatrical businessman, Philip Henslowe, describe the minimal scenery used on the Elizabethan stage: rocks, trees, furniture, Hellmouths, some kind of backcloth representing Rome; no large-scale scenic effects, however, are indicated. Machinery housed below the stage allowed for the appearance of ghosts through trapdoors in the stage floor, while cranes, ropes, and pulleys permitted objects and people to be raised to the upper stage. Resources were also available for producing fire and smoke as well as the sound of cannons, bells, thunder, and other sound effects.

Since performances took place in the daytime, lighting was not required, although torches, candles, and lanterns were used to indicate night scenes. Costumes were of two basic kinds: symbolic and contemporary. Symbolic costumes, used to represent gods, supernatural creatures, animals, exotic foreign characters, and servants in livery, were built specifically for the company wardrobes; all contemporary items (worn by the majority of actors in a production) were usually donations from the households of those nobles who sponsored the particular troupe (Figure 12–11). The troupes themselves usually included ten to twenty members, some of whom were shareholders and realized a certain percentage of the profits; all other actors and backstage personnel were hired at a fixed fee. The company also had young boys, who served as apprentices, to play all the female roles. As for the audience, it consisted of all levels of society, from the nobility in the balcony or on the sides of the stage to the "groundlings" who stood in the yard.

Public theatres in Madrid were in many ways very similar to those in London. Existing courtyards formed by the walls of houses were often remodeled so that surrounding balconies could be used to seat the nobility, while common people either stood or were seated on benches in the yard. The stage, raised on trestles at one end, did not jut out into the yard as in England, so it was observed only from one side and not from three. However, it did have a curtained inner stage and a balcony that served as an upper stage.

In both England and Spain, strong dramatic and theatrical traditions were well established before the arrival from Italy of the neoclassical ideas of writing and staging. In England and Spain, theatrical development was a logical and relatively smooth outgrowth of medieval tradition, and there was never a sharp division between entertainment for the court and that for commoners. In fact, much of

Figure 12–11.   A sketch from a production of *Titus Andronicus*, 1595. An example of the mixture of contemporary and classical dress on the Elizabethan stage. From the original drawing in the possession of the Marquess of Bath. Reproduced by courtesy of the Marquess of Bath, Longleat House, Warminster, Wiltshire, England.

the strength of the English and Spanish drama arises from the fact that it was written and performed for all classes.

In both countries, the rigid rules of neoclassicism that had developed in Italy were never fully accepted, and the idiosyncrasies of style that did develop in the drama were more natural, less self-conscious, and freer than were those that developed in Italy. Although mannerism in art and literature was an international style accepted in both England and Spain by the close of the sixteenth century, it was infinitely varied and complex, and each country expressed its cultural, political, and religious problems in a very personal, dramatic way.

Shakespeare as a Renaissance Playwright

In the nineteenth century it was assumed that the greatest playwright in the English language and the most popular playwright in the history of the Western world was a product of the Renaissance (Figures 12–12 and 12–13). This limited view of the Renaissance combined a religious outlook borrowed from medieval philosophy and the best elements of Renaissance humanism. Only in recent years, with the careful study of Renaissance mannerism as the major artistic style of the sixteenth century, have critics begun to realize the complexity of Shakespeare's genius. In the nineteenth century his work appeared to be more or less all of one piece, except for certain so-called "inferior" works. Today, when we see the fifteenth century as being primarily an age of scientific analysis of humankind and nature, we view the turn into the sixteenth century as a period in which art reached a balanced, unified peak known as the high Renaissance. Later sixteenth-century art is then seen not as a decline of Renaissance ideals but as a departure from the unified view of the outer world to the inner world of mannerism. Today we see elements of all of these shifting styles in Shakespeare's plays, just as Michelangelo's works reveal elements ranging from late medieval concepts through artistic ideals of the early and high Renaissance to mannerist ambiguities and proto-Baroque concepts. Shakespeare seems to have been endowed with the genius to absorb and make use of all the crosscurrents of cultural and artistic life available in the world in which he lived. No scientist or academician, Shakespeare could hardly have written his plays according to rigid theories of unity, proportion, and balance, but he was able to construct his plays psychologically and structur-

Figure 12–12. Mary Anderson as Juliet and Mrs. Sterling as the Nurse in an 1887 production of *Romeo and Juliet*. An example of the use of Victorian fabric textures and trim in a Renaissance play. The costume lines are as much Victorian as they are Renaissance. Photo from Gebbie and Gebbie, *The Stage and Its Stars*, Vol. I. Courtesy of the Norman Philbrick Library.

Figure 12–13. A drawing of Act I, scene 2 of *Hamlet* as presented at the Lyceum Theatre, London, 1874. An example of the romantic pageantry in Shakespearean production in the nineteenth century. From a scrapbook of Marvin Clarkson. Courtesy of the Norman Philbrick Library. Photo by Keeble and Shuchat.

ally from dramatic perspectives involving the entire spectrum of methodology from late medieval to early Baroque.

In his first chronicle plays, Shakespeare uses a late Gothic or medieval organization, allowing his material to unroll in a processional series of scenes arranged in much the same way as the individual playlets of the great religious cycles. Then, in the early dramas that follow, more form is added, and in comedies such as *Two Gentlemen of Verona* and *Love's Labour's Lost* and the tragedy *Romeo and Juliet* he seems to enter upon an early Renaissance phase. One senses the lightness of touch, the artificial pairing of figures, the balanced use of poetic line, and the foreground depth of characterization against a flat plane of two-dimen-sional background, which has the effect of destroying any "middle ground." These were all effects found in the fifteenth-century Renaissance. Even the values represented in these plays fall into symmetrical patterns of love and hate, rashness and caution, wit and grief, purity and sensuality, day and night, life and death. Although Shakespeare is too free to be described as high Renaissance or classical in his writing, his handling of the subject matter and development of mood in *Julius Caesar* (especially in the forum scene) reminds one of the balanced organization of Raphael's *School of Athens* (Figure 12–14). But Shakespeare lived in a mannerist age, and as the positive outlook of England began to fade along with the health of the aging Queen Elizabeth, Shakespeare

Figure 12–14. *The School of Athens* by Raphael, Stanza della Segnatura, Vatican Palace, Rome, 1508–1513. The balanced organization in this painting is in some ways analogous to the composition of the forum scene in *Julius Caesar*. Courtesy of Alinari/Art Resource, Inc.

came to his most brilliant period of tragic and tragicomic writing in plays such as *Hamlet, King Lear,* and *Measure for Measure.* These works have all the ambiguity, theatricality, and psychological subtlety of mannerism as an art form. Throughout the first decade of the seventeenth century, Shakespeare developed his work along mannerist lines intemingled with elements from the Renaissance past and the future Baroque. The continuous mixture of tragic and comic motifs, the contrast between the concrete and the abstract, the play of sensual language against intellectual language, the forced ornamental character of his structure, the emphasis on the contradictory and the unfathomable in life, the compulsions versus the restraints in human psychology—all these are elements linking the bulk of Shakespeare's work with mannerism. Only in the late romances, including *Cymbeline, Winter's Tale,* and *The Tempest,* do we achieve certain visual qualities, a certain calm, symphonic beauty, a progression in clear movement to a final climax that suggests Baroque characteristics within an ornamental, mannerist structure.

Romeo and Juliet

Looking at one of the most famous of Shakespeare's early plays and realizing how much his imagination and creative insight worked on a legendary tale of tragic, star-crossed lovers, we see in *Romeo and Juliet* a play filled with an instinctive understanding of the early Renaissance spirit of organization and composition. The action is confined by walls, orchards, squares, and rooms in a manner that reminds one of the geometric composition of Italian fifteenth-century painting.

PLOT AND STRUCTURE. Even at first glance, the mechanics of the plot and its compositional plan seem rather obvious and possibly too clear. The contrasting movements of the plot are arranged like the converging lines in a perspective drawing, and a heightened sense of drama is achieved by forcing the perspective a bit so that there is no middle ground in the play. There are only foreground characters and those who are part of the background. If one recalls one's first reading of the play, it is fascinating to note that the visual impression, as well as the organizational principle, reminds one of a scene from Botticelli, a bronze panel from the doors of the Florence Baptistry by Ghiberti, or a crowded scene by Fra Filippo Lippi rather than any of the paintings by Shakespeare's mannerist contemporaries, such as Tintoretto or El Greco.

The Prologue, read by the chorus, sets up the image of the star-crossed lovers. It is an objective framing device that places the story of the family feud clearly before us, suggests the ominous movement of fate, and removes the tale to the level of a legend. It is immediately followed by a clear-cut demonstration of the symmetrically conceived feud that erupts against the backdrop of a square in Verona. The balance of the opposing enmities is given a central focus in the figure of the Prince, who remains above and outside the quarrel. In the final act, all the balanced and symmetrically developed forces converge on a tableau that exemplifies the tragic beauty of the story's ending—the centrally placed bodies of the two young lovers, the flanking members of the two reunited families to right and left, and the benedictory figure of the Prince presiding over his dead kinsmen.

CHARACTERIZATION. The characters in this play are as carefully balanced against one another as are the various scenes and tableaux in the script. Romeo is scaled against Paris and Mercutio; Juliet is placed against Rosaline, the Nurse, and Lady Capulet; Tybalt against Benvolio; Capulet against Montague.

Aside from the two protagonists, the characters may be arranged in two groups. The first and largest includes all the supernumeraries, minor characters such as Peter and the Apothecary, and a few relatively important figures such as Tybalt, the Capulets, Paris, and Benvolio. These are all static, flat characters who are by nature what they are; they present a limited range of values and make the plot operable. Tybalt is choleric and determined to pick quarrels; Benvolio is equally determined to avoid them; Paris is pleasant, bland, with no surprises; the Nurse is garrulous, corruptible, and insensitive, and as long as there is no emergency she is also amusing. They all represent standard types in a representative human community, but their vitality tempts the audience with the possibility that they have more dimension than they actually possess.

The second group consists of three characters who give a doubly strong impression of life because they have qualities of real understanding and perception. The Prince knows from the beginning that keeping peace in Verona is a matter of life and death, and in the end he readily takes his share of responsibility for the tragic deaths in the tomb. Friar Lawrence, also, has from the start a clear perception of the danger and takes steps appropriate to his position to avert disaster. However, unlike the Prince, who moves openly, the Friar works in secret, and his secrecy ultimately betrays both him and the others. Mercutio, the third member of this group, is the character whose action of the moment of the play's crisis is on the threshold of accomplishing what neither the Prince nor his well-intentioned ingenuity had been able to do; but Romeo's sentimental action destroys all. It is Mercutio in his death speech who keeps this key moment in the play from becoming overt melodrama.

Finally, in Romeo and Juliet we have a full development of personality. From the beginning, Juliet is more mature; it is Juliet who leads the conversation in their two great scenes together, and it is she who knows through love what language cannot say, what cannot be expressed in words. She can conjure up the full range of the death images in the potion scene, yet when she wakes to find Romeo lifeless she cannot muster any language to help her deal with such a horror. Romeo's most mature speech is the one he delivers in the tomb, in which he gives dignity, meaning, and finality to the one act that he executes without the help of friends, the Friar, or Juliet. The courtly conventions, borrowed puns, and paradoxes of his earlier scenes are gone, and he achieves a mature directness and power to act in his last scene in the play.

THEME.   Just as the characterizations fall into balanced patterns, so do the values that one finds within the play. The theme of love versus hate, courtly love versus romantic love, rashness versus caution, tolerance versus intolerance, or the contrasted ideas of wit and grief, purity and sensuality, day and night—all of these are presented as neatly balanced opposites framed with a Prologue by the Chorus and an Epilogue by the Prince. They set up the play as a tale that exemplifies the relentless mechanics of fate. The major theme of star-crossed lovers is kept before the audience even when the plot seems to hinge on the vagaries of accident; the secondary theme of evil and tragedy that must of necessity arise from a feud between two families is kept as a backdrop or recurring motif throughout the action.

DIALOGUE.   The dialogue is noted for its poetic and lyrical values and is tightly organized by the sonnet form and the rhyming couplets at the conclusion of a scene. These give symmetrical balance, polish, and a frame to the lyrical beauty of the play. The language is also admirably adapted to the individual characters and the romantic mood of the play. Shakespeare easily catches the wide range in the social scale from the servant to the Prince: the Nurse's peasant speech, the country gentry talk of old Capulet, Mercutio's love for the sensuousness and richness of language, Tybalt's narrow and sharp-tongued insolence, Friar Lawrence's moralizing sententiousness, and even the tiny voice of the complaisant Apothecary. The personalities are simply but fully developed, and they unfold in a natural and direct way through language.

In analogy with the visual arts, it can be said that the language of the play has the lightness of touch, the clarity, the richness and sparkle of fifteenth-century painting. The dialogue in *Romeo and Juliet* is analogous to the color palette of Botticelli or Lippi.

RHYTHM.   The rhythm of the play shifts from the light, almost comedic note of the first two acts to a more somber note after the banishment of Romeo. In the changes of mood from street to orchard to ball to upper chamber, we experience shifts from the realistic to the lyrical, from pageantry to simplicity. Only after the banishment, when the scenes follow as night rather than day scenes and tightly enclosed rather than open, do we sense the play rushing to a tragic close. It is this breathless pace of action that is the dominant note in the drama; it is time that runs out in this play, and Shakespeare has used every device to make haste and speed part of the play's rhythm.

SPECTACLE.   The various scenes in the play come vividly and clearly to life in the imagination, and each setting offers a clearly marked-off space with characters in the foreground and a measured distance to the background. There seem to be no unlocalized areas; even street scenes seem to be specific. And on the Elizabethan stage much depends on a clear, localized use of the various stage areas: the inner area above for Juliet's bedroom, one of the windows for the balcony scene, the tomb placed in the study below, the doors at either side of the stage for the entrances of the two families. Although the pace of the action cannot allow for a perspective box setting for each major scene, on reading the play one envisions a series of balanced, one-point perspective scenes, and the characters always seem to be foreground accents against the changing backgrounds.

Visual Presentation of Romeo and Juliet

In staging a production of *Romeo and Juliet* in the contemporary theatre, the director is faced with a major dilemma in choosing the visual

Figure 12–15. Act III, scene 1 from *Romeo and Juliet* as produced by the Shakespeare Memorial Theatre, Stratford-upon-Avon, England, 1954, with scenery and costumes by Motley. The setting and the costumes exemplify the simple, balanced, symmetrical, planar nature of the play. Angus McBean Photograph, Harvard Theatre Collection.

background (Figure 12–15). Stopping after each scene even for backdrop changes is unthinkable because of the pace demanded in the action, and an intermission after the banishment of Romeo seems the only logical break in the forward movement of the play. Thus, the director and the stage designer must devise a method that allows for speed of action coupled with a sense of quite separate stage areas. The Elizabethan stage design provides one solution to this problem by presenting the director with clear-cut areas including the study, the inner area above, the side doors, the forestage, and the windows above the side doors. The end of a scene can take place in one area of the stage, while the following scene may begin in quite another area without stopping the action. For

example, Act II, scene 1 (which is set near the orchard and includes Mercutio and Benvolio and a hidden Romeo) is in a space that is clearly "outside" the orchard wall, yet the rhyme scheme that ends the scene is directly tied into the beginning of the following scene "inside" the orchard. Both spaces must be on stage at the same time and yet be clearly differentiated. Following the discovery of Juliet after the potion scene, it is important (for dramatic impact) that the space of her bedroom and her bed within it be visible throughout the action of mourning, and especially during the arrival of the musicians and Count Paris for the wedding. Only if the bed (with the supposedly dead body of Juliet) is clearly in evidence when Paris learns of the death, and we can see the flowers and the musicians below contrasted with the mourning in the bedroom above, can the full dramatic impact of the scene be visually accomplished. Even the short, ironic scene that follows, showing Peter exchanging pleasantries with the musicians, is more effective when it is contrasted with the visual presence of Juliet above, lying on her bed.

The director is usually forced to discard the idea of a set for each scene if he or she wishes to gain the full visual impact required by the space relationships suggested by developments in the action. This can, however, still be done within the multiple-space relationships suggested in early Renaissance painting: two places, or inside and outside, are often shown together in a single scene. The problem in trying to approach the setting in this manner is, again, one of time for scene changes, and most directors feel that it cannot be spared. A compromise is usually the result in contemporary productions of this play. The mood of early Italian Renaissance painting is often retained in the design forms and decorative elements of the production, while the space arrangements of the setting are analogous to those available on the Elizabethan stage. Some arrangement of steps, doors, windows, and platforms is often designed to give an upper area for the bedroom and the balcony while a raised area is reserved for the Prince, side doors are used for entrances to a street, a large area is available for the ballroom scene, and a small enclosed forward area can be suggested for Friar Lawrence's cell. Within this space arrangement, which does not change during the action, the designer may then work to create the symmetrical forms, simplicity of line and ornament, and the environment that suggests the architecture, painting, and sculpture of the early Italian Renaissance. Even when a period other than the fifteenth century in Italy is used as a setting for the play, the designer, if he or she is going to work from the structural nature of the script, will feel bound to treat the Renaissance elements in a simple, direct way, with stress on slenderness of proportions,

balance and symmetry in structure, lightness and clarity in color, and a delicacy in ornamentation. *Romeo and Juliet* is a play of youth, and the fifteenth century is an age of experiment and youthfulness; it is this quality that must be placed visually before the audience no matter what historical period is chosen for the production. For example, if the play is done in the same period in which it was written, that is, within the artistic styles of the late sixteenth century, the designer must strive to exclude from the designs the twisted complexities, ambiguities, and grotesqueries of mannerist art, and must use simpler architectural and costume lines to suggest a world of strict symmetry, rich simplicity, and youthful exuberance.

In considering the costume design problems in *Romeo and Juliet,* it should already be quite apparent that the most natural period in which to do this play is fifteenth-century Italian Renaissance (Figure 12–16). This period suits both the geographical setting of the story and the mood, characters, and decorative background required by the script. Choosing another period would require a search for artistic effects analogous to the costume ideals of the Italian Renaissance.

Concerning the problem of line in the costumes for this play, the demand seems to be for balance, symmetry, simplicity, and beauty of proportion. Clean-cut, simple lines seem to be necessary in the costumes, including pleated jackets, long skirts, mantles, and robes for ease and beauty of movement. Natural body lines, without grotesque exaggeration or distortion, should be stressed, and each costume should have a single central area of focus such as the neckline, collar, chest, or waist. Whatever the period, simple, clear-cut forms in collars, sleeves, hats, dresses, and jackets should be used to suggest the same simple, clear-cut, and balanced lines that are in the script. The heavy romanticism that frequently was poured into the visual presentation of this play in the nineteenth and twentieth centuries is not compatible with the nature of the script. It is the delicate romanticism of Botticelli and

Figure 12–16. Costume design for Mercutio by Motley for a production of *Romeo and Juliet* at the Memorial Theatre, Stratford-upon-Avon, England, 1954. From the Souvenir Program for 1954. Courtesy of the University of Illinois Library, Urbana-Champaign.

other early Renaissance painters that must find its way into the costumes for this play (see Figure 9–6).

Selecting fabrics for a production of *Romeo and Juliet* may take several directions. One is to choose the soft, supple movement and flat surfaces of the woolens seen in fifteenth-century Italian paintings and thus allow the beauty of the folds, accented by a minimum of well-placed ornament, to be the dominant costume effect. Another would be to use the soft, transparent effects of Botticelli's draping with soft sheen fabrics to achieve costumes that are very effective in movement under light. Another might be to use soft brocades as accents in sleeves, underskirts, and robes, keeping the brocade subordinate to the overall color tonality of the costume. This would give a rich effect

and should be carefully controlled if the simplicity and youthful freshness portrayed in the script are to be retained. No matter what the period, the fabrics should not be heavy or stiff, nor their surface texture too complex.

In color the costumes should probably incorporate the overall blond tonality of the Italian fifteenth-century painters and make little use of the complex light and dark patterns of Shakespeare's contemporaries such as El Greco and Tintoretto. The color should have the freshness, clarity, and sparkle of spring or early summer, with darker accents to give sharpness and clarity to the design. Even in the later scenes, when the tone is tragic and the scenes are set at night, the costume colors, although they might be lowered in value, should not be grayed or muddied. Clarity

Figure   12-17.   Original sketches for Paris and Tybalt by Lee Simonson for *Romeo and Juliet* as produced by the Stanford Players, Stanford University, 1949. Courtesy of the Stanford University Archives, Stanford, CA.

Figure 12-18.   Original sketch for Montague by the author, for a production of *Romeo and Juliet* by the Berkeley Shakespeare Festival, Berkeley, California, 1983. From the collection of the author.

should remain even in the darker colors required by the concluding scenes of the play (Figures 12-17 and 12-18).

The ornament for a production of *Romeo and Juliet* should be clean-cut, symmetrically placed, and used to carry the eye to the key points on the costume. Again the asymmetrical, twisted, complex ornamental patterns of late sixteenth-century mannerism, even though this is the period in which the play was written, seem completely inappropriate to this play's structure and imagery. The costume ornament should have the kind of clearcut organization, sparkle, and brilliance characteristic of the Queen Mab speech, or the paintings of Botticelli, da Cossa, and Fra Filippo Lippi. The ornament used in the costume designs must not be merely added to the costumes for decoration, but must be integral to the line of the total costume. The best ornament or trim for this play includes accents of brocade in sleeves, tiny borders of braid or gems, small amounts of jewelry, and contrasting linings in sleeves, capes, and robes. Basically, it is the simple structure of the costume itself that creates the major decorative or ornamental effect (Figure 12-19).

Figure 12–19. Costume designs for Prince Escalus and attendants by Ann Roth, for a production of *Romeo and Juliet* as presented at the American Shakespeare Festival Theatre, Stratford, Conn., 1965. From *Designing and Making Stage Costumes* by Motley, Watson-Guptill, New York, 1964. Courtesy of Ann Roth.

Hamlet

With the opening of the seventeenth century and the writing of his first great "dark tragedy," *Hamlet,* we find that Shakespeare has revised all the dimensions of his dramatic art. England after the Essex rebellion had taken on the trappings of a police state, and, as had happened more than a half-century before in the rest of Europe, a heavy disillusionment

and despair took hold of the land and its people. The national pride and patriotic excitement that had accompanied the defeat of the Armada had waned, and in Elizabeth's last few years the country had to look forward to the reign of a foreigner from Scotland. England, which had borrowed only casually from the mannerist styles of the continent since the days of Henry VIII and had used mannerist ideas only in an ornamental way, now had its own optimism shaken and began to accept the disproportions, complexities, and ambiguities of mannerism as a deeply felt expression of the social and psychological disturbances of the time. Hamlet resides in this new world; his mind is tainted, his heart is heavy, he feels there is something rotten in the state, he is obsessed with an almost medieval sense of death. It is for this character, within this tainted world, that Shakespeare devises a whole new technique of dramatic art.

PLOT AND STRUCTURE. It was Aristotle's belief that a well-constructed plot for tragedy should be single in issue, so that if any action were to be displaced or removed, the whole structure would be disjointed. The action of *Hamlet* is far from single in issue, and the principal effect of the play is to present the audience with a multiple sense of action that leaves it with a sense of ambiguity and disturbance. Everywhere there seems to be a double statement, a psychological inner world and a concrete outer world; and Hamlet certainly takes this double view of the world, seeing life as a bad dream as well as a horrible reality. Along with other characters in the later Jacobean theatre, Hamlet takes a violently dramatic view of reality. Although his acts seem to be involved with ordinary experience, they are also driven by some obsessive psychology that exists outside the usual ethical-moral world. His insecurity and psychological torment are presented within a framework of scenes shifting from comedy to horror, sanity to madness, brilliant external pageantry to almost impenetrable inner thought. There is also the shift within the same scene from inward emotion to outward action without clear transition, from foreground soliloquy to background pageantry without the usual sense of logic.

Throughout the plot all the characters, in one way or another, share a concern for the welfare of Denmark, but this is the only truth that remains constant. Generally, the truths of this play are unstable and changing, presented either at a high pitch, near hysteria, or so low that they are almost inaudible. All of this is the hallmark of mannerist composition and structure.

CHARACTERIZATION. The characterizations in this play seem ambiguous operating on two levels as psychological relationships and symbols of the state's decay. The playwriting method used allows abrupt shifts from the deeply psychological to the symbolic and has equally violent shifts of idea and personality within each of these dual levels. One of the major reasons for the sense of instability in this play stems from the character of Hamlet, who is of a mercurial temperament—outgoing yet inward, almost in the same instant. He is a compendium of the contrasts that are evident in all human nature. Even outwardly he must be interpreted both as the typical avenger in a melodrama and as the complex and introspective Prince, powerless to act. Repeatedly, we see the characterization of Hamlet developing from opposing impulses, and the only explicit line of transformation and development that recurs throughout the play is his attitude toward death as it progresses from "To be or not to be" to the Graveyard Scene and finally to the "readiness is all" speech. Throughout the play Hamlet acts as the guide for audience feeling—thinking and mirroring, as the Chorus often did in Greek drama, all the hopes and fears of humankind. In mannerist terms he is like the *Sprecher* or Speaker in paintings by Tintoretto and El Greco—a sharply accented figure in the foreground who faces the spectator while gesturing or glancing toward the background action. Hamlet, through his soliloquies at the edge of the stage, is the intermediate figure leading the audience from theatrical situation on stage to the non-theatrical world outside, from the world of events to the world of the inner mind.

Each of the other major characters is used to provide contrast to Hamlet and to give a particular view of the state's ill health. All act indirectly; all have a bias, a very partial view of the facts; and all help to define the action. In short, each has a dominant drive placed in opposition or relation to the conflicting motives that drive Hamlet forward through the play.

THEME. The themes of this play are many, but they tend to group about the psychological contrast of father-son and mother-son relationships and the political disease that saps the strength and power of a state. The themes are from many points of view strikingly like those in *Oedipus,* in which the father-son and mother-son relationships are the key to the play, and society must be purged before the plague (or the rottenness in the state) is lifted. Both plays begin with an invocation to the well-being of the state; in both the destiny of the individual and of the society are closely intertwined, and in both the suffering of the royal victim seems to be necessary before purgation and renewal can be achieved. These themes are achieved in *Hamlet* through a series of ritual scenes that are ceremonious invocations of the well-being of society, while in *Oedipus* the whole play is a ritual; and the theme of order in the Renaissance monarchy is a direct successor to the theme of order in the cosmic framework presided over by the Greek gods.

DIALOGUE. Shakespeare's dramatic poetry in this play is immensely complex. The use of blank verse allows for great flexibility, broken rhythms, and the interjection of prose, while still permitting great formality and elevation of tone when required. The most important element is the imagery developed by the figurative use of language. It provides visual associations, sharp contrasts, and ironic descriptions that portray in a mysterious, ambiguous, yet vivid way the condition of sickness that pervades the state and all who live in it. The pictorial imagination behind the imagery suggests the path of any sickness or infection that strikes, spreads, and finally devours the innocent and the guilty together.

The use of language in the play is firmly designed to create the most sensory impact possible on the audience. For example, the famous description, "What a piece of work is Man," lifts optimistic imagery to great heights, only to be turned inside out by the ironic last line, in which Hamlet indicates his own bitter point of view. Throughout the play, language is used in this same shifting way to build contrasting, changing, complicated images of life.

RHYTHM.   The forward pace and rhythm of action in a play such as *Hamlet* is very much complicated by sharp shifts in the mood, texture, and force of the action. The rhythm created by moving from intimate soliloquy to large-scale pageantry, from softly whispered dialogue to shouted verbal climaxes reveals the internal design of the play as seeming to run the gamut of contrasting emotions. The rhythm constantly changes from tension to relaxation, and the audience is never certain what rhythmic pattern will come next.

SPECTACLE.   There are three great opportunities for visual splendor and pageantry in the play: the opening court scene, the scene in which the play within the play is presented, and the final duel scene. Each of these ritual ceremonial scenes, representing the social order in the decaying state, allows for full visual splendor. The action of the play takes place in many locales, most of which are in and around the Castle of Elsinore. The play requires the suggestion of many passageways and rooms within the palace, a great hall, a parapet, a graveyard, and even a plain away from the castle. These, in Shakespeare's time, would have been placed in the various areas of the Elizabethan stage. Properties are limited to thrones, tables, chairs, a bed, a grave, and a funeral bier. In contributing to the spectacle, costumes are important in establishing the

ritual and ceremony of court life, the mystical quality of the Ghost, the horror of Ophelia's madness, the mourning of Hamlet, and the coldness of the night on the parapet.

Visual Presentation of *Hamlet*

The first choice that must be made in presenting *Hamlet* is whether to reproduce the locations found on the Elizabethan stage or to plan a new arrangement. In many ways there is a great advantage in having the upper stage for the parapet, the trap center stage for the grave, the full width from door to door with courtiers above for the large court scenes; but there is also a sense of rigidity and a lack of rhythmic flow when the stage space is not designed specifically for the structural arrangements of the play. If a choice is possible, it would seem better to retain those elements of the Elizabethan stage that really do further the rhythmic flow and structural development of the play, and incorporate them into a plan for stage space that contains the sharp contrasts and tensions of this mannerist composition. The necessity for a forestage is primary. Hamlet, acting like the *Sprecher* in mannerist painting, must come forward and commune directly with the audience and then move upstage to join the pageantry of a larger scene.

Another very important consideration is the disposition of the space available for the three great scenes of ritual pageantry. Is the area for the thrones of Claudius and Gertrude to be upstage center, to the right or left downstage, or down close to the forestage? This placement is especially important for viewing the play within the play. The director must decide whether his audience is to read through the backs of the King and Queen to the Players, glance at them on the other side of the stage while watching the play, or observe the Players performing downstage in front of Claudius and Gertrude (Figure 12–20). To solve the problem of spatial arrangement artistically and effectively is in many ways to set the artistic style and production approach for the entire

Figure 12–20. The Player King and Queen perform in a production of *Hamlet* presented by the California Shakespeare Festival, Visalia, California, 1980. Designed by John Conklin and based on the paintings of Gustav Klimt. Courtesy of the California Shakespeare Festival.

play. The mannerist qualities in the play's structure will profit most by an asymmetrical, unconventional placement that will give a sense of imbalance and discomfort to the unraveling events of the scene. And then again, the conventional symmetrical plan usually selected for the duel scene would profit from a certain sense of imbalance through placement of the thrones and the grouping of the courtiers. However, an upstage center blocking of Fortinbras would serve to conclude the play on a stable note of balance and order.

Tintoretto's *The Last Supper,* from San Giorgio Maggiore in Venice, with its tilted diagonal composition, sharp shifts in placement and focus, and strong eruptions of light against darkness, is an artistic work that affects the viewer very much like the play *Hamlet* (Figure 12–5). It stresses a ritual moment during the Last Supper that in its torchlit, sulphurous, supernatural illumination is analogous to that moment when Claudius rises and rushes from the scene calling for lights. A visual work such as *The Last Supper* cannot be used in any literal way to design this scene in

Hamlet, but it can serve as an excellent stimulus for the creative imagination and as a visual catalyst for the images and impressions suggested by the play. It can also reinforce the importance of mood, ambiguity, tension, and mystery that are more important in this play than the actual contours of the setting. It is the disposition of space, use of lighting, and establishment of mood through suggested texture and placement of forms, not a specific period style of architectural ornament, that are the keys to a good background for *Hamlet.*

The period chosen for the costumes is relatively unimportant. It is the appropriate choice of texture, line, and color to reinforce the tensions, sharp contrasts, mysteries, and shifting planes of reality that will aid in creating exciting costume designs. For example, a painting such as *The Burial of Count Orgaz* by El Greco, a contemporary of Shakespeare, might become an exciting visual inspiration for *Hamlet* costumes (Figure 12–21). Although the color in this painting has none of the ease of color transitions found in high Renaissance painting, the sulphurous yellows, heavy golds,

Figure 12–21. El Greco, *The Burial of Count Orgaz*, the Church of Santo Tomé, Toledo, Spain. A possible design source for a production of Shakespeare's *Hamlet* in a true mannerist style. Courtesy of the Spanish National Tourist Office.

acid greens, and unpleasant magenta reds against large background accents of white, gray, and black give an immediate sense of dramatic and theatrical impact. The stiff, crackling satin folds and the heavy brocaded immobility of the robes produce disturbing contrasts. The heavily ornamented armor of the Count completely contrasts with the dead black costumes of the courtiers surrounding him, and the black figure of the boy in the left foreground is in sharp contrast to the rich red and gold robes of the Saints. One can imaginatively identify this boyish foreground figure as Hamlet, while the rich, complicated, and overlarge patterns of gold brocade accented with red and white worn by the Church fathers could be used as mantles for Claudius and

Gertrude. The Count's armor could be used as inspiration for the Ghost, the black noblemen behind the dead Count as the basis for many of the Danish courtiers required in *Hamlet,* and the cowled Jesuit priests as ominous accents in the court scenes. The magentas, greens, and yellows used as accents in Heaven might be used effectively as accents in the mantles or short gowns of characters such as Rosencrantz and Guildenstern, while the Player King and Queen might be dressed in mantles of black and white to mirror the patterns in the robes of Claudius and Gertrude (Figure 12–22). This transference of images captures the inner qualities and techniques of mannerist style without depending on a specific period line. Consider, as a second example, the work of a

243

Figure 12-22. The Player King and Queen from *Hamlet* in a production by the Oregon Shakespeare Festival, Ashland, Ore., 1961; costumes by the author. Illustrates the exaggerated fabric patterns, white makeup, and sinister effects found in mannerist Renaissance fashion. Photo by the author.

painter completely removed from the period of Shakespeare, Caspar David Friedrich. A German Romantic painter of the early nineteenth century (with many mannerist tendencies), he painted lonely scenes of figures silhouetted in moonlight against gnarled and broken trees, misty harbors and rocks, open windows at sunset, all of which create a sense of pessimism, mystery, and profound melancholy. These works, although lacking the compositional distortions of mannerism, could be used as visual images for a production of *Hamlet* set in the 1820s. By stressing silhouette rather than ornamentation and accessories, using color as melancholic accents against black, exaggerating line, and trying for an ominous sense of decay in certain textural accents, a production of *Hamlet* could be placed in the early nineteenth century. With costumes related strongly to mood as well as to the structure of the play, the result would certainly be both Romantic and mannerist in its effect on the audience (Figure 12-23).

The period chosen as a setting for a production of *Hamlet* is therefore unimportant compared to the choice of the line, texture, and color in the costumes. These must suit the compositional or structural plan of the play and its overall mood of mystery and ambiguity. The play has been successfully produced in every historical period from the early medieval to the present. The measure of success is never the novelty and cleverness of the choice but the sensitivity in choosing fabrics, colors, and ornament, and the integration of these into appropriate costume lines.

The play in its color emphasis suggests a great deal of black, shot through with harsh, peculiar, misty, or offbeat accents of color. Color contrast should often be sharp and even shocking, and the color scheme should at no time be restful, easy, or relaxed. Even when little color is used and stress is placed on value contrasts created by light, these should be strong and the effects dramatic.

For texture, the range of fabrics can be

Figure 12–23.   Casper David Friedrich, *Man and Wife Gazing at the Moon,* 1819. An example of the dark and melancholy mood of this German romantic artist that could be useful in a production of *Hamlet* set in the early nineteenth century. Courtesy of the Nationalgalerie, Berlin.

great but should always be chosen for sharply varied effects and a strong tactile response. Subtle gradations in texture from a soft napped surface to one of elegantly refined fur, or from a soft woolen to a heavier one, should be put aside in favor of sharp textural contrasts and abrupt shifts in tactile effect.

If the actual texture of fabric is to be unimportant compared to the line or silhouette of the costume, then these same contrasts should be seen in the exaggeration of line or in the imbalance of silhouette. To use the normal fashion line from a particular period is to lose the

ominous mystery of the play. This is especially true of the women in the play; if one places Ophelia or Gertrude in the fashionable lines of the late eighteenth century, the early nineteenth century, or the twentieth century, the structure and the mood of the play are completely destroyed by the associations these fashions have for the audience. By abstracting the costume silhouette to its simplest form and then exaggerating those lines that will give a sense of the ambiguities, contrasts, and sharp changes in rhythm, theatrical gowns can be created to reinforce the meaning and mood of

Figure 12-24. Costume design for the Ghost in *Hamlet* by Jeannie Davidson, as produced by the Oregon Shakespeare Festival, Ashland, Ore., 1983. Photo courtesy of Jeannie Davidson.

the play, rather than illustrate or pictorialize Ophelia or Gertrude within a particular period (Figure 12-24).

Ornament in the costumes should be used as accent, a moment of textural richness in an otherwise flat costume, a point of focus in a complex area of pattern or texture. It should not be used as decoration.

Hamlet is complicated and ambivalent, and there are as many ways to design it effectively as there are designers to design it. But if the costumes are to be effective, they must not be pictorial or decorative—they must reinforce the mood of ambiguity, contrast, shifting rhythms, and ultimate mystery that lie at the heart of this drama.

13

Baroque Plays

Art and Culture in the Seventeenth Century

In an attempt to vanquish Protestants, skeptics, and heretics, the Council of Trent met for an extended period during the sixteenth century and finally closed in 1563. Having given new sanctions to dogma, reaffirmed the essentials of the Catholic Christian faith, and attempted to inspire a new piety in all Christians, the Council (which convened under the full cloud of mannerist doubt) laid the foundations for a renewal of Christian faith and a return to use of the arts in propagating the faith. When the Council had completed its work, it took another half-century for the arts to develop fully the secular richness, sensuous glory, and worldly grandeur that marked the new-found power of the Catholic Church.

While mannerist art and culture had been a universal European phenomenon, the new Baroque embraced so many different tendencies in each individual country that it is very difficult at a glance to find a universality or "oneness" of artistic style. There was, however, a certain wholeness of outlook and universality of vision in the new view of human beings in relation to the universe that stemmed from the discoveries of Copernicus, Galileo, and Kepler. With the theory that the earth moved about the sun instead of being the center of the universe, the cosmos came to be seen as an infinite continuity of interrelationships that even embraced humankind in its unbroken and systematic wholeness. Particularly, the new elliptical patterns of movement established for heavenly bodies had a direct influence on compositional patterns in art, and all of the strivings for exaggerated effect, lighting from within or from beyond, and movement leading outside the frame of a work of art may be viewed as a striving for the infinite. Although it may be an oversimplification, one might say that just as Gothic art seemed to strive for the spiritual, Baroque art strove for the infinite.

The Baroque art of courtly and Catholic circles seems totally different from the middle-class art of Protestant areas. The art of Bernini and Rubens depicts a very different inner and outer world than that expressed by Rembrandt. This art of the high Baroque, besides representing the triumph of the Counterrefor-

247

mation, indicated a renewed sense of absolutism in government. Throughout Catholic Europe, the new art from Rome was used to enhance the grandeur and power of each particular ruler and court in an attempt to erase the instabilities and insecurities of the Reformation.

An understanding of high Baroque art may be found in the following artistic concepts: (1) an *integration* of the mannerist tensions and energies of the preceding century by interweaving the elements of composition and building to an emotional release of energies; (2) a resolution of tensions and energies in the *richest of materials,* a sense of abundance, a sensuous richness of color, and a clustering of rich and varied forms; (3) *movement and energy,* and in architecture, sculpture, and painting, an excite-

ment of masses in motion; (4) *space*—the illusion of infinity, the stretching of distance, the expansion and contraction of areas controlled by artistically shifting boundaries, all used to give excitement and changing interest to the definition of space; (5) *light* as a theatrical and organizing factor in the creation of artistic works.

This art began in Italy in the opening decade of the seventeenth century in Rubens' paintings and, in the following decade, Bernini's sculpture (see Figures 9–10 and 9–13). By the middle of the century, the style dominated the Italian scene through the works of Bernini, Cortona, Longhena, and Rainaldi in architecture, Bernini in sculpture, and Cortona, Gaulli, and later Pozzo in large-scale paintings (Figure 13–1).

Figure 13–1. *The Triumph of the Name of Jesus* by Giovanni Baptista Gaulli, Church of the Gesù, Rome, 1672–1685 (ceiling fresco). An example of the extreme theatrical illusionism in decorative painting in the last half of the seventeenth century in Italy. Courtesy of Alinari/Art Resource, Inc.

Even within the courtly Catholic style, there is a major division between the sensualistic, active, monumental tendencies of Bernini and the stricter, more formal "classicistic" style that leads from the Caracci family to Poussin to the court art of Louis XIV. This classical Baroque style stresses many of the same elements that were operative in high Baroque, while reinforcing those ideals with rules and regulations: (1) The most important rule was that of *decorum,* the concept that every aspect of a painting is appropriate and correctly used in relation to another aspect of the work, with no hint of overstatement or excess. (2) The art was supposed to encompass composition on a high plane in an *elevated style.* (3) Subject matter was expected to be *mythological* or to depict scenes from *Greek, Roman, and Biblical history.* (4) The treatment of individual aspects of nature and personality were subordinated to the general, the *universal,* and the regular (as opposed to the irregular or abnormal). (5) Finally, all methods of painting were to be based on the *art of the Ancients* as revived in the classic Renaissance work of Raphael.

This art developed under the Caracci family and was continued in the work of their pupils, including Guido Reni and Domenichino; it was then introduced to France by the great classicist, Poussin, who carried this art to its highest point of achievement in the seventeenth century (see Figure 9–14).

Finally, the Baroque realism of Velazquez, Rembrandt, and Caravaggio was opposed to the grandiose subject matter and large-scale compositions usually associated with both high and classical Baroque. It made effective use of *theatrical lighting* from a single source, it was *closely focused* on its subjects without a great deal of background and accessories, and it stressed *individuality and personality* in its subject matter. It also chose *lower-class subjects* and treated historical or mythological subjects in a genre fashion.

The style developed in Italy under Caravaggio and his many imitators was carried to Holland by certain artists who formed the School of Utrecht, and was very important in the development of Rembrandt's work (Figure 13–2). It also spread to Spain through Spanish

Figure 13–2. *The Night Watch* by Rembrandt, Rijksmuseum, Amsterdam, 1642. An example of a virtuoso performance in movement and theatrical lighting effects. Photo courtesy of the Rijksmuseum, Amsterdam.

painters such as Ribera and was influential in forming the early style of Velazquez. Artists on the trade and travel routes from Italy to the north, such as Georges de la Tour, were also heavily influenced by this realistic style (see Figure 9–22).

Finally, some comment should be made on the difference between the art of Restoration England and Continental Baroque art. It should be remembered that the aristocrats who returned to England with Charles II in 1660 had spent the majority of their exile in France. Yet for all the pride that the court of the ''merry monarch'' took in things French in clothing, furniture, interior decoration, play-writing, and painting, there was still an unmistakably British tone to Restoration culture. It lacked the precise organization and neoclassical structure of the French court style of Louis XIV and the classical coolness of the paintings of Poussin (see Figure 9–14). The

culture tended to borrow from many sources: from the British past, from the classical French, from the flamboyant Italian, and from Dutch and Flemish bourgeois values. This is not to say that Restoration taste lacked a sense of grandeur and display; a room of the Restoration period appears very aristocratic and grand until it is compared with a room at Versailles. The formal coldness and rigid structuring of a French room will contrast strongly with an English room, which tends to be a rich and comfortable pastiche of decorative Baroque effects (Figure 13–3).

In the society portraits painted by Peter Lely there is much more stress on the casual and sensual than the formal and grand, and these portraits are a great help in capturing that exact mixture of sparkling brilliance, elegant sensuality, and relaxed yet organized structure that is so distinctive in Restoration comedy.

Figure 13–3. The Double-Cubed Room, Wilton House, near Salisbury, England, ca. 1649. Designed by John Webb under the influence of Inigo Jones. An example of the more eclectic and less formal Baroque style that was admired in England during the Restoration. Courtesy of the Earl of Pembroke, Salisbury, England.

Theatre and Drama in the Seventeenth Century

STAGING METHOD.   By 1650 the Italian theatre structure, which would be the dominant stage arrangement throughout the European theatre for the succeeding two hundred years, had fully developed in response to the great demands of the new theatrical form of opera. The auditorium was usually an elongated, U-shaped structure lined with boxes in tiers and a gallery at the back for servants and apprentices. Sight lines from the side boxes were, understandably, very poor. The floor area, which was filled with standees who could be removed for grand promenades and spectacular ballets, was considered an area for would-be gentlemen, ladies, and critics and cost less than the boxes but more than the gallery. The auditorium and the stage were divided by the heavy and usually ornate proscenium arch; the stage raked upward at an angle and was very deep (Figure 13–4). There was usually a considerable amount of space below the stage floor for

machinery and trapdoors, and some space above for painted sky borders; on the sides of the stage there was space only for the side wings to move out of sight behind the proscenium arch. Lighting was done with chandeliers hung in the auditorium and over the front of the stage, from footlights set behind reflectors along the edge of the stage, or by lights set against reflectors behind each set of wings (Figure 13–5).

The standard way of shifting from one setting to another (which can still be seen at the eighteenth-century Royal Theatre in Drottningholm, Sweden) was to have a series of flats covered in canvas and painted with details representing the sides of the setting, set one behind the other, in groups, up each side of the raked stage (Figure 13–6). In each group there were as many flats as would be needed to indicate all the locations required by the production. The back wall of the setting was formed of two larger flats or shutters which met in the center and, again, as many of these could be

Figure 13–4.   The Cuvilliés Theatre, Munich, mid-eighteenth century. An example of the U-shaped Baroque auditorium designed to focus attention on the royal box. Courtesy of KaiDib Films International, Glendale, California.

Figure 13–5. *Curtain Time* by Charles Coypel, showing the interior of the Petit Royal in Paris about 1700. An example of the tradition of lowered chandeliers before the beginning of the performance. From an engraving by Joulain and Gosselin as reproduced in *Theatre Pictorial* by George Altman, Ralph Freud, William Melnitz, and Kenneth Macgowan, University of California Press, Berkeley, 1953. Photo courtesy of William Melnitz.

Figure 13–6. A backstage view of the Royal Theatre, Drottningholm, Sweden, 1762. An example of the use of wings, borders, and the slotted floor system in use in the seventeenth- and eighteenth-century Continental theatre. Courtesy of the Drottningholm Theatre Museum.

set one behind the other as was required. Borders of two-dimensional framed cloths representing clouds or roofs completed the set above. At each change of scene and in full view of the audience, a set of shutters, wings, and a border were drawn away from the stage to reveal the next scene.

SCENERY.   The family of scene designers who most fully represent the development of the Baroque style in staging is the Bibiena, who operated throughout Europe from the late seventeenth to the late eighteenth century. Ferdinando Bibiena, founder of the dynasty and a great contributor to seventeenth-century scene design, introduced angled perspective in operatic settings, which gave a double vanishing point rather than the single central point of the usual wing-and-drop plan. He and his sons, Giuseppe and Antonio, developed to a high point the great descents by machine of deities from the heavens and expanded the ornamental and monumental aspects of stage setting (Figure 13–7).

COSTUMES.   The costumes for opera and classical tragedy used within these settings were rich, ornamental, formalized garments based originally on the lines of antique dress but abstracted by the seventeenth century into a very carefully structured basic silhouette with rich accessories. A plumed helmet or headdress, breastplate-shaped tunic, flaring skirt to above the knees, and a mantle and short soft boots to below the knee comprised the standard silhouette for men, although long robes were used for certain older or specialized types. The women's costumes usually consisted of a court gown with a hip-length overskirt and labels or tabs to break up the edge of the overskirt, the waist, the collar, and the shoulder. Sleeves were usually full and caught

Figure 13–7.   A design for an opera by Giuseppe Galli da Bibiena, The Metropolitan Museum of Art, 1719. An example of the grandeur and monumentality in painted perspective scenery associated with the work of the Bibiena family. From *Archittetura e Prospettiva,* Augsburg, 1740. Photo courtesy of The Metropolitan Museum of Art, New York, Harris Brisbane Dick Fund, 1931. All rights reserved, The Metropolitan Museum of Art.

Figure 13–8. Design for a theatrical costume by Jean Berain, for Hermione in Lully's *Cadmus and Hermione*, a lyric classical tragedy presented at the Académie Royale de Musique, Paris, 1674. Illustrates the plumed headdress, hanging sleeves, waist labels, long train, and heavily ornamented fabric used for the costume of a classical queen in the late seventeenth century. Photo courtesy of the Bibliothèque Nationale, Paris.

back to the elbow, and the hair or headdress was adorned with plumes. From this basic structure, ingenious designers were able to develop many subtle variations that suggested characters as varied as Turks, Indians, mythological satyrs and nymphs, classical heroes, and Arcadian shepherds. The style was highly developed in England in the work of Inigo Jones and in France by Henri Gissey and Jean Berain, as well as in the Italian opera of the seventeenth century (Figure 13–8). In comedies, such as those written by Molière and the Restoration playwrights in England, the costume style was basically that of contemporary dress with exaggerated effects for comic comment. All costumes designed for the stage had a very structured, classically organized basic silhouette overlaid with rich and decorative ornament. In this sense, stage costume was analogous to the method used in Baroque architecture whereby the basic structure was oriented toward balance and form, while the rich overlaid decoration achieved a dramatic, theatrical effect.

In Italy in the seventeenth century, the favorite dramatic form was no longer tragedy and comedy but *opera,* which had developed from the spectacular *intermezzi* of the sixteenth century. Opera was intended as a new attempt to approach Greek tragedy by stressing the music, dance, and choral dialogue long acknowledged as the essential elements of ancient Greek drama. Opera began to develop about 1597, culminating in the experiments in Venice from 1610 to 1640. By 1650, the new form was the rage throughout Italy and was rapidly spreading to all of Europe; and it was through the medium of opera that Italian ideals of spectacle and theatricality were introduced into other European courts and capitals.

In addition to opera and ballet, the third dramatic form that dominated the late seventeenth-century stage (particularly in France) was the comedies and tragedies of *neoclassicism.* It was based on the work of sixteenth-century critics in Italy who had analyzed classical Greek and Roman tragedy and set down many rules for playwriting. The drama was supposed to teach as well as please. It was supposed to have but a single action that developed in one place at one time, and the particulars and specifics of life were to be put aside in favor of the general and the universal. Characters were to be seen as representative types rather than as individuals, and all action was to conform to the appropriate expectations of the current social scene in matters of class, morality, and background. Both Molière and Racine followed this prescribed method in their plays while still adding much that was based on their own personal experience.

The so-called Restoration comedies written in England at this same time lacked the careful neoclassical structural method so much admired in France. They were known for sparkling wit, brilliant epigrammatic dialogue, sophisticated situations, and amoral characters, rather than for clear plots and direct story telling. Although some Restoration comedies derive from Molière they differ in the following ways: Molière wrote his comedies with a minimum of characters, no subplots, and within the unities of time, place, and action, whereas the Restoration playwrights, like their Elizabethan predecessors, used more characters, complicated plots with one or two subplots, and changes of setting. Molière's themes were very moral, whereas the themes of Restoration comedy were amoral—cynical self-knowledge was rewarded and foolishness punished. The plays, like the portraits of Lely, imply that people are corruptible and that their corruptibility must be accepted with a sophisticated, worldly tolerance (Figure 13–9). Molière stressed the ideals of moderation and balance; the Restoration playwrights stressed self-knowledge.

Figure 13–9.   Portrait of Anne Hyde, Duchess of York, by Peter Lely, National Gallery of Scotland, ca. 1660–1670. Illustrates the sensuous, loose silky clothing based on French styles imported to England by the aristocrats returning from exile. These fashions are much softer and lighter than the French and have overtones of boudoir sensuality. Photo courtesy of the National Gallery of Scotland, Edinburgh.

Tartuffe

Molière's comedies were greatly influenced by his exposure to *commedia dell'arte* and the classical comedies of Plautus and Terence. Through his efforts French classical comedy was accepted as equal to neoclassical tragedy in depth of insight into the human spirit. One of Molière's most controversial yet representative plays is *Tartuffe*.

PLOT AND STRUCTURE.   In this play, carefully organized form is always paramount, and the plot encompasses several distinct developments of action. The major portions of the play are clearly and logically developed, but the final change in the action that results in the arrival of the King's representative is forced and contrived. We may feel pleased that justice triumphed, but in terms of dramatic construction carefully prepared to lead to an inevitable conclusion, the resolution is opened to criticism.

The unities are strictly observed in this play, with only one room required for the action and the length of the action confined to a single day. The room requires little furniture, there are no extra characters except Mme Pernelle's maid and the guards, and all of the action is directly related to the main theme of the play. With the possible exception of its ending, *Tartuffe* is directly a part of the neoclassical tradition and can be admired for its purity of form.

CHARACTERIZATION.   All of the major characters are carefully developed to fit into the play's plot structure. Cléante is used to present the "common sense" view in the play and thus appears only in Act I, before Tartuffe has arrived, and again at the close of the play to point up the major theme of true piety versus false piety. He is not at all involved in the action of the play and acts only as a commentator.

Tartuffe, by being withheld from the action until the beginning of the third act, has had his character so fully developed by others that he is able to devote himself fully to his two love scenes. From his first speeches, urging Dorine to cover her bosom, to his later attempts to seduce Elmire, Tartuffe is portrayed primarily as a repressed sensualist. Only in the scene in which he is denounced by Damis do we glimpse some of the false humility and unctuous self-criticism that have duped Orgon. For the most part, what the audience concludes about his character is dictated by descriptions from other characters.

The maid Dorine, although appearing in each act, has her major part in the action early in the play as a foil to Orgon's extreme gullibility. Her charming candor is also used to contrast with the naiveté of the lovers and the falseness of Tartuffe. In fact, she provides most of the humor in the early part of the play through her witty and saucy exposé of all the exaggerated, self-conscious, and overly serious behavior surrounding her.

The lovers, Marianne and Valère, have one full scene in Act II that has a certain humorous charm, and thereafter they are of little importance. Marianne and Valère, like most lovers in Molière, are handsome, winning young people who deserve one another and are being kept apart by a biased, strong-willed parent.

Elmire is a worldly but moral woman who acts as the catalyst in exposing Tartuffe's rampant sensuality. Her appearances are unevenly distributed throughout the play, and she becomes crucial to the action only in those scenes in which Tartuffe pursues her. Orgon, on the other hand, is the key to the action, as it is only through the foolish good nature of men such as he that shams such as Tartuffe are able to flourish. Orgon is not really a fool, but more the typical prosperous businessman who is impulsive and stubborn and feels rather guilty about the money he has made. As in the case of many contemporary men of wealth, he wants to ease certain doubts that trouble his conscience by giving impulsively and generously to someone he feels is worthier than he. He totally misjudges Tartuffe because he does not analyze his character. Even when Tartuffe has been exposed, he misinterprets the difference between hypocrisy and piety and declares that henceforth he will turn his back on all pious people. Unlike Cléante, he cannot take a balanced view.

This play is usually viewed as a comedy in which the principal action of the plot lies in the revelation of character. Yet if the play is so dependent on character, it is surprising how little information is given about age and personal appearance. What we must realize is that Molière wrote for a specific group of actors, and that their individual characteristics would have expanded the roles as written in the script. For example, Tartuffe was played by a plump actor named Du Croisy, and because the actor looked healthy and well fed, much could be made of the dialogue about fasting and scourges. We also know that Molière, who was noted for his expressive face and body, played Orgon. Elmire was played by Molière's wife, who was only twenty-nine at the time. Mme Pernelle was played by a man and so would have been extremely comic in her exaggerated denunciations of all pleasure.

In summarizing the development of character in this play, one may say that the humor derives from the psychological relationships between character and situation. The norm of behavior is established by Cléante and Dorine, and all deviations from it are treated in a satirical manner.

THEME. As in all of Molière's plays, the basic theme is the importance of a balanced view of life. To Molière, the philosopher of moderation, true piety reveals itself through actions and not talk. A secondary theme, widely used in Roman comedy and *commedia dell'arte,* is the folly of forced marriage. The playwright insists that such marriages lead only to rebellion and adultery.

DIALOGUE. Although Molière wrote within the accepted Alexandrine form of his day, with brilliance and polish, his dialogue is essentially realistic prose. His verses, twelve feet long with a rhyme at the end, are clever, witty, and satirical, and they fully express peculiarities and idiosyncrasies of character, but they are seldom used for poetic purposes. To play Molière in prose translations is to miss the witty comment he makes on the traditional usage of Alexandrines. Only the polished symmetry and neat precision of English rhyming couplets is an approximation of the verse style.

RHYTHM. The urbane, gem-like, classical wit in Molière's plays is transmitted to an audience only when the rhythmic unrolling of the plot progresses with clear-cut precision. There is a sprightly, direct, onward movement from beginning to end, without sharp contrasts, abrupt breaks, or strong shifts of mood. The rhythmic flow is closely tied to the polished delivery of the symmetrically written rhymes of the Alexandrine.

SPECTACLE. The requirements for the visual spectacle are limited in this play, as in most Molière comedies. A place representing a room in Orgon's house, with a table, several chairs, a closet, and a door, is all that is required, although a staircase is frequently included from which Tartuffe may make an impressive first entrance. It can be produced in almost any period, but if it is placed in the time of Molière the costumes need not be complex nor richly ornamented as long as they represent the personality and social standing of each character. The lighting need not be varied at all; in Molière's time chandeliers hung over the acting area, and the effect of such constant static lighting is quite appropriate to the play.

Visual Presentation of *Tartuffe*

If one looks at a representative selection of stage settings for this play in recent years, the scenery falls into two general categories: (1) those settings that attempt to stress the structure and symmetrical balance of the play in a rather simple, abstract, decorative manner, and (2) those that attempt a more realistic portrayal of the interior of Orgon's wealthy, upper-class, bourgeois home. Each interpretation presupposes a particular approach to the

Figure 13-10. A scene from *Tartuffe* by Molière as produced by the American Conservatory Theatre, 1967. Directed by William Ball. Sets by Stuart Wurzell. Costumes by Jane Greenwood. Courtesy of The American Conservatory Theatre. Photo by Hank Kranzler.

total production. If it is considered important to stress the background of the characters, particularly Orgon's bourgeois temperament and taste, then the director may make many specific recommendations about scenery and property details that will set the mood (Figure 13-10). If the play is produced primarily to present the wit of the dialogue, the symmetry of the plot, and the universal types represented by the characters, it is often presented within an architectural suggestion of a room with balanced lines and simplified ornamentation acting as a framing device (see Figure 9-26). One approach obviously gives a more varied presentation of ornamentation, texture, and color to represent the wealth and comfort of a bourgeois home, while the other offers a setting that is as spare and simple as the structure of the play and acts only as a frame to the action. In either case, only those items that will clearly re-

veal the character and personality of the household should be used.

In costume, the difference between the two approaches will not be as striking. If a semi-realistic approach is chosen in order to stress the personality and status of the various characters, more variety in texture, line, and color will be needed; if one chooses to stress the classical nature of the script, then the designs should be simple, abstract parts of an overall pattern.

When designing a production of Molière, it could be beneficial to turn to a contemporary Dutch painter such as Vermeer for inspiration. In Vermeer's work are found both the classical spirit operative in Molière's play and the domestic bourgeois setting. A study of Vermeer's painting can be helpful even when the play is produced in a period other than the seventeenth century. His subtle and simple use

Figure 13–11. *A Lady and a Gentleman at the Virginals* by Jan Vermeer, St. James's Palace, London, ca. 1664. An example of the cool, carefully composed, classic, bourgeois interiors painted by this contemporary of Molière whose compositional method is similar to that of the French playwright. Photo courtesy of the Lord Chamberlain, St. James's Palace, London. Copyright reserved.

of color, line, and texture is similar to Molière's spare craftsmanship and can give the designer an insight into how to translate the verbal methods of Molière into the visual designs for the play (Figure 13–11).

If one is to produce the play in a domestic bourgeois setting, the choice of color should have a greater range than if one uses a more restricted and abstract approach. In either case, the colors should be clear and cool, not muddied or warm. If a designer is to relate color usage correctly to Molière's compositional method, a restriction should be made on the number of colors used in a particular costume. Usually a costume is most appropriate for a play such as this if it is primarily of one basic hue accented or complemented by another color or a neutral. Even in a bourgeois setting, the approach should be one of clarity and simplicity in the use of color. In the more abstract approach to background, the costumes can be still more sharply defined in simplicity of color

and accent. The costume can be designed in a single cool, clear color accented very sharply with ribbons, bows, or braid of contrasting hue. The placement of such accents becomes a test for the eye, since the width, the length, and the location of each such color accent must be exact.

Texture in the domestic setting may be varied, and the use of pattern can be greater than that used in a more abstract concept. However, great variety of textural surface within a single costume should be avoided. If, for example, a single rich brocade is used for a coat, the pattern of the brocade should be subordinate to the shape of the coat and to its overall color tonality (Figure 13–12). One major texture per costume is best, accented by small amounts of another texture. When a more abstract approach is taken, a clean, crisp, but not too insistent texture is best for the major fabric for each garment, with a strong minor texture used for accents. For example, a

Figure 13-12. A scene from *Le Bourgeois Gentil-homme* by Molière as produced by The American Conservatory Theatre, 1977. Directed by William Ball. Costumes by Robert Fletcher. An example of structured and controlled design achieved through limitation in color and ornamentation. Courtesy of The American Conservatory Theatre. Photo by William Ganslen.

crisp, shiny bengaline faille, accented with velvet ribbon in various widths and carefully selected amounts might be used for all the major costumes.

The line of the costume is extremely important when simplicity is used in color and texture. The silhouette of each costume must be exactly right for the character and action in the play. Every precaution in boning, corsetting, padding, and stiffening must be taken to ensure that the silhouette remains as sharp and clear as the dialogue and plot structure. The exact silhouette should be achieved before it is submitted for final approval by the director, and the designer should oversee the construction period to ensure that the costume is exactly as the designer and the director had envisioned it. In a domestic setting, the variety in line may be greater than in an abstract production. However, it will not be a great factor in the designs, since the texture and color will have as much interest as the line. In an abstract setting, texture and color are often subordinated to line; the silhouette and internal shapes within the costume will attract the most attention. The width of a cuff, the flair of a bow, the fall of a piece of lace, the size of curls on a wig—all become very important when the method of design is spare, simplified, and intellectually planned. If the comments in costume are exactly right and are complemented by polished acting, the performance will be as pleasing visually, despite its simplicity, as the play is verbally. American audiences, weaned on Shakespearean comedy, often fail to understand how Molière's plays are conceived. Many American and British designers, impressed by the richness and variety of the courtly costumes of the late seventeenth century, squander their wit and ingenuity to achieve a rich, lavish spectacle of varied costumes. This buries a Molière play, rather than projecting and reinforcing it. To design Molière in the same way that one designs Restoration comedy is a mistake. The latter has much more variety of character and scene than does Molière, and demands more complex visual effects. A careful study of Molière's comedies and a direct attempt to equate the visual approach to the literary method will produce costumes and settings that (although not lavish in themselves) will reinforce and support the play (Figure 13-13).

Figure 13–13.   Costume designs by the author for a production of *Tartuffe* by the Stanford Repertory Theatre, Stanford University, 1965. From the collection of the author.

Phèdre

The plays of Racine mark the height of French classical tragedy, and Racine is to the French tradition of tragedy what Molière is to comedy. Racine's reputation rests assuredly on *Phèdre*, which was written in 1677 and adapted from the Greek tragedy *Hippolytus*. It is a perfect example of the tragedy of reason based on a single moment of experience and a single angle of vision. In Racine's tragedies there is little external action; the drama results from internal psychological conflict centered on a single character, and this conflict is usually found in terms of passion versus reason or love versus duty.

PLOT AND STRUCTURE.   In French classical tragedy, form is more important than any other single factor. Originally, French classicists based their ideas on a misinterpretation of Aristotle; "a serious action of a certain magnitude" was construed as referring directly to an action involving people of rank whose every action had the correct measure of appropriateness, a decorum that worked itself out in good manners and high breeding. The word "action" meant the results of action, the facts, deeds, and chain of events that produce a final psychological result. Action is never physical or actual stage action. The "action" demonstrates the tragic life of the soul as it struggles with the problems of reason versus passion. It is reason that is the only value; it is reason alone that is to be obeyed. In his writing, Racine develops the gnawing power of passion to demonstrate to the audience the importance of a rational mode of action, an importance he politely assumes they will recognize.

The external action is simple, while the inner, psychological action and character relationships are very complex. Each action in the plot is thus magnified by the varied and involved emotional reactions to it on the part of each character. In its action, the play develops with absolute clarity and simplicity; the unity of time is completely observed; the action is entirely within the palace; and the development of the plot is completely focused on the consequences of a single great psychological aberration.

It is also interesting to look at the changes made by Racine in remodeling Euripides' *Hippolytus* for the seventeenth-century French court. Racine attempts, as much as possible, to eliminate reliance on the gods, even treating the death of Hippolytus as a result of the inevitability of fate rather than as the work of the sea god, Poseidon. He also eliminates the chorus, substituting confidences to a close servant or companion for the revelation of inner thoughts. The neoclassical tradition assumed that both long soliloquies and a chorus acting as if of a single mind violated the rules of "natural" or acceptable speech and action.

Finally, it is very evident that the religious, natural, and large world view of Greek dramatic ritual is missing, and a new, limited, and artificial ritual has replaced it in the guise of a strategy regulating all social functions at the court of Louis XIV. There is a lesser sense of life and ritual than in Greek tragedy, but the rational planning and polished structure are superb.

CHARACTERIZATION.   The role of Phèdre is to French drama what the role of Hamlet is to English drama. It is one of the most difficult parts to play, because there is so little external action and so much internal conflict to communicate to an audience. The shifts in mood and subtle changes of emotional climax must

be clearly projected. Resignation turning to hope in the opening scene, passion then overwhelming reason, humiliation after Hippolytus' rejection, the horror and terror of Theseus' return, the jealousy of Aricia, the bitter denunciation of Oenone, and Phèdre's final moment of greatness in death—all these emotional changes must be shown, as well as the smaller emotional shifts within each scene. In every way, it is one of the most outstanding female roles in the history of the theatre. Audiences have always both admired and pitied the Queen and suffer with her in her passion and remorse. At the play's end she has achieved a truly tragic stature (Figure 13–14).

Figure 13–14.   A photo of a costume for Phèdre in a production of *Phèdre* by Racine at the Comédie Française in 1959. Costume designed by Cassandre. Courtesy of the Comédie Française.

Other characters are confronted with less violent conflicts that are central to their personalities but not to the main line of the tragedy. Theseus, for example, is late in arriving on the scene and acts as a catalyst rather than an initiator of action. He has the natural responses expected of a king, a great warrior, a strong husband, and a stern father, and he shares fully in the tragic emotions of the play's conclusion. Hippolytus is torn by typical Racinian dilemmas: love for Aricia versus a sense of duty to his father, respect for his stepmother and her position versus the strong desire to protect his father's honor. In short, all of the major characters attempt to act rationally, but they are swayed by irrational forces that seem beyond their control. They all act within the ritual strategy or courtly game that is the basic plot of neoclassical drama. All follow the character dictums of the period; they have dignity, they act with decorum, they are of noble birth, and they live by the rules of personal honor.

THEME. The theme is so intricately bound to plotting and character that it is apparent at every moment of the play. It can be stated in several ways and viewed from a number of angles, but it basically involves the moral idea that tragic results occur when passion is allowed to usurp the position of thought, reason, decorum, and good breeding in society.

DIALOGUE. The language of the play is ordered in the most logical and musical manner, and the dialogue, even when expressing the full power of passion, is outwardly rhetorical and static while expressing the most brilliantly subtle shifts of inner emotion. The tightly controlled Alexandrine verse form can be built step by step to towering climaxes, and then be made to ebb to devastating quietness like the waves of the sea. When such great speeches or "tirades" are brilliantly performed, they can bring an audience to its feet in thunderous applause, and all actors who have essayed *Phèdre* agree that to do justice to the form takes tremendous technique, power, and emotional control.

RHYTHM. The rhythm or underlying musical progression in *Phèdre* is closely connected to the dignified rise and fall of the carefully ordered verse. Since there are no abrupt breaks in the action or sharp and unaccountable shifts in mood or personality, the progression throughout the play is as clear and ordered as the rhythm of the sea. For each climax there is a carefully controlled rise and an equally ordered fall. The ebb and flow establish the essence of the "tragic rhythm" of the drama.

SPECTACLE. The physical appearance of set and costumes is not indicated in the script at all, and the audience is aware only that the play takes place in the Palace at Troezen. Furnishings should be minimal or nonexistent in a setting of a simple, classic, monumental background. The costumes should reflect the station and the inherent decorum of the noble-spirited character, and the lighting could remain unchanged throughout the play.

Visual Presentation of *Phèdre*

What sources to use as a basis for designing the production is the major question to be faced in presenting this play to a modern public. Should the play be designed in authentic Greek styles reflecting the costume and architecture of the fifth century B.C., when the original *Hippolytus* was written, or should the production attempt to suggest the neoclassical theatrical dress of the age of Louis XIV? Since the play differs sharply in mood and story line from the original by Euripides, it may seem logical to re-create for a modern audience that interpretation of classical antiquity familiar to the seventeenth-century audience that first saw this play. However, after a closer look at the visual sources, especially for costume, the designer may despair at achieving anything but laughter from full-bodied wigs, plumed helmets, and over-ornamented breastplates. Another possibility, which has been attempted once or twice in recent years, is to use neither fifth-century sources nor those from the age of Louis XIV, but only the style of the play itself as a basis for costumes and settings, suggesting no specific period. A fourth idea is to use the modern period with as little detail as possible. With careful planning, insight, and ingenuity this great tragedy can be successfully designed in any of these major ways, as long as the essential nature of the play's composition is kept clearly in mind.

In designing the play (as it has most frequently been interpreted in the twentieth century) in modifications of Greek dress of the fifth century B.C, the designer would be wise, before turning to specific architectural or dress sources from the period, to look at the paintings of Racine's contemporary, Poussin. Both men wanted to liberate seventeenth-century art from excess, from superficial or external detail; both base their work on a central idea or moral theme, and both strip their work to a formal, organized disposition of the simplest visual or emotional effects. Racine and Poussin distill earlier Baroque masses and expanding energies into essences of pure emotion or pure feeling rationally conceived and organized. It is not so much the garments in Poussin that will help the designer of *Phèdre,* but the handling of outlines, the use of draping, the application of color, and the balance and proportions so carefully controlled in a group of people placed in front of some temple or palace (see Figure 9–14). Once the art of Poussin has been studied, the designer may turn to specific Greek sources and abstract those elements of form and line that will clearly be most appropriate for *Phèdre,* without getting involved in the intricacies of Greek ornamental detail. If this approach is taken, the designer will be able to suggest a Greek setting of time and place while developing fully the monumental, cold, heroic, artificial, artistic effects of Poussin, which contain that sense of removal and decorum needed for Racine.

However, there is one problem with this approach. Despite the most careful innovations on the part of the designer, the Greek draperies of Poussin based on fifth-century styles can never completely capture the formality, decorum, and artificiality of the court of Louis XIV. Only in the late seventeenth-century stage costume versions of classical dress do we find this. Therefore, if a designer has fully absorbed the painting of Poussin and is fully aware of how far one can proceed with seventeenth-century theatrical sources without getting a comic effect, then a carefully modified and subtly abstracted late Baroque approach to production may most closely capture the essence of the play. Full-bottomed wigs could be replaced by formally waved long hair, which gives grandeur and stature without looking ludicrously artificial. The heavy ornamentation of seventeenth-century stage dress should be avoided, complexity in color and fabric should be discarded, and the structure of the costume should be accented in exactly the right places with the appropriate ornamentation. Everything should be calculated to reinforce the formal, polished structure of the play and its characters, and nothing should be added that is merely picturesque, rich, or decorative.

Finally, if the designer and the director choose to produce the play in a more contemporary way for a modern audience, an abstract modern setting or one that attempts to suggest no particular period may be chosen. Certainly modern-dress items such as full dress formal evening wear for men have the formality and classical restraint of Racine, while simple uniforms and classically inspired gowns can be designed to capture the essence of both Poussin and Racine. Even a palace background can be designed in the modern manner to have all of the coolness and simplicity demanded by Racine's dramaturgy.

With regard to the specific problem of costume and the nature of the visual effects required by *Phèdre,* no matter what the period in which the play is being presented, the texture of the fabrics chosen for the play should not be complicated and varied (Figure 13–15). A single major texture that is not too insistent, yet not monotonous, and that will hold the carefully chosen shape and line desired throughout the action could be chosen for all the major costumes in the play, with other textures used only as accent. Woolens that do not absorb too much light and that hold their carefully

Figure 13–15. A scene from *Phèdre* by Racine as produced by the University of Kansas City in 1958 with costumes by the author. All gowns were of heavy wide-wale corduroy, breastplates were of felt, and trim was of heavy gold braid. Photo by the author.

planned line might be used; or if a richer effect is desired, a bengaline faille, velveteen velour, or wide-wale corduroy might be chosen. These could be trimmed with gold cord, jewels, small quantities of rich brocade, or heavy lace, with a single major accent or ornamental effect used throughout; various accents probably should not be mixed.

The colors could be selected from the clear, pure, rich hues of Poussin, with few subtly grayed or changeable color effects. Each cos-

tume, as in Poussin, could be primarily of a single color trimmed with neutrals or metallics and another minor color used for accent. For example, if Phèdre is costumed in a deep, rich red gown, it can be trimmed with gold and accented with white. Hippolytus might be costumed in yellow-gold trimmed with metallic gold and accented in white, while Theseus might be gowned in purple accented in metallic gold and relieved with a neutral beige (Figure 13–16).

Figure 13–16. Costume designs by the author for a production of *Phèdre* by Racine as produced at the University of Kansas City in 1958. From the collection of the author.

Most important is the choice and use of the costume line. It must be grand, imposing, formal, graceful, and theatrical, and great amounts of fabric carefully disposed are needed to give this effect. Mantles and long trains can help to achieve this sweeping line, and a variety of hanging sleeves ending in a tassel might be used to accent and reinforce the carefully planned upward-reaching gestures of Phèdre. Even if a modified or abstracted modern-dress approach is adopted, mantles and trains can be used effectively in the costume scheme. And at the beginning and end of each major costume line, the designer should create an accent through ornamentation. In the theatrical dress of the seventeenth century this frequently was a clasp, an edging in gold braid, or a tassel, but even in Greek clothing there is ample possibility for use of Greek decorative pins or fibulae and ornamental borders. In modern dress there are manifold possibilities in brooches, orders, sashes, and military buttons. The ornamentation should never be simply decorative but should act as an accent for the entire costume.

Restoration Comedy

Restoration comedies are noted for their sharp wit, sophistication, amorality, and complex plotting. They differ from neoclassic comedy in their diffusion, sensuality, and lack of strict form, and the emphasis in the plays is on rewarding a superior (if sometimes cynical) self-knowledge and on punishing foolishness (the plays imply that people are corruptible and that their corruptibility must be accepted with a sophisticated, worldly tolerance).

The Relapse

Let us look briefly at *The Relapse,* a play written in 1696 by Sir John Vanbrugh, who was a courtier and part-time architect. (He designed the famous Blenheim Palace for the Duke of Marlborough.) The play was written in answer to a play by Colley Cibber called *Love's Last Shift,* because Vanbrugh did not think that Cibber's play presented an accurate picture of human nature.

PLOT AND STRUCTURE.   *The Relapse* is based, as is so often the case in comedy, on an exchange of identities, and it has two quite separate plots. One plot follows the fortunes of the newly married Loveless and Amanda; the other follows the fortunes of Fashion and his brother, Lord Foppington, who is about to enter into an arranged marriage with the daughter of a country squire named Sir Tunbelly Clumsy. There are many complications and amours until Loveless is finally seduced by the amorous Berinthia and Lord Foppington loses his intended wife to his brother.

CHARACTERIZATION.   The plot's complications are far less interesting than the characters. Lord Foppington is a particularly outstanding example of the overweening and pretentious fop; his dressing scene is a high point in the production and a challenge to the designer. Everything about the personality and character of Lord Foppington is exuberantly excessive and overdrawn, and he is the perfect butt for commentary and satire throughout the play. The other characters are either exaggerated caricatures, such as Sir Tunbelly Clumsy and the matchmaker Coupler, or sophisticated and worldly aristocrats who know just how to play the game of love so admired by Restoration society.

THEME.   The theme concerns the decline —or "relapse"—of a supposedly true love and the discomfiture of the man of excess.

DIALOGUE.   The language is witty and clever, filled with exaggerated expletives and expressions coined by Lord Foppington and licentious and suggestive repartee from those involved in the game of love.

RHYTHM.   The rhythm of the play is dictated by the need to structure the two plot lines into intertwining and overlapping scenes; there is thus no through line of development, but a casual balance of scenes of excess with scenes of wit, and a series of individual rhythms rather than an overall rhythm.

SPECTACLE. In Restoration productions of *The Relapse,* a number of settings were necessary for scenes in town and in the country house of Sir Tunbelly Clumsy. Each setting would have been a separate room formed with wings and shutters, with occasional pieces of furniture carried on and off by servants. The costumes would have been the rich contemporary fashions of the day except for the laughably exaggerated clothes of Foppington and the country garb of Sir Tunbelly Clumsy and his daughter, Hoydon.

Visual Presentation of *The Relapse*

The play could be presented today with a certain quaintness by using the wing-and-shutter system or, more casually, with folding screens. If the presentation of full interiors is desired, then a turntable system might be used, or a series of wagons. In any production, the designer should use Restoration interiors, as well as the structure of the play, as a guide, in order to catch some of the imbalances and the subtle and casual asymmetries that make Restoration plays distinct from French comedies of the time. Costumes should take their lead from the fashion drawings of the day and the ideals expressed in the paintings of Sir Peter Lely, who stressed elegant sophistication and sensuousness, careful fit and casualness, all at the same time. Rich, slippery, sensuous fabrics with light reflective surfaces will be analogous to the sharpness of the wit, the sparkle of the dialogue, and the sensuality of the imagery (Figure 13–17).

Figure 13–17. A scene from *The Relapse* by Sir John Vanbrugh as produced by The American Conservatory Theatre, San Francisco, 1970. Directed by Edward Hastings. Costumes by Robert Fletcher. Illustrates a production approach to a late Restoration comedy. Courtesy of The American Conservatory Theatre. Photo by Hank Kranzler.

14

Eighteenth-Century Plays

Art and Culture in the Eighteenth Century

The development of courtly art and culture, which had proceeded in a rather uninterrupted fashion since the Renaissance, finally came to a standstill in the eighteenth century. It was superseded by bourgeois subjectivism and sentimentality, which are still the foundation of most popular art today. Even before one arrives at the bourgeois world that appears in the paintings of Chardin and Greuze, there is a tendency in the Rococo art of France and all of Europe in the early eighteenth century to neglect the solemn, the ceremonious, and the monumental in favor of the natural, the casual, and the intimate. Even though in certain ways the Rococo style is a continuation and a consummation of the Baroque splendor of the seventeenth century, the grand manner and the pompous taste of that style are completely foreign to the refined, elegant, intimate ideals of the eighteenth century. Only the basic sources and compositional approach remain from the earlier Baroque style.

Rococo art is an anticlimax, a dying fall in the history of art devoted to monarchy and aristocratic aggrandizement. The aristocracy began to accept middle-class patterns of thought, while clothing them in the most elegant aristocratic trappings. There was a slackening of personal discipline, a growing skepticism and even atheism in religion, and more unrestrained personal conduct among the nobility. Since Louis XV in France allowed his succession of mistresses to have more influence in social matters than he himself, the society developed a feminine bias, and the art a most feminine sensibility.

The paintings of Watteau set the tone for the new culture, and the transition from the grand Baroque "machines" of Charles Le Brun to this master of the delicate *fêtes galantes* expressed fully the change in taste. The art, in spite of its delight in the senses and joyful surrender to pleasure, was full of melancholy and nostalgia—an attempt at the age-old Arcadian ideal of merging nature and civilization, beauty and spirituality, seriousness and intelligence (Figure 14–1). The style that we call Rococo is not illustrative or even very expressive. It is ornamental, and its decorative patterns seem to be without constraint, like the shep-

Figure 14–1. *The Halt During the Chase* (detail) by Watteau. The Wallace Collection, London, ca. 1720. An example of the aristocratic and artificial dream world of this early eighteenth-century French artist who invented the *fête galante*. Reproduced by permission of the Trustees, The Wallace Collection, London.

herds and shepherdesses in Watteau, who, endowed with a natural liberty, seem to drift effortlessly in a delicate and airy landscape.

In England the transition from seventeenth- to eighteenth-century culture was not as obvious as in France. Even at the opening of the century, English power was held by a commercial aristocracy that had a more realistic grasp on the meaning of mercantile growth and middle-class power than did the aristocrats in France (Figure 14–2). The transition from the aristocratic Rococo to bourgeois romanticism in England was not affected by the violence to cultural values that occurred in France and Germany.

Trifling as it sometimes seems to be, the Rococo is the last coherent style before the final loss of style in the late eighteenth and early nineteenth centuries and the replacement of a European-wide cultural style with many individual artists' personal interpretations. Only with the birth of *art nouveau* (in many ways related to the Rococo) and the rise of modern art

in the early twentieth century is there a return to a coherent cultural style.

The decline of Rococo art and its traditions inherited from the Baroque began gradually during the middle of the eighteenth century as a result of a continuing attack on aristocratic taste by the bourgeois that took two different directions. The emotionalism and naturalism represented by the French philosopher and novelist Rousseau, the English novelist Richardson, the English painter Hogarth, and the French middle-class artist Greuze was one trend; the rationalism and classicism represented by the German philosopher and playwright Lessing, the German painter Mengs, the German historian-archeologist Winckelmann, and the French painter David is the other. Both emphasize an ideal of simplicity, earnestness, clarity, and morality over the courtly softness, ostentation, and decadence that are expressed in Rococo art. Greuze, in particular, represented the new middle-class taste in his realistic, story-telling paintings,

Figure 14–2. "After the Marriage" from the series *Marriage à la Mode* by Hogarth, National Gallery, London, ca. 1745. An example of Hogarth's moral and satirical tone in a painting from a narrative series dealing with the social evils of eighteenth-century English society. Photo courtesy of the Trustees of the National Gallery.

which project a strong bourgeois ethic. They are literary, banal, moralizing, anecdotal paintings that are the prototype for much of the inartistic work that followed in the nineteenth century. The work of Chardin was much more honest, simple, and truly artistic, yet in his day Greuze was more popular, since his weapons proved very effective in the battle against the decaying Rococo (Figure 14–3).

However, it is the painter David who represents the renewal of the classic and the rational in painting (Figure 14–4). What must be understood about art and public taste after 1750 is that picturesque romanticism and severe classicism were two sides of the same coin: the associational concept by which all art forms were chosen—not for intrinsic or structural values, but to evoke rich associations that could inspire the viewer to muse about past

history or literature. Such art appealed to middle-class sentiment, snobbishness about learning, and love of prestige and position. Architecture after 1750 swings from neoclassical commercial temples in the city to neogothic villas in the country in deference to this associational desire; painting turns from the heroic, stoical, republican virtues in works by David to the romantic, picturesque ruins of Hubert Robert (Figure 14–5). All art after 1750, even the most fully documented archeological classicism, is used for associational values. By the end of the eighteenth century bourgeois sentimentality and associationalism had spread from England to Germany and France, and by the second quarter of the nineteenth century this artistic ideal led to the tasteless eclecticism that dominated Western European culture in the nineteenth century.

Figure 14-3. *The Father's Curse: The Ungrateful Son* by Greuze, The Louvre, Paris, ca. 1765. An example of the moralistic, sentimental painting admired by Denis Diderot in the latter part of the eighteenth century. Photo courtesy of Le Directeur des Musées de France.

Figure 14-4. *The Death of Socrates* by David, The Metropolitan Museum of Art, New York, 1787. An example of the coldness and austerity in the "new classicism" of David, which stressed the stoic virtues and civic duty in classical antiquity.

Figure 14-5. *The Old Bridge;* Hubert Robert; National Gallery of Art, Washington; Samuel H. Kress Collection, ca. 1775. An example of the romantic ruins that became one of the most popular of subjects in the late eighteenth century.

Theatre and Drama in the Eighteenth Century

STAGING METHODS.   The staging methods of the eighteenth century were generally a continuation of the theatrical practices of the preceding Baroque period, although theatre size increased greatly toward the end of the century as the size of the middle-class audience expanded. On the Continent, where the forestage was relatively small and the proscenium doors of the English stage did not exist, the action took place on a rather narrow plane to the front of the raked stage, with a one- or two-point perspective arranged behind it (Figure 14–6). The grand drape within the proscenium

Figure 14–6.   The Opera House in Stuttgart by de la Guépierre. A cutaway sketch of the interior. Reproduced by permission of The Huntington Library, San Marino, California.

Coupe du nouvel Opéra de Stuttgardt esquissé pour en voir l'effet sans aucunes regles de Perspective

Plan ou Projet de la restauration de l'Opéra de Stuttgardt.

de la Guepierre Del.

Salles de Spectacles.   G G

was used only at the beginning of the evening to hide the stage until the play began, and at the end of the evening as a conclusion to all theatrical entertainment. Changes of scenery and the famous "transformation" scenes (when one set magically changed into another) occurred in full view of the audience through the use of the chariot system (on the Continent) or the wing-and-groove method (England). In the former, all flats moved on and off the stage by the turning of a single winch in the basement, while little chariots on tracks supported the wings and shutters on masts that came up through slits in the stage floor. The best single example we have today of this type of theatre in operation is the Drottningholm Theatre in the small royal palace of the same name just outside Stockholm. Here a group of full settings and all stage machinery were found intact in the early twentieth century, and today one may enjoy complete performances of many eighteenth-century ballets, operas, and plays (Figure 14–7).

SCENERY.   The eighteenth century saw a growing interest in archeology, historical objectivity, and the art and culture of the past, and by the latter part of the century there were movements in both England and France demanding scenery that had far more detail, more sense of reality, more of an illusion of the time of day or a particular weather condition. Thus, stage lighting improved, as did the quality of mood painting in wings and backdrops. New asymmetrical stage plans, the use of transparent drops, and the addition of individual set pieces not painted on the backgrounds were added.

COSTUMES.   The costumes of this period were either based on the theatrical garb developed in the seventeenth century (inspired by supposedly antique lines), which was still prevalent in opera and classical tragedies, or on the use of contemporary dress with certain modifications (Figures 14–8 and 14–9). But the eighteenth century, which showed a great interest in more archeological correctness in stage dress than had been the case in the past, saw a

Figure 14-7. Stage setting, Royal Theatre, Drottningholm, Sweden, ca. 1765. One of the few extant examples of a stage house completely equipped with stage scenery and machinery of the eighteenth century. Courtesy of the Drottningholm Theatre Museum. Photo by Hans Hammarskiold.

Figure 14-8. Costume sketches by Jean Eric Rehn for the Royal Theatre, Drottningholm, Sweden, ca. 1765. An example of the picturesque and exotic romantic effects achieved in stage costume in the late eighteenth century. Courtesy of the Norman Philbrick Library. Photo by Keeble and Shuchat.

Figure 14-9. The actor Quin as Coriolanus, 1749. The stiff skirt or "tonnelet" and the heroic plumes were the standard dress for classical tragedy at the middle of the eighteenth century. Crown Copyright Victoria and Albert Museum (Theatre Museum).

Figure 14-10. Mrs. Siddons in the tragedy *The Grecian Daughter,* ca. 1790. An example of the pseudoclassical costume at the close of the eighteenth century. From a steel engraving. Courtesy of the Norman Philbrick Library.

number of innovations and changes in theatrical costume by 1800. In England, Charles Macklin played Macbeth in plaids, David Garrick played Lear and Richard III in approximations of certain Renaissance garments, and Sarah Siddons and John Philip Kemble appeared in classical plays in garments based loosely on Greek and Roman originals (Figure 14–10). In France, a similar development occurred when Voltaire suggested a number of costume reforms at the Comédie Française; the great French actress Claire Hippolyte Clairon and her leading man Henri Louis LeKain were, with Voltaire's help, able to bring many more historically correct costume effects into the plays of the standard repertoire.

The School for Scandal

Although the art and culture of the eighteenth century have very complicated crosscurrents and continuous shifts from the classical to the protoromantic, the descriptive words that continually reappear in any assessment of the period and its drama are "sentimental" and "moralizing." And even though the best playwrights of the period, including Beaumarchais, Goldsmith, Sheridan, and Goldoni, worked to reestablish true comedy, the mark of eighteenth-century sentimentality and its accompanying moral tone appears to a greater or lesser degree in the work of every one of these major playwrights. *The School for Scandal* by Sheridan is frequently said to be the greatest comedy of manners in the English language. However, it in no way achieves the worldly wit and amoral tone of Restoration comedy, and although it avoids some of the excesses of sentimental comedy, it still has a strong note of sentiment and a very direct moral tone (Figure 14–11).

PLOT AND STRUCTURE. The play begins with a Prologue and ends with an Epilogue, as is the case with most plays written during the Restoration and eighteenth century. The Pro-

Figure 14–11. Costume sketches for Sheridan's *The School for Scandal* by Nancy Potts, as produced by the Association of Producing Artists at the Lyceum Theatre, New York, 1967. From *Theatre Crafts Magazine,* July-August 1967. Courtesy of Nancy Potts and *Theatre Crafts Magazine.*

logue was used to introduce the script, make public a quarrel between the playwright and the theatre manager, and put the audience in the appropriate mood; the Epilogue was an appeal for audience favor and a summary of the play's overall intent. Neither is essential to an understanding of the play, and both are frequently cut in modern productions.

Although the scandalmongers play only a small part within the action, they are very important in setting the background tone of the play and acting as framework for the action. The group is also used for exposition, since their gossip frequently introduces much of the information from which character conflict arises. In many ways they seem (in modern productions) to be the freshest and most humorous part of the play as we see how their commodity—scandal—is planned, cooked, and served to cause the downfall of reputations all around them. Even the hero, Charles, is all but ruined by them, and only Snake's exposure of the group's intrigues leads to the happy conclusion of the main action. Their conversation has a crisp and witty tone that supplies much of the play's humor, and their viciousness seems too superficial to be a real danger to the leading characters in the play. They are the background to the action, always available to complicate or untangle the plot and to set the correct comic tone for the play's development.

Sheridan's structural approach is inherited far more from English comic writing (dating back to the Elizabethan period) than from the French comic tradition of Molière. There is a major plot and a minor plot which at first have little connection, with a gradual entwining of the two toward a common resolution. This contrasts sharply with the single plot action that we find in a classic French comedy. If one judges a play by its story telling, then real praise is in order for this playwright, who carries his audience with ease and a sense of keen expectation from one scene to another despite the two threads of action. This sense of easy casualness wedded to a sure sense of control is even more admirable when one realizes that there are fourteen different scenes in the play, which take place in various portions of four different households.

Although the audience is prepared from the beginning for Joseph to be unmasked, Lady Teazle to come to her senses, Charles to be exonerated, and Maria to be happy, they do not know how all of this is to come about; hence, a marvelous dual sense of clearly knowing the purpose of the action while following it with curiosity and suspense is established. This particular skill on the part of the playwright has always been particularly admired in the Screen Scene. All of the preceding conflicts in the action are brought together in this scene, and a marvelous series of comic reversals ensues until Lady Teazle is revealed behind the screen. Then, like the final pieces of a puzzle fitting into place, Lady Teazle has the necessary

discussion with Sir Peter, Joseph is exposed, and Charles' basic goodness is revealed.

CHARACTERIZATION.   Before analyzing the individual characters in the play, one should be fully aware of the clarity of these characterizations and their relationship to one another and to the plot. The playwright sets the natures of Joseph, Charles, Sir Peter, and Lady Teazle clearly before us, and whenever a sense of ambiguity about their thoughts or motives arises they are allowed to make direct asides to the audience. In the case of minor characters whose personalities cannot be fully described, names are given such as Snake, Sir Benjamin Backbite, and Lady Sneerwell. As was the case in the Baroque theatre, the characters are developed with a sense of decorum or good manners and built on social types so that we expect them to act in a certain manner.

Charles is particularly important as a character type that was greatly admired in the late eighteenth century. He is the natural young man who has not been corrupted by society; a man of frankness, openness, sensibility, and filial affection, who represents an ideal of goodness despite his rashness and lack of social grace. Joseph, on the other hand, pretends to have the social graces and maturity admired in a man of class, but he is shown to be a hypocrite, a dissembler, a mere facade of manners, and is finally exposed as unnatural, corrupt, and somewhat ludicrous. Sir Peter at first place appears to be a man who fulfills the ideals of his age and class, and yet he has married someone far too youthful and so is made the recipient of much barbed satire. Maria, Old Rowley, and Sir Oliver seem to fit the norm of their ages and their positions in society, and so they are treated well at the end of the play. Only those who have deviated from the appropriate social patterns of behavior are punished.

The minor characters are differentiated only slightly through age, sex, or the way they speak. For example, Mrs. Candour can be differentiated from Lady Sneerwell only by a certain flightier tone to her chatter and gossip. It is also important to realize that all of the characters, except Old Rowley, Moses, and the servants, are of the leisure class and are not concerned about making a living. Although the author makes a great point of exposing dishonesty and hypocrisy, no doubts are raised about the social system within which the play operates. As with Molière, the social scene itself is fully accepted, and only the deviations from it are ridiculed. Thus, the play has a certain sense of sophistication and urbanity that sets it clearly within the mainstream of the comedy-of-manners tradition. Only the notes of sentimentality that reflect eighteenth-century bourgeois taste (in the characterizations of Charles and Maria) give an emotional tone to the play quite unlike that found in Molière, Restoration comedy, or the modern plays by Oscar Wilde and Somerset Maugham.

THEME.   Just as it is interesting to compare Sheridan and Molière in matters of plot and characterization, so is it instructive to look at the similarities and differences in the ideas or themes in their plays. For instance, both *Tartuffe* and *The School for Scandal* deal with the unmasking of hypocrites, but in the Molière play religious hypocrisy is a real threat to individuals and society, while the social hypocrisy of Joseph Surface, or even the scandalmongering of Sir Benjamin, Lady Sneerwell, and the others is never a serious threat. *The School for Scandal,* clearly reflecting the lighter touch in all eighteenth-century art and literature, is less serious in purpose than *Tartuffe.* The theme of this play is not so much the exposure of Joseph Surface and the members of the ''school for scandal'' as a defense of the new ''natural man'' ideal. Like Goldsmith before him, Sheridan is attacking the tearful sentimentality and complacent false morality that had been rampant in English comedy for fifty years. However, despite this clear intention of indicating the difference between true and false sentiment, his ''good'' characters still succumb to moralizing and sentiment. In fact, in the final analysis, the entire play illustrates the standard lesson of eighteenth-century senti-mental comedy—that virtue will be rewarded and evil will be punished.

DIALOGUE.   The language of the play serves admirably to give the play its tone of polish and wit. As with Restoration comedy, the characters generally make their points with polished epigrams and witty descriptions, and the idealized conversations that take place make every phrase seem spontaneous yet sparkling and apt. Such witty talk is far removed from the language of everyday living needed for buying, selling, and functioning within a broad spectrum of society. Although it shows the English language at a polished peak of conversational brilliance, it also reflects a certain aspect of society that is artificial, somewhat tarnished, and rather useless. Certainly the polished prose in much of this play demands a precise and exact technique of delivery, and when it is appropriately spoken it makes the play a dazzling stage piece—the superlative box office comedy that has been kept before the public since 1777.

RHYTHM.   The movement and rhythm of a play such as *The School for Scandal* are closely tied to the sharp, rapid, witty dialogue and to the polished gestures of the actors rather than to the vagaries and complications of the plot. Although the unraveling of the story line is interesting and helps to sustain a sense of curiosity and suspense, the movement and pace of the play are ultimately keyed to the conversational games from which the climaxes of all major scenes are built. The give and take of dialogue in such scenes creates a rhythm that is light, clear, and fast-moving.

SPECTACLE.   The play is set in London in 1777 and reflects, especially in costume, the manners and customs of late eighteenth-century society. A famous engraving of the time, which shows the Screen Scene from a performance at Drury Lane in 1788, gives some idea of the original costumes and settings, the nature of the theatre with its apron stage and proscenium doors, and the relation-

Figure 14–12.   ''The Screen Scene'' from *The School for Scandal* as produced at the Drury Lane Theatre, London, 1778. An example of the use of the forestage, proscenium doors, stage boxes, clearly defined wings, and contemporary dress in an English production of the late eighteenth century. From an engraving of the period. Crown Copyright Victoria and Albert Museum (Theatre Museum).

ship of the audience to the stage. It is important to note in this engraving that the actors' costumes closely approximate those worn by members of the audience (Figure 14–12).

By the time this play was written, more emphasis was being placed on each of the settings demanded in the action of the play, and although most of the settings are simply designated as a room in someone's house, the wings and shutters used at the time would probably have been quite detailed in their architectural adornment; also, they would have been changed in full view of the audience. Much of the action undoubtedly took place on the forestage, with entrances and exits through the proscenium doors, using the set simply as background. But in scenes such as those involving the auction of the pictures and the con-

cealment behind the screens, the action and the properties required are specifically identified, and the setting would have become more directly involved in the action.

Visual Presentation of *The School for Scandal*

In presenting *The School for Scandal* for a contemporary audience, the producer and director must decide whether to adopt the visual methods of the original production or one of a number of contemporary visual approaches. Since the scenic methods used in the eighteenth century can be used to capture a certain period charm that is also inherent in the play, it is possible to use wings and shutters to depict the various locations needed and allow the audience to observe the shifts from one scene to the next. This can give an added interest and charm to the production. If such an approach is taken, the wings and shutters obviously should not be painted in a manner that suggests historical re-creation of late eighteenth-century scene painting, but should take a contemporary artistic approach in capturing the decorative feeling of eighteenth-century architectural ornament. This approach will allow the audience to feel that the production is being presented as a contemporary interpretation of the eighteenth-century theatrical scene while still taking full advantage of the charm, style, and removal from reality inherent in observing the scenery shifted by a wing-and-shutter method. With this concept of production, the acting will be removed almost completely from the level of realism to one of artificiality and a mannered style. The costumes will support the decorative and pictorial needs of the play rather than being tied primarily to the psychological demands of characterization.

However, if quaintness is not desired, a production may be designed that contains detailed box settings for each room, with a certain sense of fullness and period correctness; hence, the characters and plot would have more reality for the audience than in a wing-and-shutter setting. If the play is designed in this manner, the details of interior decoration must be given careful attention; the costumes must be tied closely to special idiosyncracies of character and period, while the acting must be more fully based on a three-dimensional psychological interpretation of individual characters.

Finally, there is the completely contemporary approach, in which a number of modern staging methods could be used to project the script visually. A thrust-stage approach, where only the rear wall is set with eighteenth-century architectural decor and the acting takes place on the thrust stage away from the background, would be one way. (Eighteenth-century acting took place similarly on the forestage before the proscenium.) Another approach is to use a few architectural or decorative set pieces rather than a full setting to suggest the various rooms in the play; still another is to frame the entire production in a formal, permanent eighteenth-century architectural framework, with only furniture being shifted from scene to scene. In any of these approaches, the stress would be on an abstracted essence of the eighteenth-century world in which the play takes place, and in none of them would the major stress be on absolute character reality in acting and costumes.

For costume design, these varied staging methods include two basic interpretations of the stage dress to be created for this play: (1) the very detailed, psychologically based character approach to costume; (2) a much more limited, abstracted decorative approach to costume, in which the individual designs are less important than the overall effect of mood, style, and suggestion of period in modern terms. This is not to say that if the costumes are designed with great attention to personality and characterization they will lack unity or any sense of period style, but that these latter elements will remain subordinate to characterization. Neither is it easier or better to design the production in terms of decorative comment on the period, the play, and the visual style of the times. It is simply a fact that most costumes for a production of this play will assume one of these basic interpretations. Like all plays that can be interpreted several ways without violating the integrity of the play's structure, characterization, theme, and dialogue, *The School for Scandal,* unless it is produced for pure novelty of effect, will show certain elements remaining constant in the costume design, no matter how the script is presented.

First, the elements of eighteenth-century culture that have been described in this chapter and clearly lie at the heart of this play (including artificiality versus casualness, false sentiment versus honesty, and morality versus evil) should be as clearly evident in the costumes as in the characters who wear them. The light-hearted treatment of all these themes, as contrasted with the more serious interpretation in

Tartuffe, should be directly apparent in the stage dress. Since the effect of *The School for Scandal* is completely dependent on a clear interpretation of upper-class English society in the late eighteenth century, the artistic and cultural ideals of the time must be clearly presented—especially in terms of the costumes worn by characters of various ages and social levels.

The fabric textures chosen for the play should, therefore, reflect the social level and personal taste of each character and the artistic ideals of the society. The major fabric surfaces will probably be hard, shiny, and brittle, with some accents of softness. This means that taffetas, moiréd silks, satins, and hard wool gabardines will predominate over soft woolens, heavy velvets, and dull cottons. Only in collars, cuffs, and vests will the softer touches of velvet and lace be apparent. This use of texture also reflects the nature of the script, which makes its first impression through its hard, clever, witty dialogue and sophisticated urbanity, and only a secondary impression through its softer underlying accents of sentiment and subtle sermonizing. A major source of ideas could well be the work of the painter Gainsborough, who was a close friend of Sheridan and his wife. Exquisite portraits of them both show that Gainsborough was a painter adept at capturing the image of the social class that Sheridan represented. Both men lived at Bath for some time, and nowhere in England during this period was the social game more carefully and fully played for image and effect than at this lovely spa. In the work of Gainsborough one can find the transparent, soft, sentimental, casual effects in fabric side by side with the hard satins and reflective taffetas of a more brittle, formal, artificial society; one need only look at the portrait of Mrs. Graham next to one of Mrs. Richard Brinsley Sheridan to see the double effect (Figure 14–13a and b). Whether the costumes are to be quite realistic and tied to character or more abstracted and intended for comment on the period, the fabrics chosen will be similar, although they will probably be more subtle when chosen for character reality than when chosen for period comment or decorative effect.

In color, it seems quite obvious (from looking at the works of Gainsborough and the colors admired by society at this period) that heavy, dark, rich colors were not popular. The late eighteenth-century love of lightness, casualness, sentiment, and subtle decorative effects—borrowed from antiquity—meant the use of a scale of values above medium tonalities, and only occasionally does one find dark, rich colors used in accent. The lightness, the lack of seriousness in the treatment of theme, and the surface brilliance of dialogue in this play would also suggest lightness of color. Only in a minor character or in someone of a lower social order would a muddied or dark color seem appropriate. Since this play so clearly reflects the social ideals of its day, the colors chosen for the costumes should reflect the taste of the times.

Finally, the line of the costumes should reveal both the soft and sentimental lines found in younger women's costumes of the day and the more artificial, formal lines found in the costumes worn by the powerful leaders of society. Again, comparing the lines in Gainsborough's portrait of Mrs. Graham with those in his portrait of Mrs. Sheridan, one can see the contrasts possible in this same period and possible in this play if one wishes to contrast sharply the costume worn by Maria with that worn by Lady Sneerwell. The humor gained by slightly ridiculous costume effects in garments worn by Lady Teazle and the ladies of the "school for scandal" can be given full rein by even a minimal look into women's styles of the period. Lady Teazle's naive attempts to fit into society versus the crass and heavy impression created by Lady Sneerwell and Mrs. Candour can be beautifully illuminated through just the slightest simplification, exaggeration, and subtle differences in costume line.

Closely related to costume line is the use of ornament, through which much of the comic tone for the production may be suggested. The

(a)

(b)

Figure 14–13. (a) *Mrs. Graham* by Gainsborough, National Gallery, Edinburgh, ca. 1785. An example of the delicacy, elegance, and light brushwork of this portrait painter, who is described as the only Rococo artist that England produced in the eighteenth century. This portrait gives an image that might be useful in a design for Lady Teazle in *The School for Scandal.* Courtesy of the National Gallery of Scotland, Edinburgh. (b) *Mrs. Richard Brinsley Sheridan;* Thomas Gainsborough; National Gallery of Art, Washington; Andrew W. Mellon Collection 1937. This painting, ca. 1783, illustrates the new chemise gown introduced into English fashion in the 1780's, which gives a simple, sentimental, windblown outdoor look. The costume might be very appropriate for the character of Maria in *The School for Scandal.*

use of ribbons and bows, braid edging a man's coat, floral accents, and the treatment of buttons and buckles may, through their size and placement, make a distinct character point or strike exactly the correct comic note as a strong focal point in a particular costume (Figure 14–14).

One must always remember how much cos-

tumes for a comedy of manners such as *The School for Scandal* depend on a pointed and slightly satirical interpretation of high fashion of the particular period. In this play especially, the designer must strive to obtain the correct balance between those who dress in the artificialities of current fashion and those who wear more unpretentious garments (Figure 14–15).

Figure 14-14. Helen Hayes, Dee Victor, and Rosemary Harris in *The School for Scandal* as produced by the Association of Producing Artists, Lyceum Theatre, New York, 1967. Reproduced by courtesy of the APA Repertory Company, Photo by Robert Alan Gold.

Figure 14-15. A scene from *The Rivals* by Richard Brinsley Sheridan as produced by the American Conservatory Theatre, San Francisco, 1981. Courtesy of the American Conservatory Theatre. Photo by Larry Merkle.

15

Romantic Plays

Art and Culture in the Early Nineteenth Century

Romanticism, as a fully conscious Western European style, was impossible until the late eighteenth century; European society had for several centuries been based on a tightly organized caste system that placed great stress on organization and form. Not since medieval times had aspects of art and culture arisen in any full and meaningful way from subjective emotion alone. Even in the art of the sixteenth century, the subjective qualities of mannerism had been achieved primarily by very conscious manipulation of composition and form. Following the events culminating in the French Revolution, artists began to break from the strictures and inhibitions of the aristocratic and bourgeois world in which they had lived to the lonely, alienated, existential world of personal emotion and subjectivity. In this drive to break with reality, the leaders of romanticism always attempted to escape into a world that was more exciting, more fulfilling, more beautiful (or more terrible) than the world of bourgeois industrialism that was developing at the opening of the nineteenth century. The inexpressible was to be conveyed by any means possible in art and literature, but the great problem of the romantics was a lack of method, a lack of technique for expressing this personal and subjective reaction to life.

The only romanticist who was both a great representative of the style and an enemy of its formlessness and excesses was the painter Eugène Delacroix, who refused to surrender to the irrational and the emotional at the expense of form and composition (Figure 15–1). Although we know from his *Journal* that he suffered from fits of melancholia, ennui, emptiness, and discontent with his work and so was fully involved in the "sickness of romanticism," he despised the label "romantic" and protested against being called a "master" of the romantic school. It was Rubens, not the "Bohemian" romantics who surrounded him, who was his artistic and human model, and Delacroix was one of the few artistic personali-

Figure 15-1. *The Death of Sardanapalus* by Delacroix, The Louvre, Paris, 1827. An example of the exotic subject matter, violent movement, rich color, and loose, thick brushstroke in the developed romantic paintings of Delacroix. Photo courtesy of the Musées Nationaux, Paris.

ties since the early seventeenth century to combine the highest intellectual culture with the *grand seigneur* mode of life. What Delacroix lacked was a new technique with enough power to match his emotion. In England, Turner's canvases, scrubbed with a ''hot'' pigment, almost matched the romantic vision, but only van Gogh and the expressionist painters found a technique to match their subjective feeling (Figure 15-2). The Baroque, early Renaissance, and medieval techniques borrowed by most romantic artists merely indicated the many directions in which artists and even writers searched for meaning in life (Figure 15-3). These borrowings also indicate how much romantic art is based on escape, psychotic fear of the present, and a deep desire to find a haven, answer, or release in a world of the past or of the imagination.

This new, personal, subjective reaction to life and to the whole past history of the world also led to a totally new idea of history. Instead of the idea that history unfolds as a continuous drama of progress toward a fixed and discernible goal, there was a new, very subjective, and quite fearful idea that history and historical destiny are precisely tied to who we are and what we have been, that nothing is mutable in political or governmental institutions. This led to both pessimism and optimism, hope and despair. It was the basis for the whole development of nineteenth- and twentieth-century thought and institutions and is at the very heart of a present-day sense of relativity in art, morality, and science. This concept, astounding and frightening at the time, made students of history more aware of past ages than at any time in the history of the West, while at the

Figure 15–2. *Slavers Throwing Overboard the Dead and Dying: Typhoon Coming On* by Joseph Mallord William Turner, Museum of Fine Arts, Boston (Henry Lillie Pierce Fund), 1840. An example of the tempestuous, "scrubbed-in" brushwork of Turner, by which he hoped to express the cosmic power behind the elements of air, fire, and water. Courtesy, Museum of Fine Arts, Boston.

Figure 15–3. The Houses of Parliament, London, by Barry and Pugin, 1840–1860. An example of England's Gothic and medieval inheritance used as exterior dressing on a series of rectangular architectural forms for associational and emotional values. Photo courtesy of the British Travel Office.

same time it made them feel alienated from the concept of a historical continuum of Western civilization. In this way romanticism is the first awakening of the modern outlook, rooted in the torment of the "individual mind," in the personal, subjective feeling of loneliness and homelessness brought on by this new concept of history. Artists and writers now talk about the dignity of the unknown the way they used to talk about the dignity of humanity or of reason, and the new art is to become a human document in which the tormented personal confession—the baring of the personal wound —is acceptable as a complete subject in art and literature. In romanticism we see the beginnings of a complete alienation of the artist from public and patron, an autonomy that created art for other artists, an individualism that turned in horror from the crass world of bourgeois materialism. Romantic artists and writers considered themselves part of a new aristocracy raised above the rest of society, and this removal led to the modern concept of the artist as half-seer, half-Bohemian, removed from the usual moral and cultural values and devoted to art for its own sake.

This concept also led to a second concept, in which introspection and analysis of one's self created the figure of the "second self" among romantic artists and writers. This tendency to consider one's self over and over again as a being unknown, a remote stranger, was an attempt to escape the responsibilities of one's own historical and social situation. In this flight, the unconscious is the worshipped source of dreams, wish fulfillment, mystery, excitement, and grotesquerie, and the artist or writer replaces experiences in the world with self-experience and natural objects with infinite interest in the "second self."

Theatre and Drama in the Early Nineteenth Century

The period between the late eighteenth century and the latter half of the nineteenth century saw a number of changes in the theatre, most of which were developments from earlier trends. The major method of organizing theatrical productions was still the resident repertory theatre with its leading actors and supporting players presenting a rotating series of plays during any given theatrical season. The great companies on the continent were the government-supported national theatres such as the Comédie Française and the Vienna Burgtheater, while in England there were key companies such as the Royal Theatre at Drury Lane, which attracted the very best theatrical talent. Only the coming of the railroads in the 1840s led to the beginning, especially in the United States, of what was eventually known as the long tour, which used a production as a vehicle for a star performer to attract an audience by reputation and personality. The rise of the star system and the long-run "hit play" changed the entire nature of theatrical production in the late nineteenth and early twentieth century. It turned theatre into a great moneymaking investment for theatrical managers and their stables of stars.

As a result of increasing urbanization and industrialization in Western Europe and the United States, the cities became flooded with workers from the lower classes, and the audiences changed from a middle-class majority in the late eighteenth century to a truly mass audience by the middle of the nineteenth century. Thus, the total spectrum of theatrical experience was greatly enlarged, ranging from performances of mere variety entertainment to grand opera and the classics. During the early nineteenth century the theatre was in many ways an entertainment medium for the masses, just as television is today. Productions often included a play, short song and dance acts, a short light comedy, even a short light opera, and they lasted from seven in the evening until after midnight. The size of the theatre also expanded, until major theatres in large cities seated 3000 or more spectators. At first the old box, pit, and gallery arrangement prevailed, but as it became more and more difficult to see and hear from the boxes, comfortable seats were gradually placed in what had

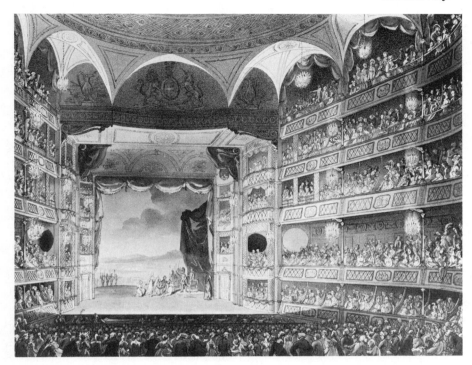

Figure 15–4. The interior of the Drury Lane Theatre by Pugin and Rowlandson, 1808. From Ackermann's *Microcosm of London,* 1808. An example of the enormous size of an English theatre in the early nineteenth century.

formerly been the pit and is now called the orchestra. In the latter part of the nineteenth century, orchestra seats finally replaced box seats in price and desirability (Figure 15–4).

STAGING. The staging methods of the entire nineteenth century were dominated by an ever-increasing drive for historical accuracy in background and costume. The neoclassical ideal that had dominated the major dramatic developments from Shakespeare's day until the late eighteenth century had always stressed universality rather than detailed reality in theatrical presentation—historical accuracy was felt to have little connection with truth in art. When an interest in archeological accuracy began to develop in all the arts in the late eigh-

teenth century, the theatre could not escape. As in literature and art, the importance of the individual in a particular time and place replaced a more generalized and cavalier attitude about past history and far-away places. In the production of plays in the early nineteenth century, actors and managers studied the architecture, sculpture, painting, literature, dress, social customs, and minor arts with as much, if not more, enthusiasm as they studied the play and its characters. Gradually plays were written that demanded many historical settings and scenes of historical pageantry, and even Shakespearean revivals became an excuse for a great museum of historical arts and facts to be paraded before the public. This trend flowered with the famous London pro-

Figure 15–5. Costume sketch for King John, second dress, by James Robinson Planché, for a production of *King John,* 1823. Another example of the stress on archeological correctness in the costumes for this British production early in the nineteenth century. Photo courtesy of The Humanities Research Center, The University of Texas at Austin.

sky or foliage borders above framed the back scene and created an illusion of foliage or architecture moving forward to the proscenium arch. Such wings were still often moved in grooves in the stage floor or on chariots whose poles came through a slit in the stage floor; but such symmetry of visual effect was undesirable for an illusion of reality, and, gradually, wings were set at asymmetrical angles by hand or were developed as partial three-dimensional pieces to frame in the backdrop. In fact, every attempt was made to create an illusion of reality, and many of the theatrical effects and visual scenes placed on the stage during these years were workable and exciting. This was due partially to the adoption of gas light for the theatre, which allowed for the dimming and raising of light on the stage; it was the arrival of

Figure 15–6. Charles Kean as Richard II in a production of Shakespeare's play at the Princess Theatre, London, 1857, directed and produced by Charles Kean. A further example of the ideal if not the fact of archeological realism in historical stage dress. Photo from Clement Scott's *The Drama of Yesterday and Today,* Vol. I, Macmillan, London, 1899, p. 240.

duction of *King John* by Charles Kemble in 1823 in which all visual details were designed with great accuracy by the antiquarian and costume historian, J. R. Planché (Figure 15–5). It reached its zenith in the early 1850s with the Shakespearean revivals of Charles Kean, for which teams of art historians and archeologists would spend months of preparation gathering the background material for a production. The program notes were pages long, and the productions were supposed to teach and enlighten more than entertain the spectator (Figure 15–6).

The scenery for these productions consisted primarily of wings and backcloths painted in perspective. A series of perspective wings with

COSTUMES. As with staging in general, costume was now based on careful research, and beauty, unity, and theatricality were prized much less than archeological authenticity (Figure 15–7). There was not, however, an overall feeling of authenticity in nineteenth-century production, but rather a sense of much detail without regard for the overall effect. For example, actresses such as Mrs. Charles Kean would wear a very authentic Greek costume over Victorian crinolines and top it with a Victorian hairdo. Few questioned the final result (Figure 15–8). The great gain for theatrical costume during these years was in careful re-

Figure 15–7. Costume sketch by Alfred Crowquill for the character of Manuel in a production of *Manfred* by Lord Byron, showing the romantic realism in stage costume that was the ideal in the early nineteenth century. Courtesy of the Norman Philbrick Library.

Figure 15–8. Mrs. Charles Kean as Hermione in a production of *A Winter's Tale* presented at the Princess Theatre, London, 1856. An example of ambiguities in costume effect achieved by an actress who continued to wear Victorian petticoats under a Greek chiton. An engraving from Joseph Jefferson's *Autobiography,* Century, New York, 1890, p. 268.

electricity for stage production, at the end of the century, that put an end finally to painted wing-and-drop scenery. Throughout the early part of the century, the stage was still sloped for perspective effect, and only when, in the 1840s, experiments with three full walls for the creation of a box set were undertaken were there strong demands for a flat platform stage.

search and planning; the great loss was in theatricality, unity, and beauty. Important theatre artists of the past, including Inigo Jones and Jean Berain, would never have deigned to occupy their time with the theatrical mass media of the nineteenth century.

Faust

Goethe is to German literature what Shakespeare is to English literature, and *Faust* is considered by many critics to be the greatest literary work in the German language. But since it is more literary than theatrical in its vast size, technique, and development, the play must be cut, condensed, and adapted to make it stageworthy. The play is really a summation of Goethe's ideals and growth as a writer throughout his life; in that he began writing Part I in 1780 and Part II was not published until 1831, the entire work literally grew with him. It is in this very personal record of the author's quest for life's meaning that the play most accurately can be called a romantic epic.

PLOT AND STRUCTURE. Romanticism, in attempting to create a picture of life on an extended scale, employs a diffuse and loosely connected plot structure that usually depends more on ideas than on form. *Faust* is very loosely structured, and although it quite obviously is modeled after Shakespeare's large-scale dramas, it has none of the economy of effect or unity of action that one finds in *Macbeth* or *Othello*. In *Faust* one can see the weaknesses as well as the virtues of romanticism. In reaching for tremendous breadth of experience and scene, it often tends to be confusing and formless. While Shakespeare, in his mature work, sets the basic dramatic situation at the beginning of his play, Goethe waits until the fourth scene of *Faust* to establish the dramatic action in the pact between Faust and Mephistopheles. The introductory material in the two prologues takes a great deal of time, the various aspects of Faust's personal search are extended or contracted at the whim of the playwright, and the amount of attention focused on each of the supporting characters is determined by the author's personal preference rather than the demands of the action. This two-part drama is held together only by Faust's quest for fulfillment and salvation. In Part I, the story of Margarete and Faust tends to hold the play together in its sequential cause-and-effect development, and it is for this reason that only Part I is usually produced. It can be played as a full-fledged tragedy despite the interruptions of many psychological and philosophical scenes that break and confuse the plot structure.

Part II continues Faust's search in the realm of ideal beauty, humanistic learning, and the relationship of the individual to society. The conclusion is one of the great positive world statements of modern times, equating salvation with an individual's work for the collective good. Only through a two-evening presentation can the entire story be staged with the full breadth of its philosophic vision. In many ways, Part I is only a prologue to Part II.

Even when Part I alone is produced, the action is spread over twenty-five scenes, two prologues, and sixteen changes of locale. Time and place shift rapidly, there are many complicated scenic effects required, and costumes and masks for the *Walpurgisnacht* scene are a challenge to any designer.

CHARACTERIZATION. The cast of *Faust* is always very large. It is composed of crowds, choruses, witches, wizards, and spirits, and only a minimal number of characters are developed with any psychological reality. Faust, Mephistopheles, Wagner, Margarete, Martha, Valentine, and Lieschen have some three-dimensionality as characters, but the large number of other characters who populate the stage are mere abstractions designated by a group label rather than by individual names.

One of the key points of characterization in romanticism is the concentration on the emotions and psychology of the leading character or hero, and in the case of *Faust* this is precisely how Goethe has developed his work. The author uses the other characters only to illustrate, give insight to, and illuminate Faust's mind

Figure 15–9. Henry Irving as Mephistopheles in his production of *Faust* as presented at the Lyceum Theatre, London, 1887. From *Art Journal,* July 1887. Courtesy of the Norman Philbrick Library.

and soul, and it is an all but impossible task for the actor playing Faust to develop fully all aspects of the character without repeating the emotions of longing, groping, and reaching upward that mark Faust's dissatisfaction with life. Mephistopheles is less complex, depending primarily on cynicism, smiling duplicity, and cunning to pose a continuous threat to the fulfillment of Faust's search (Figure 15–9). Margarete is in many ways the typically innocent heroine of melodrama brought to a sad end by naive trust and love. Although she must run the gamut of emotions from love and happiness through shame, madness, and despair, she develops primarily as a stock character, without any great subtleties of personality and character. She is individualized through emotion rather than through character. Other roles must be filled by actors who need to develop only the most limited sense of characterization, yet who must be very accomplished in movement, dance, and sometimes song. In fact, the choruses and the extras can make the difference between failure and success in a production of *Faust.*

THEME.   The theme is in many ways the most important part of *Faust* as a play. In his view of human beings as aspiring, learning, creative spirits, Goethe takes a large-scale, optimistic view of their innate strength and capability and clearly sees them as being capable of providing for their own salvation. The basic theme is established in the first prologue: although people cannot avoid loneliness, suffering, and grievous mistakes in judgment, they can hope to achieve salvation through striving for a better world. Both parts of *Faust* are a continuing dramatization of this theme. In Part I the audience is shown Faust's dissatisfaction with life, his solemn pact with Mephistopheles, and his search for salvation through enjoyment and sensual pleasure. Part II depicts the conclusion of the search and an acceptance of God's statement at the opening of the play; Faust finally rejects both poetry and beauty in favor of service to humanity as the final goal in life. Although Faust loses his wager with Mephistopheles, he has gained his own soul, and in the end it is Faust who has conquered and Mephistopheles who has been defeated.

The playwright is obviously concerned with the ageless problem of good and evil, and when Goethe indicates that God lives in eternal light and witches and evil spirits reside in eternal darkness, he is dealing with imagery in a typically romantic way. He builds on this image by posing the theory that human beings live poised between good and evil—half in the dark but longing for the light. The *Walpurgisnacht* scene, in particular, makes great use of this contrast by stressing the sinister, dark, and evil nature of the scene, while making it clear that humans are part of this scene and that it is part of them. The witches and evil creatures of darkness are part of Faust's own nature, representing the animal drives and the selfishness that he must surmount if he is to find salvation. Goethe also conceives of Faust's love for Margarete within this same image of darkness and light. Since his love is carnal, selfish, and narrow, it has been conceived in darkness and so must end in the darkness of Margarete's death and Faust's failure to find the light. In Part II Faust thinks that he has achieved the light with the attainment of Helen, only to find the light as transitory as his goal is selfish. Only in service is the true light reached and darkness banished.

DIALOGUE.   The language in this play is developed in an infinitely complex series of heavy, involved, poetic speeches. Although the poetry is often more literary than theatrical, there are many moments when the total effect of its rich imagery and soaring rhythms is very impressive, especially when spoken by experienced German-speaking actors trained in the classical tradition of the Vienna Burgtheater. Long, poetic speeches similar to the arias of an opera are frequently used to build up the philosophical themes of the drama without furthering the action or developing the characters, and key images in the play, like the opposition between light and dark already discussed, are developed to the fullest poetic extent with little consideration for the events of the plot.

RHYTHM.   The general pattern of rhythm in this huge and sprawling play consists of great sweeping crescendos and abrupt shifts and contrasts as the poetic dialogue travels from scenes of interior monologue to those of action and pageantry. The use of the spoken word, song, dance, folk festival, supernatural voices, and dramatized visions gives an endless series of stage effects that assault the senses and give great variety to the rhythmic progression of the play. At no point in the drama could one say that the rhythm becomes light-hearted, gay, or easy. Throughout the unfolding of the drama the rhythm, though rich and varied, is always heavy, sonorous, symphonic, and grand.

SPECTACLE.   The staging requirements for the two parts of *Faust* are probably as demanding as for any play ever produced on the stage. The drama was originally conceived for the stage of the imagination, and the challenge to choreographer, musicians, costumer, set designer, lighting designer, and stage director is immense. To orchestrate properly color and light, mass movement, disembodied visions, music, voice, and shifts from one locale to another is a truly stupendous task, necessitating the use of every possible theatrical effect. This assault upon the senses and imagination of the audience is a challenge to the total visual and physical resources of the theatre.

Visual Presentation of *Faust*

An epic, cosmic drama such as *Faust,* which takes place on the stage of the imagination with little reference to a particular place and time, should not be produced today as a historic recreation of how the play might have been done if both parts had been supervised by Goethe himself, in a two-evening production at Weimar. The wing-and-drop method, which has become fixed in the public mind with nineteenth-century melodrama, would have all the wrong connotations for an audience. A rich use of theatrical effects appealing to the senses would seem the logical way to bring this drama of the inner mind to life today. A realistic period approach would be much better left to the films.

Given the total forces of the modern stage, what directions might a producer and director take in presenting this epic on the modern stage? There are many possibilities, but, as in any production, structure, theme, and poetic imagery must be kept clearly in mind. *Faust* is a sweeping romantic drama, and this should not be forgotten while one is approaching a master plan for its production (Figure 15–10).

Figure 15–10. A scene in Faust's study from the 1976 Burgtheater production of Goethe's *Faust,* Part I. Note the decision to give the costumes a modern look even though they are based on early-nineteenth-century models. Photo courtesy of Elizabeth Hausmann.

One direct and quite common approach to the production of *Faust* is to use light and darkness (one of the great images from the play) as the organizing factor in the drama and to reveal only small pieces of setting rising out of a darkness symbolizing a large area or world that cannot be seen. In this way full settings do not have to be built and so can be quickly shifted. Shafts of light are used to suggest the cosmic background for the drama and are theatrically effective in concentrating attention on one figure or a small group; later they can be expanded to illuminate a full stage scene. Some producers and directors would find this approach too related to the past, tied to the design methods of Jones, Craig, and other symbolists in the visual theatre, but it is a relatively uncomplicated and appropriate way in which to approach this mammoth work.

Another more modern approach would be to admit, as so many dramatists have since Pirandello's *Six Characters in Search of an Author,* that the stage is a stage and the characters on it merely actors "describing" or "presenting" the parts they are to play. *Faust,* because of its Prologue in Heaven, obviously lends itself to this kind of interpretation, in which everything that takes place after the Prologue is a kind of cosmic charade or an acting out of a drama of search and salvation. In this approach the stage must remain a stage, a cosmic platform for events, using only stage properties to suggest a fuller reality. Changes of locale can be indicated by changes in projections, properties, and lighting, or by a combination of the three; only the costumes would have to have a certain dimension of visual effect, although they would be "costumes" and not character clothes.

Probably the most popular approach in the German theatre is a full production with full sets and costumes, using modern concepts in art to determine the use of line, form, texture, and color. Nonobjective art usually falls into two camps: (1) the abstract expressionist school, in which the strongest possible emotional effects are achieved through a heavy use of broken lines, thick textures, and rich colors; and (2) the hard-edged, smooth-surfaced, limited color effects of geometric abstraction. These modern productions, then, are often inspired by one or the other of these camps. The abstract expressionist approach might be more suitable for the romantic, subjective, emotional, sensuous grandeur of the play, but this approach neglects the intellectual, philosophical, larger-than-life monumentality of the script. However, the hard-edged, geometric approach seems to leave out the emotion and sensuous imagery of the play. In a 1967 production of Part I at the Burgtheater in Vienna, Faust's study contained a desk built of scraps of broken iron, pieces of wood, bits of burlap, and odds and ends of leather and paper against a wall that was a collage of wood framing, broken books, bits of leather, pieces of manuscript, and ends of old cloth painted, sprayed, and aged to the color and surface of an old cave interior. The concept was one of total assault on the senses through the fullest use of a very textured surface, while simultaneously symbolizing the dusty decay in Faust's mind. It was completely modern and fully in keeping with the sensuous and imaginative power of the script, which exists above and beyond real life, yet it lacked stress on the intellectual, philosophical content of the drama. In a 1966 production of Part II at the Schiller Theater in Berlin, an almost opposite approach was taken (Figure 15–11). The intellectual, philosophical aspects of the drama were stressed, with exciting minor accents of mystery and theatricality. The settings were composed of glowing, colorless shapes made of plastic and metal; the music was abstract, cosmic, and mysterious; Helen appeared inside a transparent plastic sphere; and the general impression was one of a cosmic no-man's-land between Heaven and Earth. Again, the concept was very modern and fully in keeping with the monumental philosophical and intellectual concepts in the play, while playing down its sensuous aspects.

Figure 15–11.   A scene from *Faust II* as produced by the Schiller Theater in West Berlin, 1966. Directed by Ernst Schröder. Scenery by Bernhard Heiliger. Costumes by Alexander Camaro. An example of this metaphysical drama produced in terms of extremely contemporary visual images. Courtesy of the Staatliche Schauspielbühnen, Berlin.

In the presentation of *Faust* one must be conscious of the importance of visual spectacle. The direction should take full account of stage depth, with intimate scenes in smaller areas downstage contrasting with large scenes in full depth filling the entire stage; long curving arcs and diagonal movement should be used to give epic sweep to the action, while an artistic use of space and variety is important in achieving a larger-than-life, emotional, visual effect. Also, the acting should be broad, sweeping, larger-than-life, with a great variety and range in the use of voice and gesture. Finally, in examining the costumes needed for this drama, one should realize how important a factor they are in adding to the overall effect of the play. If the play is presented in a symbolist vein, with pieces of setting looming out of darkness to suggest a fuller and larger reality, then the cos-

tumes must add to this effect and be designed in rich color and texture in order to take full advantage of the lighting. A pictorial equivalent for these effects can be seen in Delacroix' watercolor of *Faust in His Study* (Figure 15–12). Small detail and complex trim should not be used, since they will be lost in the angular shafts of light; pleating, deep folds, tacks, draping, puckering, and puffing of fabric surfaces will be the most effective ways to take advantage of the lighting. Colors should be rich but subordinate to silhouette and texture, and the full effect of the costumes should come from the sculptured form of the actor moving in light. If the play is presented on a stage that always remains a platform, then the costumes may be the major accent in the production. In this case they may be designed as simple costume props or accessories added to the basic

Figure 15–12. *Faust in His Study* by Delacroix, Fogg Art Museum, 1828. A watercolor sketch done by this famous French romantic painter after reading Goethe's great work. Courtesy of the Fogg Art Museum, Harvard University. Bequest—Grenville L. Winthrop.

clothing of the actor, or they may be full, lavish romantic costumes that read as rich accents to an otherwise bare production. In the latter case the costumes should always have the aura of theatrical stage items even when fully and richly designed to project both character and the sweeping, sensuous images of the play. Color, line, and texture could then be closely related to emotional effects, and the costumes would have the major role in carrying the visual impact of the drama. Finally, in a production designed to make full use of the shapes, lines, textures, and color of modern art, the costumes would either have to be abstractions of period dress or garments that created no illusion of period. The major stress would be placed on the texture, line, and color effects chosen from sources in modern sculpture or modern painting. If an abstract expressionist

effect is desired, then many layers of texture composed of diverse materials such as shredded rope, plastics, and melted synthetics might be used to achieve the appropriate sensuous mood. If a cooler, machine-tooled effect is desired, then costumes made of smooth surfaces in glazed, metallic, or plastic textures with hard crisp edges might be appropriate.

The textures used in costumes for a drama such as *Faust* are very important in achieving the monumental, emotional, sensuous mood that the production requires, and great thought should be given to gaining the correct strength and mood unity in the choice of these textures. The lines of the costumes, although there are no limitations of period or shape, should be strong, monumental, and grand, with a larger-than-life silhouette in the finished costume (Figure 15–13). The color may be

Figure 15–13.   Costume sketches for Valentine and Martha by Frank Bevan for the Yale University production of *Faust,* Part 1, 1949. Note the simplicity, monumentality, and strength in the mass and line of these costumes for *Faust.* From *Theatre Arts Magazine,* July 1949. Reproduced by courtesy of the Collection of American Literature, Beinecke Rare Book and Manuscript Library, Yale University.

either strong or richly muted and subordinate to texture, but in no instance should it be weak, pastel, or superficial. Even if color is almost missing and the production is designed in neutrals or in a limited range of very dark tonalities, the scheme selected should be clear and forceful, not weak and fuzzy.

In a play of this size and scope, visual prescriptions cannot be few, and because this play strains every possibility of the physical theatre, it is ever a challenge for the designer to attempt something new and exciting in order to transmit the power, infinity of experience, and vitality of Faust's quest.

16

Realistic Plays

Art and Culture in the Midnineteenth Century

About the middle of the nineteenth century the idealistic, subjective views of romanticism began to seem meaningless and overblown. Although there had been several revolutions against repressive political regimes, there had been no real reform, and the principles of liberty, equality, and fraternity, in the face of the exploitations of the Industrial Revolution, appeared outworn and passé. In the face of a factory system that drew ever more workers into urban slums, the romantic tendency to see solutions in the inner heart, soul, and imagination of humanity seemed vague and impractical. Intellectual leaders and artists began to insist that dreams and the imagination be put aside in favor of systematic research into human personality and human society. Observation, clinical analysis, and scientific study of people and institutions were to replace the subjective idealism of romanticism.

A major contribution to this new outlook was the positivist philosophy of Auguste Comte, the father of sociology, whose writings between 1830 and the early 1850s argued for the study of society in a carefully controlled scientific manner. He felt that events in society could be predicted and determined in a clear cause-and-effect relationship by using the scientific method. This concept was further reinforced by the published theories of Charles Darwin, who developed the doctrine that all forms of life had evolved from a common ancestry and that this evolution was based on the concept of the survival of the fittest. These theories, coupled with those of positivism, suddenly made heredity and environment very important to both sociologist and artist and came to be considered the principal explanation of why individuals and societies developed in a particular direction. Behavior became something beyond the control of the individual, and only improvements in heredity and environment could better the human condition.

Thus, knowledge and truth in the realistic movement were limited to scientific observation obtained through the five senses, and intuition, imagination, visions, and all forms of the supernatural were removed from art and literature. Visually, the new ideal was given great support through the invention of photography, and the objective visual reporting that the camera made possible became a tremendous influence on all the arts during the latter half of the nineteenth century. A peephole glance at life, a scene caught by a camera in the corner of a room, on a street corner, at a café, in which people and objects were framed by the edge of the film, became a way of seeing for painters and writers alike. The paintings of Edgar Degas give an excellent indication of how such seemingly accidental views of life become the framework for the carefully planned structural effects and craftsmanship to be found in realistic plays (Figure 16–1).

The very narrowness of the envelope within which a story could be developed led to a great stress on subtlety, form, and intricate charac-ter-story relationships. At a time when those opposed to realism were decrying the loss of style in art, the practice of the new method was leading novelists such as Flaubert and playwrights such as Ibsen to a new and deeper sense of style, a harsh and demanding craftsmanship, and a distilled human poetry that eventually lead to symbolism and the abstractions of modern art and literature. Forced to discard the clichés of romanticism, the realists narrowed their work and vision to go beyond outer action to a study of what Francis Fergusson calls the "movement of the psyche." At its peak, realism triumphs over its limitations of place, character, and language.

The same is true in painting; artists such as Courbet continually rise above the limitations they set for themselves and inspire subjective,

Figure 16–1.   *Interior: The Rape* by Degas, Collection of H. P. McIlhenny, Philadelphia, 1874. An example of the apparently casual "peephole" view of Parisian life, in which every item of furniture, the placement of the actors, and the use of light are very carefully selected and planned for dramatic effect. Courtesy of the H. P. McIlhenny Collection.

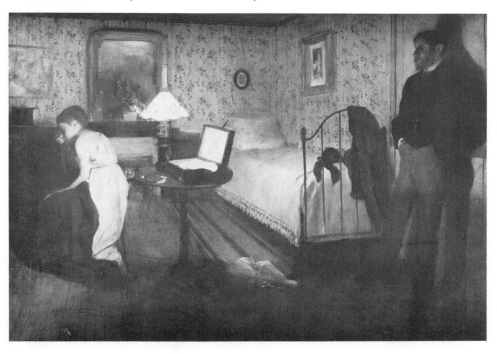

Figure 16–2. Jean-Léon Gérôme, *L'Eminence Grise (Grey Eminence),* Museum of Fine Arts, Boston, n.d. An example of the contrived "academic exercise" in painting that was admired in the salons of the nineteenth century. Note its superficial and artificially contrived subject, which enables the artist to demonstrate his technical ability. Courtesy, Museum of Fine Arts, Boston. Bequest of Susan Cornelia Warren.

Figure 16–3. *The Stone Breakers* by Courbet, formerly in the State Picture Gallery, Dresden (destroyed during World War II), 1849. An example of the new realism in subject matter and painterly detail led by the artist Courbet. Courtesy of the State Picture Gallery, Dresden.

sensuous responses rather than coldly scientific ones. In fact, it is the salon art and its "academic machines" of the latter half of the nineteenth century that produce works with a scientific objectivity. *L'Éminence Grise* by Gérôme (Figure 16-2) is superficially romantic and historical, but its painting method is more accurate in form, more technical, and more objectively rendered than a work such as Courbet's *The Stone Breakers* (Figure 16-3); and yet the latter transcends mere reporting and delves deeply into subjectively experienced personal values. In giving up the broad sweep of vision available to artists since the Renaissance for the narrow confines of the everyday scene, the realists either succeeded with sharply focused concentration and depth or failed with a superficial reproduction of certain small areas of life.

Realism in Theatre and Drama

REALISTIC STAGING.   The latter part of the nineteenth century saw an ever greater attempt at historical reality in staging, with more pieces of scenery built in three dimensions than in the past, and perspective backdrops painted, masked, and lit to give as much illusion of reality as possible. For plays requiring one or more interiors to set the action, the movement was entirely away from side wings and painted drops to the three solid walls of a box set. The plays that represented the "new drama" at midcentury were basically romantic melodramas disguised as realism, and it took the work of Ibsen, Dumas *fils,* Augier, and others to create plays in which the setting and the overall visual environment of the action were an integral part of the drama.

Along with the increasing demand for the integration of background and action came the call for the integration of all other aspects of production, and from this need arose the role of the stage director. George II, Duke of Saxe-Meiningen, is usually credited with developing the completely integrated, large-scale real-

istic production. He himself designed all the scenery and costumes, worked out blocking, picturization and movement, and organized the extended rehearsal period. Depending on no stars, his entire company was subordinated to the overall stage effect, and in his many tours to the leading cities of Europe the "Theatre Duke" spread the gospel of the realistic, ensemble performance for the stage classics of the day (Figure 16-4).

But it remained for independent noncommercial groups in Paris, Berlin, and Moscow to introduce these staging methods into productions of the new dramas of realism. André Antoine, at the Théâtre Libre (founded in Paris in 1887), stressed absolute naturalness in his stage pictures, with every property and item of set decoration taken from real life. The Freie Bühne in Berlin in 1889, the Indepen-

Figure 16-4.   An engraving of the Saxe-Meiningen Company in a performance of Shakespeare's *Julius Caesar.* An example of the dynamic and precise planning of crowd scenes that made the work of this company admired throughout Europe. Crown Copyright Victoria and Albert Museum (Theatre Museum).

Figure 16–5.   Act I of the original production of Chekov's *The Cherry Orchard* at the Moscow Art Theatre in 1904. An example of the untheatrical, everyday realism practiced by Stanislovsky and his associates in their productions of Chekov's plays. Photo courtesy of the Stanford University Drama Department Theatrical Slide Collection.

dent Theatre in London in 1891, and the Abbey Theatre in Dublin in 1904 all focused on the new realism, but the group with the most lasting influence, especially in the training of the actors, was the Moscow Art Theatre founded in 1898 by Constantin Stanislavsky and Nemirovitch Dantchenko (Figure 16–5). Stanislavsky eventually developed his theories on actor training into two books: *My Life in Art* and *An Actor Prepares,* and his basic precepts might be summed up as follows: Actors must be superbly trained in the use of body and voice, while also developing psychological techniques that permit emotional recall of personal experiences that can be related to a particular role. Actors must be able to define and outline the core of their roles, particularly the key desires that motivate their characters throughout a play, but such knowledge cannot be projected to an audience unless the actors can fuse all their onstage work into a single

purpose through concentration. Their response to other actors, their sense of the rhythmic development of the play, and their ability to work continuously toward refinement and perfection of their art are all tied to the ideal of onstage concentration. Again, as in writing and painting, the new realism led to a concentration of focus and a depth of penetration.

REALISM VERSUS NATURALISM. Of the many contributors to the drama of realism, the two greatest are undoubtedly Ibsen and Chekov—the first making use of the careful plotting of the "well-made play" to project themes of social import, the second developing the play of mood to project the hidden longings and frustrations of human nature. Ibsen stresses structure and craftsmanship in his playwriting, while Chekov is so skillful at concealing the mechanics of his work that the audience has the feeling that it has seen scenes from real life.

Before discussing plays by Ibsen and Chekov in detail, the distinction that is frequently made between realism and naturalism must be considered. The term naturalism is usually said to have originated in the essays of Émile Zola in France, who insisted that the drama go beyond the well-made problem play in which the author selects and arranges events to gain particular dramatic effects. Zola demanded a scientific, objective analysis of life presented on the stage and suggested the "slice-of-life" technique, which restricted the playwright to the recording of case studies. The importance of an absolutely accurate environment in order to show its influence on character was considered to be very important, and actors were urged to live, not play, their parts. Although no purely naturalistic drama was ever written, many playwrights reveal aspects of this form, including August Strindberg, Maxim Gorky, Gerhardt Hauptmann, Eugene O'Neill, and Elmer Rice.

Ghosts

Ibsen's *Ghosts,* which depicts the hollowness of a conventional, nineteenth-century marriage, is a typical thesis play that also includes the thrill and tricks of boulevard entertainment. On the one hand, the play pretends to be not art, but life itself; on the other, it is more artfully crafted than any acknowledged "well-made play" by Scribe or Sardou.

PLOT AND STRUCTURE. Structurally, *Ghosts* can be viewed on two levels: as a rational welding together of a series of events with a clear-cut moral, and as the "soul" or inner story of the outward action. It is actually organized as a series of debates on conventional morality between Pastor Manders and Mrs. Alving, the Pastor and Oswald, and Oswald and Mrs. Alving. There is a mounting, carefully controlled element of suspense maintained throughout, and each act ends

with an exciting moment that sets the issues to date and promises intriguing new developments. But behind the surface events of the story there is a vaguely suggested tragic form, containing a deep and brooding view of the human condition.

CHARACTERIZATION. Each principal character in the play suffers, searches for answers, and gains new personal insights with each reversal of the action. Mrs. Alving, like Hamlet and Oedipus, is involved in a search for her true human condition, but as in Greek tragedy, we are shown only the end of the search, when the events of the past are illuminated by the present. Like Oedipus, as one veil after another is removed from the past and the present, Mrs. Alving begins to realize what the past and its dead ideas have done to her. The theme of the play—the "ghosts" of the past that have come to haunt the present—follows her to the end of the drama, and she becomes both a symbol and at the same time a very real, warm, and deeply understood human being. Oswald is also both a symbol of dissolution and decline and a very pathetic individual, and Pastor Manders, representing all the clichés about bourgeois morality, is but a pathetic shell of a man. All of the major characters are thus symbols, believable human beings, and stereotypes who might appear in a boulevard melodrama.

THEME. The central idea behind this drama is a strong and vivid attack on the emptiness of a conventional bourgeois marriage and a strong demonstration of the horror that can develop when a marriage such as that between Captain and Mrs. Alving is not terminated. Within the course of the action the playwright attempts to prove that Mrs. Alving should have left the Captain twenty years before and that such a marriage is evil and wrong.

DIALOGUE. Through the fumbling phrases of everyday conversational speech, Ibsen attempts, by the use of symbolic words and phrases such as "ghosts," to suggest a half-uttered, half-hidden poetry of feelings and ideas that can be fully demonstrated not in words but in acting. There is no verbal music, only a hidden poetry masquerading as reporting, a poetry not of words but of the theatre, and the dialogue in a play such as *Ghosts* can only come alive in the theatre in the performances of outstanding players.

RHYTHM. The rhythm of the play also operates on at least two levels: (1) that of everyday life and events within the circumscribed setting of the bourgeois home, and (2) that which develops from the movement of the intrigue toward climaxes at the end of each act—a series of reversals and revelations that lead directly to the final moment of resolution.

SPECTACLE. Ibsen's realistic technique can be fully seen in the visual elements needed for *Ghosts*. A detailed description of the setting is given, and the setting is very important to the play's action, especially the photographically accurate parlor in the foreground contrasted with the large window in the background, which reveals snowy peaks and suggests the exhilarating wilderness beyond the cramped interior. The characters are heavily influenced by the physical conditions around them, and this must be made abundantly clear through an adequate and accurate representation of the environment. The characters really seem to live in the setting, and they in turn help to create the environment. Therefore, the set designer must be as subtle and aware as the playwright of the actions and characters in the drama. The movement and physical action of the play must also be based on observations from life and on the organization of effects evident in the plot structure. Furniture can be used to assist, block, or complicate the action, and it can be arranged visually to give great meaning to the personal relationships in the play. Costumes must also act on one level to provide a sense of real clothing and on another to complement and assist the relationships, mood, and action of the drama.

Visual Presentation of Ghosts

In a contemporary production of a play such as *Ghosts,* there are not many choices of staging. Any direct approach to stage realism demands a fourth-wall production, in which the audience is shown the three walls of a room with an illusion of reality in all its furnishings and accessories. This means that the designer working with realism must work with more subtlety and care than the designer working in any other style, since all the elements of mood, shape, texture, line, and color must be subordinate to the overall reality of the scene. At no time can the designer of scenery and costumes allow personal predilections or any abstract artistic ideals to dominate the visual scene; every artistic choice must be dictated by the need to develop the reality of the play's characters and the environment in which they live (Figure 16–6).

Figure 16–6. An original sketch for Hedvig in *The Wild Duck* by Henrik Ibsen designed by Laurence Irving, 1953. Courtesy of the Norman Philbrick Library.

The size of the setting for *Ghosts* need not give the illusion of size and monumentality. This is based on the intimate, private nature of the place of the action (Mrs. Alving's parlor) and on the limited, concentrated nature of the play's construction. Since the play has only five characters, it is important to establish a setting in which each character's actions illuminate their interpersonal relationships. The shape, size, texture, and color of the setting must be carefully considered in order to support the environmental mood needed at the inception of the drama. The single most important mood to be established is that of the ghost of Captain Alving, the sense of what the past twenty years of Mrs. Alving's life with this man must have been like. Unlike the effects in pure Belasco naturalism, one should avoid cluttering the walls with decorative detail, so that the primary effects of mood and environment are not blocked or obscured. In a play such as *Ghosts* a selective realism, whereby every item of set decoration is chosen to reveal the past history of a room, is far more important than merely presenting the audience with a replica of a Victorian parlor in Norway in the 1880s (Figure 16–7).

Probably the single most important item for both director and actors in a realistic play such as *Ghosts* is the furniture. It must be chosen to suit the environmental mood of the room and the character of its owners, but more important is its placement to give the strongest visual possibilities to the sharp conflicts and long debates that shape the drama. Tables and chairs must be the right height, have the right shape, and have the right weight to be used as barriers or support. More than anything else, the furniture can help to evoke the hothouse, prison-like atmosphere that has been the center of Mrs. Alving's life since her marriage to Captain Alving (Figure 16–8).

Many painters of the late nineteenth century have illuminated interpersonal relationships through the placement of the people and furniture, and none has accomplished this more brilliantly than Edgar Degas. For example, there is his painting, *The Bellelli Family,* in which the father is facing upstage and is separated from his family by the edge of the

Figure 16–7.   A scene from *Ghosts* by Henrik Ibsen as produced by the National Theatre of Oslo. The production approach is that of selective realism. Courtesy of the Oslo National Theatre. Photo by Sturlason.

Figure 16–8. A scene from *Ghosts* by Henrik Ibsen as produced by the American Conservatory Theatre, San Francisco, 1980. Directed by Allen Fletcher, scenery by Ralph Funicello, costumes by Martha Burke. An example of the strong feeling of mood that can be obtained within the narrow limitations of realism. Courtesy of the American Conservatory Theatre. Photo by Ron Scherl.

fireplace and the placement of his chair. The mother dominates one daughter by pulling the girl against her, while the other daughter shows a more independent nature, balanced between the mother and the father (Figure 16–9). Another painting by Degas, variously labeled *Interior: The Rape* or *The Seduction* (see Figure 16–1), uses the placement of the two principals within a particular furniture arrangement to achieve a heavy and ominous atmosphere. The woman is seated weeping at her dressing table, the iron bed illuminated by a small table lamp lies in the center of the painting on a diagonal, and the man, lost in shadows, is leaning on the door at the far right. It is exactly like the climactic scene in a realistic play, and a study of the so-called camera angle and ''snapshot'' effects of Degas can be of great help to a set designer and a director of any realistic play. The plays of Ibsen are as carefully devised in the logical plotting of the structure of events as are the lines and forms in a Degas painting.

It is difficult to give any secure guidelines about costume design, since each costume must be designed to fit exactly the reality of the character wearing it. The subtleties of personality and character suggested by each costume must precede any thought of overall design or atmospheric mood. At the same time, it is a mistake in realistic costume design to work so carefully for evocation of individual characters that the overall mood or atmosphere of the setting is lost.

One important distinction to make in designing costumes for a play such as *Ghosts* is that the costumes must not be laden with naturalistic detail. It is a selective realism that suits Ibsen's method of character and plot development. This means the inclusion of only those items of dress essential to illumination of character and reality, not the inclusion of busy details that suggest authentic period garments. It is important to realize that the clarity of accent and detail in costume should be as sharp as the accent and detail in the plot and development of character.

Concerning the specifics of costume, the above ideas about selective realism can readily be related to the choice of line, texture, and color. The line chosen both for costume silhouette and ornamentation should be simpler and

Figure 16-9. *The Bellilli Family* by Degas, The Louvre, Paris, 1859. An example of family relationships presented through placement of the members of the family in relation to one another, to the furniture, and to the room. Courtesy of the Musées Nationaux—Paris.

sharper than if the costumes were reproduced exactly from period sources, as the development of story and character is clearer and sharper than in real life. The textures used should be tied first to personality and character and second to the mood of the setting and the mood of the entire play. The thick, heavy, complex, oppressive textures that we associate with Victorian dress or Victorian parlor fabrics are completely right for the characters in this play. Although there is little opportunity to use any variety of these effects in individual costumes, it should be kept in mind as an image during design. It is certainly true that Pastor Manders must be in the black frock coat and clerical collar of his profession, that Regina wears a maid's costume, that Oswald dresses in a dark Victorian suit with a few Bohemian touches, and that Mrs. Alving wears a severe gown suggesting her position as the widow of Captain Alving; but in each case a very subtle difference of effect will occur with each choice of fabric if the oppressive, heavy atmosphere of the Alvings' parlor is retained as an image, and if the symbolic images suggested by the "ghosts" of the play's title are also recalled. This last point might be particularly important concerning color. The requirements of the characters' positions demand grayed, dark, oppressive color, with only tiny accents to break the monotony, but the exact tonalities can be subtly artistic.

The Cherry Orchard

If the range of realism is to be understood, then it is important to contrast Ibsen's *Ghosts* with a play such as *The Cherry Orchard* by Anton Chekov. The difference between the two writers' methods is very illuminating for the designer, especially when their individual approaches to plot and character are used as the basis for the visual design of their plays.

PLOT AND STRUCTURE. By the time Chekov wrote *The Cherry Orchard,* the ambitious machinery of the thesis thriller had begun to fade in favor of presenting the human spirit and human emotions, not in action, but in the pauses in life. This play is often said to have no plot, but by being free of the mechanical plotting of the "well-made play," it becomes a series of apparently casual incidents—a theatrical poem dealing with the pathos and suffering that accompany individual and social change. Chekov believes that those perceptions that precede rational analysis are the most true in life, and he selects those moments in his characters' lives between their rational strivings when they are most vulnerable, open, and obvious—when their personal situations are most directly felt and perceived. The action of the play is then built around four ceremonial family moments that make up the four acts of the play: the arrival back from Paris to take up the old way of life; the pause at sunset when all of the characters see themselves and their lives fleetingly for what they really are; the slightly hysterical party when the announcement about the sale of the cherry orchard is finally made; and the final departure.

CHARACTERIZATION.   In characterization there is a great difference between what we learn about the characters and the vague personal perceptions that are presented on stage. Chekov is extremely dependent on the subtle interpretive abilities of his actors, and only in a superbly orchestrated production will the poetic subtleties of characterization crystallize. For example, Lopahkin is a man of action and could have been used as a symbol of Russia's move into the future, but he is shown at moments of reflection when he is forced to examine his own motives in a rather pathetic way. Mme Ranevsky, who has traveled throughout Europe and might have been shown by another playwright with her lover in Paris, is here shown in all her pathetic, impractical, emotional immaturity, at a moment of pause in her frivolous life when she has to face herself and her past. Particularly in Act II, Chekov allows each character to reveal himself or herself within a mood that suggests that all rational processes have ceased, to allow subconscious longings their full expression.

THEME.   Unlike *Ghosts,* this play does not have a theme or thesis in a true sense of that word. In the final analysis, the play appeals to the poetic and emotional sensibilities, and all so-called themes must be read into the play or interpreted into it in production.

DIALOGUE.   The dialogue is as difficult to define as the characters. Once again, it is not the dialogue itself but the ability of the actor interpreting it that makes it have life, poetry, beauty, and meaning. The pauses, breaks, half-phrases, whispers, giggles, exclamations, tears, and laughter are as much a part of the dialogue as the words themselves; and only if

all are included can one sense the inexpressible poetry underlying modern life as evoked by the playwright. It is because Chekov says so little that he reveals so much; he knows that the poetry of modern realistic drama is to be found in those inarticulate moments when the human creature is shown responding directly to an all too human situation.

RHYTHM.   Nothing could indicate more clearly the difference between *Ghosts* and *The Cherry Orchard* than their rhythms. In the first the rhythm is tightly developed through developing conflict to crisis and denouement, while in the latter it is loosely tied to three ceremonial occasions related to the return to the estate, its sale, and the final departure. Although the rhythm is subordinated to the emotional moods of the characters and the subtle poetry of the setting, it is one of the strongest values in the play—like the inexorable flow of an underground stream occasionally observed through an opening in the ground.

SPECTACLE.   The play demands three realistic settings, two indoors and one out, and in the original production at the Moscow Art Theatre each was very literally reproduced; but it should already be obvious that photographic fact in Chekov should be put aside in favor of suggestion, and that lighting in particular will be very important in creating mood. Like music, lighting is able to define mood and atmosphere indirectly, and in this sense Chekov visually demands a production that is balanced between strict realism and symbolic impressionism. By Chekov's day, the symbolist movement in literature and the impressionist movement in art had reached full development, and much of the secondary level of effect in Chekov comes from this artistic "impressionism." The impressionist painters had begun as realists and then felt that they were deepening their realism through underlining nature's or people's moods. Only by understanding what light filtered through cherry blossoms, the sunset hours of the day, and a chandelier-illuminated party would mean to an impressionist painter can a designer have an appropriate feeling of the settings for *The Cherry Orchard.*

In the use of furniture, again the contrast between Ibsen and Chekov should be stressed. Ibsen, like Degas, uses furniture to strengthen conflict, control action, and focus movement and climax. Chekov, using a looser playwriting method, uses furniture for purposes of mood, as symbols of the past, reminders of events and feelings long forgotten. Furniture may also act to break up the usual direct patterns of movement in order to match the halting, broken rhythms of the play's development. Nothing could be more symbolic of this effect than the clumsiness of Epihodov, who is made to stumble over chairs.

In costumes, the requirements are not merely those of character, but also of mood and atmosphere. Suggestion is more important than detailed fact, and a strict realism in choice of garments is less important than the overall interplay of costume effects to establish the mood of the four semiceremonial occasions that make up the four acts.

Visual Presentation of *The Cherry Orchard*

In his stage directions, Chekov is uncomfortably bound by the realistic conventions of his time, and to fabricate in a very literal manner three settings for this play out of cyclorama, flats, cut-out silhouettes, heavy furniture, complex bits of set decoration, and strong lighting effects would be to create the interesting but unbelievable antique effect that we still amusedly associate with the settings of David Belasco. The best strategy is to pay only lip service to photographic realism and to keep all the elements as simple as possible, so that the imagination of the audience can be stimulated rather than inhibited by the number and complexity of the set decorations. Even more than Ibsen, Chekov adds the extra dimension of symbolism to his setting demands.

The textures used in the setting should appeal to a sense of association and nostalgia for a past that is rapidly drifting away. Curtains and upholstery should have a softness and a vagueness that would be in sharp contrast to the harsh effects in *Ghosts.* The cornices and mouldings, the door panels and the details of set decoration should suggest rather than state; one should have to guess when the house was built and pay little specific attention to its overall period decor. All textural effects should help to establish that poetry behind the realism that we have described in relation to the plot, characters, and dialogue of this play.

The line of setting and the colors used should also evoke the moody and indefinite. It must be a ''real'' set, not some poetic abstraction, but the suppressed mood and poetry beneath that realism can only come through if the colors are rather faded and indefinite and if the lines are not too harsh and rigid. The outdoor mood of Act II is completely enmeshed with the line of the trees that are used, and the poplars indicated in the script must have all the mournful character and mood of a ''dying fall'' that will support the nostalgic and sad ''passage of time'' indicated by this act of the play (Figure 16–10). The chandelier-lit party mood of Act III can be effective only if the drawing room is a complex mixture of fading grandeur and sad happiness. The softness of tears, which continually erupt in this act, must be in the colors of the upholstery and draperies and in the soft lines of furniture, paneling, and set decorations.

Finally, the costumes must be capable of adding to the same effect, and straightforward realism based on turn-of-the-century fashions will be quite wrong. Once again, vagueness and suggestion must be the key, and since we have mentioned Chekov's visual affinity to much of the work of the impressionist painters, a study of costume in the works of Renoir and Monet would do much to prepare the designer to make appropriate choices for *The Cherry Orchard.* Looking at costumes in impressionist paintings, the viewer is struck by the studied indefiniteness with which the artist has suggested rather than stated a suit or a gown. It is

Figure 16–10.   Act II of *The Cherry Orchard* as produced by The Stanford Repertory Theatre, Stanford University, 1967, with settings by Richard Hay, costumes by Richard Odle. An example of simplified realism to project mood through changes in lighting. Photo courtesy of Hank Kranzler.

admittedly easier to get some of these indefinite effects in women's clothes than in men's, since male clothes in the nineteenth century were so rigidly set regarding cut and line, and so devoid of ornament, that an indefinite line is almost impossible. Subtle effects can be achieved, however, through the use of soft-textured woolens for suits and coats rather than hard-surfaced gabardines, or through color choices that are muted and rather indefinite. Sometimes accessories can be used, such as a shawl or a smoking jacket, to further

soften the hard line of late nineteenth-century male attire. In the case of the women's dress the problem is simpler, although here the specific requirements of a hunting costume for Charlotta and a maid's uniform for Dunyasha do limit the design choices. Fabric choices should be in terms of changeable fibers, laces over solids, soft, absorptive textures, surfaces that suggest through light reflectivity and absorption a sense of indefiniteness, changeability, or subtlety. Lace is a particularly useful costume effect, whether in a full-lace dress over a subtle solid-color fabric beneath—an effect that is particularly close to many impressionist paintings—or as an item of trim or an element of accessory decoration. Since lace is one of the chief fashion fabrics of the period, it is also an acceptable choice without contradicting the fashion line of the times. In color, also, subtlety, indefiniteness, and suggestion should be paramount, and heavy, rich, strong colors should be avoided except as accent. Muted colors, pastels, changeable colors, mottled colors,

and broken color effects are needed to match the broken and shifting effects in the dialogue, rhythm, and characterizations in this play. The strong lines of plot organization and character delineation found in *Ghosts,* which demand equally strong and clear costume effects, are completely missing in *The Cherry Orchard.* The costumes for this play must evoke a mood, suggestion, wispiness, a sense of the passage of time and the disappearance of the past (Figure 16–11).

Figure 16–11. Costume sketches by the author for Mme Ranevsky and Gaev in Act II of *The Cherry Orchard.* An example of the use of light color tonality to create mood and to reflect changes in the lighting. From the collection of the author.

17

Symbolist Plays

Art and Culture at the Close of the Nineteenth Century

To the poets, realism seemed a betrayal of the role of the artist in society, a debasement of art from the realms of the artistic to a mere reporting of life. The artists who rejected realism as an answer to the challenge of modern industrial society were not late-blooming romantics but modernists who were probing beneath the surfaces of life and art. While the earlier romantics surrendered themselves to feeling in order to become emotionally involved in their art, the artists who followed the theories of Baudelaire had an unremitting care for composition, style, and how to turn the intuitive and the irrational into carefully planned artistic products. Art was seen as a movement, a shape, a rhythm to be imposed on feeling—a quite self-conscious attempt to impose a personal style and form on the raw materials of life. Each artist hoped to assure his or her own view of experience as the direction of a new, cohesive cultural style that would reunite the artist with the general public. Throughout the nineteenth century, with cultural absolutes all but destroyed, the true artists had been waging

war against the false prestige and historic superficialities purveyed by the great academies and salons of art and literature. Finally, in the last decade of the century they promoted a new style, *art nouveau,* which was the first great Europe-wide artistic movement since the Rococo.

In this new movement, which has been given the overall name of *symbolism,* concentration was on form over content and the inner life of the material over the outward fact. It divided itself roughly into three methods: (1) art that stresses the inner secrets of life through mood and suggestion (impressionistic symbolism); (2) art that stresses style and manner of presentation over content (neomannerism); (3) art that depicts inner emotional states of being through violent, harsh, and distorted attacks on the senses (expressionistic symbolism). All of these movements can be grouped under the title of symbolism because all turn their back on reality and the objective facts of life and use symbols to make their artistic points.

Impressionistic symbolism is an art of suggestion in which the early symbolist poets and artists such as Redon used vague symbols to sug-

Figure 17-1. *Rouen Cathedral* by Monet, The Metropolitan Museum of Art, Theodore M. Davis Collection, 1894. An example of the dissolution of reality and structural form by mist and light in the later work of Monet. Mood, atmosphere, and a personal vision take precedence over visual facts. Photo courtesy of The Metropolitan Museum of Art, New York, bequest of Theodore M. Davis, 1915. All rights reserved, The Metropolitan Museum of Art.

gest deeply buried inner states of feeling. Even impressionism in painting, originally intended to expand optical reality through the creation of momentary effect, gradually drifted in the work of Monet into vague, moody dream-like effects in which the results were often close to the sublimated reveries of the symbolist poets (Figure 17-1). In sculpture, impressionistic symbolism is exemplified in the shifting, changing surfaces in the work of Rodin (see

Figure 9-19). Like the famous descriptive phrase in the journal of the artist Delacroix, art was to be like "the memory of music" that has passed away. Odilon Redon was the painter who came closest to this ideal in works entitled *Silence, The Thought,* and *The Dream.* He used the resources of the inner mind and not the world of the senses to develop his images, and his hope was to create an art that had the uncertain, indefinite mood effect formerly possible only in music. Such an effect is exemplified in architecture by the Church of the Holy Family in Barcelona, designed by Antonio Gaudi (Figure 17-2). In drama this method was followed by Maurice Maeterlinck, while

Figure 17-2. Antonio Gaudi, Church of the Holy Family, Barcelona, begun in 1888. Gothic in outline, the design is based on the dreamlike curves and undulating shapes of the then-developing *art nouveau* style. Photo courtesy of the Spanish National Tourist Office.

in music Claude Debussy was the great exponent of the impressionist tradition of the symbolist poets. In his vague, moody, shifting evocations of the moon and sea we have in music
what the painters and poets longed for in their
art.

But impressionistic symbolism tended to be
formless, and it was to this problem that the
neomannerists addressed themselves. They used
many of the same images and symbols, but
stressed form, design, and pattern as equal to
mood in the content of their work. They developed artificiality and style as ends in themselves in much the same way as the sixteenth-
century mannerists. For example, in the work
of Gauguin, the flat poster, the woodcut, and
the Japanese print are as evident in the shaping
of the decorative pattern of the composition as
is South Seas mythology in shaping the content
(Figure 17–3).

In *expressionistic symbolism* it is the quality of

assault on the senses that is important. Its beginnings are apparent in the 1890s in the
paintings of Edvard Munch, James Ensor, and
Vincent van Gogh and in the plays of August
Strindberg, and in each case the art was due to
a very subjective development in the personality of a neurotic and tortured individual
(Figure 17–4). Patterns and symbols are used
in a distorted, explosive, violent, nightmarish
manner to depict the outward world through
the inward world of the artist. In lashing out
and attacking the suffering, horror, and injus-
tice in life, the expressionistic symbolists produced art that is often distorted to near abstraction, and eventually this led to abstract
expressionism following World War II. But in
the painting of the German expressionists and
the work of the fauvist Rouault, the artist is
specifically tied to a distorted yet recognizable
assault on the senses and an attack on the
nature of society.

Figure 17–3. *Fatata Te Miti (By the Sea);* Paul Gaugin; National Gallery of Art, Washington;
Chester Dale Collection. An example of the strong sense of mood and style through pattern that
made Gaugin a leader among the symbolists as well as among the craftsmen of the *art nouveau.*

Figure 17-4. *The Scream* by Munch, National Gallery, Oslo, 1893. An example of the swirling brushstrokes and exaggerated shapes that carry the artist's subjective and overpowering image of fear to the level of nightmare. Photo courtesy of the National Gallery, Oslo.

The Revolt Against Realism in the Theatre

The theatrical ideals of the symbolists had their origin as early as the middle of the nineteenth century in the theories of Richard Wagner, who dedicated himself to a fusion of music, dialogue, color, light, shape, and texture to give a unified theatrical mood. In his theatre at Bayreuth he used a double proscenium, a curtain of steam, and a darkened auditorium to create a mystic division between audience and stage that would allow spectators to lose themselves in the artistic magic of the production. The symbolists borrowed many of his precepts when they premiered *Pelléas and Mélisande* at the Théâtre de l'Oeuvre in 1892 with a transparent curtain in front of the action and a great stress on mood. At about the same time,

Adolphe Appia, in an endeavor to bring the ideals of Wagner to real fruition, developed stage lighting as the great unifying factor in production—defining the actor in space against simple, abstract three-dimensional forms and supporting the continually shifting moods in the action and in the music.

A few years later, the young English designer Gordon Craig further developed the same ideals, placing even more emphasis than had Wagner and Appia on the super–artist-director who would blend action, words, line, color, and rhythm into a great artistic work in which the script was only a part of a much larger whole (Figure 17-5).

The influence of Appia and Craig was immense and could be seen in most artistically designed productions before World War II.

Figure 17-5. Design for *Electra* by Gordon Craig, ca. 1905. An example of the simple and magnificent forms given mood and beauty through dramatic lighting effects that marked the work of the "new stagecraft" and the arrival of symbolism in theatrical design. From *On the Art of the Theatre* by Edward Gordon Craig, Browne's Bookstore, Chicago, 1911. Original in the University of California Library at Los Angeles. Reproduced by courtesy of Edward Carrick Craig.

The scenic philosophy of the symbolists might be condensed as follows: a simplification of means and effects; an appropriate relationship of actor to background; suggestion, by which a single candelabrum could symbolize the entire culture of the Baroque era; a synthesis of all elements of a production into a complex and rhythmic fusion of sets, costumes, lights, actors, and script.

The theatre artist who best transformed these ideals into exciting theatrical productions was Max Reinhardt, who took Craig's slogan, "Not Realism, but Style," coupled it to the concept of the director as master theatre artist and seer, and created a new meaning throughout Europe for the title *régisseur*. He paraded before the public the theatrical styles of the past and of the East in great eclectic revivals that used visual and aural symbols to unify the production, and although his eclecticism was criticized by the modernists, he did bring design back into the theatre as a major artistic form (Figure 17-6). He became the master showman of the new theatre, and his name became a household word in the United States and in Europe. It was American artist-designers such as Robert Edmond Jones, Lee Simonson, Donald Oenslager, Norman Bel Geddes, and Jo Mielziner who carried the ideals of Appia, Craig, and Reinhardt into that exciting era of American theatre that followed World War I (Figure 17-7).

Figure 17–6. A sketch of Romain Rolland's *Danton* as produced by Max Reinhardt at the Grosses Schauspielhaus, Berlin, 1920. An example of the spectacular, style-conscious productions of this master of artistic eclecticism. From *Theater Pictorial* by George Altman, Ralph Freud, William Melnitz, and Kenneth Macgowan, University of California Press, Berkeley, 1953. Courtesy of University of California Press.

Figure 17–7. A sketch for Act III, scene 4 from Shakespeare's *Macbeth* as designed by Robert Edmond Jones for a production at the Apollo Theatre, New York, produced and directed by Arthur Hopkins, 1921. An example of violent theatrical expressionism used in presenting the psychology of the protagonist. From *The Theatre of Robert Edmond Jones,* edited by Ralph Pendleton, Wesleyan University Press, Middletown, Conn., 1958. Courtesy of Robert Thirkield.

Pelléas and Mélisande

One of the most fully symbolist dramas written to exemplify the precepts of impressionistic symbolism is Maurice Maeterlinck's *Pelléas and Mélisande*. In many ways the moody tale cries out for music, and the perfect wedding of composer and author took place when Claude Debussy made the play into an opera in 1902 (Figure 17–8).

PLOT AND STRUCTURE.   Based on Dante's tale of Paolo and Francesca, the structural development of this play consists of a series of loosely connected scenes that seem to have little relation to the main story line. The opening scene, in which a group of women are vainly attempting to wash the stains from the castle steps, is typical of the scene-by-scene development. It creates a mood of mystery and hopelessness, but it has nothing to do with the story of Pelléas' love for Mélisande. There are many more such scenes: the scene in which Mélisande's doves leave her forever, the scene in which she loses her ring, symbolizing the loss

of her marriage vow, the scene in which Yniold tries to lift a stone that symbolizes the weight of sin fallen on the family. Mood and theme are the important elements in the structure of this play, not the development of a story or plot. In fact, the number of scenes between the first meeting of the lovers and their deaths could be expanded or contracted without much effect on the development of the story, although each is intricately bound to the developing mood of the play. The scenes are connected by a thread of symbolic atmosphere rather than by a cause-and-effect chain of events.

Although the playwright used the five-act play form, the act divisions are purely arbitrary and do not mark any clear breaks or high points of suspense in the action. The true unit of division in this play is the scene, and each of the sixteen scenes suggests some aspect of the theme or deepens some mood effect.

CHARACTERIZATION.   The characters are as vague and mysterious as the mood. They are embodiments of vague feelings and desires that yearn for enlightenment, yet are destined

Figure 17–8.   A scene from *Pelléas and Mélisande* by Maeterlinck and Debussy as produced by the San Francisco Opera in 1979. An example of a simple line of costumes picked out from a dark background by dramatic lighting to achieve mood and the impression required. Courtesy of David Powers for the San Francisco Opera.

to live and die governed by some inexplicable law of fate. About all we are given is their age, their social class, and their names, plus a vague stroke or two to suggest personality. Fate is the great life force that hangs over all the characters. Maeterlinck is not interested in three-dimensional, flesh-and-blood people, but in states of feeling that creep upon his characters mysteriously and lead to mysterious and inexplicable consequences.

THEME. Since his theme is that fate rules all, the playwright presents all ideas indirectly in terms of repeated motifs and symbols. For example, water is used over and over again: there is the pool by which Mélisande is first discovered, the fountain in which she loses her ring, the bottomless pits of water under the castle, the water used to wash the blood stains from the steps, and the sea, which is a soul-beckoning place of release. The same repetition occurs with darkness and light. The forests are ever dark, the characters are seated in darkness groping toward light, lamps die out and cannot be relit. There are many more, and it is difficult to assign definite meanings to them, but throughout, love, happiness, and light are in continuous struggle with fate and the forces of darkness, with the fountains and pools of water symbolizing that reflecting element into which the characters peer in vain in an attempt to unlock life's mysteries. Maeterlinck is obsessed with an even more deterministic philosophy than the realists and naturalists and sees all life as a mysterious and impenetrable unknown.

DIALOGUE. The language of the play is extremely simple and repetitive, so that words and phrases ring in the inner ear as symbols for feelings that cannot be expressed. In his long essay, *The Treasure of the Humble*, Maeterlinck speaks of this second level of language as the dialogue "for the soul"—those seemingly unnecessary and superfluous words and phrases that speak to people's deepest strivings toward beauty and truth. The playwright expects the audience to search behind the words and pauses for the play's ultimate significance.

RHYTHM. The rhythm of *Pelléas and Mélisande* is predominantly gentle, shifting, and soft and has no harsh, abrupt changes. It allows for a deepening awareness to grow within the audience, and silence amid pauses is as important as the forward movement of the play. The rhythm of this play, like symbolist poetry and symbolist painting, is close to the moods and rhythms of quiet, flowing music.

SPECTACLE. The demands for appropriate visual effects are very insistent in a play such as *Pelléas and Mélisande,* yet it is difficult to establish the visual effects required. In the original production at the Théâtre de l'Oeuvre in Paris, the stage lighting was overhead and kept low in intensity; a gauze curtain was hung at the front of the stage so that the action seemed to take place at a distance and enshrouded in a light mist. The scenery and costumes were designed in pale gray tones to emphasize the poetic removal of the action from real life; the movement and gestures were unreal and trance-like; the characters' bodies and limbs seemed to be moved by some unseen force. A key to the visual presentation of this play is the word "mist," and a key item in the design concept is the use of light.

Visual Presentation of *Pelléas and Mélisande*

It has been only a single generation since we emerged from the period in which aspects of symbolist design were apparent in almost all artistically conceived commercial productions, and we are all somewhat involved in the reaction against this style. It might be very difficult today, at a time when epic theatre is admired, to expect an audience to take a production of *Pelléas and Mélisande* seriously. In *New Theatres for Old*, Mordecai Gorelik, who opposed symbolist theatre even at the height of its acceptance, quotes a description of a mock performance in which an audience enters a theatre in 2100 A.D. and falls into a dream-like trance suffused with floating images, perfume, pulsating rhythms, seductive music, overpowering emotions, and symbolic moods. And it is true that the symbolist impulse in theatrical production, if carried to its logical conclusion, could easily remove concrete ideas, clear-cut meaning, and fully developed plots completely from the theatre in favor of the trance-like reverie, the nebulous image, and the sensual stupor. Thus, the producer of *Pelléas and Mélisande* must concentrate less on vagueness and diffuseness of effect and more on emphasizing strong mood derived from simple sets and visual images. Curtains between scenes should be removed; there should be a continuous flow of action from scene to scene, accented and focused by the lighting. Although the use of transparent gauze might still be useful in suggesting vagueness in certain settings, to place the entire action behind such a curtain is probably not possible today. The transparent drop was to symbolist theatre what the painted backcloth was to nineteenth-century romanticism.

It is very appropriate to place all aspects of the physical production on the stage at once in a simultaneous setting that demands no shifting of scenery during the course of the play. This necessitates total reliance on the lighting to lead the audience from scene to scene and place to place. In a sense, a production of *Pelléas and Mélisande* has to be orchestrated by light and developed as if it were a musical composition (Figure 17–9). Each shape and form used must be modeled to the outline and textural surface that suggest the exact mood desired. Sharp, bleak rocks, jagged branches against a dying sky, heavy, shadowed castle stones lost in a veil of mist—each specific image must be simple and direct without the clutter of detail frequently found in symbolist productions in the early twentieth century. The pattern of movement within the setting must be close to that of ballet and dance—choreographed to achieve a vague, floating, musical effect that is the essence of characterization in this play. Acting and gesture must project the total mood rather than individual characterization. Textures within the setting should be soft, vague, and light-absorbing; harshness in textural effects should be avoided. Color, if it is to be used in the setting, should be soft and grayed (never harsh or brilliant) and able to be softened and changed by the play of light. All lines within the setting should be created to give the maximum mood and symbolic effect with a minimum of means (Figure 17–10).

Specifically, in the costumes for *Pelléas and Mélisande* the designer should try not to treat the period in a direct and obvious way. The key word is "suggestion," not period education. In the original production in 1892 the costumes were modeled after those found in the paintings of Hans Memling, but to use a specific source such as this today would distract from the indefinite mood of the entire playscript. The costumes may be vaguely medieval with fairytale overtones, but the audience should not be readily able to place them as to period or place. A generalized, vague, unspecified period in the past should be the goal, with concentration on the subtle, abstract effects of color, texture, line, and movement rather than on period detail. Probably the best medieval source from which to abstract the general lines of the costumes would be the flowing, draped lines of the Romanesque or very early Gothic, rather than a choice of fourteenth- or fifteenth-century sources with the consequent stress on pattern, decoration, and rich accessories. Simplicity, as was noted in the discussion of the play's dialogue, is essential to capturing the moodiness, the vagueness, the shifting sense of reality that comprise this play.

The single most important item in designing the costumes is the choice of fabric or texture to achieve the flowing line and vague, transparent effect that will complement the play's tenuous nature. Chiffons, gauzes, and china silks are appropriate fabrics; changeable silks and soft, flowing, lightweight woolens might also be used. Costumes that are being gently waved by an unseen breeze form the important image to keep in mind when choosing the fabrics. Sometimes filmy layers of transparent fabric can be used over shimmering metallics to give an indefinite, ethereal effect, or soft and absorbent pile can be used to shift and change with the subtle play of the lights.

Figure 17–9. A sketch for Act IV, scene 3 of *Pelléas and Mélisande* by Maeterlinck and Debussy as designed by Robert Edmond Jones as a project, 1921. A further example of simple forms used in an impressionistic way to achieve mood and mystery. From *The Theatre of Robert Edmond Jones,* edited by Ralph Pendleton, Wesleyan University Press, Middletown, Conn., 1958. Courtesy of the Frances G. Wickes Collection, Yale School of Drama.

Figure 17–10. A scene from *Pélleas and Mélisande* by Maeterlinck as produced by the Belgian National Theatre, 1963. Another example of indefinite mood-producing forms and wispy or light-reflecting costumes used to create an impression through atmosphere. Courtesy of the Belgian National Theatre. Photo Carl Hensler.

Figure 17–11.   A costume sketch by Dale Hennon for Mélisande in *Pélleas and Mélisande* for a classroom project in the Department of Drama, Stanford University. An example of the transparent, wispy, mood-evoking draperies that are intended to suggest rather than create a specific costume. Courtesy of Dale Hennon.

The garments should have a suggested, indefinite effect that changes and shifts with the pattern of the movement.

In color, the key must be the pale and the indefinite. This is one reason why changeable fabrics in which the color shifts with each movement are useful. Color itself is less important in this play than value contrasts and the reflection or absorption of light from fabric surfaces.

In line, the key must again be the suggested and the indefinite. The emphasis must be on garments that float and move with the choreographed action of the play. Heavy, strong, clear-cut costume outlines should be abandoned in favor of full-flowing sleeves, floating mantles, trains, and scarves that lend themselves to arabesques of choreographed movement. The accents and points of focus achieved through ornament and accessories should be kept to a minimum. The ornamentation used should glint and shimmer vaguely in the light rather than achieve specific outline and shape; also, ornament should be seductive and suggestive of mystery rather than focusing attention on parts of the costume and specific areas of the actors' bodies (Figure 17–11).

Because of its lack of concrete effects, impressionistic symbolism, as in *Pelléas and Mélisande,* appeals to a limited audience, and as a style has produced few important and lasting plays. But as an influence in the theatre and as a way of designing and producing plays of the past, it has had a very great effect, and its heritage is still strong today.

From Morn to Midnight

From Morn to Midnight was written by the German dramatist Georg Kaiser before World War I, but it was not produced until 1917. It stands as a clear-cut example of expressionism, since it retains the personal subjective vision of symbolism while lashing out in a direct assault on audience sensibilities—depicting a world twisted and distorted by inhuman social forces. *From Morn to Midnight* obviously owes something to the medieval Morality play, since it is written in scenes rather than acts, depicts the end of modern humanity in seven steps, and uses the Cashier as a contemporary Everyman. The time span from morning to midnight also seems to symbolize man's journey from birth to death, while the Cashier's search, like that of Oedipus, Faust, and Mrs. Alving, seems to be toward personal fulfillment—a quest that ends not in hope but in the debasement of modern humanity.

PLOT AND STRUCTURE. The seven scenes that compose the structure of the play are held together by the symbolic search of the Cashier, and all attention is focused on the experiences of this central character. Unity comes not from any logical organization of the scenes or from any causally related events, but through the illumination of the play's theme by concentration on the psychological deterioration of the Cashier as a modern Everyman.

The first two scenes are primarily introductory and serve to establish the dehumanizing effects of modern materialism and the mistaken values of modern society. The Cashier, as the common person, is presented as the mechanized slave to the bank and to the system, a robot who pays out money, enters sums in a book, and taps for attention—all with the exactness and precision of a soulless automaton. With the arrival of the Lady from Italy, the Cashier's automatic routine is jarred, and in his desire to possess her he reacts as one would expect in a system in which money is success: he steals a great sum of cash.

Then begins the search of this modern Everyman. He decides that his whole life has been wasted and empty, and with his new-found freedom and his large sum of money he sets out to explore life and all its possibilities. He soon meets Death for the first time; in succeeding scenes he finds no answers in family, politics, money, sensual pleasure, or religion. His final disillusionment comes when the Salvation Army girl who pretended interest in his soul turns him over to the police for a reward. At the end a tangle of wires outlines the form of Death, and as the Cashier runs into the wires with arms spread like Christ on the cross, there is a great crackling of electricity and an exploding of lamps. The ultimate comment is given by the policeman who says that there seems to be a short circuit in the wiring.

CHARACTERIZATION. The characters in this play are given only labels, not names, and their speeches and actions are composed of a series of clichés that make them stereotypes or symbols rather than individual personalities. It is the mechanical robot quality in each character that is important in projecting Kaiser's mechanistic view of modern life. Only the Lady from Italy, who represents an older way of life, and the Cashier, who symbolizes the search for a new way of life, escape to some extent from the overall mechanistic pattern.

The responsibility for carrying the play forward falls almost entirely on the shoulders of the Cashier. After the introductory scenes he is the spokesman for the playwright and the only character who senses that there must be an escape from the machine-like existence of modern society. Although he is a symbol, he does grow in understanding as the play progresses, and his search makes him seem more and more sympathetic as the scenes pass. However, he never becomes a three-dimensional psychological character because he must ever remain a symbol of escape from the deadening effects of modern life.

THEME. The theme of this play is strongly stated, repeatedly stressed, and single-mindedly pursued through all the scenes of the drama: the mechanistic, materialistic ideals of modern life must be changed, a search must be instituted for a way out of our present social goals, and human beings must once again be human, individualized, and free. Although the ending is quite pessimistic, it does suggest that a new man was about to emerge from the soulless automaton that was the Cashier, and one is left with the suggestion that it might be possible to redeem humankind. Were this to occur, the author suggests that a complete rebirth of society could then begin.

DIALOGUE. The language as it is developed in this play has a very mechanistic quality. It is frequently intended to be hammered out in a quick, staccato pattern like a telegraph message, reflecting the violent, direct impulses of the messages transmitted by modern machines. The dialogue is often deliberately repetitious, loud, fast-paced, and harsh in its effect so that the maximum aggressive, subjective effect on the sensibilities of the audience will be achieved.

RHYTHM. The rhythm of an expressionist drama such as *From Morn to Midnight* is very strong, shows violent shifts from moment to moment, and never drops its insistent, mechanical forward drive. It seldom allows a sense of rest and relaxation for the audience. The beat established by the rhythm of the play is one of the most powerful means of suggesting the mechanized and inhuman feelings that the playwright is saying are a part of modern existence.

SPECTACLE.   The visual setting must be distorted in the same mechanistic way to indicate the unfeeling, mechanical forms the author sees all around him in modern life. Scene 3, in particular, offers one of the most standard visual clues for the design of this and other expressionist plays. A tree becomes a skeleton before the eyes of the Cashier and the audience and then returns to its normal shape, expressing the idea that the author's vision of reality as seen through the eyes of the Cashier is the distorted view of life the audience must experience. The other characters in the play would presumably see everything as normal; it is only the "awakened" Cashier who sees things as they really are. The implication is, of course, that the audience has been deadened to the truth and that only through these visual exaggerations and distortions in setting and costumes can any of the truth about modern life be expressed.

In developing settings and costumes for expressionist plays in the period between World War I and World War II, designers made great use of changing fragments of distorted form rather than complete settings; color was unnatural and exaggerated; walls, windows, and doors often leaned and tilted at unbelievable angles; sizes of things were diminished and enlarged for psychological effect; lighting was bold, unrealistic, and violent; and costumes were exaggerated or turned into uniforms to give subjective mechanized effects (Figure 17–12). The rationale behind such design is symbolism; all items are distorted and exaggerated to gain violent symbolic effects that assault the sensibilities of the audience rather than lull them into a trance-like mood in which they are receptive to subtle inner truths. Both impressionistic symbolism and expressionism work to gain an overall subjective effect through symbols, and the design principles for both are those of symbolism. Where

Figure 17–12.   A scene from *The Adding Machine* by Elmer Rice as produced by the Stanford Players, Stanford University, 1948. An example of scenery distortion to give a subjective expressionistic effect to this graveyard scene. Photo courtesy of the Stanford Collection, Stanford University Libraries.

one is attempting to reach subjective truth through inner mood, the other is trying to achieve it through violently exaggerated outer effect.

Visual Presentation of *From Morn to Midnight*

In the complicated, unsentimental, nonidealistic world of the contemporary theatre, it might be more difficult to revive *From Morn to Midnight* successfully than other plays with longer histories, because this play seems much too simplistic and naive in its analysis of human ills and in its recommendations for a brighter future. Although the world it describes is basically our world, we have come to see our world as a more complicated, many-layered compilation of problems than is evident in this pre–World War I play. Therefore, great stress should be placed on the visual production. The story and its conclusion should take second place to the texture, color, shape, and lighting effects derived from modern art and films. The simple leaning and tilting of exaggerated and distorted forms would not be enough. These effects would connect in their simple naiveté with the pre–World War I simplicities of emerging cubism and futurism, rather than with the repellent textural effects found in modern junk art, the light effects found in modern op art and psychedelic "light shows," and the forms found in modern welded sculpture. One could choose any one of these modern art forms and a number of others as a point of departure, and each of the seven scenes would then be a variation on a basic, tortured distortion of modern reality.

The basic mechanization that must lie behind any design for this play might follow either the smooth, riveted, machine-tooled surface and lack of color that we observe in industrial machinery or the corroded, broken, decaying forms and surfaces of the junk yard, dump, or waste bin of modern industry. The first approach would lend itself best to the large, mechanized scenes in the bank and at the race track; the second would lend itself best

to the scene in which Death first appears in the gnarled tree and finally reappears in the tangled wires of the last scene. However, to mix the two would take away the single, horrific, exaggerated view from which the Cashier sees the modern world, although a progression of effect might take place once the Cashier is awakened to a view of himself in relation to this world.

No matter what image or visual source is used as the basis for the various set pieces and framing devices for stage space in the production, the lighting would, by the nature of the final moments of the play when the lights go out and the skeleton of Death is outlined in a fury of sparks, be a tremendously important emotional device in unifying and projecting the script. All of the methods found in modern "light shows," such as spiraling, swirling, and bursting color, could be used with brilliant effect to support the emotional climate of each scene. This lighting would be more attuned to the sensibilities of a modern audience than the abrupt shafts of light and strong contrasts of light and dark that were characteristic of the original expressionist lighting methods. Color in light is as important to the emotional presentation of the play as the movement and shape of the lighting, and together they can set the mechanistic, staccato rhythm of the play and the mood of the Cashier's mental state (Figure 17–13).

Music would also be important in a modern production, especially if it were the new electronic music that frequently gives a strong feeling of mechanization and an inhuman rhythmic form. Amplification of the music would also be important, to make the sound even more unreal and mechanized. It would also be effective in underlining the rhythmic progression of the drama.

Exaggeration of form in costumes and a sense of uniformity in the dress of certain groups of characters may not provide enough visual comment, as they once did, to make the play acceptable to a modern audience. These effects were new and interesting at the time of World War I, but today they are often a the-

Figure 17–13. A scene from *From Morn to Midnight* by Georg Kaiser, produced at the Lessing Theater, West Berlin, 1945. Illustrates the use of exaggerated makeup, action, and groupings to gain an expressionistic effect in this drama written to exploit an expressionist view of modern life. Courtesy of the Freie Volksbühne, Berlin.

atrical cliché. What is needed is an approach in which the quality of the setting, music, and lights has completely pervaded the dress. If the smooth, polished, mechanist proach is used, then clothes could have metallic, plastic, manufactured surfaces that reflect our knowledge of the space suits of the modern age, even though the cut would still suggest the dresses and suits of current fashion. Trim could run to tubing, small spheres, prisms and cubes, and the movement within such costumes could be as labored and mechanized as it is inside a space suit. If the decaying, corroded approach to metallic and plastic surfaces is taken, then melted nylon, burned sponge rubber, and acid-eaten plastics painted to further the effect of decomposing surfaces could be effective in indicating the decay of our modern mechanized world. The principle behind either of

these seemingly opposed approaches is an attack on the sensibilities of the audience through a strong and violent statement in color, line, and texture. The effect of modern life as a destroyer of the human spirit is the key concept for the costume designs. Therefore, all visual effects must be exaggerated, violent, distorted, and horrifying for the audience.

The history of true expressionism may be limited, but the emotional effects engendered by it can be easily updated for modern production. Many plays from the past, not just the standard expressionist examples, can be presented for modern audiences in a neoexpressionist manner that will fit exactly the mood of much current theatre and will effectively make a modern point about a script that might otherwise seem to lack relevance if presented in a straightforward period manner.

18

Relativist Plays

Art and Culture in the Twentieth Century

Through its various modes of expression, including impressionism, expressionism, neomannerism, *art nouveau,* and many other related styles, the symbolist movement in art and theatre finally precipitated a crisis of subjectivism in the early years of the twentieth century. From the paintings of Turner and Delacroix to the paintings of Munch, Ensor, and van Gogh, the nineteenth century had demonstrated an inability or unwillingness to utilize science intelligently in art. Even the impressionist painters who had begun with a scientific interest in light and optics had drifted into subjectivism. The science that did arouse a response among artists was Darwinian biology, but even this appeared to sanction strong subjective impulses and romantic feelings rather than support artistic interest in analysis and intellect. During the nineteenth century art and science became alienated, and no major attempts were made to relate the great discoveries in science to the world of art. In the final analysis, the greatest of the artists in all media suffered from lack of a firm intellectual basis for their art. Rodin's sculpture, for example, was energetic, dynamic, theatrical, and highly emotional, but his late work substitutes vagueness for sculptural realization. In fact, he never found a sculptural style, and there is an abiding conflict between his cloudy implications and his inherent love of the flesh. His vagueness is reminiscent of Maeterlinck, his mass of Michelangelo, and what he lacks is an intellectual concept of simultaneous space, in which time and movement are flattened and become another dimension of space. Rodin can render only one profile at a time, and so his surfaces appear to burst and change within a succession of instants rather than in a single space-time perception. Not that anyone would want to change the sculptural work of Rodin, but it should be understood that he does lack a sound intellectual basis for his work. He is a product of the late nineteenth-century drive for energy, force, emotion, and theatricality, and in these drives he is rebelling against the static qualities of Euclidian space without finding a substitute sculptural structure (Figure 18–1).

The painter-innovator who wished to give impressionism the solidity and intellectual

Figure 18-1. Auguste Rodin, *The Gates of Hell,* bronze, 1880–1917. An example of impressionistic rather than structural vision in an architectural sculpture. Photo courtesy of the Musée Rodin, Paris.

foundation of classical art was Paul Cézanne. He wished to break down space and time so that one no longer looked at a subject from a particular point of view at a given moment in time, but observed all of its structural facets and its appearance during many moments in time in one long analytical glance (Figure 18-2).

It is from this concept that most of the great abstract movements of the twentieth century have evolved. Cubism was the first great conscious movement to break away from the idea that three-dimensional space must be seen from a fixed point of view at a particular moment, and most of the later artistic developments of the twentieth century, up until the middle of the 1960s, have been largely a return to the Renaissance coupling of art and science—the idea that the artist must think as well as feel and see (Figure 18-3).

The cubists, and the other schools of abstract art that followed, literally destroyed objects of the natural world in order to reorganize the world through the mind. Unlike the symbolists and the expressionists, who distorted life for emotional effect, the cubists and other

Figure 18-2. Paul Cézanne, *Mont Sainte-Victoire,* Philadelphia Museum of Art, ca. 1905. An example of how this artist attempted to structure and organize impressionistic art to give it the solidity of classical art. Photo courtesy of the Philadelphia Museum of Art, George W. Elkins Collection.

Figure 18-3. *Guernica* by Picasso, 1937. An example of the fragmentation and exaggeration of nature reconstituted to form a new reality. © S.P.A.D.E.M., Paris/V.A.G.A., New York, 1984.

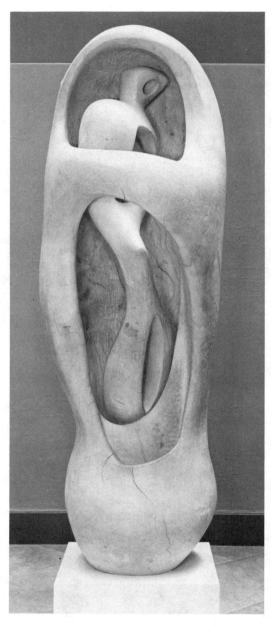

Figure 18-4. *Internal and External Forms* by Henry Moore, Albright-Knox Art Gallery, Buffalo, N.Y., 1953–1954. An example of the interpenetration of space and form in order to create a number of changing levels of reality. Photo courtesy of Albright-Knox Art Gallery, Buffalo, New York; General Purchase Funds, 1955.

abstractionists took things apart in a semi-scientific way to see how they worked, and then they reconstituted them to see both the inner and the outer dynamics simultaneously. From this process a new art was born: the collage, in which real objects and textures were juxtaposed with painted effects to underline points of intersection between levels of reality. A collage is both a painting and an object, a surface and a picture—a kind of diagram or symbol of the many diverse perspectives or realities in which modern people live and think (Figure 18-3). In a world in which there are no longer any simple absolutes and relations are multiple and complex, modern painting has attempted to show space and time as an extension of the way people live—an image of the way artists think rather than the way they see (Figure 18-4).

The same concepts and ideas also underlie much of the prose and poetry of the twentieth century. T. S. Eliot wrote that there are many simultaneous levels possible in verse writing in an age of relativity, and one can react to a word simultaneously as a word, a word among other words, a sound, a symbol, and a point in a structural development. Probably the most important literary landmark in the new style was the publication of James Joyce's *Ulysses,* in which each phrase is an intersection of meanings on three or four different levels. In Joyce's work, as in the work of Thomas Mann, Franz Kafka, Gertrude Stein, André Gide, and many others, a relationship on many levels at the same time is the structural basis of the work. There is always an ambiguity, an indeterminate quality, a feeling for multiple images, a cinema-inspired ''montage'' of effect, a shifting backward and forward in time, a compression and expansion of facts and details.

The great new form that developed along with the new perspectives in art and literature was the cinema. The twentieth-century artist or writer, like the film maker, sees reality not in an object or a sequence of causally connected events, but as a graphic conflict among slightly different recurring images and points

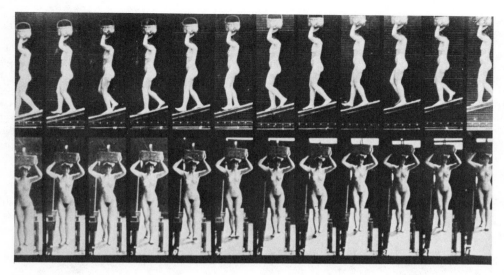

Figure 18-5. A series of photographs of a nude woman by Muybridge, George Eastman Museum of Photography, Rochester, N.Y., 1885. An example of early experiments that led to the art of the cinema and the concept of a simultaneous multiple reality. Photo courtesy of George Eastman House.

of view. Such merged images are known as a montage, and the montage has become the symbol of the new reality in art and literature. Reality is a series of changing relationships rather than a single story or event. What the box camera was to realism in the nineteenth century, the cinema is to the arts of the twentieth century (Figure 18-5).

The logical result of all this experimentation in abstract relationships was the liberation of art from subject matter in the late 1940s. Although the retreat from the real object began before World War I in the work of Kandinsky, Malevich, Severini, and others, it did not reach its climax until the triumph of abstract expressionism and neoplasticism after World War II. As practiced by Jackson Pollock and his successors, the abstract expressionism tended toward the emotional attack on the canvas that had characterized the painting of the German expressionists. However, now liberated from subject matter, the artist moved toward a physical relationship with art—drooling, dribbling, and spurting pigment onto the surface of the canvas. The texture of the field became more important than objects in the field, and the sense of the physical action of the painter more important than images, moods,

or ideas (Figure 18-6). In the neoplastic school of painting, pioneered by Kasimir Malevich and later led by Piet Mondrian, the painter dealt only with the simplest coordinates of mathematical organization—the horizontal and the vertical—and the three primary colors plus black and white. The artist aimed at an abstract expression of pure relationships without relation to a real world of objects. It was the field of relationships that was again important (see Figure 9-17).

In the art of the early 1960s, field relationships were still stressed, but variety and humor had been added to the purity of Mondrian and Pollock. Shapes, figures, and textures came back into the art of relations, not as objects but as important parts in a field of relationships. Whether one looks at the "aliterature" of Robbe-Grillet, or the antiart of pop art and op art, one seldom finds a secure point of view. Until the mid-1960s, the denial of the complexities in our culture was so strong that most artists and writers did not bother to interpret nature but merely recorded certain physical facts and relationships. It was an exhausted conclusion to the idea of multiple reality, the multifaceted levels of *Ulysses,* the early experimental cinema, and cubism.

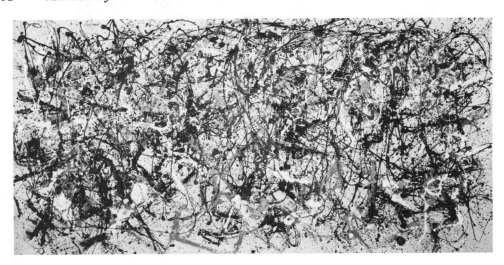

Figure 18–6. *Autumn Rhythm* by Pollock, The Metropolitan Museum of Art, New York, George A. Hearn Fund, 1950. An example of free-form action painting, in which texture rather than a defined pattern is created. Nature is reduced to the movement of forces in a field.

Theatre in the Twentieth Century

Although realist and symbolist approaches to staging have certainly not vanished from the scene of contemporary theatrical production, the major developments in the presentation of these two forms had reached their peak by the 1930s. By the beginning of World War II, several other forms of theatrical presentation related to the concept of relativism in art began to dominate Western theatre.

ELIZABETHAN STAGING REVIVED.   As early as the 1890s, a zealous devotee of Elizabethan staging methods named William Poel produced Shakespeare on a re-creation of an Elizabethan stage set up in rented halls in London and vicinity. With his largely amateur Elizabethan Stage Society, Poel dedicated his life to producing Shakespeare's plays and those of his contemporaries in the Elizabethan manner on a stage that was meant to be a close approximation of what was then known about the Globe and Fortune Theatres. His work in-

fluenced the great producer-critic Harley Granville-Barker, who also advocated producing Shakespeare on an open stage in which the division between the stage and the audience was minimized. The audience was made aware that it was seeing the reality of the stage at the same time that it was absorbing the reality of a particular play. Poel's Elizabethan staging ideals also heavily influenced the work of B. Iden Payne in his American Shakespearean productions, and a number of U.S. Shakespearean festivals continue to use modifications of Poel's staging concepts (Figure 18–7).

THE VIEUX COLOMBIER.   Another development, which took place in France just before World War I, also contributed to the idea that the fourth-wall concept of proscenium realism was passé, that the stage must remain a stage no matter what the play to be produced. In 1913, Jacques Copeau turned from a career as a critic to become a producer and director of the famous Théâtre Vieux Colombier in Paris. This theatre, which Copeau fashioned from a Parisian warehouse, had a

Figure 18-7. The Players Scene from *Hamlet* as produced by the Oregon Shakespeare Festival, Ashland, Ore., 1961. An example of a modern use of the Elizabethan stage, based on the dimension of the Fortune Theatre and inspired by the work of William Poel and B. Iden Payne in the early part of the twentieth century. Photo courtesy of the Oregon Shakespeare Festival.

permanent architectural setting for all plays on which only the essential properties and set dressings were placed. Stage and auditorium were considered to be an organic whole; there were no footlights, only a low step made the break from the audience to the stage, and the architectural background consisted of an arch with a stairway at one side leading up over the arch. Lighting came from above and from the sides, and certain sources were openly displayed within the auditorium (Figure 18-8). Once again the concept of a formal stage that remained a stage and a theatre that remained a theatre throughout all productions paved the way for the death of illusionism and an acceptance of the idea that one can be simultaneously aware of oneself, the audience, the

theatre, the actors, and the play during a theatrical performance.

Constructivism. A major breakthrough in experimentation occurred in Russia after the revolution of 1917. To reach a new audience of workers and to use the theatre as an instrument of instruction and propaganda, a number of experiments were undertaken to present plays that escaped the mood, illusionism, and sense of environment found in realism and symbolism and that stressed physical action and theatrical abstraction. The most influential exponent of this revolution in theatre was Vsevolod Meyerhold.

Meyerhold had three major concepts, all of which he used to establish his theatrical revolu-

Figure 18–8. A setting for Le Théâtre Vieux Colombier, Paris, ca. 1913. An example of the use of a basic architectural stage as developed by Jacques Copeau, in which the stage remains part of the auditorium and is changed by the minor use of props and set pieces. From *Continental Stagecraft* by Kenneth Macgowan and Robert Edmond Jones, Harcourt Brace Jovanovich, New York, 1922. Courtesy of Harcourt Brace Jovanovich.

tion: biomechanics, theatricalism, and constructivism. Like Craig and Reinhardt before him, he believed in the absolute power of the director. He shaped every element of a production to his own ideas, and insisted that all theatre personnel give him and his concepts absolute obedience.

Meyerhold believed, first, that the theatre must always remain a theatre, not a temple for dreams, a place of illusion, or a setting for reality. He wished his audiences to remain completely conscious of the fact that they were in a theatre, and he wished to use the theatre in a self-conscious, artistic way to achieve his theatrical effects. Thus, he removed the front curtain, placed lighting instruments in view of the audience, used a mechanical-gymnastic approach to acting, rewrote his plays so that elements of realism were replaced by obvious theatrical effects, and used abstract structures, which he called "constructions," as settings.

"Constructivism" had developed in the field of sculpture in Russia just before World War I, and the idea was developed to its fullest extent by two brothers, Naum Gabo and Antoine Pevsner, whose sculptural work at the close of World War I brought constructivism to the very forefront of modern art. The idea behind constructivist sculpture was that the artist, instead of working with intersecting planes and masses, constructed skeletal structures of metal and plastic in space. The aim in all of these productions and production methods was to comment on social, political, and economic problems and to incite audiences to desirable social action by strong theatrical statements (Figure 18–9).

Meyerhold's second major innovation in theatrical performance was a system of actor training that was the exact opposite of the Stanislavsky system and that he labeled "biomechanics." He was not interested in any kind

Figure 18-9. Stage design for *The Man Who Was Thursday* from the maquette by Alexander Wesnin in the Deutches Theatermuseum, Munich, ca. 1930. An example of constructivism, in which the setting becomes a structure for organizing action and space on a platform in front of an audience. Photo courtesy of the Deutches Theatermuseum, Munich.

of psychological realism but wanted an actor trained as an efficient biological machine to carry out the orders of the master director. His actors, trained in ballet, acrobatics, and gymnastics, were capable of performing on trapezes, slides, open ''constructions,'' and machinery.

Although these methods finally proved too abstract and experimental for the governmental forces in the Soviet Union, they are the first major examples in twentieth-century theatre of intellectual improvisation. This was based on the idea that the stage houses intersecting places of shifting contrasts between life and the theatre, between the reality of the actor and the reality of the role, between the reality of a play and the reality of the presentation of that play. In short, it was the first use of the simultaneous ideas of cubism in the theatre—the first use of the intellectual concept of relativity.

BRECHT AND EPIC THEATRE. Reinhardt, in his monumental productions at the Circus Schumann and later at the Grosses Schauspielhaus and in many outdoor productions, stressed the direct ''presentational'' approach to theatre, in which the proscenium was

banished and direct contact was established between actor and audience. The value of such direct contact remained with Reinhardt from the days when he had worked in the cabaret theatre Schall und Rauch in Berlin. It was this same background in cabaret theatre and this same feeling for intimacy that was to infuse the theatrical experimentation of one of the greatest playwright-producers of the twentieth century, Bertolt Brecht.

Brecht began his work in the theatre at a time when the expressionists were at the peak of their popularity. Film projections, weird lighting effects, sound effects, swirling movement on platforms and stairs—every theatrical device was used to create a total assault on the senses at the expense of critical, analytical thought. At first Brecht worked within this style, but he gradually developed a theory of theatrical production in which the intellect rather than the senses was to be aroused. He wanted his audiences to participate in a theatrical event, but he wanted this to be critical and intellectual participation rather than sentimental and emotional participation. Just as modern art had turned its back on mood, symbols, and inner emotions in order to

Figure 18–10. *Merz Construction* by Kurt Schwitters (painted wood, wire, and paper), Philadelphia Museum of Art, A. E. Gallatin Collection, 1921. An example of the so-called "trash pictures" that attempted to make interesting abstract arrangements of elements taken from a number of levels of reality. Such work was very influential in the area of stage design. Photo courtesy of the Philadelphia Museum of Art.

analyze, critically and intellectually, the nature of art in relation to modern life, so Brecht decided that the same thing must happen in the theatre. He called his work "epic"

as opposed to "dramatic," and he felt that this term (which derives from the great poetic narrative legends of the Greeks and the Germans) correctly described his ideal of a narrative rather than a dramatic theatre of emotional conflict. For Brecht both the drama and theatrical production needed to be altered and guided toward a new set of goals, which involved the key words "alienation" and "historification."

Historification to Brecht meant material chosen from other places and other times in order to obtain a sense of removal—a dispassionate look at facts and events in which we are not involved yet which have relevance to the present. Brecht hoped that by presenting events strange and removed his plays would escape the easy identification with actions and emotion that occurred in realist theatre. He hoped that his audiences would use their minds rather than their feelings to arrive at critical, intellectual conclusions about the social problems introduced in his plays.

This concept is a part of the larger concept of alienation. Although alienation is a rather inaccurate rendering of the German word *verfremdung,* it is basically a further expansion of the concept of making the stage action strange and unreal through the introduction of song, film, description, and direct address to the audience. In short, Brecht does not want his audience to confuse what it sees onstage with reality, but to view such action as a comment on life, to be watched and judged with critical detachment. Each element of the production should contribute to the "alienation" of the spectator, and, in the manner of a collage or assemblage, there should be an interdependence rather than a synthesis of the arts of theatrical production (Figure 18–10). Scenery should not create an illusion of reality, but should merely suggest locale. Costumes should comment on character, music should comment on action, lighting should illuminate but not create mood, and the actors should think of their roles in the third person. Once again, the mechanics of the theatre should remain visible at all times. The audience should be critically

Figure 18–11.   Scene from *The Threepenny Opera* by Bertolt Brecht, produced by the Stanford Players, Stanford University, 1964. Directed by Karl Weber, costumes by the author. Illustrates the separation of actor from role through exaggerated use of makeup, gesture, blocking, and properties that operate on more than one level of reality. Courtesy of the Stanford University Archives, Stanford, CA. Photo by Hank Kranzler.

aware of the various levels of reality that are created; it should not be lulled into a hypnotic, atmospheric trance (Figure 18–11).

THE CONTEMPORARY EMPHASIS ON OPEN OR THRUST STAGING.   From the time of Copeau and the constructivists to the present, the battle between the realistic or single-angle proscenium theatre and the formal, open-staging concept, which attempts a return to the precepts of the Elizabethan and Greek theatre, has been a continuing event. Only in the past three decades have more theatres been built that stress the open, thrust-stage form of produc-

tion rather than the proscenium. Many new theatre buildings have attempted to achieve both, but at major festival theatres such as the Shakespeare Theatre at Stratford, Ontario, the Guthrie Theatre in Minneapolis, and the Festival Theatre at Chichester, England, the theatre has been constructed with an open, thrust stage. Only a few popular commercial productions are still produced completely behind a proscenium arch from a single fixed point of view. The majority of productions in the Western world are produced with varying degrees of a theatrical presentational approach in which the audience is aware that it is part of

Figure 18–12.   The stage of the Stratford Festival Theatre, Stratford, Ontario, Canada, as modified in 1962 by Tanya Moiseiwitsch in association with Brian Jackson from the original 1953 version designed by Miss Moiseiwitsch and Tyrone Guthrie. An example of the thrust or apron stage in a permanent structure, it is a modern adaptation of the Elizabethan stage with seven acting levels and nine entrances. It provides close audience-actor relationship, as no seat is more than sixty-five feet from the stage. Courtesy of the Stratford Festival, Stratford, Ontario, Canada.

the theatrical event, concerned with both the reality of the stage and the reality of the story and characters presented (Figure 18–12).

Six Characters in Search of an Author

Although George Bernard Shaw is often thought of as the leading playwright of the early twentieth century, he was unable to escape the drawing-room scene for a direct approach to the stage as a platform for comic action and comic criticism. Thus, it is Luigi Pirandello who returns stage action to the direct gaze of the audience under the glare of open stage lighting; and it is *Six Characters in*

Search of an Author that should be studied to see how contemporary drama emerged from late nineteenth-century realism and symbolism.

PLOT AND STRUCTURE.   As Sypher indicates in *From Rococo to Cubism in Art and Literature,* Pirandello, like the cubist painters who preceded him, set out to show a compound image in the drama, a form of theatre in which the stage is a plane for the intersection of art and life, a place for the "collision between art and actuality."

In this stage action, which cannot really be labeled a "play," a company of actors is rehearsing a drama by Pirandello himself when six "characters" enter and ask for a completion to the drama of their lives. The author who has conceived them has not finished their play, and they beg the actors to perform their play instead of the one they are rehearsing. The action then develops on several levels: the struggle of the "characters" against the technical and commercial views of the actors and director, the struggle among the "characters" about the shape and meaning of the events of their story, the struggle in the audience's mind with the levels of reality they see before them. The effort of the "characters" to represent themselves on the stage is finally blocked when the Boy, in a fit of despair, shoots himself. The professionals interpret this as the artistic climax to the play, only to realize that it has been a genuine suicide, and the fictional characters turn out to be more real than the live members of the acting company.

By refusing the movement and forward thrust of plot, the author is left with the formal artistic problem of writing a drama about writing a drama. It is very much like the technique of collage used by the cubists to project the problems of painting or the building of a painting. In fact, the great connection between this play and the visual arts is the collage. Pirandello pieces together and arranges a number of theatrical clichés, including the director's attitude, the commercial theatre point of view, the professional actor's outlook, the stagehands' contributions, a missing playwright's concept, and a group of partially realized characters in a collage form to interpenetrate, intermingle, point up, and illuminate the many different levels of reality they represent.

CHARACTERIZATION. The six "characters" belong to life but at the same time do not belong to it. Pirandello stops the unrolling film of his "characters'" lives and allows one crucial episode or sequence to be played repeatedly, to be disputed and argued by actors, director, and even audience on a public stage. It is a fascinating philosophical-theatrical idea. The concept of the "characters" then calls into question the nature of the personal and group realities of actors and director, and finally, of

course, of the audience watching the proceedings. The director demands a single, simple illusion of reality and insists that actors are serious artists ready to project this reality, while the Father "character" insists that the actors are merely playing a game and have never found out who they really are. Thus, all characterization in the play, although it seems psychologically realistic on its own level, comes into question when pitted against another world or level of reality. Each individual on the stage is both a personality and a philosophical symbol of a certain level of reality.

THEME. Every moment of the development and every step in the intellectual discussion is used to point up and exemplify the thesis that reality is a shifting thing and that at times the reality of art and imitation may be greater than the reality of life. As research into the plural aspects of identity, the play takes every opportunity to show the many levels of reality on which events can occur.

DIALOGUE. The dialogue is primarily philosophical and argumentative as the "characters" argue the nature of their reality with the actors, and more specifically as the Father and the director debate the nature of theatrical reality. The dialogue shifts from real-life conversation to rational argument to theatrical cliché without transition or warning, to underline the multiple levels of reality.

RHYTHM. The rhythm of the play does not exist by most standards, since the movement of the play stops, starts, shifts abruptly, and changes levels without warning, in an attempt to create ambiguity, stimulate thought, and frustrate easy acceptance of a forward flow of the drama. The rhythm is closest to that of the experimental film in which story movement can go backward or forward, dissolve into multiple images, or change with the shifting viewpoint of the camera.

SPECTACLE. The demands for the visual background very consciously take on the aspects of collage as the bits and pieces of costume and scenery involved in the play being rehearsed are placed against the realities of backstage equipment and stage walls, which are the only permanent background for the action. When other bits and pieces of property and scenery are rigged so that the "characters" may act out their story, the result is a theatrical collage. Scenery and costumes are thus geared to the simultaneous presentation of theatrical reality, life reality, and "character" reality in a shifting and changing collage effect.

Visual Presentation of *Six Characters in Search of an Author*

Since Pirandello's dramas, in particular *Six Characters in Search of an Author,* are very rich intellectually and very spare visually, the design for a contemporary production cannot utilize complex visual effects. Each visual choice must be carefully selected to project a particular intellectual shift in the argument about reality without appealing to the emotions or the senses at the expense of the intellect. However, there is certainly a need to accent the theatricality of the stage effects that Pirandello does use to make his points about reality in the theatre, and these can be the visual highlights in a basically spare production. The entire ritual of actors arriving for a rehearsal on a bare stage lit only by worklights can be an interesting charade not usually seen by an audience. The arrival of the "characters," with pale faces, in an eerie and unearthly light unrelated to the worklights of the stage, and the readying of the "white parlor background with the floral decoration" as an impromptu backing for their story, can both be used as interesting visual highlights. The appearance of Madame Pace after the scene has been correctly arranged to evoke her image is a consummate visual moment—if the appearance really does seem to be a transmigration from another world. In all these examples, the lighting can obviously be very helpful in focusing and supporting the desired effect. However, it is the property or bit of setting, item of costume, or type of makeup used within or against the frame of another reality that creates the excitement.

In all matters of setting and costume there is more a problem of selection and arrangement than there is one of design. As in a collage or an assemblage, it is more important to find the right item of costume, scenery, or properties, to place it properly, and to use it at the right moment than it is to design each item as a piece of a unified visual whole (Figure 18–13).

Therefore, the costumes are better obtained from costume storage, from an actor's personal wardrobe, or from a used clothing store rather than designed and built to give a unified single artistic point of view to the production. The variety of sources suits the variety of reality levels operating in the play, while a single source and a single artistic point of view tend to give a unified visual reality that is not in keeping with the play. Clichés of theatrical costume may be placed next to items borrowed directly from the real world in an "assemblage"—an artistic arrangement based on the accents and focus indicated by the author in presenting his multilevel view of reality.

The Blacks

Jean Gênet, one of the controversial and brilliant playwrights of the absurd who appeared after World War II, created one of the most bizarre and confusing pictures of the shifting realities confronting modern people that has yet come to the modern stage. His major image in the play is that of a man caught in a maze of mirrors, trapped by the reflections of his distorted image, trying to make contact with those around him, but being rudely stopped by the barriers created by the reflecting glass. To Gênet, people are caught in the hall of mirrors of the human condition, trapped by an endless progression of images that are merely distorted reflections. In his play *The Blacks,* which the author labels a "clownerie" or clown show, Gênet presents an ingenious ritual in which a group of black ac-

Figure 18–13. A scene from *Six Characters in Search of an Author* by Pirandello as produced by the American Conservatory Theatre for the Stanford Summer Festival, 1966. An example of multiple reality, in which a scene is constructed in front of the audience from backstage properties and set pieces. Courtesy of the American Conservatory Theatre. Photo courtesy of Hank Kranzler, Palo Alto, Calif.

tors, playing both black and white roles, reenacts a ritualistic revenge on the white world.

PLOT AND STRUCTURE. There is no story line or clearly developed plot in this play, but there is a fascinating pattern of mirror images of reality that are played against one another in a most ingenious manner. The author assumes that his audience is white, and his black cast is divided into those who enact blacks' fantasies about themselves and those who enact blacks' fantasies about the white reaction to the black world. Thus, the black actors stand between an actual white audience and the white-masked, colonial, fantasy audience composed of a haughty Queen, a Judge, a Bishop, a Governor-general, a Missionary, and a Valet (who acts the part of the artist or intellectual). In front of this hierarchy of white power the other group of blacks enacts its fantasies of resentment. The central part of this is the ritual murder of a white woman enacted in elaborate detail. The white woman is presumed to be in the coffin, center stage, and the victim is first described by Village as a drunken hag found on the docks, but when the murder is actually reenacted the victim becomes an attractive white woman who had invited her black seducer to her room because of his superior physical attractions. An additional irony is added by the fact that the black appointed to portray the raped white woman turns out to be a clergyman who believes in peaceful integration and the brotherhood of humanity. Equipped with a blonde wig, an insipid carnival mask, pink knitting, and gloves, he impersonates the woman being raped and killed. When he gives birth to a number of dolls representing the figures of the "white court," the victim becomes the Mother of the White Race and the ritual murder becomes the ritual massacre of all whites.

341

After the blacks have acted out their ritual resentment and guilt, the Queen and her court descend as though to punish the blacks. They are trapped and ignominiously put to death, after which Archibald, the stage manager and master of ceremonies for the evening's events, thanks the blacks who have been impersonating the whites and concludes the play by stating that the blacks remain what whites want them to be. Early in the evening this same master of ceremonies makes it quite clear that the action on stage is a make-believe ritual, actors making the subject matter of the play palatable through the distance created by the many levels of impersonation and ceremony. The participants in the entertainment are meant to have a sense of awe, mystery, and ritual participation rather than be involved in any conceptual or rational communication. Yet by the end of the evening there is another reality, of which the audience becomes aware when Ville St. Nazaire, sent off in the first scene with a gun, returns to report an offstage revolt and the resultant conviction and death of a black traitor before an all-black court. The whole stage ritual is revealed as a blind, a diversion to distract from the deadly real problems involved in the offstage revolt. And yet because the levels of mirror reality are so complex, the offstage revolt may be still another trick, another theatrical improvisation that leaves only the reality of the black actors and the smokescreen of their various levels of diversion.

CHARACTERIZATION.   In a play written on as many shifting levels at this one, there are obviously no characters or characterizations, but merely stereotyped or ritualized images donned by the actors. Yet even the black actors on stage stand for more than blacks; they create an image of all the outcasts in a society; they stand for the author himself, who, as an outcast and thief from the age of ten, always played the role that society wanted him to play. Denied dignity as people, the outcasts, the blacks, are denied the emotions of our "real" world and so must ever play the role for which they have been cast by society. All characters are used only to create an image or make a comment on the human experience.

THEME.   Gênet's play is like an explosion of evil that breaks through the surface of rational discussion and social consciousness to the darkest reaches of the inner mind—to the level of myth, fear, masochistic fantasy, primitive ritual, and human sacrifice. As an essay on race relations it is impossible. It must be taken as an imaginative and metaphorical creation of a world underlying our own, appealing to whatever remains unconditioned and uncivilized in modern people. Gênet's purgative ritual or myth is violently subversive but also contains a sense of release and liberation. Through his direct sense of and involvement in evil and cruelty, Gênet attempts to stop the logical discussions and rational debates of the modern community through an art of crime and sacrifice, but also an art of collective ecstasy and purgation—an art about the helplessness of modern people when they realize that they are caught in an endless progression of images that are their own reflections.

DIALOGUE.   The actors, like the improvisers or "clowns" of the subtitle, are expected to manage language filled with images that continually shift from one level of reality to another. All the possible meanings and connotations of the words black and white are played off against each other, until all of our unconsciously accepted ideals are turned inside out and upside down. There is also a poetry or litany of hatred developed to fit with the ritual murder enacted onstage, and again the dialogue makes full use of the possibilities of ceremony and ritual. Like the play as a whole, the language or dialogue operates on the level of imagination, symbol, metaphor, and subconscious feelings and fantasies.

RHYTHM.   Like all plays that are deeply involved with shifting realities that change and interpenetrate during the course of the action, the rhythm is like the visual movement of a kaleidoscope, rising and falling with the blending and pulling apart of the various levels of reality. The rhythm of the masked blacks must differ from that of the unmasked ones; the rhythm of statements to the audience and the statements of the blacks among themselves must differ markedly from the rhythm of the ritualistic sacrifice. Each level, each reflection of the human condition must seek its own rhythm rather than an overall rhythm devised for the entire evening.

SPECTACLE. All that is required for the staging is a large hall or room in which a stage has been set up for the reenactment of a ritual murder. It must be easy for the master of ceremonies to address the audience, even to hand things to persons in the front row or bring a member of the audience onto the stage. There must also be a coffin at the center of the stage and a range of seats, platforms, or ramps behind, on which the blacks playing whites can range themselves to view the action below. The costumes are selections from theatrical storage that can suggest both the primitive ritual elements and the black's view of the power figures of the white establishment. Lighting also must be obvious and theatrical, able to move from the white audience to the black ritual forestage to the blacks as whites ranged to the back of the stage, uniting all locations or isolating them as needed.

Visual Presentation of *The Blacks*

In a play that has as many shifting levels of reality and as many reflecting mirrors revealing the human condition as does *The Blacks,* it is very difficult to come to any coherent or logical plan for the visual presentation of the script. In fact, the logic that must be used is the logic of the illogical and the irrational. None of the usual rules or guides to a unified production is possible, and the design must shift and change from moment to moment as the script does.

In essence there is no setting at all, merely a place for actors to present their ceremonial ritual murder. In planning the ramps and platforms for the blacks playing whites, the designer should let his or her personal reaction to the structure and the shifting images of the play be a guide in obtaining a construction in space that is primitive and sophisticated, handmade and machine-tooled, something that is organic yet constructed in material modules of form. In terms of proportion, the setting should have the same ambivalent quality: it should be part stage property, part primitive symbol, and part polished ''product.'' The coffin can be at the same time a box from backstage, a sinister primitive hand-hewn container, and a highly tooled modern mortuary product. The challenge to the designer is in suggesting all such levels simultaneously (Figure 18–14).

In designing the costumes, one cannot think of each character as a single unit to be designed in a unified way from top to bottom. Differing levels of reality must be combined within the same costume. This is particularly true of those costumes and masks worn by the blacks playing whites, and the costumes for the Queen, the Bishop, the Governor-general, the Missionary, and the Valet. Obviously, the white stereotype each black portrays must be presented in all its overdrawn caricature as seen through the hatred of the blacks: the exaggerated sexuality and accouterments of the Queen, the massive uniform and hat of the Governor-general, the poetic qualities of the Valet, the mitre and cope of the Bishop, and the false purity of the Missionary. But from under and within these exaggerated outward labels could escape the fearful symbols that we associate with the rituals of tribal Africa: bangles, bracelets, claw-like nails, painted bodies, animal teeth, for example. These would suggest to the actual white audience how they still see blacks in their subconscious. Still another level of reality that can be suggested in the costumes is the reality of the stage and of the black actors presenting the various intersecting levels of reality. Underneath the ironic paraphernalia of white colonialism and

Figure 18–14. A scene from *The Blacks* by Jean Gênet as produced by the Akademie der Kunste, Berlin, 1964, as part of the Berlin Festwochen. An example of the many layers of reality that must be suggested in the play by the settings and costumes. Photo courtesy of Heinz Köster, Berlin.

black primitivism could creep the worn shoes, the dirty trousers, or the old wrist watch of the actor, although such things might be hidden through much of the action and allowed to appear only at certain dramatic moments.

The blacks preparing the ritual murder may also wear ridiculous outfits of fake elegance as they dance the minuet around the coffin covered with flowers, again keeping the audience guessing about who they are and what they represent. When Diouf must be done up in yellow wig, cheap mask, and white gloves holding knitting, the bitter caricature must be vicious and unsettling.

The costume designer must deliberately keep the audience unnerved and guessing about the planes of reality represented visually, and must create mixtures of reality from items laden with symbolic values that will violate and upset the white audience's usual feelings and preconceptions.

Textures must not be chosen to give any overall or generalized impression; they must be chosen for symbolic contrasts of reality. The velvet of the Queen's gown may turn abruptly into grass or reeds, a richly sophisticated crown may suddenly sprout teeth, claws, or feathers, or the Governor-general's rich uniform may stop at the knees and his feet turn into those of an ape. It is the designer's talent for putting two incompatible and incongruous textural effects together that will give the play bite and disturb the usually accepted canons of visual taste.

Colors can, in the same way, shift in mid-figure or midcostume from one level of reality to another without any regard for the usual rules of visual choice. The line of a costume may move in one direction and then turn com-pletely in another direction to get the right symbolic visual contrasts across to an audi-ence. A scepter that changes to a shrunken head at the top, medals and orders that turn to claws and shells, animal horns that grow from a mitre or a helmet—these are the shifts in line from one symbolic level of reality to another that can make the costume designer's work a real contribution to the harrowing effect this play can have on a modern, sophisticated au-dience (Figure 18–15).

Figure 18–15. Costume sketches of Felicity and Archibald by Jean Schultz Davidson for *The Blacks* by Jean Gênet. Prepared as a class assignment in the Department of Drama, Stanford University. Note the intermingling of African and Western European reality in costume. Courtesy of Jean Schultz Davidson.

19

Contemporary Plays

Contemporary Art and Culture

In the past twenty years culture has moved away from many of the cultural images that were still so much a part of the Western European and American way of life through the decade and a half that followed the close of World War II. The limited outlook of the Eisenhower 1950s, with its images of men in gray flannel suits and women in black A-line shifts, began to break down in the early 1960s. The somewhat narrow and rather complacent outlook of those earlier Cold War years were gradually eroded by the arrival of the civil rights movement, the founding of the Peace Corps, the explosion of the "hippie" movement, and the new philosophical view of the world as a great global village. National interdependence has become a fact rather than an idea as the entire Western industrial world has come to terms with a truly international capitalism and a far greater interdependence in natural resources than ever before.

The first decade of this new outlook was marked by naive idealism and optimism about the possibilities of change, despite the deepen-

ing involvement of the United States in the Vietnam War. Many young people wore buttons bearing slogans such as "We shall overcome," "Legalize Spiritual Discovery," "Suppose they gave a war and nobody came," and "I am a human being: do not fold, spindle, or mutilate." Such messages proclaimed recognition that a mechanized, profit-oriented, conformist approach to life deadens feelings, physical responses, moral values, and the individual's basic humanity. There followed mass congregations of the young in the Haight-Ashbury section of San Francisco in 1967, in New York's East Village, on Boston Common, in the Pennsylvania farmlands and New England woods, and at mass rock festivals such as the one held near Woodstock, New York, in 1969. Almost an entire generation of young people copied the clothing, hairstyles, sexual freedom, taste for rock music, and general outlook fostered in these mass congregations, and they seemed to find the "establishment society" plastic and dull. The new ideal was to leap into the freedom and experience of life without societal restrictions.

But the gentle love preached by the hippies

gave way to violence in 1968 with anti-Vietnam War demonstrations, the clashes between protestors and police at the Democratic Convention in Chicago, and the student riots in Paris and Tokyo. In the next few years violence dominated college campuses throughout the world, and only with financial recession, an energy shortage, and a gradual disengagement from Vietnam in the early 1970s did confrontation wane. The group ideals of the 1960s began to recede into a concern for self, although the basic affirmation of human values over organizational values, of openness over duplicity and deceit, carried over into the furor over Watergate and led to individual commitment to such causes as Amnesty International, the human rights organization, and the development of Third World nations.

Another phenomenon of the past two decades has been the growth of interest in the occult in Western society as an antidote to an excessive interest in the scientific method. Bookstores and the media continue to be filled with tales of ancient astronauts, exploits of psychokinetic key benders, movies of creatures from outer space, advertising for biorhythm calculators, reports of after-death experiences, documentaries on the Abominable Snowman and the Loch Ness monster, and articles on every aspect of extrasensory perception. In short, though the high tide of the personal and sexual freedom movement has waned, much of the distilled thinking of the 1960s is still a part of our culture in the early 1980s. Like the explosive cultural revolution of 1830, in which the nineteenth-century romantic movement reached its peak, thereafter to continue in a quieter, tighter, more distilled manner, so the cultural revolution of the 1960s continues in a subdued, subterranean fashion. The cool-hip defiance of the 1960s with its scorn for sentiment has given way to a new nostalgic romanticism. Films like the heart-grabbing *E. T.* and the moralistic parable *Star Wars* are great successes. Dinner and tea dances have returned, full-dress Viennese balls are in vogue, and nostalgia for the simpler and optimistic values of the American past is rampant.

In art a movement developed that heralded a break from the fascination with nonobjective painting and the intellectual values of hard-edged abstraction: the "happening." As much theatre as it was art, the "happening" attempted to involve the spectator emotionally and physically in the artistic event or exhibition. Allan Kaprow was one of the leaders in this new art form, and in his *18 Happenings in Six Parts* in 1959 he divided a gallery into three compartments; events went on simultaneously in each while images were projected on various surfaces, music and sounds provided background, and viewers carried out instructions given them at the door (Figure 19–1).

The idea was that participants would participate physically and sensually in the artistic event rather than respond with their intellects or critical faculties, would become awakened to a whole new dimension of nonintellectual, nonverbal communication in a society in which many artists felt that such neglected human values had all but died. To single out but one now established cultural ritual based on the happening that did not exist in the United States before the 1960s, one need only look at an arts fair held at a shopping mall, fairground, or schoolyard (Figure 19–2). At such a gathering, there are all kinds of handcrafted items on display that are based on primitive and folk crafts from around the world, representing a great unspoken celebration of the physical and emotional involvement of the human body and spirit in natural, nonmachine-made products. At a typical arts fair one can find dancing, jewelry making, pottery demonstrations, musical improvisations, mime shows, poetry readings, and embroidery lessons. In this modern version of the Eastern bazaar there is an escape from our technological society and a determined effort to feel, touch, and work with the hands as a direct response to what is natural, emotional, and physical in life.

In sculpture it was the tableaux of artists like Edward Keinholz that celebrated the physical and emotional in art. In *The State Hospital* Kienholz shows us a ward for senile

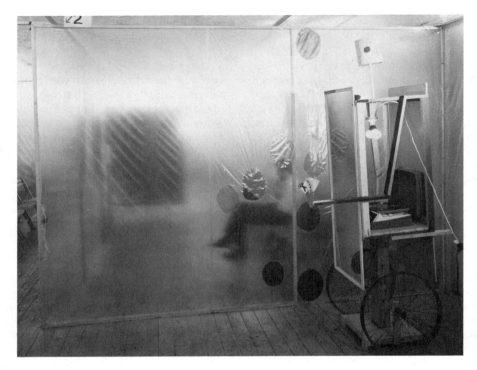

Figure 19–1. Scene from *18 Happenings in Six Parts* by Allan Kaprow, 1959. Illustrates a new artistic form in which the spectators at an artistic exhibition are involved in the process of creation. Photo by Scott Hyde, courtesy of Allan Kaprow.

Figure 19–2. Arts Fair, Inverness, California, 1977. A bazaar-like atmosphere in which dancing, jewelry making, pottery crafting, ballet exhibitions, poetry readings, blue jeans embroidery lessons, and various crafts stalls mix and vie with each other to create an open, non-structured, tactile, emotional experience. Photo by the author.

patients with a naked man strapped to the lower bunk (Figure 19–3). His skin is leathery and discolored, his head is a fishbowl with fish inside, and when the work was originally exhibited a sickly odor pervaded the scene. Thus, the work is vividly, physically real, demanding a direct involvement of our emotions and senses while deepening the experience with the unrealistic device of the fishbowl head. The brilliant metaphor of having live fish inside the fishbowl makes the viewer shockingly aware of how such a patient feels.

The idea that art is now free from the boundaries of the studio and the categories of sculpture, painting, and architecture has also led to massive artistic enterprises involving the natural world. These so-called ecological art projects are usually ephemeral in character and recapitulate the concept of the art "happening," with the gallery replaced by the natural world. As an example, in 1976 the artist Christo erected a cloth sail-like fence that covered over twenty miles of the landscape of Sonoma County, California, before dipping into the sea (Figure 19–4). It was in place for less than a month, and yet it drew crowds of spectators and photographers, creating a great media event. *Running Fence* made a gallery of nature, forcing the public to take a new look at the land in relation to the fence and to reevaluate the area after the fence was removed. Implicit in such a project was an emphasis on size and upon art as a part of the natural process of growth and decay. Related to this ecological art are folk or "lay" artworks—such as barn, billboard, and fence paintings—by groups and individuals often without professional artistic training.

Thus, the key artistic and cultural ideals of the past two decades have been involved in the physical, even the violent, breaking of barriers between the various arts, the probing of the inner and outer worlds of the individual through physical-emotional rather than intellectual

Figure 19–3.   *The State Hospital* by Edward Keinholz, 1966. A realistic tableau showing two senile patients strapped to their beds. They have goldfish bowl faces, within which real goldfish swim to dramatize the patients' experience of themselves. Photo courtesy of the Moderna Museet, Stockholm.

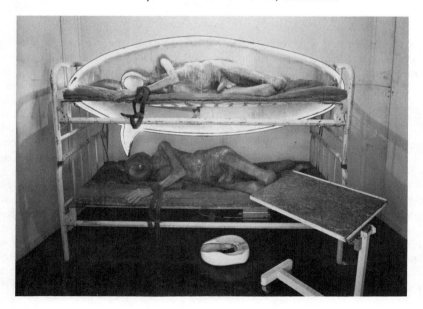

Figure 19–4.   *Running Fence* by Christo, Sonoma County, California, 1976. An example of ecological art. Courtesy of the *San Francisco Chronicle,* © Chronicle Publishing Company, 1976.

processes, and the gradual acceptance of the interdependence of all life and nature throughout the globe.

Contemporary Theatre and Drama

The contemporary scene of playwriting and production—the so-called "new theatre" that has been in the process of formation for twenty years—has turned its back both on the intellectualism of the absurdists and the emotionalism of the psychological realists.

For half a century, at least, it was accepted that the theatre is a unity and all elements should blend under the absolute control of the director. But this was largely a matter of external unity, and today, when no conventional forms stand firm, the author who cares more about content and substance than about the external methods of production, must work *with* a director and a cast until what is said is fresh, honest, and direct. A stable and harmonious society need only look to the theatre for reflection and reaffirmation of its harmony, but a shifting, chaotic world must often choose between a playhouse that offers a unified but spurious "yes" and one that offers a provocation so strong that the audience is fragmented into hundreds of vivid and different "no's."

It is obvious and banal to say that sacred, spiritual, or holy art has been destroyed by bourgeois values, but it is also foolish to allow revulsion for bourgeois forms to include reaction against the spiritual and artistic needs common to all people. If the need for true contact with a sacred mystery through the medium of theatre still exists, then all possible vehicles for the projection of this invisible world must be reexamined.

Artists dedicated to this goal are often accused today of wanting to destroy everything admired in the theatre of the past century, particularly the spoken word. There is actually a grain of truth in this assertion, since the word is not the same tool for the dramatist that it once was. Possibly it is because we are living in an age of images that we must go through a period of image saturation before language can reemerge; but dramatists today seem less interested in making ideas and images meld through words than they were in the great dramatic eras of the past. The great prophet of this new theatre of images was the French genius Antonin Artaud, who wrote just before World War II. He railed against the sterility of the bourgeois theatre and described from the depths of his imagination and intuition another theatre—a holy theatre whose blazing core was to speak through the forms closest to it; a theatre working like the plague through intoxication, infection, and magic. He saw a theatre in which the play, the event itself, stood in place of the text.

It was the influence of this mad genius, carried forward in the work of Peter Brook in productions of such plays as *Marat/Sade, A Midsummer Night's Dream, King Lear, Timon of Athens, USA,* and *The Ik,* and through workshops devoted to the "theatre of cruelty," that has made such an impact on the contemporary playwriting and theatre scene (Figure 19–5).

Figure 19–5.   A scene from the Royal Shakespeare Theatre production of *A Midsummer Night's Dream,* directed by Peter Brook at Stratford-upon-Avon, 1970. An example of Shakespeare designed and directed to make strong, direct physical communication with the audience without the interference of illustrative or pictorial material; a production with strong emphasis on physical and even acrobatic presentation of the script. Photo courtesy of Joe Cocks.

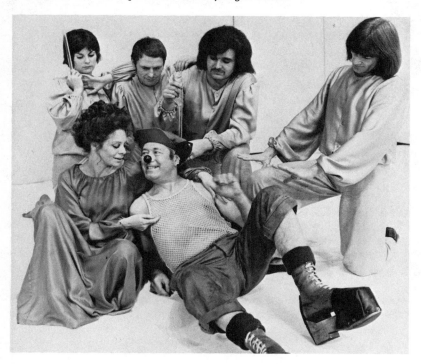

In American works such as *Hair, Tom Payne,* and *Futz* in the 1960s and the work of Sam Shepard in the 1970s, and in much of the experimental work going on in theatre centers such as Prague, Paris, and Rome, this new theatre of image and action has taken a strong hold (Figure 19–6). By making words secondary to movement and gesture, by limiting the alternatives of expression, this theatre trains actors to summon all of their reserves, all of their concentration, all of their will to communicate to express a true dramatic action. The leaders of this movement speak of making the invisible visible through the mere presence of the performer. Masks, makeup, and the traditional properties and accessories of the theatre are rejected in favor of silence, noise, the ritual use of repeated patterns, the climaxes and denouements of group action. To the followers of Artaud, Brook, Planchon, and others, the surprise element and surrealistic incongruity of absurdist drama is as dead as the psychological drama of naturalism. From the "theatre of cruelty" these artists developed a theatre more violent, less rational, more extreme, less verbal, more dangerous than the theatre of the immediate past. Though these exciting ideals have been somewhat eroded during the past decade by the growth of nostalgia theatre and a return to many of the plays and styles of the past, experimental theatre still looks to the ideals of the "happening" for inspiration, and all the arts, not just theatrical art, are brought together in avant-garde productions.

Figure 19–6.   Eron Tabor (center) and the Tribe in a scene from the San Francisco production of *Hair,* presented by Michael Butler, Marshall Naify, and the American Conservatory Theatre, 1969. An example of the new theatre of image and action, in which verbal communication is secondary to ritual communication through group action. Photo courtesy of the Press Representative of the American Conservatory Theatre.

The Persecution and Assassination of Jean-Paul Marat as Performed by the Inmates of the Asylum of Charenton under the Direction of the Marquis de Sade

One of the most influential plays of the 1960s to combine a relativist reality with a physical-theatrical event is Peter Weiss's 1964 play known by the abbreviation *Marat/Sade*. The play is set in the year 1808 in the insane asylum of Charenton, where the Marquis de Sade is confined and where he passes the time writing and directing playlets performed by the patients for the amusement of the fashionable audience from Paris.

PLOT AND STRUCTURE. One of de Sade's productions is a play about the assassination of the radical Jacobin Jean-Paul Marat by Charlotte Corday in 1793, at the height of the French Revolution. De Sade participates in this play-within-a-play as a philosophical antagonist to the patient who plays Marat. Both the play and the play-within-a-play are based on historical fact; the Marquis de Sade did direct plays while confined at Charenton (not because he was insane but because he was regarded as a debauched criminal), and Marat was in fact assassinated by Charlotte Corday.

Peter Weiss prepares the audience for an intellectual debate between Marat and de Sade by using many of Brecht's distancing effects, such as spoken and musical commentary on the events, while treating the audience as if it were part of the fashionable audience of 1808 invited to the asylum by its Director, Coulmier. But Weiss also takes from Artaud the use of a chorus of patients who create a horrifying and very powerful and immediate physical background action. Four of these patients are separated from the background to comment musically and physically on each forward step in the argument, while the background patients create a physical-vocal atmosphere that is overpowering in its image of distraught, oppressed humanity. They are kept in order by nurses who have the "appearance of butchers" and by nuns "played by athletic-looking men." It is this secondary level that brings the play into the contemporary theatrical scene as a major example of the "theatre of cruelty." The structure itself is Brechtian: the play is composed of a series of short scenes, each with a separate title. The play was popularized by Peter Brook in his London and New York productions, was made into a film, and has been widely performed in amateur and semiprofessional productions. It has become the most outstanding example of the transition from the theatre of ideas and relativist reality to the "theatre of cruelty."

CHARACTERIZATION. Marat and de Sade are fully developed characters (though Marat is actually two characters, Marat and the patient who plays him). The Herald acts as a moderator-prompter and comments on the action in the Brechtian manner, while the remainder of the characters are largely one-dimensional, each projecting a specific mental patient's aberration.

THEME. The major argument of the play is devoted to the continuing debate between those who espouse private, selfish interests and those who espouse communal, revolutionary ideals. De Sade argues that the strong always dominate the weak, that human beings are essentially selfish, and that it is useless to attempt to improve the human condition. Marat argues that only through revolution and change can humans invent new meanings for life and develop a mutual respect that will better their condition.

DIALOGUE. The dialogue is a mixture of debate, commentary, songs, symbolic verse, and cryptic imagery, but the part that makes the strongest impact is almost irrational and nonverbal, expressing the frustration, suffering, and torture of the patients who symbolize the human condition.

RHYTHM. The play's rhythm is a disjointed one, broken by the interruption of the songs and commentary as well as by the background distractions of the patients' distorted and violent actions.

SPECTACLE. The play plunges the audience into the atmosphere of the asylum and forces them to participate in the mental suffering of the patients.

Visual Presentation of Marat/Sade

At first reading one would think that the visual approach would follow the same precepts as those of a Brechtian drama—overdone realistic caricatures for Coulmier and his family, bits and pieces of French Revolutionary garb placed over the patients' smocks, and de Sade set aside in the middle of the action as a simple and severe center around which the action swirls. But as one comes to recognize the theatrical possibilities presented by the inmates, one comes to understand how important their visual contribution is to the underlying "theatre of cruelty" imagery embedded in the play. The setting needs to be as bleak and cold and deadly as a morgue or mortuary with enough levels to give the director ample variation in the placement of the twisting, writhing, suffering inmates. The changing spectacle comes not in the setting but in the choreographed movements and groupings of the actors. The death of Marat in the bathtub is one conscious moment of spectacle that is often designed and blocked to mirror or comment on the famous painting of the subject by Jacques-Louis David.

In matters of costume the designer has great opportunities for some striking effects. First, one can overdesign in an almost expressionist manner the caricatured richness and decadence of Coulmier and his family as these Empire aristocrats enter and are seated to watch de Sade's play. They should probably be seen as if through the eyes of the inmates. De Sade should be simply dressed in ballet shirt and knee pants with powdered hair, and the patients should be dressed in dirty loincloths and hospital gowns distorted by the patients

into weird shapes and defaced with scrawled messages of an obscene or antisocial character. Over these garments can be added bits and pieces of the garb of the French Revolution, possibly with color held to blacks, whites, and grays plus the tricolor motif of the Revolution. The guards should look like nightmare images from a Nazi death camp, while the nuns should have heavy boots and headdresses that combine the qualities of a helmet and a nun's coif. Ugliness, violated textures, obscene messages, excrement-smeared gowns, shredded fabrics, and the harsh accent of the Revolutionary colors should mingle to assault the senses in a physical way; only thus can the essential character of the "theatre of cruelty" be achieved (Figure 19–7).

Gilles de Rais

Another example of this new approach to theatre is a production written and produced by Roger Planchon for the Théâtre Nationale Populaire in France. Since Planchon develops his own scripts or theatrical collages as he works with his company, his ultimate theatrical event is much more important than the historical material on which the production is based.

PLOT AND STRUCTURE. In the mid-1970s Planchon presented in collage form the life of the medieval personage Gilles de Rais, a late Gothic Charles Manson who was an orgiast, blasphemer, and child killer. De Rais was also a wealthy and powerful noble, a marshal of France who kept a private retinue of priests, a dabbler in alchemy and black magic, and a theatrical angel who financed the performance of a famous Mystery play at Orléans in 1434. He fought beside Joan of Arc in the battle to liberate France from the English, and he later became an important figure in the struggle between the King and the Dauphin for the control of France.

In the play the historical material is conjured up as a shifting nightmare or dream in

Figure 19–7.   Scene from *Marat/Sade* by Peter Weiss, produced by the Stanford Players, Stanford University, 1976. Directed by Robert Egan, costumes designed by the author. In this play, the playwright fuses the ideas of Brecht and Artaud to create an environment that combines multiple reality and intellectual debate with a violent physical-vocal theatre of cruelty. Photo by the author.

which the characters speak and act not as embodiments of thoughts and ideas, but as vehicles for the subterranean feelings of the medieval world. The specific action involves the last six months of Gilles' life—he died in 1440—and includes his exploits as the head of a gang of sadists, whores, bullies, procurers, and fallen priests; his capture and torment of adolescent boys; his attempts to preserve his chateau and lands from rival nobles; his seizure of a high-ranking priest and his subsequent arrest by the Duke of Brittany; and his trial and incineration at the stake.

The play is presented in a striking manner. The first images signal the complexity and ambiguity of Planchon's vision. The audience is presented with a large rectangular box surrounded by coarse, unpainted white tarpaulins. Inside are rocks like those painted by Giotto, and thrown across the rocks and into the auditorium are gangways made of three massive planks on which are placed what appear to be clusters of bushes. These suddenly turn into young boys who are holding foliage to hide themselves and who jump up and run off as Gilles' gang comes to hunt them. The strangeness and dislocation of this opening image, which is visual rather than verbal, stresses the turbulence of the medieval world. Images of the uncertain political and spiritual reality of the times are everywhere: Gilles clings to the opinions of his Florentine alchemist as if seeking in black magic support for his violent and scandalous actions; a wandering soldier turns out to be a girl in disguise, thus echoing the Joan of Arc story; Gilles' arraignment and trial become a medieval Mystery play; and the wife of the Duke of Brittany delivers an ecstatic speech about boar hunting that is both imaginative and fanciful and deeply vicious and ugly at the same time.

CHARACTERIZATION.   The characters seem to shift and change as in a dream and take on new facets as the action requires. At the close of the first act a figure appears who is a man but also an archetype of Vice or the Devil. As the subsequent trial of Gilles is transformed into a Mystery play set against a backcloth containing the signs of the zodiac, the characters are also transformed: the adolescent victims become a host of winged angels, the wandering soldier becomes the Virgin Mary, the Inquisitor becomes Abel, and the Unknown Man becomes God the Father.

THEME.   Planchon's deeply serious point in this surrealist spectacle is that society when confronted with violently heretical and defiant personalities must somehow find a place for their opposition and antagonism before putting them to death. This theme is not just stated but is embodied before the audience in a bewildering mixture of physically felt realities.

DIALOGUE.   The lines that the characters speak form a collage (as does the visual presentation). They are part character speeches, part lines borrowed from medieval dramas, and part actual speeches made by Gilles de Rais at his trial.

RHYTHM.   The rhythm of such a play can best be described as surrealistic, shifting and dissolving as if in a dream. Such rhythm is a product of the visual kaleidoscope presented by the production rather than being tied to the play's language.

SPECTACLE.   Though the spectacle is not excessive, it changes from moment to moment by having foliage turn into boys, blank backgrounds change into the mansions of a Mystery play, props that begin as one thing turn into something else. As with Brecht, the stage is treated as a collage, but there is a difference: here the collage is intended to produce a direct physical and tactile effect upon the audience, whereas in Brechtian drama the collage makes a rational, relativist comment on the action.

Visual Presentation of *Gilles de Rais*

Probably the easiest way to view the visual presentation of this play or performance piece is as a kaleidoscope of the inner mind—a kind of dream landscape of mixed realities held together by the strength and physical power of the theatrical imagination. The rough box surrounded by unpainted canvas and bridged by rough plank gangways to the audience is transformed by the addition of props and costumes into other places and other images. When the drop with the zodiac signs from *The Book of Hours* is brought in and costume and prop images change to those of a medieval Mystery play, the entire stage in the mind of the audience is transformed into a medieval Mystery theatre.

The costumes are basically rough, physical, tactile-textural actors' clothes that can be transformed by the addition of a costume prop, a piece of clothing, or the way some bit of clothing is worn into an image of an entirely different world. By adding a mitre and halo and reversing his mantle, the Unknown Man becomes God; by wrapping a cloak tightly about an actor's body, it becomes a shroud; by adding simple wings, young boys become angels; and by removing his official church mantle, the Inquisitor becomes Abel. Texture is always tactile, physical, and personal; color is used to provide focus and symbolic effect and to make a flash of emotional, physical color in a neutral scene. In short, the style is simple, unrealistic, and suggested rather than presented, and changes are immediate and done in view of the audience. Costume is thus used to underline the physical movement of the actors and to underline surrealistic shifts of reality and focus (Figure 19–8).

Figure 19–8.   Scene from *Gilles de Rais,* produced at the Théâtre National Populaire, Villeur-banne de Lyon, France, 1976. Written and directed by Roger Planchon. Another brilliant, theatrical collage in which modern and medieval philosophy and theatrical techniques are intercut and merged. Photo courtesy of the French Cultural Services, New York.

20

The Problem of Style: Summary and Conclusion

The Meaning of Style

It should be evident by now, even with the cursory treatment of style development in the Western world in the preceding chapters, that to study "style" is to study the complex path of human beings transforming their reactions to life into artistic creations such as dramas, novels, paintings, and sculptures. It is the "style" of these artistic works that both tells us about the spiritual and physical reactions of the artists to the societies in which they lived and provides a glimpse of one or more aspects of the cultures of their times. In short, to understand the development of cultural history, one must understand the meaning and operation of "style" in the history of all the arts.

During the early history of art, when the formal elements of art seemed to evolve in an inevitable and spontaneous way, artists were not nearly as conscious of the problem of style as they are today. The Renaissance gave Western Europe a mixed bag of stylistic self-consciousness as artists returned to the classical past, and the neoclassicism of the eighteenth century and the eclecticism of the nineteenth century compounded the issue. Only in the twentieth century were many of the confusions and distractions cast aside. As a result of the confusion of the nineteenth century, we adopted the word "style" to describe superficial, whimsical preferences such as are seen in the annual showings of fashions; what the concept of "style" should summarize is something deep and significant about a person or society. It should be a word associated with mature personal and cultural decisions rather than frenzied improvisation and constantly shifting fashion.

The artist who is the product of a society that cooperates for its own well-being and advancement will have a socially oriented self-confidence and a feeling of belonging, while the artist who identifies with a group that is condescending or antagonistic to the surrounding society will view the world egotistically and place great stress on fantasy, caprice, accidental effects, and sensationalism. Order versus accident, logic versus sensation, analysis versus intuition, production versus consumption, humanism versus egotism—all are extreme opposites that cluster about the two poles of human personality, and style is that recording point on the graph of time that marks the wavering line between them. It sums up the meaning, records the dominant attitudes, and presents an overall picture of the historical, economic, and cultural forces that may be operating at any given point.

The Various Style Labels in Relation to Life

If the many style ''isms'' that have been pinpointed and labeled in the past two centuries could all be arranged in relation to the polar opposites in human life (that is, between the logical and the spontaneous, between the sensational and the rational), much of the confusion caused by the many modern style ''isms'' might be removed. The common labels that usually describe the two poles in art are classical and romantic, but these are very confusing since they also refer to specific period developments. In the art of the theatre, the words classical and romantic tend to be used far more than any other labels to denote the contrasting poles of human experience. The average student *does* tend to think of these words as both period labels and general labels that describe two major kinds of theatrical products. To say the word ''romantic'' to a student of theatrical design is to conjure up a production that stresses emotions, richness, sensuous appeal, physical action, and all the design elements that can be coupled with the word sensation. To use the word ''classical'' is to conjure up a production that stresses order, structure, logic, humanism, simplicity, careful analysis, and beauty of form. It is only when students have this distinction clearly in mind and can quickly respond to these two poles of artistic development that they can begin to place labels such as expressionism, impressionism, symbolism, surrealism, naturalism, and mannerism in some kind of relation to these two basic stylistic poles.

Another very important distinction that students of the theatre tend to understand and use is the distinction between representation and presentation—between a theatrical production that will be accepted as a picture of real life or a production that will be accepted as an abstraction from reality. Although all productions are, by their nature, unreal or abstracted to some extent from reality, there is a whole spectrum of theatrical production that attempts to represent some aspect of real life in such a way that the audience will accept what they see as a picture of reality. The point at which the artists of the theatre begin to abstract and organize this reality in an obvious way cannot be defined, but there is a point at which an audience will be aware that what they see on stage is an artistic abstraction. Thus all productions, whether they lean toward the romantic or the classical, toward the sensational or the rational, can be divided at some point into those that an audience will accept as ''real'' and those that will be viewed as ''abstractions from reality.'' Many a theatre artist thinks that he or she has conceived a production as a very obvious abstraction from reality, only to have an audience accept it as a ''real'' picture of life in a particular period, thus proving that the division between representation and abstraction is closely allied to artistic knowledge, cultural sophistication, and historical information.

These two areas, romantic-classical and representational-presentational, cut across each other when one is attempting to place a theatrical production on a diagram of style, and although diagrams that attempt to relate ''isms'' of style to the ''life'' from which they come can give us little definitive information, such as diagram can help the student visualize the relationships of one style to another better than words can (Figure 20–1).

A diagram such as this makes it clear that a modern style such as *expressionism* will almost always be accepted as an abstraction from reality, will usually tend more toward the emotional and the sensational than the logical and rational, and can be thought of as a direct de-

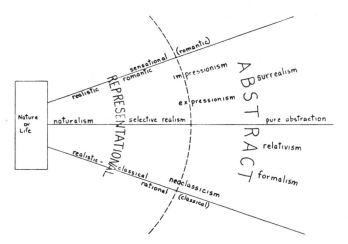

Figure 20–1. A diagram showing an arbitrary placement of styles in relation to reality or life.

velopment from representational realism, since the artist is using the subconscious reality of an individual as the rationale for his or her art. *Impressionism* will, at times, be acceptable as a representation of reality but is far more likely to move out to the level of abstraction—usually with a strong element of subtle, intuitive romanticism in its composition. *Surrealism* (which is not well represented in the drama) makes use of the reality of dreams and sensations of the inner mind, usually has sensational or romantic overtones, and would almost always be accepted as an abstraction rather than as a representation of reality. *Naturalism* as a stylistic form hugs close to the actual "life" from which it is taken and has few clearly defined characteristics, while *realism* tends to be more logically, rationally, and selectively formed while still attempting to capture the shifting balance between the sensational and the rational in life. Both of these stylistic forms are, of course, representational in intent and never allow an audience to be aware of the organizations and abstractions that are taking place in the production. *Symbolism* may stress either the rational or the sensational aspects of life, and by the nature and strength of the symbols used it can be thought of as either representational or abstract. *Mannerism* is such a loose stylistic term and covers so much artistic ground that it is impossible to tie down easily,

but it tends more toward the sensational and the mystical than toward the rational and logical, even when it is most preoccupied with structural effects and rational ideas. It speaks to the spirit rather than the mind, and although it can be representational at times, it is usually viewed as a clear abstraction from reality.

Many more minor stylistic labels can be placed on the diagram if one wishes, but one point is very clear: the great unifying cultural styles (such as the Romanesque, the Gothic, and the Baroque) produce such variety that one cannot tie them down to any single area on a diagram; they take in such wide balances of artistic effect in all directions that one can only discuss this variety, one cannot diagram it.

How the Various Style Labels Affect the Costume Designer

The terms representation and abstraction, when applied to the clothing of the past or present from which the designer is to create costumes, must mean the difference between costumes that an audience will accept as "real" garments based on the historical fashions of an era and costumes that an audience will accept as "abstractions" created by the designer from historical sources. This difference can apply to plays in any "style," and a majority of plays can be interpreted either abstractly or representationally. In one mode the designer is using source material as a way to comment on the period in terms of the play and its characters; in the other the designer is deliberately abstracting costume effects so that the audience will concentrate on things in the production other than the cultural background of the period. There has been a tendency in the theatre to stress the representational in costume even when settings move toward the abstract, simply because the body of the actor does not lend itself to abstraction as well as do stage sets; but the costume designer should not allow his or her creative vision to become narrow. If the play and the director's approach allow for an abstract expression of life, the designer should not be afraid to work in this direction.

The terms romantic and classical, which are the common opposites in theatre terminology, mean to the costume designer the difference between colors, fabrics, and costume lines that possess richness, variety, sensuous appeal, and decorative effect or colors, fabrics, and costume lines that stress balance, overall form, simplicity, logic of structure, and limitation of effect. A stage costume is usually balanced somewhere between the two poles, leaning toward one effect or the other. The costume designer instinctively knows when to work in one direction or the other, although there has been a tendency in the past century to equate all theatre and things theatrical with the intuitive, sensational, romantic outlook on life. This leads the costume designer to "dress up" all productions in essentially romantic costumes. This is obviously a limitation that does not allow the full breadth of our artistic inheritance to be expressed in stage costume.

The Problem of Costume Design in Our Present Culture

One of the great problems of the theatre in the twentieth century is that it has become (or at least it thinks it has become) so well versed in the theatrical styles of the past that its producers are only too ready to display their knowledge and theatrical prowess by presenting each play in its original, distinctive style. Like the great Reinhardt, who attempted to unify all the visual effects in his productions in order to capture the stylistic feeling of the period in which the play was written, many students of costume design become enamored of the idea of presenting each play in a style based on the play's original production. Although this is a commendable idea, it leads to an eclecticism that may eventually have only the academic flavor of a museum display. The costume designer who takes pride in being able to design equally well in all styles runs the risk of being superficial—of operating as a dilettante instead of as an artist.

On the other hand, the preceding chapters on style have emphasized the importance of understanding the cultural, historical, and artistic background within which a play was written as well as having a clear idea of the play's compositional structure before setting about the design of costumes. Since the costume designer, unlike the painter and the sculptor, is an interpreter of another person's artistic product, the concept of a designer having an individual style and forcing it on each production with which he or she is associated is untenable, if not dishonest. What is needed is a fusion of all that can be learned about a play and its background with the visual sources and design concepts that are prevalent today and will speak to the audiences of our own time. In short, the costume designer must make full use of the latest "breakthroughs" in the visual arts for interpreting the plays of the past, without doing violence to the original stylistic concept of that play. This is a large order, but costume designers must commit themselves to it if they intend to be honest to playwrights as well as to themselves as theatre artists.

The costume designer, like the set designer, the actor, and the director, always works within the limitations set by the script, and only when designing for some entertainment or ceremonial occasion that does not include a play script is he or she free to create like a painter, sculptor, or architect. There are occasions, however, when even painters, sculptors, and architects are required to work under quite strict limitations; we might take example from such limitations to illustrate how the costume designer may solve artistic problems within the limitations of a script.

Take, for example, the limitations given an architect who must fit a design into a group of buildings constructed in an earlier era. No self-respecting architect today would create a structure that re-created all the attributes of some historical style, even though this was the *beaux arts* architectural method of the nineteenth century. The architect would study the style of the other buildings very carefully and then, using the abstract attributes of line, texture, and color that they incorporated, would design a structure that would harmonize with the older buildings, would contain many of the same ideas of space, form, and surface texture, but would be conceived according to present-day visual usages. At Stanford University, several rather interesting structures have been built in which the red tile roofs, the sandstone texture, the round arches, and the cloister-like porticos have been retained from the Richardson Romanesque style that was adopted for the earliest buildings of the University (Figure 20–2). In each of these structures the basic characteristics of the older buildings have been retained

while new visual modes have been introduced. The arches are simpler, smoother, and unornamented; the surfaces are smooth plaster or poured concrete rather than cut stone; there is more sense of thrust and balanced weights than in the piled-up block-like forms of the original, and an overall cleanness and lack of ornament replaces the variety of carved stone effects in the earlier buildings. Yet with all the simplifications, expansions, and contractions of form in relation to space, the basic idea of a tile-roofed sandstone-colored structure surrounded by round arches has been maintained in one way or another. The architects, given strong limitations in their design approach, have succeeded in bringing the past and the present together without doing violence to either.

Costume design today should take advantage of the same dual effect. In a Shakespearean production, for example, one may spatter or spray the costumes to bring them closer to the patina of age or the sense of exposure to the elements that one finds prized in much modern art; one may treat raised ornament and jewelry in terms of the melted-metal, free-form look of much modern sculpture and jewelry; fabrics may be treated and dipped and dry-brushed to get a strong statement of surface that has a contemporary look yet is closely derived from historical fabric surfaces; while lines of costumes may be accentuated by out-

Figure 20–2.   The Lou Henry Hoover Pavilion of the Hoover Institution, Stanford University. An example of the tile roofs, columns, and arches found in the Richardson Romanesque architecture of the old campus used in a contemporary architectural design. Photo by the author.

lining contrasts in order to point up the contemporary interest in the structural lines behind an artistic presentation. There are no rules, no way to know how little or how much to change and develop your sources; it depends on sensitivity, intuition, a feeling for the original source as well as for modern artistic ideals, and a great sense of communication with the director of the particular production.

A Production of *Prometheus Bound*

To conclude this discussion of how to bring costume design for the theatre into the mainstream of contemporary art without violating the visual ideals found in an analysis of the script, let us briefly review the thinking and planning that went into a production of Aeschylus' *Prometheus Bound* at the Stanford Repertory Theatre.

The director wanted a visual production that would stress the sense of primitive ritual and ceremony that he hoped to bring to the play, and since none of the characters is specifically human, the director wished the costumes to suggest natural, organic, universal forces rather than people. A book on precious stones led to a design for the chorus costumes based on a cross section of a piece of malachite. The blues and greens with touches of white suggested the sea as it laps against rock, and this seemed an appropriate image for the chorus, who represent Daughters of the Ocean. The shape of the rock also suggested a series of overlapping circular capes, and this gave the conical silhouette eventually used in the chorus costumes, culminating in monumental masks based on primitive votive images from Africa and the South Pacific. The final chorus costume was made of overlapping petals of melted nylon, which gave a broken and coruscated texture of rock and seaweed, and with the use of the mask it suggested the primitive origins of the Greek drama while making an appeal to contemporary visual sensibilities (Figure 20-3).

Figure 20-3. A scene from *Prometheus Bound* by Aeschylus as produced by the Stanford Repertory Theatre, Stanford University, 1966. An example of the use of the traditional Greek mask and costumes interpreted in terms of primitive, ritualistic evocations of natural organic forms. Photo courtesy of Hank Kranzler.

Io's costume had to suggest not only her intense suffering but also that Zeus had transformed her into a cow, and the finished design made use of a great pink gown suggesting raw membranes covered with pasture grass, hemp garlands, webs at neck and wrists, symbolic horns on the forehead, and claws instead of hands (Figure 20-4). The costume was fabricated from melted nylon, sisal hemp, shredded rope, and liquid plastic, and although the basic shape of a Greek gown and mask were suggested, the primitive symbolic character of the role was forcefully presented, and the contemporary love of organic surfaces and textures utilizing current synthetics was stressed.

The final costumes for this production were mysterious, primitive, new, exciting, and made a fresh comment using new synthetic textures within the original visual demands of the play. Although most plays will not allow this much abstraction or textural display, many plays that are produced as re-creations of period dress can profit by the right subtle touches of contemporary visual usage.

Figure 20-4. Io from *Prometheus Bound* by Aeschylus as produced by the Stanford Repertory Theatre, Stanford University, 1966. An example of pastoral textures and imagery used to create a ritualistic ceremonial costume. Photo by Hank Kranzler.

Outline History of Western Costume

This outline may be used by students wishing to refresh their memories about the major developments in costume during the history of the Western world. It is in no way meant to take the place of or to be used in place of the standard texts in costume history, but is appended here merely as an aid to students who need to keep their period, dates, and costume silhouettes clearly in mind as they read the body of the text. It has, however, been coordinated with the chapters in *Costume History and Style* by the same author and publisher.

Recommended Sources on the History of Western Costume

(These references appear in abbreviated form in the outline history of Western costume. The numbers in parentheses before multiple items by the same author indicate which book by the author is included in the sources listed for each period.)

Barton, Lucy. *Historic Costume for the Stage.* Boston: W. H. Baker, 1935.

Batterberry, Michael and Ariane. *Mirror Mirror: A Social History of Fashion.* New York: Holt, Rinehart & Winston, 1977.

(1) Battersby, Martin. *The Decorative Twenties.* New York: Walker & Co., 1971.

(2) ———. *The Decorative Thirties.* New York: Walker & Co., 1971.

Bazin, Germain. *The History of World Sculpture.* Greenwich, Conn.: New York Graphic Society, 1968.

Berenson, Bernard. *Italian Painters of the Renaissance,* 2 vols. London: Phaidon, 1957.

Blitzer, Charles. *Age of Kings.* The Great Ages of Man Series. New York: Time-Life Books, 1967.

Blum, André. *Histoire de Costume: Les Modes aux XIXième Siècle.* Paris: Hachette, 1931.

Boas, Franz. *Primitive Art,* New ed. New York: Dover, 1955.

(1) Boehn, Max von. *Die Mode: Menschen und Moden in achtzehnten Jahrhundert.* ... Munich: Bruckmann, 1909.

(2) ———. *Die Mode: Menschen und Moden im Mittelalter.* ... Munich: Bruckmann, 1909.

(3) ———. *Die Mode: Menschen und Moden im neunzehnten Jahrhundert.* ... Munich: Bruckmann, 1907–1919.

(4) ———. *Die Mode: Menschen und Moden im sechzehnten Jahrhundert.* ... Munich: Bruckmann, 1923.

(5) ———. *Die Mode: Menschen und Moden im siebzehnten Jahrhundert.* ... Munich: Bruckmann, 1913.

(6) ———. *Modes and Manners* (trans. by Joan Joshua), 4 vols. London: Harrap, 1932–1935.

Boucher, François. *20,000 Years of Fashion.* New York: Harry N. Abrams, 1967.

Bowra, C. M. *Classical Greece.* The Great Ages of Man Series. New York: Time-Life Books, 1965.

Brantl, Ruth (ed.). *Medieval Culture.* The Culture of Mankind Series. New York: Braziller, 1966.

Brion, Marcel. *Art of the Romantic Era: Romanticism, Classicism, Realism.* New York: Holt, Rinehart & Winston, 1966.

(1) Brooke, Iris. *History of English Costume.* New York: Theatre Arts, 1968.

(2) ———. *Western European Costume.* London: Harrap, 1939, Vol. I. London: Theatre Arts, 1964, Vol. II.

(3) ———. *English Costume in the Age of Elizabeth.* London: A. & C. Black, 1933.

(4) ———. *English Costume of the Early Middle Ages.* London: A. & C. Black, 1936.

(5) ———. *English Costume of the Eighteenth Century.* London: A. & C. Black, 1931.

(6) ———. *English Costume of the Later Middle Ages.* London: A. & C. Black, 1935.

(7) ———. *English Costume of the Nineteenth Century.* London: A. & C. Black, 1929.

(8) ———. *English Costume of the Seventeenth Century.* London: A. & C. Black, 1934.

(9) ———. *Medieval Theatre Costume.* New York: Theatre Arts, 1967.

(10) ———. *Costume in Greek Classical Drama.* New York: Theatre Arts, 1961.

(1) Brown, H. C. *The Golden Nineties.* New York: Valentine, 1928.

(2) ———. *New York in the Elegant Eighties.* New York: Valentine, 1927.

Burchell, S. C. *Age of Progress.* Great Ages of Man Series. New York: Time-Life Books, 1966.

Burckhardt, Jakob C. *The Civilization of the Renaissance in Italy* (trans. by S. G. C. Middlemore), 3rd rev. ed. London: Phaidon, 1950.

Canaday, John. *Mainstreams of Modern Art.* New York: Holt, Rinehart & Winston, 1959.

Carcopino, J. *Daily Life in Ancient Rome.* New Haven, Conn.: Yale University Press, 1940.

(1) Casson, Lionel. *Daily Life in Ancient Egypt.* A Horizon Book. New York: American Heritage, 1975.

(2) _____. *Daily Life in Ancient Rome*. A Horizon Book. New York: American Heritage, 1975.

Colton, Joel. *Twentieth Century*. The Great Ages of Man Series. New York: Time-Life Books, 1968.

Connoisseur, The (1901–1927. In 1927 merged with International Studio). London.

Contini, Mila. *Fashion*. New York: Odyssey Press, 1965.

Courthion, Pierre. *Romanticism* (trans. by Stuart Gilbert). New York: Skira, 1961.

Crankshaw, Edward. *The Hapsburgs: Portrait of a Dynasty*. New York: Viking, 1971.

(1) Cunnington, C. Willett. *English Women's Clothing in the Nineteenth Century*. London: Faber, 1937.

(2) _____, and Cunnington, Phillis. *Handbook of English Costume in the Eighteenth Century*. London: Faber, 1957.

(3) _____. *Handbook of English Costume in the Seventeenth Century*. London: Faber, 1955.

(4) _____. *Handbook of English Costume in the Sixteenth Century*. London: Faber, 1954.

(5) _____. *Handbook of English Medieval Costume*. Philadelphia: Dufour, 1952.

(6) _____. *A Picture History of English Costume*. London: Longacre, 1960.

Davenport, Millia. *The Book of Costume*. New York: Crown, 1948.

Dewald, Ernest T. *Italian Painting 1200–1600*. New York: Holt, Rinehart & Winston, 1961.

Enlart, Camille. *Manuel d'Archaeologie Française. Tome III, Le Costume*. Paris: Auguste Picard, 1916.

Esquire Magazine (1937–   ). New York.

(1) Evans, Joan. *Art in Medieval France*. New York: Oxford University Press. 1948.

(2) _____. *Dress in Medieval France*. Oxford: Clarendon Press, 1952.

Evelyn, Sir John. *Diary (1641–1705)*, 2 vols. Washington, D.C.: Dunne, 1901.

Faniel, Stephanie (ed.). *French Art of the Eighteenth Century*. New York: Simon & Schuster, 1957.

Fletcher, Sir Bannister. *A History of Architecture on the Comparative Method*, 17th ed. New York: Scribner's, 1965.

Frankfort, Henri. *The Art and Architecture of the Ancient Orient*. Baltimore: Penguin, 1955.

Frankl, Paul. *The Gothic*. Princeton, N.J.: Princeton University Press, 1960.

Freedberg, Sydney J. *Painting of the High Renaissance in Rome and Florence*, 2 vols. Cambridge, Mass.: Harvard University Press, 1961.

Freemantle, Anne. *Age of Faith*. The Great Ages of Man Series. New York: Time-Life Books, 1965.

Friedlander, Walter F. *Mannerism and Anti-Mannerism in Italian Painting*. New York: Columbia University Press, 1957.

Galerie des Modes, La (1778–1787). Paris.

Gallery of Fashion, The (1794–1803). London.

Garbini, Giovanni. *The Ancient World*. Landmarks of the World's Art Series. New York: McGraw-Hill, 1966.

Gay, Peter. *Age of Enlightenment*. The Great Ages of Man Series. New York: McGraw-Hill, 1965.

Gentleman's Magazine of Fashions, Fancy Costume, and Regimentals of the Army, The (May 1828–December 1894). London.

Gernsheim, Helmut. *The History of Photography from the Earliest Use of the Camera Obscura in the Eleventh Century up to 1914*. London: Oxford University Press, 1969.

Ghorsline, Douglas. *What People Wore*. New York: Viking, 1952.

Godey's Lady's Book (1830–1898). Philadelphia.

Gonzalez-Palacios, Alvar. *The French Empire Style*. London: Homlyn Publishing Group, 1970.

Good Housekeeping (1885–   ). New York.

Green, Frederick C. *Eighteenth Century in France*. New York: Ungar, 1965.

Greenberg, Clement. *Art and Culture: Critical Essays*. Gloucester, Mass.: Peter Smith, n.d.

Hale, John R. *Renaissance*. The Great Ages of Man Series. Baltimore: Time-Life Books, 1965.

Hamilton, George Heard. *Painting and Sculpture in Europe, 1880–1940*. The Pelican History of Art Series. Baltimore: Penguin, 1967.

(1) *Harper's New Monthly Magazine* (1850–   ). New York.

(2) *Harper's Weekly* (1857–1916). New York.

(3) *Harper's Bazaar* (1867–   ). New York.

Hartley, Dorothy. *Medieval Costume and Life*. New York: Scribner's, 1931.

(1) Hartley, Dorothy, and Elliot, Margaret M. *Life and Work of the People of England (The Eleventh to the Thirteenth Century—A.D. 1000–1300)*. New York: Putnam's, 1931.

(2) _____. *Life and Work of the People of England (The Eighteenth Century)*. New York: Putnam's, 1931.

Heuzey, Léon and Jacques. *Histoire du Costume dans L'Antiquité Classique de l'Orient*. Paris: Les Belles Lettres, 1935.

Hibbert, Christopher. *Daily Life in Victorian England*.

A Horizon Book. New York: American Heritage and McGraw-Hill, 1975.

Hildebrand, Alice (ed.). *Greek Culture*. The Cultures of Mankind Series. New York: Braziller, 1966.

(1) Houston, Mary G. *Ancient Egyptian, Assyrian and Persian Costume*. London: A. & C. Black, 1920.

(2) ⸺. *Ancient Greek, Roman and Byzantine Costume*. London: A. & C. Black, 1931.

(3) ⸺. *Medieval Costume in England and France*. London: A. & C. Black, 1939.

Howell, Georgina. *In Vogue: Sixty Years of Celebrities and Fashion from British Vogue*. London: Penguin Books, 1978.

Illustrated London News (1842–   ). London.

Illustration, L' (1843–   ). Paris.

International Studio (1897–   ). New York.

Janson, H. W. *History of Art*, 2nd ed. Englewood Cliffs, N.J.: Prentice-Hall, 1977.

Journal des Dames et des Modes (1797–1839). Paris.

Kahler, Heinz. *The Art of Rome and her Empire* (trans. by J. R. Foster). New York: Crown, 1963.

Kelly, Francis M. *Shakespearean Costume for Stage and Screen*. Boston: W. H. Baker, 1938.

Kidson, Peter. *The Medieval World*. Landmarks of the World's Art Series. New York: McGraw-Hill, 1967.

Kimball, Sidney Fiske. *The Creation of the Rococo*. Philadelphia: Philadelphia Museum of Art, 1943.

Kitson, Michael. *The Age of Baroque*. New York: McGraw-Hill, 1966.

Köhler, Carl. *A History of Costume*. New York: Dover, 1963.

Ladies' Home Journal (1883–   ). Philadelphia.

Larkin, Oliver. *Art and Life in America*. New York: Holt, Rinehart & Winston, 1949.

Lassus, Jean. *The Early Christian and Byzantine World*. Landmarks of the World's Art Series. New York: McGraw-Hill, 1967.

(1) Laver, James. *Costume*. London: Hawthorn, 1964.

(2) ⸺. *Costume Through the Ages*. London: Thames & Hudson, 1963.

(3) ⸺. *Style in Costume*. New York: Oxford University Press, 1949.

(4) ⸺ (ed.). *Costumes of the Western World*. New York: Harper & Row, Pub., 1951.

(5) ⸺ (ed.). *Costume in Antiquity*. London: Thames & Hudson, 1964.

Leloir, Maurice. *Histoire du Costume*. Paris: Henri Ernst, 1933.

Life Magazine (1883–   ). New York.

Linthicum, M. Channing. *Costume in the Drama of Shakespeare and His Contemporaries*. Oxford: Clarendon Press, 1936.

Lloyd, Seton. *The Art of the Ancient Near East*. New York: Holt, Rinehart & Winston, 1961.

Lynton, Norbert. *The Modern World*. Landmarks of the World's Art Series. New York: McGraw-Hill, 1965.

Mâle, Émile. *Religious Art in France in the Thirteenth Century*. New York: Dutton, 1913.

Marinatos, Spyridon. *Crete and Mycenae*. New York: Harry N. Abrams, 1960.

Martindale, Andrew. *Man and the Renaissance*. New York: McGraw-Hill, 1966.

Mates, Julian, and Cantelupe, Eugene (eds.). *Renaissance Culture*. The Cultures of Mankind Series. New York: Braziller, 1966.

Mee, Charles L., Jr. *Daily Life in Renaissance Italy*. A Horizon Book. New York: American Heritage and McGraw-Hill, 1975.

Men's Wear (1937–1950). New York.

Mode Illustrée, La (1869–1873). London.

Modes Parisiennes, Les (1843–1875). Paris.

(1) Morey, Charles Rufus. *Christian Art*. New York: Longmans, Green, 1935.

(2) ⸺. *Medieval Art*. New York: W. W. Norton & Co., Inc., 1942.

Morse, Harriet K. *Elizabethan Pageantry*. . . . London: Studio, 1934.

Newton, Eric. *The Romantic Rebellion*. New York: St. Martin's Press, 1966.

(1) Norris, Herbert. *Costume and Fashion*. London: Dent, 1925, Vol. I; 1940, Vol. II. New York: Dutton, 1938, Vol. III.

(2) ⸺. *Church Vestments*. London: Dent, 1949.

Norris, Herbert, and Curtis, Oswald. *Costume and Fashion*. Vol. VI. London: Dent, 1933.

Novotny, Fritz. *Painting and Sculpture in Europe, 1780–1880*. Pelican History of Art. Baltimore: Penguin, 1960.

Payne, Blanche. *History of Costume*. New York: Harper & Row, Pub., 1965.

Pepys, Samuel. *Diary and Correspondence of Samuel Pepys*. 10 vols. New York: Dodd, Mead, 1885.

Peterson's Magazine (1846–1898). Philadelphia.

Petit Courrier des Dames (1822–1865). Paris.

Pevsner, Nikolaus. *An Outline of European Architecture*. Baltimore: Penguin, 1963.

Piton, Camille. *Le Costume Civile en France du XIIIième au XIXième Siècle*. Paris: Ernest Flammarion, 1913.

Powell, T. G. *Prehistoric Art*. New York: Holt, Rinehart & Winston, 1966.

Praz, Mario. *An Illustrated History of Furnishing from the Renaissance to the Twentieth Century*. New York: Braziller, 1964.

Racinet, Albert C. A. *Le Costume historique*, 6 vols. Paris: Firmin-Didot, 1888.

Reynolds, Graham. *Victorian Painting*. London: Studio Vista, 1966.

Rice, David Talbot. *The Art of Byzantium*. New York: Harry N. Abrams, 1959.

Richter, Gisela. *A Handbook of Greek Art*, 2nd rev. ed. London: Phaidon, 1960.

Robertson, Donald A. *A Handbook of Greek and Roman Architecture*. Cambridge: Cambridge University Press, 1954.

Schneider, Isador (ed.). *The Enlightenment*. The Cultures of Mankind Series. New York: Braziller, 1965.

Sears Roebuck Catalog, The (1894–). Chicago.

Selz, Peter, and Constantine, Mildred (eds.). *Art Nouveau: Art and Design at the Turn of the Century*. New York: MOMA and Doubleday, 1960.

Sherrard, Philip. *Byzantium*. The Great Ages of Man Series. New York: Time-Life Books, 1966.

(1) Skira, Albert (ed.). *The Great Centuries of Painting: Roman Painting*. Geneva: Editions Albert Skira, 1953.

(2) _____. *The Great Centuries of Painting: Byzantine Painting*. Geneva: Editions Albert Skira, 1953.

(3) _____. *The Great Centuries of Painting: Early Medieval Painting*. Geneva: Editions Albert Skira, 1957.

(4) _____. *The Great Centuries of Painting: Romanesque Painting*. Geneva: Editions Albert Skira, 1958.

(5) _____. *The Great Centuries of Painting: Gothic Painting*. Geneva: Editions Albert Skira, 1954.

(6) _____. *The Great Centuries of Painting: Italian Painting of the Renaissance*. Geneva: Editions Albert Skira, 1951.

(7) _____. *The Great Centuries of Painting: The Sixteenth Century*. Geneva: Editions Albert Skira, 1954.

(8) _____. *The Great Centuries of Painting: The Seventeenth Century*. Geneva: Editions Albert Skira, 1951.

(9) _____. *The Great Centuries of Painting: The Eighteenth Century*. Geneva: Editions Albert Skira, 1952.

Soehner, Halldor, and Schonberger, Arno. *The Rococo Age*. New York: McGraw-Hill, 1960.

Speltz, Alexander. *The Styles of Ornaments, etc.* (trans. and rev. by R. P. Spiers). London: Batsford, 1910.

Squire, Geoffrey. *Dress and Society, 1560–1970*. New York: Viking, 1974.

Strommenger, Eva, and Hirmer, Max. *5000 Years of the Art of Mesopotamia*. New York: Harry N. Abrams, 1964.

Strong, Donald. *The Classical World*. Landmarks of the World's Art Series. New York: McGraw-Hill, 1965.

Studio, The (1893–). London.

Sullivan, Mark. *Our Times, 1900–1914*. Vol. I, *The Turn of the Century;* Vol. II, *America Finding Herself;* Vol. III, *Prewar America;* Vol. IV, *The War Begins*. New York: Scribner's, 1927–1932.

Swarzenski, Hanns. *Monuments of Romanesque Art*. Chicago: University of Chicago Press, 1954.

Tapié, Victor L. *The Age of Grandeur*. New York: Holt, Rinehart & Winston, 1960.

(1) *This Fabulous Century: Prelude 1870–1900*. New York: Time-Life Books, 1970.

(2) *This Fabulous Century: 1900–1910*. New York: Time-Life Books, 1969.

(3) *This Fabulous Century: 1910–1920*. New York: Time-Life Books, 1969.

(4) *This Fabulous Century: 1920–1930*. New York: Time-Life Books, 1969.

(5) *This Fabulous Century: 1930–1940*. New York: Time-Life Books, 1969.

(6) *This Fabulous Century: 1940–1950*. New York: Time-Life Books, 1969.

(7) *This Fabulous Century: 1950–1960*. New York: Time-Life Books, 1969.

(8) *This Fabulous Century: 1960–1970*. New York: Time-Life Books, 1970.

(1) Tilke, Max. *The Costumes of Eastern Europe*. London: Benn, 1926.

(2) _____. *Orientalische Kostüme in Schnitt und Farbe*. Berlin: Wasmuth, 1923.

Tilke, Max, and Bruhn, Wolfgang. *A Pictorial History of Costume*. London: A. Zwemmer, 1955.

(1) Tissot, James. *The Life of Our Savior, Jesus Christ* (trans. with notes and drawings by Mrs. Arthur Bell). New York: Doubleday-McClure, 1899.

(2) _____. *Old Testament Selections*. Paris: M. de Brunoff, 1904.

Vecellio, Cesare. *Habiti Antichi et Moderni*. Venice, 1598.

Vingt Ans (1947–). Paris.

Vogue (1892–). New York.

Volbach, Wolfgang F., and Hirmer, Max. *Early Christian Art*. New York: Harry N. Abrams, 1961.

Waterhouse, E. K. *Painting in Britain 1530–1790*. Pelican History of Art Series. Baltimore: Penguin, 1966.

Weinstein, Leo (ed.). *The Age of Reason*. The Cultures of Mankind Series. New York: Braziller, 1965.

(1) Wilcox, Ruth Turner. *The Mode in Costume*. New York: Scribner's, 1946.

(2) ———. *The Mode in Furs*. New York: Scribner's, 1951.

(3) ———. *Five Centuries of American Costume*. New York: Scribner's, 1963.

Wildeblood, Joan. *The Polite World*. London: Davis-Poynter, 1973.

Wills, Garry (ed.). *Roman Culture*. The Cultures of Mankind Series. New York: Braziller, 1966.

(1) Wilson, Lillian May. *The Clothing of the Ancient Romans*. Baltimore: Johns Hopkins University Press, 1938.

(2) ———. *The Roman Toga*. Baltimore: Johns Hopkins University Press, 1924.

Winston, Clara and Richard. *Daily Life in the Middle Ages*. A Horizon Book. New York: American Heritage and McGraw-Hill, 1975.

Wittkower, Rudolf. *Art and Architecture in Italy, 1600–1750*. Pelican History of Art. Baltimore: Penguin, 1958.

(1) Wölfflin, Heinrich. *Classic Art,* 2nd ed. London: Phaidon, 1953.

(2) ———. *Principles of Art History* (trans. by Mary D. Hottinger). New York: Holt, Rinehart & Winston, 1932.

Worth, J. P. *A Century of Fashion*. Boston: Little, Brown, 1928.

Prehistoric

What little we know about Early Stone Age people comes from the amazingly naturalistic images they incised upon the walls of caves as a form of sympathetic magic by which they tried to trap or control the animals depicted. The few extant images of women, such as the famed fertility figurine known as the *Venus of Willendorf*, are little more than images to invoke procreation—a merging of breasts, hips, and genital areas rather than realistic depictions of female figures. The few extant images of men are much the same, with great concentration on the genital area. The image of the human figure was thus far less realistic than the animal images depicted by Old Stone Age humans, but this is to be expected in an age when far more time was spent tracking animal herds than relating in a human way to other human beings.

Then, in about 8000 B.C., with the gradual opening of the New Stone Age era known as the Neolithic Revolution, primitive people began to settle down in villages, to till the soil and engage in animal husbandry. As in the story of the Garden of Eden, humans who had been children of nature, dealing with instincts and sensations rather than facts, began to gain self-knowledge and to use the intellect to categorize and organize life. There was now a dualistic view of a real world and a supernatural one—an inner and an outer reality—and there were complex rituals devised to connect human beings with the spirit world. At the same time the visual arts turned from natural images to signs and symbols that eventually led to pictographs and hieroglyphs. These abstract, geometric forms represented a more organized, disciplined, intellectual, and dualistic religious outlook that continued into historical times.

THE OLD STONE AGE (PALEOLITHIC). Since animal hides were a by-product of hunting, skins became the logical basis for simple loin cloths, wraparound skirts, and shawls in southern Europe during late Paleolithic times, while in warmer climates plaited grasses and leaves were used for similar clothing shapes. Also, skin decoration must be included as a form of clothing, not just as decoration for the body but as having important ritual-symbolic associations. Beyond the simple use of shawls and loin cloths, we know that Old Stone Age people often punched holes in skins and laced these skins to the legs or torso with leather thongs. In general, most clothes made of skin, except for shawls, remained close to the body and were laced to give the wearer the feeling of a second skin.

THE NEW STONE AGE (MESOLITHIC AND NEOLITHIC). With the development of weaving, garments became square and rectangular. The basic garments were skirts, coats, T-shaped tunics, and wraparound shawls. Woven garments were not as tightly fitting as skins; skirts or kilts were hung from the waist, complemented by T-shaped coats and tunics. A wide range of animal and mineral dyes was developed to give color to clothing, and a wide range of jewelry and ornament was developed to give accent to dress. Sandals and slipper shoes were also added, as were a variety of caps and headdresses. Due to the primitive nature of weaving and sewing in the New Stone Age, garments were much the same in Africa, Europe, and the Orient, with allowance for changes in climate, terrain, and available materials.

PREHISTORIC

DATES
Paleolithic 600,000–8000 B.C.
Mesolithic 8000–6000 B.C.
Neolithic 6000–50 B.C.
Bronze Age 2100–1000 B.C.
Iron Age 1000–50 B.C.
COMMON TERMS (FOR OTHERS SEE GLOSSARY)
plastron
sagum

RECOMMENDED SOURCES
Boas
Boucher: Chapter I
Norris (1): Volume I, Chapter I
Payne: Introduction
Powell
Strommenger and Hirmer

Paleolithic

Neolithic

Typical Figures

Egyptian

The earliest civilization of the Western world arose along the Nile River in Egypt and the Tigris and Euphrates Rivers in Mesopotamia several thousand years before Christ; both flourished for roughly 3000 years, but because the Egyptians built their temples and pyramids of stone, Egypt left many more remnants of their civilization than did Mesopotamia, where brick was used.

The Egyptian style is characterized by severity, regularity, order, and rhythmical repetition. Flowers and plants such as the lotus and the papyrus were incorporated into the rigid patterns used on columns, capitals, wall decorations, and costume accessories. Costuming, like the other arts, was sophisticated, symbolic, removed from the level of the natural to a formal, frozen, unchanging silhouette that would always suggest the triumph of humans' organizing powers over their natural subordination to nature.

THE OLD KINGDOM.   In the first period of Egypt's prosperity, the major masculine garment was a short, plain *loin cloth* of linen wrapped tightly around the hips and secured by a belt with a loop. Loin cloths of the Pharaohs were often woven with gold thread and were formed into carefully arranged folds at the front of the figure. This stress on many stiffened, lightweight, even, transparent folds is characteristic of most Egyptian costume. The feminine dress was also a single garment: a close-fitting *skirt* or *kalisiris* covering the body from under the breasts to the ankles and supported by two shoulder straps. As time progressed, the skirt was often overlaid with a girdle with all emphasis drawn to the front of the figure, and a stiffly starched and pleated triangle of fabric at the front of the figure was added to the male loin cloth.

THE MIDDLE KINGDOM.   In the next period of prosperity, men's dress was complicated by the addition of a skirt. The skirt was often semitransparent, over a loin cloth frequently finished with a girdle and again stressing a decorative emphasis at the front of the figure. The head was often covered with a stiffened cloth such as we see on the Sphinx. Women's clothing, though more richly adorned, did not change appreciably during this time.

THE NEW KINGDOM.   After a period of disruption caused by foreign raids, a period of great expansion and wealth developed. At this time the seamed tunic became a part of Egyptian dress, with men wearing it either over or under a skirt, while women used it as a principal garment coupled with a short cape knotted on the breast; the fabric chosen was so thin and fine in texture that it was almost completely transparent. These tunic dresses, especially at the time of the artistic naturalism of Akhenaten or Amenhotep IV, were often finely pleated and followed the line of the body without the severity of line found in earlier Egyptian dress. The great rectangular robe with a hole in the center for the head was also used at this time. There are many artistic depictions of such well-known symbolic accessories as the sacred *uraeus* or asp, the *scarab* or beetle symbol, the vulture headdress, the combined red and white crown of Upper and Lower Egypt, the winged solar disk, and the famous Queen's Headdress of the Empress Nefertiti. Flowers and jewelry were used extensively in geometric patterns of decoration, the most vivid decorative accessory being the richly colored round collar used by both men and women. Cosmetics were used extensively. Women's eyes were outlined with kohl and shadowed in green, while the body and false wig were bathed in sweet-smelling oils. Men of the nobility frequently used false wigs and beards.

In the long history of Egyptian dress the basic costume ideal underwent very few modifications, because in Egyptian culture respect for tradition was far stronger than the need for change.

EGYPTIAN

DATES
   Old Kingdom 2980–2160 B.C.
   Middle Kingdom 2160–1580 B.C.
   Empire or New Kingdom 1580–1090 B.C.
   Saite Period 1090–332 B.C.

COMMON TERMS (FOR OTHERS SEE GLOSSARY)
   kalisiris
   sacred uraeus
   mitre of Osiris
   vulture headdress
   schenti
   postiche
   pectoral
   ankh

RECOMMENDED SOURCES
   Casson
   Garbini
   Houston (1): Section I
   Payne: Chapter I
   Köhler: Chapter on Egypt
   Boucher: pp. 91–103
   Fletcher: Chapter on Egyptian architecture
   Speltz: Chapter I
   Barton: pp. 3–18
   Davenport: pp. 15–35
   Contini: pp. 15–26
   Tilke: Plates 1–5

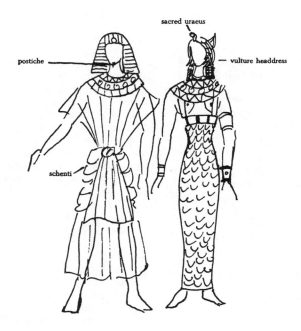

Typical Figures

Mesopotamian

The Tigris–Euphrates Valley and the surrounding areas, which include Persia, southern Turkey, and Palestine, gave birth to a highly developed series of civilizations at approximately the same time that Egyptian culture developed. However, since the major architectural structures were of brick rather than stone and the transition from one culture to another was quite rapid, we have far fewer artifacts from which to judge each succeeding culture than is the case in Egypt. The most consistent image left to us from these various cultures is that of fierce and war-like conquerors whose major interests were hunting and fighting. Their physical image, draped in fringed woolen shawls over woolen tunics surmounted by heavy beards and headdresses, is far heavier, less sophisticated, and less carefully ordered than the Egyptian figure.

SUMERIAN CIVILIZATION. The few artistic representations of dress from this period show the men in what must be shaggy sheepskin skirts wrapped around the waist. Women wore a simple tunic. Toward the end of this early period the famous fringed shawl was introduced, worn either diagonally over the shoulder and under the other arm or (usually for women) fastened about the neck with a brooch.

ANCIENT BABYLONIAN EMPIRE. The decline toward the end of the third millennium of the Sumerian empire of Ur allowed the city of Babylon to become the center of a new Mesopotamian empire, which further developed the use of thick, richly decorated garments. There was a great emphasis on the use of fringe. The basic garments for both men and women were a fringed shirt or tunic surmounted by the diagonally draped shawl. Headdresses tended toward metal circlets or truncated metal cones, while footwear included an open sandal and a partially closed and laced shoe.

ASSYRIAN EMPIRE. The period of Northern ascendency under the rule of the Assyrians at Nineveh lasted about 600 years, and it is from the reigns of the great kings such as Ashurbanipal and Ashurnasirpal that we get the most striking and best-preserved artistic representations of Assyrian dress. The square-cut hair and beard, the long tunic, the heavy, diagonally draped, fringed shawl, the heavy metal ornaments at wrist and waist, and the truncated cone headdress all make it easy to distinguish male Assyrian figures. Women wore a modification of these garments.

SECOND BABYLONIAN EMPIRE. This brief period of resurgence of the city of Babylon lasted only from 612 B.C. until the invasion of the Persians in 539 B.C. and produced no marked change in dress except for added richness and decoration.

THE PERSIAN EMPIRE. The Persians, who swept into the Tigris–Euphrates Valley from the East in 539 B.C., accepted much of the architecture and artistic decoration of those they conquered, but they did bring with them a longer-sleeved and tighter tunic or coat, sometimes open down the front, and also trousers for covering the legs; both of these were worn by men. The *candys*, a great rectangle reaching from wrist to wrist with a hole for the head and seamed together up the sides, was used as a ceremonial garment. Beards were pointed rather than square; crowns flared out instead of tapering in, and feet were covered with slipper-like shoes. Women still wore the tunic and shawl with the addition of head veils.

HEBREW DRESS. The Hebrews were originally desert people. When they settled in Palestine they kept the enveloping, striped, woolen garments and draperies that protected head and body from the sun. The basic garments for men were the long-sleeved tunic, a short, wide-sleeved overtunic, and the very wide-sleeved coat or *aba*, a rectangular robe similar to the robe used by the Egyptians and the shawl used by the Assyrians. Women usually wore a sleeveless tunic, often covered with the wide-sleeved aba or a shawl. Priests wore the tabard-like *ephod* with its jeweled purse over their tunics and a dome-shaped mitre on their heads.

MESOPOTAMIAN

DATES
- Sumerian Civilization 4000–2232 B.C.
- Ancient Babylonian Empire 2232–1275 B.C.
- Assyrian Empire 1275–612 B.C.
- Second Babylonian Empire 612–539 B.C.
- Persian Empire 539–331 B.C.

COMMON TERMS (FOR OTHERS SEE GLOSSARY)
- aba
- ephod
- candys
- caftan
- kidaris
- kilt
- kaunakes
- Phrygian bonnet

RECOMMENDED SOURCES
- Houston (1): Sections II and III
- Tissot (1)
- Tissot (2)
- Heuzey
- Lloyd
- Frankfort (background)
- Köhler: pp. 64–85
- Strommenger and Hirmer

kidaris

Assyrian ca. 1300 B.C.

Typical Figures

Greek

In certain Egyptian tomb paintings we see long-legged ambassadors from Crete wearing costumes that have a freer and more lightly decorative aspect than those worn by the Egyptians. But it was not until Heinrich Schliemann excavated Mycenae and Sir Arthur Evans uncovered the royal palaces of Crete that historians became aware of the brilliant civilization that existed in the vicinity of the Aegean centuries before the rise of classical Greece. The most astonishing things about the clothing of the Cretan and Mycenaean civilizations were their tight-fitted, artificial lines and light, gay, ornamental, decorative patterns. The beautifully draped garments of classical Greece developed slowly, as Greek art developed a more natural, relaxed, idealized beauty. During the transitional period from roughly 500 to 460 B.C., we find all manner of experimentation with soft fabrics, draped lines, and pins instead of seams, to gain subtlety, beauty, and gracefulness in the form and manner of wearing garments.

CRETAN DRESS. Since the ideal Cretan man and woman were tall and supple with slender waists, costume was calculated to emphasize these lines. For men, a loin cloth was often the only covering, resting high on the hips and held in place by a corset belt. Women's dress was a two-piece costume consisting of a bell-shaped tiered skirt and a small jacket, the skirt having a pattern of bright colors running in alternating squares and stripes over the tiers. The waist was constricted by a tight belt, while the short-sleeved jacket was very tight, with the breasts completely exposed. Both men and women wore their hair over the forehead in loose spiral curls, a characteristic motif of Cretan art.

MYCENAEAN DRESS. The inhabitants of the city of Mycenae on the Greek mainland were of a different race than the Cretans. The women copied Cretan styles; the men tended to wear short, tight-fitting tunics copied from those worn in Asia Minor. This tunic eventually became the basis for the looser, draped *chiton* of the Greeks. Mycenaean color and ornament were heavier and less playful than Cretan.

ARCHAIC GREEK DRESS. Greek immigrants overwhelmed the Cretan-Mycenaean civilization between 1200 and 1000 B.C. The strongest tribes participating in these invasions were the Dorians and the Ionians, the former settling in the mainland,

the latter along the coast of Asia Minor. The new civilization is known as Archaic Greek and stretched from the eighth century B.C. to the time of the Persian invasions.

The standard garment for men was the close-fitting *chiton* or tunic, either full length or short with a decorative pattern border. Overgarments were the short, rectangular cloak or *chlamys* and the rectangular shawl or *himation*. The major garment for women was the tubular *peplos,* with an overfold at the top held at the shoulders by two pins. Toward the end of the period, light, pleated linen chitons from Ionia began to replace the tubular peplos, and the move toward the draped beauty of classical Greek costume began. Ornament during this period was rigidly geometric, and the general feeling of the costume was one of tightness and geometric formality.

THE CLASSICAL PERIOD. The basic garment for men during the fifth century B.C. was the *Ionic chiton,* formed without seams from a rectangle whose center fold was placed on the left side of the figure, leaving the right side open. It was supported at the shoulder with *fibulae* or safety pins. Most Ionic chitons were short, the length adjusted by belting, but a long, pleated chiton of linen or soft wool was worn by charioteers, musicians, and old men. The outergarment was the rectangular *himation,* which was draped over the left shoulder, under the right arm, and back over the left shoulder. The short cloak or *chlamys* was fastened on the right shoulder with a brooch to leave the right arm free.

The women of the classical period usually wore the *Doric peplos* or *chiton* with an overfold at the top. It was full and fell in graceful folds with a woven border but no overall pattern. It was left open on the right side. It could be fastened with pins all the way down the arm or loosely draped, with a cord at the waist and hips to allow a blousing of fabric called the *kolpos.* Sometimes women wore the Ionic chiton without the overfold, and the draped himation was the standard outergarment.

HELLENISTIC PERIOD. After the conquests of Alexander the Great, Greece was brought into contact with the East, and cotton and silk were imported and woven into a variety of fabrics. Costume displayed more orientalized embroidery techniques, with much use of metallic threads, and in general was richer and more ostentatious.

GREEK

DATES

- Cretan–Mycenaean,
  - early 2800–2200 B.C.
  - middle 2200–1600 B.C.
  - late 1600–1104 B.C.
- Archaic Greece 1104–490 B.C.
- Age of Pericles or Classical Greece 490–429 B.C.
- Fourth Century 429–338 B.C.
- Hellenistic 338–146 B.C.

COMMON TERMS (FOR OTHERS SEE GLOSSARY)

- Doric chiton
- Ionic chiton
- kolobium
- himation
- chlamys
- fillet
- stephanie

petasos
peplos
kolpos
fibula
cothurnus
buskins
Phrygian bonnet

RECOMMENDED SOURCES

- Fletcher: pp. 69–113
- Houston (2): Chapters I and II
- Heuzey: Parts I and II
- Norris (1): Volume I, Chapter II
- Laver (5): pp. 39–103
- Bowra
- Brooke (10)
- Hildebrand
- Richter: Section I
- Strong: pp. 9–102

Cretan   Classical

Typical Figures

Roman

The Etruscans inhabited that part of Italy that is now called Tuscany from about 1000 B.C. until they were finally conquered and merged with Roman civilization about 300 B.C. At the height of their power they influenced a region extending from the Alps in the north of Italy to the Greek colonies in the south.

Rome, founded about 700 B.C. according to tradition, quickly expanded in all directions, asserting its power over the entire Italian peninsula by 300 B.C., conquering Greece by 146 B.C., and controlling the entire Mediterranean Basin by the end of the first century B.C. Octavian proclaimed the Empire in 27 B.C. Rome remained at the height of its power until the rise of Christianity and barbarian invasions weakened the imperial system in the third century A.D. The Emperor Constantine recognized Christianity in 313 A.D. and moved his capital to Byzantium in 323 A.D. Thereafter, there was rapid decline until the final collapse of Rome in 476 A.D. Throughout its rise and fall, Roman culture was strongly influenced by the Greeks, often adding to and improving on Greek ideals and forms for more practical ends.

ETRUSCAN DRESS.   Masculine dress was either a long *chiton* resembling Greek ceremonial garb, or a short chiton like a tunic or doublet. The rectangular cloak could be worn transversely below the right arm and across the left shoulder, wrapped over the lower part of the body, or draped over both arms.

Feminine dress was at first a tight, tunic-like chiton, later a loosely hanging, beltless chiton of transparent spotted material. Footwear for both men and women was either sandals or closed shoes with pointed, turned-up toes.

ROMAN DRESS.   The Greek chiton reappears in Roman feminine costume as the *tunica,* but over it was worn the *stola* or outer chiton with the rectangular *palla* or cloak draped over all. The head was usually covered with a *flameum* or veil, and the hair was built up in a halo of curls across the front of the head.

Fabrics ranged from very fine woolens to the most precious of silks at the time of the empire.

The male *tunica* could be sleeved or sleeveless, short or long, the long-sleeved version being known as the *tunica talaris.* The key Roman garment was the half-circle cloak or *toga.* There were many versions: the *toga praetexta* of white wool with a purple border for senators; the cream-white *toga pura* or *virilis* for the ordinary citizen; the dark-colored *toga pulla* for mourning; the bleached white *toga candida* for those running for office; the embroidered *toga picta* for triumphal occasions; and the particolored *toga trabea* for ceremonial occasions. It was folded down its length, then placed on the left shoulder with a fold against the neck. The front material reached the left ankle or toe, while behind the material was passed across the back, under the right arm, across the chest, and once more over the left shoulder. The remaining material fell down the back. The great toga of Imperial Rome evolved from the semicircular to an elliptical shape four to five yards long, about three yards wide, and folded lengthwise before draping. The top layer of this fold was frequently brought up over the head and was called the *sinus,* while the bottom layer or fold on the left side was lifted over the material across the chest to form a pouch or *umbo.* Late in the imperial period the toga was folded lengthwise several times, was diminished in size, and was no longer draped but fastened rigidly in place with brooches. Also in the late imperial period, it became the practice to wear several sleeved tunics one over the other; the top one, with very wide sleeves, was called the *dalmatica.*

Besides the toga, other cloaks worn by the Romans included the *pallium,* which was worn like the Greek *himation;* the *sagum,* which was a short military cloak; and the *paludamentum,* which was a larger officer's cloak fastened with a brooch at the neck or shoulder. Footwear consisted of sandals (*solea*) or the military boot (*caligula*). Soldiers wore a breastplate (*lorica*) of solid metal, metal strips, or metal studs on leather over a short tunic; a crested metal helmet protected the head.

ROMAN

DATES
 The Age of Monarchy 753–500 B.C.
 The Age of the Republic 500–27 B.C.
 The Age of Empire 27 B.C.–323 A.D.

COMMON TERMS (FOR OTHERS SEE GLOSSARY)
 tunica
 balteus
 augustus clavus
 latus clavus
 toga praetexta
 toga pura or virilis
 toga candida
 toga pulla
 toga picta
 toga trabea
 tunica talaris
 tunica palmata
 sinus
 pallium
 lacerna
 sagum
 paludamentum
 paenula
 solea
 calcaeus
 crepida
 lorica
 caligula
 bracchae
 palla
 stola
 flameum
 dalmatica

RECOMMENDED SOURCES
 Houston (2): Chapter IV
 Norris (1): Volume I, Chapter III
 Wilson (1)
 Wilson (2)
 Heuzey: Part III
 Skira (1)
 Strong (background)
 Carcopino (background)
 Casson
 Kahler
 Wills

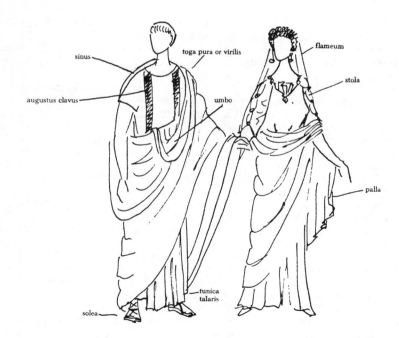

Typical Figures

Early Christian and Byzantine

The dress worn in the western lands of the former Roman Empire in the fourth century A.D. continued to be based on the conventions of the late Empire until the rise of Charlemagne at the beginning of the ninth century A.D. It was during those centuries that the liturgical dress of the Roman Catholic church began to form. By the ninth century A.D. the basic ecclesiastical garments—the *dalmatic,* the *chasuble,* the *stole,* the *pall,* the *cope,* and the *alb*—had been separated from lay dress as church vestments.

Byzantium, later called Constantinople and today Istanbul, became the second capital of the Roman Empire in 323 A.D.; after the division of the Empire into two parts, it was the capital of the Eastern section and the center of Eastern Orthodox Christianity. After Rome fell to the Teutonic armies and Odoacer dethroned the last of the Roman emperors in 476, the Eastern Empire held out until it fell to the Turks in 1453.

Byzantine culture was a combination of the richness and ornamental formality of the Orient, the beauty and proportion of the Greeks, and the practical outlook of the Romans. As in Egypt, hierarchy and tradition played a great part in preserving Byzantine culture for over a millennium.

ECCLESIASTICAL VESTMENTS. One of the first vestments to appear was the *pall* or *pallium*—originally a folded, draped strip derived from the Roman *toga* and *pallium*—which eventually developed into a circle dropped over the shoulders, with long tabs front and back decorated with four crosses. It is part of a bishop's full vestments for the Mass. The *stole,* a long narrow silk strip with fringe on the ends and decorated with three crosses, was also an early vestment used by priests, deacons, and bishops during the Mass. It may have derived from the fringed *orarion* waved by the Emperor Aurelian in the third century to applaud the games. The Roman rain cape, the *paenula,* was transformed into a clerical garment called the *chasuble* by the fourth century, and continued as the basic overgarment for priests and bishops officiating at the Mass. By the sixth century, the *dalmatic* with its wide sleeves became the official outer tunic for priests and bishops, while the *cope* or half-circular cloak fastened at the front of the neck by a brooch called a *morse* became the standard processional outer garment for priests and bishops. The *alb,* derived from the Roman *tunica alba,* became the standard undertunic, worn over the cassock and under other liturgical vestments by bishops and priests. The embroidered patches at the center front and back of the hem, at the wrists, and sometimes at the breast and back, were known as *apparels* or *orphreys.* The *cassock,* which developed into the everyday wear of all clerics, derived from the basic tunic of the Roman common people, while clerical footwear developed from Roman *sandals* and *buskins.* The Roman *mappula* or folded linen napkin, which symbolized service when worn over the arm of a Roman consul, was adapted by the Church into the *maniple* or silken band decorated with three crosses that was hung over the left forearm during Mass. The *mitre,* a liturgical and processional headdress worn by the bishops of the church, developed from the cone-shaped caps of the early popes, perhaps derived from the headdresses of Hebrew priests.

Most of these items are still a part of Roman Catholic clerical garb, though fabrics, shapes, and colors have changed over the centuries.

SECULAR DRESS. The basic decorative qualities of court dress can best be seen in the famous Ravenna mosaics of the Emperor Justinian and the Empress Theodora, with their richly oriental, jeweled decoration. The masculine costume usually began with a belted, long-sleeved *tunica* with embroidered *segmentae* on the shoulders, worn over *hosa* or leg coverings cut to fit close to the body, and with soft shoes or slippers on the feet. The outergarment was a cloak derived from the *paludamentum* and fastened with a buckle or brooch on the right shoulder. A large embroidered rectangle known as the *tablion* appeared on the front and back of the mantle. Later emperors placed greater stress on the long *dalmatic* worn over a long-sleeved tunic, and a heavy jeweled *lorum,* a kind of "sandwich board" garment, was used in place of a mantle.

Feminine dress, also based on the long-sleeved *tunica* or sometimes on the Roman *stola,* dropped to jewel-studded slippers and was heavily embroidered and set with jewels. Women also wore the great mantle fastened on the right shoulder, but without the *tablion.* In later Byzantine women's costume, the dalmatic was completely encrusted in jewels, and embroidery was frequently added, tending to make the figure look like a walking mosaic. Wigs set with crowns or diadems and covered with jewels were used, and jeweled collars reminiscent of the Egyptians were worn.

The two things that made Byzantine costume quite different from the Roman were the use of silk and metallic fabrics and the excessive use of jeweled decoration.

EARLY CHRISTIAN AND BYZANTINE

DATES

Early Christian 323–604 A.D.
Proto-Byzantine 323–565
Early Byzantine 565–726
Period of Iconoclasm 726–843
Early Byzantine Renaissance, Macedonian
    Dynasty 843–1067
High Byzantine Renaissance, Comenian
    Dynasty 1067–1185
Late Byzantine 1185–1453

COMMON TERMS (FOR OTHERS SEE GLOSSARY)

cassock
alb
surplice
pallium
dalmatic
chasuble
orphreys
apparels
mitre
cope
stole
maniple
tunicle
segmentae
tablion
paenula
paludamentum
hosa
camisa
colobium
superhumeral

RECOMMENDED SOURCES

Houston (2): Chapters IV and V
Norris (1): Chapter IV
Norris (2)
Skira (2)
Rice (background)
Davenport: pp. 93–103
Morey (1) (background)
Volbach and Hirmer (background)
Lassus (background)
Sherrard (background)
Mosaics, ivory carving, manuscripts,
    sculpture

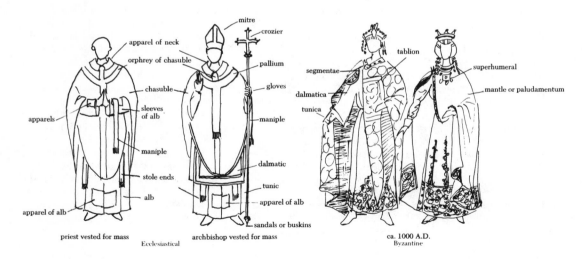

priest vested for mass   archbishop vested for mass   ca. 1000 A.D.

Ecclesiastical   Byzantine

Typical Figures

Barbaric, Carolingian, and Romanesque

About 150 years ago, when a critical historical sense began to develop in Westerners, the period of the early Middle Ages was labeled Romanesque since it was thought of as being a culture derived from a Roman heritage, in much the same way that Romance languages derived from Latin. Unfortunately this is a misleading term, since the culture that developed from the fall of Rome to the end of the twelfth century in Western Europe was more Germanic in inspiration than Roman. Although the style flourished only from the time of Charlemagne to the beginning of Gothic style, its heritage reaches back well beyond the times of the Teutonic invasions of Rome. Its major characteristics are heaviness, weight, distortion, and rigidity, with strong accents of the primitive, the geometric, and the supernatural.

BARBARIC DRESS. The major garment worn by barbarian men that was not a part of Graeco-Roman dress was trousers or *bracchae*, which had been worn by mountainous northern tribes since before the Christian era. Roman troops in Gaul had worn short versions of these trousers, and the Byzantine *hosa* were a refinement of the idea. In Germany and France during the period before Charlemagne, they became the symbol of the barbarian. They were usually laced with thongs and covered with leggings. A short, coarsely woven tunic covered the body, and a cloak of animal skins or coarse wool was fastened on the shoulder with a huge metal clasp. Hair was long, the face bearded, and metal helmets set with wings and horns were worn on the head. The women's hair was very long and frequently braided; they wore a long coarse tunic, often woven in stripes or squares, and a mantle was again pinned on the shoulder.

CAROLINGIAN DRESS. At the time that Charlemagne united the petty tribal kingdoms of Western Europe, the standard male dress was a linen undershirt and drawers, a long-sleeved tunic bloused over a girdle that extended to the middle of the thigh, and close-fitting leggings. A half-circular mantle was fastened with a large metal *fibula* on the right shoulder. A metal circlet held the hair, and soft leather shoes completed the dress. The *dalmatic* was in evidence for all ceremonial occasions, and the longer tunic was used by older men. A metal helmet with noseguard was used for battle, and a shirt of mail formed of leather sewn with metal disks or constructed of tiny interlocking metal circles was worn. By the time of Charlemagne, women wore a *chemise* or *camisa* as an undergarment, a long-sleeved undertunic, and a wide-sleeved overtunic or *dalmatic,* with a semicircular or circular mantle fastened on the right shoulder. The hair was often completely covered by the *couvrechef* or large kerchief.

ROMANESQUE DRESS. The basic lines of dress changed very little, aside from refinements in cutting and fitting, over the three centuries from the rise of the Ottonian emperors to the beginning of the Gothic style. The most stylish male tunic was laced and lifted at the sides of the waist to give a play of draped folds at the front of the figure and was known as the *bliaut.* The feminine version of this garment was floor length, with a slight train, laced to the body at the sides or back, and gave a smooth fit to the hips without special darting or complex cutting. The older, loose tunic of floor length for men and women was now called the *cote,* and the overtunic with wider sleeves was called a *surcote.* A woman's neck and chin were now frequently covered by a kerchief or *gorget,* while the kerchief over the head was called a *wimple.* For men, a distinctive new outer garment developed at this time—the hooded cloak, which also became an important item in the dress of monks. Originally worn by the common man, the hood eventually became a separate item for court dress, with a long tail at the back of the head and a full collar-cape over the shoulders.

BARBARIC, CAROLINGIAN, AND ROMANESQUE

DATES
    Barbaric 400–752 A.D.
    Carolingian 752–1000
    Romanesque 1000–1150
COMMON TERMS (FOR OTHERS SEE GLOSSARY)
    bliaut
    cote
    corsage
    surcote
    hauberk
    wimple
    couvrechef
    mantle
    fibula
    capuchon
    gorget
RECOMMENDED SOURCES
    Brooke (4): pp. 10–58
    Brooke (9) (theatre costume)

Norris (1): Volume I, Chapters V–VII;
    Volume II, Chapter I
Enlart: Part I
Evans (2): Part I
Houston (3): Chapter I
Cunnington (5): Part I
Skira (3)
Skira (4)
Morey (2): Chapter IV
Swarzenski (background)
Brantl (background)
Freemantle (background)
Hartley and Elliot (1) (background)
Kidson (background)
Hartley
Sculpture, manuscripts, mosaics,
    frescoes

ca. 1000 A.D.

Typical Figures

Early and High Gothic

During the Renaissance, when enthusiasm for things classical had reached a peak, Giorgio Vasari, artist and art historian, called the art and architecture of the preceding period Gothic. He assumed that it had been invented by the so-called Goths, the Germanic tribe that sacked Rome in 410 and destroyed the architectural wonders of antiquity. Although the Gothic style that was invented in France at the close of the twelfth century had nothing to do with the Goths of the great migration, the name has remained and today refers to art from the twelfth to the fifteenth centuries. Entirely opposed to most classical conceptions of style, the Gothic is vertical, strongly linear, stresses open framework rather than solid form, and is highly and complexly decorative. The figures in illuminated manuscripts indicate the active decorative aspects of Gothic dress as opposed to the static and rigid effects of Byzantine dress, as well as the tendency to go beyond the limits of the human body to achieve verticality of form.

MASCULINE DRESS.   The long Byzantine tunic, which before had been worn only on special occasions and by royalty, now became the standard dress for men, having been popularized by the Crusaders who had passed through Byzantium on the way back from the Holy Land. Known as the *cote,* it usually had very wide sleeves cut in one with the shoulder and narrowing to the wrist. It was usually covered by a second, sleeveless tunic or *surcote,* which was often left open up the sides to the hips. Sometimes the *surcote* had hanging sleeves and was known as a *gardcorps,* or it had flaring cape sleeves to the elbow and was known as a *ganache.* When it was fur lined, it was frequently known as a *peliçon.* As a military garment, the *surcote* with a coat of arms emblazoned on it was worn over a *hauberk* of chain mail. With the long tunic that stressed the vertical line of the human figure were worn pointed shoes or boots of soft leather. Separate leg coverings or hose worn over underwear were of cloth or leather shaped like long stockings and fastened to a belt around the waist. The hood was also a prominent accessory, with *scalloped* or *dagged* edges around the bottom of the cape-collar giving a strong decorative accent.

At the close of this period in the early decades of the fourteenth century, a close-fitting tunic to the hips, known as a *cotehardie,* came into fashion for younger men. It was usually worn with a decorative caped hood, a jeweled hip girdle, and long pointed shoes, all related to the slim decorative lines of late Gothic art.

FEMININE DRESS.   At first, feminine dress was the same as in the Romanesque period, with the use of the undertunic or *cote,* the overtunic or *surcote,* and the *wimple* and *gorget* for covering the head. Sometimes the hair was placed into a pillbox cap or *toque* with chin strap, sometimes coiled over the ears and held by jeweled nets, or loosely confined by a circlet or coronet. Gradually, the lines of the costume became more fitted to the body; the surcote was cut away under the arms and opened up the sides to show more of the figure. At the end of the period the name *cotehardie* was applied to a close-fitting princess-line gown with a low neckline and a full skirt.

PARTICOLORING AND HERALDIC DEVICES.   In the early Gothic period, costumes were frequently divided in color down the center to tie the color usage in dress to that found in a family's coat of arms; this particoloring became one of the most characteristic effects of the period. It was also fashionable to have a coat of arms or a crest embroidered on the costume, or at times to have the entire costume constructed as if from a large coat of arms.

EARLY AND HIGH GOTHIC

DATES
> Early Gothic 1144–1194
> High Gothic 1194–1248
> Later High Gothic 1248–1325

COMMON TERMS (FOR OTHERS SEE GLOSSARY)
> ganache
> gardcorps
> surcote
> cotehardie
> couvrechef
> wimple
> gorget
> doublet
> jupe
> cyclas
> toque

RECOMMENDED SOURCES
> Norris (1): Volume II, Chapters I–III
> Brooke (4): pp. 58–86
>
> Brooke (6): pp. 10–24
> Morey (2): Chapter V
> Evans (1): Part II
> Evans (2): Part II
> Houston (3): Chapters II–IV
> Frankl: Part I (background)
> Mâle (background)
> Hartley and Elliot (1) (background)
> Hartley
> Boehn (2)
> Brantl (background)
> Cunnington (5)
> Freemantle (background)
> Kidson (background)
> Winston (background)
> Sculpture, manuscripts, frescoes (especially Giotto)

ca. 1250

Typical Figures

Middle Gothic

In the middle Gothic period, the classical semi-draped lines of the early Gothic gave way to extravagant fashions. They moved from the close-fitting contours of the *cotehardie* to the flamboyant lines of the *houppelande,* just as architecture, sculpture, and manuscript illuminations moved from simple, clear-cut vertical lines of structure to highly decorative, graceful, curvilinear lines of design. Throughout Western Europe, the Age of Faith was giving way to an age of worldly power and material prosperity, despite the terrible plagues that stopped artistic and cultural development in the middle of the fourteenth century. The Renaissance that had been in preparation in Italy in the late thirteenth and early fourteenth centuries through the work of Dante, Giotto, Petrarch, and Boccaccio was slowed by many decades, and the full fruition of the early Renaissance in Florence did not occur until the first two decades of the fifteenth century.

In general, the costume of the last half of the fourteenth century and the early years of the fifteenth century was composed of slim, close-fitting body garments overlaid with flowing draperies, with the edges of all things scalloped, dagged, and foliated until the human figure in movement was all aflutter. Particoloring, emblazonment, and the powdering of garments with family crests increased, giving a far more sophisticated and decorative look to the general costume silhouette.

MASCULINE COSTUME. The hip-length, tight-fitting *cotehardie* remained a basic body garment throughout the period, usually worn with a hip girdle and a hood or *capuchon* with cape-collar and richly cut edges, the hood now having a long tail or *liripipe.* Often the cotehardie had cuffs on the sleeves that flared into hanging *foliations* or hung in long bands called *tippets.* Later in the century, a voluminous overgown with trailing bell sleeves and a high collar made its appearance. This *houppelande,* with all its flamboyant movement of foliated edges and flowing fabric, was worn over the cotehardie.

The hood was now frequently worn with the band of the face opening placed around the head, the dagged edges of the collar falling to one side, and the long tail or liripipe wrapped about the head or draped over the shoulder. This fantastic headdress was known as a *chaperon.* Shoes were now exaggeratedly pointed; in the more advanced fashions, the toes were even fastened to the knee by a chain. Hair was worn shoulder length or in an allover bowl cut; mantles were often made the ground for a complete coat of arms; and jewelry and jeweled accessories included bells, hanging baubles, tassels, and chains.

FEMININE COSTUME. Women also continued to wear the cotehardie, but it was soon covered with various overgowns. The first was the famed *cyclas* or *sideless gown,* in which the entire gown was cut away to the hips on each side, leaving only a central panel or *plastron* with fur or embroidered edges over the breast. Sideless gowns, often completely emblazoned with the family coat of arms, continued as official court wear throughout the fifteenth century. At the end of the fourteenth century the houppelande was also added to the female wardrobe, as were the foliated and dagged edges that made for flamboyant effects in sleeves, collars, and gown edgings. The *reticulated headdress,* with its metal cages for holding the hair coiled over the ears, was the most prominent form of hairdressing, while the wimple and gorget arrangement continued to be worn by older women. Larger horned and cone-shaped headdresses known as *hennins* began to develop in the early years of the fifteenth century. With their veils, jeweled decoration, and heavy metallic net accessories, they were to become the major headdress of the late Gothic period. Women shaved their brows and temples and completely concealed their hair under headdresses. All movement was flowing and graceful, and skirts were often as long in front as the train in back; the lady was expected to lift her skirts and hold them over her abdomen in movement.

MIDDLE GOTHIC

DATES

    Middle Gothic 1325–1425
        Reign of Edward III in England 1327–1377
        Reigns of Richard II, Henry IV, and Henry V in England 1377–1422

COMMON TERMS (FOR OTHERS SEE GLOSSARY)

    chaperon
    liripipe
    coif
    capuchon
    jupe
    pourpoint
    jacquette
    courtepy
    houppelande
    foliated
    bagpipe sleeve
    dagged
    castellations
    jupon
    reticulated headdress
    corset
    plastron
    sideless gown
    tippet
    particolored
    caul

RECOMMENDED SOURCES

    Norris (1): Volume II, Chapters IV–VI
    Skira (5)
    Houston (3): Chapters IV and V
    Cunnington (5): Part II
    Evans (1): Part III
    Evans (2): Part III
    Brooke (6): pp. 24–46
    Boehn (2)
    Brantl (background)
    Brooke (9)
    Freemantle (background)
    Kidson (background)
    Winston (background)
    Sculpture, book illuminations, frescoes, panel paintings (especially the Lorenzetti brothers)

ca. 1350-1360

ca. 1415

Typical Figures

Late Gothic and Early Italian Renaissance

The late Gothic period was a time of rich and sophisticated effects in art and in costume—a final complex and flamboyant use of all the decorative elements in the Gothic vocabulary. It was also an era divided between two great cultural and artistic centers—Flanders in the north and Florence in the south. The styles and the art that dominated each area were radically different. In the south, all the elements of a revived classicism and a renewed interest in antiquity prevailed, while in the north, the final rich, decorative, flamboyant effects of the late Gothic achieved fulfillment. In the fifteenth century the towns of Ghent and Bruges were two of the greatest centers of European trade and industry. Flemish cloth was famous throughout Western Europe, and the court of Burgundy shared the leadership in fashion with the court in Paris. Simultaneously with the dawn of the Renaissance in Florence and later throughout northern Italy, Gothic costume reached its final phase of richness and splendor in Ghent, Bruges, and Brussels.

MASCULINE DRESS. In aristocratic Burgundian costume, all the sartorial variations that had gradually appeared during the medieval period were combined into a final magnificent flourish. Shoes were elegantly pointed, and doublets, which had replaced *tunics, cotehardies,* and the sweeping *houppelande,* were tight-fitting, often pleated, and had large padded sleeves that increased the width and height of the shoulders. The long gown was now slim and elegant, again stressing the height of the wearer through padded sleeves and raised shoulders. Sometimes hanging sleeves were used on both doublets and gowns, with an undersleeve coming through a slit in the outer sleeve. Padded, carefully placed pleating in gowns and doublets added to height and elegance, while fur was a preferred trim on collars, sleeves, and hemlines. Hats were divided between the *roundlet*—a stuffed, donut-shaped piece of headgear with a wide strip of material still called a *liripipe* draped over the shoulder—and the tall, bag-shaped sugarloaf hats that complemented the pleated lines and padded shoulders of the male figure. Hose, sometimes particolored, covered both legs and were tied with points to the belt of the underdrawers. A voluminous mantle occasionally lined in fur was the chief outer garment, although loose gowns were also worn for this purpose. Armor was now of solid plate in carefully planned overlapping and interlocking pieces and finished with a heraldic tabard.

FEMININE DRESS. The woman's gown now had a slightly lifted waistline, a train that was more voluminous than ever, a deep V-shaped neckline in front partially filled in with the top of the undergarment or *corset,* and a wide belt just above the waist. The wide shawl collar rolled back from the bare neck was usually trimmed in fur, as were the cuffs of the tight sleeves that came down over the hands. The *cotehardie,* covered by a *sideless gown,* usually emblazoned with family or national arms, was still the formal ceremonial dress for women, as was the emblazoned, half-circular mantle. Over the heads of the women rose the steeple-shaped headdress or *hennin* with its floating veil, the most typical headcovering of the period. Variations of it were the *heart-shaped headdress;* the *escoffion,* a padded and embroidered high-rising round headdress set with jewels; the *horned hennin* with its two or three conical points; and the *butterfly hennin* with its wired wing-like veils. In fact, the women's headdresses of the middle of the fifteenth century are some of the most exaggerated and flamboyant headdresses seen in the entire history of female costume. As with men, any loose upper garment might, on occasion, become an outdoor wrap—especially if it were fur-lined. Shoes were tiny slippers worn over stockings or hose.

NORTHERN ITALIAN DRESS. During these same years, in styles emanating from Florence, Italian dress projected a simpler, natural silhouette with a stress on pleated short and long gowns, natural headdresses, and very limited ornamentation.

LATE GOTHIC
AND EARLY ITALIAN RENAISSANCE

DATES

    Late Gothic and Early Renaissance
        1425–1485
    Flemish-Burgundian Renaissance 1419–
        1477
    Early Italian Renaissance 1422–1485

COMMON TERMS (FOR OTHERS SEE GLOSSARY)

    hennin
    escoffion
    journade
    roundlet
    poulaine
    crackowe
    pourpoint
    plastron
    liripipe
    sideless gown
    houppelande

RECOMMENDED SOURCES

    Houston (3): Chapters V–VII
    Norris (1): Volume II, Chapters V and VI

Skira (5)
Skira (6)
Brooke (6): pp. 46–86
Brooke (9)
Boucher: Chapter VII
Contini: pp. 74–110
Brantl (background)
Cunnington (5)
Freemantle (background)
Hale (background)
Kidson (background)
Martindale (background)
Mates and Cantelupe (background)
Winston (background)
Book illuminations, paintings (especially Van
    Eyck, Van der Weyden, Masaccio, Fra
    Lippo Lippi, Piero della Francesca),
    sculpture

ca. 1460 Burgundian

Typical Figures

Renaissance

While Gothic costume was reaching its final phase at the court of Burgundy, the first stirrings of the Renaissance brought a new concept of dress—or rather a revival of a classical concept—to Italy. The Gothic style had never really been "at home" south of the Alps, and early in the fifteenth century Florence became the center for a revival of interest in the art of antiquity. The new style in clothing that developed by the end of the century was a fresh exploration of certain Roman ideals and artistic effects integrated with garments inherited from the late Gothic style. The new artistic style stressed the horizontal over the vertical, the simple and geometric over the complexly decorative, blond color over the strong color of heraldry, and richly patterned fabrics of silk, velvet, and brocade over woolens. The new Renaissance concept of style stressed that perfection lay in the rational and harmonious relationship of all of the separate parts; nothing could be added, subtracted, or changed without impairing the overall effect.

MASCULINE DRESS. The undergarment was usually a sleeveless doublet to which two long stockings or hose could be fastened with points. These hose, of cloth or leather, were sometimes sewn together to form one garment with a *codpiece* that tied in over the front opening, or they remained separate and were pulled loosely up over the underdrawers. The collarless shirt under the doublet was now much in evidence, with sections of outer sleeves laced over it or slashed to show the shirt sleeve beneath. The doublet front was laced loosely across the shirt, which bloused casually at the waist between hose and doublet. Eventually, the doublet was cut low enough to display the shirt at the neck, the edge being finished with embroidery in gold or silk or with a ruffle. Overgowns were loose, rather short, worn casually and often open up the front, the general line being horizontal and somewhat square, with a wide collar falling over the shoulder. Very long gowns were now worn only by the elderly; these too were wide and square, with emphasis placed on a wide collar, large cuffs, and thick pleats. The headgear of the period turned to wide, flat, slightly turned-up brims decorated with feathers and jewels, or to small skull caps, truncated cones of heavy felt, large soft fur hats with turned-up brims, and tiny felt pillboxes. Hair was usually shoulder length, either falling loosely or curled under at the bottom. Shoes were like slippers, without the heavy accent on a pointed toe.

FEMININE DRESS. The lacing characteristic of masculine dress also appeared in women's dress at the breasts, under the arm, and at the shoulder, where the long, often tight, and sometimes slashed sleeves were laced to the armhole of the bodice over the looser sleeves of the chemise. Whereas elderly women still wore long, loose, trailing gowns under a cloak, younger women followed the male trend toward shorter gowns, sometimes without a train. The gown was often divided into bodice and skirt and was frequently worn under a sleeveless outer gown slit below the waist on each side or in the front. Sometimes the outer gown was loose and flowing, but more frequently it was fitted smoothly to a slightly raised waistline. The neckline of the undergown was square, in contrast to the pointed Gothic neckline, although the outer gown often showed a V-shaped outline. On the head, elderly women still wore kerchiefs, but younger women preferred to leave the hair uncovered and to knot and twist it into complex hairdos that could be adorned with pearls or nets of gold. Sleeves were the key area for complex lines of trim, with tiny slits in the outer sleeve allowing many interesting effects when the fabric of the chemise was pulled through the slits from underneath. This fashion for slashes was to grow and become more complex and rigid in the early sixteenth century. The loose, casual effect of its original design was to change to restriction, tension, and complexity in both masculine and feminine dress in the later Renaissance.

RENAISSANCE

DATES
    1485–1520
        Early Renaissance in France
        Early Tudor in England
        High Renaissance in Italy

COMMON TERMS (FOR OTHERS SEE GLOSSARY)
    bases
    points
    slashing
    simarre
    caul
    codpiece
    jerkin
    kirtle

RECOMMENDED SOURCES
    Norris (1): Volume III, Book I, pp. 1–232
    Vecellio (patterns)
    Martindale (background)

Laver (4)
Berenson (background)
Burckhardt (background)
Dewald (background)
Freedberg (background)
Hale (background)
Mates and Cantelupe (background)
Mee (background)
Statues and relief sculpture
Brass rubbings
Useful painters: da Vinci, Carpaccio, Bellini, Mantegna, Messina, Botticelli, Filippino Lippi, Ghirlandaio, Raphael, Pinturicchio, del Sarto, Fra Carnavale, Signorelli, Gozzoli, Baldovinetti, Verrocchio, the two Pollaiuoli, Perugino, Rosselli, di Credi, di Cosimo, Ercole Roberti, Cosimo Tura, Dürer

Italian ca. 1500

Typical Figures

Early Mannerist Renaissance

After the crest of optimism and artistic accomplishment was achieved in Italy during the first two decades of the sixteenth century, foreign invasions, loss of morale, the rise of the Reformation, and the decline of Italian artistic and cultural nationalism brought about a change in art and culture today referred to as the rise of mannerism. Heavily influenced by German and Spanish artistic ideals brought to Italy by the forces of the Emperor Charles V, the new style was heavier, more complicated, more distorted, and, in general, reflected the new malaise and loss of faith that was to mark the development of all European culture during the sixteenth century. From roughly 1520 to 1560, the German influence in fashion was predominant, while from 1560 into the second decade of the seventeenth century, Spanish styles tended to be the major source of inspiration in dress.

MASCULINE DRESS. The major artistic development of this period took place in puffs and slashing. One colored fabric was placed over another, the top one was slit to show the fabric underneath, and the two fabrics were then puffed out so that all slashes spread to the fullest extent. The major points of usage were on legs and sleeves, although in German military costume they covered the entire costume. The effect of the interpenetration of two planes of fabric was similar to the scroll work on contemporary ornament, in which tongues from one scroll passed through slits in another.

The predominant male silhouette of the period was square, the major garment being a short gown, usually fur-lined with hanging sleeves. It was loose, with ample folds; a large collar covered the shoulders, making them appear wide and square. The open front showed the jerkin, which had a gathered or formally pleated knee-length skirt (sometimes called *bases*) and was frequently cut very low to show the doublet. At the beginning of the period the neckline was low, but later the shirt fitted closely around the neck and ended in a ruffle. By the end of the period the doublet also rose to a standing collar. At first the tops of the hose were slashed, later the tops were covered with loose, often slashed breeches fitted with an ornamented *codpiece*. These puffed breeches reached their greatest excess in the extravagant *pluderhose* of the German *Landsknecht* or mercenary soldier. Shoes were broad at the toe with slashes. The headdress was a wide-brimmed flat cap trimmed with ostrich feathers, usually worn at a rakish angle and sometimes over another cap. Hair was relatively short, and beards were popular. Full, heavily ornamented plate armor was still worn by the nobility for war.

FEMININE DRESS. At the beginning of the sixteenth century the now stiffened bodice of the gown had a low-cut square neckline, but the neckline gradually moved upward and frequently ended in a standing collar finished with a ruffle. The fabric was voluminous and heavy, with a tendency to width. Skirts were pleated to the bodice over a funnel-shaped, boned *farthingale* and a V-shaped front panel of rich ornamentation. Sleeves were fur-lined, bell-shaped appendages open or folded back over a series of slashed puffs that made up the undersleeve, or were alternately puffed down the entire length of the arm. Headdresses included flat caps, wide turbans, or complicated *coifs* or *hood* structures derived from the Flemish and German middle-class headgear of the late fifteenth century. While Italian ladies continued to prefer their hair caught only by a jeweled net or *caul* (or at the most, partially hidden by a slashed turban), northern ladies preferred the *gable kennel* or pedimented headdress or a crescent-shaped variation. In all of these headdresses a heavily stiffened and ornamented frame outlined the face, while a rich fall of fabric or *hood* covered the back of the head. Outer garments consisted of the large circular mantle or a loose, often fur-lined gown.

EARLY MANNERIST RENAISSANCE

DATES
 1520–1560
  Period of First-Generation Mannerism in
   Italy
  Tudor Period in England
  Renaissance Period in France and Germany
COMMON TERMS (FOR OTHERS SEE GLOSSARY)
 chamarre
 duck-billed shoes
 morion
 basquine
 farthingale
 gable headdress
 barbe
 fall
 cale
 bombast
 pomander
 panes
RECOMMENDED SOURCES
 Norris (1): Volume III, Book I, pp. 232–377
 Brooke (3): pp. 10–56

Laver (4)
Morse: Part I
Skira (7)
Berenson: Volume II
Boehn (4)
Cunnington (4)
Hale (background)
Martindale (background)
Mates and Cantelupe (background)
Waterhouse (background)
Friedlander (background)
Sculpture on tombs, statuary, engravings,
 painting, miniatures
Useful painters: Giulio Romano, Titian, Tin-
 toretto, Holbein, Brueghel, Bronzino,
 Giorgione, Mor, Pontormo, Rosso, Pin-
 turicchio, Jean and François Clouet,
 Vasari, Michelangelo, del Piombo,
 Bordone, Primiticcio, Parmigianino,
 Baroccio

Typical Figures

Elizabethan–Jacobean (Late Mannerist Renaissance)

Shortly after the middle of the sixteenth century, Spain achieved European dominance in matters of taste and fashion, and the nature of mannerist art and culture began to be more formal, more elegant, and more reserved but still stressed tension, distortion, and exaggeration. Art, as well as fashion, turned its back on nature in favor of the "mannered," the charmingly contrived, or the deliberately grotesque. In the paintings of El Greco and Tintoretto, in the sculpture of Bologna, and in the architectural inventions of Zuccaro, broken rhythms, elongated forms, tense lines, and rich, often grotesque ornamentation characterize this late sixteenth-century style. In fashion, the complex Spanish tailoring that elongated the figure, exaggerated the shoulders and hips, extended the waist, and held the whole body in a tense, elegant, and overly formal envelope was the admiration of all Europe.

In the Spanish style the body was stiff and motionless—a mannequin on which was mounted a richly ornamented case, following its shape on the inside, but showing exaggerated contours on the outside. The wearer was encased in an armor of ornament, adorned like an idol with gold, pearls, and precious stones, while the fabrics used were often black or dark-colored silks and velvets, like the soft lining of a jewel case.

MASCULINE DRESS. The Spanish fashion replaced the wide-brimmed hat with a high-crowned, sometimes bag-shaped hat with a narrow brim, and the short gown now became a circular short cloak with a collar. The short puffed upper hose breeches, ornamented with slashings or strips of fabric called *panes,* were called *trunk hose, melon hose,* or *pumpkin hose* and were stuffed with horsehair *bombast* or straw to hold their distended shape. The *codpiece,* rarely noted after 1575, all but disappeared by the early seventeenth century. At the same time, stuffed shoulder wings were sewn around the armhole, and a peplum or *picadils* were added to the *doublet,* which was very long waisted, sharply pointed in the front, and frequently padded into a *peascod* below. The legs were enclosed in tight hose of soft cloth, although knitted silk stockings became more prevalent as the century wore on; they were pulled up and gartered over tight breeches called *canions* worn under the trunk hose. These were sometimes referred to as *up-per stocks,* in contrast to *nether stocks* or knitted hose. Wider breeches to the knee were known as *Venetians.* Shoes became narrower, covered more of the foot, and had a firmer sole than in the past. With the introduction of the starched circular *ruff* (supporting the head like a platter), the high standing doublet collar became the central point of focus in the costume. The *jerkin* was still used as an outer garment over the doublet, usually sleeveless or with sleeves tied in with *points* under a *shoulder wing.* After 1600 the ruff was often replaced by a flat collar or *whisk* (golilla in Spain); sleeves were tightened, breeches became squarer and often full to above the knee, and heels appeared on shoes with rosettes over the instep. Hats had higher, stiffer, sloping crowns and wider brims.

FEMININE DRESS. Women's costume followed men's in the use of padding, exaggeration of the width of the hips, and the emphasis on the horizontal line of the shoulders. Two new garments made their appearance under the gown: the corset of stiff material with steel stiffeners in the lining to flatten the bust completely, and the *farthingale* or *vertugale,* which was a cone-shaped cage first of felt and later of hoops to hold out the distended lines of the skirt. The skirt usually had a triangular opening in front to show the rich underskirt. As in men's fashions, the waist was elongated and pointed in front and known as a *stomacher;* the hips were frequently distended, with a sausage roll or stuffed *bolster* under the petticoat; and the shoulders were frequently finished in *crescents* or *wings.* Sleeves were padded into great tapering "demi-canons," slashed, tucked, embroidered, and stitched with precious stones, while necklines were either low-cut, filled in with a soft *partlet,* or finished in a great platter-shaped ruff. Hair was done in a heart-shaped roll away from the face, frequently framed by a heart-shaped cap or covered with jewels. Versions of men's headgear were reserved for riding or outdoor occasions.

After 1600 the wide wheel farthingale all but replaced the Spanish farthingale in England, and the sleeves were less padded. The fan-shaped lace collar was very popular, lace cuffs replaced wrist ruffs, heeled shoes became the standard fashion, and coiffures were higher. A relaxation in mannerist stiffness finally began after 1615.

ELIZABETHAN-JACOBEAN (LATE MANNERIST RENAISSANCE)

DATES
- 1560–1590
  - England: Early Elizabethan
  - France: Late Valois
  - Italy: Late Mannerist
  - Spain: High Renaissance or Golden Age
- 1590–1620
  - Italy: Late Mannerist
  - France: Early Bourbon
  - Germany: Late Renaissance
  - England: Late Elizabethan and Jacobean
  - Spain: Decline of the Golden Age

COMMON TERMS (FOR OTHERS SEE GLOSSARY)
- canions
- Venetians
- ruff
- peascod
- codpiece
- jerkin
- doublet
- pumpkin hose
- round hose
- trunk hose
- galligaskins
- bell farthingale
- slops
- upper stocks and nether stocks
- underproper or supportasse
- picadil
- aiglet
- bombast
- panes
- mandilion
- falling band
- vertugale
- bolster
- partlet
- stomacher
- whisk
- golilla
- baldric
- kirtle
- pantofles
- shoe roses
- shoulder wings or crescents
- cross gartering
- cartwheel vertugale or farthingale
- chopines

RECOMMENDED SOURCES
- Norris (1): Volume III, Book 2
- Morse: Part II
- Kelly (theatre costume)
- Linthicum (theatre costume)
- Laver (4)
- Boehn (4)
- Dewald (background)
- Brooke (3)
- Cunnington (4)
- Hale (background)
- Martindale (background)
- Mates and Cantelupe (background)
- Vecellio
- Waterhouse (background)
- Sculpture, miniatures, paintings, engravings
- Useful painters: El Greco, Veronese, Tintoretto, Brueghel, late Bronzino, Moroni, late Titian, late Mor, François Clouet, Eworth, Federigo Zuccaro, Gheeraerts, Sanchez Coello, Pourbus, Rubens, Caravaggio, the Caracci, Visscher, early Callot

Elizabethan ca. 1585   **Typical Figures**   Jacobean ca. 1610

Early Baroque (Cavalier)

The Counterreformation reached its full stride in Italy during the second quarter of the seventeenth century, and the Church gave its full support to art as one of the great weapons to be used in glorifying God. Art, following many of the precepts of Michelangelo, threw off the tensions, ambiguities, and distortions of the past in favor of vigorous movement, sensuous richness, and theatrical effects. The name Baroque, meaning extravagantly ornamental, was eventually given to this expansive new artistic ideal. In architecture, straight lines gave way to curved, oval, and elliptical forms, and focus was placed on great central portals or domes. In painting, figures were shown in violent motion or in strong contrasts of artificial light, while in sculpture, figures expanded out into space in dramatic, momentary movement. Ornament became massive and voluminous, with lines that curled and twisted like the cartilage of the ear. In fashion, as in art, a dashing flamboyance superseded the stiffness and tension of mannerism. Although the richest art and fashion effects were to be found in Italy, France, and southern Germany, more sober but none the less theatrical effects were achieved in Holland, Flanders, northern Germany, and England. Spain in many ways remained outside the major lines of development, creating an artistic style that retained many mannerist effects.

MASCULINE COSTUME. The overall line of the male costume by 1630 was relaxed, easy, dramatic, and quite simple in comparison with the complexities that had preceded. The doublet was now un-stiffened, with a slightly raised waist and skirts that were either cut in one with the top or casually set on as loose overlapping tabs. The waistline was frequently decorated with metal-tagged ribbons or *points* made into bows, which had originally been drawn through eyelets in the waist to hold up the breeches, but were now merely decorative. Breeches lost their padding and, after being baggy and loose, became long and tapering, had buttons or bows on the sides, and finished in loose garter bows at the bottom. Sometimes breeches were loose at the bottom, finishing in points or bows, and this style grew in importance after the middle of the century. High, soft leather boots were frequently worn indoors as well as outdoors over silk boot hose that fell in a lace cuff over the top of the boot. If shoes were worn, they had a raised heel and rosettes. The smooth white collar, trimmed or made entirely of lace, replaced the pleated ruff and now fell softly over the shoulders. Sleeves were full, usually with one or more slashes the length of the arm in order to show the rich shirt beneath. Such slashes were frequently set with a full line of buttons and holes down the length of the sleeve, and cuffs were of rich lace. Circular, calf-length cloaks were worn over one shoulder and fell diagonally down across the back. Hats were soft and wide-brimmed, of felt or beaver, decorated with ostrich plumes and worn at a jaunty angle. Military wear continued the use of a helmet and a metal *cuirass* over a leather jerkin.

FEMININE DRESS. During this period both the corset and the *farthingale* disappeared, the waistline rose and no longer dipped in front, and several skirts, the top one usually draped up over the one beneath, gave a healthy, homey, slightly pregnant look. The dress was usually low-cut, and a rich lace collar either framed or covered the bosom. The sleeves, which ended in wide, turned-up lace cuffs, were large, elegant, sometimes slashed, and often gathered in at the elbow with silk ribbons finished in bows. A similar silk ribbon sash with a bow emphasized the waistline above the tabs of the peplum. The hair was worn shoulder length, often with a fringe of bangs on the forehead and two long ringlets falling forward over the ears. Masculine hats were reserved for riding, while the hooded cloak was used for travel.

EARLY BAROQUE (CAVALIER)

Dates
1620–1660
England: Cavalier
France: Louis XIII
Italy: Early Baroque
Germany: Thirty Years' War
Spain: Reign of Philip IV

Common terms (for others see glossary)
casaque
canons
la modeste
la friponne
falling band
la secrète
pinners
boot hose
beaver hat
galants
lovelock
quatre-foil spur leathers

Recommended sources
Laver (4)
Brooke (8): pp. 10–58
Kitson (background)
Skira (8)
Boehn (5)
Wittkower (background)
Tapié (background)
Wölfflin (2) (background)
Blitzer (background)
Cunnington (3)
Waterhouse (background)
Weinstein (background)
Sculpture, paintings, engravings, drawings
Useful painters: Rubens, Hals, Callot, Van Dyck, Brose, Hollar, Inigo Jones, Vouet, Champaigne, Terborch, Rembrandt, Ostade, Brouwer, Jordaens, Velázquez

Typical Figures

Late Baroque (Restoration)

After the middle of the seventeenth century, the Baroque style became more sumptuous and dignified, and a new Baroque classicism began to develop in France under the leadership of Louis XIV and his artistic dictator, Le Brun, based on the work of the great French artist Poussin. For the first time since the middle Gothic period, France took the lead in art and fashion, and after Louis XIV became king in his own right in 1661, every aspect of French culture was organized under the central government. All European fashion emanated from the palace at Versailles after the Sun King and his court moved there in 1664. In England after the restoration of Charles II, French styles in art and fashion were predominant, since the majority of the court had spent the years of the Commonwealth in France. Later, as Louis XIV and his regime grew older and more conservative, a heavy-handed formality dominated art and fashion. French painters such as Le Brun, Mignard, and Rigaud set a style that was a heavy, ponderous echo of the flamboyant, dramatic work of Rubens; sculptors such as Coysevox and Girardon echoed the excitement of Bernini only vaguely in their formal, dignified statues; and architects such as J. H. Mansard stressed formality and weight over curves and movement in structures built in Paris and at Versailles. All of the petty courts of Germany, the imperial court in Vienna, and the conservative court of William and Mary and Queen Anne in England followed suit. Only in the very last years of the Sun King's reign did the early work of Watteau and other younger artists foreshadow the lightness and gaiety of the Rococo.

MASCULINE DRESS.   During the early years of Louis XIV's reign the doublet became an open bolero jacket with sleeves only to the elbow, so that the wide shirt sleeves, edged with lace and tied with ribbons in several places, were visible. Boot hose disappeared, but their lace tops survived as wide lace ruffles below the knee, while breeches, decorated at the top with bunches of ribbon loops or *galants,* hung low on the hips and revealed the shirt at the waist. Open and very wide, so that they resembled a short skirt, they sometimes were an actual skirt worn over full, bloused knee breeches. Called *rhinegrave breeches* in Paris and *petticoat breeches* in England, they were worn from 1655 to 1680. Shoes were high-heeled, square-toed, and finished with stiff bows over the tongues, while stockings were of pale colored silk. Necks were dressed with a lace-edged, box-pleated collar under the chin known as a *rabat,* or a lace fall or *cravat.* Hair was worn shoulder length, often with curls caught into ribbons, and by 1665–1670 this long hair was replaced by wigs. Hats were usually tapered and had tall crowns, and the stiff wide brims were trimmed with ostrich, though lower crowns were more in evidence after 1670. Also by 1670, the short bolero jacket had given way to the long jacket or coat known as a *casaque,* which became the fitted *justaucorps* or formal coat after 1685. This garment was the key to military wear along with high boots, breastplate, baldric, and sash. The formal coat was heavy, fitted, had partially flared skirts slit at the sides and center back to the waist, and had large turn-back cuffs. Wigs were large and long, waistcoats extended to the knee, and breeches were tight to the leg with stockings rolled over them and gartered above the knee. Hats began to be three-cornered about 1690.

FEMININE DRESS.   In the early years of Louis XIV's reign, women's dresses were low-cut in a boat-shaped neckline and were worn either with a collar or with a lace edging falling from the top of the bodice. Sleeves were three-quarter length and full, often of lace or material contrasting with the dress, and puffed many times with ribbon bows. The bodice, with its vertical row of bows *à l'echelon,* was pointed in front and had a natural waistline in back; the corset underneath kept the figure smooth and trim from bustline to waist. The open *manteau* or overskirt was frequently looped up slightly at one or two points with ribbon bows to show the *jupe* or underskirt, or it opened naturally in a triangle. The necklace at the throat was frequently replaced by a small brooch on a chain known as a *lavallière,* named after the mistress of Louis XIV. Hair was done in full hanging curls over the ears. Hats and coats were reserved for riding, while the hooded mantle was still used for travel.

After 1685 the hair was built up with a cap, ribbons, and lace fans into the *Fontanges* coiffure, while the overskirt was looped back in great swags to the back of the waist, revealing a rich underskirt heavily decorated at the base with trim known as *pretintailles.* Flounces or *falbalas* were also popular as trim, as were lace aprons. Necklines were square with bows down the bodice front.

LATE BAROQUE (RESTORATION)

DATES
- 1660–1685
  - England: Restoration
  - France: Louis XIV
  - Italy: Middle Baroque
- 1685–1715
  - England: Late Restoration or Queen Anne
  - France: Classic Baroque or Late Louis XIV
  - Italy: Late Baroque
  - Germany: Period of the Great Elector

COMMON TERMS (FOR OTHERS SEE GLOSSARY)
- petticoat breeches
- rhinegrave breeches
- rabat
- cassock
- lavallière
- echelon
- manteau
- galants
- cravat
- boot hose
- canon
- perruque
- culottes
- justaucorps
- steinkirk
- Fontanges
- commode
- spatterdashes
- falbalas
- mante
- habit à la française
- Ramillies wig
- pretintailles

RECOMMENDED SOURCES
- Pepys (background)
- Evelyn (background)
- Brooke (8): pp. 58–82
- Cunnington (1)
- Cunnington (2)
- Leloir: Section on seventeenth century
- Skira (8)
- Tapié (background)
- Wittkower (background)
- Blitzer (background)
- Kitson (background)
- Waterhouse (background)
- Weinstein (background)
- Boehn (1)
- Boehn (5): Part I
- Piton: Part VI
- Boucher: pp. 291–318
- Contini: pp. 165–191
- Faniel (background)
- Racinet: Section on eighteenth century
- Sculpture, paintings, engravings, illustrations
- Useful painters and illustrators: Lely, Kneller, Mignard, Champaigne, de Hooch, Terborch, Vermeer, Van Tilborgh, Jan Steen, Van Oost, Le Nain, Largillière, Careño, Murillo, Hollar, Bérain, late Rembrandt, Le Brun, Van der Helst, Dolci, late Jordaens, Rigaud, early Watteau, early Nattier, Van Loo, A. S. Belle, de Troy

Typical Figures

ca. 1660   ca. 1690

Rococo

On the death of Louis XIV in 1715, the Duke of Orléans became regent during the minority of Louis XV; these transitional years between the Baroque and Rococo are referred to as the Regency. From 1730 to 1774—the high period of the Rococo style—the elegant tastes of Louis XV dominated art and fashion. Aristocratic society now stressed the virtues of individuality, relaxation, delicacy, naturalness, and intimacy as opposed to the heavy formality of the previous reign. Painters such as Watteau, Boucher, and Fragonard formulated the pastoral, the *fête galante,* with its shimmering aristocrats amorously disporting themselves amid the delicacy of forest glades. Sculptors such as Clodion and Pigalle created creamy, rounded figures in pink stone, and architects scaled down the size of their structures and lavished their knowledge on the delicate, gay, playful, and extravagant interiors that they designed for their aristocratic patrons. Rococo decoration made great use of asymmetrical shell ornament, S- and C-shaped forms, and motifs such as bat wings and palm branches; straight lines and right angles were systematically avoided. The enthusiasm for the Far East was reflected in ornamental effects from the Orient known as "chinoiserie." This style, as well as the major attributes of the Rococo, were avidly copied throughout Europe.

MASCULINE DRESS. In the early Regency period, the man's coat and waistcoat were narrow at the shoulders and longer than in the past and the coat was left open; the wig was powdered white and not as full as in the past, and the general silhouette was of a conical or funnel shape expanding toward the knees. After 1730 the silhouette changed to a dome shape as the skirts of the slightly shorter coat as well as those of the knee-length vest were stiffened with canvas and horsehair. Sleeves were full length, ending in large cuffs over the shirt frill, while knee breeches were still tight and fastened over the stockings or rolled and gartered over the breeches above the knee. Shoes were less heavy than in the past, had a lower heel, and invariably finished with a buckle over a much shorter tongue. Fashion required that the head appear small despite the wig, and the hair, now powdered white, was drawn back into a bag and tied with a silk bow or *crapaud.* From this, another ribbon, the *solitaire,* frequently came around the neck and tied over the *jabot,* which was a ruffle attached to the shirt. The neck itself was wrapped in a *stock* of plain linen. Hats, though somewhat smaller than in the past, were still three-cornered and often trimmed in ostrich or embroidered in gold. Suits were heavily embroidered with gold, silver, or silk thread. Pale color harmonies were subtle and exquisite, and silk fabrics were preferred. Uniforms were braided and often of a set color for entire regiments or armies.

FEMININE DRESS. During the early Regency period, the *contouche* or loose-fitting housecoat became the most prevalent style, laced loosely over an underdress in front with flowing box pleats in back. These were referred to as *robes volantes* (flying gowns) or *robes battantes* (ringing gowns) because of their bell shape when worn over the wicker-basket *panier* or hoop that appeared about 1719. After 1735 these hoop *paniers* gave way to the lateral-spreading collapsible baskets that often stretched gowns after midcentury to as much as four yards at the hem. The gown or *robe à la française* had a square neckline; the bodice was tightly fitted over a corset; sleeves were narrow and reached to the elbows, where lace flounces still appeared, while the spreading lines of the open skirt showed a richly decorated underskirt or *jupe.* The fanciful, asymmetrical festoons of wall decorations were repeated on the tightly stretched silk of the dress in the form of gathered lace, gathered silk ribbon, or garlands of artificial flowers. The gown was edged with ruching, and large bows on the sleeves matched the ladder-like *bows à l'échelle* on the breast. The coiffure was set close to the head and powdered white, and cosmetics were heavily applied.

ROCOCO

DATES
    1715–1774
        England: Early Georgian
        France: Rococo or Louis XV
        Italy: Rococo

COMMON TERMS (FOR OTHERS SEE GLOSSARY)
    polonaise
    jabot
    solitaire
    tricorne
    paniers
    robe à la française
    parapluie
    perspective
    modestie
    robe volante
    Watteau sacque
    cadogan

RECOMMENDED SOURCES
    Brooke (5): pp. 10–56
    Gay (background)
    Green (background)
    Hartley and Elliot (2) (background)
    Kitson (background)
    Waterhouse (background)
    Schneider (background)
    Faniel (background)
    Soehner and Schonberger (background)
    Cunnington (2)
    Skira (9)
    Boehn (1)
    Kimball (background)
    Sculpture, paintings, illustrations
    Useful painters and illustrators: Watteau, Boucher, Fragonard, Chardin, Lancret, Nattier, Perroneau, Quentin la Tour, Drouais, Coypel, Van Loo, Hogarth, Gainsborough, Reynolds, Zoffany, Longhi, Tiepolo, Guardi, Pater, Moreau le Jeune, Cochin Chadowiazchi

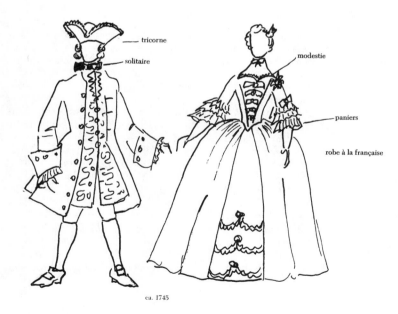

ca. 1745

Typical Figures

Neoclassicism and Revolution

Halfway through the eighteenth century the ruins of Herculaneum and Pompeii were rediscovered, and Europe developed a passion for classical antiquity. In a history of the fine arts published in 1775, the German archeologist Winckelmann emphasized the classical qualities of "noble simplicity and tranquil grandeur." The style of Louis XVI, or the neoclassical style, mixed Rococo elements with the simpler "English style" based on the new classicism. It was not an authentic Greek or Roman revival, but a "dream of the antique"—a charming, delicate, refined use of antique ornament and, after the excesses of the Rococo, a return to horizontal and vertical lines. In painting, the passion for the picturesque in the work of Fragonard and Robert changed to an admiration for the stark, cold, stoical compositions of David; in sculpture, the direct simplicity of Houdon was admired; and in architecture, a severe structure such as the Panthéon in Paris was the ideal. This period saw Rococo costume ideals reach their final form and then merge into the new modes that crossed the Channel from England.

MASCULINE DRESS.   Men's dress in the 1770s consisted of the *justaucorps*—with large cuffs, pocket flaps, and a cutaway line to the coat skirts in front—or the more closely fitting frock coat. With this was worn a waistcoat that now reached only to the top of the thighs, tight-fitting knee breeches or *culottes* that fitted over white silk stockings, and black shoes with buckles and low red heels. The material used was usually silk in delicate shades, and the edges as well as the front of the coat were richly embroidered in gold, silver, or silk thread. The hat was still three-cornered, but smaller. The wig, which was dusted with white or gray powder, was dressed into elegant side curls brushed steeply up from the forehead in front and caught either into a bag or by a ribbon bow in back. At home, the wig was replaced by a soft turban or hat and the coat by a silk dressing gown. Only after 1780 did the man's costume *à l'anglaise*, in which shoes and silk stockings were often discarded for close-fitting riding breeches and boots, become

fashionable. The *tricorne* was replaced with a low- to medium-crowned, flat-brimmed traveling hat, a smaller jockey hat, or a *bicorne*. Wool was now preferred to silk for men's coats, standing turnover collars were added, coat skirts were either cut back even more sharply or stepped back at the waist, and cuffs either disappeared or were merely marked by a bit of horizontal trim on the sleeve. Waistcoats were short and frequently double-breasted, uniforms were usually double-breasted and garded with braid and buttons.

The garb of the French revolutionaries usually consisted of the red *Phrygian cap;* a sleeveless, loose-fitting jacket called a *carmagnole,* worn by peasants; and the long, wide trousers worn by sailors.

FEMININE DRESS.   In feminine fashion the *panier* and *robe à la française* were used only in formal wear, and for all other occasions the knee-length hoop was used. With this the underskirt or *jupe* was usually ankle length, and the gown or *robe* was often caught up *à la polonaise* in three large loops over the skirt. Shoes were of silk with high heels, and when ladies went walking they always carried parasols or long walking sticks. In the early 1770s, coiffures were enormous—built up over frames and pads, held with pins and pomade, and often culminating in flowers, fruit, or a frigate in full sail. But new ideas were arriving from across the Channel by 1780, and for a time England became the leader in European fashion. Corsets were still worn, but hoops disappeared and the dress fell softly around the body—held in position by a wide sash. Instead of an elaborate coiffure, the hair was arranged in loose curls down the back, and the shoulders were covered by a small scarf or *fichu*. Long, close-fitting sleeves covered the arms to the wrist, while large, broad-brimmed straw hats made a charming frame for the face. A masculine touch was added by the use of the double-breasted *redingote,* similar to a man's riding coat, with skirts to the floor, and the *lévite* gown— tight and double-breasted to the waist, with a trailing skirt over a bustle pad at the rear.

NEOCLASSICISM AND REVOLUTION

DATES
    1774–1795
        France: Louis XVI or Neoclassical
            (1774–1789); Revolution (1789–1795)
        England: Late Eighteenth Century or
            Late Georgian
        Italy: Neoclassical
        U.S.: Colonial
COMMON TERMS (FOR OTHERS SEE GLOSSARY)
    lévite gown
    Gainsborough hat
    redingote gown
    pelisse
    calash
    dormeuse bonnet
    mobcap
    hedgehog hairdo
    circassienne gown
    cadogan hairdo
    caraco gown
    carmagnole
    cockade
    fichu
    bicorne
    stock
    thérèse

RECOMMENDED SOURCES
    Brooke (3): pp. 56–85
    Skira (9)
    Kitson (background)
    Lynton (background)
    Schneider (background)
    Gay (background)
    Cunnington (2)
    Canaday (background)
    La Galerie des Modes
    Green (background)
    Hartley and Elliot (2) (background)
    Boehn (1)
    Faniel (background)
    Novotny (background)
    The Gallery of Fashion
    Sculpture, cameos, medallions, engravings,
        illustrations
    Useful painters and illustrators: Reynolds,
        Gainsborough, Romney, late Fragonard,
        David, Greuze, Vigée le Brun, early
        Goya, Guardi, Canaletto, Boilly, prints of
        Moreau le Jeune, Copley, Stuart, Trum-
        bull, Charles Wilson Peale

Typical Figures

ca. 1780

Directoire and Empire

With the coming of the French Revolution, the Republican virtues of classical antiquity triumphed in society. The artist David became the leading painter of the new Republic. During the early years of the Napoleonic Empire, David was dictator of the arts for the Emperor. The Romans, in particular, provided the models for literature, art, and oratory; in every way, Napoleon hoped to create a modern equivalent of the Roman empire. The Church of the Madeleine and the Arc de Triomphe are architectural examples, the busts and statuary of Canova are the sculptural models, and the efforts of David and his pupils Gérard, Girodet, and Prud'hon were the painting ideals of the period. But this was also an age of a growing romanticism, and after the Egyptian campaign many oriental and Near Eastern elements, along with historical touches from the medieval, Renaissance, and Baroque, mingled with the classical.

MASCULINE DRESS. England remained the source of masculine tailoring during this period despite some exciting aberrations in dress brought on by the Revolution and Empire in France. During the Directoire the most radical fashion figures were referred to as *incroyables,* and they were judged by the elegance of their extravagant disarray. They carried heavy, knotted sticks, sported unruly hair to the shoulders, and hid their jaws in enormous neck cloths. They wore tight, striped trousers, riding boots, square-cut waistcoats with high waistlines, and coats with huge lapels and high, turned-down collars. With this ludicrous outfit was worn a *beaver* or cocked hat. As the Directoire merged into the Empire, men's costume saw the development of the long trousers of today, some very snug, others somewhat looser in fit. Leather and knitted breeches, fitted and ending in knee-high boots, were also popular. Knee breeches and stockings were now worn only with court dress. The fashion in England during the period of the Regency, which coincided with the Empire in France, was set by Beau Brummel, who prided himself on spotless linen—a two-pointed collar now rose above the carefully wrapped *stock.* Frills still decorated the shirt front and sleeve cuffs,

waistcoats were usually double breasted and often showed below the buttoned coat front, and coats had a high, rolled collar, slightly gathered sleeves at the armseye, and *clawhammer* tails. Hair imitated the windblown Roman look, headgear was based on variations of the top hat, and caped overcoats were worn for travel. Slipper pumps, or *escarpins,* were the appropriate footwear for evening, and boots under trousers became the standard daytime style. Uniforms were heavily braided, and heads were covered with tall *shakos.*

FEMININE DRESS. At the end of the Revolution, the only changes in female dress came in the casual disarray of the hair, fichu, and muslin gowns, plus the addition of cockades and sashes of the red, white, and blue of the Republic. At the beginning of the Directoire the antique garb of the ''new classicism'' appeared. The waistline moved up to just below the breast, all corseting disappeared, and the dress, cut very simply in white muslin or batiste or some other quiet color, was held by a ribbon under the breast. Flat slippers replaced high-heeled shoes, the large brim of the straw hat was turned down and extended in front of the face to form the *coal-scuttle bonnet,* and the hair was done in a loose series of corkscrew curls clustering down to the shoulders. During the Directoire those wearing exaggerations of this costume were referred to as *merveilleuses.* By 1800 the upper part of this chemise dress became a small, separate bodice with a square neckline, a tunic was frequently worn over the dress like a Greek *peplos,* and the hair was arranged to imitate a Greek coiffure. After Napoleon was crowned in 1804, heavier fabrics such as silk and satin were reintroduced, small puffed sleeves came in, and for court wear a heavy, separate train or *courrobe* of dark colored velvet was fastened and trailed from the waist. The short *Spencer jacket* and the longer *redingote* were worn outdoors, shawls or stoles were still popular, and the poke bonnet that fitted close to the face was fashionable. Toward the close of the Empire, long sleeves returned, along with ruffles and bows, and heavy trim adorned the bottoms of skirts.

DIRECTOIRE AND EMPIRE

DATES
> 1795–1815
>> England: Regency
>> France: Directoire (1795–1803) and Empire (1803–15)
>> Germany: Biedermeier
>> Italy: Empire
>> U.S.: Federal

COMMON TERMS (FOR OTHERS SEE GLOSSARY)
> merveilleuses
> incroyables
> muscadine
> redingote
> clawhammer tails
> chemise à l'anglaise
> escarpins
> cherusse
> Spencer jacket
> courrobe
> shako
> Carrick greatcoat
> coal-scuttle bonnet

RECOMMENDED SOURCES
> Blum (background)
> Norris and Oswald: Part I
> Brooke (7): pp. 8–24
> Laver (2): pp. 70–81
> Cunnington (1): Part I
> Novotny (background)
> Canaday (background)
> *The Gallery of Fashion*
> Gonzalez-Palacios (background)
> *Journal des Dames et des Modes*
> Lynton (background)
> Paintings, sculpture, engravings, illustrations, fashion plates
> Useful painters: David, Ingres, Gros, Prud'hon, Gérard, Géricault, Le Brun, Raeburn, Opie, Lawrence, Isabey, Goya, Hoppner, drawings by Vernet and Debucourt, Stuart, Copley, Trumbull, Earle

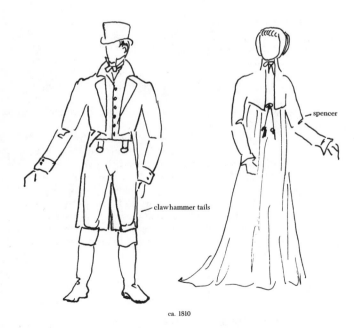

clawhammer tails

spencer

ca. 1810

Typical Figures

Romantic

The nineteenth century was an age of revival. As much more became known about the styles of the past than ever before, architects, sculptors, and painters drew unceasingly on the riches catalogued by art historians and archeologists. The major reaction to the classicism of the Empire was in the direction of Baroque movement, Gothic mystery, and Rococo elegance and charm—the latter being especially influential in the arts of costume. In painting, the Baroque borrowings of Delacroix and Géricault tended to take precedence; in architecture, the Gothic style of the English Houses of Parliament was given great emphasis; while in sculpture, the dramatic effects of Rude and Barye reflected admiration for the work of Bernini. This was a new age of capitalism and the machine, and with the expanding middle class, which had little taste and much money, factory imitations superseded the quality craftsmanship of individual artisans.

MASCULINE DRESS.   Although the long trousers, coat, and waistcoat had by now become permanent features of men's dress, the masculine silhouette echoed the women's silhouette in its wasp waist and fullness in chest and hips. The trousers fastened under the instep and were padded at the hips, the coat and overcoat were fitted very closely with *leg-o'-mutton* sleeves joined to the coat below the shoulder, and the cap or shawl collar gave the shoulders a rounded appearance. Coats were fitted either with tails or the flaring skirts of the frock coat, and a corset or *Basque belt* was often used to pinch in the waist under the pigeon-breasted waistcoat. Short jackets were used only for sport. Height was given by the tall, flaring top hat that was worn for all formal occasions except court appearances, when the cocked *bicorne* was carried. Men wore full side whiskers and clustering curls around the ears, and toward the close of the period beards and mustaches began to make their appearance. The crisp points of the shirt collar were still held in place by a wide *stock* that usually tied in a bow in the front, and rich ruffles still showed at the chest above the waistcoat. The mantle and the caped overcoat were standard wear for travel, knee breeches and slippers were used only for court presentation, and pointed boots were now worn under the trousers except for riding or sporting occasions. In uniforms, the braided *frock coat* superseded tails, and long trousers often replaced high boots.

FEMININE DRESS.   Under the Empire, dresses had already become shorter at the hem and were closed around the neck, but now the girdle moved down from below the bust to the slimmest point of the waist, the corset returned, and skirts flared out in many folds over full petticoats. Appliqué trimming, ruching, and many ruffles came back in force. The *poke bonnet* was still in use, but now it flared out into a huge brim decorated with plumes and ribbons framing a hairdo that had great sausage curls at the temples and a complexly curled top knot at the back. Flat shoes, fastened with cross lacings up the ankles, continued to be worn, and shawls of all sizes continued to be carried or worn. As the width of this costume expanded at shoulders and hips, the collar of the low-cut bodice increased in size and formed a kind of roof over the greatly distended *leg-o'-mutton sleeves,* which were attached to the bodice well below the shoulder line. From about 1835 on, the upholsterer, rather than the cabinet maker, dictated in matters of interior decoration, and just as the basic shape of furniture was lost under padded fabric, tassels, and fringe, so women's fashions ceased to have the lightness of the ballet line, and the female figure was gradually covered in heavy fabric and decoration. The skirt lengthened to the floor and was further extended with petticoats. The leg-o'-mutton sleeve disappeared in favor of snug-fitting sleeves, exaggerated hairdos were modified to ringlets over the ears and a smooth part across the forehead, and bonnets closed in about the face. The hourglass silhouette gave way to the tea-cozy look, and heavier fabrics and trim replaced light ruffles and flowers.

ROMANTIC

DATES
    1815–1848
       England: Period of William IV and the
          Young Victoria
       France: Romantic or Restoration and the
          July Monarchy
       Italy: Restoration
       Spain: Restoration
       Germany and Austria: Biedermeier
       U.S.: Early Republic

COMMON TERMS (FOR OTHERS SEE GLOSSARY)
    stock
    crinoline
    robe d'intérieur
    bertha
    beret sleeve
    pèlerine
    canezou
    bishop sleeve
    leg-o'-mutton sleeves
    Byron collar
    mackintosh
    nankeen trousers
    pelisse
    mantelette

RECOMMENDED SOURCES
    Laver (2): pp. 81–92
    Norris and Oswald: Part I
    Brooke (5): pp. 24–48
    Canaday (background)
    Courthion (background)
    Cunnington (1)
    Illustrated London News
    Journal des Dames et des Modes
    Lynton (background)
    Newton (background)
    Petit Courrier des Dames
    The Gentleman's Magazine
    Les Modes Parisiennes
    Novotny (background)
    Gernsheim (background)
    Boehn (3)
    Paintings, sculpture, illustrations, engrav-
       ings, drawings, fashion plates
    Useful painters: Delacroix, Sully, Samuel
       Morse, Cruikshank, Ingres, Lawrence,
       Raeburn, Bouguereau, Meissonier,
       Horace Vernet, Daumier, Gavarni, Fried-
       rich

stock or cravat

bertha

crinoline underneath

ca. 1830

Typical Figures

Late Nineteenth Century: Victorian and Second Empire

The revolts and pressures against the status quo that had erupted throughout the romantic period reached their culmination in 1848. Revolutions arose in all the capitals of Europe and many changes began to take place in intellectual and artistic circles, if not in the mass middle-class taste of the European bourgeoisie. A new interest in social problems, urban living, and the increasing misery caused by industrialization led to the development of realism in art and literature. In France, Dumas *fils,* Augier, Flaubert, the Brothers Goncourt, and others pioneered in the new style, as did Ibsen in Norway and Dickens in England. In painting, Courbet and Millet pioneered new subjects and new ways of viewing based on the world around them. However, taste at the court of the Emperor Napoleon III was still imitative of styles of the past, particularly the Rococo.

MASCULINE DRESS. At the beginning of this period the romantic silhouette still retained a tight-fitting, slim-waisted line, but without the previous exaggeration in shoulder and hips. The top hat was still obligatory, but in 1848 the beaver was supplanted by the silk hat. The hair was still full, although not as tightly curled around the ears, and beards were now becoming more and more prevalent. The most fashionable was the pointed "imperial," worn with side whiskers and a mustache. By 1860 a man's daily outfit tended to be uniform in color, and was now known as "a suit of clothes." Trousers, though narrow, were no longer tight-fitting and fastened under the shoe, frock coats and tail coats were no longer as snug at the waist, and standing collars and cravats were replaced by starched collars and ties. Special suits of clothes for different occasions also began to be used at this time: the frock coat and top hat for formal afternoon wear, the bowler and short sack suit—usually with waistcoat, pants, and matching coat—for business wear, and short hunting or fishing jackets with leggings and straw hats for country wear. The full black outfit of tails with a white vest was established at this time as the standard for formal evening wear. Overcoats now superseded the cloak for outdoors, and uniforms stressed long trousers, braided frock coats, and visored caps or *shakos.*

FEMININE DRESS. About midcentury the weight of the many petticoats that had achieved the tea-cozy silhouette brought about the reintroduction (for the third time in the history of dress) of a frame to hold out the skirts. This *crinoline* or *cage américaine,* was made of bamboo, whalebone, or metal hoops suspended from tapes and increasing in width toward the bottom, and with it came the possibility of extra width in the skirt—a fact that was exploited to the full. The hair was now either parted in the middle, waved over the forehead and caught in a bun or bunch of curls over the ears, or drawn in soft waves from center part to the back of the head and held in a *chignon* or soft roll. The former style was preferred by Queen Victoria, the latter by the Empress Eugénie, who was Spanish by birth, married Napoleon III in 1853, was considered by many the most beautiful woman in Europe, and who, with the help of her couturier, the House of Worth, was the leader of European fashion until 1869. Under the influence of the Empress Eugénie, the poke bonnet was replaced by the small straw hat with a ribbon at the back and the *capote,* a tiny bonnet at the back of the head. In the new style, based in many ways on the Rococo, the lower part of the skirt could be divided into horizontal layers of ruching or garlands of flowers. It might consist of several layers of different lengths, or there could be a major use of overlapping flounces at the hem. The effect of the flouncing on the skirt was repeated in the *bertha* around the shoulders and spread also to the sleeve, which became funnel-shaped—the famous *pagoda* sleeve—with undersleeves of white tulle. For evening wear, short cap sleeves and low decolletage were the fashion, while daytime wear required long sleeves and a high neck, except in certain summer frocks. Fabrics ranged from silk taffetas, damasks, brocades, and velvets to light muslins, gauze, and crêpe de chine, which made women look like floating clouds. Stockings were now colored; cloth boots were used by day, slippers at night. At the close of the period the crinoline changed to an oval shape with emphasis at the back.

LATE NINETEENTH CENTURY:
VICTORIAN AND SECOND EMPIRE

DATES

1848–1890

England: Victorian

France: Age of Realism in Painting;
Period of Second Republic and Empire

Italy: Age of Revolution and Independence

Germany: German Confederation

U.S.: Antebellum and Civil War

COMMON TERMS (FOR OTHERS SEE GLOSSARY)

frock coat
tails
morning coat
sack suit
bowler
burnous
raglan coat
paletot
cage américaine
shirtwaist
Dundreary
imperial
muttonchops
pagoda sleeve
zouave jacket
princess gown
pork-pie hat
Empress Eugénie hat
Prince Albert coat
Inverness cape

RECOMMENDED SOURCES

Godey's *Lady's Book*
Les Modes Parisiennes
L'Illustration
Illustrated London News
Burchell (background)
Canaday (background)
Crankshaw (background)
Gernsheim (background)
Harper's (1)
Harper's (2)
Hibbert (background)
Lynton (background)
Peterson's Magazine
Petit Courrier des Dames
Reynolds (background)
Worth (background)
Cunnington (1)
Boehn (3)
Norris and Oswald: Part II
Brooke (7): pp. 48–64
Laver (2): pp. 92–100
Larkin (background)
Paintings, illustrations, photographs
Useful painters and illustrators: Manet, Delacroix, Ingres, Millet, Courbet, Daumier, Guys, Gavarni, Phiz, Winterhalter, Lami

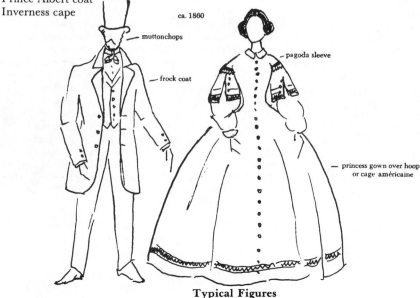

ca. 1860

— muttonchops

— frock coat

— pagoda sleeve

— princess gown over hoop
or cage américaine

Typical Figures

Late Nineteenth Century: The Gilded Age

During the last decades of the nineteenth century, the imitation of the past produced a confusion of styles, each applied to a different purpose. Studies and dining rooms were Renaissance, smoking rooms oriental, girls' rooms Rococo. Coziness was everything, and heavy door hangings, thick upholstery, elephantine furniture, and accessories that ran to wax flowers, lacquered bulrushes, and peacock feathers created a crowded chaos of confused ornamentation. It is no wonder that true art moved outdoors into the light and air as the impressionists, using the new art of optics and a sensitive eye, made people see things "as if for the first time." Even a sculptor such as Rodin gave an "impressionistic" immediacy to his work through the surging, flickering line of tactile surfaces, while other artists experimented with pattern and form at the expense of subject matter.

MASCULINE DRESS. Dress, like interior decoration, followed the mass taste of the times, and men's costume became very conservative in line and color and very organized as to what should be worn when. Formal dress in the morning now consisted of stiff-bosomed shirt, wing collar, bow tie, light gray vest, cutaway morning coat, gray striped trousers, pearl gray gloves, and a top hat—all items still a part of daytime formal wear. Afternoon formal wear consisted of starched shirt, standing collar, *four-in-hand* or *ascot* tie, a rich but sober waistcoat, a dark double-breasted frock coat with matching or lighter trousers. Informal evening wear saw the introduction of the black *tuxedo* or satin-lapeled dinner jacket of fingertip length, while formal evening wear still consisted of white tie and waistcoat with black tails and trousers. For business wear, the bowler hat and the sack suit, the latter frequently in checks and narrow stripes, was the standard. For sports there was a variety of belted *Norfolk jackets* and knee-length knickerbockers worn with billed caps, fore-and-aft caps, and straws. These sporting suits were usually worn with collar and tie, and with buttoned leggings over long woolen stockings. The *Inverness cape* and the *Chesterfield overcoat* were used against rain and cold, faces still sported beards, side whiskers, and full mustaches, hair was moderately full, and shoes were buttoned to the ankle and frequently worn with spats. Uniforms showed innovations in headgear but remained much the same in silhouette.

FEMININE DRESS. The material in dresses was now cut into complex small pieces before being sewn to fit the female figure, in order to demonstrate the masterful art of dressmaking. Folds were draped across pleats, drapings draped over drapings, and velvets were used with dull silks and glossy satins. Everything seemed to strive toward a complex juxtaposition of lines, fabrics, and colors. With the transition from the crinoline to the bustle, the fullness in the 1870s moved firmly to the back. This bustle was either a small pad of horsehair or a small metal cage with the overskirt draped up over it. All draping was as imaginatively contrived as in the portières and curtains of the day. The upper part of the figure was firmly encased in a corset that pushed up the bust and pushed out the abdomen, necks were high, and sleeves were full length during the day, décolleté and short for evening. Long white or pastel gloves were worn with evening wear to cover bare arms. By the late 1870s, the bustle began to disappear as the draped outer skirt wrapped more tightly about the lower part of the body. In this *fish-tailed* style, which reached its peak in 1880, the hips, waist, and bust emerged with a magnificent flourish owing much to corsetry and padding; a long row of buttons down the front emphasized the central line of the figure. In the early 1880s, the bustle returned, now worn higher on the waist and giving the female silhouette the look of a centaur. A skirt with a bustle was worn with tailored jackets, skating outfits, and topcoats, all of which were cut to accommodate this exaggerated line at the rear of the figure. Hair was built up toward the back of the head with tight curls falling down the back; small hats with flowers, ribbons, and feathers were perched atop this hairdo, kept on by a ribbon or a hatpin. Shoes were ankle-high, buttoned affairs except for evening, when the heeled slipper was worn.

LATE NINETEENTH CENTURY:
THE GILDED AGE

DATES
    1870–1890
        England: Victorian
        France: Third Republic and Age of Impressionism
        Italy: Age of Nationalism
        Germany: German Empire
        Spain: Carlist Wars
        U.S.: The Gilded Age

COMMON TERMS (FOR OTHERS SEE GLOSSARY)
    Norfolk jacket
    tuxedo
    spats
    wing collar
    monocle
    knickerbockers
    windsor tie
    fore-and-aft cap
    Chesterfield overcoat
    ascot
    fedora
    homburg
    frou-frou
    four-in-hand tie

RECOMMENDED SOURCES
    Brooke (7): pp. 64–80
    Godey's Lady's Book

Harper's (1)
Harper's (2)
Harper's (3)
Peterson's Magazine
Burchell (background)
Canaday (background)
Crankshaw (background)
Cunnington (1)
Gernsheim (background)
Hibbert (background)
Larkin (background)
Lynton (background)
Reynolds (background)
This Fabulous Century (1) (background)
Sullivan (background)
Brown (2): (background)
Norris and Oswald: Part III
Laver (2): pp. 101–111
Boehn (3)
La Mode Illustrée
Paintings, illustrations, photographs
Useful painters and illustrators: Manet,
    Monet, Degas, Toulouse-Lautrec, Renoir,
    Thomas, Nast, Homer, Whistler, Sargent,
    Eakins, du Maurier

ca. 1875

Typical Figures

Late Victorian and Edwardian: *Art Nouveau*

With the last decade of the nineteenth century, the first modern mass style began to make itself felt in design and decoration. Artists such as Monet, Gauguin and Whistler, who throughout the last half of the nineteenth century had stressed design, pattern, and form over subject, saw their ideals vindicated in a Europe-wide style variously labeled *art nouveau* or *Jugendstil*. As it spread, eclecticism went out of fashion and the pattern and lines of decoration and ornament, which were based primarily on "organic" growth lines, influenced architecture, painting, sculpture, and interior decoration. As art stressed a strong sense of style, so clothing made the Edwardian years synonymous with a sense of style. Women looked like pastel birds of plumage, while men looked like elegant dandies.

MASCULINE DRESS.   Male fashions changed only slightly during this period, with casual clothing for outings and the sack suits for everyday wear becoming more prevalent. The fashionable ideal was the subtly tailored, square-shouldered, smooth-waisted elegance of the dandy or "dude." Hair was now most frequently parted in the middle, cleanshaven faces began to return, and many varieties of soft *homburgs, fedoras,* and billed caps began to replace the rigid "topper" and bowler. Very high, stiff collars were still the rule, whether they were winged, turnover, or standing, and the *ascot* and *four-in-hand* ties were rivaled in popularity by the bow tie. Shirts were stiff-bosomed for all formal occasions and buttoned up the back, while with all informal outfits the soft, often striped shirt with separate collar was worn. There were still the formal *morning coat,* the square-skirted *frock coat, tails,* the *tuxedo,* and the *sack coat,* with informal *blazers,* knitted *cardigans, Norfolk jackets,* and pullover sweaters for sporting. There was great variety in both double- and single-breasted waistcoats, either matching or contrasting with the coat and trousers, sometimes in rich patterns. Trousers were slim and often pressed into a crease, sometimes turned up into a cuff, while knee-length *knickers* worn with woolen stockings were also

still seen in sports wear. Ankle-length button shoes were worn in winter, low *oxfords* in summer, and *spats* were fashionable. Heavy or light overcoats, sometimes in plaid, with a shoulder cape, at other times with fur lining and trim, were worn. Field uniforms moved to khaki brown jackets, riding pants, and leggings.

FEMININE DRESS.   By 1890 the bustle disappeared, leaving behind a certain amount of residual drapery in the skirt, but this did not remain, and by the mid 1890s the skirt became a smooth, many-gored, flaring skirt with extra fullness at the back; large *leg-o'-mutton sleeves* and a tiny waist helped give an hourglass figure. The dresses were still high-necked and long-sleeved for day wear, décolleté with short capped sleeves for evening. A feminine version of the male suit appeared in the 1890s, consisting of a tailored jacket and ankle-length skirt worn with a shirt blouse and tie. This blouse, smothered in every conceivable kind of trimming—lace, buttons, frills, and flounces—influenced dress styles toward having a great fullness of material in front. This, coupled with the introduction in the late 1890s of a new corset that pushed the bust forward and the hips backward, produced the famous sway-backed S-curved figure of the opening years of the new century. Hair, which had been drawn up fairly close to the head in the style of Mme de Pompadour, became fuller and surrounded the temples, ears, and forehead with a massive halo of hair. Flowered and beribboned hats, which had small brims in the 1890s, expanded into great, broad-brimmed creations saturated with plumes. By 1908 the silhouette was taller and slimmer, the bust had become higher and more prominent, and the hips were held in tightly by the corset; hats were even larger and the silhouette was that of a triangle standing on its point. There was a brief revival of pseudo-Empire styles with a slightly raised waistline and slim lines to the floor, but the real revolution in women's clothing did not arrive until the height of the woman's suffrage movement in 1912–1913.

LATE VICTORIAN AND EDWARDIAN:
ART NOUVEAU

DATES
    1890–1911
        England: Late Victorian and Edwardian
            Age of Imperialism
        France: Third Republic
        Germany: German Empire
        U.S.: Gay Nineties and Age of Immigra-
            tion
COMMON TERMS (FOR OTHERS SEE GLOSSARY)
    boater
    Gibson Girl blouse
    leg-o'-mutton sleeves
    bloomers
    châtelaine bag
    Windsor tie
    street sweepers
    Panama hat
    string tie
    beehive hat
    Buster Brown collar
    dog collar
    duster
    knickers
    Lillian Russell dress
    mackintosh
    oxford
    Peter Pan collar
    marcel wave
    wrapper
    Merry Widow hat
    pompadour
RECOMMENDED SOURCES
    Vogue
    Life Magazine
    Ladies' Home Journal
    Sears Roebuck Catalog
    Wilcox (2)
    Brooke (7): pp. 80–89
    Burchell (background)
    Colton (background)
    Crankshaw (background)
    Cunnington (1)
    Greenberg (background)
    Hamilton (background)
    Harper's (1)
    Harper's (2)
    Harper's (3)
    Hibbert (background)
    Larkin (background)
    Lynton (background)
    Peterson's Magazine
    Reynolds (background)
    Selz and Constantine (background)
    This Fabulous Century (1)
    This Fabulous Century (2)
    Worth (background)
    Good Housekeeping
    Sullivan (background)
    Brown (1) (background)
    Gernsheim (background)
    Paintings, sculpture, photographs, engrav-
        ings, drawings
    Useful painters and illustrators: Sargent, Gib-
        son, Henri, Eakins, Toulouse-Lautrec,
        Maillol, Bonnard, Boldini, Bottini, Pi-
        casso, Beardsley, Klimt, Munch, Matisse,
        Van der Velde

Typical Figures

ca. 1902

ca. 1894

World War I and the Twenties: Early Art Deco

During the years just before World War I and during the 1920s the revolution in art and culture that had begun in the last decade of the nineteenth century finally became an integral part of life in the Western world. The new concept of relativity influenced thinking in art, morals, science, literature, and world outlook. Particularly in the arts, with the invention of the motion picture and the establishment of cubism, reality was seen changing from moment to moment, varying widely when seen from different points of view, and capable of being presented as a simultaneous view from many angles. This led to the simultaneous inner and outer levels of reality in the work of James Joyce, to the many visual angles and points of view of Picasso, and to the interpenetration of space and object in the work of Gabo, Pevsner, Le Corbusier, and others. A second major concept was that of functionalism, wherein beauty lay not in ornament and decoration but in the practical function for which a house, a gown, a chair, or an automobile was designed.

MASCULINE DRESS. Masculine dress changed only very slowly and subtly during this period, becoming more functional and less formal. The frock coat finally disappeared altogether, leaving only morning coats and tails as leftovers from the nineteenth century in formal wear. Collars, except for the formal winged collar, became moderately soft turnovers; the soft felt *slouch hat* or *fedora* finally came to dominate the *derby, bowler,* and *top hat*—the latter remaining only for formal wear. High laced and buttoned shoes gave way to the low *oxford*. In the 1920s the male silhouette tended to have rather a slim and boyish look, with the exception of the *Oxford bags* or knee-length *plus fours* for golfing and sports. In the 1930s the silhouette became very broad-shouldered and the trousers quite wide and pleated, while hat brims increased in width. Bright-colored sport shirts made their appearance, double-breasted coats were very popular, white tuxedo jackets for summer wear were introduced, and there was great emphasis on swimming trunks, beach wear, and walking shorts. In outergarments the unique items of the 1920s were the raccoon coat and the trench coat. Throughout the whole period the sack suit was dominant, while in uniforms the khaki brown color became standard and lapel jackets replaced high-collared tunics.

FEMININE DRESS. About 1912 the one piece *kimono dress* began to predominate, with much draping about the legs to give a diamond-shaped silhouette or the *hobble skirt* effect. Large floral and oriental patterns based on Russian ballet designs became fashionable, hats became smaller, and hair simpler, softer, and shorter. Gradually functionalism began to triumph over the complexities of line and superfluous decoration. After the first introduction of the draped kimono lines, dresses and coats fell loosely about the body and showed a marked tendency to become shorter, to reveal that a woman, like a man, had two legs to walk on. After the War, straight lines began to become the ideal, and by 1923 women's costume had developed into a short, absolutely straight dress hanging from the shoulders, usually sleeveless, with the waist around the hips. The curves of the body were ignored, the female form was presented as a sort of tube without hips or breasts. The low waist marked the tops of the legs, and more and more of the leg, clad in light silk stockings, was exposed until the dress reached minimum length in 1928. At the same time, the *Eton crop* and bobbed hair appeared along with the *cloche hat*—the result was a youthful figure of indeterminate sex. The dress of this period was a clear expression of a sober, practical functionalism in design.

WORLD WAR I AND THE TWENTIES: EARLY ART DECO

DATES

- The Age of Relativity (1911–1929)
- World War I Era (1911–1919)
- Twenties (1919–1929)

COMMON TERMS (FOR OTHERS SEE GLOSSARY)

- Oxford bags
- plus fours
- polo coat
- blazer
- raccoon coat
- cummerbund
- trench coat
- dolman wrap
- cardigan
- shingled and bobbed hairdos
- arctics or galoshes
- jodhpurs
- monkey-fur coat
- bandeau
- Eton crop
- kimono dress
- hobble skirt
- lampshade dress
- peg-top skirt
- Hoover apron
- saddle shoe
- T-shirt
- black tie

RECOMMENDED SOURCES

- *Harper's* (1)
- *Harper's* (2)
- *Harper's* (3)
- *Vogue*
- *Life Magazine*
- *Illustrated London News*
- *International Studio*
- *Connoisseur*
- *The Studio*
- *Esquire*
- *Men's Wear*
- *Sears Roebuck Catalog*
- *Ladies' Home Journal*
- *Good Housekeeping*
- Wilcox (1)
- Wilcox (2)
- Contini: pp. 283–306
- Battersby (background)
- Canaday (background)
- Colton (background)
- Greenberg (background)
- Hamilton (background)
- Lynton (background)
- *This Fabulous Century* (3)
- *This Fabulous Century* (4)
- Paintings, illustrations, photographs, drawings, fashion plates
- Useful illustrators and painters: Grosz, Chagall, Benton, Kirchner, Kokoschka, Marsh, Schmidt-Rotluff, Sloan, Shahn, Wood, M. Parrish, Van Dongen, Dufy, Leyendecker

Typical Figures

ca. 1925

The Thirties and World War II: Late Art Deco

The 1930s were born prematurely and disastrously in October 1929 with the New York stock market crash, and what followed was to affect millions of people throughout the world for over a decade. The 1920s bubble of hectic gaiety and the delusion of prosperity for all was completely exploded, and a decade of hardship and depression ensued. The arts survived under federal government and private patronage, but made few forward strides. Abstraction and relativity continued in the fine arts, while the popular arts continued the slick, polished, streamlined machine product that had become known as *art deco*. This art, in clothing, interiors, furnishings, advertising, and artifacts, led from a period of austerity at the start of the 1930s to a moment of escapist fantasy and romanticism in the spectacular movies made in Hollywood just before the outbreak of World War II. In fact, for this entire period Hollywood was the source of style ideas in clothing, interiors, and artifacts. But with the outbreak of war, there was a complete break in style, with most new style ideas stemming from the military. The mammoth undertaking of winning the war drained all inspiration away from the arts. When World War II ended in 1945 with the dropping of the atomic bomb, the world was both exhausted and shocked by the terrible power released upon Japan.

MASCULINE DRESS. In general, men's clothing during the 1930s and the years of World War II changed only slightly from the styles of the 1920s. The major change was in bulk and squareness. Suit shoulders were padded, there was much more use of the double-breasted suit, pants were wide with deep pleats at the top and large cuffs at the bottom, and felt *fedora* hats had very wide snap brims. The major additions during the Depression were in sports clothing and evening dress. For example, the white dinner jacket for evenings was introduced, usually with a *cummerbund* to replace the tuxedo vest, and with all tuxedos the wing collar gave way to the slightly starched turnover. For sports there were *Bermuda shorts;* open-necked, short-sleeved, patterned shirts with or without silk scarves; casual slacks; many varieties of cardigan and pullover sweaters; checked and plain sports jackets; and the new swimming trunks without tops. The most fashionable new overcoat was the *trench coat,* which was adapted from the World War I officer's raincoat, and the *polo coat* of camel's hair, which derived from the coat thrown over the shoulders of players after a polo match.

FEMININE DRESS. With the Depression, the saucy, boyish look came to an end. Fashion seemed to say that the party was over, and a more conservative image, although still within the sleek, efficient, streamlined contours of the machine age, set in. About 1930 evening dresses became much longer again, first at the back and then all the way around; and they were frequently cut on the bias so as to shape themselves over the bust, hips, and thighs in a clinging series of subtle curves. The new form of body emphasis in many of these dresses was backlessness, a style probably related to the new swimming suits. For daytime the waist was again normal, skirts were long, and suits copied the broad male line with padded shoulders. Toward the close of the 1930s skirts began to rise to knee length; hats were either felts with tiny brims, pillboxes, or turbans; and the hair was generally parted in the middle and waved and rolled up and to the back. There was also great experimentation in wide slacks, playsuits, tennis dresses, bathing suits, ski costumes, low and platform sandals, and shirtwaist frocks. With the coming of the War, the new synthetic fabrics began to appear, especially as sources of silk were closed, and the utility and convenience of the new fabrics were recognized in both military and civilian situations. The all-out war effort also made itself felt in what was left of the fashion industry, and designers like Mainbocher created military uniforms for women that were both practical and fashionable. Women factory workers now found freedom in zippered coveralls, *Levis,* and practical slacks, eliminated metal accessories, and accepted substitutes for all those dress items that were now scarce or needed in the war effort.

THE THIRTIES AND WORLD WAR II: LATE ART DECO

DATES

Depression through World War II 1929–1945

COMMON TERMS (FOR OTHERS SEE GLOSSARY)

argyles
beanie
Bermuda shorts
borsalino
crew cut
culottes
Palm Beach suit
Eisenhower jacket
halter
loafer
lodencoat
polo coat
polo shirt
shirtwaist dress
snap brim
snood
swing skirt
windbreaker

RECOMMENDED SOURCES

Battersby (2)
Canaday (background)
Colton (background)
Esquire
Good Housekeeping
Greenberg (background)
Hamilton (background)
Harper's Bazaar
Ladies' Home Journal
Sears Roebuck Catalog
This Fabulous Century (5)
This Fabulous Century (6)
Vogue
Boucher pp. 413–418
Contini pp. 301–311
Paintings, illustrations, photographs, drawings, fashion plates
Useful illustrators and painters: Chagall, Benton, Kokoschka, Shahn, Bérard, de Chirico, Dufy, Erté, Grosz, Lavery, Picasso, Rivera, Sheringham, Hopper

ca. 1939

Typical Figures

The Cold War

Culture changed radically in the years after World War II. Through improved methods of communication, the threat of destruction by a "super" bomb, and the greater speed and efficiency of travel, the world seemed to grow smaller. The two greatest technical influences were the transmission of information to all parts of the world via communications satellites, and the lurking fear in every country in the world of atomic and hydrogen bombs. Together, these caused a continuing growth in uniformity of culture from place to place throughout the world, plus a growing anxiety neurosis felt in every aspect of contemporary culture. Acceptance of the *avant garde* in painting, sculpture, architecture, theatre, and the arts of fashion was widespread; there was a greater breakdown of boundaries among all the arts; and there was a kind of Cold War mentality in culture that led to a great conformity in attitudes, clothing, and outlook.

MASCULINE DRESS. The basic form of male dress established at the time of Napoleon has varied in sympathy with the times but has not changed substantially in 150 years. Various new items have been added to it, it has been considerably modified for sport, new fabrics have been introduced, but the basic construction is so practical that it has remained the same. Formal dress such as tails and morning coats diminished in use, and dinner jackets in black, white, checks, and velvets, often without vests, were more and more acceptable for formal occasions. The major changes in cut were toward slimmer lines, smaller lapels, less padding, and a closer fit. Hats narrowed to much smaller brims, sandals began to return for men as well as women, and colors and patterns finally brightened for men (at least in sportswear), so that sport shirts equaled some female clothing in brilliance. Wash-and-wear fabrics, creaseless and stainless materials, and longer-wearing synthetics of all kinds made men's clothes ever more efficient and practical, while in sportswear the variety of fabrics, shapes, and numbers of garments greatly increased.

FEMININE DRESS. During World War II military wear influenced fashion, and many forms of the male and female uniforms of the time made their way into civil dress, but it was not until 1947 that a great change came to the short-skirted, tubular, square-shouldered look that had been in vogue since 1939. The "new look," established by the House of Christian Dior in Paris, stressed narrow shoulders, smooth bust, normal waist, and a long skirt with a wide hem. This dress silhouette was not really new at all, but merely a return to past styles, and in the years that followed, it was modified, especially in the length and width of the skirt. In the early 1950s, not too many years after the "new look" appeared, the House of Balenciaga was first in the field with a chemise or sack dress, and by 1956 Dior produced his H-line and A-line dresses. After Chanel revived boxy suits in the mid-1950s, clothes often resembled the straight lines of the mid-1920s, except when skirts were abandoned altogether in favor of trousers. The simple, geometrically shaped basics for women in the late 1950s dramatized the concept of unemotional efficiency as the key to middle-class clothing at the moment that the "beat" generation was challenging the whole cultural outlook. To them the straight sheath, sack, and chemise dresses of plain fabric worn with simple pearls seemed to symbolize the mechanized efficiency of the "establishment."

In general, after World War II, fashion, like art, became more geometric, often taking its color and line from paintings of hard-edged abstractions by Mondrian and his imitators.

THE COLD WAR

DATES

    Cold War Period 1945–1963

COMMON TERMS (FOR OTHERS SEE GLOSSARY)

  weskit
  waspie belt
  ballerina skirt
  capri or pirate pants
  chukka boot
  cocktail dress
  dirndl
  gaucho pants
  halter top
  huarache
  page-boy hairdo
  parka
  pedal pushers
  sloppy joe
  toggle coat
  toreador pants
  trapeze line
  tent dress
  duffle coat
  Eisenhower jacket
  car coat
  shift
  blue jeans
  new look
  A-line
  sack dress
  Teddy boy

RECOMMENDED SOURCES

  Harper's (1)
  Harper's (2)
  Harper's (3)
  Vogue
  Life Magazine
  Ladies' Home Journal
  Illustrated London News
  Esquire
  Connoisseur
  The Studio
  Vingt Ans
  Contini: pp. 306–317
  Boucher: pp. 415–421
  Wilcox (1)
  Wilcox (2)
  Canaday (background)
  Colton (background)
  Greenberg (background)
  Lynton (background)
  In Vogue
  This Fabulous Century (6)
  This Fabulous Century (7)
  Newspaper photographs, magazine illustra-
    tions, drawings, fashion plates, catalogues
  Useful illustrators and painters: Kokoschka,
    Chagall, Picasso, Bérard, Koudine

Typical Figures

ca. 1955

Contemporary

The tired and complacent American culture of the 1950s with its image of the man in the gray flannel suit, suburban living, and Cold War politics began to change in the mid-1960s. There arose a new feeling of commitment to human concerns. From those at the bottom of the economic pyramid to others at the top there was a stirring of humanistic values in place of the organizational and analytical—people were placed above societal structure. There was also a new sense of the interconnectedness of all peoples—the world was seen as an interdependent global village. Even after the shock of the Kennedy assassination and the escalation of the war in Vietnam, there was no retreat from idealism, but a more violent and militant support of the new outlook. Lapel buttons carried such phrases as "Legalize Spiritual Discovery," "Suppose they gave a war and nobody came," "I am a human being: do not fold, spindle or mutilate." There was a feeling that the cold, mechanized, profit-oriented, conformist approach to life deadens feeling and dulls individual moral and human values. But the new movement had a violent side, and by 1968 there were violent clashes with the authorities at the Chicago Democratic Convention, in Paris and Tokyo, and on college campuses. After 1970, when the war in Vietnam began to wind down and financial recession set in, confrontation receded, and young people retreated into private goals and concern for self. There was a new conservatism and a quiet distillation of the explosive ideals of the 1960s. In films, heart-grabbing parables of good triumphant, such as *Rocky* and *Star Wars,* became popular along with a growing nostalgia for the past—particularly the 1930s, 1940s, and even the 1950s. There was a growing interest in the irrational and the occult, and romantic escapism became a major factor in popular culture.

MASCULINE DRESS. The youthful rebellion of the 1960s was strongly represented in dress, and clothes became a weapon in the struggle with the "establishment." The key to dress was personal choice at the expense of what was left of the concept of the gentleman. Though the three-piece suit made a dramatic comeback in the 1970s, younger men no longer thought it necessary to wear the traditional capitalist uniform, and wore instead leather jackets, boots, tight trousers, open-necked shirts, long hair, beards, and turtlenecks. The explosion of the sensuous and physical was reminiscent of the 1490s as seen in the famous Dürer self-portrait. Many fashions came from cycling, riding, hiking, and skiing outfits, and thus the art of tailoring became less important than texture, variety, and romantic eroticism. The greatest symbol of the 1960s was the blue-jean material used in *Levis*. Derived from miner's pants and cowboy outfits, the faded, tight-fitting jeans and jackets became a symbol of protest against the "establishment"—they were romantically physical garments that seemed to have faded and weathered to conform to the contours of the body. They were frequently embroidered and decorated, and when the idea was later coopted by high fashion there developed designer *jeans,* mechanically produced photographic patterns, and new dyed colors. Though the mid-1970s brought more conservatism in color, texture, and line, there still remains today a great variety in male fashions, and the ideal remains personal rather than merely traditional choice in dress.

FEMININE DRESS. Although clothing was remarkably similar for men and women, there was an even greater variety of shapes and textures in feminine dress. First came the *mini skirt,* which was even shorter than the skirt of the 1920s; then came boots, leather pants, tight jeans with flared bottoms, and long straight hair that made young males and females look much alike. There was also a rich variety of clothing sources—Russian, Indian, African, Gypsy, and oriental. These were often mixed in the same outfit to create the "funky" look, and furs, leathers, rough knits, colorful woolens, exotic silks, capes, shawls, jackets, and scarves created a textural display that stressed the sensuous and romantic. In the 1970s some of this display decreased, and with the rise of the women's movement there developed the pants suit for the business look as well as soft knit outfits to give a sense of romantic femininity. As recession and inflation increased and nostalgia for the recent past developed, women's fashions borrowed from the classic suits, dresses, shoes, and hats of the 1930s and 1940s, especially in the use of broad shoulders and hats.

CONTEMPORARY

Dates
1963–
The Rebellious Sixties and Nostalgic
Seventies
Common terms (for others see glossary)
Afro hairdo
braless look
caftan
flower children
hot pants
Levis
maxi coat
midi skirt
mini skirt
mod clothing
moon girl style
Nehru jacket
Op Art
pants suits
poncho
Pop art
punk
Sassoon cut
trouser suits
turtleneck
Velcro
vinyl
Recommended sources
Colton (background)
Esquire
Good Housekeeping
Harper's Bazaar
Connoisseur
Illustrated London News
The Studio
In Vogue
Ladies' Home Journal
Sears Roebuck Catalog
This Fabulous Century (8)
Vingt Ans
Vogue
Newspaper photographs, magazine illustrations, drawings, fashion plates, catalogues
Useful illustrators and painters: Peter Max, Lichtenstein, Warhol, Wyeth, Bacon

ca. 1968

Typical Figures

Glossary of Terms
Relating to the History of Costume

PREHISTORIC
(ca. 600,000–50 B.C.)

Mesolithic: The scientific name for the transitional age between the Old and the New Stone Ages.

Neolithic: The scientific name for the New Stone Age, in which humans settled down in tribes, cultivated the land, and domesticated animals.

Paleolithic: The scientific name given to the Old Stone Age, when people were nomadic hunters.

Plastron: The name given to a leather, metal, or ornamental piece laced to the front of a woman's tunic or bodice.

Sagum: A coarse woolen cloak worn by Iron Age Britons.

EGYPTIAN
(ca. 2980–332 B.C.)

Ankh: A decorative piece symbolizing life, in the shape of a cross and appearing on the crown or carried in the hand.

As: Prince's Lock, which hung down one side of the head.

Crook and Flail: Symbols of the Pharaoh were a crook, originally the boomerang, a flail with three lashes, and a tall animal-headed staff.

Henna: Hand and nail dye, from a shrub or tree whose leaves give a red-orange dye.

Horus Lock: A braid of false hair worn behind the right ear by fashionable women.

Kalisiris: A tightly molded body-fitting sheath or tunic that stopped underneath the bosom when worn by women.

Kilt: Pleated wraparound skirt worn by men.

King's Apron: A colored triangular apron worn by the Pharaoh; usually carefully decorated.

Klaft: A kerchief that wrapped around the front of the head and fastened at the back of the neck, usually horizontally striped. Later, it was cut away so that it fit over the shoulder, and was decorated heavily with beads and trim.

Kohl: A black cosmetic substance used in Egyptian makeup for eyes and eyebrows.

Menyet: A necklace composed of a hank of green beads, balanced by a gold plaque of equal weight at the other end, which could be carried and waved during religious ceremonies.

Mitre of Osiris: The white crown of the South, or Upper Egypt. Also called *Atef.*

Pectoral: A trapezoidal-shaped piece of metal jewelry worn about the neck by nobility.

Postiche: False beard, made of leather, felt, or metal. Reserved for royalty.

Pschent: The red crown of Lower Egypt, worn on the white crown when the two kingdoms of Egypt united.

Sacred Uraeus (Asp): Crowns were often decorated with the uraeus, a rearing viper, the symbol of royalty.

Schenti: A loin cloth; a rectangular piece tied in front in a knot and made of linen.

Stibium: A mixture used for staining eyelids and eyebrows.

Vulture Headdress: A headdress reserved for royalty, symbolic of Maati, Goddess of Truth.

Was and Tsam: Two staffs or scepters, carried by dignitaries to signify support of heaven. Was—straight; Tsam—wavy.

MESOPOTAMIAN
(3400–331 B.C.)

Aba: A robe resembling Egyptian or Persian garments, still worn in Palestine today. Folded rectangle, left unseamed at the sides and held in place by cords under each arm. A garment of virtually the same shape, seamed at the sides and open up the front, was put on like a coat.

Breastplate of Judgment: A 9-inch rectangle, doubled over to form a 4½-inch pocket, ornamented with four rows of jewels, three in a row, which stood for the twelve tribes of Israel.

Caftan: A close-sleeved, long-skirted tunic, trimmed with fringe or tassels on the edges.

Candys (Kandis): A long, flowing cloth gown, looped up to a belt at the sides; with or without voluminous sleeves, widening from shoulder to cuff as the garment itself widened from shoulder to hem; worn by the Persian King.

Catogan: Male or female hair, arranged in a ball at the nape of the neck, sometimes decorated with pins and bands. The hair was often looped or braided.

Ephod: A kind of scapular (two rectangles about 30 inches by 10 inches, fastened together by shoulder straps about 10 inches long), worn on top of the robe. Attached to it was a girdle like that of the Levites, wrapped around the waist and tied in front.

Kaunakes: A long, shaggy skirt, probably closed in front. It was made of hanks of wool fastened in horizontal lines like coarse fringe on cloth, or perhaps twisted locks of wool still fastened to the hide. Sometimes it covered the left shoulder.

Kidaris: Ribbed tiara or embroidered hat, worn by a king.

Kilt: A short wraparound skirt, made of strings or grass; worn by fishermen for protection.

Kulah: High, cylindrical felt hat.

Kyrbasia: A hat similar to the Phrygian bonnet, worn in the Persian Empire. It also included Median caps with a soft, high crown that fell forward; usually there were flaps at the neck and at either side that could be fastened under the chin.

Petasos: A brimmed sun hat or traveling hat.

Phrygian Bonnet: A segmented conical casque or hat worn by heavily armed Parthian and Sarmathian cavalry.

Phylacteries: Small leather boxes containing sacred texts written on parchment; they are attached to long leather bands that are bound around the forehead and left arm by devout Jewish men during prayer. Hebrew name *tefillin*.

Tiara: A king's headdress—a truncated conical shape of white felt with a spiked top and purple infulae (two narrow tabs hanging almost to the waist in back).

Tyrian Purple: Purple dye, made from a sea creature, the murex; very rare and very expensive, originally manufactured in the Phoenician city of Tyre. Color most probably a blue-red, a rich plum, or garnet.

GREEK
(2800–146 B.C.)

Aegis: Animal skin worn with a slit for the head, with the head of the animal, usually a goat, on the breast.

Ampyz: A diadem, female headdress.

Apodesme: Bands of leather used as a brassiere.

Apotygma: The overfold of the Doric chiton or peplos.

Boss: Point on shields and knees (armor).

Buskins: Commoners had feet or legs bound or swathed in skin or cloth, called buskins.

Carabitina: A sandal with a large toe, worn by peasants.

Causia: A Thessalonian traveling hat for men or women, worn also by actors to indicate an arduous journey.

Ceryphalos: Bandage-shaped fillet that fitted snugly about the head.

Chlamydon: Short wrap, pleated over a band, that ran from the right shoulder under the left arm. Mainly for women.

Chlamys: A woolen rectangle smaller than the himation, of Macedonian or Italian origin; sometimes bordered, pinned at right shoulder or front; worn with a short chiton or alone, by younger, more active men.

Chloene: Like the chlamys, of coarse wool, worn hooked on one shoulder, running below the other breast; often folded over before fastening; originated in Macedonia or Thessaly.

Cothurnus: Boots to midleg, with platform soles, worn by tragic actors.

Diplax: The female equivalent of the chloene.

Doric Chiton or Peplos: A garment worn by all Greek women after the sixth century B.C. It was of wool dyed indigo, madder, or saffron, frequently patterned, especially at the turn of the fifth century; used also as a blanket. Its upper edge was folded over to hang down on the breast; it was folded around the body, caught together on each shoulder by pins, leaving the arms uncovered, and though open down the right side, was held in place by the girdle, over which it bloused. In Corinth and Attica it was sewn together down the side below the waistline. With time, the garment grew wider and the overfold deepened so that it was included in the girdling or hung over and concealed the girdle. When not girded, the overfold could be raised over the head in back as a shawl.

Exomia: An intermediate form of sleeveless chiton, caught on one shoulder, worn by athletes and workmen; often of sheepskin or leather.

Fibula: Pin or brooch of ancient Greece and Rome that resembled in form the modern safety pin. Often richly decorated.

Fillet: Piece of fabric bound around the head, as a sweatband.

Himation: A rectangle of wool with weighted corners, slung over the left shoulder, leaving the right arm free; or worn by married women with the corner over the head like a shawl. Dorian men wore it as their only garment (as did the Athenians in their return to an earlier simplicity, in the third to the second century B.C.). A man wearing the himation alone was always adequately dressed. It served also as a blanket. The colors were gamut (natural wool colors), white, natural, brown, and black, or dyed scarlet, crimson, and purple; woven patterns, selvages, and embroidery were also used.

Ionic Chiton: Of Phoenician origin. It was worn first by men, later by women. It was made of thin woolens, probably crepe-like, similar to materials still woven in Greece; also of linen, or the gauzy materials from Cos in Asia Minor, patterned in murex (Tyrian) purple. It was cut with ample width from two pieces, then sewn together, frequently pleated, and was long, sometimes trailing. It was often sewn or caught together all the way down the arm, into the equivalent of sleeves, and sewn up the right side. It was worn in a number of ways by both men and women. The chiton was often worn with a short wrap, the chlamydon.

Kolobus: Another form of chiton, which came into use around the beginning of the fourth century B.C. In shape it was two pieces of fabric, cut square and sewn together on the shoulders, leaving an opening in the middle for the head, and sewn down the sides with sufficient space left at the top for the arms to pass through. When the kolobus was girded at the waist, it had very much the same appearance as the chiton, the difference being that the arms emerged at the top edge of the chiton and at the side edge of the kolobus.

Kolpos: The bloused part of the chiton, made by pulling up the chiton over the girdle to make it the proper length from the ground.

Nimbus: A linen headband embroidered with gold.

Peplos: The Archaic name for the Doric chiton.

Petasos: Wide-brimmed traveling hat, worn also by peasants and shepherds.

Pharos: Linen equivalent of the himation, worn only by nobles on special occasions.

Phrygian Bonnet: See *Mesopotamian.* Shows Scythian, Persian influence.

Pilos: Cape worn by workmen, shepherds, sailors.

Saccus: A completely enveloping form of hair binding.

Soccus: Comic actor's boot.

Sphendone: A felt, leather, or metal sling, holding up the hair.

Stephanie: A tiara-like crown worn as a headdress by women.

Strophion: A type of corset made of linen, wool, or soft skin, consisting of shoulder straps and three supporting bands, one for the bust, one for the waist, and one for the hips.

Tellex: Hair binding for athletes; refers to segmented windings around the hair, which was clubbed at the neck. Also called *Cricket.*

Tribon: A small oblong cloak of Balkan origin, worn by Spartan males over the age of twelve as the only garment.

ROMAN
(753 B.C.–323 A.D.)

Abolla: A Roman military cloak similar to the Greek *chlamys.*

Balteus: A form of baldric or sash that went over one shoulder and down to the waist on the opposite side.

Bracchae or Braeis: Northern English breeches, tied with strings, worn by Roman provincial soldiers.

Bulla: Medallion put around a male child's neck to ward off evil until he became an adult.

Byrrus or Birrus: A heavy woolen cloak with a cowl.

Calcaeus: Strapped, cut-out, and laced sandals, varying in height from ankle to well up the calf. Senators wore black, patricians and magistrates wore purple.

Caligula: Heavy, often hobnailed, military boots, rising well up on the leg.

Chlamys: Semicircular cape, hung over the left arm and fastened by a fibula or clasp at the right shoulder. It continued for many centuries as the outer garment for the upper classes of Western Europe.

Clavi: Purple bands on the tunica indicating the wearer's rank. With time, the clavus lost distinction, and by the first century it was worn by everyone. The clavi then became more elaborately decorative in character, broken into spots of decoration and amalgamated with borders at the hem of the garment. *Augustus Clavus:* For equestrian knights; narrow bands running up over each shoulder and down to the hem or tunic or ungirded dalmatic. *Latus Clavus:* Single wide clavus worn by senators down the center of the tunica.

Colobium: The Greek kolobus. It was like the tunica although sleeveless. When more than one tunica was worn, the undertunic was called the tunica interior or subucula.

Crepida: Half-shoes, soles to which a piece of leather or fabric was attached to enclose the heel and sides of the foot. Fastened across the instep by straps or bands laced through eyelet holes set in the sides.

Cuculla: An overdress without sleeves, practically an oblong piece of cloth with a hole in the middle for the head. Used by all classes as a protection from weather and when traveling. Later prescribed for monks of the Benedictine order. (About 1500, given the name of scapular as an ecclesiastical garment.)

Dalmatica: An outer garment, originally for males. Introduced ca. 190 A.D. from Dalmatia. Prominent in Rome by the third century A.D., it was cut like a tunic, but wider, with wide sleeves to the forearm. It went on over the head, was worn without a girdle, and was characteristically decorated by the clavus.

Feminalia: Knee-length breeches for men.

Fibula: See *Greek.*

Flameum: Veil of the Roman matron.

Lacerna: Cloak similar to the chlamys, but light and short, worn by everyone in the last century of the Republic. Even senators wore it, in place of the toga, although this was frowned upon.

Lorica: A cuirass of brass or bronze, molded to the shape of the body with perfect fit and following the line of the abdomen. Frequently enriched with reliefs and ornaments in metal work.

Mappa: Napkin used at table before and after meals for wiping the mouth and hands after washing in a basin brought by a slave.

Orarium: Large napkin, carried by servants and slaves over the left shoulder and used for cleaning vessels of all sorts.

Paenula: A hooded, bell-shaped, weatherproof garment of leather or wool. It was already in use by the Etruscans in the fourth century B.C. It was worn by everyone, civil and military, particularly by centurions.

Pallium (Palla, f.): Roman outdoor garment that could also be used as a bed covering. It was originally Greek, and in Rome it was draped like a Greek himation, held by a fibula, not hooked as in Greece. It was a rectangle as wide as from the wearer's shoulder to the floor, about three times as long, and was worn by men, women, children, civil servants, and military. Women wore the palla outdoors, often draped over the head but always in conjunction with a veil or cap. The pallium was the characteristic garment of the scholar and philosopher (as the sole garment, it was the conventional mantle of Christ).

Paludamentum: A purely military mantle, used as the official military mantle of the general in command, or the Emperor while in the field. Used particularly in the earlier years, before the first century A.D. In cut, it resembled the chlamys or lacerna, with two corners truncated to form an elongated, primitive semicircle.

Sagum: Gallic in origin. Became the military wrap of the Roman army, used also as a blanket. Generals wore it in red and purple. "Putting on the sagum" was the equivalent of declaring war. Square in shape, of thick, heavy, tightly woven wool.

Sapparum: A shawl for women.

Sinus: That part of the toga draped over the head for religious ceremonies.

Solea: Strapped slippers, like sandals.

Stola: Woman's garment. Worn over the tunica interior (which was of similar cut, might or might not have sleeves, and which served as a house dress). The stola had sleeves like the men's tunica, or was pinned along the shoulder line and down the arms. It was girded once under the breast and often girded again at the hips.

Sublagaculum: Small garment or piece of cloth, worn bound around the hips as a loin cloth. This was worn under the toga, or frequently without any other covering. It was a fashion copied from the Greeks, who themselves derived it from the Egyptians and Assyrians.

Sudarium: Small piece of fine linen, often embroidered with silk or gold and equivalent to the modern handkerchief.

Tebenna: The cloak of the ancient Etruscan man; it was usually semicircular and thus became the basis for the later Roman *toga.*

Toga: General: Outergarment; the badge of the Roman citizen, rich or poor. Originally, the rectangular Greek pallium made into an ellipse, the draping of which was infinitely complicated. Of wool, it was characteristically a bleached white.

    Toga Candida: Worn plain by candidates for public office.

    Toga Picta: Purple embroidered official robe of the Emperor, worn over the tunica palmata; in the second century A.D., became part of the official garb of Roman consuls. Essentially a ceremonial dress, it constituted the correct costume of the court during the whole of the Empire period, until the center of government was transferred to Constantinople, where it was superseded by the paludamentum. From the toga picta all imperial and regal robes have descended.

Toga Praetexta: Had a purple hem; worn by senators, certain officials, and priests.

Toga Pulla: Black, worn as a mourning robe, or for sacrifices; of darker colored wools, worn draped over the head.

Toga Pura: Natural-colored wool, not a bleached white; worn by the Roman citizen.

Toga Trabea: Worn by the equestrian knights, small toga striped in scarlet; basically white for soldiers.

Toga Umbo or Contabulatum: The ordinary toga, with a red or purple band, draped so that a pocket or pouch was formed. Came into fashion among high dignitaries toward the end of the second century A.D.

Toga Virilis: An all-white toga, worn by young males, fourteen to sixteen years of age.

Tunica: Wide, shirt-like undergarment, the indoor dress of the Roman; worn outdoors without the toga only by working people. It was not, like the toga, distinctly Roman. Originally sleeveless and woolen, usually white, it acquired sleeves and was later made of linen and cotton as well. The tunica was girded with meticulous care to the exact length considered correct for the rank and sex of the wearer.

Tunica Alba: Bleached white tunic later transformed into the clerical *alb*.

Tunica Interior or Subucula: Woolen undertunic worn beneath the regular tunic.

Tunica Palmata: Part of the official garb of emperors. With the toga picta, it constituted part of the ornamenta triumphalia. Decorated richly and elaborately with gold embroideries of conventional foliage. It was also usual to have the tunica embroidered all over with the same design as that used on the toga picta, in circular, square, and lozenge-shaped motifs, with a border at the neck, wrists, and bottom.

Tunica Talaris: Fell to the feet and had long, loose sleeves; it was the marriage dress for men, but was looked down upon by the citizens of Rome and did not compete with the short tunic until the fourth century A.D.

Tutulus: A stiff, pointed Etruscan headdress for women with a tiara-like brim.

EARLY CHRISTIAN AND BYZANTINE (323–1453 A.D.)

Alb: A liturgical vestment of the Catholic church; derived from the tunica alba, which passed out of Roman civil use in the sixth century. Of white linen, narrow-sleeved; slit for the head to pass through, and girded to clear the ground. Worn over the cassock and under other liturgical garments.

Amice: The first liturgical vestment to be assumed by the priest vesting himself for Mass. Developed out of the Roman neckcloth, it is a strip of linen laid hood-like over the head, dropped to the shoulders, and tied in position around the upper body with tapes sewed to two corners, forming a collar.

Bracco or Braies: Semiclose-fitting leg covering sometimes worn over hose; used with or without cross gartering.

Camisa or Chemise: An undergarment with long sleeves that showed beneath the sleeves of the outergarment for women.

Cassock: Originally derived from the daily wear of the dignified and elderly, it was retained by the Catholic church after the change in lay fashions in the seventh and eighth centuries. It is now the ordinary dress of the Roman Catholic and, to a more limited extent, the Church of England clergy; eucharistic and processional vestments and monastic habits are superimposed on it. Its color is black, purple, red, or white, all of which indicate rank: priest, bishop, cardinal, or pope. Monks' cassocks are the color of the order.

Chasuble: One of the most important liturgical garments of the Catholic church. Its shape has varied by period and country, but it is essentially a cape of silk or metallic cloth (never linen or cotton), with a hole for the head, shortened at the sides to the shoulder to leave the arms uncovered, and falling down the front and back. Derived from the Roman paenula or casula, it was originally a garment worn by barbarians to ward off bad weather.

Colobium: A garment similar to the Greek kolobus; made of linen or wool and sewn on the sides and at the shoulder if not woven all in one piece.

Cope: A liturgical vestment of the Catholic church and a choir vestment of some Anglican churches; it is a semicircular cape embroidered or brocaded and fastened across the chest by a wide ornamental band. This is sewn to one edge and hooked or pinned by a jeweled morse to the other. It has a vestigial hood or embroidered flap hanging down the back. It usually substitutes for the chasuble in all ceremonies aside from the Mass.

Dalmatic: A knee-length, wide-sleeved gown slit up the sides, it derives from the Roman dalmatica and is decorated with two vertical stripes over the shoulder to the hem—taken from the augustus clavus of Roman dress. The dalmatic of a bishop is fringed on both sides and sleeves, and that of a deacon is fringed on the left side and left sleeve only. Since the fourth century, the dalmatic has been a vestment worn as a festal garment during Mass, benedictions, and processions. It can be worn under the chasuble, never under the cope.

Dalmatica: One of the most important garments of the Byzantine Empire, it had the same general wide-sleeved shape as in Roman days but with far more embroidery and decoration.

Hosa: A close-fitting covering for the leg.

Lorum: A long, narrow scarf originating from the pallium and worn with Byzantine court costume from the eighth to the twelfth centuries.

Maniple: A narrow strip of silk three feet long, decorated with three crosses hung or fastened over the left forearm. It is one of four distinctly Roman contributions to liturgical costume, originally a linen handkerchief or cloth derived from the folded consular mappula. It is part of liturgical vestments of all orders above subdeacon.

Mitre: A liturgical headdress of the Catholic church specifically worn by bishops but occasionally worn by abbots and other church dignitaries. It is a high hat composed of two identical stiffened pieces that fold flat against each other when not spread horn-like around the head; from the back hang two narrow fringed strips. It seems to have developed out of the cone-shaped caps of the early popes, which in turn may relate back to the mitres of the Hebrews.

Orb: A celestial sphere usually topped with a cross, carried by the emperor and empress.

Orphreys or Apparels: Embroidered squares and bands used on the ecclesiastical *alb, dalmatic,* and *chasuble.*

Paenula: A hooded, bell-shaped, weatherproof garment of wool or leather. In the fourth century B.C. it was gradually transformed into the chasuble.

Pallium: A vestment worn by Catholic archbishops, it is a woven band of white lamb's wool "three fingers broad," worn over the chasuble. Derived from the Roman pallium, it was originally a longer strip draped over both shoulders and pinned to the left one; now it is a strip decorated with four crosses and made into a circle, which is dropped on the shoulders and pinned front and back.

Paludamentum: The Roman general's cloak became a half-circular imperial mantle of rich material, often of purple silk embroidered in gold or gold and jewels.

Pastoral Staff: A five-foot staff that is the insignia for cardinals, bishops, and abbots of the Catholic church. Heads were originally of four kinds: shepherd's crook, the knobbed crook, the bent crook, and the cross or crozier top. Today, either the crozier or the pastoral shepherd's crook is seen.

Pedule: Short hose usually turned down at the knee.

Sarcenet: A fine, thin silk cloth originating in the Orient and named from the Saracen.

Segmentae: Embroidered circular decorations worn on the sleeve of a tunica or dalmatica.

Stole: A liturgical vestment of the Catholic church for Mass, never for processional use. It is a long strip of material, usually silk, now decorated by three crosses at the ends and middle, and frayed at the hem. It is worn over the shoulder in different ways and is characteristic of deacon, priest, or bishop. It probably descended from the *orarion,* adopted by the Emperor Aurelian in the third century to be waved in applause at games.

Sudarium: A handkerchief, often embroidered with silver or gold.

Superhumeral: A jeweled collar, usually worn by the empress or ladies of the court.

Surplice: Originally, as the Latin name indicates, it was worn over fur-lined garments. Made of white linen like the alb, it was initially long, then became much shorter after the thirteenth century. It is usually trimmed in lace or embroidery.

Tablion: The very elaborate oblong decoration embroidered in red and gold on the back and front of the imperial mantle. For other high officials and courtiers it varied in color.

Tunicle: A garment peculiar to deacons at Mass; bishops wear it under the dalmatic, but always under the chasuble, never under the cope. It is basically a plainer, narrower-sleeved dalmatic without clavi and usually fringed.

BARBARIC, CAROLINGIAN, AND ROMANESQUE
(400–1150 A.D.)

Amusse: A hood with a small cape worn by monks and the nobility.

Barbe or Barbette: A piece of linen, often pleated, worn under the chin, especially by a widow or a person in mourning.

Beguin, Biggon, or Biggin: A head covering for men and women, worn from the twelfth century into the Renaissance. It was worn in Byzantine times by the Beguines, a religious order of women, and the name remained. It was a three-piece cap made of linen for aristocrats, coarse wool for commoners, and leather for underhelmets for soldiers. It was also worn under crowns, by nobles under hats, and by the clergy. It is a close relation of the *coif* (see *Early and High Gothic*).

Bliaut: A garment worn by men and women, it originated about 1130 in the East and was brought to Europe with the end of the First Crusade. As worn by the upper classes at the end of the twelfth century, it consisted of a snug-fitting torso, often wide embroidered sleeves, a low skirt pulled into elegant pleats across the hips, and snug lacing up the back or under each arm. It is one of the first garments to depend on a fitted torso line for its effect.

Broigne: A metal cuirass from the time of Charlemagne.

Cagoule: A semicircular cape of cloth or fur, with a hood; usually worn by peasants.

Cainsil or Chainsil: A very fine, lightweight or heavyweight cloth of simple weave.

Capuchon: A hood usually attached to a cape, often with a long tail later known as a liripipe.

Caul: Close-fitting gold hairnet worn by ladies of the aristocracy.

Chainse: A body garment for men and women that later developed into the shirt or chemise. It was made of hemp, linen, wool, and sometimes silk, with the fabric varying according to the wearer's station in society.

Chape: Similar to the mantle, sometimes slit at the sides, with cap-like or long, loose sleeves.

Chaplet: A headband of gold or silver filigree, set with jewels, flowers, or leaves.

Chausses: Leg coverings of cloth, shaped and sewn to fit.

Chemise: A long feminine undergarment with tight sleeves and a skirt frequently showing from beneath the underdress.

Corsage: A tight-fitting, sleeveless jacket resembling a corset, worn over the bliaut.

Corse: A tight-fitting, sleeveless jacket of leather or metal disks laced up the front and worn under a man's tunic or bliaut.

Cote, Cotte, or Cotta: A long tunic with the sleeve cut in one piece with the garment. The length varied from the calf to the instep.

Couvrechef: A woman's veil.

Crispine or Crispinette: A headdress of gold net and pearls.

Diaper: Silk, linen, or cotton cloth of one color woven in a sprinkled ornamental pattern.

Fibula: The heavy metal or jewel-encrusted brooch used to fasten the mantle at the shoulder.

Girdle: A type of waistband or belt that encircles the hips.

Gorget: A wimple or couvrechef worn under the chin and tucked under the neckline of the gown.

Gown: A "gunn" (from the Anglo-Saxon) was a tunic for women somewhat like the Roman and Byzantine stola.

Guimpe: A chemise worn with a low-cut dress.

Gypsire: A pouch or bag worn at the hip from which alms were given.

Hauberk: A coat of chain or linked mail used as body armor.

Head Rail: A colorful rectangular veil draped over the head and shoulder from left to right, passed around the neck and tied under the chin.

Heaume: A military helmet from the time of Charlemagne.

Jube or Jupe: An undergarment or shirt, sometimes fur-lined; worn by both men and women.

Kirtle: Anglo-Saxon for tunic.

Liripipe: The long, pointed tail on a hood.

Mantle: A half-circular cape, usually fastened on the right shoulder.

Rheno: A mantle without a hood.

Sherte: A straight, knee-length garment with slits at front, back, and sides, resembling a modern shirt.

Smock: Innermost garment of fine linen worn by women.

Surcote or Surcoat: A loose, lightweight garment originally worn by crusaders over their armor as a protection against the sun. It soon became an overtunic worn over the cote, sometimes unseamed, sometimes sleeveless, sometimes with wide-open sleeves like a dalmatic. It could be belted or unbelted, and the length varied from the knee to the ankle.

Torque: A neckband or armband, usually of gold or bronze, worn by the ancient Gauls, Britons, and Germans. It was a twisted spiral of metal shaped into a hoop and open at the ends, which were crafted into knobs or serpent's heads. When taken as spoils by the Romans, these *torques* were awarded to soldiers as a symbol of their valor.

Wimple: See *Early and High Gothic.*

EARLY AND HIGH GOTHIC (1144–1325)

Aglet, Aiglet, Point, or Poynt: A metal tag or point used to fasten pieces of plate armor, or various parts of other garments such as sleeves and paltock.

Bateau Neckline: A boat-shaped neckline.

Button: A solid, dome-shaped top, with an eye at the base, used as trimming at the beginning of the Middle Ages; used as a fastening with buttonholes from the middle of the thirteenth century on.

Castellated, Dagged, or Foliated: Deep-cut scallops at the hem or other edges of a garment, shaped in triangles, half-circles, squares, or leaf-like foliations.

Coif: A close-fitting cap of silk, linen, or cotton, tied under the chin. A circlet or band of jewels might be worn over the coif by royalty.

Cointise or Quintise: Cut-out decoration of the cyclas; also applied to a garment so decorated.

Coronet: An ornamental circlet worn about the head.

Cotehardie: A shaped garment, tight-fitting around the shoulders, waist, and hips. When worn by a woman it had a circular skirt; when worn by a man it usually ended at the hips or slightly below, often with dagged or scalloped edges. It could be hooked or laced up either the front or the back.

Couvrechef: See *Wimple.*

Cyclas: An overgarment cut from a single piece of cloth, with a hole in the center for the head, sometimes lined with fur or silk.

Doublet: See *Middle Gothic.*

Emblem or Badge: The distinguishing symbol worn by crusaders; the various emblems developed into the system of heraldry.

Ganache or Garnache: A surcoat or robe with short, caped sleeves, worn for extra warmth.

Gardcorp: A surcoat or robe with hanging sleeves slit to allow the arms to pass through.

Gorget: See *Barbaric, Carolingian, and Romanesque.*

Gueules: A small, fur-lined shoulder cape with the lower corners of the cape turned back in front; it was usually attached to the peliçon.

Herlot or Lachet: A string used to tie the hose to the paltock or the sleeve to the armhole of the paltock.

Jupe: See *Middle Gothic.*

Paltock: A short jacket to which undersleeves and hose were attached; later called pourpoint.

Particolored or Pied: A two-colored garment, often with one side embroidered.

Passemente: Gold, silver, and colored braid.

Peliçon: Any fur-lined garment of robe length.

Plastron: A type of garment that later became the stomacher. It was most frequently of fur and was worn as a decorative front to a female costume.

Surcote: See *Barbaric, Carolingian, and Romanesque.*

Toque: A pillbox-shaped headdress worn by women in the thirteenth century, attached either to a barbe or barbette, or worn with a caul or crispinette.

Wimple or Couvrechef: A fine silk or linen covering for the head, usually brought under the chin and pinned to the gown and to the head; frequently worn with a separate gorget under the chin.

MIDDLE GOTHIC (1325–1425)

Bacinet or Basinet: A light helmet made of a single piece of steel with a conical shape. It was usually worn over a chain-mail hood.

Barbute: A helmet of fourteenth century Italian origin that first had a high pointed crown and later a round one. Its large cheek pieces almost completely covered the face.

Bellows or Bagpipe Sleeve: A gathered sleeve with a cuff and a long vertical slit through which the hand could pass.

Capuchon: See *Barbaric, Carolingian, and Romanesque.*

Castellations: Square or rectangular dagges or cuts in the hem or edge of a garment; named after the wall tops of castles.

Caul: See *Barbaric, Carolingian, and Romanesque.*

Chaperon: A caped hood with long liripipe, worn with the face opening around the head and the tail or liripipe wound about the head and then draped under the chin.

Coif: See *Early and High Gothic.*

Corset: A fitted garment worn over the chemise with skirt attached and usually laced up the front.

Courtepy or Jacquette: A very short overgarment or cotehardie, often particolored or embroidered with gems. It usually had a high collar.

Cracow or Poulaine: A long-tipped hose and shoe introduced during the reign of Richard II and named after the city of Cracow in Poland; later the length of the toe became so long that it had to be tied to the knee.

Dagged: Edges of garments cut in tooth patterns.

Doublet or Doblet: A short jacket or variety of pourpoint, sleeved or sleeveless, worn under a close-fitting pourpoint. When used as an outer garment it was padded and had a short skirt.

Foliated: Edges of garments cut in a leaf pattern.

Galoche: A wooden platform with an ornamental strap fastening the base beneath the heel and ball of the foot; elevated to varying heights.

Hennin or Cornet: A truncated cone or steeple headdress with veil completely covering a woman's hairdo.

Houppelande: A loose and comfortable gown of great size introduced during the reign of Charles VI in France that became very fashionable during the reign of Richard II in England. One style worn by men had long, flowing, bell-shaped sleeves, a long, fitted waist, and a floor-length skirt slit to the knees; another style, known as the "bastard houppelande," was only knee to calf length. A high standing collar was usually part of this flamboyant costume. The woman's version of this robe had a soft, open collar, a short waist, a full skirt, and long, flowing sleeves.

Journade: A short, circular garment that at first had large, full sleeves and later had long, slit sleeves. It was often worn for riding.

Jupe: A form of shirt or undertunic, sometimes furlined; worn by both men and women.

Jupon: An overgarment having armorial blazonry, worn over armor in the fourteenth century; the term sometimes was also used to refer to a petticoat.

Liripipe: See *Barbaric, Carolingian, and Romanesque.*

Mahoitres: The name given to the shoulder padding of a gown or jacket.

Particolored: See *Early and High Gothic.*

Patten: Iron support worn under a shoe.

Plastron: A stomacher-shaped appendage, usually of fur or embroidered fabric, worn at the front of the sideless gown as both support and decoration.

Pomander: A ball or hollow ornament, often made of filigree, containing a sponge of perfume suspended from a necklace or a girdle.

Pourpoint: A short jacket with tight sleeves buttoned from elbow to wrist, worn under the cotehardie and formerly known as a paltock.

Reticulated Headdress: Headdress with decorative metal cages that confined the hair at the side of a woman's head.

Roundlet: A headdress made of a doughnut-shaped roll of material with a scarf or liripipe hanging down one side and draped over the shoulder.

Sideless Gown: A woman's overgown cut away at the sides from under the arms to the hips to show the cotehardie or kirtle underneath; it was usually worn with a plastron at the front of the figure.

Tippet: A band sewn around the elbow of the sleeve with the end hanging as a streamer.

Tressure or Tressour (also referred to as *caul, crepine, crestine,* and *crispinette*): A woman's medieval headdress in which the hair was concealed in two silken, half-spherical cases on either side of the head and covered with a heavy net of reticulated gold or silver cord interspersed with pearls and beads.

Tussoire: A chain and clasp that hung from the girdle and held up one side of a long skirt.

LATE GOTHIC AND EARLY ITALIAN RENAISSANCE (1425–1485)

Bag Cap: A cloth or velvet brimless cap with fur band and ornament that resembled a turban.

Bevor or Beaver: A movable face piece of armor attached to helmets in the fifteenth and sixteenth centuries. When lowered it protected the face from swords and lances.

Biliment: An elaborate women's headdress of the late fifteenth and early sixteenth centuries of gold-threaded lace worked with beads, jewels, ribbons, gauze, and sometimes a feather. Usually seen in Italy.

Biretta: A stiff, square cap with three or four points projecting from the crown. It was worn by the clergy as well as by academics. Today birettas are worn in purple by bishops, red by cardinals, and black by priests on informal occasions.

Brigandine: A sleeveless, armored jacket of overlapping metal plates or scales sewn to linen, leather, or canvas, fitting to the waist with a short peplum below the waist.

Butterfly Headdress: Made of semitransparent linen, it was draped and wired to resemble a butterfly and was worn over a tall hennin.

Cracowe or Poulaine: See *Middle Gothic.*

Escarelle: A pouch or purse, attached to the waist on a hip belt, into which a knife was frequently inserted.

Escoffion: A tall, richly brocaded headdress, sometimes shaped like two horns, sometimes like a narrow, tall turban; it usually had a veil of fine lawn about a yard wide.

Hennin: See *Middle Gothic.*

Houppelande: See *Middle Gothic.*

Journade: See *Middle Gothic.*

Kirtle: A dress that evolved from the cotehardie after 1450. It was close-fitting at the shoulder, waist, and hip and had a very full skirt. The neckline, edged in fur, velvet, or brocade, was very low in front, on the shoulders, and in the back.

Liripipe: Still retained from the chaperon as a tail of material coming from the doughnut shape of the roundlet, draping under the chin and over one shoulder.

Plastron: See *Middle Gothic.*

Pourpoint: The name usually given to the short, fitted jacket with a pleated skirt during this period. Sleeves were either full at the top and tapering to the wrists, open and hanging behind a tight undersleeve, or slashed to allow the arm to come through.

Roundlet: The doughnut-shaped, turban-like headdress worn by most men of fashion until the latter part of the fifteenth century.

Sideless Gown: This gown, cut away under the arms to the hips, was usually covered with armorial bearings and remained the ceremonial dress for women during this period.

RENAISSANCE
(1485–1520)

Barret: A flat Spanish cap of gorgeous material that was slashed, puffed, and embroidered.

Bases: Sixteenth-century cartridge-pleated skirts for men, worn separate from the doublet. To be noted in many portraits of Henry VIII.

Breeches or Hosen: Leg coverings, either cut from fabric or knitted, all in one piece.

Calotte: A cape or coat, usually of expensive material, over which the barret was worn.

Caul: Developed from the crispinette. A meshwork covering for the hair, sometimes edged with jewels in a border.

Clog, Chopine, or Patten: A wooden-soled platform attached to the shoe, worn as a protection from mud and to gain height.

Codpiece: A pouch-like appendage made from the same fabric as the jerkin or upper stocks and fastened by ties or buckles as a decorative covering for the opening in the front of breeches.

Jerkin: A short velvet or leather jacket, usually sleeveless.

Kirtle: See *Late Gothic and Early Renaissance.*

Little Hennin: A headdress shaped like a truncated cone.

Mancheron: A false, hanging sleeve.

Pantoffle: A mule or slipper with a cork sole, worn as a protection for the shoe.

Points: Metal-tipped ribbons or lacings sewn in corresponding pairs to sleeves and armseyes or to doublet and hose.

Simarre: A robe for men, derived from chimer or chimere, an ecclesiastical garment very much like it in shape. The neck part is shaped somewhat on a double-breasted line with no collar in back, but with wide revers turned back from the front edge of the robe. The robe is worn either ungirded or confined at the waist by a narrow silk scarf, knotted with one loop and two ends.

Slashing (Puffs and Slashes): Vertical, horizontal, or diagonal slits in the fabric of the garment through which appeared a different fabric. Often the shirt was the garment that puffed through.

Solleret: A shoe with a rounded toe.

Tabard: A military tunic with short wing sleeves; usually emblazoned with a coat of arms.

Upper Stocks: See *Early Mannerist Renaissance: trunk hose.*

EARLY MANNERIST RENAISSANCE
(1520–1560)

Barbe or Barbette: Pleated neck and shoulder covering with a hood (or béguin) worn by widows until the time of Catherine de Médicis, when it was replaced by a wired-out hood, dipping low over the forehead or carried out into a beak. For the white mourning of a young queen (i.e., Mary of Scotland), a veiled hood over a wired cap and a pleated barbe under the chin was worn.

Basquine: A fitted restraining underbodice of heavy material used in the late fifteenth century. Origin of the term Basque.

Beefeater's Hat: A black beaver hat with red, black, and white ribbon bows around the crown worn by British Yeomen of the Guard and the Wardens of the Tower of London in the sixteenth century.

Bombast: Stuffing of wool, flax, or hair.

Bongrace or Attifet Headdress: A short headdress of silk, velvet, or chiffon that hung free in back but dipped over the forehead in a peak in the front. It was often finished on the forehead with a single pearl or other jewel.

Braguette: The French word for *codpiece.*

Buckram: A coarse open weave of linen or cotton sized with glue and used as early as the sixteenth century as a stiffening for parts of dress. The name comes from the floor coverings used under fine rugs in Bukhara.

Busk: A rigid piece of wood set in the fake front or stomacher, which gave a straight line effect.

Cale: Bag of black velvet to conceal the hair; for the gable headdress or for the French hood.

Cappa Magna: The long, trailing, luxurious cloak-vestment worn by ecclesiastics on ceremonial occasions. Usually of watered silk, hooded in ermine; worn in red by cardinals, violet by bishops.

Chain or Order: A heavy chain worn by a man as decoration across the chest and neckline that often denoted an order or organization to which the man belonged.

Chamarre: Large, square piece of fabric, slit up the front vertically and into a T-shape to leave a neck opening; a collar was attached to the top of the T-shaped slit and the sides folded back into revers. Worn as a coat and principally a French style.

Cordelière: A long chain, usually of gold, that hung from the girdle.

Duck-Billed or Splay-Footed Shoes: Very wide, square-toed, slipper-like shoes, usually decorated with jewels, puffs, and slashes.

Fall: Like the cale, for the gable headdress, of black silk or velvet.

Farthingale: Hoops of graduated size inserted in a petticoat. Of several types. See *Elizabethan.*

Fraise: A small ruff that edged the standing collar. It is said that Henry II adopted the neckline to hide a scar.

Gable, Kennel, or Pedimental Headdress: Resembled in outline the pediment of a Greek temple. Its essentials were a piece that went over the front part of the head and covered the ears and a veil or bag cap covering the rest of the head; the forehead was covered with rolls or folds of cloth. With the formal styles of this headdress, no hair was visible. There were, however, linen coifs shaped in the same outline that left the parted hair visible on the forehead. The front

roll was of diagonally striped material or velvet. The kennel consisted of a stiff plane covered with rich material, pieces of which extended down the sides and might be pinned back on themselves. The cap at the back, joining the kennel, was like a bag with a square bottom. One side was turned back and pinned to the other at the back of the head. The bag was generally of black velvet.

Lower Stocks or Bas de Chausses: Silk or cloth stockings showing beneath upper stocks or trunk hose.

Mary Stuart Cap: A heart-shaped cap worn by the Scottish queen.

Medici Collar: The lace-edged ruff that opened into a standing fan-shaped frill, high in the back with low decolletage. Accompanied by cuffs to match.

Morion: Brimmed helmet; English, Spanish.

Panes: Loose, vertical bands used on sleeves, doublets, and trunk hose.

Partlet: See *Elizabethan.*

Pomander: A small apple-shaped ball of gold or silver filigree that held ambergris, musk, or other perfumes. It was usually worn suspended by a chain from a lady's girdle, although sometimes it was worn around the neck. Men sometimes carried it in the hand, often hidden in a hollowed-out orange. The pomander was particularly used at outbreaks of the plague to ward off infection.

Shakefold: A stiffened pad on a wire frame, an early form of *farthingale.* The name was given to this part of the garment because it swayed back and forth as the wearer moved.

Simarre or Simarra: A man's long, sumptuous robe of rich brocade that originated in Venice in the early sixteenth century. It flared from neck to floor with wide Dalmatian sleeves and was sometimes worn by ladies of fashion with a long train.

Solleret or Bear's Paw: Italian footwear of the sixteenth century that resembled the long-toed *poulaine* of the fifteenth century. Gradually the point disappeared, and it changed to the square toe with padding that became the standard male shoe shape from 1520 to 1550. The name *bear's paw* was given to the shoes worn by the German mercenary soldiers (Landsknechte) of the period, whereas in England they were called *duckbilled* shoes.

Stomacher: False front or ornamental covering on front of bodice.

Trunk hose, mellon hose, or haut-de-chausses: Upper hose or full trunks that extended from upper thighs to waist.

ELIZABETHAN-JACOBEAN
(LATE MANNERIST RENAISSANCE)
(1560–1620)

Aglet, Aiglet, Point, or Poynt: A metal tag or point used to fasten armor or various parts of other garments, including sleeves and hose to a paltock or underdoublet.

Attifet Coiffure: A heart-shaped style with a point dipping over the forehead, often supporting a cap of heart shape stiffened by a wire frame. The style was first favored by Catherine de Médicis and Mary Queen of Scots and was popular throughout the remainder of the sixteenth century.

Baize: A coarse woolen cloth used for servants' clothes. During the reign of Queen Elizabeth it was made at Colchester, England, but was originally from Baza, Spain.

Baldric: Some kind of band, ribbon, or leather, usually to hold a sword; worn through several centuries. Here, a shoulder sash of satin, the fashion for both men and women; white was reserved for the King.

Basquine: A boned bodice resembling a corset.

Bavolet: A woman's headdress worn by the European middle class and peasants during the sixteenth century. It was a towel-like piece of white linen about 2 yards long and about 18 yards wide with fringed ends, folded and pinned to a cap. Later the deep back ruffle on any bonnet was called by this name.

Bell Farthingale: A skirt shaped like a bell, held out by a hooped petticoat.

Bolster: A doughnut-shaped pad worn at the waist under a petticoat.

Bombast: Padding for shaped breeches, composed of flock, rags, or any other serviceable material. Also used to stuff the peascod belly.

Busk: A rigid piece of wood set in a fake front or stomacher to give a straight line effect.

Canions: Tight knee breeches. The lower edges were covered by the nether stocks or stockings, usually rolled above the knee and secured by garters.

Cartwheel Vertugale or Farthingale: The circular wheel support worn under the full, drum-shaped hoop skirt, also with underskirt.

Chopines: High clogs, worn by Spanish women, serving both to increase their stature and to protect them from the surfaces of dusty roads. They were usually made of cork covered with leather or velvet. They came to Europe from the Middle East by way of Venice.

Codpiece: The stuffed and slashed appendage at the front opening of male hose.

Cross Gartering: Criss-crossed bands, ribbons, or cords tied below the knee.

Doublet: Sleeved, short padded jacket for men, with a pointed waistline.

Falling Band: Wide, flat collar, known as the Louis XIII collar, of sheer white fabric, with or without lace edge. Bands diminished in size from about 1640.

Fers: Metal buttons used by a woman of rank, worn as decoration on costume.

Galligaskins: Loose knee trousers that remained wide and open at the knee.

Gauntlets: Elbow-length gloves of velvet or satin, silk- or gold-fringed, with backs embroidered or sewn with jewels; for courtier wear.

Golilla: The starched, dish-like neckband introduced by Philip IV of Spain. It remained in favor for some fifteen years after his pragmatic of 1623 against the large ruff (gran gola). It was worn usually in conjunction with plain turned-back wristbands.

Jerkin: An outergarment, often of leather, that had a shoulder puff or wing, sometimes hanging sleeves or tied-in sleeves; it was worn over the doublet.

Kirtle: Fundamental woman's garment of the period, often composed of the two separate parts that make up its form—the bodice and the skirt. For most of this period these two elements of the kirtle had emphatically contrasting forms, the bodice tapering to a sharp point at or below the waistline, the skirt in the shape of an upright cone, bell, or drum. The skirt derived its form from the shape of the farthingale.

Mahoîtres: A high, standing, padded sleeve or shoulder puff worn during the late sixteenth century.

Mandilion: A type of tabard (see *Late Gothic*). Worn by common folk in inclement weather since the early Gothic period, but in the later sixteenth century transformed into a straight-hanging, hip-length garment with open hanging sleeves. Worn as servants' livery or as a loose jacket by heralds and soldiers. Also often worn as a kind of cape thrown over the shoulders and fastened with one button or tied across the chest.

Marlotte: A loose-bodied dress robe that many European women wore with slight variations during the late sixteenth century. It was cut in a full funnel shape from neck to floor in rich brocade with a small standing collar and short puffed sleeves. It usually fastened only at the neck and flared out over the extended *farthingale* shape of the undergown.

Medici Collar: This was shaped like the male falling band but was pleated and wired, rising from a low decolletage and standing high at the back of the head. It originated in Italy and was most popularized by Queen Marie de Médicis of France, 1573–1642.

Morion: A helmet that appeared in Europe about the middle of the sixteenth century; it was introduced by the Spaniards who had copied it from the Moors. It was worn by foot soldiers and had a crown shaped like two halves of a shell that met to form a crescent crest at the top. The brim was also in a crescent shape with a great curve like the line of a ship, and articulated earpieces covered the ears.

Mules: Slippers without heels or heel counters worn in the sixteenth century by men and women, often as a second slip-on covering over other footwear in wet weather.

Neck Whisk: A standing, fan-shaped, wired collar for women.

Nether Stocks: Hose that covered the lower leg.

Panes: Strips of fabric that covered trunk hose or puffed sleeves.

Pantofles: Shoes or pumps of crimson, red, or violet velvet, cut in the shape of a lobster tail.

Partlet: A fine linen or lawn insert placed inside a round or square neckline that was gathered into a neckband or drawn closed by a cord.

Peascod: A padded doublet with a front shaped like a peascod.

Picadil: The tabbed finish on the edge of a garment; also a collar support or underprop at tabs.

Plunderhose: Huge German hose bloused to below the knee.

Pumpkin Hose: Padded trunks in the shape of pumpkins.

Round Hose: See *Pumpkin Hose.*

Ruff: A starched figure-eight pleated collar for the neck.

Shoe Roses: Large ribbon ties in the form of rosettes for men's shoes; worn at the buckle, with heeled shoes, during the reign of James I.

Shoulder Wings or Crescents: Decorative pieces extending outward at the shoulder of the doublet.

Slops: Unpadded trunk hose, termed Spanish slops. Very full breeches, bagging at the knees, were termed full slops. Small, very short trunk hose were called pansid slops.

Stomacher: See *Early Mannerist Renaissance.*

Supportasse: See *Underproper.*

Trunkhose: See *Pumpkin Hose.*

Underproper or Rebato: A frame to hold up ornate, starched lace collars.

Venetians: Full, loose breeches without codpieces, fastening below the knee.

Vertugale: Another term for a hooped petticoat or *farthingale.*

Whisk: A starched, flat collar that framed the neck like a dish. Similar to the golilla.

EARLY BAROQUE (CAVALIER) (1620–1660)

Balagnie Cloak: An elegant cloak of the early seventeenth century from the reign of Louis XIII with a deep collar, usually draped over only one shoulder and held in place by cords attached under the collar.

Balandrana or Supertotus: A traveler's raincoat of the seventeenth century that had a hood and enveloping sleeves buttoned back on the arm.

Baldric, Bandoleer, or Bandolier: A wide silk sash or leather belt, often richly decorated, worn over the right shoulder and fastened on the left hip to carry a sword.

Basquine or Vasquine: A fitted, boned, hip-length garment with a petticoat, in which a bolster tied around the waist over the petticoat and under the outerskirt created the drum-shaped silhouette seen in many of the Spanish court ladies painted by Velázquez. The male *basquine* was a fitted, padded doublet fastened tightly down the center front.

Batts: A popular women's shoe of the early seventeenth century that resembled the men's, with a medium heel and latchets tied over the tongue. These are the shoes we associate with many women's outfits in early New England.

Beaver Hat: A fur hat that was fashionable for both men and women in the seventeenth century. It was a costly item with a thick nap and usually broad-brimmed.

Boot Hose: Ornamental topped stocking worn under boots, the decorated edge of which fell over the top of the boot.

Bows à l'Échelle: See *Late Baroque: echelon.*

Bucket-top Boot: Wide-topped boot, sometimes turned in a large cuff.

Buffcoat: The military coat of the seventeenth century, originally made of buffalo hide and worn with buff gauntlets. It had a body formed of four pieces with deep skirts and was often thong-laced up the front. Those worn by officers were often richly decorated with braid, loops, buttons, and lace.

Cadanette: Lovelock, a long curl or strand over one shoulder, tied with a ribbon or a string with a rosette.

Canons: A lace flounce attached just below the knee to the stocking that was drawn up over the breeches.

Casaque: A loose greatcoat, with big sleeves, usually three-quarter length, with turned-back cuffs.

Falling Band: A collar of fine white lawn edged with lace, later developed into the pleated *rabat.* It is the wide collar spreading out over the shoulders that is seen in the later portraits by Anthony Van Dyck, and in this width is sometimes known as a *rabatine.*

Galants: Ties or loops of ribbons used on sleeve, bodice, or skirt.

Lovelock: Plait or curl of hair near left ear and tied with a ribbon; worn by both men and women.

La Modeste, la Friponne, la Secrète: The modish woman of the period wore a chemise, a corset, then several petticoats over the *vertugale,* or hoop. The hoop had grown smaller but continued to be worn until 1630. Over that was the gown, consisting of skirt and bodice or stomacher, with sleeves of light-colored satin or other fabric. Over that, a robe or sort of redingote of darker or contrasting colored material opened the full length in front. The robe usually had slashed sleeves showing the undersleeves. This robe was generally worn until 1645. The outer robe was called *la modeste,* and when there were two skirts the outer one was called *la friponne* (hussy, in English), the under one *la secrète.*

Pantoffle: Type of soft slipper.

Pinners: In women's dresses, aprons of exquisite workmanship, with matching lingerie accessories, such as sheer lingerie cuffs and collar.

Points: See *Elizabethan: aglet.*

Quatre-Foil Spur Leathers: Worn by early-seventeenth-century cavaliers on the insteps of their boots to hide the fastenings of the spurs. The shape was that of a broad quatre-foil, or four-leafed petal.

LATE BAROQUE (RESTORATION) (1660–1715)

À la Maintenon: A coiffure with hair parted in the center, trimmed in graduated lengths, curled and fluffed; designed by Mme Martin, hairdresser to Mme de Maintenon.

Apron: A length of cloth hemmed and usually ornamented, gathered into a waistband having long, ornamental strings; worn at the front of a full court gown.

Boot Hose: Hose with lace tops, worn over silk hose inside boots.

Brandenberg Greatcoat: An overcoat adapted from the coats of Prussian soldiers.

Busk: See *Elizabethan.*

Canons or Cannons: Bunches of ribbon loops affixed at the knee, worn between 1660 and 1670.

Cassock: Between 1650 and 1670 the *doublet* of Charles I's reign was sometimes lengthened almost to the knee. Like its predecessor it could be worn either belted or beltless, but following the new trend it had a lower waistline; its skirts flared slightly. Except for length, it was essentially like the modern clerical cassock.

Commode: See *Fontanges.*

Cravat: Any type of neck dressing other than a collar. Of various types through several periods. Here the *rabat* or lace *falling band* with round corners became broad and long, and the *jabot,* or frill on the shirt front, frequently appeared with it. By the end of the 1670s the ends of the cravat became full lace tabs, tied under the chin with a *cravat string* of ribbon or lace.

Culottes: Breeches tied below the knee and trimmed in braid.

Echelon: Bowknots (or bows à l'echelle) of graduated size on the *stomacher.* The bodice often laced in back, but when fastened in front it had jeweled clasps, buttons, or many bowknots with which to fasten it.

Falbalas or Furbelows: Heavy ruffles gathered up the center; used as decoration on women's garments, particularly at the end of elbow-length sleeves.

Fontanges: In 1680 the Duchesse de Fontanges, having her hat blown off at a royal hunting party, tied her curls in place with her garter, arranging a bow with ends in front. From that incident a new fashion evolved—a cap of tier upon tier of upstanding wired and pleated ruffles of lawn, lace, and ribbons. The hair dressed in that fashion was called *coiffure à la Fontanges,* and the cap with its narrow rising front was known as *le bonnet à la Fontanges*. The cap often had two floating pieces of ribbon or lace in back, and over the whole arrangement was often worn a black silk hood or kerchief. In 1691 the head-dress was reduced to two tiers of pleats and became known as the *commode*.

Galants or Favors: Bunches of ribbon loops of variegated colors. Extravagant ornamentation in a braid of gold or silver, laces, and ribbons became the standard decoration for women's dress.

Habit à la Française: Adhering to the three fundamentals of coat, vest, and breeches, the style began in the reign of Louis XIV, was perfected in design during the Regency, and then became the formal attire of European gentlemen for a century. The coat retained its name *habit à la française* to the end of the eighteenth century with very little change in cut.

Hurluberlu: Short curls worn over the entire head; introduced by Mme de Maintenon, 1670.

Jackboot: A knee-high boot of heavy black leather with broad heel worn by cavalrymen during the seventeenth century.

Justaucorps: A long, fitted coat with full skirt, buttoned down the front with sleeves usually turned back in large cuffs; replaced the cassock about 1675–1680. It was slashed up the center back to the waist, originally necessary for riding. The sleeves, usually split partway up the back, were straight with wide cuffs. The skirt of the coat, reaching to the knees, was reinforced with linen, buckram, or whalebone and cut to flare when buttoned at the waist.

Lavallière: A necklace with a pendant. Style introduced by Louise de La Vallière, first mistress of Louis XIV.

Mante: A short scarflike cape, edged with ruffles or lace. This popular wrap for women and the *manteau* were probably made of Mantua silk imported from Italy. *Mantes* of gold or silver tissue, were worn only by women of high rank at court.

Manteau: The formal women's gown of the period of Louis XIV. The overskirt was looped back and held by ribbon bows. The looped-up folds were often bunched in back over an underskirt of taffeta; the looped-up outerskirt of brocaded silk ended in a train, the length of which was determined by the lady's social position. The train was carried over the left arm, except in the presence of royalty, when it trailed on the floor.

Monmouth Cockade: A cocked hat of beaver with feather fringe made popular by the Duke of Monmouth about 1670.

Montero: A round fur cap with a turned-up brim.

Mouches: This French word for *flies* was used to denote beauty patches of black silk court plaster cut in diamond, crescent, star, or other shapes and applied to the face, often to cover unsightly pockmarks.

Palatine: A small shoulder cape introduced in 1671 by the Princess Palatine to avoid exposing her shoulders.

Passecaille: The ribbon on which a muff was hung.

Pelerine: A short shoulder cape, usually with long ends hanging down in front.

Periwig or Perruque: Wig for men that gained favor during the period of Louis XIV; hair at this time was worn shoulder length and in flowing curls. The head was then regularly shaved, the wig taking the place of the man's own hair. At first it was made to look like natural hair, but eventually an artificial effect was cultivated. Masses of ringlets fell over the shoulders and down the back. By 1660 wig-making in France reached such a stage of perfection that the French periwig was in demand all over Europe.

Petticoat Breeches or Rhinegrave Breeches: Full breeches, ending in deep ruffles or *canons*. There were two styles of petticoat breeches—one resembled a kilt, the other a divided skirt. By about 1660 the breeches were so wide that it is not always easy to distinguish between *rhinegrave* breeches and a short skirt. Sometimes the legs of these garments attained a width of six feet.

Pretintailles: Cut-out motifs of lace or gold embroidery, appliquéd or gummed to the bottoms of skirts, making elaborate ornamentation.

Rabat: Type of cravat, with a vertically pleated front fall. See *Early Baroque: falling band*.

Ramillies Wig: Of English origin, named in honor of the Battle of Ramillies, won by the Duke of Marlborough. The wig had one or two hanging braids, tied top and bottom with black ribbon. Later the end of the braid was often looped under and tied.

Spatterdashes: High leather leggings, introduced about 1700. The joining of legging and shoe was covered by spur leathers.

Steinkirk: A scarf of lace or lawn, loosely tied with the ends casually twisted into the vest or shirt front or drawn through a buttonhole or ring. Black silk steinkirks were introduced in the 1690s and were named after the Battle of Steinkirk, where the hurriedly garbed French, unable to tie their cravats, twisted the ends through buttonholes in their coats.

Taure: A hairdress resembling a bull's head, introduced in 1673.

ROCOCO
(1715–1774)

Bagnolette: Hood wired away from the face.

Bag Wig or Crapaud: A wig with a bag in the back that held loose ends of the hair, tied at the nape of the neck with a bow.

Banyan: Men's eighteenth-century dressing gown, same cut as the coat.

Cadogan: In the catogan or cadogan wig, the back hair was looped under and tied with a concealed string or solitaire. The name of the wig is attributed to the first Earl of Cadogan.

Calash: Eighteenth-century hat, attached to capes, to cover women's high wigs; folded back like a baby-buggy cover.

Festoons: Decorative elements on women's gowns; pieces of sheer fabric or flowers.

Frills: Decorative ornamentation with fabric gathered on one side, in contrast to furbelows, which are fabric strips gathered down the center.

Furbelows: See *Late Baroque: falbalas.* Decorative ornamentation for gowns.

Jabot: The military tied the ends of the large, flat collar in front with a band, and from the loose ends the jabot was later developed as a falling lace ruffle, which filled in the opening of the shirt.

Jupe: Richly decorated petticoat.

Leghorn: Large, straw picture hat.

Mantle: The long winter cloak for women fully lined throughout and buttoned down the length of the front.

Modestie: When the neck in front was low on a woman's dress, often the stomacher was ornamented with graduated ribbon loops or lacings of narrow ribbon, finished with gauze or lace, known as the modestie. In English, the "modesty bit."

Monterro: Skull cap, often fur-trimmed, worn with banyan.

Paniers: These baskets to hold out the skirt returned in 1717 to France, by way of England, where they had already been in fashion for six or seven years under the name of hoop skirt. They did not really take hold in France until 1730. The hoops were of reed or whalebone, held together with basket-like ribbons, thus the French name, panier, meaning basket. The framework was covered with taffeta or brocade. The hoop was first funnel-shaped, but from the 1730s to 1740s it grew very broad at the sides and flat in front and back.

Parapluie: Rain umbrella, made with a folding frame.

Perspective: Women carried the lorgnette, men the single glass, or perspective.

Polonaise: An overgown for women, with fitted back and front and a draped skirt. It lasted from 1776 to 1787, and its special feature consisted of three *paniers,* one back and two side sections, which rounded away in front. The paniers of the *polonaise* were drawn up on cords and could also be let down to form a flying gown. The cords were run through slots and were finished with tassels and rosettes. Later the paniers were sewn in position, with the cords merely serving as ornament.

Quizzing Glass: Looking glass on a stick.

Robe à la Française: In the 1730s the Watteau gown became the "robe à la française," and by 1770 this loose gown was the formal dress for court functions, six box pleats stitched flat to the back, and ending in a train. Under the upper part of the gown, attached to the bodice, was a fitted lining that was laced in back.

Robe Volante or Flying Gown: A variation of the gown with the Watteau pleat. The soft pleats flowed from shoulder to hem, both back and front. Usually ankle length, worn over a wide hoop that created an undulating movement during walking.

Roquelaure or Roquelo: Knee-length cloak, first worn in the eighteenth century by the Duke of Roquelaure, made of heavy woolen cloth in bright colors with a hood and buttoned down the front.

Skimmer: A wide, soft-brimmed, leghorn straw hat faced with silk, worn over a white lawn cap and tied under the chin with velvet ribbons. It developed in England about 1750.

Solitaire: A concealing string of black taffeta, satin, or velvet, which tied the back hair of the cadogan wig. The solitaire, which no doubt is the origin of the black tie, was the black ribbon tied to the wig in a bow at the back, with the ends brought around under the white cravat and tied in a bow in front. Sometimes the solitaire was held in front by a diamond pin or a barrette.

Tricorne: The standard three-cornered hat worn by gentlemen of the period.

Watteau Sacque: The gown named after Watteau was the principal style of the Regency. The original Watteau gown was a loose sack or dress, worn over a tight bodice and very full underskirt. The loose folds falling from the shoulders in back became part of the skirt. The front of the gown varied in design, either hanging loose or fitted at the waist, worn closed or open, and, if open, revealing a bodice and underskirt. The elbow-length sleeves had vertical pleats and soft, wide cuffs. But from the 1740s on, the pagoda-shaped sleeve took hold, tight from shoulder to elbow, where it spread into flaring ruffles headed by ribbon bows.

NEOCLASSICISM AND REVOLUTION (1774–1795)

Bicorne: A type of man's hat having a front and back flap, with the highest point or corner in center front caused by a pinching of the front flap, thereby resembling a tricorne. Developed from a variation of the Swiss military hat.

Bowknot: A flat black ribbon that secured the *cadogan* coiffure worn by men in the later eighteenth century.

Cabriolet: A bonnet shaped like a cabriolet carriage top and tied under the chin. It was similar to the *calash* and could also be collapsed at will.

Cadogan hairdo: See *Rococo.*

Calash: A cage covering huge hairdos and therefore very large. Had reed or whalebone hoops that could be raised or lowered by a ribbon like the hood of a carriage. See *Rococo.*

Caraco gown: A gown with long *basque*, finished with a peplum ruffle and often a train called a *Figaro*, which was attached under the peplum.

Carmagnole: A short jacket worn by French Revolutionists. Originally worn by workers in Piedmont who came from Carmagnole, Italy; deputies from Marseilles introduced it to Paris in the early 1790s. It buttoned down the front, had revers and a high turned-down collar.

Circassienne Gown: A variation of the *polonaise*, it also had three *paniers* run on cords, but was very short and of even length. The gown had double sleeves—that is, the outerbodice had short cap sleeves worn over the longer sleeves of the underbodice.

Cockade: A rosette or similar ornament worn on the side of the hat.

Dormeuse Bonnet or Sleeping Bonnet: So named because it was also worn at night, it hugged the head tightly covering the cheeks, and was threaded with a ribbon tied into a bow on top of the head. For daytime wear it was worn higher on the head, revealing the ears and back of the head.

Fichu: Piece of lightweight, almost transparent fabric, worn like a shoulder scarf with the different styles of gowns. It was bunched above the small, tight waist, giving a pouter-pigeon look to the figure.

Gainsborough Hat: A type of wide-brimmed hat, decorated with ribbons or ostrich plumes, that appears in Gainsborough's paintings.

Le Gilet: Copy of the English sleeveless waistcoat, with a laced back of lining material, which fitted the figure.

Hedgehog Hairdo: A woman's hairdo that appeared in 1778. Resembled a short male hairdo, cut fairly short in front, frizzed to the ends, and brushed up high off the face with long, loose curls or the cadogan in back.

Hessian Boots: Worn by the Hessian mercenaries hired to fight the American colonists, this boot came to a heart-shaped curve at the top and finished with a tassel that hung from the dip in the top of the boot.

Kevenhüller or Androsmane: A Swiss military hat that was more a bicorne than a tricorne. Named after a famous Austrian field marshal. It was built high in front and back with a gentle crease in front. When used by generals in the Continental army it was known as the *continental hat.*

Lévite Gown: A type of *redingote* with train. Its creation was inspired by the Englishman's *redingote*, or riding coat, of the same period.

Liars, Menteurs, or Trompeurs: Wires that supported the *fichu.*

Macaroni: Member of a London club who dressed in extreme fashions. The costume consisted of a bobtailed coat and a foot-high wig topped by a small *tricorne* hat.

Mobcap: Large cap with soft, full crown and wide brim that almost hid the face; usually trimmed with ribbon bands and loops; known in England and therefore not restricted to use in the French Revolution.

Nivernois: A diminutive *tricorne* worn by the English fops known as *Macaronies* on top of their high *cadogan* wigs in the 1770s. Named for the Duke of Nivernois, Louis-Jules Mancin Mazarani.

Pelisse: A woman's fur-trimmed, capelike wrap, with armholes and broad collar.

Polonaise: See *Rococo.*

Pouf: Huge headdress with ornaments that were attached to a framework of gauze.

Redingote: A man's double-breasted, long coat with turned-down collar and two or three shoulder capes; of English origin.

Redingote Gown: A gown for women which had a double-breasted jacket with wide lapels and an overskirt with a train behind. This costume was considered very mannish.

Robe à la Française: See *Rococo.*

Robespierre Collar: A high, turned-down collar worn with a frilly jabot and stock tied in a bow in front. Made popular by the famous French statesman about 1790.

Sans Culottes: Name given to the French Revolutionists or Jacobins to distinguish them from the aristocrats, who wore knee breeches. Since they wore the long trousers that had been used only by the lowliest of peasants in centuries past, they were literally without culottes or breeches.

Stock: A neckcloth or *cravat.*

Thérèse: A huge cage of fine gauze worn over a high-dressed coiffure and kept in shape by fine wire. Popular in France in the 1780s.

Tricorne: See *Rococo.*

Directoire and empire (1795–1815)

À la Titus or à la Victime: Coiffure resembling the hairstyle worn by a condemned person before execution; worn with a red shawl and red necklace.

Austrian Knots: Heavy black silk braid ornamentation on military uniforms appliquéd in looped designs. It originally decorated Austrian uniforms and was then copied by Napoleonic armies as well as other armies.

Barouche Coat: Tight-fitting, three-quarter-length coat having full sleeves, fastened down front with gold, barrel-shaped snaps and confined at the waist with elastic girdle and buckle.

Blücher: A half-boot or shoe invented by Field Marshall von Blücher, commander of the Prussian forces at Waterloo. A laced shoe in which the quarters reach to the front over the instep and are laced together over the tongue.

Bonaparte Helmet: A gathered white silk bonnet with a forehead band of black velvet embroidered with gold laurel leaves and mounted with a panache of white ostrich.

Cabriolet: Huge hat with elaborate silk trimming.

Canezou: A bodice with a high neckline and long sleeve.

Carrick Greatcoat or Capote: Overcoat of the period, with several capes over the long-skirted *redingote.* It had originally been a coachman's coat.

Chemise à l'anglaise: A soft, full lingerie gown with crushed satin sash; it was worn both summer and winter, and it originated in England.

Cherusse: A small ruffle or ruff of lace worn by women during the early nineteenth century.

Circassian Wrapper: A dress similar to a night chemise, with very low-laced bodice and sleeves of lace and muslin in alternate stripes.

Clawhammer Tails: Any male coat with stepped-back front at the waist and very long tails at the rear.

Coal-Scuttle Bonnet: A bonnet with a huge, shovel-like lip in front, worn during the Directoire period.

Courrobe: Sleeveless court outergown.

Curricle Cloak: A half- or three-quarter-length shaped cloak with sloping sides, edged with fur or lace. Worn 1801 to 1816.

Escarpins: Pumps of soft leather with pointed toes, worn with silk stockings, either plain white or striped on white.

Hussar Breeches: Skintight breeches, often in canary yellow and bottle green, and usually worn with a frock coat.

Incroyables: A group of young dandies who went to extremes in their dress, right after the French Revolution. The *incroyables* strove for a careless, wrinkled appearance. Their coats, which sloped away in front from the waist when buttoned, had a high, turned-down collar, very wide lapels, and were usually worn open. Sometimes the coat had bulky pleats across the back, giving the effect of a hump. With this coat was worn a waistcoat of contrasting colored satin and a very full, sheer white cambric cravat. The cravat or neckcloth was loosely wound around the neck several times, often over padded cushions so that it rose up over the chin with ends tied in front.

Mameluke Sleeve: A long woman's sleeve done in a series of puffs down the arm. Named after a squadron of Mamelukes created by Napoleon.

Merveilleuses: The feminine counterpart of the *incroyables.* The neck of a *merveilleuse's* short, tight bodice was very low, the fabric diaphanous. A sheer lingerie muffler resembling the masculine neckcloth was often added and worn in the same fashion. The woman either went bareheaded or wore an extreme style of hat, frequently a bonnet with a very large brim, rising high off the forehead—an exaggerated version of the English jockey hat.

Muscadine: A pastille scented with musk. The name was applied to effeminate men who overdressed and used quantities of this scent. The muscadine carried a short or long stick weighted with lead.

Pantalettes: A separate leg covering of lace and ruffles that extended below the hem of the dress.

Redingote: The long cloth or velvet coat that became a fashion for women ca. 1812. It was high-waisted, was at first knee length and later reached to 9 to 10 inches above the hem of the dress. By the end of the decade, the coat was full length and edged with wide bands of fur.

Reticule: A small drawstring purse used in lieu of pockets.

Roguelo Dress: A morning dress with a loose back and bias front.

Rotonde: Short cape of the same material as the dress.

Shako: A military headdress with a high stiff crown finished in front with a brush or plume. It was of Hungarian origin and was much the same in most European and American armies during the Napoleonic period. The tall, black, polished felt with a leather pompon on the left side was prescribed by the U.S. Congress in 1810.

Spencer: A very short-waisted jacket, worn by women with the Empire dress. Named after Lord Spencer.

Talma: A man's cloak, sometimes hooded, named after the French tragedian François Joseph Talma.

Wellington Mantle: Garment that resembled a Spanish cloak of merino lined with sarcenet.

Witzchoura: A feminine *redingote* of about 1808 in a long Empire line and usually fur-lined. It was probably of Russian origin.

Yeoman hat: A triangular hat turned up in front and ornamented at the top with button and tasseled cord.

ROMANTIC
(1815–1848)

Angoulême Bonnet: Bonnet with a high crown and tied at the side.

Banditti: A small panache of feathers on a feminine bonnet in the early 1800s.

Basque Belt: A waist-pinching girdle.

Bateau Neck: A boat-shaped straight neckline reaching from shoulder to shoulder and equally high in front and back.

Beehive Bonnet: A lady's simple straw cottage bonnet of the early nineteenth century made in the shape of a beehive and trimmed with a ribbon tied under the chin.

Beret Sleeve: After 1813 the sleeves of evening gowns were short, puffed, and stiffened and called the *beret* or *pancake sleeve.*

Bertha: Wide collar on women's gowns of the period, which accentuated the dropped-shoulder look.

Bishop Sleeve: A wide, long sleeve gathered at the cuff.

Bottine or Jemima: A lady's gored boot of beige fabric with black leather tip and elastic inserts. It was first designed for Queen Victoria in 1836, since the first cloth or webbing made with stretchable rubber was invented in England shortly before this. The shoe was designed by J. Sparkes Hall, bootmaker to the queen. It usually had leather or cloth uppers with the elastic gussets set in at the sides. *Jemima* was the British term for the style, and it was soon worn by both men and women.

Byron Collar: An unstarched collar left open at the throat and held together by a silk scarf carelessly tied.

Canezou: Refers to Canezou Spencer. A short, separate, transparent jacket with sleeves, its two scarf-like ends held in place by the dress belt. Usually of sheer muslin with embroidery, it was worn over the bodice. The false canezou was a deep ruffle or bretelle, falling over the short puffed sleeves.

Crinoline: Made its appearance in the early 1840s and was, at first, a band or braid of horsehair—crin is the French word for horsehair. The crinoline was a petticoat, corded and lined with horsehair and finished with a braid of straw at the hem.

Donna Maria: A full sleeve puffed to below the elbow and then tighter to the wrist.

D'Orsay Pump: A gentleman's shoe with cutaway sides and a low broad heel introduced by Count D'Orsay, a society dandy who began his fashion reign in Paris but came to have most influence in London in the 1830s. The masculine evening pump of the twentieth century is an outgrowth of the style.

Frock Coat: A double-breasted coat having long skirts of equal length in front and back.

Frog Fastening: Ornamental fastening with cord loops and suspended buttons.

Hessian Boot: A rather tight-fitting high boot.

Leg-o-Mutton Sleeve: See *Donna Maria.*

Macfarlane Cloak: A cloth topcoat with separate sleeve capes and side slits to permit the hands to reach inner pockets. About 1846.

Mackintosh: A cloak of rubber-coated, waterproof fabric invented by Charles Macintosh.

Mantelette: Shaped scarf. Covered the back almost like a jacket and descended to the knees in front, being sloped off and narrow from the shoulders down.

Montespan: A sleeve with the upper part full, a band at the elbow, and a ruffle extending over the forearm.

Nankeen Trousers: A strong, buff-colored, cotton trouser named after the Chinese city of Nanking. It was introduced in America from Sicily in 1828 and became especially popular for summer wear.

Opera Cloak: A man's knee-length cloak of velvet or fine woolen with a standing collar fastened by tasseled silk cords. It was worn by men with formal evening wear in lieu of an overcoat to give a dashing effect.

Pantalettes or Drawers: Leg coverings of lace and ruffles that extended below the knees. They were sometimes false, being ruffles held at the knees with tapes.

Pelerine: A short, separate cape deriving its name from the shoulder cape of the medieval pilgrim; often of fur.

Pelisse: A fur-lined or fur-trimmed cloth coat, used in France, although the English applied the name to any long outercoat.

Quizzing or Perspective Glass: A single round lens carried on a black silk cord or ribbon, on a chain around the neck, or on a long handle of gold, tortoise shell, or ivory. It became fashionable among male dandies in the 1830s and women often set the lens into their painted fans.

Robe d'Intérieur: At-home wear for men; robe of brilliantly figured silk or velvet. Also worn were lounging clothes or smoking suits with a velvet cap.

Sautoir: A silver or gold chain upon which women carried a watch.

Stock: During the 1840s a fashionable, wide neck covering. As before, it was often neatly shaped to the neck, whaleboned at the sides, and secured by a strap and buckled in back. Often was plain across the front or had a piece

brought around the back and fastened in a knot or bow.

Studs: Jeweled shirt fasteners for formal and semiformal wear in gold, pearls, or cut stones. They were used to fasten collars and shirts and first appeared in the 1840s.

Taglioni Overcoat: A short, braid-bound overcoat used in the 1840s. Named after the Italian dancer Taglioni.

Tam-o'-Shanter: A jaunty bonnet-cap named after a poem by Robert Burns. It was usually of heavy brushed wool and varied colors, the number varying according to a man's status. It became popular as a sporting cap during the Romantic Period and has remained a popular style until today.

Zouave Jacket: A bolero jacket with round corners in deep blue Arabian cloth without collar or buttons but ornamented with braid and worn with full red pantaloons. It was the uniform of the Zouave regiment formed by the French in Algiers in the early 1830s which in 1838 became a unit in the French army.

LATE NINETEENTH CENTURY:
VICTORIAN AND SECOND EMPIRE
(1848–1870)

Antimacassar: An ornamental washable covering used to protect chair backs from the oil used on men's hair.

Armenian Cloak: A fashionable gentleman's cloak of the 1850s and 1860s. It was cut in one piece without inserted sleeves, but side seams formed loose armcoverings. Had a deep velvet collar.

Balmacaan: A loose, flaring coat of Scottish origin with flaring sleeves, usually of tweed, gabardine, or raincoat fabric with a military standing collar and slashed pockets.

Balmoral: A laced-up shoe or half-boot with closed throat introduced by Prince Albert in 1853. Everything new and smart at the time was named *Balmoral* after the royal castle in Aberdeenshire, built by the prince and Queen Victoria.

Basque: The outer part of a dress sewn onto a boned bodice.

Bavolet: A flounce sewn at the back of a bonnet.

Bertha: A cape-like collar of cloth or lace.

Bloomers: Loose oriental trousers gathered at the knee; popularized by Amelia Bloomer in 1851.

Bolero: A small jacket with rounded corners in front.

Bournouse or Burnous: A fringed, knee-length,

Arabian-style mantle with hood worn in the 1850s.

Bowler or Derby Hat: A stiff felt hat with a low round crown and narrow brim; the bowler, which is the British term for derby, has a slightly wider brim and roll at the sides.

Braces: Suspender straps extending from the waist belt in the front over the shoulder to support trousers.

Cage Américaine: Another term for the whalebone, metal crinoline, or hoop skirt.

Canezou: At first a sleeveless outdoor garment developed from the Spencer jacket; later it referred to a neckpiece on a dress.

Capote: Elaborate mid-Victorian bonnet with ribbon bows tied at the side or front.

Cardigan: Originally a short military jacket of knit worsted designed and worn by the Earl of Cardigan, a British general during the Crimean War. Trimmed in fur, braid, and buttons. Later the name for a knit sweater jacket of hip length.

Chignon: A heavy twist or knot of real or false hair worn high or low at the back of the head.

Chimneypot or Stovepipe Hat: A tall, cylindrical hat with very little brim, worn by men.

Crinoline: A stiff or unpliable material used to stiffen a costume, but at this time was the name also given to the spring steel hoops set into a petticoat or onto cloth strips to hold the petticoats and skirts away from the body in a bell shape.

Dundrearies, Dundreary Whiskers, or Piccadilly Weepers: Long side whiskers worn by Lord Dundreary in *Our American Cousin* by Tom Taylor, 1858.

Empire Jupon: A petticoat with gores and two or three steel frames at the bottom.

Empress Eugénie Hat: A flat-crowned straw with a rolled brim and ribbons falling down the back, used by the Empress Eugénie for riding and traveling.

Figaro Jacket: A close-fitting short jacket with epaulets on the shoulder and cut away at the side in a bolero style.

Forage Cap or Képi: In the mid-1800s replaced the military *shako.* A cap with a hard front brim and a soft, low crown often raised a bit at the back. It was first adopted by the French in 1857 and by the American forces during the Civil War.

Frock Coat: A double-breasted coat having long skirts of equal length in front and back; the skirts had less flare than in the Romantic Period.

Four-in-Hand Tie: See *Late Nineteenth Century.*

Garibaldi Jacket: A shirt of bright scarlet merino wool, decorated on the front with black braid and buttons. Named after the popular Italian hero.

Gladstone Collar: A comfortable standing collar with flaring points worn with a silk scarf in a bow-knot. Worn in the 1850s by William Ewart Gladstone who later became prime minister of Great Britain.

Imperial: A small, tufted beard on the chin, usually worn with a waxed mustache; named after the style worn by the Emperor Napoleon III.

Inverness Cape: A full, sleeveless cape that fitted closely around the neck; from Inverness in Scotland.

Morning Coat: The swallowtail or curved, cutback, skirted coat worn by gentlemen for formal morning wear.

Muttonchops: Heavy sideburns.

New York Surtout: A man's fashionable, short, black overcoat with straight-cut skirts and a wide collar to the waistline finished with black silk braid. Popular in the 1850s.

Pagoda Sleeve: A sleeve shaped like a funnel, tight above and gradually widening at the bottom, often finishing in several ruffles over a soft lawn undersleeve.

Paisley Shawl: A copy of an Indian shawl made in Paisley, Scotland.

Paletot: A capelike outdoor garment hanging in stiff pleats from shoulder to flounce of dress, with a flap over the armhole and a number of still shorter shoulder capes.

Pea Jacket: A heavy, short coat worn by sailors from 1850 on. Made of heavy, tightly woven cloth in dark blue. Sometimes used as a model in lighter fabric for young boys' coats.

Peignoir: A dress with a boneless bodice and bishop sleeve.

Pork-pie hat: A hat worn with a dish-shaped fold in the crown.

Prince Albert: Another name for the double-breasted frock coat with satin lapels, named after the consort of Queen Victoria who favored the style.

Princess Gown: A full-length gown cut in one from shoulder to waist with a number of gores and full enough in the skirt to go over a hoop. Usually it buttoned up the front.

Raglan Coat: A coat with sleeves cut to fit into the shoulders all the way to the neckline of the garment. Named after Lord Raglan.

Russian Jacket: A sleeveless short coat.

Russian Vest: A loose blouse resembling the Garibaldi jacket.

Sack Suit: A loose-fitting combination of vest, coat, and trousers of the same material, with the coat ending at the finger tips and having high, short lapels. It was used in commerce and in sports.

Shirtwaist: A style of bodice that looked like a man's shirt with high collar and cuffs.

Tails: Men's evening coat stepped-back in front with tails in back.

Victoria Mantle: A knee-length mantle with collar and wide, hanging sleeves; usually with a deep-colored border.

Waistcoat: The forerunner of the present-day vest.

Waterproof Coat: An outdoor garment with or without a cape, worn as a protection from the rain.

Zouave Jacket: See *Romantic.*

LATE NINETEENTH CENTURY:
THE GILDED AGE
(1870–1890)

Ascot Tie: A scarf with horizontal ends, tied in a knot and then crossed diagonally; the whole usually held in place with a jeweled stick pin.

Balayeuse, Dust Ruffle, or Street Sweeper: A ruffle on the inner side of the hem of a skirt to protect it from the ground.

Basque: A short, skirt-like termination of an upper garment (originally on the male doublet) that was adopted by women in the 1870s. The style is said to have developed when the Princess of Wales wore a fisherman's jersey pulled tightly over her rigidly corseted figure.

Blazer: A lightweight sport jacket.

Boater: A man's hard straw hat coated with shellac from India that became popular for summer outings and sporting events in the 1870s. The English wore it boating (hence the name). Standard summer wear in America from June to September.

Braces: See *Late Nineteenth Century: Victorian and Second Empire.*

Bustle: Whalebone or steel strips placed in the top back of the petticoat or in a separate panier puff in order to hold out the elaborate draping at the back of the overskirt.

Camargo: A jacket with a built-in panier.

Camisole: The light cloth cover worn over the corset.

Cardigan: A collarless sweater with a front opening.

Chesterfield Overcoat: A fitted dress overcoat with hidden buttons and a velvet collar, worn in the late nineteenth century.

Dolman: A three-quarter-length, out-of-doors wrap

made of brocade, silk, or woolen fabric with sleeves cut in one with the body of the wrap.

Eton Jacket: A short jacket with side lapels first worn by the students at Eton in England.

Fedora: A velour hat with a fairly high, tapering crown that was usually creased in the middle.

Fore-and-Aft Cap: A cap having a visor front and back, worn with an Inverness cape.

Four-in-Hand: A type of necktie tied in a slip knot.

Frou-Frou Dress: A dress with a low corsage and a light pink underskirt covered with many small flounces.

Homburg: A carefully blocked, stiff felt hat with a medium tapering crown creased in the middle and a brim that was rolled up on the sides and finished in grosgrain ribbon.

Hussar Jacket: A jacket with braiding and frog fastenings; it was worn with a waistcoat and heavily influenced by military uniforms of the English in Egypt.

Jersey Sweater: A slipover sweater, fairly close-fitting, copied from a fisherman's sweater.

Knickerbockers: Full, knee-length breeches gathered in at the knee; named after Father Knickerbocker, who came to New Amsterdam in 1674.

Langtry Bonnet: A small, close-fitting bonnet.

Monocle: A single glass with a ribbon, fitted into the eye socket to help the wearer both to improve the vision of one eye and to appear aristocratic.

Mousquetaire Glove: A heavy leather glove with wrist extensions fringed in silk from the seventeenth century was adapted in the 1870s by Sarah Bernhardt into the long forearm evening glove with a tiny wrist opening fastened with small pearl buttons. It soon became *de rigueur* for formal evening dress.

Norfolk Jacket: A jacket with box pleats or straps of the same material passing over the belt and extending from shoulder to hem in front and back; usually worn for sport occasions.

Polonaise: See *Rococo.*

Pompadour: Hair style formed by drawing the hair straight up and back from the forehead.

Reefer: A double-breasted, close-fitting jacket.

Rubbers: Low overshoes of rubber worn to protect regular shoes from wet weather. The style developed for men during the 1870s.

Russian Bonnet: A type of bonnet with a large bow tied under the chin with steel embroidered crown and a lace brim.

Spats: Short coverings for the ankles and instep, usually made of felt and buttoned on the outside.

Swallowtail Coat: Formerly a riding coat with skirts buttoned back, it now had the skirts cut back in a gentle curve to behind the knees.

Tam-o'-shanter: A round, flat cap with a tight-fitting headband. See *Romantic.*

Toque: A small, close-fitting female hat without a brim.

Tucker: Fabric used to cover the neck above a very low bodice.

Tuxedo: An informal dinner jacket introduced from England, but the name is of American origin.

Ulster: A fitted, double-breasted coat having several capes; at first made of frieze, a coarse woolen cloth with shaggy mat on one side made in Ulster, Ireland.

Windsor Tie: A large, flowing tie.

Wing Collar: A high, stiff collar with turned-back corners.

LATE VICTORIAN AND EDWARDIAN:
ART NOUVEAU
(1890–1911)

Aigrette: A feather or plume from the egret, a kind of heron.

Alpaca: The long hair of the Peruvian llama that was woven into woolen cloth for men's and women's suits during the last years of the nineteenth century and the first years of the twentieth. Thus one often reads references to "my alpaca jacket or coat" in literature of the time.

American Shoulders: Known in France as *épaules américaines* because of the broad shoulders worn by American male tourists about 1905. This style was popular for men's fashions from 1905 to 1909 and again in the later 1930s.

Balaclava: A heavy woolen helmet crocheted or knitted for British soldiers as a winter cap in the years before World War I. Its name came from the seaport village in the Crimea that was the site of the Charge of the Light Brigade in 1854.

Balkan Blouse: A low-bloused bodice with a belt girding the hips.

Bateau Neck: A wide, fairly low female neckline.

Beau-Catcher: The coquettish curl in the middle of a woman's forehead that was popular as a coiffure accent at the turn into the twentieth century.

Beehive Hat: A large hat shaped like a beehive that came down well over the head and was fashionable from 1910 to 1914.

Bertha: A capelike collar of varying length and usually of lace that was popular in the early years of the twentieth century for women and recalled the Palatine capes of the seventeenth century.

Bishop sleeve: See *Romantic.*

Bloomers: Loose underdrawers usually gathered at the knee.

Boa: A long or short cylindrical neck scarf of fur or feathers.

Boater: A stiff-brimmed, flat-crowned straw hat worn by young men with summer sporting outfits.

Brassière: A band worn around th ust, usually as a support.

Bulldog Toe: The high, rounded, and blunt toe of a shoe.

Bungalow Apron: A simple, straight-line dress.

Bust Improver: A device used to make the bust appear larger.

Buster Brown Collar: A wide, starched collar wo with a Windsor tie and identified with the character, Buster Brown, in the comic strip of the period.

Châtelaine Bag: A pouch bag of pin-s al attached to a belt.

Chemisette: An underbodice of lawn and lace with short or long sleeves. It was often worn to supply sleeves and cover the cutaway neck of a jumper dress. The style was popular for women and girls from about 1890 to 1910.

Deerstalker Cap: See *Late Nineteenth Century: The Gilded Age: fore-and-aft cap.*

Diadem: A form of tiara or small jeweled crown for evening.

Dog Collar: A close-fitting necklace that hugs the throat; also known as a *choker.*

Duster: A coat of panama, pongee, alpaca, or natural linen used for driving and motoring.

Fascinator: A lacy woolen square or triangular head covering.

Friendship Bracelet: Consisted of similar links given by various friends and later put together to form a bracelet.

Gainsborough Hat: A velvet, beaver, or straw hat having a low crown and a broad brim, trimmed with feathers.

Gibson Girl Blouse: A blouse with a single pleat that extended over each shoulder front and back, hiding the armseye of the shirtwaist.

Gigot Sleeve: A full sleeve with more fullness at the elbow than at the shoulder or wrist.

Godet Pleats: Fluting held in place by a fine steel in the hem; used on the back and sides of a skirt.

Harem Skirt: A divided skirt.

Knickers: Full breeches gathered or pleated into

kneebands and buckled at the knee; based on the knickerbockers of the preceding period.

Leggings: Fitted coverings for the legs, usually fastened with a strap under the shoe and extending above the knee or to the waist.

Leg-o'-Mutton Sleeves: A sleeve that is extremely wide at the top and tapers to the wrist.

Lillian Russell Dress: The fashion identified with the American actress (1861–1922) who had a buxom figure and loved form-fitting gowns with a train. Her marcel-waved pompadour was topped by a large black velvet hat of Gainsborough style with ostrich plumes.

Mackintosh: A waterproof coat bearing the name of the originator of rubberized cloth garments, Charles Macintosh.

Marabou: Trimming made from the feathers of a certain species of stork; also a kind of raw silk or fabric made from it.

Marcel Wave: A type of artificial waving of the hair devised by Marcel of France in 1907.

Merry Widow Hat: An extremely large hat named from the musical comedy of the same name.

Mesh Bag: A bag made of interwoven metal links.

Morning Glory or Serpentine Skirt: A skirt that fitted snugly at the hip and flared bell-like at the hem.

Mother Hubbard: A loose-fitting housedress worn for comfort when doing housework.

Mushroom-Style Hat: A large hat suggesting the shape of a mushroom; worn by women between 1908 and 1913.

Napoleon Costume: A woman's dress of 1905 having a straight standing collar with deep turnover, wide revers, and braid trimming.

Opera Hat: A tall silk hat that folded flat.

Orby Cutaway: An American-designed man's single-breasted walking cutaway that eliminated the waistline seam. The seam down the center back ended at the waistline.

Oxford: A low shoe for men, women, and children laced or tied over the instep. The first oxford was a half-boot of heavy black leather dating from seventeenth-century England. It finally developed into a lightweight dress shoe at the beginning of the twentieth century. There were also button oxfords with a leather piece over the instep that buttoned to one side.

Pajama: Loose trousers and jacket, usually of silk, that were beginning to be worn for sleeping and lounging.

Panama Hat: A handwoven hat of fine straw from Ecuador and Colombia.

Peek-a-Boo Waist: A very thin blouse.

Peg-Top Skirt: A skirt with fullness of drapery around the hip and very narrow at the hem.

Peg-Top Trousers: Trousers that are wide and pleated at the top and very narrow at the ankles. The name peg-top originally applied to a boy's cone-shaped spinning top.

Permanent Wave: The vogue of the marcel wave in the 1890s and early 1900s led to the invention of the permanent wave in 1906 by Charles Nestlé, a fashionable coiffeur in London. The wave was first applied by an electric heat machine, but a later method used lotions instead of heat and was called a *cold wave.* This was much faster than the heated machine method.

Peter Pan Collar: A small, soft, turnover collar, named from the costume worn by Maude Adams in the stage production of *Peter Pan.*

Pettibockers: Related to bloomers, these were ankle-length, silk jersey pantaloons worn by women.

La Pliant: An invention of 1896 consisting of pieces of steel enclosed in cotton or silk ribbon tapes that held out the stiff and heavy skirt in the back and was much lighter than numerous petticoats. It was possible to transfer the steels to different skirts.

Pompadour: Full, upswept hair over a padded roll; loosely based on 18th century style of Mme de Pompadour.

Prince Rupert: A velvet or plush jacket worn open at the front and resembling a Louis XV coat.

Rainy Daisy Skirt: The nickname given to the skirts of women who belonged to the Rainy Day Club; a walking skirt, 2 to 3 inches off the ground in rainy weather.

Rat: Padding worn to make the hair extend outward from the head.

Rough Rider Shirt: A khaki shirt similar to that worn by Theodore Roosevelt and his cavalry in Cuba in 1898.

Street Sweepers: Ruffles worn under the hem of a skirt to protect it from dust and dirt.

String Tie: A very thin tie tied in a small bow with long ends; worn by Western types.

Sun-Ray Skirt: A skirt with accordion pleating.

Switch: A separate tress of real or artificial hair bound at one end.

Ulster: A heavy overcoat originally worn by men and women in Ulster, Ireland. In the early 1900s it was a loose-fitting overcoat, usually double-breasted with a full or half belt. The coat was originally made of Ulster frieze (a stout woolen cloth with a shaggy pile).

Umbrella Skirt: A full, bell-shaped skirt.

Windsor Tie: A loosely tied large bow tie.

Wrapper: An unshapely housedress of about 1905.

Yoke Skirt: A skirt that had a shaped piece in front and two side pieces that extended around the hips and joined in the back. The lower part of the skirt was attached to this yoke.

WORLD WAR I AND THE TWENTIES:
EARLY ART DECO
(1911–1929)

Algerian Purse: A purse made of Algerian leather, usually tooled and embossed in colors or gold.

Apron Tunic: A tunic having an overskirt, cut away in the back and forming an apron in front.

Arctics or Galoshes: A rubberized overshoe worn as a protection against rain and snow.

Babushka: A scarf worn around the head and tied under the chin. Babushka is the Russian word for grandmother.

Balkan Blouse: A blouse with full, loose sleeves gathered into a wide band around the waist; came into fashion after the Balkan Wars.

Balmacaan: A type of loose-fitting, flaring overcoat with raglan sleeves.

Bandeau: A band worn around the head to hold the hair tightly to the head.

Bed Jacket: A short jacket worn while resting in bed.

Beer Jacket: A simple, straight jacket of flannel, cotton, or linen that male students wore to beer parties in the 1920s and 1930s.

Black Tie: A popular term given to men's semiformal evening wear, which consisted of tuxedo dinner jacket, black waistcoat or cummerbund, and a black bow tie worn with a soft white shirt. The term is often used in opposition to *white tie,* which refers to formal evening wear.

Blazer: A bright-colored sport jacket, originally vertically striped.

Bobbed Hair: The style had originally been for boys wearing a Dutch haircut with bangs and straight hanging hair to the top of the neck, but in the 1920s the designer Paul Poiret adopted a coiffure for his female mannequins in which the hair was swept back from the face and lightly waved to the bottom of the ears and upper part of the neck. Later even shorter bobbed hair developed to complement the head-hugging cloche hat. After that came the boyish bob or shingle, which was almost like a male cut except for the curved points of hair that came forward from the ears, and the tousled bob cut.

Boutonnière: A real flower or an artificial nosegay worn in the buttonhole of the left lapel.

Box Coat: A loose, short, fingertip-length coat of a boxy cut.

Bush Jacket: A belted, hip-length jacket with tailored collar and two sets of pockets, worn by a hunter in the African jungle.

Camisole Neckline: An evening dress with a neckline resembling that of a camisole-top slip, which was straight above the bustline with a strap over each shoulder.

Cardigan: A knitted sweater-jacket that opens up the front.

Chemise Dress: A one-piece dress slipped over the head. It had short sleeves, a long waist, and a narrow belt, and became the basic style for all dresses in the 1920s. It was also called the tube or pillowslip dress.

Cloche: A close-fitting, bell-shaped hat.

Compact: A small ornamental box containing powder and rouge.

Cowl Neckline: The loose neckline of a dress falling in graceful curves across the chest; the draping of the fabric resembled the soft folds of a monk's cowl.

Crew-Neck Sweater: A sweater with a flat, close, round neckline.

Cummerbund: See *The Thirties and World War II.*

Dolman Wrap: A coat with sleeves cut in one with the body and the whole tapering toward the ankles.

Eton Crop: Very short hair for women that made them have a boyish look.

Fedora: See *Late Nineteenth Century: The Gilded Age.*

Ferris-Waist: The trade name given to a fitted waist that had buttons on tabs to hold the supporters. It was worn mainly by young girls.

Foulard: A thin, soft material of silk, or silk and cotton.

Harlequin Hat: A hat with wide, turned-up brim and oblique at the sides.

Helmet: A close-fitting cap worn toward the back of the head and with sides extending over the ears.

Hobble Skirt: A narrow skirt that inhibited walking and was popular from about 1912 to 1914.

Hoover Apron: A wraparound, coverall apron with sleeves. It originated in World War I when Herbert Hoover was Food Administrator.

Irene Castle Bob: A haircut, loosely waved and combed back from the forehead. It was introduced by the dancer Irene Castle.

Jodhpurs: Breeches used for riding; designed with fullness above the knee, a close fit below, cuff at ankle, and often with a strap under the instep.

Kiki Skirt: An extremely tight, knee-length skirt that appeared after it was worn by Leonore Ulric in the play *Kiki.*

Kimono: A loose Japanese robe or gown of silk tied with a sash and with sleeves cut in one with the body that was used as a dressing gown or negligee robe in the 1920s.

Kimono Dress: A loose gown with sleeve with body cut in one piece that was popular about 1910 when there was a great interest in Japanese art.

Lampshade Dress: A two-tiered skirt with the top tier flared out in the shape of a lampshade. The style was popular just before World War I.

Lindbergh Jacket: A heavy, warm, woolen or leather jacket with large pockets and elastic, fitted waist and wrist bands. It was worn by Charles Lindbergh on his 1927 flight over the Atlantic.

Middy Blouse: A young girl's straight blouse with a braid-trimmed sailor collar, bearing the nickname of the English midshipman; the three stripes on the collar represent the three great naval victories of Lord Nelson.

Monastic Silhouette: A dress resembling a monk's robe, hanging loosely from the shoulder, with fullness held in place by a belt at the hips.

Monkey-Fur Coat: A woman's outercoat actually made of monkey fur or to imitate monkey fur.

Off-the-Face or Halo Hat: A hat worn to the back of the head with the brim framing the face.

Oxford Bags or Plus Fours: These loose knee trousers were an exaggeration of the earlier knickers and were usually reserved for golf.

Pajamas: Loose trousers and jacket, usually of silk, used for sleeping by both men and women during the 1920s.

Patch Pocket: A pocket sewn on the outside of a garment and made of the same material.

Peg-Top: A skirt with a fullness of draping around the hip and very narrow at the hem that was popular in the years just before World War I.

Peter Pan Hat: Small hat with a feather at the side, similar to that worn in the play of the same name by Maude Adams.

Pinch-Back Coat: A coat with inverted pleats at the back that were stitched into a belt.

Planter's Punch: A firm straw hat, shaped like a fedora, that originated in Jamaica about 1923; it had a creased crown and a wide, pleated ornamental band.

Pocket Cascade: A pocket formed in the fold and draped section at the side of the skirt.

Polo Coat: A light-colored, soft-surfaced topcoat for informal wear and sports.

Polo Shirt: A sport shirt, usually knitted, with an open collar and short sleeves.

Profile Hat: A hat worn on one side of the head, forming a background for the profile of the wearer.

Raccoon Coat: A very bulky outercoat or overcoat of raccoon fur, worn for display as well as for warmth at sporting events, particularly at football games.

Saddle Shoe: A two-toned oxford with an ornamental strip of leather across the instep.

Shawl Collar: An attached collar having a rounded, unbroken outline, often extending to the waistline.

Shingle Bob: A mode of cutting the hair very close to the head in the back to show the natural contour of the head.

Skimmer Sailor: A flat-crowned sailor hat with a heavy and wide straight brim.

Tonneau Silhouette: A skirt similar to the peg-top style in shape that developed briefly about 1914.

Trench Coat: A tan-colored topcoat with a belt, a double yoke at the shoulder that was loose at the bottom, and epaulet straps at the shoulder; resembled a military coat and was used as a protection in bad weather.

T-Shirt: A tennis or sports shirt of knitted lightweight cotton (or wool) with a crew or V-neck and usually white. It was usually sleeveless but could have long sleeves and sometimes a mock turtleneck. The style developed in the 1920s.

Turtleneck Sweater: A slip-on, knit sweater with a high turnover collar.

Tyrolean Hat: A hat with a feather usually of soft, fuzzy felt similar to those worn in the highlands of Bavaria and Austria.

THE THIRTIES AND WORLD WAR II:
LATE ART DECO
(1929–1945)

Aloha Shirt: A brilliantly colored printed silk shirt that was a copy of the Hawaiian man's shirt or tunic that hung down over his trousers. Its breezy comfort made it a style that appealed to men on vacation from the 1930s until today.

Argyles: A multicolored diamond pattern in woolen socks and sweaters. Argyll is the name of the clan whose tartan is imitated by this pattern.

Beanie, Beany, or Calotte: This skullcap was originally Greek and worn by all classes, but particularly the lower classes, and the fabric varied according to the position of the wearer. Later as a small round skullcap it was worn under a priest's hood to cover his *tonsure,* and gradually in varying colors it came to denote ecclesiastic rank among churchmen. In the 1930s under the name *beanie* instead of *calotte* it became a popular female fashion as well as a cap for young boys.

Bermuda Shorts: Knee-length shorts for summer sportswear.

Borsalino: An Italian-made felt hat in which the fibers are aged for several years and the detailing is done by hand; supposedly the finest of men's hats.

Crew Cut: A haircut developed during World War II and often favored by young men in the late 1940s and early 1950s. The hair was cropped very close to the head except on top where it made a bristly stand of less than an inch. Although also known as the *G.I. haircut,* it was really a collegiate style that originated among varsity rowing crews to differentiate them from other undergraduates. When the top was slightly longer and tousled, it became a *feather crew* or *Ivy League cut.*

Culottes: A trouserlike garment that has the fullness to make it look like a full skirt when the wearer is not in motion. It was originally the name given to aristocratic knee breeches in the eighteenth century, but in the 1930s came to be used specifically to describe divided skirts.

Congo and Palm Beach Suits: Originally summer suits of white cotton and mohair, later applied to all white summer suits.

Cummerbund: A wide cloth band worn around the waist to imitate the same item worn by Spanish and Latin American men as a first waist sash. The term comes from the Hindu word *kamarband*—a wide, soft sash worn around the waist with little pockets for carrying small possessions. In the hot summer of 1893 it was adopted by Europeans to replace the waistcoat, and by the 1930s it had become a standard replacement (in black silk or faille) for the black waistcoat usually worn with a tuxedo dinner jacket.

Eisenhower Jacket: A waist-length military tunic in khaki worn by General Eisenhower during World War II and adapted for civilian use after the war.

Halter: A more or less triangular piece of sturdy material made to tie at the back of the neck and at the back of the waist. In the 1930s for women's beach wear it was often the only garment above the waist, leaving the arms and back bare for tanning.

Halter Neckline: A neckline new in the 1930s that was high in the neck at the center front, leaving the shoulders and the back completely bare. It was

first designed for beachwear, but a version for afternoon and evening soon followed.

Handkerchief Tunic: A tunic made from a square of material, the center of which was cut out for a waistline, the corners falling in graceful folds at the sides of the skirt.

Hollywood Top Slip: A fitted slip with a single or a double V top.

Levis: See *Contemporary.*

Loafer: Heel-less Norwegian slipper shoe introduced in 1940.

Lodencoat: A coat made of waterproof green Tyrolean woolen fabric with wooden toggles and loops instead of buttons. See *The Cold War: toggle coat.*

Montgomery Beret: A dashing military beret associated with the British general Montgomery.

Polo Coat: See *World War I and the Twenties.*

Polo Shirt: See *World War I and the Twenties.*

Saddle Shoe: See *World War I and the Twenties.*

Sash Blouse: A blouse with wide pieces that crossed in front like a surplice with attached ends forming a sash or girdle, which was tied or fastened in the back.

Sequin Calotte: A small beanie-like cap covered in sequins—a style fashionable in the 1930s.

Shirtwaist Dress: A one-piece belted and tailored dress having a tucked shirtwaist.

Slacks: Loose trousers worn for informal wear.

Snap Brim: A soft felt hat having a medium crown and brim pulled down in front in a jaunty manner.

Snood: Originally a ribbon or *fillet* worn by unmarried Scottish maidens. Later it signified the coarse hairnet or fabric that was attached to the back of a Victorian hat to hold the hair—a style that had its origins in the use of the medieval *caul* or hairnet of gold thread. The snood returned to fashion in the 1930s, sometimes with a tiny hat attached.

Swagger Coat: A coat having a very loose skirt or flared from shoulder to hem.

Swing Skirt: A circular skirt with gores that gave a swinging motion when the wearer was walking. The skirt was also popular in the 1930s when swing music was popular.

Tab Collar: A collar with a long point on each side extending down the front.

Teddies: A straight garment, combining a shapeless brassiere and a straight skirt, with a wide strap separating the garment into two separate parts or legs.

Windbreaker: A lined leather or closely woven cloth

jacket with a zipper that was used as a protection against the weather in place of a longer or a heavier coat when a sport shirt and slacks were worn.

THE COLD WAR
(1945–1963)

A-Line: A triangular or **A**-shaped dress, either belted or unbelted and usually sleeveless.

American Blade: A coat with a broad shoulder and with fullness at the upper arm and back to prevent strain.

Ballerina Skirt: A very full, usually ankle-length, gored or flare skirt, sometimes made of three or four tiers of ruffles, resembling the type worn by a Spanish dancer.

Ballet Slipper: A flat, low slipper laced around the ankle and worn for casual or evening wear.

Beach Coat: A short, loose coat of terry cloth, plain cotton, or synthetic fiber used for beach wear.

Blücher: A shoe with a long vamp and a strap across the instep, derived from the style of boot worn by General Blücher during the Battle of Waterloo.

Blue Jeans: Trousers made of denim, a heavy, twilled cotton cloth; formerly worn by cowboys and workers, they had become the standard day-to-day wear of many young people and students by the early 1960s.

Boy Coat: A short jacket with collar and cuffs that resembled the jackets worn by small boys.

Butcher Linen: A strong, heavy cloth made of long-fiber flax and used for the aprons worn by butchers; in white it was used for dresses and suitings. Made of either rayon or rayon and cotton.

Cabin Boy Breeches: Short, tight-fitting knee pants laced at the knee.

Cache-chignon: A velvet bow used to catch loose ends of hair.

Capri or Pirate Pants: Similar to pedal pushers but loose and tapered, ending at midcalf.

Car Coat: A fingertip-length coat with patch pockets and a turned-up collar; used for traveling in an open sports car.

Chukka Boot: A two-eyelet, ankle-high shoe of suede or smooth leather with rubber or leather soles. Related to the *jodhpur boot,* which fastened with a strap. The name *chukka* is of East Indian origin and is the name for a period of play in polo.

Cinch Belt: A tight, wide, elastic belt.

Cocktail Dress: A party dress appropriate for wear in the late afternoon; often longer than a daytime dress.

Cobbler's Apron: A sleeveless, hip-length, belted apron with huge pockets across the front, worn for dress or for utility.

Convertible Jumper: A sleeveless dress worn with a sweater for sportswear, with a dressy blouse for daytime, and without a blouse for evening.

Cowichan or Siwash Sweater: A sweater with a striking Indian pattern in black on white or grey background, made by the Siwash Indians of Vancouver Island, B.C.

Desert Cloth: A relatively stiff and medium-coarse-weave cotton in bright colors that was used for sport-skirts in the 1950s.

Directory Suit: A suit with high midriff and very short cutaway jacket; in general followed the silhouette of the French Directoire.

Dirndl: A very full, gathered skirt resembling the skirt of Tyrolean peasants.

Duffle Coat: A warm woolen coat of fingertip length with hood attached, having frogs of wood and rope. It came into use on ski lifts after World War II when surplus English Navy coats were made available to civilians. Worn by men and women and children, they are frequently of Tyrolean cloth with wooden toggles and hemp loops. See *The Thirties and World War II: loden coat.*

Duvetyn: A type of cotton suede cloth with a soft, fuzzy right side and a hard underside; used for skirts during the 1940s and 1950s.

Eisenhower Jacket: A waist-length military tunic popularized by General Eisenhower.

Flyaway Collar: A collar with points that flare to the side in the manner of a winged collar.

Flyaway Jacket: A very short jacket with a very full back.

Gaucho Pants: Calf-length pants, wrapped across the front, with trouser leg tapered below the knee; resembling pants worn by the cowboys of Argentina.

Halter Top: A blouse with bare back, having the neckline continued around the back of the neck.

Harem-Hem Skirt: A soft hem, draped to give a bloomer effect.

Hippies: A cult of young people of the 1960s devoted to a primitive look through the use of old or worn clothes and accessories; they are usually associated with long hair, mysticism, beards, *bare* feet, and alienation from conventional society.

Huarache: A sandal woven of leather or raffia strips; used by the Mexican Indians.

Lumber Jacket: Short, heavy, plaid woolen jacket, belted and with patch pockets.

Mandarin Jacket: A loose-fitting jacket resembling a Chinese tunic-coat.

Martingale Belt: A half-belt in back of a jacket or coat. The word has been long applied to a leather strap extending from the bit of reins in a horse's bridle to the girdle.

Mixed-Match Separates: A jacket and skirt of unlike but harmonizing fabrics that can be worn interchangeably with other garments.

Moat Collar: A narrow standing collar worn around a high, broad neckline.

Monk Shoe: A low shoe, plain across the instep and fastened with a buckle.

New Bold Look: An organized program of manufacturers and retailers to assist men to coordinate an ensemble and to create a demand for new male styles.

New Look: Styles for women introduced in 1947 by Christian Dior.

Page-Boy Hairdo: A medieval hair style adopted by women in the 1940s. It involves shoulder-length hair with the ends turned under.

Paratrooper Boot: A Blücher-style boot of stout, oiled, brown leather, water-resistant and laced with leather thongs over hooks on either side of the front opening. Later in World War II the dangerous hooks were replaced by the eyelets used on the *chukka boot.*

Parka, Anorak, or Amout: A hip-length hooded garment of sealskin worn by Eskimos. The name comes from the Aleutian Islands. The modern parka used in Europe and the United States developed in Scandinavia. It was made of lightweight cotton or silk, was very wind-resistant and water-repellent, and had allowance for ventilation when used for sports such as skiing or sailing.

Pedal Pushers: Close-fitting pants extending below the knee, made in various colors, frequently of blue denim, and with or without a cuff.

Poodle Cloth: A woolen material with a surface of thickly woven loops, popular in 1952.

Poodle Haircut: A woman's hairdress in which the hair was cut uniformly to about 1½ inches and loosely curled.

Puggree: Wide, soft band arranged in a fold around a hat.

Reefer: A single- or double-breasted tailored coat.

Sack Dress: A straight dress with no shape, cut from shoulder to hem like a bag or sack.

Sarong: A short, wraparound skirt of colorful fabric, usually with Polynesian designs.

Sheath dress: A tight-fitting dress.

Shift: Another straight dress without shape that was worn without a belt at the waist and that rode on shoulders and hips.

Shrug Jacket: A very short jacket or sweater with sleeves cut in one with the body.

Sleeveless Blazer: A short, sleeveless jacket with pockets, knitted or made of fabric.

Sleeveless Look: A dress or a blouse without sleeves or decorations at the armhole.

Sling Neckline: A pointed neckline that extended diagonally and joined the side opening of a dress.

Sloppy Joe: A costume including a man's shirt, usually several sizes too large and worn on the outside over blue jeans carelessly rolled up at the knee; also the name given to a loose, baggy sweater, also worn too large.

Square Dance Dress: A dress with a full blouse, sleeveless or puff sleeve, and a full skirt.

Stocking Bodice: A knitted woolen tube, to be pulled over the head and fastened with a drawstring or shirred on elastic, worn with shorts, skirts, or dinner dress.

Sundress or Sunback Dress: A cotton dress with the back cut out.

Teddy Boy: Exaggerated outfits worn after the war in England by young boys who were trying to attract attention by their dress and gang behavior.

Tent Dress: First launched in 1951 by Balenciaga in a wonderfully simple, black, woolen coat flaring widely from a low standing collar. It was followed in the early 1960s by Yves St. Laurent's **A**-*line silhouette.*

Toggle Coat: A coat that fastened with wooden blocks and loops instead of buttons and buttonholes. The toggle of smooth wood about an inch long and the thickness of a wide pencil was secured to the coat by a cord around a groove in the middle and was pushed through a loop on the opposite side for fastening.

Toreador Pants: Short, tight-fitting pants buttoned at the knee, resembling those worn by the Spanish toreador.

Trapeze Line: In 1958 Yves St. Laurent, the protégé and successor of Christian Dior, was acclaimed for his *trapeze* line, which later evolved into the **A**-*line.*

Tremont Hat: A man's hat with a tapered crown,

center crease, and a fairly narrow brim worn up or down; sometimes with a pinched crown and a snap brim.

Trumpet Coat Dress or Trumpet Skirt: Garments that were fairly tight over the hips with pleating or fullness from just above the knee.

TV Lounging Jacket: A loose-fitting jacket for watching television.

TV Sets: Lounging separates worn while watching TV programs.

Vicuña: A wild animal of the Andes mountains that lives in herds in Ecuador and Bolivia. Its soft wool and fur was made into the softest, most expensive woolen overcoats (often with fur collars) sold in Europe and America; also used in suitings and fine sweaters. Became famous in the 1960s as the political gift that brought scandal to the Eisenhower Administration and the resignation of Sherman Adams, the president's chief aide.

Waspie Belt: A very wide, shiny, imitation leather belt that both raised the waist and lowered the belt line in the period from 1957 to 1959.

Wedgie: A shoe having a very thick sole and a wedge-shaped heel.

Weskit: A waist-length, tight-fitting, sleeveless jacket.

CONTEMPORARY
(1963–1980)

Afro Hairdo: A frizzed-out halo of hair that surrounded the head in a great bush. First worn by American blacks in the 1960s to establish connection with their roots in Africa; later adopted by both male and female whites to give an anti-establishment look. The style was achieved by a heavy backcombing of the hair.

Braless Look: During the revolution in styles that erupted among young people in the 1960s, with its stress on natural, sensuous bodies, there was a movement to throw out the *brassiere* as a symbol of establishment repression. The braless look was sometimes achieved by not wearing a brassiere; at other times it was simulated as much as possible by wearing a thin, flexible, barely existent bra.

Caftan: Originally a long, coat-like garment worn by both sexes in the Levant and adopted as a robe by members of the Muslim clergy. The variation introduced in the 1960s, more like the Egyptian robe, consisted of a great square of material front and back reaching from wrist to wrist and sewn on the shoulders and sides to make a great flowing gown to be worn belted or unbelted by women wishing to give a luxuriant, sensual, exotic, Eastern flavor to their dress.

Flower Children: A name given to the anti-establishment young in the late 1960s who left their homes to congregate in places like the Haight-Ashbury in San Francisco. They were so called because they often adorned their deliberately shabby jeans and T-shirts with flowers.

Hot Pants: A style intermittently seen in the late 1960s and early 1970s in which very tight-fitting short shorts were worn by women with tights and boots or even with just the bare leg showing from boot tops (often vinyl) to the crotch.

Levis: A tight-fitting blue denim trouser with a U-shaped crotch, worn by boys and younger men (there are also Levis waist-length jackets); originally part of a western cowboy outfit, the trousers were and still are manufactured by Levi Strauss of San Francisco. During the 1960s they became a symbol of the natural, outdoor, shabby look of the "hippies" and "flower children" who often cut, fringed, and remade the jackets and pants as well as insetting them with colored fabric and embroidering them with colored thread and yarn.

Maxi Coat: Huge, blanket-like overcoats in tightly woven wool that reached to the ankles and were worn with mufflers, knit caps, and boots in winter. Often worn over the *mini skirt.*

Maxi Skirt: Very full, long, gypsy skirts worn with boots in the late 1960s and early 1970s. The length was ankle or floor length.

Micro Skirt: The shortest of the *mini skirts,* this one came to just a little below the crotch and was usually worn with tights and boots in the 1960s.

Midi Skirt: A brief and erratic reaction to the *mini skirt* in which designers (fairly unsuccessfully) attempted in the late 1960s to lower skirts to the mid-calf and below. They were usually intended to be worn with boots.

Mini Skirt: A very short skirt that ended well above the knees. Popular between 1963 and the early 1970s.

Mod Clothing: A contraction of "modern clothing"; applies to the exaggerated, smartly cut clothes for young people that came out of Carnaby Street, London, since 1963.

Moon Girl Style: In 1963 and 1964 Courrèges in Paris introduced this style as a reflection of the great interest in the space program, which was supposed to reach the moon by the end of the decade. Representative styles, always in whites or silvers, were made of silver sequin pants, white jackets, and white vinyl boots.

Nehru Jacket: A fitted tunic with a low standing collar instead of lapels worn by East Indian men of the Punjab and Kashmir. Introduced into London and Paris styles for men in the 1960s and made of all manner of fabrics from velvet to brocade, from wool and cotton to silk. The name comes from Prime Minister Nehru of India who popularized the style in the 1950s.

Nouveau Classique: A style introduced in 1963 by Emmanuelle Khanh that revived the classic architectural lines of Chanel but with many carefully planned curves instead of angles. The jackets had a drooped, ''no-shoulder'' look, and the outfits were usually worn with a Sassoon haircut.

Op Art: Designs based on optical illusions created through playing with simple geometric forms in primary colors. Often used in dress design in the 1960s.

Palazzo Pajamas: Evening outfits with soft jackets, tunics, and trousers that were introduced for evening wear in the early 1960s. An updated version of the at-home silk pajama outfits developed in the 1920s.

Pants Suits: In the late 1960s and early 1970s acceptance of trouser suits for women coincided with the rise of interest in the women's liberation movement and the support for the Equal Rights Amendment. Such suits had fitted jackets that were tailored much like the men's suit with matching or contrasting vest and matching trousers. The style waned in the late 1970s.

Poncho: A large square or rectangular piece of material, often in gay colors, with a hole cut out of the middle for the head. Originally worn by Mexican peasants, the style became very popular in the United States as a rain garment or a colorful outerwrap in soft hand-woven woolens in the 1960s and early 1970s.

Pop Art: Paintings and designs based on photographs or cartoons or on the advertising art of the day. Designs based on Pop Art were often incorporated in fashions of the 1960s.

Punk: Name given to excessive makeup, clothing, haircoloring, and attitudes that were meant to violate every expected social norm. The name comes from Punk Rock music and the styles were worn by nihilistic followers of the Punk Rock bands in the 1970s and 1980s.

Sassoon Cut: A hair style named after Vidal Sassoon, who became the most fashionable hairdresser in London in the 1960s. In his hands the permanent wave straightened into a *fall* that stood high over the forehead with the long ends on the shoulders. Often he curtained the forehead with a deep fringe of straight hair.

Tent Shape: This full spreading line for women, first introduced by Balenciaga in 1951 as the *A-line,* came back in full force in 1967 in the tent-silhouetted evening gowns of Madame Grès.

Trouser Suits: Another name for the pants suits of the late 1960s and early 1970s. *Trouser suit* was the name more frequently used during the mid-1970s.

Turtleneck: Originally a masculine or feminine knitted or jersey sweater with a long, straight, tube-like collar that was rolled down to the height desired. In the 1960s such pullovers in very soft jersey came into fashion for men with suits and sports jackets and have continued in popularity as a replacement for a shirt and tie.

Velcro: The trade name of a nonmetallic overlapping fastener of two strips of fabric faced with tiny nylon hooks which when pressed together hold fast. To undo the strips they are simply pulled apart. The closing was invented by Georges de Mestral of Switzerland and was first used in the early 1960s.

Vinyl: A trademarked American-made couture fabric introduced about 1965. Originally used for waterproof umbrellas and raincoats, it was soon seen in boots, jackets, belts, and even drapes. It takes dye and prints in bright colors and is often seen in simple geometric patterns as well as in its original semitransparent form.

Bibliography

This bibliography lists some of the more useful works to be consulted in costume, theatre, and art in connection with the study of this text. The bibliography is divided into categories that correspond to the divisions in the text.

GENERAL

Altman, George, et al. *Theater Pictorial, A History of World Theater as Recorded in Drawings, Paintings, Engravings, and Photographs*. Berkeley: University of California Press, 1953.

Anthony, Pegaret, and Arnold, Janet. *Costume, A General Bibliography* (rev. and enlarged). London: Costume Society, Victoria and Albert Museum, 1974.

Beaumont, Cyril. *Ballet Design: Past and Present*. New York: Studio, 1946.

Berthold, Margot. *A History of the World Theater*. New York: Ungar, 1972.

Brockett, Oscar. *The Theatre: An Introduction,* 4th ed. New York: Holt, Rinehart & Winston, 1979.

————. *History of the Theatre,* 4th ed. Boston: Allyn & Bacon, Inc., 1982.

Burris-Meyer, Harold, and Cole, Edward C. *Scenery for the Theatre: The Organization, Processes, Material, and Techniques Used to Set the Stage,* 2nd ed. Boston: Little, Brown, 1972.

Cheney, Sheldon. *The Theatre: Three Thousand Years of Drama, Acting and Stagecraft* (rev. ed.). New York: Longmans, Green, 1972.

————. *Stage Decoration*. New York: Day, 1928.

Cohen, Robert. *Theatre*. Palo Alto, Calif.: Mayfield Publishing Co., 1981.

Corrigan, Robert W. *The World of the Theatre*. Glenview, Illinois: Scott, Foresman, 1979.

Fuller, Edmund. *A Pageant of the Theatre*. New York: Harper & Row, Pub., 1941.

Gascoigne, Bamber. *World Theatre: An Illustrated History*. Boston: Little, Brown, 1968.

Gassner, John, and Allen, Ralph. *Theatre and Drama in the Making*. Boston: Houghton Mifflin, 1964.

Hartnoll, Phyllis. *The Oxford Companion to the Theatre,* 3rd ed. London: Oxford University Press, 1967.

———. *The Concise History of the Theatre.* New York: Harry N. Abrams, 1968.

Macgowan, Kenneth, and Melnitz, William. *The Living Stage.* Englewood Cliffs, N.J.: Prentice-Hall, 1955.

Molinari, Cesar. *Theatre Through the Ages.* New York: McGraw-Hill, 1972.

Nagler, Alois. *Sources of Theatrical History.* New York: Theatre Annual, 1952.

Nicoll, Allardyce. *The Development of the Theatre,* 5th ed. London: Harrap, 1966.

Odell, G. C. D. *Annals of the New York Stage,* 15 vols. New York: Columbia University Press, 1927–1949.

Oenslager, Donald. *Scenery Then and Now.* New York: W. W. Norton & Co., Inc., 1936.

Pickering, Jerry. *Theatre: A History of the Art.* St. Paul, Minn.: West Publishing Co., 1978.

Roberts, Vera Mowry. *On Stage: A History of the Theatre,* 2nd ed. New York: Harper & Row, Pub., 1974.

Sachs, Curt. *World History of the Dance* (trans. by Bessie Schoenberg). New York: W. W. Norton & Co., Inc., 1937.

Simonson, Lee. *The Stage Is Set.* New York: Harcourt Brace Jovanovich, 1932.

Sobel, Bernard. *The Theatre Handbook and Digest of Plays.* New York: Crown, 1948.

CHAPTER 1

Adams, J. Donald. *Naked We Came.* New York: Holt, Rinehart & Winston, 1967.

Albright, H. D., Halstead, W. P., and Mitchell, Lee. *Principles of Theatre Art.* Boston: Houghton Mifflin, 1955.

Bell, Quentin. *On Human Finery,* 2nd ed. New York: Schocken Books, 1976.

Broby-Johansen, R. *Body and Clothes* (trans. by Erik I. Friis and Karen Rush). New York: Van Nostrand Reinhold, 1968.

Burris-Meyer, Elizabeth. *This Is Fashion.* New York: Harper & Row, Pub., 1943.

Burris-Meyer, Harold, and Cole, Edward C. See *General.*

Cremers-van der Does, Eline Canter. *The Agony of Fashion* (trans. by Leo Van Witsen). Poole, Dorset, England: Blandford Press, 1980.

Flügel, John Carl. *The Psychology of Clothes.* London: Hogarth, 1950.

Hollander, Anne. *Seeing Through Clothes.* New York: Avon Books, 1975.

Jones, Robert Edmond. *The Dramatic Imagination.* New York: Theatre Arts, 1941.

Komisarjevsky, Theodore. *The Costume of the Theatre.* London: Bles, 1931.

Laver, James. *Costume in the Theatre.* New York: Hill & Wang Dramabook, 1965.

———. *Drama, Its Costume and Decor.* London: Studio Publications, 1951.

———. *Taste and Fashion.* London: Harrap, 1945.

Lurie, Alison. *The Language of Clothes.* New York: Random House, 1981.

Newton, Stella Mary. *Health, Art and Reason: Dress Reformers of the Nineteenth Century.* London: John Murray, 1974.

Rudofsky, Bernard. *The Unfashionable Human Body.* New York: Doubleday, 1974.

Young, Stark. *The Theatre.* New York: Doubleday, 1927.

———. *Theatre Practice.* New York: Scribner's, 1926.

CHAPTER 2

Anderson, Barbara and Cletus. *Costume Design.* New York: Holt, Rinehart & Winston, 1983.

Arnheim, Rudolph. *Art and Visual Perception.* Berkeley: University of California Press, 1954.

Clark, Kenneth. *The Nude: A Study in Ideal Form.* New York: Pantheon, 1956.

Doten, Hazel R., and Boulard, Constance. *Fashion Drawing: How to Do It.* New York: Harper & Row, Pub., 1939.

Edwards, Betty. *Drawing on the Right Side of the Brain.* Los Angeles: J. P. Tarcher, Inc., 1979.

Emerson, Sybil. *Design: A Creative Approach.* Scranton, Pa.: International Textbook, 1962.

Gombrich, E. H. *Art and Illusion: A Study in the Psychology of Pictorial Representation.* New York: Pantheon, 1965.

Gordon, Conni. *You Can Paint.* New York: Conni Gordon, 1965.

———. *You Can Draw.* New York: Conni Gordon, 1963.

———. *You Can Watercolor.* New York: Conni Gordon, 1962.

Gutierrez, Jose, and Roukes, Nicholas. *Painting with Acrylics.* New York: Watson-Guptill, 1962.

Hale, Robert Beverly. *Drawing Lessons from the Great Masters.* New York: Watson-Guptill, 1964.

Hill, Adrian. *The Beginning Book of Watercolor Painting.* New York: Emerson, 1964.

Loomis, Andrew. *Figure Drawing for All Its Worth.* Cleveland, Ohio: Collins Publishers, 1943.

Mayer, Ralph. *The Painter's Craft: An Introduction to Artists' Methods and Materials* (rev. ed.). Princeton, N.J.: D. Van Nostrand, 1966.

————. *The Artist's Handbook of Materials and Techniques* (rev. ed.). New York: Viking, 1957.

Motley. *Designing and Making Stage Costumes.* London: Studio Vista, 1965.

Mugniani, Joseph. *The Hidden Elements of Drawing.* New York: Van Nostrand Reinhold, 1974.

Pope, Arthur. *The Language of Drawing and Painting.* Cambridge, Mass.: Harvard University Press, 1949.

Raynes, John. *Human Anatomy For the Artist.* New York: Crescent Books, 1979.

Sloan, Eunice Moore. *Illustrating Fashion.* New York: Harper & Row, Pub., 1968.

Sotto, Marilyn. *The Art of Costume Design.* Laguna Beach, Calif.: Walter Foster, n.d.

Taylor, Joshua C. *Learning to Look.* Chicago: University of Chicago Press, n.d.

Yochim, Louise Dunn. *Perceptual Growth in Creativity.* Scranton, Pa.: International Textbook, 1962.

Zinkeisen, Doris. *Designing for the Stage.* London: Studio, 1945.

CHAPTER 3

Anderson, Donald M. *Elements of Design.* New York: Holt, Rinehart & Winston, 1961.

Bay, Howard. *Stage Design.* New York: Drama Books, 1974.

Cole, Michael, and Scribner, Sylvia. *Culture and Thought, A Psychological Introduction.* New York: John Wiley, 1974.

Fry, Roger. *Vision and Design.* London: Chatto & Windus, 1920.

Horn, Marilyn J. *The Second Skin,* 2nd ed. Boston: Houghton Mifflin, 1975.

Lowry, Bates. *The Visual Experience: An Introduction to Art.* Englewood Cliffs, N.J.: Prentice-Hall, 1961.

Motley. See *Chapter 2.*

Oxenford, Lyn. *Playing Period Plays.* London: Miller, 1958.

Panofsky, Erwin. *Meaning in the Visual Arts.* Garden City, N.Y.: Anchor, 1955.

Rowell, Kenneth. *Stage Design.* New York: Van Nostrand Reinhold, 1968.

Sheringham, George, and Laver, James. *Design in the Theatre.* London: Studio, 1927.

Teague, Walter Dorwin. *Design This Day: The Technique of Order in This Machine Age* (rev. ed.). New York: Harcourt Brace Jovanovich, 1949.

Watkins, Charles Law. *The Language of Design.* Washington, D.C.: Philips Memorial Gallery, 1946.

Weismann, Donald L. *The Visual Arts as Human Experience.* Englewood Cliffs, N.J.: Prentice-Hall, 1970.

CHAPTER 4

Albers, Josef. *Interaction of Color* (rev. pocket ed.). New Haven, Conn.: Yale University Press, 1975.

Birren, Faber. *Creative Color: A Dynamic Approach for Artists and Designers.* New York: Van Nostrand Reinhold, 1961.

Burris-Meyer, Elizabeth. *Color and Design in the Decorative Arts.* Englewood Cliffs, N.J.: Prentice-Hall, 1935.

Burris-Meyer, Harold, and Cole, Edward C. See *Chapter 1.*

Bustanoby, J. H. *Principles of Color and Color Mixing.* New York: McGraw-Hill, 1947.

Ellenger, Richard G. *Color Structure and Design.* Scranton, Pa.: International Textbook, 1961.

Graves, Maitland. *The Art of Color and Design,* 2nd ed. New York: McGraw-Hill, 1951.

Green, Joyce Conyngham. *Planning the Stage Wardrobe.* London: Nelson, 1941.

Itten, Johannes. *The Art of Color: The Subjective Experience and Objective Rationale of Color* (trans. by Ernst von Haagen). New York: Van Nostrand Reinhold, 1961.

Jacobson, Egbert. *The Science of Color.* Chicago: American Photographers Association, 1937.

Küppers, Harold. *Color: Origin, System, Uses.* London: Van Nostrand Reinhold, 1973.

Luckiesh, Matthew. *Visual Illusions: Their Causes, Characteristics and Applications.* New York: Dover, 1965.

Motley. See *Chapter 2.*

Pope, Arthur. *See Chapter 2.*

Pye, David. *The Nature of Design.* New York: Van Nostrand Reinhold, 1971.

Sargent, Walter. *The Enjoyment and Use of Color.* New York: Dover, 1964.

CHAPTER 5

A. F. Encyclopedia of Textiles, 3rd ed. Englewood Cliffs, N.J.: Prentice-Hall, 1980.

Denny, G. G. *Fabrics and How to Know Them.* Philadelphia: Lippincott, 1947.

du Pont de Nemours. *A Brief History of Dyes.* Wilmington, Del.: E. I. du Pont de Nemours, n.d.

Fernald, Mary, and Shenton, Eileen. *Costume Design and Making.* London: A. & C. Black, 1958.

Finch, Karen, and Putnam, Greta. *Caring for Textiles.* New York: Watson-Guptill, 1977.

Gostelow, Mary. *The Complete International Book of Embroidery.* New York: Simon & Schuster, 1977.

Green, Joyce Conyngham. See *Chapter 4.*

Healy, Daty. *Dress the Show: A Basic Costume Book.* Evanston, Ill.: Row, Peterson, 1948.

Hess, Katharine. *Textile Fibers and Their Use.* Philadelphia: Lippincott, 1941.

Jacobsen, E. A., and McCullough, H. E. *Fundamentals of Textiles: A Workbook.* New York: John Wiley, 1941.

Kafka, Francis. *The Hand Decoration of Fabric.* New York: Dover, 1973.

Mathews, J. M. *Textile Fibers.* New York: John Wiley, 1947.

Potter, David M., and Corbman, Bernard P. *Textiles: Fiber to Fabric,* 4th ed. New York: McGraw-Hill, 1967.

Prisk, Berneice. *Stage Costume Handbook.* New York: Harper & Row, Pub., 1966.

Wingate, Isabel. *Textile Fabrics and Their Selection,* 7th ed. Englewood Cliffs, N.J.: Prentice-Hall, 1976.

Woolman, M. S., and McGowan, E. B. *Textiles.* New York: Macmillan, 1934.

CHAPTER 6

Arnold, Janet. *Patterns of Fashion: English-women's Dresses and Their Construction* (2 vols.: 1660–1860, 1860–1940). Washington, D.C.: Hobby House Press, 1965.

Barton, Lucy, and Edson, Doris. *Period Patterns.* Boston: W. H. Baker, 1942.

Bernstein, Aline. *Masterpieces of Eighteenth and Nineteenth Century Women's Costumes.* New York: Crown, 1959.

Bradford, Nancy. *Costume in Detail.* Boston: Plays, Inc., 1970.

Brooke, Iris. *Medieval Theatre Costume.* New York: Theatre Arts, 1967.

Burnham, Dorothy K. *Cut My Cote.* Toronto: Royal Ontario Museum, 1973.

Croonberg, Frederick. *The Blue Book of Men's Tailoring.* New York: Van Nostrand Reinhold, 1977.

Evans, Mary. *How to Make Historic American Costumes.* New York: A. S. Barnes, 1942.

Fernald, Mary, and Shenton, Eileen. See *Chapter 5.*

Gassner, John. *Producing the Play* (Including *The Scene Technician's Handbook* by Philip Barber). New York: Holt, Rinehart & Winston, 1953.

Healy, Daty. See *Chapter 5.*

Hill, Margaret Hamilton, and Bucknell, Peter A. *The Evolution of Fashion: Pattern and Cut from 1066 to 1930.* New York: Van Nostrand Reinhold, 1968.

Houston, Mary G. *Technical History of Costume,* 2nd ed. London: A. & C. Black, 1954.

Köhler, Carl. *A History of Costume.* New York: Dover, 1963.

Norris, Herbert. *Costume and Fashion.* London: Dent, 1941.

Payne, Blanche. *History of Costume.* New York: Harper & Row, Pub., 1965.

Prisk, Berneice, See *Chapter 5.*

Prisk, Berneice, and Byers, Jack. *The Theatre Student, Costuming.* New York: Richard Rosen Press, 1970.

Singer Sewing Machine Company. *Métado Singer de Corte y Costuma.* New York: Singer Sewing Machine Company, 1955.

Smith, C. Ray (ed.). *The Theatre Crafts Book of Costume.* Emmaus, Pa.: Rodale Press, 1973.

Tilke, Max. *Costume Patterns and Designs.* New York: Holt, Rinehart & Winston, 1957.

Walkup, Fairfax Proudfit. *Dressing the Part.* New York: Appleton-Century-Crofts, 1950.

The Vogue Sewing Book. New York: Vogue Patterns, 1975.

Waugh, Norah. *The Cut of Men's Clothes 1600–1900.* New York: Theatre Arts, 1964.

———. *The Cut of Women's Clothes 1600–1930.* New York: Theatre Arts, 1968.

———. *Corsets and Crinolines.* New York: Theatre Arts, 1970.

CHAPTER 7

Anderson, Barbara and Cletus. See *Chapter 2.*

Belfer, Nancy. *Designing in Batik and Tie-Dye.* Englewood Cliffs, N.J.: Prentice-Hall, 1977.

Barton, Lucy. *Historic Costume for the Stage* (new ed.). Boston: H. Baker, 1961.

Dryden, Deborah. *Fabric Printing and Dyeing for the Theatre.* New York: Drama Books, 1982.

Emery, Joy Spanabel. *Stage Costume Techniques.* Englewood Cliffs, N.J.: Prentice-Hall, 1981.

Fernald, Mary, and Shenton, Eileen. See *Chapter 5.*

Green, Joyce Conyngham. See *Chapter 4.*

Healy, Daty. See *Chapter 5.*

Hillhouse, Marian S., and Mansfield, Evelyn A. *Dress Design, Draping and Flat Pattern Making.* Boston: Houghton Mifflin, 1948.

Hollen, Norma R. *Pattern Making by the Flat Pattern Method,* 4th ed. Minneapolis: Burgess Publishing Co., 1975.

Ingham, Rosemary, and Covey, Elizabeth. *The Costumer's Handbook.* Englewood Cliffs, N.J: Prentice-Hall, 1980.

Ingham, Rosemary, and Covey, Elizabeth. *The Costume Designers Handbook.* Englewood Cliffs, N.J.: Prentice-Hall, 1983.

Jackson, Sheila. *Simple Stage Costumes and How to Make Them.* London: Studio Vista, 1968.

Jackson, Sheila. *Simple Stage Costumes and How to Make Them.* London: Studio Vista, 1968.

Lippincott, Gertrude (ed.). *Dance Production: Music, Costumes, Staging, Decor, Lighting, Photography, Makeup, Planning and Rehearsing.* Washington, D.C.: American Association for Health, Physical Education and Recreation, 1957.

Moulton, Bertha. *Garment Cutting and Tailoring for Students* (rev. ed.). London: Batsford, 1967.

Prisk, Berneice. See *Chapter 5.*

Young, Agnes Brooks. *Stage Costuming.* New York: Macmillan, 1927.

CHAPTER 8

Barton, Lucy. See *Chapter 7.*

Bowman, Ned A. *Handbook of Technical Practice for the Performing Arts.* Wilkinsburg, Pa.: Scenographic Media, 1972.

Bryson, Nicholas L. *Thermoplastic Scenery for the Theatre:* Vol. I, *Vacuum Forming.* New York: Drama Books, 1972.

Corson, Richard. *Stage Makeup,* 6th ed. New York: Prentice-Hall, 1981.

Healy, Daty. See *Chapter 5.*

Heffner, Hubert; Selden, Samuel; and Sellman, H. D. *Modern Theatre Practice,* 5th ed. New York: Prentice-Hall, 1973.

Macgowan, Kenneth, and Rosse, H. *Masks and Demons.* New York: Harcourt Brace Jovanovich, 1923.

Motley. *Theatre Props.* New York: Drama Books, 1975.

Nicoll, Allardyce. See *General.*

Prisk, Berneice. See *Chapter 5.*

von Neumann, Robert. *Design and Creation of Jewelry* (rev. ed.). Radnor, Pa.: Chilton, 1972.

Winter, Garry. *Crafts and Hobbies.* New York: Arco, 1965.

Zarchy, Harry. *Creative Hobbies.* New York: Knopf, 1953.

CHAPTER 9

Aristotle. *Aristotle's Theory of Poetry and the Fine Arts,* 4th ed. (critical text and trans. by S. H. Butcher). New York: Dover, 1951.

Bowman, Walter P., and Ball, Robert H. *Theatre Language, A Dictionary of Terms in English of the Drama and the Stage from Medieval to Modern Times.* New York: Theatre Arts, 1961.

Clark, Kenneth. *Civilization: A Personal View.* New York: Harper & Row, Pub., 1969.

Cole, Toby, and Chinoy, Helen K. (eds.). *Directing the Play: A Sourcebook of Stagecraft.* Indianapolis, Ind.: Bobbs-Merrill, 1953.

Edman, Erwin. *Arts and the Man.* New York: W. W. Norton & Co., Inc., 1939.

Fergusson, Francis. *The Idea of a Theatre: A Study of Ten Plays.* Princeton, N.J.: Princeton University Press, 1949.

Fleming, Arthur. *Arts and Ideas.* New York: Holt, Rinehart & Winston, 1974.

Fry, Roger. *Vision and Design.* New York: Brentano's, 1924.

Hauser, Arnold. *The Social History of Art,* 4 vols. New York: Vintage, 1959.

Heffner, Hubert. *The Nature of Drama.* Boston: Houghton Mifflin, 1959.

Holt, Elizabeth. *A Documentary History of Art,* 2 vols. Garden City, N.Y.: Doubleday, 1957.

Langer, Susanne K. *Problems of Art: Ten Philosophical Lectures.* New York: Scribner's, 1957.

Laver, James. *Style in Costume.* New York: Oxford University Press, 1949.

Levy, Mervyn. *Pocket Dictionary of Art Terms.* Greenwich, Conn.: New York Graphic Society, 1961.

Read, Herbert. *Art and Society.* London: Faber & Faber, 1945.

Rothschild, Lincoln. *Style in Art: The Dynamics of Art as Cultural Expression.* New York: Yoseloff, 1960.

Squire, Geoffrey. *Dress and Society, 1560–1970.* New York: Viking, 1974.

St. Denis, Michel. *Theatre: The Rediscovery of Style.* New York: Theatre Arts, 1960.

Wildblood, Joan. *The Polite World.* London: Davis-Poynter, 1973.

Wöfflin, Heinrich. *Principles of Art History: The Problem of the Development of Style in Later Art.* New York: Dover, 1950.

————. *The Sense of Form in Art: A Comparative Psychological Study*. New York: Chelsea, 1958.

CHAPTER 10

Allen, James T. *Stage Antiquities of the Greeks and Romans and Their Influence*. New York: Longmans, Green, 1927.

Arnott, Peter D. *An Introduction to the Greek Theatre*. London: Macmillan, 1959.

Bieber, Margarete. *The History of the Greek and Roman Theater*. Princeton, N.J.: Princeton University Press, 1939.

Brooke, Iris. *Costume in Greek Classic Drama*. New York: Theatre Arts, 1965.

Casson, Lionel. *Daily Life in Ancient Rome*. New York: American Heritage, 1975.

Gaster, Theodor. *Thespis: Ritual, Myth, and Drama in the Ancient Near East*. New York: Abelard-Schuman, 1950.

Hamilton, Edith. *The Greek Way*. New York: W. W. Norton & Co. Inc., 1952.

————. *The Roman Way*. New York: W. W. Norton & Co., Inc., 1932.

Harsh, Philip W. *A Handbook of Classical Drama*. Stanford, Calif.: Stanford University Press, 1944.

Havemeyer, Loomis. *The Drama of Savage Peoples*. New Haven, Conn.: Yale University Press, 1916.

Hunningher, Benjamin. *The Origin of the Theatre: An Essay*. New York: Hill & Wang, 1961.

Jaeger, Werner. *Paideia: The Ideals of Greek Culture*, 3 vols. (trans. by Gilbert Highet). New York: Oxford University Press, 1939–1944.

Strong, Donald. *The Classical World*. New York: McGraw-Hill, 1965.

Webster, T. B. L. *Greek Theatre Production*. London: Methuen, 1956.

CHAPTER 11

Brooke, Iris. See *Chapter 6*.

Chambers, E. K. *The Medieval Stage*, 2 vols. Oxford: Clarendon Press, 1903.

Fremantle, Anne. *Age of Faith*. New York: Time-Life Books, 1965.

Kernodle, George. *From Art to Theatre*. Chicago: University of Chicago Press, 1944.

Kidson, Peter. *The Medieval World*. New York: McGraw-Hill, 1967.

Nicoll, Allardyce. *Masks, Mimes and Miracles*. New York: Harcourt Brace Jovanovich, 1931.

Southern, Richard. *The Medieval Theatre in the Round: A Study of the Staging of The Castle of Perseverance and Related Matters*. London: Faber & Faber, 1958.

Wickham, Glynne. *Early English Stages 1300–1660*, 2 vols. New York: Columbia University Press, 1959–1962.

Williams, Arnold. *The Drama of Medieval England*. East Lansing: Michigan State University Press, 1961.

Winston, Richard. *Daily Life in the Middle Ages*. New York: American Heritage, 1975.

Young, Karl. *The Drama of the Medieval Church*, 2 vols. Oxford: Clarendon Press, 1933.

CHAPTER 12

Beckerman, Bernard. *Shakespeare at the Globe 1599–1609*. New York: Macmillan, 1962.

Bentley, Gerald E. *The Jacobean and Caroline Stage*, 5 vols. Oxford: Clarendon Press, 1941–1956.

Burckhardt, Jakob C. *The Civilization of the Renaissance in Italy*, 3rd ed. Vienna: Phaidon, 1937.

Campbell, Lily Bess. *Scenes and Machines on the English Stage During the Renaissance*. Cambridge: Cambridge University Press, 1923.

Hale, John R. *Renaissance*. New York: Time-Life Books, 1965.

Hewitt, Barnard (ed.). *The Renaissance Stage: Documents of Serlio, Sabbattini, and Furttenbach*. Coral Gables, Fla.: University of Miami Press, 1958.

Hodges, C. W. *The Globe Restored*. London: Benn, 1953.

Hotson, John Leslie. *Shakespeare's Wooden O*. New York: Macmillan, 1960.

Joseph, Bertram. *Elizabethan Acting*. London: Oxford University Press, 1951.

Kennard, Joseph S. *The Italian Theatre*, 2 vols. New York: Rudge, 1932.

Kernodle, George. See *Chapter 11*.

Martindale, Andrew. *Man and the Renaissance*. New York: McGraw-Hill, 1966.

Mee, Charles. *Daily Life in the Renaissance*. New York: American Heritage, 1975.

Nagler, A. M. *Shakespeare's Stage*. New Haven, Conn.: Yale University Press, 1958.

Nicoll, Allardyce. See *Chapter 11*.

————. *Stuart Masques and the Renaissance Stage*. London: Harrap, 1937.

Symonds, John A. *The Renaissance in Italy*, 7 vols. London: Murray, 1909–1937.

Sypher, Wylie. *Four Stages of Renaissance Style:*

Transformation in Art and Literature. Garden City, N.Y.: Doubleday-Anchor, 1955.

Wickham, Glynne. *Early English Stages, 1300–1600,* 2 vols. New York: Columbia University Press, 1959–1962.

Wölfflin, Heinrich. *Classic Art: An Introduction to the Italian Renaissance.* New York: Phaidon, 1952.

CHAPTER 13

Baur-Heinhold, M. *Baroque Theatre.* New York: McGraw-Hill, 1967.

Beijer, Agne. *Court Theatres of Drottningholm and Gripsholm* (trans. by G. L. Frölich). Malmo, Sweden: Kroon, 1933.

Blitzer, Charles. *Age of Kings.* New York: Time-Life Books, 1967.

Campbell, Lily Bess. "A History of Costuming of the English Stage Between 1660 and 1823," *University of Wisconsin Studies in Language and Literature, 1918,* pp. 187–223.

Hathaway, Baxter. *The Age of Criticism: The Late Renaissance in Italy.* Ithaca, N.Y.: Cornell University Press, 1962.

Hotson, John Leslie. *The Commonwealth and Restoration Stage.* Cambridge, Mass.: Harvard University Press, 1928.

Kitson, Michael. *The Age of the Baroque.* New York: McGraw-Hill, 1966.

Lockert, Lacy. *Studies in French Classical Tragedy.* Nashville, Tenn.: Vanderbilt University Press, 1958.

Lough, John. *Paris Theatre Audiences in the Seventeenth and Eighteenth Centuries.* London: Oxford University Press, 1957.

Mayor, A. H. *The Bibiena Family.* New York: Bittner, 1945.

McBride, Robert. *Aspects of Seventeenth Century French Drama and Thought.* Totowa, N.J.: Rowman & Littlefield, 1980.

Summers, Montague. *The Restoration Theatre.* London: Macmillan, 1934.

Sypher, Wylie. See *Chapter 12.*

Tapié, Victor. *The Age of Grandeur.* New York: Holt, Rinehart & Winston, 1957.

Thaler, Alwin. *Shakespeare to Sheridan.* Cambridge, Mass.: Harvard University Press, 1922.

Wiley, W. L. *The Early Public Theatre in France.* Cambridge, Mass.: Harvard University Press, 1960.

Wittkower, Rudolf. *Art and Architecture in Italy 1600–1750.* Baltimore: Pelican, 1958.

Wölfflin, Heinrich. *Principles of Art History.* See *Chapter 9.*

CHAPTER 14

Beijer, Agne. See *Chapter 13.*

Boas, Frederick. *An Introduction to Eighteenth Century Drama 1700–1780.* Oxford: Clarendon Press, 1953.

Burnim, Kalman. *David Garrick, Director.* Pittsburgh: Pittsburgh University Press, 1961.

Campbell, Lily Bess. See *Chapter 13.*

Faniel, Stéphane (ed.). *French Art of the Eighteenth Century.* New York: Simon & Schuster, 1957.

Gay, Peter. *The Age of Enlightenment.* New York: Time-Life Books, 1965.

Hawkins, Frederick. *The French Stage in the Eighteenth Century,* 2 vols. London: Chapman & Hall, 1888.

Kimball, Sidney Fiske. *The Creation of the Rococo.* Philadelphia: Philadelphia Museum of Art, 1943.

Odell, George C. D. *Shakespeare from Betterton to Irving,* 2 vols. New York: Scribner's, 1920.

Scholz, János. *Baroque and Romantic Stage Design.* New York: Dutton, 1962.

Schneider, Isador (ed.). *The Enlightenment.* New York: Braziller, 1965.

Sypher, Wylie. *Rococo to Cubism in Art and Literature.* New York: Vintage, 1963.

Thaler, Alwin. See *Chapter 13.*

Theatrical Designs from the Baroque Through Neo-Classicism, 3 vols. New York: Dutton, 1962.

CHAPTER 15

Abrams, M. H. *The Mirror and the Lamp: Romantic Theory and the Critical Tradition.* New York: Oxford University Press, 1953.

Brion, Marcel. *Art of the Romantic Era: Romanticism, Classicism, Realism.* New York: Holt, Rinehart & Winston, 1966.

Clement, N. H. *Romanticism in France.* New York: Modern Language Association of America, 1939.

Courthion, Pierre. *Romanticism* (trans. by Stuart Gilbert). New York: Skira, 1961.

Delacroix, Eugène. *The Journal of Eugène Delacroix* (trans. and ed. by Walter Pach). New York: Crown, 1948.

George, A. J. *The Development of French Romanticism: The Impact of the Industrial Revolution on Literature.* Syracuse, N.Y.: Syracuse University Press, 1955.

Lucas, F. L. *The Decline and Fall of the Romantic Ideal.* Cambridge: Cambridge University Press, 1936.

Newton, Eric. *The Romantic Rebellion.* New York: St. Martin's Press, 1966.

Novotny, Fritz. *Painting and Sculpture in Europe 1780–1880.* Baltimore: Penguin, 1960.

Odell, George C. D. See *Chapter 14.*

———. See *General.*

Rowell, George. *The Victorian Theatre.* Oxford: Clarendon Press, 1956.

Scholz, János. See *Chapter 14.*

Vardac, Nicholas. *Stage to Screen: Theatrical Method from Garrick to Griffith.* Cambridge, Mass.: Harvard University Press, 1949.

Walzel, Oskar F. *German Romanticism* (trans. by Alma E. Lussky). New York: Putnam's, 1932.

Watson, Ernest B. *Sheridan to Robertson: A Study of the Nineteenth-Century London Stage.* Cambridge, Mass.: Harvard University Press, 1926.

Willoughby, Leonard A. *The Romantic Movement in Germany.* London: Oxford University Press, 1930.

CHAPTER 16

Brockett, Oscar, and Findlay, Robert R. *Century of Innovation: A History of European and American Theatre and Drama 1870–1970.* Englewood Cliffs, N.J.: Prentice-Hall, 1973.

Burchell, S. C. *Age of Progress.* New York: Time-Life Books, 1966.

Gassner, John. *Form and Idea in Modern Theatre.* New York: Holt, Rinehart & Winston, 1956.

Gorelik, Mordecai. *New Theatres for Old.* New York: Dutton, 1962.

Hibbert, Christopher. *Daily Life in Victorian England.* New York: American Heritage, 1975.

Hunter, Sam. *Modern French Painting 1855–1956.* New York: Dell, 1956.

Macqueen-Pope, W. *Nights of Gladness.* London: Hutchinson, 1956.

Melcher, Edith. *Stage Realism in France from Diderot to Antoine.* Bryn Mawr, Pa.: Bryn Mawr College Press, 1928.

Nicoll, Allardyce. "History of Late Nineteenth Century Drama," *A History of English Drama, 1660–1900,* Vol. V. Cambridge: Cambridge University Press, 1930.

Rowell, George. See *Chapter 15.*

Sloane, Joseph C. *French Painting Between the Past and Present: Artists, Critics and Traditions from 1840 to 1870.* Princeton, N.J.: Princeton University Press, 1951.

Stone, Edward. *What Was Naturalism? Materials for an Answer.* New York: Appleton-Century-Crofts, 1959.

Sypher, Wylie. See *Chapter 14.*

Vardac, Nicholas. See *Chapter 15.*

Waxman, S. M. *Antoine and the Théâtre-Libre.* Cambridge, Mass.: Harvard University Press, 1926.

CHAPTER 17

Appia, Adolphe. *The Work of Living Art: A Theory of the Theatre.* Coral Gables, Fla.: University of Miami Press, 1960.

Bergson, Henri. *The Creative Mind* (trans. by Mabelle L. Andison). New York: Philosophical Library, 1946.

Cole, Toby (ed.). *Playwrights on Playwriting: The Meaning and Making of Modern Drama from Ibsen to Ionesco.* New York: Hill & Wang, 1960.

Cornell, Kenneth. *The Symbolist Movement.* New Haven, Conn.: Yale University Press, 1951.

Craig, Edward Gordon. *On the Art of the Theatre.* New York: Theatre Arts, 1957.

Fuerst, Walter, and Hume, Samuel. *Twentieth Century Stage Decoration,* 2 vols. New York: Knopf, 1929.

Gorelik, Mordecai. See *Chapter 16.*

Jones, Robert Edmond. See *Chapter 1.*

Lehmann, Andrew G. *The Symbolist Aesthetic in France, 1885–1895.* Oxford: Blackwell, 1950.

Macgowan, Kenneth, and Jones, Robert E. *Continental Stagecraft.* New York: Harcourt Brace Jovanovich, 1922.

Madsen, Stephan T. *Art Nouveau.* New York: McGraw-Hill, 1967.

Moussinac, Leon. *The New Movement in the Theatre. A Survey of Recent Developments in Europe and America.* London: Batsford, 1931.

Schmutzler, Robert. *Art Nouveau* (trans. by Edouard Roditi). New York: Harry N. Abrams, 1962.

Simonson, Lee. *The Art of Scene Design.* New York: Harper & Row, Pub., 1950.

———. See *General.*

Stein, Jack M. *Richard Wagner and the Synthesis of the Arts.* Detroit: Wayne State University Press, 1960.

Sypher, Wylie. See *Chapter 14.*

Vardac, Nicholas. See *Chapter 15.*

Willet, John. *Expressionism.* New York: McGraw-Hill, 1970.

CHAPTER 18

Arnason, H. H. *History of Modern Art.* New York: Harry N. Abrams, 1968.

Artaud, Antonin. *The Theater and Its Double* (trans.

by Mary C. Richards). New York: Grove, 1958.

Barr, Alfred H. Jr. (ed.). *Masters of Modern Art.* New York: MOMA, 1954.

Brustein, Robert. *The Theatre of Revolt.* New York: Atlantic-Little, Brown, 1964.

Clurman, Harold. *The Fervent Years: The Story of the Group Theatre and the Thirties.* New York: Hill & Wang, 1957.

Cole, Toby (ed.). See *Chapter 17.*

Colton, Joel. *Twentieth Century.* New York: Time-Life Books, 1968.

Esslin, Martin. *The Theatre of the Absurd.* Garden City, N.Y.: Doubleday-Anchor, 1969.

Fuerst, Walter, and Hume, Samuel. See *Chapter 17.*

Goldwater, Robert. *Primitivism in Modern Painting.* New York: Harper & Row, Pub., 1938.

Haftmann, Werner. *Painting in the Twentieth Century,* 2 vols. (trans. by Ralph Manheim). New York: Holt, Rinehart & Winston, 1965.

Hainaux, René (ed.). *Stage Design Throughout the World Since 1935.* New York: Theatre Arts, 1956.

————. *Stage Design Throughout the World Since 1950.* New York: Theatre Arts, 1964.

Rickey, George. *Constructivism: Origins and Evolution.* New York: Braziller, 1967.

Ritchie, Andrew C. *Sculpture of the Twentieth Century.* New York: MOMA, 1952.

Roters, Eberhard. *Painters of the Bauhaus.* New York: Holt, Rinehart & Winston, 1967.

Soby, James Thrall. *Modern Art and the New Past.* Norman, Okla.: University of Oklahoma Press, 1957.

Southern, Richard. *The Open Stage.* New York: Theatre Arts, 1959.

Sypher, Wylie. See *Chapter 14.*

CHAPTER 19

Battcock, George (ed.). *The New Art: A Critical Anthology.* New York: Dutton, 1968.

Biber, Pierre. *The Living Theatre,* 2nd ed. New York: Horizon Press, 1972.

Brook, Peter. *The Empty Space.* New York: Atheneum, 1968.

Clark, Brian. *Group Theatre.* New York: Theatre Arts, 1971.

Grotowski, Jerzy. *Toward a Poor Theatre.* New York: Simon & Schuster, 1968.

Kirby, Michael. *Happenings.* New York: Dutton, 1965.

Lesnick, Henry. *Guerrilla Street Theatre.* New York: Avon Books, 1973.

Lippard, Lucy R. *Pop Art.* New York: Holt, Rinehart & Winston, 1966.

Pasolli, Robert. *A Book on the Open Theatre.* Indianapolis, Ind.: Bobbs-Merrill, 1970.

Schechner, Richard. *Public Domain: Essays on the Theatre.* Indianapolis, Ind.: Bobbs-Merrill, 1969.

Seitz, William C. *The Responsive Eye.* New York: MOMA, 1965.

Taylor, John R. *The Angry Theatre* (rev. ed.). New York: Hill & Wang, 1969.

Trewin, J. C. *Peter Brook.* London: McDonald & Co., 1971.

CHAPTER 20

Langer, Susanne. See *Chapter 9.*

Richman, Robert (ed.). *The Arts at Mid-Century.* New York: Horizon Press, 1954.

Rothschild, Lincoln. See *Chapter 9.*

St. Denis, Michel. See *Chapter 9.*

Smith, C. Ray (ed.). See *Chapter 6.*

Sources of Theatrical Supplies

Zauder Bros., Inc., 902 Broadway, New York, N.Y. 10010

CELASTIC

Maharam Fabric Corporation, 420 N. Orleans St., Chicago, Ill. 60610; 1113 S. Los Angeles St., Los Angeles, Calif. 90015

HEXALITE

Hexel Corporation, Rexolin Div., 20701 Nordhoff St., Chatsworth, Calif. 91311

ARMOR

The Armory, American Fencing Supply, 2122 Fillmore St., San Francisco, Calif. 94115

Costume Armor, Inc., Shore Rd., P.O. Box 325, Cornwall-on-Hudson, N.Y. 12520

Tobins Lake Studios, 2650 Seven Mile Road, South Lyon, Mich. 18178

DANCE FOOTWEAR AND DANCE COSTUME SUPPLIES

Baum's Inc., Dance Wear, 106–112 S. 11th St., Philadelphia, Pa. 19107

Capezio, 745 Seventh Ave., New York, N.Y. 10019; 116 E. Walton St., Chicago, Ill. 60602; 126 Post St., San Francisco, Calif. 94102

Custon Theatrical Shoes, 4 W. 62nd St., New York, N.Y. 10023

Lew Serbin Company, 1217 Sutter St., San Francisco, Calif. 94102

COSTUME RENTAL

Broadway Costumes, Inc., 932 W. Washington, Blvd., Chicago, Ill. 60607

Chicago Costume Company, Inc., 1120 W. Barry St., Chicago, Ill. 60657

Costume Collection, 601 W. 26th St., New York, N.Y. 10001

Costume Crafters, 2979 Peach Tree St. N.E., Atlanta, Ga. 30305

Costumes Unlimited, 814 Franklin St., Chicago, Ill. 60610

David's Outfitters, Inc., 117 W. 46th St., New York, N.Y. 10036

Eaves-Brooks Costume Company, 21–07 41st Ave., Long Island City, N.Y. 11101

Hooker Howe Costume Company, 46 S. Main St., Haverhill, Mass. 01830

Krause Costume Company, 2439 Superior Ave., Cleveland, Ohio 44114

Malabar, 14 McCaul St., Toronto, Canada M5T 126

New York Costume Company, 10 Hubbard St., Chicago, Ill. 60610

Norcostco, Inc., 3203 North Highway 100, Minneapolis, Minn. 55422

Rubie's Costume Company, 1 Rubie Plaza, Richmond Hills, N.Y. 11418

Stagecraft Studios, 1854 Alcatraz Ave., Berkeley, Calif. 94703

Western Costume Company, 5335 Melrose Ave., Hollywood, Calif. 90038

COSTUME SHOP SUPPLIES

Automatic Steam Products Corporation, 43–20 34th St., Long Island City, N.Y. 11101

David Kaplan and Company, Inc., 210 S. DesPlaines St., Chicago, Ill. 60606

Fine Brand, Inc., 411 Hall St., Los Angeles, Calif. 90013

Fox Sewing Machine Company, 307 W. 38th St., New York, N.Y. 10001

Greenburg and Hammer, 24 W. 57th St., New York, N.Y 10019

Industrial Sewing Company, 333 Market St., Paterson, N.J. 07501

Lion Notions, Inc., P.O. Box 2468, South San Francisco, Calif. 94080

Pam Tailor Supply, 625 Adam St., Dorchester, Mass. 02122

Sewing Notions Div., Scoville Manufacturing Company, 90 Hatch St., New Bedford, Mass. 02745

Troy Thread and Textile Corporation, 2300 W. Diversy Ave., Chicago, Ill. 60625

Wolf Form Company, 39 W. 19th St., New York, N.Y. 10011

DYESTUFFS

Almore Dye House, 442 S. Wentworth St., Chicago, Ill. 60609

Calusa Chemical Company, 801 E. Macy St., Los Angeles, Calif. 90012

Crescent Bronze Powder Company, Western Div., 1841 S. Flower St., Los Angeles, Calif. 90015

Keystone Aniline and Chemical Company, 321 N. Loomis St., Chicago, Ill. 60607

Pearl Paint Company, 308 Canal St., New York, N.Y. 10013

Putnam Dye Company, P.O. Box 1267, Galesburg, Ill. 61401

Western Solvents and Eaton Chemical Company, 13395 Huron Dr., Romulus, Mich. 48174

INDUSTRIAL FELT

A. B. Boyd Company, 8033 N.E. Holman St., Portland, Ore. 97218

Metric Felt Company, 135 S. Peoria St., Chicago, Ill. 60607

Standard Felt Company, 115 S. Palm Ave., P.O. Box 871, Alhambra, Calif. 91802

Index